Clinician's Guide to Self-Renewal

Clinician's Guide to Self-Renewal

Essential Advice From the Field

Edited by

Robert J. Wicks

and

Elizabeth A. Maynard

WILEY

Cover image: @istockphoto.com/ooyoo
Cover design: Wiley

This book is printed on acid-free paper.

Published by John Wiley & Sons, Inc., Hoboken, New Jersey
Published simultaneously in Canada

ISBN: 978-1-118-44381-1 (pbk)
ISBN: 978-1-118-84103-7 (ebk)
ISBN: 978-1-118-84106-8 (ebk)

Printed in the United States of America

10 9 8 7 6 5 4 3 2 1

For the Students and Faculty of Loyola University Maryland: In gratitude for being the recipient of your graciousness, wisdom, good humor, and friendship for over 25 years.

Robert J. Wicks

To all who offer comfort and sustenance to those in need: May you be renewed each day.

Elizabeth A. Maynard

Contents

Part V Spirituality and Self-Renewal

Part VI Topics in Self-Renewal

About the Book

The goal of this book is to *begin* a more in-depth and broader discussion as to how using the lens of self-renewal can enrich the psychotherapy process as well as the clinician's personal and professional life.

The emphasis on the clinician's own self-renewal in the early chapters of the book is an outgrowth of the belief that while technique and the therapeutic relationship are of paramount importance in the treatment encounter, there is a third element that is of profound import as well: the modeling by the therapist of a respect for, and involvement in, seeking a healthier lifestyle. In this light, a clinician's self-care is not viewed solely as benefiting the therapist alone, although the direct benefit to the helper is certainly a goal. It is also seen as having a subtle but powerful impact on the therapy process itself.

With clinician self-care and mindfulness as a bedrock of self-renewal, the remainder of the subsequent sections of the book are designed to provide new insights and perspective on self-renewal in terms of client growth and healing, therapeutic techniques, spirituality, different populations, ethics, and other challenges.

Specific key features in *Self-Renewal Themes in Psychotherapy* include:

- Self-care for clinicians in the disaster context.
- Clinical supervision and self-renewal.
- Mindfulness, silence, solitude, and reflection in the life of the clinician.
- Zen therapy and renewal.
- Self-renewal among gay and lesbian adults.
- Posttraumatic growth.
- Intergenerational trauma and healing.
- Patience, forgiveness, and courage in the process of self-renewal.
- Renewal in marital, family, and group settings.
- Spirituality, religion, and renewal.
- Self-renewal with African Americans in psychotherapy.
- Growth, love, and work in psychotherapy.

The positive impact of this information is not simply limited to a present *specific* benefit (i.e., how can I put this knowledge in play with my caseload?) alone. In a broader sense, the topics covered are designed as well to draw on the experience and wisdom of the clinicians reading this material by prompting them to also ask such questions as:

- How can I more productively use the frame of "self-renewal" with different populations and presenting problems?
- What topics were *not* covered in this initial effort at discussing self-renewal and clinical practice that you might develop more clearly going forward?
- What are the most pressing issues that intrigue, challenge, and reward you in your own personal and professional journey that would significantly enhance your self-renewal process?
- How can your own self-renewal plan be developed further—not as a duty in being healthier but as part of a pilgrimage in enjoying life—including one's clinical practice in a much fuller way *now*?

These are but a few questions that, if truly, honestly, nonjudgmentally, and comprehensively faced, may well lead to alter and enrich how clinicians can involve themselves in the process of therapy. The impact, and living out, of insights achieved from grappling with such questions and the different approaches in this book can change the clinician and how therapy is undertaken. The lyrics (theory and technique) of the treatment may remain fairly unaltered. However, the music (modeling, relational aspects, and sense of mindfulness in play) of the clinical work may be profoundly changed, ending in surprisingly gratifying results. Once again, self-renewal is a gift therapists can give themselves. But, in the end, it is a gift that can open up those they treat to open up so much more in their lives as well and, in its essence, isn't this what therapy is truly about?

About the Editors

Robert J. Wicks, PsyD

Dr. Wicks, who received his doctorate in psychology from Hahnemann Medical College and Hospital, is a professor emeritus of Loyola University Maryland. He has published more than 50 books for professionals and the general public. They include: *Bounce: Living the Resilient Life*; *Riding the Dragon*; *The Inner Life of the Counselor*; and *Streams of Contentment*. Dr. Wicks has lectured on the importance of resilience and possessing a healthy perspective in Hanoi, Bejing, Budapest, Belfast, and Johannesburg as well as at the Mayo Clinic, Harvard's Children's Hospital and Harvard Divinity School, at the Johns Hopkins School of Medicine, and on Capitol Hill to Members of Congress and their Chiefs of Staff. He received the Humanitarian of the Year Award from the American Counseling Association's Division on Spirituality, Ethics, and Values and in 2006 was recipient of the first annual Alumni Award for Excellence in Professional Psychology from Widener University.

Related Books by Dr. Wicks . . .

Bounce: Living the Resilient Life (OUP)
Streams of Contentment (Sorin Books)
Riding the Dragon (Sorin Books)
The Inner Life of the Counselor (Wiley)
Primer on Posttraumatic Growth—Written with Mary Beth Werdel (Wiley)

Elizabeth A. Maynard, PhD

Dr. Maynard is associate professor of psychology and director of clinical mental health counseling programs at the University of St. Thomas in Houston, Texas. Trained as a clinical psychologist at Fuller Theological Seminary, she is a licensed clinical psychologist who serves professional helpers, including both clergy and mental health professionals and those in training for helping careers. Her research focuses on the themes of sexuality, religious coping, and prejudice.

About the Authors

Jeffrey E. Barnett, PsyD, ABPP

Dr. Barnett is a professor and associate chair of the Department of Psychology at Loyola University Maryland. He is a licensed psychologist in Maryland, board certified in clinical psychology and clinical child and adolescent psychology by the American Board of Professional Psychology, and is a distinguished practitioner in the National Academies of Practice. He specializes in ethics and professional practice issues for mental health professionals to include self-care, psychological wellness, and burnout prevention.

Jodi L. Bartley

Jodi is a doctoral student in the Department of Counseling and Educational Development at the University of North Carolina at Greensboro. She holds master's degrees in both Mental Health Counseling and Educational Psychology. Her current research interests include relational depth and spirituality.

Amber E. Blews

Amber is a doctoral student in the clinical psychology program at Fuller Graduate School of Psychology in Pasadena, California. She holds an MA in Educational Counseling from the University of Redlands and an MA in Psychology from Fuller Theological Seminary. Blews studies the effects of religion and spirituality, goals, and virtue/character development in adolescent and young adult populations.

Virginia Brabender, PhD, ABPP

Dr. Brabender is a professor at Widener University's Institute for Graduate Clinical Psychology. She has authored or coauthored five books, four on group psychotherapy. Her most recent contribution is a volume coedited with April Fallon titled *Working with Adoptive Parents: Research, Theory, and Therapeutic Interventions.*

David Brazier, PhD

Dr. Brazier is an authority on Buddhist psychology, is current president of Instituto Terapia Zen Internacional, a Buddhist priest, psychotherapist, head of the Amida

Order, and founder of the Eleusis project. Author of *Zen Therapy* and eight other books, he lectures regularly in Europe, Asia, and North America.

Gina M. Brelsford, PhD

Dr. Brelsford is an associate professor of psychology at Penn State Harrisburg and a licensed clinical psychologist with a specialization in working with children and families. Her research agenda focuses on the psychology of religion and spirituality and the family, positive psychology, and cognitive-behavioral work with children and adolescents.

Craig S. Cashwell, PhD

Dr. Cashwell is professor in the Department of Counseling and Educational Development at the University of North Carolina at Greensboro. He is a fellow of the American Counseling Association and maintains a part-time private practice specializing in couple counseling and addiction counseling.

Sharon E. Cheston, EdD

Dr. Cheston is a full professor in the Pastoral Counseling Department at Loyola University Maryland. Her more than 30 years of experience as an educator, supervisor, mental health counselor, and author has led to her attaining an expertise in trauma, the integration of spirituality in counseling, and counselor education and supervision. Dr. Cheston distinguished herself as a leader in the counseling field both at the state and national levels, serving in leadership roles in the Association for Spiritual, Ethical, and Religious Values in Counseling (ASERVIC) and with her gubernatorial appointment to the Maryland Board of Professional Counselors and Therapists where she served as chair, spearheading the process of obtaining licensure for professional counselors in Maryland.

Patricia A. Engert, PhD

Dr. Engert is a licensed clinical psychologist at Psychology Resource Consultants in South Pasadena, California, where she specializes in psychological assessment and individual, group, and family therapy. Additionally, she works as an adjunct lecturer at the California School of Professional Psychology at Alliant International University and the Graduate School of Psychology at Fuller Theological Seminary.

Robert D. Enright, PhD

Dr. Enright is a professor in the Department of Educational Psychology at the University of Wisconsin–Madison and a board member of the International Forgiveness Institute, Inc. He has been researching the psychology of forgiveness in clinical contexts since 1985.

Melissa D. Falb

Melissa is a doctoral student at Bowling Green State University. She holds MA degrees in theology and psychology. Her primary interests include coping, positive psychology, Buddhism, and mindfulness, especially the interpersonal benefits of mindfulness and relational practices.

Jaelyn R. Farris, PhD

Dr. Farris is an assistant professor of Human Development & Family Studies at Penn State Harrisburg. Dr. Farris earned an MSEd in Community Counseling from Youngstown State University, and an MA and PhD in Developmental Psychology from the University of Notre Dame. Her work as a clinical counselor with impoverished urban children and adolescents provided the foundation for her primary research interest in the onset, progression, and prevention of psychopathology among at-risk youth. Dr. Farris has more than 20 scholarly publications, including numerous journal articles and two books. She maintains a general interest in the promotion of positive development among at-risk youth and is currently pursuing research on the delivery of interventions in the context of after-school programming.

Jessica A. Foss

Jessica Foss is a doctoral student in the Fuller Theological Seminary Graduate School of Psychology. Her clinical interests include working with adolescents, college students, couples, and adults. To meet the unique needs of each client, Jessica incorporates attachment theory as well as person-centered, family systems, and developmental approaches into her therapeutic work.

Paul Giblin, PhD

Dr. Giblin is associate professor of pastoral studies and pastoral counseling at Loyola University of Chicago, the Institute of Pastoral Studies, where he began and directs the master's program in pastoral counseling. He is a clinical member and approved supervisor in AAMFT and fellow in AAPC. His research interests have focused on healthy marital and family functioning and the psychology and spirituality of men. He especially finds renewal in alpine skiing and instruction.

Cheryl A. Giles, PsyD

Dr. Giles is a licensed clinical psychologist and the Francis Greenwood Peabody Senior Lecturer on Pastoral Care and Counseling at Harvard Divinity School. She has extensive experience in the treatment of children, adolescents, and families with significant mental illness, high-risk behaviors, and traumatic stress. Her primary research interests are identifying the role of risk and resilience in developing healthy adolescents in the lives of queer youth, health care disparities in African Americans, and fostering sustainable resilience in caregivers who practice contemplative care for the dying. Professor Giles is a core faculty member of the Buddhist Ministry Initiative at Harvard Divinity School and coeditor of *The Arts of Contemplative Care: Pioneering Voices in Buddhist Chaplaincy and Pastoral Work* (Wisdom Press, 2012).

Rev. Kaye N. Glennon

Kaye was a pastor in the United Methodist Church for 14 years before beginning an independent, inclusive progressive Christian community in 2011 in Racine, Wisconsin. Currently she pastors the new congregation, Sacred Journeys Spiritual Community, and teaches courses on religion and women's spirituality at Carthage College in Kenosha, Wisconsin.

Kathleen Gregory, PhD

Dr. Gregory is course convener of the master of counseling program in the School of Public Health and Human Biosciences at La Trobe University, Melbourne. She is a counseling psychologist and holds a PhD in Comparative Philosophy. She has been a Buddhist practitioner in the Tibetan Tradition for 20 years. Her current research focus is to extend the psychotherapeutic application of Buddhist principles and practices.

Deborah G. Haskins, PhD

Dr. Haskins is assistant professor and director of counseling programs at Trinity Washington University (DC). She specializes in and publishes in the areas of cultural competency, service delivery to cultural communities, and gambling addiction treatment. She has a PhD in pastoral counseling from Loyola College (now Loyola University Maryland).

Matthew J. Hirshberg

Matthew is a graduate student in the Department of Educational Psychology at the University of Wisconsin–Madison. He is interested in interventions to reduce negative affect and promote well-being and prosocial behaviors, particularly in educational contexts.

Katie E. Katuzny

Katie is a doctoral student at the California School of Professional Psychology at Alliant International University, San Francisco, and senior research assistant at the Rockway Institute for LGBT Psychology and Public Policy. Her dissertation is focused on heterosexuals' attitudes toward same-sex marriage. Previously,

Katie was the public policy assistant at Equality Florida where she worked to promote LGBT-affirmative legislation.

Suzanne Mayer, IHM, PhD

Dr. Mayer is the coordinator of pastoral and theological studies and a full professor in the pastoral care counseling program at Neumann University. Nationally certified [NBCC], with a small practice as a pastoral counselor, she also works with a number of groups as a teacher of formation and human development, consultant, retreat director, lecturer, and team builder. Licensed as a professional counselor in Pennsylvania and Delaware, Sister has served on numerous committees for various professional organizations, including American Association of Pastoral Counselors, American Counselors Association, and Chi Sigma Iota. She has contributed to many publications and journals including *Weavings, Human Development, Spiritual Life, Counselling et Spiritualité, The Journal of Pastoral Care and Counseling*, and *Lectionary Homilectics* and two books edited by Dr. Robert Wicks.

Maria Mouratidis, PsyD

Dr. Mouratidis is a licensed psychologist and is currently an associate professor and chair of the Department of Psychology at Notre Dame of Maryland University. Dr. Mouratidis has received extensive training in dialectical behavior therapy (DBT), provides training and supervision in the area of DBT, and has developed and coordinated dialectical behavior therapy programs. Dr. Mouratidis was previously a faculty member at Yale University School of Medicine and served the Department of the Navy by providing clinical services and developing programs for returning service members with posttraumatic stress disorder and traumatic brain injury.

Geoffrey Newbegin

Geoffrey has been a practicing counselor and psychologist for 12 years and is currently completing his doctorate of counseling psychology at La Trobe University, Melbourne. His doctoral thesis is examining the effects of mindfulness and loving kindness meditation on health professionals. He has had a long-term interest in Buddhist philosophy and has been practicing Buddhist meditation for 20 years.

Helene Nissen-Lie, PhD

Dr. Nissen-Lie is a clinical psychologist and researcher at the University of Oslo, Norway. Her work has focused on the relationships between therapist variables and client outcomes in psychotherapy. Her work emphasizes the importance of ongoing therapist self-care and development.

David E. Orlinsky, PhD

Dr. Orlinsky is Professor Emeritus of Human Development at the University of Chicago and a clinical psychologist and social scientist internationally recognized as an expert in the field of psychotherapy and psychotherapy research. His interests focus broadly on the nature and functions of close interpersonal relationships in the context of personality development, and on the social and cultural domain of "personal life" in modern and postmodern societies where these relationships are most significant.

Kenneth I. Pargament, PhD

Dr. Pargament is professor of psychology in the Department of Psychology at Bowling Green State University and Distinguished Scholar at the Institute for Spirituality and Health of the Texas Medical Center in Houston. He is editor-in-chief of the recently published two-volume *APA Handbook of Psychology, Religion, and Spirituality*.

Cynthia L. S. Pury, PhD

Dr. Pury is a professor of psychology at Clemson University in Clemson, South Carolina. Her research on emotion and cognition, particularly fear, led her to explore courage in the early 2000s, and this research has continued to today. She is the author of numerous publications on courage, and, along with Shane Lopez, edited *The Psychology of Courage: Modern Research on an Ancient Virtue* (published by the American Psychological Association).

Jonathan D. Reeves

Jonathan is a clinical psychology doctoral student at the Fuller Graduate School of Psychology in Pasadena, California. His research and clinical interests include sexuality, relationships, anthropology, and the integration of psychology with religion, literature, and the other sciences. Originally from the Pacific Northwest, he spends his free time searching for trees and clean air.

Rev. Thomas E. Rodgerson, PhD

Dr. Rodgerson is director of the MA program in Spiritual and Pastoral Care, Loyola University Maryland. He completed his PhD at Loyola with a focus on research in the area of clergy burnout. He is currently the Clergy and Congregational Care Coordinator for Centrepointe Counseling, and is both a Diplomate with the American Association of Pastoral Counselors and a Licensed Clinical Professional Counselor in the state of Maryland.

Sarah A. Schnitker, PhD

Dr. Schnitker is an assistant professor in the Thrive Center for Human Development at Fuller Graduate School of Psychology in Pasadena, California. She holds a PhD and an MA in personality and social psychology from the University of California, Davis, and a BA from Grove City College. Dr. Schnitker studies virtue and character development in adolescents and emerging adults, with a focus on the role of spirituality and religion in virtue formation.

Margot J. Schofield, PhD

Dr. Schofield is professor of counseling and psychotherapy in the School of Public Health and Human Biosciences at La Trobe University, Melbourne, and head of the Department of Counseling and Psychological Health. Her current research focuses on the development of psychotherapists and counselors, process and outcome evaluation of counseling and clinical supervision, couple counseling and family mediation, art-based approaches in mental health and cancer recovery, and women's health.

Stephen W. Simpson, PhD

Dr. Simpson is the director of clinical training and an assistant professor of clinical psychology at the Graduate School of Psychology at Fuller Theological Seminary. In addition to articles in scholarly journals, he is the author of *Assaulted By Joy: The Redemption of a Cynic* (2008), *What Women Wish You Knew About Dating: A Single Guy's Guide to Romance* (2008), and *What Wives Wish Their Husbands Knew About Sex* (coauthored with Ryan Howes and Richard Rupp, 2007). He explores the intersection of sexuality and religion in his writing, research, and clinical work. He and his wife, Shelley, live in Southern California with their quadruplets and three dogs.

Courtney Slater, PhD

Dr. Slater is a licensed clinical psychologist. She completed her master's and doctorate degrees at the Rosemead School of Psychology, where she developed a specialization in the integration of spirituality/religion and psychology. Dr. Slater currently serves as an assistant professor at Widener University's Institute for Graduate Clinical Psychology where she conducts research and teaches on the topics of spirituality and religion, attachment, diversity, and psychodynamic psychotherapy. She also sees therapy patients in Newark, Delaware.

Rev. Jill L. Snodgrass, PhD

Dr. Snodgrass is assistant professor of pastoral counseling at Loyola University Maryland and an ordained minister in the United Church of Christ. Dr. Snodgrass' interests include spiritual care and counseling with traditionally marginalized populations, with specific emphasis on individuals experiencing homelessness and women transitioning from incarceration. In addition to her work as a teacher, researcher, and minister, Dr. Snodgrass has served as a pastoral counselor in churches, shelters, transitional programs, and community centers. From 2008 to 2011, Dr. Snodgrass served as associate director of the Clinebell Institute for Pastoral Counseling and Psychotherapy in Claremont, California.

Mary Beth Werdel, PhD

Dr. Werdel is an assistant professor of pastoral counseling and spiritual care in the Graduate School of Religion and Religious Education at Fordham University. She is also a licensed mental health counselor. She earned a doctorate in pastoral counseling from Loyola University Maryland. She is the coauthor of *A Primer on Posttraumatic Growth: An Introduction and Guide* (Wiley, 2012) and author of *As Faith Matures: Beyond the Sunday God* (Liguori Press, 2012). Her research interests center on images of God, positive and negative forms of religious coping, and growth following stress and trauma.

Rick Williamson, PhD

Dr. Williamson is a consulting psychologist with the Headington Institute where he works with humanitarians responding to suffering across the globe. He is also a clinical psychologist in Los Angeles with the Emmada Psychology Center, specializing in providing culturally responsive psychotherapy. He is a board member and chair-elect of the California Psychological Association's Training and Education Division.

Self-Renewal Themes in Psychotherapy: An Introduction

Elizabeth A. Maynard and Robert J. Wicks

The goal of this book is a simple one: to begin an in-depth discussion of the ways in which self-renewal themes enrich the psychotherapy process and the clinician's own personal and professional development. To that end, the editors have assembled a talented group of authors from a wide variety of settings to speak to the themes of self-renewal in direct service to clients, in the training and supervision of those entering the field, and in the life of the clinician both within and beyond the clinical hour.

It is often noted that the primary tool of the clinician is her or his own self. Thus, the clinician not only supports and encourages the self-renewal of the clients with whom she works, but also returns to the habits and processes of self-renewal so that she may both personally thrive and be of aid to clients. Technique and the real therapeutic relationship built between the client and clinician are key to effective helping relationships. The therapist's own modeling of a healthy way of being in the world is also a powerful force to inspire clients seeking greater health, well-being, or personal transformation.

The clinician's engagement in self-renewal practices often allows him or her to be more fully present and alive in the work with the client, shaping the ways in which the clinician is able to be present in the therapeutic context. Further, attention to self-renewal themes and paradigms allows the clinician to assess the client's current habits of self-renewal while also identifying where she or he may be stuck. Finally, understanding the importance of self-renewal themes, rather than simply attending to themes of remediation or repair, allows the clinician to join with the client in interventions that go beyond "fixing" a perceived problem, to engaging in lifelong growth.

At its most fundamental level, self-renewal may be understood as those processes and practices that support the ongoing well-being of the client or clinician. They are processes focused primarily within the individual, recognizing her or his interpersonal and cultural context and the important ways in which the individual may be enlivened by these connections. Renewal also implies a return and a new beginning. In this sense, self-renewal refers to processes that return the client or clinician to those values and practices that are most essential to her or his well-being. These may include attention to physical well-being through healthful eating, sleeping, exercise, and sexuality. Further, they may include processes to refresh one's psychological well-being, such as thinking in new ways, expressing gratitude, practicing courage, or cultivating forgiveness. Self-renewal is often a social enterprise as well, as we seek to strengthen, revise, or discover new territory in our most important relationships. Finally, self-renewal is a spiritual process in the broadest sense, as individuals reflect on their most cherished values, beliefs, and connections, and commit to what is most meaningful.

The authors in this volume have approached the self-renewal themes from a number of these perspectives, each attending to a particular theme, practice, or community. It is the hope of the authors and editors that, taken together, this tapestry of perspectives invites the reader to consider those self-renewal themes most relevant to the reader's personal and professional growth. Further, it is hoped that the reader will be inspired to attend to self-renewal themes in work with clients and supervisees, not only in the manifest content of what is discussed in sessions, but also in the deeper and more subtle threads of one's professional work.

The focus of this volume is most often on the self-renewal process of the individual, though the reader is also encouraged to consider the implications of these themes for the renewal of the communities of which she or he is a part. Thus, what might it mean for a community to renew its courage, to cultivate patience, or to engage in forgiveness? How might these individual themes inspire broader cultural renewal?

Self-renewal may be understood both as a project and as a process. By this we mean that self-renewal activities are often undertaken as projects ("I must spend more time in the sun," or "I must learn mindfulness skills"), which we and our clients quantify and measure. This may be a very effective way to proceed, and the measurement of the effectiveness of our interventions (with ourselves and others) has been an important priority in the field in recent years. At the same time, self-renewal is also a process that often unfolds in ways that surprise both the clinician and client. That is, renewal is not always the result of our concerted efforts, but often also the fruit of serendipity, auspicious events, or what some term "grace." Psychotherapy is both a science and an art. Self-renewal may be understood in this way, too, as the outcome of carefully planned and measured interventions, and often riotous flowering that is neither controlled nor expected.

OVERVIEW OF THE PRESENT VOLUME

Because the growth and self-renewal of the clinician is essential to both his well-being and his ability to be of aid to others, this volume begins with work from authors who address several common self-renewal themes for clinicians. The authors in this section address the dynamic interplay among growth, love, and work in psychotherapy, the themes of self-care and self-renewal in high-stress clinical work, and the ways in which clinical supervision can be used as a means for self-renewal of both the professional and the clinician-in-training.

As the reader begins the second section, she will encounter chapters focused on self-renewal practices such as silence, solitude, taking a Sabbath, and the cultivation of empathy and loving kindness. Each of these practices prepares the clinician to be more fully present to herself and others, both in the clinical setting and outside it. The readings in the third section invite the reader to consider self-renewal in the context of trauma and posttraumatic growth, as well as exploring the psychological virtues of patience, forgiveness, and courage.

In the fourth section of the book, authors invite the reader to explore theoretical approaches to self-renewal, including group work, family systems perspectives, self-renewal themes in dialectical behavior therapy (DBT) work, and the use of the "Ways" paradigm to explore self-renewal themes with clients. Spiritual themes are explored in the fifth section, with emphasis on spiritual coping and spiritual resources for both individuals and families. Finally, the work ends with exploration of special topics in self-renewal, including self-renewal themes for African American clients and clinicians, clergy, and queer adults. The renewal of one's ethical sensibilities and addressing sexual attractions in clinical work round out the volume.

Much like an abundant banquet comprising small dishes, it is the editors' hope that the reader will find a number of enticing offerings here. We further hope that readers will be inspired to select those themes and practices that most resonate with them to include in their own self-renewal and care of clients.

PART I

Self-Renewal and the Clinician

CHAPTER

1

Growth, Love, and Work in Psychotherapy

Sources of Therapeutic Talent and Clinician Self-Renewal

Helene Nissen-Lie and David E. Orlinsky

Successful psychotherapy can be seen as a process that essentially involves self-renewal. This is most apparent in the lives of clients, where self-renewal implies the restoration of normal development for those whose personal growth had been limited or distorted by adverse life circumstances. In therapy, that restoration is accomplished through the client's *personal* involvement in a *professional* relationship that combines meaningful challenge with support and encouragement. This requires a commitment of emotional energy reflected in the client's motivation for therapy and hopeful morale about eventual positive outcome—an investment of energy that must be sustained and renewed through experiencing the therapist's personal interest, empathic responsiveness, and effective interventions.

Less apparent, perhaps, is the fact that psychotherapy also requires and relies on the clinician's experiences of self-renewal, because clinicians too need to participate *personally* (in a special but essential sense) in their *professional* relationships with clients. Therapists invest and expend a significant amount of emotional and intellectual energy in order to be personally present—alert, attuned, and empathically responsive to clients—and to provide each client with realistic challenges and meaningful support in ways well suited to the client's level of need, state of mind, and stage of progress.

Providing psychotherapy is demanding work, both intellectually and emotionally. Maintaining one's morale can be difficult when working with clients who are in deep emotional turmoil, often having experienced traumatic childhoods or devastating life circumstances. Clients who have experienced disruptive breaches of trust on the part of those they once depended on often exhibit defensive behavior in therapy, criticizing therapists for perceived slights and rejecting well-intended interventions, or else idealizing them and burdening them with insatiable neediness, or yet again engaging in distressing destructive or self-destructive behaviors.

Coping constructively with conditions like these requires a high level of interpersonal skill on the part of psychotherapists, and a resilient core of emotional equilibrium. Some of those interpersonal skills are acquired or enhanced through professional training and experience in practice, but the basic interpersonal skills and capacities that therapists need to deal effectively with challenging clients derive in large part from formative experiences in their own personal development that can be described as *therapeutic talent*—abilities that therapists already have when they come for professional training, and which undoubtedly can be refined and augmented by training and experience but probably cannot be produced by training alone if they are not already present (Orlinsky, Botermans, & Rønnestad, 1998). Similarly, the motivations that lead therapists to apply for professional training, and need in order to engage in therapeutic work, stem in large part from formative personal experiences in their own development, and are renewed and maintained both by successful practice and by personal experiences of current life satisfactions that help them maintain a positive emotional equilibrium.

This chapter is devoted to exploring some sources of clinicians' talents and motivations for psychotherapeutic work, and some of the long- and short-term self-renewal that work to maintain them. The first of its two main sections (by Orlinsky) presents a theoretical model of personal development that explores the interconnected themes of personal growth, love relationships, and the development of capacities that define *therapeutic talent*. The second section (by Nissen-Lie) reflects on therapists' private lives with respect to the personal factors that motivate therapists to pursue their profession and the resources in their private lives that sustain them in their work.

I. PERSONAL GROWTH, LOVE, AND THE DEVELOPMENT OF THERAPEUTIC TALENT

David E. Orlinsky

This section explores the idea that therapeutic talent is rooted in the personal development of the psychotherapist. The talent itself consists of the therapist's personal ability to engage clients in a supportive and challenging professional psychotherapy relationship. Research on therapeutic process and outcome has amply documented that the client's experience of a strong positive therapeutic bond consistently predicts improvement in clinical outcome (Horvath, Del Re, Flückiger, & Symonds, 2011). This personal/professional therapeutic bond reflects and depends to a significant degree on the interpersonal skills and capacities of the therapist that are initially developed in the course of the therapist's personal growth. The following section offers a conception of personal development and suggests distinctive aspects of therapeutic talent traceable to that development.

Personal Growth

Personal growth can be defined as the progressive *differentiation* and subsequent *integration* of experience (e.g., Angyal, 1941; Lewin, 1935; Werner, 1942) that alternately distinguish the self from others (*individuation*) and intimately connect the self with others (*interdependence*). The result is a cumulatively more complex set of *self-other experiences* (e.g., Sullivan, 1949) that constitute the interrelated spheres of ego-identity and object-world, which composes the individual's *personality*.

Alternating and successive phases of individuation and interdependence generate a dialectical pattern of development mediated through a person's close relationships with others—relationships in forms and ways that are appropriate to each specific stage of life. Accompanied by newfound pleasures as well as growing pains and eventual experiences of loss, the close relationships that emerge in each phase of development promote personal growth by alternately stretching the individual's capacities for asserting a clear self-presence, and for merging in mutual and mutually beneficial interdependence with others.

Individuation occurs through relationships of self-assertion that frequently result in contentious interpersonal behaviors. Examples of this are the *willfulness* shown by toddlers in their "terrible twos," by the oedipal and sibling *rivalries* of early childhood, and by later *competition* for dominance when relating with peers. Growth through successive phases of self-assertion and self-realization involves putting together and putting forward a distinct, and distinctive, socially viable identity—pushing others, sometimes *against* others, to recognize and respect one's presence.

Growth through successive phases of interdependence occurs through involvement in age-appropriate love relationships (Orlinsky, 1972). Each new phase of growth-through-love thrusts the individual into experiencing a relationship that transcends the self, and that evokes a new aspect or facet of self through which the individual can connect with other persons.

The alternating phases of growth serve as prerequisites for subsequent phases of development. Thus, each phase of individuation generates *a new aspect of self-experience* that incorporates the experience of the person in the most recent phase of love attachment, and integrates that with aspects of self that had been generated in prior phases of individuation. In a similar way, each phase of interdependence generates *a new capacity for involvement in close relationships* that incorporates the experience of self in the most recent phase of individuation, and integrates that with capacities for closeness that had been generated in prior phases of interdependence.

Table 1.1 presents a highly schematic chart showing the alternating successive phases of personal growth as socially and culturally configured in late 20th century Western societies (cf. Kakar, 1981, for an example of a contrasting cultural pattern). This conception is based largely on ideas advanced by writers like Freud (1917/1963), Erikson (1950, 1959a), Piaget (Piaget & Inhelder, 1969), Sullivan (1953), and Bowlby (1969). Before commenting on specific phases, it is important to note that Table 1.1 shows an *ideal* pattern—a societally specific cultural normative pattern that *empirically*, in the lives of real individuals, is traceable only more or less clearly due to the influence of many circumstances. It is also important to note that phases of growth may overlap and interfere with one another, especially when one phase is closing and the next is starting.

Mastery of the developmental challenges in each phase may be abbreviated and incomplete, leaving the persons in question unprepared for challenges that their future holds. Adaptations in each phase may be distorted or disrupted by traumatic experiences that leave the survivor overly sensitive and potentially vulnerable in later life. Real persons always grow imperfectly, often deficiently, and occasionally defectively, according to an ideal cultural pattern of development.

Growth Through Love and the Accrual of "Therapeutic Talent"

The first phases of individuation and interrelatedness take place in the context of the child-parent relationship ("parent" understood as caregiver), which extends over many years and changes in character and tone as the child grows physically, cognitively, and emotionally. Interrelatedness and individuation start within the womb on a biological level, the first phase of interdependence being one of umbilical attachment, and the first phase of individuation culminating in birth.

Infancy

For the parent, this phase in the child-parent relationship represents an intensely focused and extremely conscious experience of love. For the infant, the attachment is initially reflexive, and unfolds a diffuse and pervasive but essentially *unself-conscious* embodied experience of hunger, distress, and discomfort, followed more or less reliably by satisfaction, safety, and pleasure—which, if not yet experienced distinctly as a love relationship, is the ground and foundation of all later love relationships (Bowlby, 1969; Erikson, 1950; Stern, 1985).

Table 1.1 Phases of Personal Growth

	Personal Growth through successive alternating phases of		
Life Phase	**Individuation** ***Separation > Self-Realization***	and	**Interdependence** ***Involvement > Love Attachment***
Embryonic	*Separate Male/Female Gametes* [bisexual reproduction]	>	*Umbilical Attachment* [intrauterine physiological dependence]
		V	
Infant	Unself-conscious-Postnatal Being [progressive physiological autonomy]	>	Preverbal *Body-Hunger* Love [reflex-based behavioral attachment]
		V	
Baby	Sensorimotor-Embodied "I" [distinct self *vis-à-vis* other awareness]	>	Reciprocal-Joyful "*I-Thou*" Love [perceived self-other attachment]
		V	
Toddler	Articulate-Imaginative "I" [actively willful/willing self]	>	Entrusting-Dependent *Reliant* Love [attention-affection-approval attachment]
		V	
Nursery/ Pre-school	Assertive-Engendered "I" [little-boy-self/little-girl-self]	>	Possessive Family-Complex Love [self-centered "oedipal" attachments]
		V	
Juvenile	Normative-Familial "I" [concrete operational self-system]	>	Idealizing *Hero-Worship* Love [avid apprentice-disciple attachments]
		V	
Pre-adolescent	Inner-Conceptual "I" [abstract self-reflective identity]	>	Peer-Intimacy *Philia* Love [confiding "best-friend" attachment]
		V	
Adolescent/ Youth	Erotic-Attractive Adult-Sexual "I" [self-identity as a "sexual person"]	>	Erotic-Ecstatic *Romantic* Love [personal-sexual inseparability]
		V	
Young Adult	Committed Adult-Vocational "I" [recognized economic self-identity]	>	Mutual-Collaborative *Conjugal* Love [committed intimate-erotic attachment]
		V	
Mature Adult	Generative-Parental "I" [productive-prolific "successful" self]	>	Nurturing-Guiding *Parental* Love [fostering/protective attachments]
		V	
Senior	Contextual Life-Historic "I" [life-in-historic-perspective self]	>	Caring-Compassionate *Caritas* Love [generic life-affirming attachment]

Babyhood

The baby's ability to consciously experience love as an active exchange in attachment with a caregiver depends on the psychological development of a "self"—the first *psychological* individuation—made possible as a result of the child's sensorimotor, cognitive, and affective maturation during the first six to nine months of postnatal life. One becomes increasingly able to differentiate between "inner" experiences of more or less urgent need and "outer" experiences of a world in which Others who gratify (but sometimes also frustrate, irritate, and frighten) recurrently appear to attend to it.

This step in self-realization makes possible and introduces a phase of genuine attachment-love for the infant-child, an encompassing holistic experience of recognition and affirmation by—and deep and wholehearted affirmation of—a powerful, responsive, and benignly sustaining presence. This phase reflects the development of love in a primal "I-Thou" relationship, an intimacy that can only be felt rather than spoken because it is grounded more deeply in experience than words (Buber, 1965).

Later, in the lives of therapists, this early experience enables them to be present to clients in a steady, deeply affirming way—to engage with, witness, and comfort their distress—and enables clients to receive this as a healing gift. The aspect of relational talent that derives from it is well described as "therapeutic presence."

Toddlerhood

The next cycle of individuation and attachment also occurs in the context of the child-parent relationship as the child becomes more mobile, verbally articulate, and socially discriminating between 18 months and 3 years of age. Now possessing a stable/continuous sense of self, the toddler begins to employ and practice its new capacities for self-direction, self-expression, and self-assertion in relating with others. They walk away on their own to explore, and return when they want to rather than when summoned. The first simple sentences that children speak typically are No! and I want—and the child-parent relationship is modified accordingly.

Parents must learn to tolerate and find ways to lovingly affirm, support, and contain the child's actively individuated toddler-self even when it is challenging the parent's ability to engage in caregiving activities. The evolution of our species supports parents in this by making toddlers as physically adorable (cute), as "charming" as they will ever again be in their lives; and it supports the survival of oppositional children because they are still physically, emotionally, and socially highly dependent. Even though experiencing and exercising a newfound sense of autonomy, the toddler-self is physically and emotionally far from self-sufficient or self-confident, setting the stage for a new form of love attachment within the parent-child relationship.

The toddler-self needs and seeks reliable support—support on which it can depend, physically and emotionally. Toddlers seek attention, affection, and approval, and learn to act toward their caregivers in ways that are appealing, endearing, and pleasing. Caregivers need to experience themselves as attentive, encouraging, and sufficiently protective; and they find validation of themselves as such in the toddler's attachment behaviors. The complementary growth-needs of toddler and caregiver lead them to engage in a form of love-exchange that facilitates developmentally relevant aspects of personal growth for both.

Later, in the lives of therapists, these early experiences enable therapists to engage with clients in personal attachment that is reliably and sensitively supportive, reassuring as needed but fostering the client's independent self-exploration. This personal bond is at the core of the therapeutic alliance.

Boyhood/Girlhood

This second phase of love attachment produces conditions required for a further phase of self-realization, as the child continues to grow in cognitive abilities and social skills to become a safe and appropriate partner in social interaction for others (i.e., a child who is "no longer a baby"). This requires mastering certain bodily disciplines (e.g., toilet-training) and interpersonal disciplines (e.g., rules of etiquette like "minding" or "paying attention" to others, "answering when spoken to," and "taking turns"), together with learning family-transmitted culturally defined gender identities that mark their becoming "little-boy-selves" or "little-girl-selves" from autonomous but still limited "little-selves."

The sphere of interpersonal relations also expands to include other members of the "familiar group" consisting of the nuclear family and other regular members of the household (e.g., nannies, grandparents, aunts and uncles, neighbors). This entails potential rivalries with others who have claims on the attention, care, and affection of parents; for example, younger siblings (the new baby), older siblings, and the other parent.

The emergence of the "concrete-operational" level of cognition (cf. Piaget & Inhelder, 1969) enables children to understand the existence of the family as an ordered group rather than a series of overlapping and potentially conflicting one-to-one relationships, and thus to understand their place (i.e., their status and role) within the group, as the son or daughter of mother-*and*-father, and as the brother or sister of brothers and sisters who are also sons or daughters of the *same* mother-*and*-father dyad. The personal growth that follows ideally from this new development is the ability to love in ways that are role-appropriate and, thus, to love-within-boundaries; and the appropriate forms of gendered parental love toward children involves a positive but playful (i.e., "virtual") acceptance and affirmation—within the bounds of family order (the "incest taboo")—of the real growth needs expressed in the child's flirtatious, seductive, suggestively erotic behaviors.

Later, in the lives of therapists, having learned from these experiences will make it possible for them to offer patients an emotionally warm, open, and responsive yet safe relationship, in which the sublimated (virtual) erotic attraction can unfold within role-appropriate boundaries.

Pupil/Apprenticeship

Learning one's place in the family is the step forward in self-realization that allows one to interact with others in the wider community (e.g., school classes, peer groups, religious congregations, voluntary interest groups) as a responsible representative of one's family (of its social status and honor). This in turn widens the scope for idealizing attachments to new role models, personal mentors, and cultural heroes who can become sources of character-shaping identity formation as well as valuable instrumental and social skills. The idolization of such "master teachers" by their young devotees—whether real persons in their lives or just iconic posters pinned to their bedroom walls—must be recognized as a mode of love relationship (especially as it will have an important function as an element of "romantic" love attachments later in life). Youthful devotees seek and obtain a self-congruent sense of bigness and potency by experiencing themselves (through identification) as one with their idols. Socially and culturally (and usually before puberty), they grow from being the boys and girls of their families to become young men and young women in their communities. On the other hand, the charismatic idols or "masters" (and peer leaders who emerge as first among equals in their juvenile peer groups) who are prized and venerated by disciples receive a precious gift of validation for their own personal growth and importance as responsible sources of generativity (Erikson, 1959a).

Both sides of this idealization-love contribute to the therapist's interpersonal resources: as idealizers, a capacity to perceive the ideal growth potential within the distressed and in some ways personally limited patients who come to them; and, as figures who are frequently idealized by clients, self-validation of themselves as generative persons, together with a sense of humility based on the difference between what they see themselves taken to be by others and what they well know themselves to be as limited, imperfect human beings.

Adolescence. The preadolescent begins to recognize that other persons are also unique and distinctive selves, each an "I" capable (like oneself) of reflective thought about who and what sort of person they are and aspire to be. This self-realization in turn creates the groundwork for a new phase of intimacy between pairs of peer-group friends who are now able to view each other essentially as "alter-egos." When further developed, this capacity blossoms into a special type of love attachment between comrades called *philia* by the Greeks (e.g., Aristotle). Distinguished from ordinary social friendships, this relationship between best friends involves a constant sharing of confidences, personal secrets, and true feelings about every event in their lives; and these confidential exchanges create a new form of self-confidence for each partner. While other, earlier forms of love attachment tend to be retired or subsumed in later stages of personal growth, these best friendships often become lifelong attachments of the kind that can be easily resumed even after lengthy separations.

Later, in the lives of therapists specifically, the interpersonal skills acquired through experiences of philia-love with best friends enables therapists to approach their clients as existential fellow-travelers (Yalom, 2002) in search of healing, wholeness, and meaningfulness in their lives.

Youth and Adulthood

Since Erikson's (1959a, 1959b) groundbreaking work, the idea that personal growth continues across the entire lifespan has become widely accepted. With respect to development through interdependence in close relationships, these include phases in which the dominant forms of closeness involve romantic love (e.g., De Rougemont, 1983; Paz, 1995), marital love (e.g., Coontz, 2005), and parental love (e.g., Benedek, 1959; Bowlby, 1969). The first two of these are explicitly sexual, although in different ways: first, as defining the behavioral content and emotional intensity of romantic attachments; second, as providing a basis and emotional sustenance for marital partnerships.

Due to the central role of adult sexuality in both, those forms of love are normatively proscribed or taboo as emotional resources for psychotherapeutic work, and their intrusion into therapy is seen as disruptive and widely condemned (e.g., Gabbard & Lester, 2003; Pope & Bouhoutsis, 1986). Thus, unlike earlier phases of growth-through-love attachments in psychotherapists' lives, these adult love relationships and the needs they seek to satisfy are most constructive for therapeutic work when they are well satisfied in the therapist's private life, and there is a clearly bounded separation between therapists' personal and professional lives.

The empathy and rapport of therapeutic relationship often creates a climate of intimacy between patient and therapist that may evoke an erotic transference in the patient that can potentially elicit a similar countertransference in the therapist. If the therapist's own personal life has not provided sufficiently for the growth-needs seeking fulfillment in romantic love or conjugal love, the therapist may be tempted to respond in kind to the patient's transference, rather than using the countertransference more correctly as an essential "receiver" in therapy of "unconscious to unconscious communications" from the client (Freud, 1912/1958). This emotional vulnerability is amplified to the extent that the therapist's personal growth was left incomplete or conflict-bound during preadult phases of development, without being successfully resolved in the therapist's own therapy. By contrast, the therapist's sense of meaningful involvement and emotional satisfaction through love relationships in private life is a source of stability and self-renewal that enables therapists to safely offer a personal attachment within the professional framework of the therapeutic relationship.

Parenthood. The last stage of development in love attachments that is relevant for understanding the emotional nuances of therapeutic work is the years-long process through which parental love is recurrently evoked, challenged, and evolves as one's children grow from infancy to adolescence. Ideally, the developmental process in parental love constructively complements each of the alternating phases of love and self-realization through which children grow—although every parent knows, at some level, that they fall short of this ideal in practice. What is unique to parental love is the fact that, if it is true to itself, it must preserve its essential character as love even during the child's self-realization or individuation phases that often involve resistant, oppositional, or competitive efforts to be separate. In other words, a parent must learn how to love in response, not only to the different modes of love expressed and sought by the child, but also to actions and expressions by the child that appear to be *against* love (Tillich, 1954). Moreover, the parent needs to learn how to love in ways that foster and support the child's growth toward emotional independence, toward the time in young adulthood when the child will be setting out to establish his/her own life—a life in which, in modern societies, the parent is likely to have a relatively peripheral role.

Clearly, it is also essential for psychotherapists to withstand opposition from their clients, and stimulate their autonomy, as the clients become more and more able to live meaningful and satisfying lives independently of the therapist's support and guidance.

Summary

Success in psychotherapy is consistently predicted by and reflects the development of a strong, positive therapist-client relationship. Effective therapists are able to find ways to create and sustain a positive therapeutic bond with a broad range of clients, many of whom experience difficulties or limitations in forming and managing close interpersonal relationships. The ability of therapists to engage varied clients in a *personally* close yet *professionally* bounded relationship defines the nature of therapeutic talent—a talent that has roots in the therapist's own personal growth from childhood onward. Experience in each successive type of love adds another dimension to the therapist's expanding capacity for close relationships, and each successive era of individuation constructs new boundaries of self-experience that enable therapists to engage closely with clients in a disciplined professional context. The motivations and capacities that therapists have to apply their personal talents professionally, and the resources to help renew that motivation and capacity, are topics to be explored in the next sections.

II. WHAT IT TAKES TO BE A THERAPIST

Helene A. Nissen-Lie

For much of the century since Freud's initial work, clinical theory and psychotherapy research have focused predominantly on therapeutic techniques and procedures as the effective agents of change, whereas the therapeutic relationship and the influence of the therapist as a *person* were long neglected as primary change mechanisms. Many proponents of such different theoretical orientations as psychodynamic and cognitive-behavioral therapy still hold that if psychotherapists are properly trained, they should be *interchangeable* in performing the same therapeutic task with a client in a treatment process which would take the same course independently of *who* the therapist is.

That idea is rooted in the "medical model" of psychotherapy, which assumes that psychological treatment methods are analogous to drugs that exert their effects on the client regardless of the administrator. Such a basically technical or procedural view of therapy not only fails to account for the inherently personal nature of the therapeutic relationship, but also ignores the fact that patients' responses to drugs often are individually quite varied, and is inconsistent with findings from six decades of psychotherapy research that indicates that clients' experiences of the therapeutic relationship, and the respective interpersonal capacities of the client and therapist, are among the strongest predictors of outcome in psychotherapy (Del Re, Flückiger, Horvath, Symonds, & Wampold, 2012; Orlinsky, Rønnestad, & Willutzki, 2004).

To the extent that the therapists' ability to provide the best of their interpersonal skills and sensitivity, and offer a healing relationship to the clients, are vital influences in renewing and repairing the client's growth, we may ask what it takes psychologically as a person to be a therapist. The question has two aspects: What kind of natural skills or *talent* must a person have to be a psychotherapist, and what kind of *motivation* must a person have to practice psychotherapy?

Therapeutic Talent: Relational Skills and Reflectivity

The kind of skills that constitute therapeutic talent, which candidates for professional training ideally should already have and bring with them to the training institutes and programs that accept them, are both interpersonal and intrapersonal. The main *interpersonal* skills include empathy, genuineness or authentic presence, and expressive tact; the main intrapersonal skills may be described as *reflectivity*.

In Freud's view (1910/1957), *Einfühlung* (empathy) was not an active technique but a nonjudgmental, tactful attitude in the analyst, which served as an important basis for the clients' preconscious positive transferences, which enabled them to benefit from the analyst's interpretations. Rogers (1957) was probably the first to place "accurate empathy" in the center of therapeutic interventions, and to empirically demonstrate its positive therapeutic effect. Empathy was also considered to be a curative factor in its own right by Heinz Kohut (e.g., 1984), the founder of psychoanalytic Self-Psychology. Kohut defined empathy as "vicarious introspection," or "more simply as one person's (attempt to) experience the inner life of another while simultaneously retaining the stance of an objective observer" (Kohut, 1984, p. 175). Empathy is such a powerful therapeutic tool because it can help reduce the clients' emotional isolation and their fear of or shame toward their own feelings; it fosters the attachment between client and therapist, and can validate and provide meaning to the client's experiences.

Much empirical research over the years has demonstrated that therapists' empathic abilities contribute significantly to a beneficial therapeutic alliance and to positive psychotherapy results (Bohart, Elliot, Greenberg, & Watson, 2002). Typically, empathy is seen as having an *affective* base (the process of *feeling* like someone else, which is seen as an immediate and involuntary process) and a *cognitive* base (taking someone else's perspective and understanding someone using voluntary cognitive control). Affective empathy may have a clear biological foundation in the functioning of "mirror neurons" (e.g., Decety, 2002; Decety & Jackson, 2004; Preston & de Waal, 2002). It appears to be universal, and to play a major role in learning processes as well as in the development of stable attachment patterns between people.

By contrast, cognitive empathy is a skill that probably requires training to be refined in those who already possess a fundamental (affective) empathic capacity. Understanding someone "as if" one was the other person requires an advanced capacity for *mentalization* (e.g., Bateman & Fonagy, 2012), and represents a very challenging task for most people, including psychotherapists. To listen and gather information from another person *in his own right* in the therapeutic encounter is an art of interpersonal skill that few people are able to practice without special training and experience (Nerdrum & Rønnestad, 2002; Rønnestad & Skovholt, 2013). It requires the ability to avoid getting caught up in the immediate emotional responses or associations that are evoked in meeting the client's experiences, to *de-center* and reflect on how it is experienced by clients—given their unique history, life circumstances, personality, coping style, and defensive strategies.

The therapist's ability to be genuinely *present* or personally respond to others nondefensively, affectively, and cognitively complements empathy as a basic aspect of therapeutic talent. Therapists must be able to bear witness to traumatic suffering and intensely expressed emotions of clients, whether positive or negative, without withdrawing self-protectively or minimizing the impact by hastening to "interpret" or "reconstrue" the experience; or, on the other hand, becoming overwhelmed and incapable of responding. This requires a sense of comfort and safety in direct face-to-face contact with other persons, as well as honesty, courage, and compassion.

Related to this is the concept of emotional "containment" advanced by Wilfred Bion (1962), which was transferred to therapy from observations of early mother-child communication. In optimal circumstances, the parent contains a child's difficult emotions by withstanding them and providing meaning to them at a time when children are unable to do so themselves. This "containing function" is vital for the development of emotional maturity and may also be seen reflected in the attitude of therapists toward their clients. By using their own emotional reactions to contain the undifferentiated and often disturbing emotions projected by the client, therapists help increase the client's own ability to tolerate and integrate emotions.

The final basic interpersonal skill worthy of comment is a capacity for lucid, timely, and tactful *expression*; that is, generally having an understanding of what to say, how to say it, and when to say it, especially in situations where strong feelings are involved. It includes as well a willingness to accept others as they are rather than as one might wish they would be, yet also to perceive what they might become if they grow further, and help as appropriate to allow or promote that development. These interpersonal skills or talents reflect social intelligence that is partially rooted in inborn temperament and developed during childhood through socialization in primary relationships with parents, siblings, other family members and caregivers, as well teachers, peers, and companions.

The *intrapersonal* skills that persons who would work as professional psychotherapists need include the ability to be self-aware, self-accepting, and open-minded; a capacity to reflect on their own feelings and motives nondefensively, and consideration of the meaning that others have for them and that they have for others. It includes a capacity to hold beliefs confidently but nondogmatically, to question their beliefs with respect to experience, and to recognize the particularity and limitations of their own experience with respect to the experience of others. This implies a willingness to entertain the possibility of being wrong, to recognize and correct errors as they occur, and to feel and express appreciation for gaining deeper understanding, and includes a capacity for self-compassion as well as compassion for others. Many theoretical constructs have been advanced to describe this quality of self-relatedness (e.g., psychological-mindedness, mentalization capacity) but, however conceptualized, it is clearly a personal quality that psychotherapists ideally already possess substantially when entering professional training—talents to be further refined and developed through training and practice.

Wanting to Help: Personal Roots of Therapeutic Motivation

Without a strong desire to help other persons, the skills and qualities constituting therapeutic talent would benefit only those persons who have it and those others who may be directly involved with them in private life. To have their talent serve more broadly, therapists need the motivation to refine it through professional training and apply through careers in psychotherapy or counseling; and, like the capacities and skills constituting therapeutic talent, these motivations have roots in personal development through childhood.

Many authors have studied and discussed the various motives that have inspired people to enter psychotherapy practice, and suggest that some motives are more functional and healthy; others are more "infantile" and rooted in the therapists' own unresolved issues. All therapists probably have both functional (adult) and infantile motivations that led them to choose their career. Examples of functional or healthy motives that are frequently mentioned in the literature are a deep interest in other people or the human condition; a sense of compassion or desire to help people in distress; intellectual curiosity; the search for meaning and love of truth (e.g., Kottler, 2010; Norcross & Farber, 2005). When people (including therapists) have been the beneficiaries of love, care, and empathy from parents, teachers, and others as they grew up, they tend naturally to develop an expectation of similar behaviors from new persons, which Freud (1912/1958) described as the preconscious positive transference that, for example, predisposes patients to trust and hope in their therapists. Similarly, help received from others while growing up naturally predisposes people (including therapists) to develop a general sense of *gratitude* (Simmel, 1964), which Aristotle (in his book *Nicomachean Ethics*; see Aristotle, 1999) described as *goodwill* or the inclination toward *philia*—the intimate rapport and sense of care that, in the context of their professional relationships, therapists consciously experience as the *therapeutic bond*.

On the other hand, the infantile and potentially dysfunctional motives of psychotherapists are often unconscious and may remain unconscious for the larger part of the therapist's career. For some, they may only become conscious looking back over a long career. For others, these motives remain hidden but may still fuel and influence their daily therapeutic work, and may, if unresolved, become harmful to the therapy process and to their own development as therapists. Data accumulated in a large international study of therapists suggest that a substantial proportion of therapists in 12 countries (ranging from 25% to 45%) report having experienced moderate to very serious trauma or abuse during childhood (Orlinsky, Rønnestad, Schröder, Schofield, & Jacobsen, 2014). It seems plausible to suppose that therapists who grow up as children in emotionally demanding or disturbed families often develop a sensitivity that can be a great asset for them in grasping their clients' emotional states, needs, and defense or coping strategies, and to appreciate the pain and insecurity associated with disclosing such experiences. Indeed, they may well be strongly motivated to become therapists by a determination to correct and prevent such experiences happening to others. The concept of the "wounded healer" (e.g., Guy, 1987; Rice, 2011) is a reminder that therapists who have suffered certain emotional problems may be more sensitive and compassionate toward their clients, and more able to emotionally identify and put themselves in their clients' position.

Yet, such emotionally challenging experiences may also lock the therapist into certain ways of thinking that will not benefit the client. Growing up in an emotionally dysfunctional family may tend to evoke unconscious feelings of inadequacy and anger in therapists toward themselves and their parents that can develop into guilt and anxiety rooted in the child's feeling of having *caused* the difficulties or suffering in the family of origin. To complicate matters, this feeling of guilt combined with a positive experience of being needed as "negotiator" and helper in the dysfunctional family can lead a person into the field psychotherapy. Authors such as Alice Miller (1981), who draw on the thoughts of Melanie Klein (e.g., Klein & Riviere, 1964), suggest that by "repairing" the client, therapists also engage in symbolical reparation for themselves. Another source of unconscious motivation not uncommon among therapists is "rescue fantasies" rooted in unresolved oedipal feelings (Freud, 1910/1957)—which, if "acted out" as a countertransference response to the client's "transference-love" (Freud, 1914/1958), may lead to serious boundary violations in therapy (e.g., Kächele, 2012; Pope & Bouhoutsis, 1986; Yalom, 1989). Even when mutually felt, this kind of love most often has destructive consequences for both the client and the therapist.

These processes can develop in a positive direction if a successful experience in personal therapy for therapists lessens their need to be reconciled with their own background and troubled self through their work with clients in therapy. However, such unconscious motives can also increase in intensity and take the form of a "compulsion to help" that for its satisfaction needs a constant source of relatively helpless and dependent clients. Practicing psychotherapists need to continually improve their ability to separate their own needs from those of the client, providing themselves what they need and providing their clients what the clients need. In order for "wounded healers" to be effective therapists, their own emotional pain would need to be acknowledged, reflected on, and resolved in personal therapy (e.g., Geller, Norcross, & Orlinsky, 2005; Rønnestad & Skovholt, 2003, 2012). To initiate a process by which it is possible to separate one's own needs from that of others seems to be one of the most essential and wise reasons to enter personal therapy for practicing or training therapists.

Personal Therapy: Self-Repair and Self-Renewal

Personal psychotherapy is clearly the prime vehicle that psychotherapists rely on to discover and resolve the problematic and potentially countertherapeutic residues of their own development. Empirical research reported by Norcross and Guy (2005) and Orlinsky, Norcross, Rønnestad, and Wiseman (2005) has established that therapists of all theoretical persuasions seek personal therapy. For example, in their study of nearly 5,000 therapists worldwide, Orlinsky, Rønnestad, Willutzki, Wiseman, and Botermans (2005) found overall that 84% of those surveyed had undertaken at least one course of personal therapy, and that approximately half had engaged in more than one. There were some variations according to therapists' theoretical orientation, country, and career level; e.g., almost 90% of psychodynamic therapists had personal therapy as compared with 58% of CBT therapists. Moreover, most therapists in 14 countries regarded their personal therapy as a strong positive influence on their professional development as therapist (Orlinsky, Rønnestad et al., 2005).

In a synthesis of more than 25 years of research, Norcross (2005) summarized the benefits of the therapists' personal therapy as including a better understanding of the perspective of clients, the opportunity to experience and assess the impact of clinical methods, improved self-insight, improved emotional and mental functioning, and the potential reduction of stress related to the work as a therapist. Having direct experience of being at the receiving end of a therapeutic intervention teaches therapists that therapy is a demanding process, that personal change takes time and effort, makes them aware of the vital importance of the therapeutic relationship and the (surprisingly strong) impact of subtle, nonverbal signals from the therapist.

Studies have shown that therapists through personal therapy acquire an increased awareness of the significance of showing warmth and empathy and the significance of the therapist-client relationship, as well as the need to develop therapeutic tolerance and patience in the work, which in turn benefit their patients (Norcross, Dryden, & DeMichele, 1992). Therapists may also become more *humble* in the face of the complexities of therapeutic work as a result of experiencing how it feels to be a client. Recent studies by Nissen-Lie, Monsen, and Rønnestad (2010) and Nissen-Lie, Monsen, Ulleberg, and Rønnestad (2013) in Norway suggest that a modest and humble attitude on the part of therapists allows them to admit their self-doubts and shortcomings, which facilitates the development of the alliance and client growth.

Early in the history of modern therapies, Freud (1910/1957) grew aware that even "approximately normal" therapists have blind spots, and provided a strong rationale for therapists to seek personal therapy. Those blind spots represent areas of therapist functioning that prevents them from clearly seeing clients' conflicts and other problematic aspects of client experience due to similar issues of their own that have remained untreated, and his experience led him to state that no therapist "can reach further with a client than what his own resistance permits" (Freud, 1910/1959, pp. 144–145).

Relations Between the Private Life and Professional Work of Therapists

From a certain point of view, the widespread practice of therapists' undertaking their own personal therapy may be viewed as an act of reparative love by the profession at large toward its individual members and practitioners, and through them for the clients who come for help. Beyond this, we may ask what therapists need from their *personal lives* to sustain themselves as practitioners and to replenish their energy and zest for work with clients.

Like other human beings, psychotherapists need close, loving, and mutual relationships to find support, trust, and relief of distress (Norcross & Guy, 2007). An important principle is that psychotherapists need to find the sources of a "holding environment" for themselves outside the therapy consulting room (Guy, 2002). Through the acceptance, love, and reciprocity of friends, partners, and family members, a sense of self-worth is affirmed. Moreover, partners and children can serve to counteract any tendencies to omnipotence or grandiosity that therapists may experience through their work as benevolent providers of help to supplicant clients. Although the therapeutic relationship is one of mutuality, therapeutic work itself is unilateral in that it focuses on the problems and vulnerabilities belonging to the client, while the therapist is responsible for providing help and support and the protection of boundaries. However, therapists are human beings and we will now discuss how two related studies illustrate the *interdependence* between psychotherapists' private and personal selves.

As part of the international study of psychotherapist development previously mentioned (Orlinsky & Rønnestad, 2005), several thousand clinicians of varied professions, theoretical orientations, and career levels were asked a series of questions about the quality of their personal lives. Among these were the following: How satisfying is your own life at present? How frequently do you experience moments of unreserved enjoyment? How frequently do you experience a sense of being genuinely cared for? How frequently do you feel a satisfying sense of intimacy and emotional rapport? How frequently do you freely express your private thoughts and feelings? In a study being readied for publication, the authors found that the responses to these questions were highly correlated and could be combined into a reliable multi-item Quality of Life scale (Orlinsky & Rønnestad, 2004). The core of this scale clearly reflects the therapist's current personal experience of intimacy, love, and emotional satisfaction. Moreover, when this new variable was analyzed in relation to positive and negative aspects of therapists' current work with clients, a significant and highly positive correlation was found with the facet of therapeutic work experience called Healing Involvement ($r = .42$), and a smaller significant negative correlation was found with the facet of therapeutic work experience called Stressful Involvement ($r = -.19$). Although correlations do not allow an inference of causality, it is plausible to interpret these correlations as reflecting a reciprocal influence between therapists' personal and professional experiences. More specifically, it appears that feeling loved, cared for, and emotionally satisfied in private life may be a source of the therapist's ability to provide a positive therapeutic experience for clients, and a factor that also helps to mitigate stresses that may arise in the course of practice. Insofar as influence may flow in the opposite direction, it is possible that having a very positive experience of work as a therapist enables clinicians to participate more happily in the relationships of private life.

In a recent study, psychotherapists' responses to the Quality of Life scale described above were examined in relation to both patients' and therapists' evaluations of the working alliance over time in a study of public outpatient care in Norway (Nissen-Lie, Havik, Høglend, Monsen, & Rønnestad, 2013). The authors demonstrated that positive and negative experiences in therapists' personal lives influenced both the therapists' and clients' experiences of the working alliance, but in divergent ways depending on the rater's perspective. While the therapists' personal satisfactions were associated with their positive view of the therapeutic alliance, clients' views of the therapeutic alliance were not related to the therapists' personal well-being. By contrast, clients' views of the therapeutic alliance were inversely related to therapists' reports of experiences of stress and burden in their personal lives, even though therapists' own views of their alliance with clients were not related to feeling stressed and burdened in their private lives. Thus, we may interpret that the "glow" of therapists' personal well-being seems to enhance their own view of the alliance and make them more optimistic in evaluating their bond with clients, without actually seeming to influence their clients. Yet, on the other hand, the "shadow" of therapists' personal conflicts, losses, and disappointments seems somehow to seep into the client's experience of the relationship, possibly through the process of "unconscious-to-unconscious" communication noted by Freud (1912/1958) among others, without being consciously recognized by therapists.

While these studies represent the bare beginnings of research into the complex relationships between therapists' personal and professional lives, they serve to indicate the importance of this area for understanding the processes and impacts of psychotherapy. Given its central position in human growth (as explored in the beginning of the chapter), as well as its strong association to therapeutic outcomes (Horvath et al., 2011; Orlinsky et al., 2004), the emotional bond between therapist and client is a central common factor of successful therapy.

CONCLUSION

This chapter has presented a model of personal growth through a series of self-in-relationship experiences that alternately emphasize self (individuation) and relatedness (interdependence in love), and has sought to connect the varied types of love experienced in the course of development both to therapeutic talent and professional motivations. This chapter also reflected on how therapeutic talents are refined and how professional motivations are made most constructive through training, supervision, and personal therapy, aided by self-reflection; and noted how nurturing mutual relationships in personal life may contribute to the clinician's work with clients and self-renewal as a therapist. The concepts advanced and research described point in the same direction: The effect of psychotherapy is deeply embedded in the *person* of the therapist. Therapists need to become aware of the impact exerted by their own personal backgrounds and their interpersonal styles, their motives for entering one of the therapeutic professions, the personal satisfactions and burdens they experience in private life, their emotional well-being and self-renewal, on their therapeutic work. Experiences of love, past and present, are surely a central part of these concerns.

REFERENCES

Angyal, A. (1941). *Foundations for a science of personality*. New York, NY: Commonwealth Fund.

Aristotle (1999). *Nicomachean Ethics* (Martin Oswald, Trans.). Upper Saddle River, NJ: Prentice Hall (Library of Liberal Arts).

Bateman, A. W., & Fonagy, P. (2012). *Handbook of mentalizing in mental health practice*. Washington, DC: American Psychiatric Association.

Benedek, T. (1959). Parenthood as a developmental phase. *Journal of the American Psychoanalytic Association, 7*, 389–417.

Bion, W. (1962). *Learning from experience*. London, England: Heinemann.

Bohart, A. C., Elliott, R., Greenberg, L. S., & Watson, J. C. (2002). Empathy. In J. C. Norcross (Ed.), *Psychotherapy relationships that work*. New York, NY: Wiley.

Bowlby, J. (1969). *Attachment: Vol. I. Attachment and loss*. New York, NY: Basic Books.

Buber, M. (1965). Elements of the interhuman. In M. Friedman (Ed.), *The knowledge of man: Selected essays*. New York, NY: Harper & Row.

Coontz, S. (2005). *Marriage: A history*. New York, NY: Viking.

Decety, J. (2002). Naturaliser l'empathie [Empathy naturalized]. *L'Encéphale, 28*, 9–20.

Decety, J., & Jackson P. L. (2004). The functional architecture of human empathy. *Behavioral and Cognitive Neuroscience Reviews, 3*, 71–100.

Del Re, A. C., Flückiger, C., Horvath, A. O., Symonds, D., & Wampold, B. E. (2012). Therapist effects in the therapeutic alliance–outcome relationship: A restricted-maximum likelihood meta-analysis. *Clinical Psychology Review, 32*, 642–649.

De Rougemont, D. (1983). *Love in the western world* (Rev. ed.). Princeton, NJ: Princeton University Press.

Erikson, E. (1950). *Childhood and society*. New York, NY: Norton.

Erikson, E. (1959a). Growth and crises of the healthy personality. In *Identity and the life cycle: Selected papers by Erik H. Erikson*. *Psychological Issues, 1*(1), 50–100.

Erikson, E. (1959b). The problem of ego identity. In *Identity and the life cycle: Selected papers by Erik H. Erikson)*. *Psychological Issues, 1*(1), 101–164.

Freud, S. (1957). A special type of choice of object made by men (Contributions to the psychology of love I). In J. Strachey (Ed), *Standard edition of the complete psychological works of Sigmund Freud* (Vol. XI). London, England: Hogarth Press. (Original work published 1910)

Freud, S. (1959). Future prospects of psychoanalytic psychotherapy. In J. Strachey (Ed.), *Standard edition of the complete psychological works of Sigmund Freud* (vol. XI). London, England: Hogarth Press. (Original work published 1910)

Freud, S. (1958). The dynamics of the transference. In J. Strachey (Ed.), *Standard edition of the complete psychological works of Sigmund Freud* (Vol. XII). London, England: Hogarth Press. (Original work published 1912)

Freud, S. (1958). Recommendations to physicians practicing psychoanalysis. In J. Strachey (Ed.), *Standard edition of the complete psychological works of Sigmund Freud* (vol. XII). London, England: Hogarth Press. (Original work published 1912)

Freud, S. (1914/1958). Observations on transference-love. In J. Strachey (Ed.), *Standard edition of the complete psychological works of Sigmund Freud* (vol. XII). London, England: Hogarth Press.

Freud, S. (1917/1963). Introductory lectures on psychoanalysis, Part III: General theory of the neuroses. In J. Strachey (Ed.), *Standard edition of the complete psychological works of Sigmund Freud* (vol. XVI). London, England: Hogarth Press.

Gabbard, G. O., & Lester, E. (2003). *Boundaries and boundary violations in psychoanalysis*. Arlington, VA: American Psychiatric Publishing.

Geller, J. D., Norcross, J. C., & Orlinsky, D. E. (2005). *The psychotherapist's own psychotherapy: Patient and clinician perspectives*. New York, NY: Oxford University Press.

Guy, J. D. (1987). *The personal life of the psychotherapist: The impact of clinical practice on the therapist's intimate relationships and emotional well-being*. New York, NY: Wiley.

Guy, J. D. (2002). Self-care corner: Holding the holding environment together: Self-psychology and psychotherapist care. *Professional Psychology: Research and Practice, 31*(3), 351–352.

Horvath, A. O., Del Re, A. C., Flückiger, C., & Symonds, D. (2011). Alliance in individual psychotherapy. *Psychotherapy, 48*, 9–16.

Kächele, H. (2012). *False happiness—A misplaced fantasy of rescue*. Unpublished paper, International Psychoanalytic University of Berlin.

Kakar, S. (1981). *The inner world: A psychoanalytic study of childhood and society in India*. New Delhi, India: Oxford University Press.

Klein, M., & Riviere, J. (1964). *Love, hate and reparation*. New York, NY: Norton.

Kohut, H. (1984). *How does analysis cure?* A. Goldberg & P. E. Stepansky (Eds.). Chicago, IL: University of Chicago Press.

Kottler, J. A. (2010). *On being a therapist* (4th ed.). San Francisco, CA: Jossey-Bass.

Lewin, K. (1935). *A dynamic theory of personality*. New York, NY: McGraw.

Miller, A. (1981). *Prisoners of childhood*. New York, NY: Basic Books.

Nerdrum, P., & Rønnestad, M. H. (2002). Changes in therapists' conceptualizations and practice of training following empathy training. *Clinical Supervisor, 22*, 37–61.

Nissen-Lie, H. A., Havik, O. E., Høglend, P. A., Monsen, J. T., & Rønnestad, M. H. (2013). The contribution of the quality of therapists' personal lives to the development of the working alliance. *Journal of Counseling Psychology, 60*(4), 483–495. doi: 10.1037/a0033643.

Nissen-Lie, H. A., Monsen, J. T., & Rønnestad, M. H. (2010). Therapist predictors of early patient-rated working alliance: A multilevel approach. *Psychotherapy Research, 20*(6), 627–646.

Nissen-Lie, H. A., Monsen, J. T., Ulleberg, P., & Rønnestad, M. H. (2013). Psychotherapists' self-reports of their difficulties and interpersonal functioning in practice as predictors of patient outcome. *Psychotherapy Research, 23*(1), 86–104.

Norcross, J. C. (2005). The psychotherapists' own psychotherapy: Educating and developing psychologists. *American Psychologist*, 60(8), 840–850.

Norcross, J. C., Dryden, W., & DeMichele, J. T. (1992). British clinical psychologists and personal therapy: What's good for the goose. *Clinical Psychology Forum*, *44*, 29–33.

Norcross, J. C., & Farber, B. A. (2005). Choosing psychotherapy as a career: Beyond "I want to help people." *Journal of Clinical Psychology*, *61*, 939–943.

Norcross, J. C., & Guy, J. D. (2005). The prevalence and parameters of personal therapy in the United States. In J. Geller, J. C., Norcross, & D. E. Orlinsky (Eds.), *The psychotherapist's own psychotherapy. Patient and clinician perspectives* (pp. 165–176). New York, NY: Oxford University Press.

Norcross, J. C., & Guy, J. D. (2007). *Leaving it at the office: A guide to psychotherapist self-care*. New York, NY: Guilford Press.

Orlinsky, D. (1972). Love relationships in the life cycle: A developmental interpersonal perspective. In H. Otto (Ed.), *Love today: A new exploration*. New York, NY: Association Press.

Orlinsky, D. E., Botermans, J-F., & Rønnestad, M. H. (1998, June). *Psychotherapeutic talent is the skill that therapists have already when they start training: An empirical analysis*. Paper presented at the annual conference of Society for Psychotherapy Research annual conference, Snowbird, Utah.

Orlinsky, D. E., Norcross, J. C., & Rønnestad, M. H., & Wiseman, H. (2005). Outcomes and impacts of the psychotherapists' own psychotherapy: A research review. In J. Geller, J. C., Norcross, & D. E. Orlinsky (Eds.), *The psychotherapist's own psychotherapy. Patient and clinician perspectives* (pp. 192–200). New York, NY: Oxford University Press.

Orlinsky, D. E., & Rønnestad, M. H. (2004). *The psychotherapist's quality of life*. Unpublished manuscript.

Orlinsky, D. E., & Rønnestad, M. H. (2005). *How psychotherapists develop: A study of therapeutic work and professional growth*. Washington, DC: American Psychological Association.

Orlinsky, D. E., Rønnestad, M. H., Schröder, T. M., Schofield, M., & Jacobsen, C. H. (2013). *The experience of childhood trauma and abuse by psychotherapists: An international survey*. Manuscript in preparation.

Orlinsky, D. E., Rønnestad, M. H., & Willutzki, U. (2004). Fifty years of psychotherapy process-outcome research: Continuity and change. In M. Lambert (Ed.), *Bergin and Garfield's Handbook of Psychotherapy and Behavior Change* (5th ed., pp. 307–389). Hoboken, NJ: Wiley.

Orlinsky, D. E., Rønnestad, M. H., & Willutzki, U., Wiseman, H., & Botermans, J-F. (2005). The prevalence and parameters of personal therapy in Europe and elsewhere. In J. Geller, J. C. Norcross, & D. E. Orlinsky (Eds.), *The psychotherapist's own psychotherapy. Patient and clinician perspectives* (pp. 177–191). New York, NY: Oxford University Press.

Paz, O. (1995). *The double flame: Love and eroticism*. New York, NY: Harcourt Brace.

Piaget, J., & Inhelder, B. (1969). *The psychology of the child*. New York, NY: Basic Books.

Pope, K. S., & Bouhoutsis, J. C. (1986). *Sexual intimacy between therapists and patients*. Westport, CT: Praeger.

Preston, S. D., & de Waal, F. B. M. (2002). Empathy: Its ultimate and proximate bases. *Behavioral and Brain Sciences, 25*, 1–72.

Rice, C. A. (2011). The therapist as "wounded healer": A modern expression of an ancient tradition. In R. H. Klein, H. S. Bernard, & V. L. Schermer (Eds.), *On becoming a psychotherapist: The personal and professional journey* (pp. 165–189). New York, NY: Oxford University Press.

Rogers, C. R. (1957). The necessary and sufficient conditions of therapeutic personality change. *Journal of Consulting and Clinical Psychology, 21*, 95–103.

Rønnestad, M. H., & Skovholt, T. M. (2003). The journey of the counselor and the therapist: Research findings and perspectives on professional development. *Journal of Career Development, 3*, 5–44.

Rønnestad, M. H., & Skovholt, T. M. (2013). *The developing practitioner. Growth and stagnation of therapists and counselors*. New York, NY: Routledge.

Simmel, G. (1964). Faithfulness and gratitude. In K. Wolff (Ed.), *The Sociology of Georg Simmel* (pp. 379–395). New York, NY: Free Press.

Stern, D. N. (1985). *The interpersonal world of the infant*. New York, NY: Basic Books.

Sullivan, H. S. (1949). Psychiatry: Introduction to the study of interpersonal relations. In P. Mullahy (Ed.), *A study of interpersonal relations: New contributions to psychiatry*. New York, NY: Grove Press.

Sullivan, H. S. (1953). *The interpersonal theory of psychiatry*. New York, NY: Norton.

Tillich, P. (1954). *Love, power and justice*. New York, NY: Oxford University Press.

Werner, H. (1942). *Comparative psychology of mental development*. New York, NY: International Universities Press.

Yalom, I. D. (1989). *Love's executioner and other tales of psychotherapy*. New York, NY: HarperCollins.

Yalom, I. D. (2002). *The gift of therapy: An open letter to a new generation of therapists and their patients*. New York, NY: HarperCollins.

CHAPTER

2

Renewing One's Self-Care Sensibilities

Distress, Burnout, Vicarious Traumatization, and Self-Renewal

Jeffrey E. Barnett

Helping professionals provide valuable services to their clients in a wide range of roles and settings, frequently making a significant difference in the lives of those with whom they work. Although this work may be tremendously gratifying and rewarding, it may also be quite emotionally demanding and stressful. Despite their best intentions, helping professionals may be adversely impacted by the many challenges associated with their work, resulting in problems with professional competence (Elman & Forrest, 2007). This may result in adverse effects on their own emotional and physical well-being as well as on the ethical and competent provision of ongoing professional services.

Each of the helping professions' ethics codes acknowledges these facts and each emphasizes the need to self-monitor, to be vigilant for the development of problems with professional competence, and to take corrective actions when needed. This focus on our professional functioning is consistent with the theme of self-renewal. Because of the nature of the work we do and the many demands and challenges associated with it, to be able to function ethically and competently over time we each need to engage in an ongoing process of self-examination, self-monitoring, and self-renewal.

THE CHALLENGES OF BEING A HELPING PROFESSIONAL

Helping professionals face a number of unique challenges, both professional and personal, making our work especially demanding. Failure to be aware of and address these factors places us at increased risk for adverse consequences. Yet, awareness of and attention to these issues not only provides us with the chance to proactively address them and have the best possible chance of competent and ethical practice, it can be seen as being the beginning of our personal self-renewal process and journey.

While extremely gratifying and rewarding, work as a helping professional may be challenging, demanding, and emotionally draining at times. Factors that may contribute to these adverse effects may include the professional isolation many helping professionals experience. While this is most pronounced for those who work in independent or private practice, even professionals who work in group practices, for agencies, and even within large health-care systems may experience the pressures and effects of professional isolation. Because of the ethical and legal obligations we have regarding confidentiality, we may have only a limited ability to talk about our work with others and to vent or gripe. We carry the weight of the many secrets we keep and we often are the receptacles of very distressing information.

Helping professionals also may work with clients who have chronic and debilitating conditions who either may not improve despite our best efforts or for those who do, may experience significant relapses. Professionals working with seriously troubled individuals may have to cope with the effects of client behaviors such as suicide attempts, homicidal behavior, and other violent behavior such as being the victim of assault by a client. Each of these situations may be extremely stressful for the helping professional. The effects of having a client commit suicide are described as "emotionally devastating" (Baerger, 2001, p. 359). Studies have found that between 18% (Pope & Tabachnick, 1993) and 39% (Guy, Brown, & Poelstra, 1990) of helping professionals surveyed have been assaulted by a patient or client. Additionally, 80% acknowledged living with the ongoing fear of an assault by a patient or client occurring and 97.2% reported living with the fear of a client committing suicide (Pope & Tabachnick, 1993). Even the day-to-day pressures of feeling responsible for treatment outcomes and adverse client events can be very distressing for helping professionals.

Other challenges can include administrative requirements, such as increased paperwork and documentation requirements, being asked to do more with fewer resources due to budgetary constraints, and other bureaucratic demands. Helping professionals who work within the insurance or managed care environment may have to cope with utilization review requirements, having to appeal adverse utilization review decisions, decreased reimbursement rates, and even long delays in receiving payment for services rendered (Murphy, DeBarnado, & Shoemaker, 1998). Further, the possibility of being sued or having an ethics or licensing board complaint filed against oneself can be a significant ongoing stressor for helping professionals. To have a malpractice suit or a complaint filed against us, even if unfounded, can be especially stressful and emotionally demanding for helping professionals (Baerger, 2001).

Each helping professional also brings with him or her certain vulnerabilities that conspire to make the work we do even more stressful and demanding. Many who enter the helping professions have personal histories of family distress and dysfunction in which we played a caregiver or peacemaker role. As O'Connor (2001) describes, there is often:

> [. . .] a possible link between a history of abuse, alcoholism, or parentification in family of origin, and a desire to enter a helping profession. Such a profession allows a continuance of the caretaking role, as well as the potential for mastery of chaotic environments, more generally. In essence, the mental health professional may be drawn to the role in part because they have been well prepared for it. A traumatic childhood may allow greater identification with the client and an opportunity to repair or master old wounds. (p. 346)

Having such a history can help make an individual quite well-suited to a career as a helping professional due to a great sensitivity to, and compassion about, similar issues in their clients. But these same strengths also create vulnerabilities for the helping professional, perhaps making us more vulnerable to being retraumatized and increasing the likelihood of the resurfacing of unresolved issues from the past.

Each helping professional also experiences the many stresses, challenges, and demands of his or her personal life, each of which interact with and compound the effects of professional challenges and the effects of any reactivated personal vulnerabilities that may be present. Like all other individuals, helping professionals must deal with relationship difficulties and challenges, family illness, financial stressors, death and other losses, caring for elderly parents or for children, and the many other typical stressors associated with our personal life (Lee, Reissing, & Dobson, 2009).

While we might wish otherwise, it is impossible to keep our professional and personal lives separate (Pipes, Holstein, & Aguirre, 2005). As Stevanovic and Rupert (2009) describe, experiences in our professional and personal lives present as a "bidirectional phenomenon" (p. 67), in which the effects of these experiences move back and forth unhindered. Just as experiencing a client's suicide attempt will likely impact our mood and ability to cope with stresses at home that evening, we cannot help but be impacted in our professional roles such as through decreased focus and concentration by preoccupying worry about a loved one in critical condition in the hospital. The personal and professional aspects of our lives impact each other, and at times, this may result in decreased functioning in both domains. This reality highlights the importance of ongoing self-renewal; without it we are destined to experience increased levels of distress and as a result, problems with professional competence and problems in personal functioning.

DISTRESS

Each helping professional will experience distress to varying degrees over the course of our careers. Distress is described as the "emotional reactions of the clinician in response to ongoing challenges, stressors, or demands in one's life" (Barnett, Johnston, & Hillard, 2006, p. 257). As has been highlighted, these challenges, stressors, and demands are naturally occurring and may be experienced in both the professional and personal realms of our lives. Distress is the subjective emotional response to these ongoing stressors. Distress is a naturally occurring phenomenon, but if not attended to and managed effectively through our ongoing process of self-renewal, it can increase to the point where it begins having deleterious consequences for us, for those we serve professionally, and for those we care about personally.

While each of us will experience distress in varying amounts and intensities over the course of our careers, actively attending to its presence through self-awareness and honest self-reflection will enable us to take needed corrective actions so that the distress does not lead to decreased professional competence. When not addressed as is needed, distress can over time lead to anxiety, depression, and even suicidality (Gilroy, Carroll, & Murra, 2002). Further, helping professionals have been known to attempt to manage their distress through alcohol and other substance use (Good, Thoreson, & Shaughnessy, 1995), further compounding their difficulties.

It is important to note that many helping professionals not only acknowledge the presence of distress, but also its deleterious effects. In one large early study of helping professionals, Guy, Poelstra, and Stark (1989) found 75% of those surveyed to report experiencing distress over the previous 3 years. But, of greater significance is the fact that 36.7% of these helping professionals acknowledged the distress resulting in a decreased quality of care provided to clients and 4.6% acknowledging their distress resulting in the provision of inadequate care to clients.

In one recent study (Cooper, 2009), helping professionals were found to significantly underestimate their ongoing level of distress when their self-appraisals were compared to objective measures of ongoing distress. This finding is consistent with the work of Dunning, Johnson, Ehrlinger, and Kruger (2003) who found that as one's distress increases, the ability to accurately self-assess our level of distress decreases. This contextual view of self-assessment highlights how the presence of distress adversely impacts our ability to self-assess. Numerous studies (e.g. Barnesly et al., 2004; Davis et al., 2006; Weinstein, 1980) have found helping professionals to overestimate their abilities and to underestimate the presence and effects of distress.

These findings have clear implications for each helping professional's self-renewal process. They highlight that professional isolation and a reliance on self-assessment may have a pernicious effect on our competence and effectiveness. We must include colleagues in ongoing discussions of the stresses we face, the distress we experience, and their impact on our functioning and be open to our colleagues' assessments of our distress levels and how they may be impacting our functioning. Failure to openly and honestly engage in this process may result in distress, leading to the experience of burnout.

Burnout

Burnout is described as "the terminal phase of therapist distress" (Baker, 2003, p. 21). In many ways, it can be considered the antithesis of self-renewal. It is composed of three components that we each have experienced to varying degrees at different points during our lives and careers. These three components of burnout are: emotional exhaustion, a feeling of emotional depletion and fatigue; depersonalization, the loss of caring and empathy for others; and decreased sense of accomplishment, the loss of feelings of fulfillment and satisfaction that come from assisting others in our work (Maslach & Jackson, 1981). Freudenberger (1984) additionally described burnout as "a depletion or exhaustion of a person's mental and physical resources attributed to his or her prolonged, yet unsuccessful striving toward unrealistic expectations, internally or externally derived" (p. 223). When these challenges result in distress and this distress is not adequately addressed, burnout may occur.

While each of us has experienced symptoms of burnout to some degree at different times throughout our careers, when they are present to a significant degree for a prolonged period of time both the helping professional and those we serve professionally will suffer. As Rupert and Morgan (2005) emphasize:

> The costs of burnout among human service professionals are potentially high, involving not only the personal toll on the individual who experiences burnout but also costs to organizations from employee turnover and possible harm to clients as a result of decline in the quality of service provided by burned-out professionals. (p. 544)

Thus, prevention of burnout is of primary importance, as working to ameliorate it after its effects have already been experienced would clearly not be optimal. It is the prevention of the harm to those we serve that is at stake. Further, as has been highlighted, unchecked distress that leads to burnout can have devastating effects in the helping professional's personal life and relationships as well.

Burnout has been documented to be present to varying degrees in all helping professions. In one survey of helping professionals in the community setting, to include psychologists, social workers, and psychiatric nurses, Lasalvia et al. (2009) found that almost 20% of the respondents met the criteria for severe burnout with rates ranging from over 30% for social workers to 12% for psychologists, with many more professionals experiencing moderate and low levels of burnout. These authors found emotional exhaustion to be the component of burnout most frequently experienced. This is consistent with Rupert and Morgan's (2005) finding that helping professionals experiencing symptoms of burnout are most likely to exhibit symptoms of emotional exhaustion.

Because the development of burnout is a gradual process, it may progress without the helping professional being aware of its presence. It is especially challenging to catch because of the intermittent and low level symptoms of burnout that all individuals experience during times of stress and overwork. Every helping professional has at some time experienced feelings of frustration, a lack of patience, or lapses in interest in and focus on our clients. Each of us has at times felt exhausted at the end of an especially long or challenging day and perhaps thought to ourselves, "I just can't listen to another person's problems today."

Because of burnout's gradual development over time and the fact that we each experience its symptoms to some extent every now and then, it is easy to overlook the developing symptoms of burnout. Yet, even low to moderate symptoms of burnout may have a negative impact on the helping professional's clinical competence and therapeutic effectiveness (Skorupa & Agresti, 1993). It is therefore essential that we not minimize or overlook the presence of symptoms of burnout, but rather, reach out to colleagues and share with them what we are experiencing as part of our ongoing process of self-renewal. Failure to do so can yield undesirable results, results that could possibly have been prevented. It is through self-reflection, self-awareness, candor, and a willingness to openly share with caring colleagues that we may engage in the self-renewal process.

Being sensitive to the factors and circumstances that contribute to the development of burnout is important as well. While all the factors associated with the development of distress are still relevant, additional factors include working long hours, failure to take regularly scheduled breaks and vacations, having an especially challenging caseload such as providing treatment to very demanding or high risk clients, and experiencing high administrative demands (Rupert & Morgan, 2005). One's practice setting also impacts the risk of developing burnout. Acker (2010) found that helping professionals employed at hospitals and public agencies reported significantly higher levels of burnout than those in private practice. Issues such as perceived control over one's work environment, the ability to control one's scheduling and caseload, fewer administrative demands, and feeling fairly compensated for one's work efforts are all relevant factors that help to lower the incidence of burnout in private practitioners. But practice setting is just one factor associated with the risk of developing burnout and each of us should keep in mind that no one is immune to burnout, regardless of our practice setting or circumstances.

VICARIOUS TRAUMATIZATION

An additional challenge of great relevance to many helping professionals is that of vicarious traumatization, also known as secondary traumatic stress, compassion fatigue, or secondary traumatization (Figley, 1995). Helping professionals who provide clinical services to clients who were victims of trauma may find themselves experiencing symptoms of trauma themselves. This may occur with clients who are victims of violence, rape or sexual assault, abuse and torture, and even natural disasters. During the treatment of these clients it is common for clients to repeatedly share detailed and emotionally charged accounts of these traumatic events as well as the impact of these experiences on them. Empathic helping professionals may easily begin experiencing the emotional effects of this as though they were subject to the original trauma themselves.

This vicarious or secondary trauma can have profound effects on the helping professional. Symptoms experienced may include significant emotional arousal to include anxiety and interrupted sleep and appetite, intrusive thoughts and dreams and a pre-occupation with the client's traumatic experiences, somatic complaints, avoidance responses such as making a concerted effort to avoid thoughts or reminders of the client's trauma, and feelings of hopelessness and depression (Figley, 1995; O'Halloran & Linton, 2000). Additional symptoms often experienced are consistent with those of burnout to include emotional numbness, cynicism, and becoming emotionally distant from clients (Saakvitne, 2002). Taken together, these symptoms clearly can reduce the helping professional's clinical effectiveness and functioning and impact his or her personal life and functioning as well. One can easily see that the experience of vicarious trauma can not only hinder our ability to effectively help the traumatized client in question, but all our other clients as well.

While not all helping professionals provide clinical services to victims of trauma and abuse, those who do so must be cognizant of the risks involved. This type of clinical work should be considered high risk and only those with relevant training and high levels of clinical competence should attempt it. Pearlman and Mac Ian (1995) found that helping professionals with less than 2 years of professional experience and those with personal histories of trauma or abuse were at markedly higher risk for developing symptoms of vicarious traumatization when providing treatment to clients who are victims of trauma.

Those in training must exercise caution and be sure to have ongoing clinical supervision and oversight that includes careful monitoring of the trainee's emotional status and functioning, regularly assessing for the presence of secondary trauma symptoms, and taking active steps to try to prevent them from developing. Such active steps may include openly discussing in supervision sessions one's emotional reactions to the client's trauma, attending to relevant issues in one's personal history that may increase one's vulnerability to secondary trauma and make clinical work with a particular client more challenging, and when it is indicated, participating in personal psychotherapy to address these issues as well as any symptoms of vicarious traumatization that may be present.

Because experienced helping professionals will not likely be receiving ongoing clinical supervision, the use of colleagues for consultation, monitoring, and support is essential as elements of our self-renewal process. Just as with distress and burnout, it is essential not to overlook, ignore, or minimize developing symptoms of vicarious trauma. Even low to moderate levels of traumatization can be debilitating and result in harm to both ourselves and our clients. Establishing a self-care constellation of colleagues (Johnson, Barnett, Elman, Forrest, & Kaslow, 2012) before difficulties arise is vital for maintaining our emotional and physical health and well-being. Further, helping professionals should also consider participation in personal psychotherapy both to address factors and patterns in our histories that may make us vulnerable to experiencing vicarious trauma and to assist us to work through and resolve any symptoms of vicarious trauma that may be experienced.

Consistent with the process of self-renewal, Saakvitne (2002) recommends that helping professionals who treat victims of trauma regularly ask themselves "How am I doing?" (p. 447). This also includes being cognizant of our personal vulnerabilities and triggers for vicarious trauma based on our personal histories and actively monitoring each client's impact on us emotionally and behaviorally (Figley, 1995). Failure to adequately engage in this process on an ongoing basis will place us at increased risk for developing symptoms of vicarious trauma and experiencing its deleterious effects on our emotional functioning and on our professional competence.

PROBLEMS WITH PROFESSIONAL COMPETENCE

Professional competence is described by Epstein and Hundert (2002) as "the habitual and judicious use of communication, knowledge, technical skills, clinical reasoning, emotions, values, and reflection in daily practice for the benefit of the individual and the community served" (p. 226). Helping professionals obtain knowledge from formal course work and other educational experiences and we develop our clinical skill through supervised training experiences. Professional competence is not a singular or unitary entity; one can be competent in one area of practice and not another, one can be competent at one point in time and not at another, and one is never completely competent or incompetent. Professional competence falls along a continuum and it must actively be developed, maintained, and expanded over time. We may forget knowledge learned in the past, we may lose skills not practiced regularly, and new developments regularly advance our field, rendering previously accepted treatments obsolete (Haas & Malouf, 2005). Thus, attention to our professional competence is a dynamic process that requires our ongoing attention and effort.

Each of the helping professions' codes of ethics places an emphasis on the development and maintenance of professional competence. For example, the American Counseling Association's (ACA's) Code of Ethics (2005) states in Standard C.2.a., Boundaries of Competence, "Counselors practice only within the boundaries of their competence, based on their education, training, supervised experience, state and national professional credentials, and appropriate professional experience" (p. 9). The National Association of Social Workers' (NASW's) Code of Ethics (2008) has competence as one of the social work profession's six core values. Further, this value is explained as an overarching principle of the profession, stating "Social workers practice within their areas of competence and develop and enhance their professional expertise" (para. 23). Further details are then provided in Ethical Standards 1.04, Competence, and 1.05, Cultural Competence and Social Diversity. Similar guidance is provided in the American Nurses Association's (ANA's) Code of Ethics (2008) in Standard 5.2, Professional Growth and Maintenance of Competence, which emphasizes an active lifelong approach to learning and the maintenance of professional competence. Additionally, each of the codes of ethics includes a standard similar to the American Psychological Association's (APA's) Standard 3.04, Avoiding Harm (2010), which makes a clear connection between maintaining professional competence and its impact on those we serve.

Yet, possessing clinically relevant knowledge and skills is not sufficient for being a competent professional. It is possible for helping professionals to possess superior knowledge and skills in their area of practice, but still not be competent due to interference with clinical reasoning and emotional functioning, what Knapp and VandeCreek (2006) refer to as emotional competence.

Consider for example a helping professional who is well trained in the treatment of depression, has extensive knowledge, skill, and supervised clinical experience in treating depression, and even is a well-respected researcher of the treatment of depression. Yet, what if this helping professional has suffered a recent loss in his or her life, such as the death of a loved one following a long battle with a chronic illness? Or, perhaps, what if this helping professional has a predisposition for depression and despite the absence of any significant losses has been struggling with periods of depression recently? What if, despite all this professional's extensive knowledge and skills relevant to the treatment of depression, he or she does not seek out professional assistance? Instead, the professional thinks "I can handle this myself. I treat my clients' depression every day and I know all about the treatment of depression."

Knowledge and skills are not enough. Epstein and Hundert (2002) include reflection as a component of professional competence. The need to conduct ongoing self-assessments of our professional competence is emphasized in each of the helping professions' codes of ethics such as in the ACA (2005) Code of Ethics' Standard C.2.d., Monitor Effectiveness, which states, "Counselors continually monitor their effectiveness as professionals and take steps to improve when necessary. Counselors in private practice take reasonable steps to seek peer supervision as needed to evaluate their efficacy as counselors" (p. 9).

Failure to honestly and nondefensively engage in self-reflection places the helping professional at great risk for problems with professional competence. Further, this failure to engage in a legitimate self-reflection process can lead to impairment of two other elements of professional competence emphasized by Epstein and Hundert (2002), emotions and reasoning. As is illustrated in the above example, the helping professional's emotional status and functioning are essential aspects of professional competence. Failure to adequately attend to and address our emotional functioning can easily lead to a reduction in professional competence even for those with outstanding clinical knowledge and skills. It can also be seen how a debilitating emotional state can lead to impairment of reasoning, resulting in the helping professional continuing to provide clinical services when an objective analysis would likely indicate the need to seek professional assistance and even to limit or restrict one's clinical practice.

An expanded view of the professional competence components of knowledge and skill is essential for helping professionals to ensure that they are providing the highest quality of services possible, while also working to avoid harm to those we serve. Beyond the knowledge and skills needed in the clinical realms in which we provide professional services, we must each have knowledge of the importance of self-reflection, how our personal histories may render us vulnerable to distress in certain situations and with certain types of clients, what our warning signs of burnout are and how burnout may impact our clinical effectiveness, how vicarious trauma may impact our emotional functioning and lead to problems with professional competence, and how we must actively engage in an ongoing process of self-renewal, never minimizing, avoiding, or denying the reality of these issues, but proactively addressing each of these risks for problems with professional competence. We must possess and actively implement skill in the self-reflection process, honestly and accurately assessing our self-care needs, and in the utilization of colleagues to promote our own wellness and competence. Without competence in the self-reflection and self-renewal processes we may not consider ourselves to possess true professional competence and what professional competence we do possess may be tenuous at best.

THE ETHICAL MANDATE TO MONITOR AND PROMOTE OUR WELLNESS

Each of the helping professions' codes of ethics make a clear connection between self-reflection, awareness of and attention to our emotional competence and ongoing self-care, and the maintenance of the professional competence needed to provide clinical services effectively. Each of these codes of ethics places emphasis on maintaining an awareness of emotional and physical factors that may impact our professional competence. The codes of ethics of the helping professions are clear in emphasizing that stresses, challenges, and conflicts in our personal lives may adversely impact our professional functioning. We are further guided to consult with colleagues to help determine what actions should be taken in response to these situations, such as limiting our scope of practice, seeking ongoing clinical supervision, and receiving treatment to address the challenges we are experiencing.

Each of the helping professions makes it an ethical requirement to be alert to signs of impaired functioning that can negatively impact our professional competence. Helping professionals are required to attend to their own wellness on an ongoing basis and to be alert to signs of difficulties in our colleagues. While minimal standards for addressing these issues are mandated in the helping professions' codes of ethics, it is hoped that each helping professional will endeavor to address them as thoughtfully and comprehensively as is possible, for their own sake and for the welfare of their clients and patients.

SELF-CARE AND WELL FUNCTIONING

Self-care is the practice of those actions and habits that help to maintain our emotional, physical, relational, and spiritual wellness, and what Coster and Schwebel (1997) call well functioning. Self-care activities should be seen as integral to the process of self-renewal, a process whose ultimate goal is our ongoing well functioning. For, without positive and preventive activities, we are at risk of burnout, vicarious traumatization, and problems with professional competence developing. It is vital that helping professionals do not see self-care as an optional activity, but as essential for maintaining our professional competence. As Baker (2003) highlights, "Responsibly taking care of ourselves, as well as our patients, may be the most important thing we do, not just for ourselves, but ultimately for our clients, and for our own families" (p. 10).

Yet, unfortunately, not all helping professionals are trained to integrate a focus on self-care into their day-to-day lives. As Sapienza shared, "I have never learned how to care and how to nourish myself, for I had been trained to believe that this would be selfish or that there is no time for this when there is so much else to handle" (as cited in Baker, 2003, p. 39). Unfortunately, helping professionals with this belief are at greater risk for the negative consequences described above. Recent studies have supported the notion that training programs may not be emphasizing the importance of self-care to their students and that a focus on self-care may not adequately be integrated into the professional identities of those entering the helping professions. Roach and Young (2007) found that 52% of graduate students preparing to enter the counseling field reported that their training programs did not offer any wellness-related programs or activities. Similarly, Munsey (2006) found that over 64% of psychology graduate students reported that their training programs did not offer any self-care related activities and that 59.3% reported that their training program did not actively promote self-care.

Yet, we must not minimize the importance of ongoing self-care but should see it as an ethical obligation for helping to ensure our competent professional functioning as well as our own emotional, physical, relational, and spiritual wellness (each of which is relevant to maintaining professional competence). An essential aspect of self-care is balance, both within our professional roles and between our professional and personal lives. Balance is essential for preventing the development of burnout, especially its emotional exhaustion component (Rupert, Stevanovic, & Hunley, 2009).

Balance within our professional roles may include working to ensure a balance between professional activities (e.g., treatment, assessment, individual clients, and groups) and workload to include the number of hours worked and types of clients treated (e.g., suicidal clients, clients with personality disorders, and violent clients). We may also consider other professional activities to promote balance in our professional roles such as providing supervision, consultation, and other professional services, teaching, conducting research, doing writing for publications relevant to our profession, and becoming active in one's professional association. These suggestions may also help to reduce professional isolation and to promote enhanced professional functioning. With regard to the number of hours we work, while we all may enjoy earning more money, there are limits to how many hours we can work before our clinical effectiveness begins to suffer. We must be honest with ourselves about this and utilize colleagues for their input and expert opinions on what workload would generally promote optimal professional functioning.

Self-care can also include attention to how many hours are worked before taking a break, providing oneself free time between appointments to relax, recover, check telephone messages, and complete needed documentation. Although one can have more billable hours per day by not scheduling any breaks, again, this practice likely will result in problems with professional competence over time. To combat professional isolation and to achieve the benefits of the input and support of colleagues, participation in peer supervision and support groups, receiving clinical supervision, participating in personal psychotherapy, and seeking out social interactions with colleagues may all be helpful.

Balance between one's professional and personal lives is an important element of self-care as well. This may include not bringing work home with us each evening, making shared emergency coverage arrangements with colleagues so that we are not on-call 24 hours each day and 7 days each week, taking time for vacations, participating in hobbies and other enjoyable leisure time activities, and taking the time to focus on the relationships in our lives, on our spiritual side, and on our physical health.

Thus, self-care can include such basic activities as getting enough rest each night, maintaining a healthy diet, exercising regularly, and maintaining a healthy lifestyle in general. It can also include activities that help us to release the stressful effects of our work to include meditation, yoga, massage, and related activities. Helping professionals also need to make the effort and take the time to focus on the important relationships in our lives and to have an enriching and meaningful life outside of our work. One study of 400 helping professionals' self-care activities found that engaging in meditation and prayer, socializing with friends, participating in relaxing activities, maintaining good relationships with one's family of origin, and maintaining a diversity of professional roles were all helpful for promoting wellness and minimizing the effects of distress and burnout (Case, 2001).

Hopefully, it is clear that active engagement in ongoing self-care is an essential aspect of each helping professional's ethical obligations. Additionally, it should be seen that self-care is essential to self-renewal. Without it, we may become stale in our clinical work, be at risk for experiencing symptoms of burnout, and develop decreased professional competence. Also relevant to our process of self-renewal are the effects of failure to engage in these positive processes on our personal lives and functioning. Further, as has been emphasized, since the professional and personal domains in our lives interact with and impact each other, the self-care activities in which we participate should fall within both of these domains.

MALADAPTIVE COPING STRATEGIES

At times we may lose our self-care focus and fall into maladaptive or self-destructive coping patterns despite our best efforts. Awareness of the presence of these patterns is a clear sign for the need to reengage in the process of self-renewal. The most common maladaptive coping strategy used across the helping professions is self-medication. This may range from the use of comfort food as a form of self-nurturing and the use of caffeine to get through long and challenging days, to the use of alcohol and other substances in response to the stresses of our work and lives. These practices are a part of a pattern that Cushway (1997) referred to as *avoidant coping*, something quite different than the proactive process of self-renewal. If left unchecked, these behaviors may lead to great harm to ourselves, to those we serve, and to those in our personal lives.

Other maladaptive coping practices may include continuing to work harder such as working through lunch, during evenings, and even weekends; failing to get adequate sleep; and having a poor diet to include relying on fast food rather than planning ahead and preparing healthy meals and snacks. When under stress and pressure at work it may seem that the only available alternative is to work harder, letting other important aspects of our lives slip away. Thus, we may spend our evenings and weekends dictating and editing reports for work, giving up exercise, time for family and friends, hobbies, and other enjoyable leisure time activities. While these choices may seem necessary, they are not sustainable in the long run and over time only compound our difficulties. These maladaptive temporary efforts at managing the stressors in our lives only serve to further degrade our functioning and, over time, result in even more negative outcomes.

Instead, we must learn to engage in effective time and stress management, to know our personal limits, and to maintain good balance within and between our professional and personal lives. Rather than compare ourselves to others and what they *appear* able to competently do, it is important to honestly reflect on our strengths, weaknesses, and personal needs. Regardless of external pressures we may feel, it is vital that we recalibrate our balance on an ongoing basis, never letting it get far off the mark. We must know and accept how many hours we can work while still maintaining our clinical effectiveness (and how many hours of sleep we need each night, how much downtime we need each day, etc.), and we must remain self-aware of our ongoing levels of distress.

SELF-AWARENESS, RISK FACTORS, AND WARNING SIGNS

An important aspect of this process is to know and be alert to our personal risk factors and warning signs. Failure to practice self-awareness on an ongoing basis can leave us at greater risk for developing symptoms of burnout and resultant problems with professional competence. Barnett, Johnston, and Hillard (2006) highlight examples of warning signs a helping professional may become aware of. These include:

> Hoping that certain clients do not show up for their sessions, daydreaming or fantasizing about being elsewhere during treatment sessions, ending sessions early, missing or canceling treatment sessions, becoming bored or losing interest in clients' difficulties and what they have to say, becoming easily irritated by clients, feeling increasingly fatigued as the workday proceeds, and prematurely terminating clients' treatment. (p. 262)

These are but a few of the many warning signs that are possible, but each of us should have an acute awareness of our possible personal warning signs. While prevention is far better, if any warning signs are present, it is important that we not ignore or minimize their presence or implications. Instead, it is essential that we take one or more of the corrective actions that have been highlighted earlier. At a minimum these should include reaching out to trusted colleagues with whom we openly and honestly share about our current stressors, challenges, and functioning. Then, with our colleagues' input, we must make important decisions about the need to seek professional assistance for ourselves, cut back on the number of hours we are working, alter the type of work we are doing, take time off from work to recover and regenerate, and even participate in ongoing peer consultation and support. If maladaptive coping strategies are being used we may need to participate in a formal colleague assistance program, and if substance abuse is present, participation in formal treatment, a self-help program such as Alcoholics Anonymous, and a diversion program run by our professional association or licensing board may be necessary.

The importance of nondefensively and honestly participating in this process of remediation and professional help cannot be overstated. This is necessary to overcome professional blind spots we may each have. It is easy to see ourselves as individuals who help others with such difficulties, but perhaps very challenging to see ourselves as in need of the very same assistance. Our professional identity as a caregiver may place us at risk for missing the above-mentioned warning signs, and the fear of embarrassment and loss of professional status can add to a tendency to avoid and minimize such difficulties. We may be so focused on our role as one who helps others that we may lose sight of the fact that we each at times need help ourselves. Each helping professional will hopefully accept that we are each vulnerable to the many challenges and demands of our profession, to the challenges and demands of our personal lives, and to our own personal histories, issues, and blind spots. These do not make us weak or defective, just human. And as humans, we must engage in a career-long process of prevention and when needed, we must respond appropriately for our own sake and for the sake of those we serve.

SELF-CARE AS SELF-RENEWAL

It is hoped that it can be seen that self-care and self-renewal are inextricably intertwined for the ethical helping professional. Failure to engage in effective ongoing self-care may, in essence, be the same as a failure to engage in self-renewal. Throughout our careers, helping professionals face a wide range of stresses, challenges, and demands. While the work we do can be infinitely rewarding, at times it can also be demanding, challenging, emotionally and physically draining and exhausting, and at times downright frustrating. In addition to the many challenges of our professional work and roles, each helping professional brings with him or her a personal history, personality, and coping style that can at times put us at greater risk for experiencing the negative effects of the work we do. We each also have our personal lives and the many challenges and demands they bring. Each of these, our professional work, our personal attributes and histories, and our personal lives all interact and impact each other.

Failure to attend to this makes the experience of distress inevitable and makes the risk of developing burnout and problems with professional competence ever more likely. It is therefore important that we each actively engage in a process of self-renewal. We must regularly engage in self-reflection and consider how well we are functioning, assessing if we are maintaining a good balance in our professional and personal lives, if we are utilizing adequate self-care strategies on an ongoing basis, and if we have slipped into reliance on maladaptive coping strategies. We may be assisted in this process through activities such as journaling and personal psychotherapy as well as by utilizing colleagues as more objective sounding boards that can provide feedback that we might otherwise tend to avoid or hide from ourselves.

The process of self-renewal must go beyond theoretical discussions with colleagues and promises to make changes tomorrow, next week, or next month. Self-renewal is a tangible process that we implement through honest introspection, hard work, and behavioral change. It is important that helping professionals remain conscious of our blind spots and use of defense mechanisms such as minimization, avoidance, and denial. Additionally, rather than project blame onto an unreasonable boss or supervisor, a particularly challenging client, an unsympathetic partner or spouse, or a recalcitrant child, helping professionals must each take personal responsibility for our self-renewal throughout the course of our careers and lives. Doing so will assist us to achieve clinical competence, professional success, and personal happiness, each of which is much more desirable than distress, burnout, and the consequences of maladaptive coping strategies.

CONTINUING YOUR SELF-CARE (SELF-RENEWAL) JOURNEY

It may seem that there is never a right time to initiate living a balanced life in which we integrate ongoing self-care on a daily basis. There are always challenges, demands, and stressors present. Perhaps a good time to initiate your own process of self-renewal will be after you complete your professional training, or after you are licensed, or after you have established your practice, or after you receive that promotion, or after your children are all in school full time, or after your children are out of college, or after you have saved for retirement, or perhaps even after you have retired. Delay in initiating this process is ill-advised. There is a right time to being in the process of self-renewal and that time is now.

It does not matter what stage of your career you are in. There is always more work to do; there are always more challenges to address and more obstacles to overcome. If we wait for when it feels right, we may not engage in this important process until it is too late. Self-renewal, like self-care, is a lifestyle. It is a set of habits that we integrate into our professional identity and into our very being, and it is not optional. Self-renewal should be seen as an essential component of what it means to be a helping professional. Failure to engage in self-renewal will leave us at risk for and vulnerable to burnout, problems with professional competence, unethical practice, and personal distress and unhappiness. So, the time for your professional and personal self-renewal process to begin is *now*.

REFERENCES

Acker, G. M. (2010). The challenges in providing services to clients with mental illness: Managed care, burnout and somatic symptoms among social workers. *Community Mental Health Journal*, 46, 591–600. doi:10.1007/s10597–009–9269–5

American Counseling Association. (2005). ACA *code of ethics*. Retrieved from http://www.counseling.org/Resources/CodeOfEthics/TP/Home/CT2.aspx

American Nurses Association. (2008). *Code of ethics for nurses*. Retrieved from http://ana.nursingworld.org/MainMenuCategories/EthicsStandards/CodeofEthicsforNurses.aspx

American Psychological Association. (2010). *Ethical principles of psychologists and code of conduct*. Retrieved from http://www.apa.org/ethics

Baerger, D. R. (2001). Risk management with the suicidal patient: Lessons from case law. *Professional Psychology: Research and Practice*, *32*, 359–366. doi:10.1037//0735–7028.32.4.359

Baker, E. K. (2003). *Caring for ourselves: A therapist's guide to personal and professional well-being*. Washington, DC: American Psychological Association.

Barnesly, L., Lyon, P. M., Ralston, S. J., Hibbert, E. J., Cunningham, I., Gordon, F. C., & Field, M. J. (2004). Clinical skills in junior medical officers: A comparison of self-reported confidence and observed confidence. *Medical Education*, *38*, 358–367.

Barnett, J. E., Johnston, L. C., & Hillard, D. (2006). Psychotherapist wellness as an ethical imperative. In L. VandeCreek & J. B. Allen (Eds.), *Innovations in clinical practice: Focus on health and wellness* (pp. 257–271). Sarasota, FL: Professional Resources Press.

Case, P. W. (2001). Spiritual coping and well-functioning among psychologists. *Journal of Psychology and Theology*, *29*, 29–41.

Cooper, N. A. (2009). *A closer look at distress, burnout, stressors, and coping in psychologists today* (Unpublished doctoral dissertation). Loyola University Maryland, Baltimore.

Coster, J. S., & Schwebel, M. (1997). Well-functioning in professional psychologists. *Professional Psychology: Research and Practice*, *28*, 5–13. doi:10.1037/0735–7028.28.1.5

Cushway, D. (1997). Stress in trainee psychotherapists. In V. P. Varma (Ed.), *Stress in psychotherapists* (pp. 11–23). New York, NY: Routledge.

Davis, D. A., Mazmanian, P. E., Fordis, M., Harrison, R. V., Thorpe, K. E., & Perrier, L. (2006). Accuracy of physician self-assessment compared with observed measures of competence: A systematic review. *Journal of the American Medical Association, 296*, 1094–2009.

Dunning, D., Johnson, K., Ehrlinger, J., & Kruger, J. (2003). Why people fail to recognize their own incompetence. *Current Directions in Psychological Science, 12*, 83–87.

Elman, N. S., & Forrest, L. (2007). From trainee impairment to professional competence problems: Seeking new terminology that facilitates effective action. *Professional Psychology: Research and Practice, 38*, 501–509. doi:10.1037/0735–7028.38.5.501

Epstein, R. M., & Hundert, E. M. (2002). Defining and assessing professional competence. *Journal of the American Medical Association, 287*, 226–235.

Figley, C. R. (1995). Systemic traumatization: Secondary traumatic stress disorder in family therapists. In R. Mikesell, D. Lusterman, & S. McDaniel (Eds.), *Integrating family therapy: Handbook of family psychology and systems theory* (pp. 571–581). Washington, DC: American Psychological Association. doi:10.1037/10172–033

Freudenberger, H. J. (1984). Impaired clinicians: Coping with burnout. In P. A. Keller & L. Ritt (Eds.), *Innovations in clinical practice: A source book* (Vol. 3, pp. 223–227). Sarasota, FL: Professional Resource Exchange.

Gilroy, P. J., Carroll, L., & Murra, J. (2002). A preliminary survey of counseling psychologists' personal experiences with depression and treatment. *Professional Psychology: Research and Practice, 33*, 402–407. doi:10.1037//0735–7028.33.4.402

Good, G. E., Thoreson, R. W., & Shaughnessy, P. (1995). Substance use, confrontation of impaired colleagues, and psychological functioning among counseling psychologists: A national survey. *Counseling Psychologist, 23*, 703–721. doi:10.1177/0011000095234010

Guy, J. D., Brown, C. K., & Poelstra, P. L. (1990). Who gets attacked? A national survey of patient violence directed at psychologists in clinical practice. *Professional Psychology: Research and Practice, 21*, 493–495.

Guy, J. D., Poelstra, P. L., & Stark, M. J. (1989). Professional distress and therapeutic effectiveness: National survey of psychologists practicing psychotherapy. *Professional Psychology: Research and Practice, 20*, 48–50.

Haas, L. J., & Malouf, J. L. (2005). *Keeping up the good work: A practitioner's guide to mental health ethics* (4th ed.). Sarasota, FL: Professional Resource Press.

Johnson, W. B., Barnett, J. E., Elman, N. S., Forrest, L., & Kaslow, N. J. (2012). The competent community: Toward a radical reformulation of professional ethics. *American Psychologist, 67*, 557–569.

Knapp, S. J., & VandeCreek, L. D. (2006). *Practical ethics for psychologists: A positive approach*. Washington, DC: American Psychological Association.

Lasalvia, A., Bonetto, C., Bertani, M., Bissoli, S., Bristofalo, D., Marrella, G., . . . Ruggeri, M. (2009). Influence of perceived organisational factors on job burnout: Survey of community mental health staff. *British Journal of Psychiatry, 195*, 537–544. doi:10.1192/bjp.bp.108.060871

Lee, C. M., Reissing, E. D., & Dobson, D. (2009). Work-life balance for early career Canadian psychologists in professional programs. *Canadian Psychology, 50*, 74–82. doi:10.1037/a0013871

Maslach, C., & Jackson, S. E. (1981). The measurement of experienced burnout. *Journal of Occupational Behaviour, 2*, 99–113.

Munsey, C. (2006, November). Questions of balance. *Gradpsych, 4*(4). Retrieved from http://www.apa.org/gradpsych/2006/11/cover_balance.aspx

Murphy, M. J., DeBernardo, C. R., & Shoemaker, W. E. (1998). Impact of managed care on independent practice and professional ethics: A survey of independent practitioners. *Professional Psychology: Research and Practice, 29*, 43–51.

National Association of Social Workers. (2008). *Code of ethics of the National Association of Social Workers*. Retrieved from http://www.naswdc.org/pubs/code/default.asp

O'Connor, M. F. (2001). On the etiology and effective management of professional distress and impairment among psychologists. *Professional Psychology: Research and Practice, 32*, 345–350.

O'Halloran, T. M., & Linton, J. M. (2000). Stress on the job: Self-care resources for counselors. *Journal of Mental Health Counseling, 22*, 354–364.

Pearlman, L. A., & Mac Ian, P. S. (1995). Vicarious traumatization: An empirical study on the effects of trauma work on trauma therapists. *Professional Psychology: Research and Practice, 26*, 558–565. doi:10.1037/0735–7028.26.6.558

Pipes, R. B., Holstein, J. E., & Aguirre, M. G. (2005). Examining the personal-professional distinction: Ethics codes and the difficulty of drawing a boundary. *American Psychologist, 60*, 325–334. doi:10.1037/0003–066X.60.4.325

Pope, K. S., & Tabachnick, B. G. (1993). Therapists' anger, hate, fear, and sexual feelings: National survey of therapist responses, client characteristics, critical events, formal complaints, and training. *Professional Psychology: Research and Practice, 24*, 142–152. doi:10.1037/0735–7028.24.2.142

Roach, L. F., & Young, M. E. (2007). Do counselor education programs promote wellness in their students? *Counselor Education and Supervision, 47*, 29–45. doi:10.1002/j.1556–6978.2007.tb00036.x

Rupert, P. A., & Morgan, D. J. (2005). Work setting and burnout among professional psychologists. *Professional Psychology: Research and Practice, 36*, 544–550. doi:10.1037/0735–7028.36.5.544

Rupert, P. A., Stevanovic, P., & Hunley, H. A. (2009). Work-family conflict and burnout among practicing psychologists. *Professional Psychology: Research and Practice, 40*, 54–61. doi:10.1037/a0012538

Saakvitne, K. M. (2002). Shared trauma—The therapist's increased vulnerability. *Psychoanalytic Dialogues, 12*, 443–449. doi:10.1080/10481881209348678

Skorupa, J., & Agresti, A. A. (1993). Ethical beliefs about burnout and continued professional practice. *Professional Psychology: Research and Practice, 24*, 281–285. doi:10.1037/0735–7028.24.3.281

Stevanovic, P., & Rupert, P. A. (2009). Work-family spillover and life satisfaction among professional psychologists. *Professional Psychology: Research and Practice, 40*, 62–68. doi:10.1037/a0012527

Weinstein, N. D. (1980). Unrealistic optimism about future life events. *Journal of Personality and Social Psychology, 39*, 806–820.

CHAPTER

3

Self-Care for Clinicians in the Disaster Context

Rick Williamson and Patricia A. Engert

April 1995: A bomb blast tore through an Oklahoma City federal building, shattering the lives of residents and shocking the entire country. This act of violence claimed the lives of 168 adults and children and injured 700. Therapists and counselors across the region responded by providing mental health support to the impacted community. A majority of these caregivers would later report experiencing greater stress in this context compared to their other work in nondisaster contexts (Myers & Wee, 2002).

August 2005: Hurricane Katrina devastated 90,000 square miles of the U.S. Gulf Coast. New Orleans' levees burst and for weeks the metropolis sat inundated with seawater. The storm resulted in more than 1,500 deaths and displaced tens of thousands of Americans. Amid the aftermath, mental health professionals across the country proved a tremendous comfort and help to survivors. Yet, experiential accounts from these professionals also conveyed the immense emotional toll of their work (Dass-Brailsford, 2008; Mitchell, Witman, & Taffaro, 2008).

January 2010: A 7.2-magnitude earthquake struck Haiti's densely populated capital city Port-au-Prince. Within minutes, more than 250,000 people lay dead or dying beneath the rubble. Another 1 million were left homeless while disease and violence would continue to claim lives in the subsequent months. This time, mental health professionals across the world deployed to Haiti to assist its affected community. My personal experience in this context would confirm the heavy emotional demand of work in the context of disaster.

As the number of human-engineered and natural catastrophes rises, more people are experiencing their impact (International Federation of Red Cross and Red Crescent Societies, 1998). As a result, clinicians are recognizing trauma's increasing relevance to their clinical work. Even in our nonprofessional lives we are bombarded with vivid, empathy-evoking media coverage of suffering and catastrophe. Consequently, more and more clinicians are responding to the call to assist survivors in disaster situations. Since 2002 in the United States alone, more than 100,000 persons have joined disaster response teams focused on health and mental health specifically (Rosser, 2008). Disaster mental health is indeed an area of growing interest in the mental health field and among trainees at the graduate level as well (Novotney, 2008). Consequently, we can expect that more clinicians will work in a disaster context at some point in their career. However, as we seek to prepare clinicians for this context, we are also discovering a great deal about the psychological impact of this work on the care professional.

Clinicians who work in the disaster context can pay a hefty price psychologically for their efforts. In addition to reports of greater stress in disaster mental health work, there is also evidence that prolonged involvement in this work results in ever-increasing stress on the clinician (Myers & Wee, 2002). Therefore, as more care professionals encounter this work, there will be a greater need for strategies of self-care and renewal among our ranks. To develop effective self-care strategies, it is helpful to first understand how the disaster context can affect clinicians.

CLINICIAN STRESS IN DISASTER—AN EXAMPLE FROM HAITI

The following case illustrates some of the stress factors associated with mental health work in the disaster context:

> In the aftermath of Haiti's 2010 earthquake, a series of training workshops and groups were conducted with Haitian field staff tasked with providing psychosocial support to the affected community. As local residents, these caregivers had themselves suffered through the disaster. Many had no previous professional training, and they described any extant supervision for their work as tenuous at best. As a result, most felt unprepared for the level of trauma they encountered in their work. A consistent theme voiced over the course of the training concerned their emotional reactions to the recounts of the severely traumatized. One caregiver tearfully conveyed her intense distress in response to a particular female survivor. The earthquake had not only traumatized this survivor, but it claimed the life of her child. Additionally, all of this

> subsequently disrupted the woman's compliance with her HIV medication regimen. The worker recounted how the child, when alive, served as the mother's motivation for compliance with her medication. Tragically, however, this woman discovered her child's crushed body beneath the quake's rubble. The mother's grief was inconsolable. The very presence of the caregiver only seemed to exacerbate this grief given that the focus of their meetings concerned her HIV treatment. The provider felt a tremendous emotional burden for this woman, but with each subsequent visit felt increasingly powerless to console her. This caregiver emphatically conveyed how all of her thoughts grew to revolve around this woman in her grief. She admitted that consequently she could often think of nothing else. "Kisa pou m fè?" [*What do I do?*], she pleaded.

When working with disaster survivors, caregivers are exposed to a variety of stressors. Beyond the stress of witnessing the devastation itself, there is also the emotional impact this work has on the caregiver. In the above case, the caregiver experienced emotional strain due to a combination of personal, work-specific, and environmental factors. For example, how she herself experienced the quake is an unknown factor that may be associated with feelings of helplessness and fear. Thus, her trauma history is relevant in this context (Tosone, Nuttman-Shwartz, & Stephens, 2012, view such experiences as "shared trauma"). In addition, the caregiver felt that she had been inadequately prepared for the nature of this work. This likely resulted in a psychological assault on her self-image as a helper/healer given her inadvertent exacerbation of the woman's grief. Thus, the degree to which the provider held her supervisors or organization responsible for sending her out ill-equipped was an additional source of her stress. However, even beyond the personal and work-specific stress factors, a subtler negative change process was also in operation. This process, termed *vicarious traumatization* (McCann & Pearlman, 1990), emerged from the caregiver's relationships with the traumatized people she served. Thus, difficulties can result from empathic engagement with survivors' trauma narratives (i.e., both on the part of the caregiver and on my part in my discussions with her). The impact of these various types of stressors and forms of traumatization exact a steady toll on clinicians in the disaster mental health context. The ultimate expression of these can be problems that take forms that may not be readily apparent to the clinician at the onset. Thus, awareness of the signs of stress and trauma is a necessary start to any self-care strategy.

ACUTE STRESS

Truly, all who experience destruction and suffering on a massive scale are impacted to some degree. Some stress symptoms that clinicians experience are intermittent and temporary (i.e., irritability or anxiety, muscle tension, difficulty falling asleep, stomach pains and appetite disturbance, heart palpitations). These reactions are commonly a result of acute stress (American Psychological Association, n.d.). In acute stress, the body's natural responses are triggered by the challenges we face. To deal with these challenges, our bodies mobilize so that we can either adapt to them, flee from them, fight against them, or freeze in the face of them (Levine, 1997). If the challenge is of sufficient magnitude, it can overwhelm our ability to manage, resulting in distress. In the above illustration, the worker's own critical incident and trauma exposure history is unknown, but she, too, had experienced the earthquake. The degree of distress produced by these types of experiences varies by person. However, the sheer devastation of this particular event affected so many persons that practically every survivor was in some manner connected to someone killed or maimed in the event. Given all of this, the caregiver likely faced adjustment to personal loss from the quake, and she perhaps experienced bereavement of relatives or friends. The stress of this experience, compounded by the other stressors she also endured, may eventually emerge as indirect trauma in the worker. One possible manifestation of this can be conflicted feelings in the caregiver that result from her own experience contrasted against the great loss experienced by others such as the bereaved woman.

Acute stress responses can also occur in disaster mental health workers deploying from outside the affected region. For example, most clinicians deploying to disaster regions know to anticipate widespread destruction and difficult environmental conditions; yet, many will still experience surprise on witnessing these scenes firsthand. The physical and psychological demands of having to quickly adjust in these environments should not be downplayed. In addition to initial shock, clinicians go on to confront many other stressors. These are likely to include long work hours, time zone adjustments, changes in diet, the need for role-flexibility in a chaotic environment, "filling in" where needed, and so on. These factors exert a physical and psychological strain on clinicians and must be managed while simultaneously doing mental health work.

Self-care strategies for persons in acute stress are numerous. However, concerning psychotherapists' self-care, Norcross and Guy (2007) emphasized having a broad arsenal of self-care strategies from which different techniques can be selected and implemented based on one's changing context as opposed to relying on a specific technique across all circumstances. Offered here are a few such approaches chosen because we believe them to be relatively easy to appropriate over to the disaster context.

There is ample evidence of the physical and emotional benefits of exercise (Stathopoulou, Powers, Berry, Smits, & Otto, 2006). A bio-behavioral view of the stress response posits that hundreds of chemical changes occur within the body as it copes with challenges and threats. Under stress, the brain releases the chemical cortisol that helps our muscles mobilize for a fight or flight response.

However, when prolonged or chronically recurring stress coincides with a chronic lack of physical exertion (exercise), cortisol accumulates and produces many of the problems we commonly associate with stress (Hays, 1995). Therefore, exercise provides an intuitive benefit to us in that it activates our muscles and processes accumulated cortisol. It follows then that increased exercise processes greater amounts of cortisol, thereby offsetting the effects of a greater amount of stress. Such exercise promotes our mood and physical stamina (Norcross & Guy, 2007). There is even new evidence that exercise may promote our mental capacity in ways we did not previously think possible. Exercise in animals has now been found to cause the release of proteins in the brain that support the growth of dendrites and synapses, increase brain plasticity, and promote the new growth of neurons in the hippocampus (Aamodt & Wang, 2008). These are the very brain structures negatively affected by prolonged stress and trauma and increased levels of cortisol. In this way, physical exercise can bring literal renewal to our brains!

In our experience, disaster workers who maintain regular self-care usually manage to creatively incorporate some form of regular physical exercise into their routines despite the lack of gym facilities in disaster regions. For those workers who are new to self-care, we recommend they purchase and travel with a jump rope. This simple piece of equipment can function as a portable gym that offers a number of exercise possibilities that can be performed within a circumscribed indoor area.

We also suggest a psychological strategy that targets the acute stress brought on by shocking sights on arriving in a disaster zone. Promoting clinicians' sense of control may be particularly helpful in the disaster context because a hallmark of most disaster zones is an elevated level of chaos. Clinicians deploying to these environments have expressed that the chaos is a particular challenge on arrival (Rosser, 2008). Clinicians may be able to avoid becoming overwhelmed with acute stress by consciously exerting control in some aspect of their task or actions. For example, during times of high stress clinicians may respond by temporarily focusing away from their emotional strain and instead channel their attention into a particular work task over which they can exercise control. Some disaster workers have intuitively developed this as a coping strategy when confronting the immediate aftermath of a disaster. However, if this coping technique is adopted, then we recommend they intentionally make the time to process the emotions that they temporarily fend off when using this technique (Pearlman, 1995). Taking regular downtime away from the stress becomes essential as the counterbalance to this technique. By respecting downtime, workers train their brains to anticipate regular breaks from the stress of work. The brain learns to anticipate these stress-free intervals during which it is better able to rest and recharge. This anticipation also facilitates the ability to process emotions with regularity and thereby avoids a buildup of unprocessed feelings.

BURNOUT

A related stress situation that clinicians must guard against is burnout. Burnout is an endpoint manifestation after accumulated stress has depleted our coping resources over time, leaving us in a state of physical, emotional, and mental exhaustion (Maslach & Goldberg, 1998). In addition to the previously mentioned stressors, burnout also includes stress from the work environment, particularly if it is unsupportive, chaotic, or seems unfair (Maslach & Leiter, 2008). Burnout is associated with the experience of long-term emotional exhaustion, a reduced sense of personal accomplishment, and cynicism or depersonalization (Maslach, Schaufeli, & Leiter, 2001). In the illustration earlier, organizational factors may have resulted in the caregiver's lack of preparedness, and therefore these factors could be a source of burnout. An important factor of resilience in the domain of our professional lives involves having a sufficient level of competence when entering into situations of adversity and challenge, which, after resolving, can result in subsequent professional growth (Caza & Milton, 2012). Yet, in disaster contexts even seasoned clinicians are surprised at their reactions to seeing suffering on a grand scale. In the illustration, most of the caregivers were acutely aware of their lack of training and preparedness for the severity of trauma they were sent to address. This lack of preparedness in combination with a myriad of other stress factors can deplete their coping reserves. If they are unable to refuel their reserves at the pace that these are depleted, then eventual burnout or vicarious trauma may result. Workers may disengage from the work and find it difficult to connect with clients. They may begin to lack specificity in their approach to clients, responding to and treating each the same as the next. Their experience of exhaustion may not be contained to their work life, but its symptoms may be noticeable by family and friends outside of the work context (Maslach & Leiter, 2008).

Burnout may occur even among highly competent clinicians in the disaster context. The combination of personal and other stressors that confront clinicians in the disaster context can also apply to highly competent master clinicians. This clinician like any other may also experience limitations imposed by their respective sending organization. Rosser (2008) found that many clinicians felt hampered in their clinical work by their sending organization. These organizations are numerous and differ regarding their designated role for clinicians. Some allow only basic supportive counseling to be offered to survivors. In these situations, clinicians with extensive expertise in trauma and disaster work may feel particularly inhibited by the organization based on their great level of clinical ability to do more. In this regard, this potential frustration is minimized if clinicians understand the limitations of their sending organization before they deploy. If burnout does occur, it may appear as a reluctance to engage with the work or as an emotional distancing from those served. It may also appear as an increase in mental stress effects such as moodiness, concentration difficulty, carelessness in a dangerous environment, and the inability to distinguish between which tasks are important and which are not (McKay, 2007). Emotional exhaustion and fatigue may become an everyday experience. Ultimately, clinician burnout is related to depletion of coping resources often associated with demanding work and workplace conditions. The inability of the clinician to get sufficient downtime away from the stressors ensures that the demands of the work will ultimately lead to emotional depletion. Given the challenges of the disaster context, clinicians are often motivated to work longer hours in the face of mass suffering and become inattentive to their own emotional needs while focused on helping the traumatized. It is therefore intuitive that burnout is an inherent occupational hazard of prolonged work in disaster contexts. The same self-care techniques and approaches that are helpful for addressing daily demands and acute stress may also apply to situations of burnout. Particularly, because burnout is a factor of the inability to restore one's emotional vitality and reserves, we emphasize the importance of regular downtime in these instances.

In some cases of burnout, the sufferer may be unable to take or make use of downtime sufficiently. However, if the person is able to take an extended time away from the work, then this may be helpful because they remove themselves from the chronic stress and depletion process. This time away affords them a chance to experience a less demanding context for an extended period of time and to recharge. If vacations and extended time off are not possible, then it can be helpful to establish a balance between time spent in the stressful aspects of the work and time spent in those aspects of the work that are engaging, different, and certainly less stress inducing. Countering burnout involves regaining balance between the demands of the work that deplete us and those aspects of work and life that refuel us.

As illustrated earlier, many of the psychological demands faced by disaster mental health workers are a function of their coping resources and the environmental challenges. These stressors and their manifestations are recognizable and thus relatively easy to delineate. However, the stress that stems from clinicians' engagement with their traumatized clients is subtler and often unrecognized among the more salient stress factors in the disaster context, and it therefore deserves clinicians' special attention.

VICARIOUS TRAUMATIZATION

Clinicians undergo significant changes as a result of working with traumatized survivors of disasters. Over time, psychological and spiritual changes impact clinicians' perceptions of themselves and the world. These changes are the result of empathically engaging with the trauma narratives of survivors. When the result of this change is positive, clinicians' connection to humanity may be deepened, their sense of meaning and purpose in clinical work may be enhanced, and they may have a greater capacity for empathy. This positive change process is referred to as *vicarious transformation* (Pearlman & Caringi, 2009) and it connotes the deeply meaningful rewards of trauma work. Alternatively, exposure to survivors' trauma material over time may also result in negative changes that can leave potentially permanent scars in the clinician. McCann and Pearlman (1990) call this negative transformation *vicarious traumatization* and it connotes the hazards of trauma work. The changes, whether positive or negative, are an inevitable reality in disaster mental health because clinicians empathically connect with survivors and listen to their traumatic experiences and are committed to helping them. Thus, if clinicians are to continue providing treatment and support to the traumatized that is effective, then they must facilitate their change in the positive direction. Saakvitne (2009) finds this to be among the most important factors for successful clinical work with traumatized persons.

However, awareness of these changes may be more difficult for clinicians to recognize because they do not result from one contact with a traumatized person, in contrast to acute stress, which is more immediate. Instead, vicarious trauma results from the cumulated effect of contact with traumatized survivors (McCann & Pearlman, 1990). In addition, while we readily perceive the physical and emotional impact of other types of stress, the hallmark of vicarious trauma is disrupted spirituality (Pearlman, 1995), which means that over time, the clinician may experience changes in their worldview (e.g., disruptions in their moral principles and ideas of causality); decreases in their capacity to maintain hope and see meaning in life; and decreases in connection to the transcendent. Additionally, the clinician may undergo changes in their view of self (e.g., disruptions in their identity as a helper, healer, mother/father). Because these changes occur over time and are manifested spiritually, the clinician may be less cognizant of this process in operation compared to other, more salient forms of stress.

Spiritual disruption is an ever-present threat for clinicians who repeatedly encounter horrendous events through their engagement with the traumatized. How then do clinicians facilitate a process of positive transformation from their clinical experiences? Again, awareness is an important part of an approach to addressing this kind of stress. The example below offers a picture of how this stress could affect clinicians. The self-care recommendations that follow from the example assume that the clinician also engages in general self-care behaviors. Therefore, all the self-care recommendations delineated above are also applicable to vicarious traumatization. The subsequent recommendations are additional strategies that specifically address the spiritual disruption that is the mark of vicarious traumatization.

Perhaps a clinician exposed to the trauma material of survivors begins to create images of these horrific events as happening to himself, or to his children or to his partner. Over time, this ongoing and disturbing imagery adds to the clinician's distress (Batson, Fultz, & Schoenrade, 1987). Furthermore, as this clinician encounters a seemingly endless stream of victims in his work, the mounting distress gives way to an egoistic motivation to shield himself from the pain of his traumatized clients. A messianic drive emerges in this clinician. He attempts to "save" victims through his increasingly driven efforts. He wants to see his clients well but circumvents delving with them into their trauma experience. His efforts fail to be therapeutic and the traumatized survivors show little improvement. Recognizing their unending pain, he begins to question life's meaningfulness. His belief in a greater benevolence in the world is shattered, and he grows disconnected from the transcendent.

Strategies for spiritual self-care presume to be applied alongside general self-care strategies. As a general rule, all self-care strategies are best when engaged preventatively prior to clinician distress. However, the strategies can certainly be applied at any point in a clinician's experience.

In the case mentioned earlier, it is important that the clinician empathically engage his clients around the range of their experiences, but in a way that does not exacerbate his own distress (i.e., creating disturbing images of his own suffering). Because this is indeed occurring, he must become willing to process his counterproductive imagery. Seeking therapy can be helpful in this regard. If therapy is not available in his context, then consultation with colleagues can be beneficial. His process of the imagery should help to decrease subsequent negative ruminations and their resultant distress. It would have been ideal if he had established and maintained a disciplined engagement in a spiritual life from the outset. In support, Follette, Polusny, and Milbeck (1994) found that clinicians reported using meditation, yoga, and prayer as spiritual coping strategies. If the clinician is nonreligious, then activities such as engaging in art and journal writing have been found to be helpful in developing an awareness of the more ephemeral aspects of experience (Pearlman, 1995). Mindfulness practices are another helpful technique used by many (Goodman & Calderon, 2012). Additionally, it may be helpful for him to create an environment that helps him to appreciate meaning in both his professional and nonwork life. For example, he should be encouraged to intentionally acknowledge and celebrate even the small triumphs in a day's work (Pearlman & Saakvitne, 1995). These acknowledgments can keep the rewards of doing this work salient and increase his capacity for appreciation and gratitude.

Perhaps this clinician experienced a disruption in his worldview whereby he became disillusioned with how the world works and should work. His broken schema may be restored by his investing time with nontraumatized individuals. Thus, reestablishing balance between his engagement with others in their pain and with others in their wellness may keep him from an overfocus on life's difficult aspects. Balance may also be restored through activities such as travel vacations. In an unpublished study, Gamble, Pearlman, Lucca, and Allen (as cited in Pearlman, 1995) found that among a sample of trauma therapists, 69% reported travel as helpful. The clinician should be encouraged to implement activities, like travel, that can provide him enriching experiences of the world and thereby re-expand his worldview.

Narrowing is one effect that vicarious trauma can have on the clinician over time. Narrowing in this case resulted in the clinician's overfocus on work to the exclusion of important other things. In this regard, the clinician's commitment as a helper to survivors was transformed into a messianic drive to save them. This subtle shift in identity resulted in more stress through his experience of therapeutic ineffectiveness and ultimately disillusionment. Possible strategies for renewal in this instance may include engaging the clinician in activities that will expand his identity beyond his professional work role. He should regularly engage in social activities that reconnect him with others. By expanding his social life, he can reassert his identity as someone's good friend, or as a parent, or as a partner, which can bring forgotten aspects of his life and humanity back into salience (Pearlman & Saakvitne, 1995). Put simply, reestablishing a balance in work and life will enable the clinician to reclaim important parts of himself, thereby nurturing himself more holistically and preventing his preoccupation with his therapist role.

In sum, self-care and renewal strategies for the disaster context tend to align with general factors of resilience. The specific approaches recommended in the examples above all presume general self-care behaviors as a prerequisite. The specificity and creative application of the recommendations above may or may not fit every clinician's context and situation, but we believe that most of them are likely to generalize across contexts as they represent approaches employed by resilient disaster workers, who by the transient nature of their occupation, find themselves in constantly changing and challenging environments. Yet, they continue to appropriate their self-care and renewal practices in new and creative ways.

CAUTIONS FOR CARE PROFESSIONALS WITH SIGNIFICANT TIES TO IMPACTED COMMUNITIES

Before concluding this topic of self-care in disaster mental health, we offer a few specific recommendations for clinicians who may find themselves deploying to an impacted region to which they have a special connection. These therapists are likely members of the affected community and may respond out of a deep commitment to it and bring a special knowledge of and proficiency with the culture and language. These clinicians may not have received the formal training in disaster mental health afforded their fellow deploying colleagues. However, their deep personal connection to the community and knowledge and understanding of its culture are invaluable to the community. We hope that none need ever confront disaster in their community. Yet, for those who will, it is our hope that they receive support in their service and that this writing offers them something helpful in this regard.

Some clinicians encounter the disaster context compelled to respond to a particular affected community to which they have a special tie. On the positive side, this tie can be a significant motivator throughout the care response. In addition, the quality of the care may be enhanced given the professional's familiarity with the community and its culture. However, these ties may also magnify the emotional impact of the disaster on the clinician. Regarding professionals who conduct disaster counseling within their own communities, Wee and Myers (2002) state that regardless of whether the individual had sustained any personal loss in the disaster, he or she was likely to be affected simply by being a part of the affected community. Hartsough and Myers (1985), in discussing the impact of disaster on community members, note that disaster is such an awesome event that it elicits strong reactions in even the residents spared any personal loss. Everyone who sees such an event is, in some sense, a victim. This caution extends to care professionals who respond to disaster in communities to which they have a personal connection.

Professionals with ties to an impacted region or group are among the first to respond in the aftermath of disaster. Consequently, they may arrive to the locale before significant restoration or cleanup efforts have begun. In such a scenario, the professional may witness mass tragedy firsthand and at its most acute. The emotional toll of this experience may be magnified if the professional strongly identifies with the suffering survivors. This identification can occur around life status (e.g., professionals with young children responding to others bereaved of their children in a mass tragedy) as well as culture.

Clinicians responding to disaster in environments in which they themselves had resided or been reared may be emotionally impacted by the physical destruction of once familiar places. The buildings, streets, and landmarks that served as monuments to their memories and personal histories may have been eradicated in the destruction. The destruction of one's community can impact self-identity and feelings of safety even if one was spared direct personal loss in the disaster (Wee & Myers, 2002). The nostalgia that arises upon recognition of familiar and significant places of one's community can evoke emotions of grief and loss when this occurs in a disaster context. This experience may be made all the more painful by the sense of isolation that can happen when the clinician works side by side with colleagues who have no history or experience in the community. In these instances, it becomes all the more important for the clinician to connect with other persons with similar connections to the environment. It may be helpful for the clinician to develop a social network of persons who are also keepers of the memories of the community. They may find it beneficial to take the time to share recollections and old stories together.

In addition, the residential accommodations provided to care professionals responding to disasters are usually rudimentary living quarters. While varying security concerns and priorities for staff care are determinants for the style of living accommodations in each situation, most all of them will be relatively luxurious compared to those of the impacted community. Clinicians deploying from abroad may experience their accommodations as basic or at best rudimentary. However, a clinician connected to the affected community and aware of the worse living conditions of people on a large scale may not be comfortable in their relatively "nicer" accommodations, resulting in dissonance or guilt, which can therefore be an added source of stress for the clinician. This guilt may be accentuated if the clinician is witness to the daily plight of his or her community due to abject conditions that can typically arise following a disaster.

Finally, clinicians must be able to process threats to their self-image and role as a caregiver and healer. Because mental health professionals generally honor these roles and qualities, clinicians can experience great dissonance and demoralization in situations where their efforts result in the exacerbation of suffering. For example, uncoordinated disaster response efforts in Haiti resulted in persons being directed away from the community's indigenous networks for care and healing toward the "free" help and programs coming in from abroad. Some of these well-intentioned efforts resulted in interventions that were culturally inappropriate for the community. They also undermined the indigenous infrastructure for care and healing by directing resources and community engagement toward temporary foreign interventions and programs. When problems such as these are eventually recognized, the emotional toll on the clinicians who participated in these institutional processes of revictimization of survivors can be quite significant (Dutton & Rubinstein, 1995).

Self-care strategies for a clinician in this context would likely involve social support. In response to distress and trauma many people may seek out others as a source of comfort (Taylor, 2012). When traumatization occurs at the community level, we may find similar reactions and mobilization attempts by the community as a whole (Wicke & Silver, 2009). As a response to trauma, community members may come together in an effort to seek and provide comfort to each other. The clinician who is a part of the community may also experience the desire to be among the community. Barring any safety concerns that would contraindicate engaging the community, we are in agreement with Norcross and Guy (2007) who encourage clinicians to "luxuriate" in relationships. Clinicians should avail themselves to the fullest and broadest, most meaningful social network they can. There is probably no other factor more germane to life satisfaction and overall happiness than the quality of one's social connectedness.

In conclusion, the disaster context presents clinicians with a number of challenges. In an effort to help clinicians who will encounter this context we have presented examples meant to raise awareness about how these challenges can manifest as problems in the clinician. We have offered strategies for clinician self-care and renewal that we hope can be applied in the most challenging contexts. This book contains many more offerings for this purpose. We recommend that you use these chapters to develop your repertoire of self-care techniques and approaches. However, old wisdom says that the best approach is ultimately the one that you actually use. So try out something new and creative from these pages. Now is the perfect time to invest in your self-care. Therefore engage life, live well, and take care of yourself.

REFERENCES

Aamodt, S., & Wang, S. (2008). *Welcome to your brain: Why you lose your car keys but never forget how to drive and other puzzles of everyday life*. New York, NY: Bloomsbury.

American Psychological Association. (n.d.). *Stress: The different kinds of stress*. Retrieved from http://www.apa.org/helpcenter/stress-kinds.aspx

Batson, C. D., Fultz, J., & Schoenrade, P. A. (1987). Distress and empathy: Two qualitatively distinct vicarious emotions with different motivational consequences. *Journal of Personality*, 55, 19–39.

Caza, B., & Milton, L. P. (2012). Resilience under adversity. In K. S. Cameron & G. M. Spreitzer (Eds.), *The Oxford handbook of positive organizational scholarship* (pp. 895–908). New York, NY: Oxford University Press.

Dass-Brailsford, P. (2008). After the storm: Recognition, recovery, and reconstruction. *Professional Psychology: Research and Practice*, 39(1), 24–30. doi:10.1037/0735-7028.39.1.24

Dutton, M. A., & Rubinstein, F. L. (1995). Working with people with PTSD: Research implications. In C. R. Figley (Ed.), *Compassion fatigue: Coping with secondary traumatic stress disorder in those who treat the traumatized* (pp. 82–100). New York, NY: Brunner/Mazel.

Follette, V. M., Polusny, M. M., & Milbeck, K. (1994). Mental health and law enforcement professionals: Trauma history, psychological symptoms, and impact of providing services to child sexual abuse survivors. *Professional Psychology: Research and Practice*, 25(3), 275–282. doi:10.1037/0735–7035–7028.25.3.275

Goodman, R. D., & Calderon, A. M. (2012). The use of mindfulness in trauma counseling. *Journal of Mental Health Counseling*, 34(3), 254–268.

Hartsough, D. M., & Myers, D. G. (1985). *Disaster work and mental health: Prevention and control of stress among workers*. Rockville, MD: National Institute of Mental Health.

Hays, K. F. (1995). Psychotherapy and exercise behavior change. *Psychotherapy Bulletin*, 30(3), 29–35.

International Federation of Red Cross and Red Crescent Societies. (1998). *World disasters report*. Oxford, England: Oxford University Press.

Levine, P. A. (1997). *Waking the tiger: Healing trauma: The innate capacity to transform overwhelming experiences*. Berkeley, CA: North Atlantic Books.

Maslach, C. & Goldberg, J. (1998). Prevention of burnout: New perspectives. *Applied & Preventative Psychology*, *7*, 63–74.

Maslach, C., & Leiter, M. P. (2008). Early predictors of job burnout and engagement. *Journal of Applied Psychology*, *93*(3), 498–512. doi:10.1037/0021–9010.93.3.498

Maslach, C., Schaufeli, W. B., & Leiter, M. P. (2001). Job burnout. *Annual Review of Psychology*, *52*(1), 397–422.

McCann, I., & Pearlman, L. A. (1990). Vicarious traumatization: A framework for understanding the psychological effects of working with victims. *Journal of Traumatic Stress*, *3*(1), 131–149. doi:10.1007/BF00975140

McKay, L. (2007). *Understanding and coping with traumatic stress* [Training Module]. Retrieved from http://headington-institute.org/Default.aspx?tabid=1783

Mitchell, M. J., Witman, M., & Taffaro, C. (2008). Reestablishing mental health services in St. Bernard Parish, Louisiana, following Hurricane Katrina. *Professional Psychology: Research and Practice*, *39*(1), 66–76. doi:10.1037/0735–7028.39.1.66

Myers, D., & Wee, D. F. (2002). Strategies for managing disaster mental health worker stress. In C. R. Figley (Ed.), *Treating compassion fatigue* (pp. 181–211). New York, NY: Brunner-Routledge.

Norcross, J. C., & Guy, J. D. (2007). *Leaving it at the office: A guide to psychotherapist self-care*. New York, NY: Guilford Press.

Novotney, A. (2008, January). Postgrad growth area: Disaster mental health. *gradPsych*, 12–14.

Pearlman, L. (1995). Self-care for trauma therapists: Ameliorating vicarious traumatization. In B. Stamm (Ed.), *Secondary traumatic stress: Self-care issues for clinicians, researchers, and educators* (pp. 51–64). Baltimore, MD: Sidran Press.

Pearlman, L. A., & Caringi, J. (2009). Living and working self-reflectively to address vicarious trauma. In C. A. Courtois & J. D. Ford (Eds.), *Treating complex traumatic stress disorders: An evidence-based guide* (pp. 202–224). New York, NY: Guilford Press.

Pearlman, L. A., & Saakvitne, K. W. (1995). *Trauma and the therapist: Countertransference and vicarious traumatization in psychotherapy with incest survivors*. New York, NY: Norton.

Rosser, B. R. (2008). Working as a psychologist in the Medical Reserve Corps: Providing emergency mental health services in Hurricanes Katrina and Rita. *Professional Psychology: Research and Practice*, *39*(1), 37–43. doi:10.1037/0735–7028.39.1.37

Saakvitne, K. W. (2009). *What clinical supervisors need to know about vicarious traumatization*. Washington, DC: American Psychological Association.

Stathopoulou, G., Powers, M. B., Berry, A. C., Smits, J. J., & Otto, M. W. (2006). Exercise interventions for mental health: A quantitative and qualitative review. *Clinical Psychology: Science and Practice*, *13*(2), 179–193. doi:10.1111/j.1468–2850.2006.00021.x

Taylor, S. E. (2012). Tend and befriend theory. In P. M. Van Lange, A. W. Kruglanski, & E. Higgins (Eds.), *Handbook of theories of social psychology* (Vol. 1, pp. 32–49). Thousand Oaks, CA: Sage.

Tosone, C., Nuttman-Shwartz, O., & Stephens, T. (2012). Shared trauma: When the professional is personal. *Clinical Social Work Journal, 40*(2), 231–239. doi:10.1007/s10615–012–0395–0

Wee, D. F., & Myers, D. (2002). Stress responses of mental health workers following disaster: The Oklahoma City bombing. In C. R. Figley (Ed.), *Treating compassion fatigue* (pp. 57–83). New York, NY: Brunner-Routledge.

Wicke, T., & Silver, R. (2009). A community responds to collective trauma: An ecological analysis of the James Byrd murder in Jasper, Texas. *American Journal of Community Psychology, 44*(3–4), 233–248. doi:10/1007/s10464–009–9262–8

CHAPTER

4

Clinical Supervision and Self-Renewal

Craig S. Cashwell and Jodi L. Bartley

The process of engaging in psychotherapy is a daunting undertaking for client and therapist alike. The client enters into a relationship with a previously unknown person and begins sharing highly personal information, often things never before disclosed. He or she enters into a process where there is agreement, either explicit or implicit, to explore the painful places in her or his life, often entering into a level of psychological intimacy that is virtually unparalleled outside of the therapy room. The client explores her or his struggles, sets goals with the therapist, takes risks both inside and outside of the therapy room, examines and begins to deconstruct core beliefs, comes into psychological contact with painful emotions and memories, and engages in between-session tasks.

Whew! Quite an undertaking. When one stops to think about it, though, therapists do all of the above *and* do this multiple times each day. Therapists respond to a range of clients with different presenting issues, cognitive styles, counseling goals, and relationship styles/strategies (some of which can be rather challenging). Additionally, there is the stress of sitting with other people who are in psychological pain, all of whom are in distress in some way, and many of whom face unsolvable problems. Each therapist also faces her or his own limitations and human struggles, many of which may be triggered or exacerbated by certain clients. For example, all therapists are confronted at some point in their development with their own sense of inadequacy when working with a particularly difficult or challenging client. As if this were not enough, many therapists also must deal with third-party reimbursement groups and the associated paperwork and challenges. It is within this context that therapists can experience vicarious trauma, compassion fatigue, and burnout.

Additionally, we must acknowledge the importance of the self of the therapist. In decades of research on counseling outcomes, researchers have focused on variation in outcome across methods. What this body of research primarily has taught us, however, is that variation in outcome across methods is smaller than outcome variation across *therapists* within a given method. That is, method accounts for less variance than does the individual therapist. It is this unit of analysis, the person of the therapist, that emerges as most salient to therapeutic outcomes for clients (Rønnestad & Skovholt, 2003). This highlights the importance of therapist development, growth, and renewal.

If the developmental process was organic, however, all therapists would evolve through a predictable series of developmental tasks and we might expect that all therapists with equivalent experience would be equally skilled. Such is clearly not the case, though. In fact, meta-analyses have found weak relationships between therapist experience and therapy outcomes (Crits-Cristoph & Mintz, 1991; Stein & Lambert, 1995). Although graduate training lays an important foundation, much of a therapist's most significant growth occurs after graduation *if* the therapist has the appropriate and necessary supervision and remains open to learning and growth (Borders & Brown, 2005). If experience, in and of itself, does not make you a better therapist, then what does? This is a complex question but there are some clear developmental themes that researchers have established that will be discussed throughout this chapter. By jointly considering these themes, supervisors can work with their supervisees to establish effective contracts for their work together. Such efforts arrest negative professional development such as incompetence, impairment, burnout, and disillusionment with the profession (Rønnestad & Skovholt, 2003), and maximize growth and renewal.

Simply stated, the "business" of doing therapy is stressful and can be depleting. Topics such as compassion fatigue (and associated decreases in empathy), vicarious trauma, and burnout are explored more fully in other chapters within this volume. For our purposes here, suffice to say that it is quite possible to give oneself away in the business of doing therapy to the point that there is nothing left for clients, family, and self.

Further, it is one of the great professional ironies that the process of doing therapy can be a lonely process. Although therapeutic relationships often have great psychological intimacy and depth, they are one-sided and lack the type of "give and take" found in intimate friendships. Additionally, many therapists work in settings where they are somewhat isolated from other counseling professionals. This may be due to a hyperfocus on billable hours (leading to a de-emphasis on nonbillable tasks such as case consultation and supervision) or the lack of proximity of other professionals. While clinical supervision is required prior to licensure, postlicensure requirements vary by state and professional discipline. Without an external mandate, many therapists discontinue supervision, an unfortunate truth as good clinical supervision is one of the best buffers against work-related stress, burnout, and compassion fatigue. Good clinical supervision is about more than buffering stress, however, as it can support ongoing growth, development, and renewal for the clinician.

Each time we enter into a new therapeutic relationship, doubtless it is our hope that the process will be one of renewal and transformation for the client. But what of the therapist? Is it possible that this work can be more than a "daily grind" of frustrations, difficult clients, and bureaucratic red tape? Mild levels of compassion fatigue and burnout are familiar to any experienced therapist. What separates the long-term successful therapist from the therapist who changes careers after only a few years or, far worse, the therapist who should change careers but does not? This likely is a complex question, but one common theme in therapist development and renewal is a commitment to lifelong learning and growth (Skovholt, 2005). There are many ways in which this occurs, but one of the most common and important is clinical supervision.

WHAT IS CLINICAL SUPERVISION?

It is likely that somewhere in your training program, you received poor clinical supervision. If you have never received any bad clinical supervision in your career, consider yourself among the lucky few who escape unscathed. Ineffectual supervision shows up in many ways, including:

- The "expert" supervisor who is far more interested in demonstrating her or his expertise than in maximizing supervisee development.
- The "hidden" supervisor who is unwilling to share knowledge with the supervisee; while there is a time and place for the supervisor to help the supervisee explore her or this thoughts on a subject, as will be discussed more fully below, one of the traits of a good supervisor is knowing when the supervisee most needs direct information that the supervisor already has.
- The "critical" supervisor who does not affirm the good skills and attributes of the supervisee to build self-efficacy, but focuses solely on deficits and inadequacies.
- The "judgmental" supervisor who tends to focus solely on the client in a highly judgmental and critical way, failing to model the important attributes of compassion, empathy, and positive regard.
- The "ivory tower" supervisor who functions as a clinical supervisor despite not having worked with clients in many years and/or the supervisor who is not perceived by the supervisee as having clinical skills.

The list above certainly is not exhaustive, as there are many factors that can negatively impact counselor development. What is clear empirically is that bad supervision is not only unhelpful, but also may be counterproductive and cause stagnation in supervisee development (Gray, Ladany, Walker, & Ancis, 2001; Ladany, Hill, Corbett, & Nutt, 1996). Supervision can be threatening under the best of circumstances. Being a good supervisee is a vulnerable process, one that can trigger one's feelings of shame and struggle with the complexities of the therapeutic process, further underscoring the importance of good clinical supervision.

What, then, is effective clinical supervision? Broadly defined, clinical supervision is characterized as a regular meeting between two therapists where one is tasked with facilitating the professional development of the other. Typically, the supervisor has more experience than the supervisee and has specific training in clinical supervision. The supervisor is focused primarily on the professional development of the supervisee, including behavioral skills, assessment conceptualization skills, therapist self-awareness, and therapist self-care. Additionally, a clinical supervisor is tasked with monitoring client care and welfare and, when necessary, serving as a professional gatekeeper. *Development* refers to the normal developmental progression from new graduate student to new professional to experienced professional. Along this developmental path, there are *many* opportunities for self-renewal.

Because there is huge variance in the process and quality of clinical supervision, it is helpful to distinguish what clinical supervision is *not*. Clinical supervision is not:

- Case management/case staffing: Clinical supervision often is confused with case management/case staffing. The primary difference is in focus. Case staffing is solely concerned about client care and supervisee development is not a consideration. Accordingly, virtually all (if not all) of the time in case staffing is spent focusing on case conceptualization and treatment strategy. In contrast, clinical supervision focuses on both the supervisee and the client (as well as the supervisor and both the supervisory and counseling working alliances), with decisions made strategically on when and where to focus the supervision sessions.
- Administrative supervision: Administrative supervision is focused solely on administrative details, such as time sheets, appropriateness and timeliness of case notes, and whether therapists are meeting their job requirements. In many instances, supervisors are tasked with both clinical and administrative supervision responsibilities, but it is important nonetheless to recognize that these are not the same thing.
- Teaching: Although the supervisor may engage, at times, in a teacher role to confer knowledge to the supervisee, supervision involves more than simply teaching and is flexible in goals and interventions (as opposed, for example, to classroom teaching, which follows a syllabus).
- Counseling/therapy: Although good supervision will examine ways in which the supervisee's personal issues are influencing the therapeutic

process, it differs from counseling. For example, the focus of supervision might be on helping the supervisee learn about managing her or his emotions in session, overidentifying with clients, therapist cognitive distortions, therapist values, or therapist beliefs about change. The primary focus, however, is on how the self of therapist is impacting the client and/or the therapeutic process. When more work on these issues is needed, the supervisor might refer the supervisee for therapy to address these issues in more depth.

- Consultation: Often, supervisors engage in a consultation process with supervisees (e.g., brainstorming client conceptualization). True consultants provide information and have no vested interest in whether their recommendations are carried out. Because of vicarious liability (i.e., the fact that supervisors can be sued for the work of their supervisees), supervisors often have more investment, authority, and responsibility over how supervisees carry out decisions that are made in supervision.

Effective supervisors are intentional in their work and pay close attention to the developmental level of their supervisee, selectively choosing roles and foci for supervision that support the growth and renewal of the supervisee. Effective supervisors recognize the need to stretch supervisees to grow within a supportive environment by mismatching the supervisory environment about one-half step beyond the supervisee's current functioning in a way that balances challenge and support (Stoltenberg, 1981). When supervisees feel competent and challenged, the resulting experience in supervision and counseling sessions might be characterized as a flow experience (Csikszentmihalyi, 1997). Insufficient challenge, however, can lead to boredom with the supervision process and therapist stagnation. Stagnation also may occur if therapists become overwhelmed by supervision that is overly challenging and insufficiently supportive. This often leads supervisees to engage in a process called *premature closure* (Skovholt & Rønnestad, 2003), characterized by defensiveness, misattribution, distortion, or unhealthy reduction of phenomena encountered in response to an inability to handle the challenges of developing as a therapist. That is, if overchallenged and undersupported, the supervisee may become emotionally dysregulated, defensive, frustrated and, subsequently, lose self-confidence and self-efficacy as a therapist. This developmental balance of challenge and support will evolve and vary over the course of the therapist's development but is always critical to self-renewal.

Similarly, attention to supervisor roles and foci characterize effective clinical supervision. Bernard (1979, 1997) developed the Discrimination Model, which has strong empirical support (Ellis & Dell, 1986). Bernard originally established three primary roles (teacher, counselor, and consultant) for the supervisor and three primary foci: process issues, conceptualization issues, and personalization issues. Lanning (1986) added a fourth focus, that of professional issues.

The expanded Discrimination Model, then, offers a 3 (role) × 4 (foci) grid, one that has many nuances and subtleties (Borders & Brown, 2005). Supervisors take on the role of teacher when they directly instruct and provide information. Supervisors function in the role of counselor when they assist the supervisee in exploring how personal issues, such as blind spots or countertransference, are impacting the supervisee's work. Supervisors function in a consultant role when they provide support by helping the supervisee explore various foci of their work with clients.

Each of these three roles can be used with the various foci of supervision. The focus of process issues involve the use of discrete behavioral skills, including timing and pace. A focus on conceptualizations skills includes client conceptualization skills and integration of theory to practice. Personalization issues involve a focus on how therapists integrate their own experiences, thoughts, and feelings to establish a therapeutic presence with clients. Professional issues, added by Lanning (1986), include issues such as legal and ethical issues that can be stressful in the day to day work of the therapist.

So, supervision can best be characterized as an *intentional* process whereby two helping professionals come together for the purpose of facilitating growth and development within the supervisee. When therapists practice in isolation, without the support of others, they are more likely to get into the proverbial "rut" in their work and may soon feel compassion fatigue, loss of empathy for others and, ultimately, stagnation and burnout. We turn our attention now to the importance of self-renewal among therapists and then to how supervision can facilitate this process.

Self-Renewal

Pondering the words *self-renewal*, what comes to mind? The denotative definition of *renew* hovers around words such as *revive*, *restore*, *replenish*, and *begin again*. The connotative definition, however, is most likely colored by one's own experience. For some, the idea of renewing oneself may take the shape of a staircase, a linear step-by-step process for optimal functioning. These individuals may be prone to create plans for exercising, eating healthfully, and obtaining enough sleep. For others, the idea of self-renewal could simply take the shape of a closed door, a gentle escape from the demands of everyday life. In a bolder form, self-renewal could stir up images of a desired vacation, perhaps a week gazing at ocean waves or shopping for souvenirs in another country.

Self-renewal may look different for different people. At its core, however, self-renewal represents bringing color back into what may feel like a gray world. The use of the color metaphor is intentional, for self-renewal is not a black or white construct. Just as people cannot be lumped into dichotomous categories of good versus bad, self-renewal cannot be pigeonholed into perfect

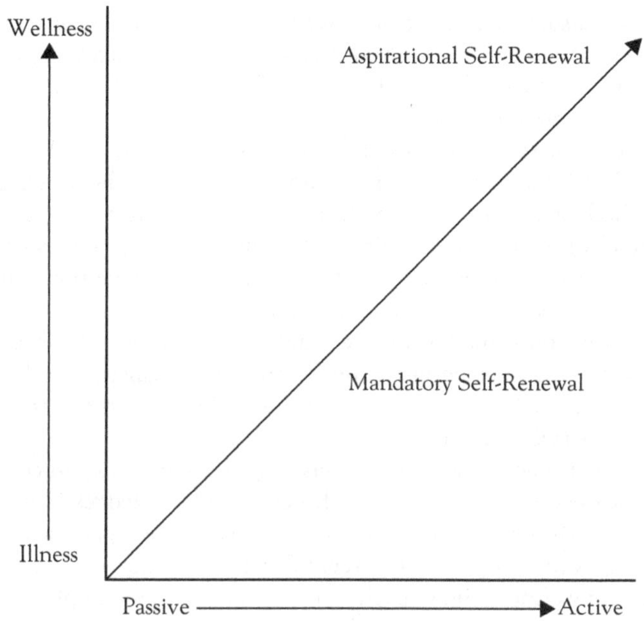

Figure 4.1 Self-Renewal Model

versus imperfect, or even right and wrong. Rather, people's relationship with self-renewal resides on a continuum of many shades. While there are many ways of conceptualizing self-renewal, we use a model that juxtaposes two continua: (1) illness to wellness and (2) passive to active. From these continua, we propose that a larger continuum emerges, from mandatory to aspirational forms of self-renewal. This model can be used to inform clinical supervisors' interventions with therapists.

FIRST CONTINUUM: ILLNESS TO WELLNESS

It is difficult to discuss the concept of self-renewal without discussing wellness. Wellness can be defined as "a way of life oriented toward optimal health and well-being in which body, mind, and spirit are integrated by the individual to live more fully within the human and natural community" (Myers, Sweeney, & Witmer, 2000, p. 252). From a holistic framework, wellness touches on many areas of a person's life, including the physical, emotional, occupational, spiritual, and social, among others. Individual wellness may vary in each of these individual facets, such that a person is well in one domain but not another. For example, a person who is "well" physically may eat nutritious foods and exercise regularly. However, he or she may be "unwell" socially in that he or she isolates and feels disconnected from others.

Complicating matters further, wellness does not automatically exist in the *absence* of illness. That is, wellness is far more than simply the absence of illness. After all, nobody is perfectly well and, in fact, attempts to be *perfect* at wellness (or anything else) likely indicate illness. This may show up in supervision when either the supervisor or supervisee (or both) attempt to have the other perceive her or him as perfect or without faults. When supervisors "act" perfect, they are setting a very poor model for their supervisees. When supervisees portray themselves as having no supervision needs, they are engaging in self-protection, but also remain closed to the growth and renewal opportunities that can occur within a safe supervisory context.

A far healthier space in which supervisors and supervisees can co-construct a supervisory process is one in which each person acknowledges their limitations and struggles, with appropriate boundaries. This creates space within supervision for struggles to be openly and freely discussed. When this occurs, the orientation toward wellness allows each to recognize those incomplete parts of self, explore them, and use them to develop greater compassion. One of therapists' greatest gifts is humanness. In his book *The Wounded Healer*, renowned priest and author Nouwen (1972) writes that our capacity for healing others is sometimes born from our own wounding. Thus, *perfect* wellness is not only unlikely, but it may even distance us from the aching parts of ourselves that allow us to experience true empathy for and with others. While it is not encouraged that counselors remain mired in their own suffering, the ability to access those tender parts may foster greater compassion and acceptance for others. Imagining that self-renewal resides on a continuum allows therapists to embrace both ends of the spectrum from wellness to illness, and furthermore, to develop greater understanding of and compassion for others in their struggle.

Second Continuum: Passive to Active

In addition to the continuum between illness and wellness, we propose that self-renewal can be pursued on a continuum ranging from passive to active. A therapist who is active in self-renewal recognizes when he or she is feeling stressed and subsequently takes active steps to course correct. If the person fails to recognize the stress (passive approach), however, he or she may become less effective with clients. Taken one step further, a supervisor or coworker may inquire about stress levels only to hear the supervisee emotionally react that they are *not* stressed. In such cases, the passive approach has elevated to an *active avoidance* approach, in which the supervisee is actively working to deny the stress.

Similar to our earlier discussion of wellness, active, passive, and active avoidant approaches to self-renewal can vary in different areas of a person's life. For example, a person may actively seek out professional trainings and attend conferences in order to maintain his or her passion for doing therapy. However, he or she may be reluctant (passive) to address issues from his or her past that are triggered when working with clients. When a supervisor asks about possible countertransference issues with a particular client, the supervisee may become defensive about this being supervision and not their own counseling (active avoidance). In many cases, this may be unconscious for the supervisee. A good supervisor will gently point out areas in which the supervisee is passive to make this more conscious and recognize that active avoidance likely is a fear response from the supervisee. Such responses from the supervisee must be addressed accordingly, that is, with attention to psychological safety and compassion, rather than an approach that says, "I am the supervisor and I say you have to do this."

CLINICAL SUPERVISION AND SELF-RENEWAL

While the process of engaging in clinical supervision may not seem like a vacation, it can be a form of self-renewal. Metaphorically, clinical supervision could be conceptualized like a fountain, perhaps the fountain of *professional* youth. Often, a therapist's professional world is steeped with ache, listening to heartbreaking stories day after day. Furthermore, counselors, by nature, are often sensitive and empathic souls. These traits allow them to sense what exists in the space between themselves and their clients—not only with regard to what's being said, but also with regard to the hidden white space of what is *not* being said. Day in and day out, they allow themselves to brush upon the depths of the human condition, all the while attempting to facilitate healing. Furthermore, with the bounds of confidentiality that therapists abide by, this whole process is often a solitary endeavor. After a while, therapists may simply feel parched. It is during these instances where clinical supervision serves as the fountain of renewal. Now we can better examine how clinical supervision aids in this process.

Skovholt (2005) delineated vital characteristics of effective therapists. This list of characteristics highlights the complexity of being a therapist and the need for a competent, wise, and caring supervisor to help navigate the evolution of these characteristics. Skovholt's list includes:

Cognitive Characteristics

- Flexibly embrace complex ambiguity
- Accumulate wisdom
- Understand the human condition
- Make learning a lifelong adventure

Emotional Characteristics
- Acceptance of self
- Genuine humility
- Self-awareness
- Willingness to grow and gain competence
- Passion for life
- Quiet strength
- Appreciation for life in the moment

Relational Characteristics
- Ability to intensively engage with others
- Keen interpersonal perception
- Being led by the well-being of the client
- Expressing compassion within limits
- Making accurate judgments
- Remaining open to learning from others

While Skovholt listed these characteristics as indicators of "expertise," we believe also that development of these characteristics indicates ongoing self-renewal and growth and accordingly, can provide a map for supervision efforts. First and foremost, a good supervisor must model these attributes for their supervisee, highlighting the importance of continued growth and development. Through the dialectic process of supervision, these characteristics can be supported and, indeed, imbued in the supervisee to promote optimum development and therapist well-being.

The establishment of these attributes is most assuredly a developmental process. That is, no student comes to graduate school possessing all of these characteristics. Good supervisors support therapist development, meeting, accepting, and encouraging the supervisee where he or she is currently functioning, while also conceptualizing the supervisee's developmental needs and working accordingly. On the supervisee's part, openness to learning is a vital aspect of self-renewal and development as a therapist (Skovholt & Jennings, 2005).

Skovholt and Rønnestad (2003) empirically established themes in therapist development. The full list of developmental themes is beyond the scope of this chapter, but themes highly salient to supervision and self-renewal are highlighted below.

Continuous Reflection Is Necessary for Optimal Growth at All Levels of Experience

Regardless of experience level, the process of continuous reflections on clients, self, the human condition, the etiology of mental health issues and suffering, and the therapeutic process are all necessary for self-renewal. Without the ongoing structure of some type of supervision (which may include less formalized arrangements such as peer supervision or group consultation), it is difficult for the therapist to engage in this type of continuous reflection and, over time, the lack of continuous reflection may result in deteriorating processes or negative development. Clinical supervision provides a structure and the space for this process of continuous reflection.

Many Beginning Practitioners Experience Anxiety in Their Work

Often, the nuanced complexities of being a therapist are overwhelming. Many students enter graduate school with a dualistic mind-set that they will be trained in *the* right way to do therapy. Once they encounter the myriad of therapeutic approaches that are available, this dualistic mind-set gives way to a multiplistic mind-set, which commonly includes confusion, anxiety, and fear of inadequacy as a therapist. Each supervisee enters into this complex developmental process with her or his own wounding and coping strategies, which often are elicited amidst this complex and sometimes ambiguous developmental process. Supervisors occasion negative development with attitudes of "this is just what therapists do, so get over it." Instead, gently validating and normalizing the anxiety and sense of being overwhelmed is important. Supervisors of less experienced therapists also must ensure that their supervision is sufficiently concrete to not simply create more ambiguity. When supervisees have extremely high levels of anxiety that do not seem to improve after gaining some clinical experience, a referral to a therapist to work specifically on the anxiety might be warranted as this can become a long-term barrier to optimal growth and renewal.

Clients Serve as a Major Source of Influence and Are Therapists' Primary Teachers

Experienced therapists, particularly those who are most effective with clients and energized by their work, recognize the above statement to be an unquestionable truth. Beginning therapists, however, often enter this work expecting to be the "expert" in the room who functions in the role of teacher. Whether born of naiveté about the therapeutic process or personal needs, beginning therapists must go through a process of deconstructing this perspective, and evolving to a place of valuing clients as our teachers. Supervisors can help by modeling both an openness to learn from their supervisee *and* helping supervisees consider what an individual client has to teach the therapist.

Interpersonal Sources Are Most Effective at Propelling Professional Development

Although therapists at all experience levels are encouraged to engage in study and ongoing continuing education, the most salient evolutions in work emerge from interpersonal interactions, with clients, peers, and supervisors. Meaningful dialogues and contact with key others inevitably serve as the "fuel" for professional development and growth. Although a clinical supervisor is but one person who may hold such interpersonal influence, he or she is a key player in the ongoing dialectic for the developing therapist.

Beginners Have Strong Affective Reactions to Professional Elders

Students, in particular, are faced with a complex dilemma in which they often feel inadequate at the complex process of becoming a therapist, and want to learn from and model after more seasoned therapists. At the same time, these "elders" serve necessary gatekeeping functions, which create a power differential, regardless of how the supervisor may work to create a co-constructed and collaborative relationship. There are multiple potential pitfalls in the supervisory process here that might impede student development. First, supervisees may be so anxious about the evaluative component of the supervisory process that they are unable to move beyond a "please the supervisor" mind-set. Such a mind-set does not support optimal growth in the supervisee. Similarly, the supervisee may idealize the supervisor and see the work that he or she does as unattainable. Many supervisors are "seduced" by this idealization and present themselves in a way to perpetuate this myth rather than humanizing themselves as therapists who make mistakes in their professional and personal lives. Other supervisees may be just as intensely engaged in scrutinizing and critically judging the supervisor. Effective supervisors must be willing to model openness and transparency in explicitly processing and working through supervisees' efforts to idealize or devalue them as professionals.

Suffering Broadens Acceptance and Appreciation of Human Variability

Supervisors and supervisees alike are prone to allow critical judgment to replace empathy and compassion for others. Some supervisors become overly enthusiastic in "figuring out" the client, often with a critical and judgmental tone. This provides a negative model for the supervisee that potentially stagnates renewal and growth. Similarly, supervisees may present clients in overly critical and judgmental terms, at times wholly devoid of compassion for their situation or struggles. We believe this is most often due to experiential avoidance in an attempt to avoid the natural suffering that is part of the human condition. At times, the supervisor and supervisee may even implicitly and unconsciously collude in working together to "conceptualize" the client, but do so in a manner that is highly critical of the client. In such cases, the supervisor and supervisee may actually be saying, "I struggle in my life, but one way to avoid this is to project this on to others and to judge them for their struggles." Effective supervisors recognize their own struggles and suffering and accept this as part of the human condition. In so doing, they can model this for supervisees and, perhaps, support supervisees in a greater acceptance of their own struggles and suffering, which inevitably leads to a more accepting and valuing reflection on client conditions.

Realignment From "Self as Hero" to "Client as Hero"

This theme, in particular, may serve to delineate those therapists who thrive professionally and personally and those who experience compassion fatigue and burnout. In our experience, virtually all students have a "self as hero" orientation at the outset of their studies. This may be motivated by the helpful desire to help others or an unhealthy motivation that the therapist has to prove her or his self-worth by helping others. In either case, though, the "self as hero" model leaves the therapist thinking that he or she is most important person in the room and may create an unnecessary and potentially harmful hierarchy in the therapy room. It also leaves the therapist in the unhealthy place of feeling "responsible for" clients, a poorly boundaried position. Recognizing the hero's journey in the client's story, however, leaves a therapist feeling "responsible to" rather than "responsible for"; that is, the therapist who recognizes the client as the hero in the room prizes the client, holds great compassion and empathy for her or him, and comes beside the client in a small portion of her or his journey. Rather than constantly depleting the self through an often unboundaried generosity in an effort be the "hero" in the room, the therapist is energized and heartened by the amazing resilience shown by the client, who often has survived many difficult circumstances.

Taken together, these examples illustrate the challenges inherent in fully describing the continual structure of self-renewal. In essence, there is no perfect, clear definition of self-renewal. It becomes even more complicated when describing *how* clinical supervision nurtures self-renewal. Before launching into the ways in which this can be accomplished, though, it is advantageous to discuss *why* it is important.

Referring back to the model, we infuse the smaller continua of self-renewal (i.e., illness to wellness and passive to active) into an overarching continuum ranging from mandatory development to aspirational self-renewal in order to describe how clinical supervision may nurture growth. Basically, as a counselor more actively attends to wellness, he or she will move closer to aspirational self-renewal. Clinical supervisors would then be wise to intervene in ways that promote optimal growth (i.e., encourage a person to attend more conferences and trainings, try new methods of psychotherapy). On the other hand, if a therapist is "ill" in any area of his or her life and either passively accepts or actively avoids this aspect of the personal life, clinical supervisors would be wise to intervene on a mandatory level to safeguard clients' well-being. In this situation, the clinical supervisor may encourage the counselor to enter into personal counseling, refrain from seeing a particular type of client who is too triggering to their personal situation until this can be worked through or, in extreme cases where there is client harm, discontinue seeing clients.

MANDATORY DEVELOPMENT

Mandatory development is necessitated when a therapist is ill or unwell and is not taking active measures to correct this, which then endangers the welfare of clients. To differentiate clinical supervisors' interventions on the mandatory development versus aspirational self-renewal continuum depends on how *clients* are affected by counselors. When clients' well-being is jeopardized, it is *mandatory* that clinical supervision aid in promoting therapist development. If clients are not being harmed, clinical supervision focuses on an *aspirational* level. Mandatory development is perhaps most common with less experienced supervisees but may be necessary with supervisees at any experience level. To better illustrate how this occurs developmentally, we discuss mandatory self-renewal as it exists for all counselors, and then distinguish forms of mandatory self-renewal specifically for those who are novices and for those who are more experienced.

All Counselors

There are three primary instances where it becomes mandatory for all counselors to engage in supervision to promote self-renewal, specifically when they (1) lack awareness, (2) need support, and (3) are suffering from professional competence problems. With each instance, clinical supervisors' interventions are crucial.

Self-Awareness

From the beginning of their careers, therapists are encouraged to know themselves. Faced with a myriad of issues from a variety of clients, it is highly likely that counselors will be emotionally triggered at some point. For example, imagine that a female therapist's unhealthy marriage is affecting her health, and yet, because of her strong religious beliefs about the sanctity of marriage, she refuses to consider divorce. Concurrently, this therapist is counseling a married couple who are contemplating divorce. Without the awareness of the effects of her marriage on her health and of her own strong religious beliefs about marriage, the counselor may unduly influence the couple toward a certain decision. Referring to the Self-Renewal Model, the counselor in this instance is unwell on the illness-wellness continuum in that her health is declining due to her marriage. Additionally, she is passive (or perhaps even avoidant) on the passive-active continuum in that she is not actively dealing with the state of her marriage, her declining health, and her religious beliefs.

It is for this reason that clinical supervision is crucial; it alerts counselors to their blind spots. When highly emotional situations brush up against therapists' unresolved issues, it is difficult for them to remain objective. Clinical supervision aids in helping therapists identify those intrapersonal barriers of clinical effectiveness and take steps to remove them. In this situation, a clinical supervisor may recommend mandatory forms of development, such as engaging in personal therapy, visiting her doctor for a physical, or reflecting on the effects that her religious beliefs may have on her practice.

Support

In addition to raising awareness of their blind spots, all counselors need support from time to time. As mentioned earlier, the nature of the counseling career is to listen to and digest some of the most heartbreaking stories of the human condition. Furthermore, after each clinical hour, therapists are expected to compartmentalize the emotions that are triggered by their clients and proceed as if life is normal. Taken at its most absurd, a counselor can literally go from sitting with a client grieving over her child's death to buying eggs at the supermarket in the short space of an hour. It is no wonder that therapists suffer from such issues as vicarious trauma (Jordan, 2010), job-related stress (Eunha, 2007; Sterner, 2009), isolation (McMahon & Patton, 2000), and burnout (Lloyd, King, & Chenoweth, 2002). Clinical supervisors can intervene in such situations in order to provide support in the form of actively listening to the supervisees' struggles and validating and normalizing these experiences.

To expand on this and incorporate the Self-Renewal Model, imagine that a male therapist is counseling veterans who recently returned from war. Day in and day out, the therapist listens to and attempts to process veterans' traumatic stories of loss. Bound by confidentiality, he holds these stories close to his chest and thinks about them even when away from his office. The counselor then begins to notice that he has trouble falling asleep at night, his appetite has decreased, and he experiences little interest in hobbies that previously interested him. This therapist may be suffering from vicarious trauma and need support from a clinical supervisor in order to process the veterans' stories.

Using the Self-Renewal Model, the therapist is slowly becoming unwell on the illness-wellness continuum (as evidenced by the effects these traumatic stories are having on his everyday life). In this situation, it is difficult to determine where the counselor resides on the passive-active continuum. If he is passively allowing the traumatic stories to affect his everyday life without seeking support in clinical supervision or if he is actively avoiding his experiences related to hearing these difficult emotion saturated stories, mandatory interventions to promote self-renewal become more crucial. In this case, a clinical supervisor may attempt to promote self-renewal by offering his or her support and normalizing the therapist's reactions to such traumatic stories. If support proves unsuccessful in correcting the issue, the clinical supervisor may suggest that the therapist seek his own personal counseling, modify his practice so that he is seeing clients other than veterans, or even take a leave of absence. It is assumed that taking these steps toward self-renewal will better protect clients' well-being.

Professional Competence Problems

It is probably safe to assume that all counselors lack self-awareness and need support from time to time. When a therapist suffers from professional competence problems, though, the situation has become more severe. Problems of professional competence (historically deemed "impairment") can be defined as:

> An interference in professional functioning that is reflected in one or more of the following ways: (a) an inability and/or unwillingness to acquire and integrate professional standards into one's repertoire of professional behavior, (b) an inability to acquire professional skills in order to reach an acceptable level of competency, and (c) an inability to control personal stress, psychological dysfunction, and/or excessive emotional reactions that interfere with professional functioning. (Lamb et al., 1987, p. 598)

In essence, then, problems of professional competence involve harm to clients. To illustrate this further and incorporate aspects of the Self-Renewal Model discussed earlier, imagine that a female therapist has just lost a loved one and is coping with this by abusing alcohol and denying the severity of her abuse. In this example, she is suffering from an illness (addiction) and actively avoiding it (denying the issue). Within the Self-Renewal Model, the therapist resides on the illness end of the illness-wellness continuum and on the extreme passive end of the passive-active continuum. This requires mandatory intervention on the part of the clinical supervisor to protect clients and promote the welfare of all involved parties. The supervisor must help the therapist develop awareness of the problem and how it is affecting her practice. At its most severe, the supervisor may require the counselor to take a leave of absence and attend personal counseling, or if refused, the clinical supervisor has a duty to report this to the appropriate ethics board (depending on one's area of practice). All of these interventions seek to promote development at the mandatory level by addressing the counselor's problems of professional competence.

As discussed thus far, clinical supervision can support mandatory development for all counselors by promoting greater self-awareness, providing support, and addressing problems of professional competence. However, some forms of mandatory self-renewal tend to be more specific to the experience level of counselors.

Novice Counselors and Skill Development

Described earlier, the task of a beginning counselor is to develop his or her counseling skills. Interestingly, this can be linked to mandatory forms of self-renewal. Often, students are admitted to graduate training programs based on their intellectual acumen in academic classes. This skill set does not always translate well, however, to the interpersonal nuances and complexities of being a therapist. For example, such students, when faced with academic challenges in the past, have responded to these challenges by working harder. In some cases, though, the student therapist is already working too hard and is, in essence, getting in the way of the therapy process. "Working harder" is actually the opposite of what needs to transpire for development and growth. Accordingly, Skovholt and Rønnestad (2003) found seven major stressors for novice therapists that impact their development:

- Acute performance anxiety
- Scrutiny of professional gatekeepers
- Porous or rigid emotional boundaries
- Fragile and incomplete practitioner-self
- Inadequate conceptual maps
- Glamorized expectations
- Acute need for positive mentors

From this, it is not difficult to see the importance of good clinical supervision for the novice therapist. Any of these seven stressors can impede development and renewal if not addressed and it often is the clinical supervisor who supports the student in exploring these stressors in a nonthreatening manner. Particularly given that novice therapists are acutely aware of the gatekeeping function of supervisors, supervisors must adopt a developmental orientation to supervision that emphasizes and builds on strengths and normalizes the developmental nature of becoming an effective therapist.

At the same time, there is a time and place for the gatekeeping function to be made explicit. Consider, for example, a student in his first semester of counseling internship at a community mental health center. His skills at reflecting feelings, paraphrasing, summarizing, and questioning are strong; however, he has trouble confronting clients when needed. Furthermore, he becomes nervous in supervision when considering the possibility of confronting clients. Over time, this anxiety leads to feelings of ineffectiveness as a therapist, which leads to uncertainty about his decision to enter this career field. Passively accepting this anxiety and uncertainty, the novice counselor starts calling in sick and leaving his clients without a therapist. Using the Self-Renewal Model, the counselor's anxiety and uncertainty place him on the unwell side of the illness-wellness continuum, and without actively confronting (no pun intended) his fear of confrontation, he remains on the passive side of the passive-active continuum.

In this situation, it is mandatory that the counselor's clinical supervisor intervene to promote development. Without doing so, the therapist may become so anxious about his effectiveness as a counselor that he abandons his clients. To prevent this, the clinical supervisor may act as a teacher and model and role-play the skill of effective confrontation. Furthermore, it likely is important for the clinical supervisor to examine the therapist's anxiety around confrontation, focusing on how this hinders the therapeutic process. Each of these strategies is aimed to intervene with the therapist in order to safeguard clients' well-being. Once the counselor becomes comfortable and proficient with all of the basic skills, the role of the clinical supervisor may be to *enhance* these skills in order to develop even greater self-confidence and effectiveness as a therapist.

Experienced Counselors and Stagnation

Skill development may not be an issue that experienced counselors face. It is presumed that by the time therapists are experienced, they are comfortable with and confident in their skills. However, professional stagnation is an issue that experienced counselors may face. Working in isolation without someone to brainstorm ideas with, counselors can become "stuck in their ways" (McMahon & Patton, 2000, p. 347). Without exploring new counseling theories and interventions, therapists suffering from stagnation may apply the "cookie-cutter" method to all clients rather than developing individualized treatment plans for each. Clients could be harmed by participating in treatment interventions that do not coincide with their specific needs. This concept of stagnation overlaps with the discussion on burnout described earlier.

Referring to the Self-Renewal Model, a counselor suffering from stagnation is presumably occupationally unwell on the illness-wellness continuum. Without actively seeking ways to invigorate her or his passion for counseling, he or she remains on the passive side of the passive-active continuum. It then becomes mandatory that clinical supervisors step in and promote self-renewal in order to protect clients' welfare. In this case, supervisors may encourage the counselor to reinvigorate his or her passion by attending professional conferences and trainings, taking a leave of absence, or even reexamining his or her commitment to the profession. Engaging in one or all of these may prevent professional stagnation and safeguard clients' well-being.

To summarize, this section discusses mandatory interventions that clinical supervisors can use in order to promote therapist development. Development is mandatory for all counselors when they lack self-awareness, need further support, or suffer from problems of professional competence. Novice therapists may need to pursue focused development when poor clinical skills impair their ability to be effective counselors. Therapists who are more experienced may need to focus on self-renewal in order to ward against professional stagnation. In all of these situations, clinical supervisors serve as guides in helping counselors embrace forms of self-renewal.

ASPIRATIONAL SELF-RENEWAL

Aspirational self-renewal, in contrast, is oriented toward therapists' optimal development. Maslow's (1998) hierarchy of needs has application here. A developing therapist who has developed a clear conceptual map (theory) of change and a solid integration of the foundational skills is like the person whose basic physiological and safety needs are met. This person now becomes aware of higher level needs, including the longing toward occupational self-actualization as a master therapist.

Such higher level needs can never be met in isolation. Each of us as a therapist can recount important others, including supervisors, peers, clients, students, our own therapists, and others who have greatly impacted our evolution as a therapist. Clinical supervisors, in particular, can use a road map of master therapists to support optimal development among supervisees.

Skovholt, Jennings, and Mullenbach (2003) discussed paradoxical characteristics of master therapists, that is, areas where there is inevitably a dynamic tension in the therapist's life. One way that supervisors facilitate aspirational self-renewal is by working with supervisees to "hold" this dynamic tension consciously. For example, Skovholt et al. (2003) found that master therapists hold the following paradoxes:

- Drive to mastery *and* sense of never having fully arrived.
- Ability to enter another's world *and* often prefers solitude.
- Can create a safe environment *and* can create a challenging environment.
- Skilled at therapy *and* humble about self.
- Personal/professional integration *and* clear boundaries between the two.
- Excellent at giving of self *and* excellent at nurturing self.
- Open to feedback *and* not destabilized by feedback.

Many therapists do not develop optimally because they are unable to balance these various paradoxes. For example, a therapist may be excellent at nurturing clients and giving of self, but lack the skills to challenge/confront clients and nurture the self. Such a therapist is unlikely to be highly effective because of an inability to confront others and care for the self, and is notably at risk for compassion fatigue and burnout.

Beyond these paradoxes, Skovholt et al. (2003) also discussed identifying characteristics of master therapists that reflect ongoing growth, development, and renewal. Although the full list of identifying characteristics is beyond the scope of this chapter, it is important to note that master therapists can be identified by a high level of self-acceptance, including an acceptance of both personal and professional limitations. Clinical supervisors can be hugely influential here, as some supervisees need help not only grasping what they *can* do, but also what they cannot do. Additionally, the experience of reverence and awe for the human condition provides a foundation for an optimum level of empathy and positive regard to be an effective therapist (Skovholt et al., 2003). Supervisors may certainly teach supervisees about this experience, but more likely teach by modeling this reverence not only for the supervisee's struggles, but also the struggles of clients.

CONCLUSION

Being a voracious learner with a commitment to lifelong learning characterizes an ever-renewing, evolving therapist. While some of this learning certainly comes from reading and attending trainings, much of this learning can only come from the dialectic inherent in the clinical supervision process. Conscious and intentional clinical supervision that balances challenge and support in the supervision process will support optimal therapist development and renewal. Supervisee openness to the supervisory process can greatly enhance their self-efficacy, effectiveness, and professional vitality.

REFERENCES

Bernard, J. M. (1979). Supervisory training: A discrimination model. *Counselor Education and Supervision*, *19*, 60–68.

Bernard, J. M. (1997). The discrimination model. In C. E. Watkins, Jr. (Ed.), *Handbook of psychotherapy supervision* (pp. 210–327). New York, NY: Wiley.

Borders, L. D., & Brown, L. L. (2005). *The new handbook of counseling supervision*. Mahwah, NJ: Erlbaum.

Crits-Christoph, P., & Mintz, J. (1991). Implications of therapist effects for the design and analysis of comparative studies of psychotherapies. *Journal of Consulting and Clinical Psychology*, *59*, 20–26.

Csikszentmihalyi, M. (1997). *Finding flow: The psychology of engagement with everyday life*. New York, NY: Basic Books.

Ellis, M. V., & Dell, D. M. (1986). Dimensionality of supervisor roles: Supervisors' perceptions of supervision. *Journal of Counseling Psychology*, *33*, 282–291.

Eunha, K. (2007). Occupational stress: A survey of psychotherapists in Korea and the United States. *International Journal of Stress Management*, *14*(1), 111–120. doi:10.1037/1072–5245.14.1.111

Gray, L. A., Ladany, N., Walker, J. A., & Ancis, J. R. (2001). Psychotherapy trainees' experience of counterproductive events in supervision. *Journal of Counseling Psychology*, *48*, 371–383.

Jordan, K. (2010). Vicarious trauma: Proposed factors that impact clinicians. *Journal of Family Psychotherapy*, *21*(4), 225–237. doi:10.1080/08975353.2010.529003

Ladany, N., Hill, C. E., Corbett, M. M., & Nutt, E. (1996). Nature, extent, and importance of what psychotherapy trainees do not disclose to their supervisors. *Journal of Counseling Psychology*, *43*, 10–24.

Lamb, D. H., Presser, N. R., Pfost, K. S., Baum, M. C., Jackson, V. R., & Jarvis, P. A. (1987). Confronting professional impairment during the internship: Identification, due process, and remediation. *Professional Psychology: Research and Practice*, *18*(6), 597–603. doi:10.1037/0735–7028.18.6.597

Lanning, W. (1986). Development of the supervisor emphasis rating form. *Counselor Education and Supervision*, *25*, 191–196, 207–209.

Lloyd, C., King, R., & Chenoweth, L. (2002). Social work, stress and burnout: A review. *Journal of Mental Health*, *11*(3), 255–266. doi:10.1080/09638230020023642

Maslow, A. H. (1998). *Toward a psychology of being* (3rd ed.). New York, NY: Wiley.

McMahon, M., & Patton, W. (2000). Conversations on clinical supervision: Benefits perceived by school counsellors. *British Journal of Guidance and Counselling*, *28*(3), 339–351. doi:10.1080/713652301

Myers, J. E., Sweeney, T. J., & Witmer, J. (2000). The wheel of wellness counseling for wellness: A holistic model for treatment planning. *Journal of Counseling and Development*, *78*(3), 251–266. doi:10.1002/j.1556–6676.2000.tb01906.x

Nouwen, H. J. M. (1972). *The wounded healer: Ministry in contemporary society*. Garden City, NY: Doubleday.

Rønnestad, M. H., & Skovholt, T. M. (2003). The journey of the counselor and therapist: Research findings and perspectives on professional development. *Journal of Career Development*, *30*, 5–44.

Skovholt, T. M. (2005). The cycle of caring: A model of expertise in the helping professions. *Journal of Mental Health Counseling*, *27*, 82–93.

Skovholt, T. M., & Jennings, L. (2005). Mastery and expertise in counseling. *Journal of Mental Health Counseling*, *27*, 13–18.

Skovholt, T. M., Jennings, L., & Mullenbach, M. (2003). Portrait of the master therapist: Developmental model of the highly functioning self. In T. M. Skovholt & L. Jennings (Eds.), *Master therapists: Exploring expertise in therapy and counseling* (pp. 125–146). Boston, MA: Allyn & Bacon.

Skovholt, T. M., & Rønnestad, M. H. (2003). The hope and promise of career life-span counselor and therapist development. *Journal of Career Development*, *30*, 1–3.

Stein, D. M., & Lambert, M. L. (1995). Graduate training in psychotherapy: Are therapy outcomes enhanced? *Journal of Consulting and Clinical Psychology*, 63, 182–196.

Sterner, W. R. (2009). Influence of the supervisory working alliance on supervisee work satisfaction and work-related stress. *Journal of Mental Health Counseling*, *31*(3), 249–263.

Stoltenberg, C. (1981). Approaching supervision from a developmental perspective: The counselor complexity model. *Journal of Counseling Psychology*, *28*, 59–65.

PART II

Alonetime, Mindfulness, the Sabbath, Natural Empathy: Loving Kindness, Zen Therapy, and Self-Renewal

CHAPTER

5

Valuing and Accessing Alonetime

*Silence, Solitude, and Reflection in the Life of the Clinician**

Robert J. Wicks

Spending time in silence and possibly solitude at the beginning and end of the day, as well as between client contacts, may seem like a luxury for many of us with busy practices, heavy teaching schedules, and involved lives. Yet, even though such realities no doubt exist, taking whatever steps necessary to incorporate and access such spaces is still a necessity for both quality clinical work and, for that matter, a rich personal life. If we are not to be "psychologically contaminated" by the darkness or drivenness people bring into our interpersonal space, we must be able to step back in quiet solitude—not just for reflection, but also to emotionally breathe.

We may not feel as dramatically as writers and poets who feel they must be in total silence for long periods of time or they cannot write. However, as clinicians we must have the time and space to recognize, debrief, and free ourselves from the unrealistic negative thinking, unexamined distorted schemata or countertransferences that may have been stirred up so we do not carry them over into our next therapeutic encounter or bring them back to our families when we

*Adapted from material in Wicks, R. (2012). *The inner life of the counselor*. Hoboken, NJ: Wiley.

return home. More than this though, when we create the space to reflect, meditate, and simply be, therapy becomes part of the entire flow of our life—not simply the clinical "work" we do, which stands alongside the rest of our personal life. To accomplish this, one of the initial steps is to intentionally enjoy both the scheduled and unscheduled "crumbs of mindfulness" in our life and this process can be logically initiated by how we begin our day.

I used to tease clinicians that if in your mind the day ahead was going to be a boring one, an easy way to change all that was to leave home for the clinic, hospital, school, or wherever you work, an hour late! The problem is that for some of us this is a regular style of living.

A colleague of mine at a clinic I worked in years ago would always be late—even for meetings she called. She always appeared to be chasing her schedule like a gargoyle on roller skates. Part of her seemed to enjoy this. It made things seem exciting, she always made an auspicious entry, and she seemed to have the feeling because of it, that her day was truly filled with many important things and people whom she needed to attend. And, because she was such a lovely person to interact with, people tended to give her the room to do this and simply wink at her behavior so she did not have to deal with the negative reactions of others as many of us less gentle persons would. However, this style of behavior started to wear on her as she began to age. She felt the exhaustion more and the unconscious payoffs less. In addition, it became more at odds with her value system because she was also a pastoral counselor and valued pacing, mindfulness, and respect for those she was scheduled to be with at a certain time.

Although we may not have this particular style (or at least to this extent), most clinicians do feel at certain points that their lives are out of control. The practice is busy. They may be working in a number of geographic settings. The paperwork seems enormous. Family pressures seem to temporarily be outweighing the joys of relationships at home. Difficult colleagues and extremely demanding clients all seem to be lined up for attention. So, the simple question whose answer may still seem incredibly elusive at the time for them is:

> How can I find and nourish myself with alonetime and enjoy at least "the crumbs of mindfulness" as a way to begin to nourish my inner life and, in turn, then have real availability for my family, friends, coworkers, and clients?

ALONETIME

For more than 30 years I have dealt with an unusual type of darkness. When physicians, nurses, or international relief workers found themselves on the edge of burnout, counselors, social workers, or psychologists found themselves losing perspective, or priests confessed to feelings of despair at the abuse crisis in their church, I was often called in to consult, mentor, or present information on the topics of resilience, self-care, and the prevention or limitation of secondary stress—the pressures experienced in reaching out to others. The goal in all cases was to aid these helping and healing professionals to regain a healthy perspective.

Of all the approaches I offered, the most important one I feel I shared with them is the one also essential for all of us as clinicians to attend to: Namely, how can I better appreciate, expand, and explore the spaces in my life? These inner spaces—when we are physically alone or spending time reflectively within ourselves—are not simply about personal renewal or for the purpose of reengagement (as important as both of these are). They are about recognizing the scaffolding of expectations that are tyrannizing our lives. Even more importantly, they are also about having a more healthy perspective, being more mindful, and free from the invisible puppeteers in our life that are present when dysfunctional thinking or unrecognized schemas (beliefs) lay unrecognized and unexamined.

Time alone or within ourselves or "alonetime" needs to be appreciated in the broadest sense (not just in the extreme where someone goes off by him- or herself to an isolated spot) in the living opportunities that present themselves during our current normal daily routine. When alonetime is appreciated, explored, and enjoyed in the right way, we can lessen our projections, become easier on ourselves, and do not become as discouraged when immediate gratification or success is not granted. Instead, we may feel a sense of inner ease and intrigue about the life we can live that is before us *right now* rather than constantly being postponed into some uncertain future. As we can see in the following reflection by Peterson (2006), the author of *A Primer in Positive Psychology*, life need not, *should not*, be postponed—even for apparently practical reasons:

> Like many academics, I spent my young adult years postponing many of the small things that I knew would make me happy, including reading novels for pleasure, learning to cook, taking a photography class, and joining a gym. I would do all of these things when I had time—when I finished school, when I was awarded tenure, and so on. I was fortunate enough to realize that I would never have time unless I made the time. And then the rest of my life began. (p. 22)

Consequently, we need to explore silence and solitude to unearth, appreciate, and fathom the value of such spaces in our life, as a way of ensuring that the rest of our life will be more centered, rich, and renewing. And, as was previously emphasized, this will not simply be a wonderful gift to us, but also for those with whom we relate each day, be it only for a few moments or—as in the case of clients—for a single session or an entire therapy.

Spending time in silence, and possibly at times in solitude, can dramatically impact—for good or for bad—the way we live the rest of our lives. Certain fortunate people have some natural sense of this and say they are attracted to these "spaces" whether they be for a few moments or, on occasion, a few days. We can see this even in little children when they step back from being active with others to go and play with their toys by themselves, regroup, and feel once again a sense of inner ease.

When high school counselors report back on the process of a senior retreat, their comments also often echo a shown appreciation for quiet time by adolescents who are used to a daily diet of stimulation. The one thing that most often surprises the adult chaperones since they are used to dealing with the obvious intensity of young people's lives is the gratefulness they express for these silent periods. These times are often rated as the most beneficial and appreciated aspect of the retreat experience, especially when the stage was properly set for these quiet periods.

The same is true for young adults. In an email I received from a friend in the Netherlands, he reported how his spiritual community was trying to support the need for periodic silent spaces that are desired and needed by those entering adulthood today.

> We have a building which is called the Stiltehuis—the "House of Silence," where weekends are run to introduce young people to the practice of learning how to be present to self through silence and meditation. A small group have also come together on a regular basis, and there is an interest in creating a community or house for some of these people who are committed to building this into their lives. Some young people come to Stiltehuis or the community house for individual time with one of the brothers and a woman who works there. They both offer individual mentoring. It has been remarkably successful and speaks powerfully of the thirst for a life of the spirit of what is good, renewing, and refreshing among young people.

Adults, as well, demonstrate an appreciation for open moments of silence, the opportunity for some solitude and time to withdraw into themselves to regroup and regain a healthy perspective. These free moments can be captured even when flying on a plane, sitting in a group, or walking down a busy city street. They offer a chance to take a breath, center, and allow the process of meaning-making to be examined anew so they can see if and how their living is congruent with their hopes. There is clearly a desire in many adults to have the space to be comfortable in their own skin, to have an opportunity to sit with themselves peacefully, to take stock, renew, and achieve a sense of inner ease that translates into the ability to have healthier relationships with themselves and others.

Yet, *how* we seek and approach the spaces in our day and life can make all the difference. The process is not the same as in our search for success in the other areas of our life. From psychologists, writers, contemporary and classic spiritual guides, and secular journeyers we can see a sampling of what some of those attitudes and approaches might be and how significant periods of solitude and even small "crumbs of time" spent alone can alter the most intense of lives.

Probably no other group has been as articulate as writers and poets have been about the need to be alone so creativity can flourish. And nowhere has this need been more dramatically reflected than in the response of Franz Kafka (1974) to his intended wife. In her letter she said she was looking forward to the time when she could sit and watch him write. After Kafka had time to reflect on this letter, you could tell by the tone and wording of his response that this was in his eyes quite impossible. (As a matter of fact, you could also tell from his words that the subsequent possibility of this marriage, given his "unique personality," was doomed from this point on!)

> You once said that you would like to sit beside me while I write. Listen, in that case I could not write at all. For writing means revealing oneself to excess; that utmost of self-revelation and surrender, in which a human being, when involved with others, would feel he was losing himself, and from which, therefore, he will always shrink as long as he is in his right mind—for everyone wants to live as long as he is alive—even the degree of self-revelation and surrender is not enough for writing. Writing that springs from the surface of existence—when there is no other way and the deeper wells have dried up—is nothing, and collapses the moment a truer emotion makes that surface shake. That is why one can never be alone enough when one writes, why there can never be enough silence around one when one writes, *why even night is not night enough*. (emphasis added; pp. 155–156)

Another writer known for his love of silence and solitude is minimalist poet Robert Lax who spent the past 30 years of his life living alone on Patmos and other Greek Isles. When interviewed by former BBC correspondent Peter France (1996) in his book *Hermits*, his comment on the need for solitude—though much less dramatic—follows the same theme as Kafka's words. Lax says, "I haven't actually consciously looked for solitude. All I've looked for are decent working conditions. I think if I didn't like to write, to do something that works best without interruptions, I might not be so interested in being alone for most of the day" (p. 200). (I might add at this point that the same is the case of counselors whose work requires periods of quiet if balance and quality therapy are to be truly possible.)

This valuing by Lax of a place of solitude in which to create was further explored years later in an interview with him by Steve Gregoriou (2002) in his book entitled *Way of the Dreamcatcher*. In it, he asks Lax why Patmos was so important as an environment of solitude (and a limited form of relationship because Lax did leave his house so was not strictly a hermit). Lax replied that the isle of Patmos was important because it offered him:

> A timeless serenity. Generative silence. Awe. The quiet imposed by the volcanic mountains and stones, a real love moving over the face of the waters. In a more familial sense, I did feel like someone might if they had run into their long-lost parents or grandparents—as if everything you've heard in your life, up till then, had just been an echo of something that all along had been planted right here. And the echoes of that something could still be heard. . . . The feeling of sanctuary is quite evident. But I think the island is simply a place where strangers may more easily become friends . . . it's a wholesome place that naturally fosters self-discovery and genuine *agape*. There's a living tradition here. I felt a great wave of peace when I came to Patmos, and I still sense these peaceful rhythms. (p. 82)

Although few of us could escape to an island, the value of "a place" where we can be quiet and alone is immeasurable. Writers have much to teach us about the creative power of the "place" of solitude. Writers and poets such as Rilke (1934) and Thoreau (1853), Grumbach (1994) and Sarton (1973), as well as other artists of the word can help us appreciate time alone in ways that will encourage us to eke out such spaces in our own schedule and maybe take occasional periods of extended time by ourselves that in the past we might have thought impractical or unnecessary.

Psychologists and psychiatrists also help in the explanation of the value and appropriateness of time spent in silence, solitude, and reflection even though it is true that they, in the main, have been one of the last groups to recognize and discuss the importance of time spent alone. In possibly his finest work, *Solitude: Returning to the Self*, psychiatrist Edwin Storr (1988) sought to begin rectifying this by noting the lack of appreciation by clinicians—including himself—for periods by oneself. He partially addresses this by citing the early work of psychoanalytic writer Donald Winnicott:

> Modern psychotherapists, including myself, have taken as their criterion of emotional maturity the capacity of the individual to make mature relationships on equal terms. With few exceptions, psychotherapists have omitted to consider the fact that the capacity to be alone is also an aspect of emotional maturity.

One such exception is the psychoanalyst Donald Winnicott. In 1958, Winnicott published a paper on "The Capacity to Be Alone" which has become a psychoanalytic classic. Winnicott wrote:

> It is probably true to say that in psycho-analytic literature more has been written on the fear of being alone or wish to be alone than on the

> ability to be alone; also a considerable amount of work has been done on the withdrawn state, a defensive organization implying an expectation of persecution. It would seem to me that a discussion of the positive aspects of the capacity to be alone is overdue. (p. 18)

Following Storr, psychologist Estes Schuler Buchholz (1997) published a book-length work *The Call of Solitude: Alonetime in a World of Attachment.* In it she also made the point that a balance is needed between being alone and in relationship. She wrote: "We are born wanting and needing time and space alone to process the stimulation around us, as we also learn quickly to revel in and long for attached and related times" (p. 49).

From a developmental standpoint, psychologist Barbara Powell (1985) pointed as well to the longstanding value solitude has for many cultures.

> In many societies, voluntary isolation from others is considered necessary for the completion of certain phases of personal growth. Adolescent males entering adulthood in certain tribal cultures are expected to wander alone in the forest, mountains, or desert for as long as several months at a time. During this period the solitary wanderer is instructed to communicate with the [divine], compose a song, or experience a magic dream. Those who return without their dream may be sent back into the mountains and told to return when they are successful. (p. 35)

Following this, time in silence—and possibly solitude—was also emphasized in writings on mindfulness meditation. This information looked at formal alonetime as meditation in which persons could fruitfully spend time within themselves. Such writings by psychologists and psychiatrists also expressed the value of informal mindfulness as an ideal psychological and/or spiritual partner (depending on how you view this process) during daily activities. In terms of mindfulness meditation, Christopher Germer (2005) notes:

> [Mindfulness] can be compared to a *searchlight* that illumines a wider range of objects as they arise in awareness, one at a time. The benefits are greater awareness of the personal condition of our minds and an understanding of the nature of mind itself. . . . Mindfulness meditation helps us to develop the capacity for relaxed, choiceless awareness in which conscious attention moves instantly and naturally among the changing elements of experience. . . . Meditation can be practiced sitting, standing, lying down, or moving. Mindfulness meditation is not hard to learn; and anyone can practice it. (pp. 15–16)

And so, the psychology of meditation now has much to offer us on the need for, and dynamics of, spending time alone as well as—in Germer's (2005) words again—"[developing] a skill that allows us to be less reactive to what is happening in the moment. [Mindfulness] is a way of relating to all experience—positive, negative, and neutral—such that our overall level of suffering is reduced and our sense of well-being increases" (p. 4). Given this, being familiar with both formal mindfulness (meditation) and informal mindfulness (being attentive and open in the moment) can significantly enhance our well-being.

Many classic and contemporary spiritual figures have also been proponents of spending time quietly and reflectively whether individually or in groups. Christian spirituality, for instance, has an established history of prizing leaning back from the bustle of activity. It not only sees that time alone provides an opportunity for refreshment and renewal but also is necessary so we can find our true identity. Kenneth Leech (1985) traces this appreciation of solitude in his book *Experiencing God* in the following way:

> Elijah, who journeyed into the desert for forty days and forty nights, and, arriving at Horeb, lodged in a cave . . . has been seen as a key figure for those seeking God in solitude and stillness . . . Jesus too was led by the spirit in the wilderness where he experienced temptations . . . and throughout his ministry he is described as having sought solitude in deserts and lonely places, instructing his disciples to follow his example. . . . In the New Testament, the Judean wilderness was the context for the preaching of John the Baptist, identified as "a voice crying in the wilderness." . . . The desert experience was one with which the early Christians too were familiar, for they saw themselves as a pilgrim people seeking a better country. . . . The sense of belonging nowhere, of having no continuing city, is one which comes across powerfully in the literature of early Christians. (pp. 129–130)

Included in this group of early Christians who sought solitude were the fourth-century women (Ammas) and men (Abbas) who fled to the desert to find and preserve their true identities. In the following realistic but challenging words of Trappist contemplative Thomas Merton (1960) about these desert Ammas and Abbas, we can see their journey is valued to this day by those who wish to be true to themselves and become persons who hold fast to serious values:

> We cannot do exactly what they did. But we must be as thorough and as ruthless in our determination to break all spiritual chains, and cast off the domination of alien compulsions, to find our true selves, to discover and develop our inalienable spiritual liberty and use it. . . . Let it suffice for me to say that we need to learn from these [persons] of the fourth century how to ignore prejudice, defy compulsion and strike out fearlessly into the unknown. (p. 24)

Psychologist and spiritual writer Henri Nouwen (1981) also valued these desert dwellers and wrote *Way of the Heart* to encourage his contemporaries to value both solitude and silence. To his fellow spiritual seekers he wrote: "In solitude I get rid of my scaffolding. . . . It is this nothingness that I have to face in my solitude, a nothingness so dreaded that everything in me wants to run to my friends, my work, and my distractions so that I can forget my nothingness and make myself believe that I am worth something" (p. 27). He then adds about silence: "Silence completes and intensifies solitude. . . . [It] protects the inner fire" (p. 43).

Jewish spiritual guides also address alonetime. Abraham Joshua Heschel's (1951) book *The Sabbath: Its Meaning for Modern Man* does it eloquently by encouraging weekly separation from the daily grind of our work week. (What I refer to as *alonetime* may not simply be separation from other people but from a way of existence and a habitual style of interacting that can be destructive if it goes uninterrupted or is not broken up.)

In *The Sabbath* he notes, "In the tempestuous ocean of time and toil there are islands of stillness where man may enter a harbor and reclaim his dignity. The island is the seventh day, the Sabbath, a day of detachment from things, instruments, and practical affairs" (p. 29).

Orthodox rabbi Aryeh Kaplan (1982), on the other hand, addresses a more formal type of time spent in silence: meditation. In his book *Meditation and Kabbalah* he goes out of his way to tie meditation to a number of sources, indicating the later 18th century and early 19th century as its most popular period in Judaism. He also acknowledges the fact that the techniques used are similar throughout the different world religions and points out that in Judaism there is often a lack of awareness of this tradition of meditation among practicing Jews:

> With the spread of the Hasidic movement in the Eighteenth Century, a number of meditative techniques became more popular, especially those centered around the formal prayer service. This reached its zenith in the teachings of Rabbi Nachman of Breslov (1772–1810), who discusses meditation in considerable length. . . . Many people express surprise that the Jewish tradition contains a formal meditative system. (p. 3)

Exploring the work of Kaplan then is very revealing as is further examining the writings of Heschel who will draw on past figures who knew how to distance themselves from everyday activity. They were also open to renewing, reflective time to the extent that it is defined not just as time in solitude but also time *within* oneself.

It is no surprise that contemporary Buddhist and Zen masters also value time in quiet reflection as well. Pico Iyer (2008) in his book on the Dalai Lama noted that "his public virtues were really just symptoms of the private practices and stillness that underlay them" (p. 58). This is not surprising because from a Buddhist perspective, the practitioner's enemies are internal ones: ignorance, anger, attachment, and pride. In this respect, then, time alone in meditation or performing a spiritual ritual is not simply something to add on to an already overbooked schedule but something that will make it and your life more meaningful.

According to Sandy Johnson (1996) in *The Book of Tibetan Elders*, "Shambala," which has been portrayed in both novel and movie as an exotic place of peace and joy, is really seen as a "metaphor for one's own inner spiritual journey and [many Tibetans] dedicate their lives to finding it within themselves" (p. 5). In this regard, time alone allows people to examine their mind, see their behavior and intentions for what they truly and totally are, so they can refocus on what is both growthful and compassionate.

So, for the Buddhist then, alonetime has a purpose. In the words of one of the leading contemporary American spokespersons for Buddhist spirituality (who is also a psychologist), Jack Kornfield (2000):

> We live in disordered times, complicated, distracted, and demanding, yet to sustain a spiritual practice demands our steady attention. The first task, then, in almost any spiritual voyage, is to quiet ourselves enough to listen to the voices of our hearts, to listen to that which is beyond our daily affairs. Whether in prayer or meditation, in visualization, fasting, or song, we need to step out of our usual roles, out of the busy days on automatic pilot. We need to find a way to become receptive and open. (p. 25)

Kornfield then broadens the value of alone time beyond the Buddhist tradition to point out that most major religions and philosophies value being apart, and follows this with a recognition of the potential challenges this can offer:

> In entering solitude one does not necessarily find silence. At first solitude can be noisy, filled with the conflicts of the body and the mind's ongoing commentary that Chögyam Trungpa called "subconscious gossip." Meditation practices help us to find a way to genuine stillness. In them we find that there are many levels to silence. The first is simply external silence, and absence of noise. Then there is the silence of the body, a growing physical stillness. Gradually there comes a quieting of the mind. Then we discover the silence that comes as witness to all things, and then twenty other levels of silent absorption in prayer and meditation. Still deeper we come to the indescribable silence beyond the mind, the silence that gives birth to all things. To enter silence is a journey, a letting go into progressively more profound levels of stillness until we disappear in the vastness. (p. 83)

Consequently, Buddhism as well as Jewish, Christian, and other world spiritualities seem to have much to offer in appreciating the value and challenges of silence, solitude, and time alone—whether we are religious or not.

There are also numerous, what I would term, *secular adventurers* in the exploration and appreciation of quiet time alone or with others. They help us appreciate that silence and solitude can sometimes seem like a different world to us when we experience it in the extreme. Gertrude Bell, ally of Lawrence of Arabia, noted having this experience in a letter to her father. In commenting on one of her encounters with the desert she wrote to him: "Shall I tell you my chief impression [of the desert]—the silence. It is like the silence of mountain tops, but more intense, for there you know the sound of wind and faraway water and falling ice and stone; there is a sort of echo there, you know it, Father. But here *nothing*" (emphasis added; Wallach, 1996, p. 54).

Bell is one of the many secular searchers and adventurers who have experienced the power of silence, possibly at times along with solitude. And there are many others who join her—some with a more intentional sense of spending time in meditation or being with others with a deep sense of presence and awareness—in other words, *mindfulness*. One of the most recent such practitioners is Clark Strand (1998), a former Buddhist monk. In his book *The Wooden Bowl* he sets out the desire for, and response to, formal periods of being alone or meditation.

He began this book by explaining his former commitment to Buddhism and his subsequent mindful practices when alone after leaving participation in this way of life as a leader in his temple. He then poses the question: "Was there a way for people to slow down and experience themselves, their lives, and other people in the present moment without adopting a new religion or philosophical ideology" (Strand, 1998, p. 2)? He felt that if it were possible it would result in a person maintaining "a spirit of lightness and friendliness with regard to what you are doing" and that meditation "ought to be an area of your life where you can let go of the obsessive desire to improve yourself, to get ahead, or to do better than anyone else. . . . Meditation ought to decrease the drivenness of our lives, not make it worse" (p. 12).

In his encouraging us to spend part of our time alone in meditation, he is asking us to experience "brief glimpses of a freer, more spacious world" (p. 21), whether we meditate briefly for a few moments or an extended period of time. He believes that through sitting with a comfortably erect posture (after all, meditation is not a rigid "charm school") and through the use of a simple counting procedure (1 to 4) of our breaths, we can remind ourselves to take life as it is and comes to us.

Designated times of silence as it is experienced by Strand in formal or informal meditative approaches to life, according to him, are essential if we are to have life and live it abundantly. In his sense of viewing it, a meditative approach to our alonetime will help people see more fully the "fundamental *enoughness*, *sanity*, and *beauty* of the world" (p. 14).

Less formal in his approach than Strand's to time in silence—but this time with the added element of solitude—are those informal periods that are described by Richard Bode (1993), author of the simple, elegantly written book, *First You Have to Row a Little Boat*. In this book, using sailing as a metaphor for how we appreciate or ignore how life should be lived, he makes the point that we need to learn to make adjustments in life as a sailor tacking his sloop is called to do.

> The truth is that in our daily lives we constantly make similar migrations from land to water and back to land again—and we don't always do so with the fluency of the sailor. Time flips us rapidly from place to place and role to role. We shuttle from suburb to city, from home to job, from business meeting to dinner party. Each milieu has its own conventions and makes its own demands. Sometimes the changes occur so fast we lose our bearings. We behave like parents to our colleagues and executives to our kids. We lack a sure sense of the appropriate because we haven't taken the time to figure out where we are. (pp. 12–13)

From his time sailing alone, he sees the need for us to have time to breathe, reflect, respect the currents of life, and respond to our hopes rather than inadvertently kill them.

> When we kill the dream within us, we kill ourselves, even though the blood continues to flow within our veins. We can see the signs of this living death about us everywhere: in shopping malls, in discount and department stores. . . . We see people scurrying compulsively, buying compulsively, as if they hoped through the expenditure of money, the acquisition of goods, to deaden the pain they don't even know they have. (p. 24)

In addition to his time on his sloop alone, Bode also had an enforced idleness because of an accident. During this time he reflected: "I thought deeply about who I was, where I came from, and what I wanted to be. What I had lost in physical motion I had gained in insight, which is movement of another kind. I learned the interior life was as rewarding as the exterior life and that my richest moments occurred when I was absolutely still" (p. 70). Bode's simple words typify the experiences and comments of other secular adventurers in alonetime as well as those from writers, psychologists, and spiritual authors who show respect for a formal "Sabbath" and the informal spaces in our lives.

RECOGNIZING, HONORING, AND APPRECIATING MORE FULLY THE SPACES IN DAILY LIFE

As in anything valuable for our welfare and, by natural extension, our clients and the persons who are part of our interpersonal community, time spent in silence, solitude, and some form of formal or informal mindfulness needs to be respected and fully understood if it is to have a positive impact. Otherwise, such spaces in our lives run the risk of being relegated to being no more than useless empty holes within "the real action" of life or simply represent those times when we merely brood about what we may have said to someone or resent what happened to us yesterday or yesteryear.

Given this, it is essential—*especially* as clinicians—to address the questions that will help us to uncover and enhance the spaces in our life. To accomplish this, such questions need to be addressed as: How can time alone and within ourselves become a more fruitful, enlightening, challenging, and renewing place? What pitfalls might we encounter? How can we meet such perils in ways that actually result in their paradoxically being an advantage to us?

The dynamics of enjoying and benefiting more from the spaces one recognizes or creates may hold some surprises since solitude and reflective time are often taken for granted or seen as needing no introduction. The feeling often is "What's the big deal about being alone? Anyone can step aside or become reflective when in a group." Yet, as psychologists, poets and writers, spiritual figures, and other searchers have recognized, there is so much to learn about time in silence, solitude, and mindful presence. This includes:

- Uncovering the resistances to and reasons for seeking space in our active life.
- Appreciating the expectations we have for time alone and the surprises it can offer us.
- Determining how we can make it a priority.
- Experiencing how time in silence and solitude can "positively contaminate" the rest of our day.
- Knowing the differences between alone and lonely.
- Understanding the simplicity that periods of quiet time can foster in our life.
- Recognizing the conduit free time can be for "unlearning" as well as new learning for us.

And so, part of the goal of nurturing one's inner life is to provide a panoply of approaches to how silence, solitude, and mindfulness can be viewed from different, possibly surprising angles. Free, quiet moments will never again be seen as being merely the interruptions or stopgaps in a life of activity and function. Instead, very brief informal periods and formal lengthy times when we are physically alone or within ourselves (even when surrounded by others) will be something else, something more, something into which we can enter to alter our whole life in some very significant ways.

APPRECIATING THE CRUMBS OF ALONETIME

Alonetime already exists throughout much of our day, no matter how hectic our schedule is. And so, one of the first steps in leaning back so we can capture moments of silence, solitude, and reflection is to recognize them. Crumbs of silence and solitude are easily ignored or swept away. This often results in a vision of being at peace and alone as being in the purview of pure fantasy for most of us. Consequently, while we love to read about a hermit's experience, we let the available spaces in our own day lay unnoticed and unfathomed for what they might be.

If anything, then, free time needs to be appreciated first for what it is now in our life—not for what we would like it to be. Just as people would starve if they continued to read extravagant menus or recipes and didn't eat the simple meal before them, so too would the inner life be starved if we didn't actually experience the quiet, solitude, and a chance to explore one's interior terrain that is already available to us but for some reason is presently being left unnoticed and not fully experienced.

Writer Sara Maitland (2008) recognized this in her search for deeper and broader silence. She wrote:

> One of the things I discovered at this point was that there were bits and pieces of silence woven into the fabric of each day and I began to try to keep an eye out for them and move into them as swiftly as possible. Some of these moments I had to create for myself . . . but some were just there, waiting for me. (p. 154)

When we seek small moments of silence and solitude with a sense of fervor, it is a fallacy to think that in doing this we are merely settling for less. Instead, we are moving with our present busy reality in seeking the space that is already available, but being left not fully accessed, to breathe, reflect, renew, learn, and relax, just be. From another perspective, Annie Dillard (1989) recognized how the larger periods begin with a love of the smaller and symbolic. In her classic work, *The Writing Life*, she told a story to illustrate this with respect to being a writer:

> A well-known writer got collared by a university student who asked, "Do you think I could be a writer?"
>
> "Well," the writer said, "I don't know. . . . Do you like sentences?"
>
> The writer could see the student's amazement. Sentences? Do I like sentences? I am 20 years old and do I like sentences? If he had liked sentences, of course, he could begin, like a joyful painter I knew. I asked him how he came to be a painter. He said, "I liked the smell of paint?" (p. 70)

Using this approach with the goals for this book in mind, the question is simple then: As clinicians, do you like the crumbs of silence and solitude you already have and can discover? If you do, you can begin to become someone who will enjoy a deep sense of alonetime.

WHAT ARE SOME OF THE CRUMBS OF ALONETIME?

For most of us there are periods in life that are already open. They might include early morning before the rest of the house rises, at the end of the day after everyone turns in for the night, when driving in the car to and from the clinical practice, when walking to the restroom, the few seconds before answering a ringing cell phone, during a lunchtime walk, while jogging or at the gym, or waiting on a line or in a doctor's or dentist's office. On the other hand, it may be an even longer period of time such as when one is home alone or during a scheduled day of renewal.

As clinicians we also have additional built in opportunities for alonetime (though for some reason we may not recognize them as such). They include:

- Client cancellations
- Quiet periods before or after client hours
- The space between clients
- Time after attending a CEU
- Client cancellations are perfect times to take 15 minutes to:
  - Close door to office;
  - Sit up in a chair or on a cushion;
  - Simply count our breaths from 1 to 4;
  - Gently look a few feet in front of us at an object that inspires us; and
  - Simply *be* . . . how hard can that be?

There are also other times when we can take a nice walk to increase our oxygen exchange and stretch our legs given all the sitting that is part of a clinical practice. During such times a good exercise is to "simply" look at and experience your surroundings. In this way we are truly taking an energizing walk instead of merely "taking a think"—in other words, walking around, slightly hunched over, pondering things in our life while the experiences of life and all that is around us passes us by while we remain in a psychological envelope of preoccupation and concern. When we are involved in such cognitive self-centered functions we miss so much. Buddhist Pema Chödrön (1997) used to refer to such involvement as tantamount to wearing ear plugs while walking up to a tree filled with birds singing.

During quiet periods before or after client hours as well as between each of them there are other opportunities presented to us for a few moments of silence and solitude. In addition to this, another opportunity can present itself if you: (a) leave for work a bit earlier so you are not racing the first client to your practice; (b) close your door so no one comes to chat; and (c) take a few breaths before the intensity of counseling begins. This allows us then to be mindful (alert, present, and open) to the first client and the day. Otherwise, we run the risk of contaminating the first session and the rest of the day with elements involved in our home life. Moreover, not having a space before and between sessions also increases the chances that you will be less open to what is actually happening to the client in the room and causing you to rely more on the diagnostic box you may have put the client in.

Time after a CEU is another one of many periods that clinicians have to not only digest what they have learned but also to lean back and relax from the cognitive input received. This allows us to be open to all that lies below and beyond our thought processes and analytic skills. There is more to us than the cognitive so why not enjoy that part of ourselves as well?

Small crumbs of silence and solitude when they are recognized and enjoyed do two things: one, they help nourish us immediately and two, they inspire and call us to seek more and lengthier periods of alonetime. When this happens we can then see how such periods bring us to life and help us to feel fresher and more open. We will also begin to more deeply appreciate such important realities as *impermanence* and the *fragility of life* so we value what little time we have here in the world and in the process respect others who also are here on this earth for a short time as well. This will also help us to see more clearly how often we are "mindless," which need not be the source of self-castigation but, instead, can be turned into places where we can profitably attend to in both our professional and personal life. With this in mind, in closing this brief discussion of this topic here, some questions to consider at this point are:

- Where in your life does quiet time already exist?
- In what parts of your life is it realistic to create some new space where you can relax and practice mindful breathing?
- Image in your mind's eye people in your life that you admire because they are more reflective and relaxed than you are. What are some basic ways to emulate them?
- In what ways can you create an environment in your home and office that is conducive to sitting meditation and mindful breathing?
- How can you develop a list of triggers to help you be mindful so you don't just run to your grave thinking that once this task is done you will take time? (These reminders can and should include common daily triggers such as: the ring of phone, entering your car to drive to work or on an errand, your morning alarm clock, entering the shower, sitting down to a meal, etc.)
- How might you create significant time and occasionally a day or longer in which you have nothing on the schedule? (This may require that you leave the house or office because sitting there may remind you of what you still have left unfinished but whatever needs to be done to create such a leisure space is worth it.)

REFERENCES

Bode, R. (1993). *First you have to row a little boat*. New York, NY: Warner.

Buchholz, E. (1997). *The call of solitude: Alonetime in a world of attachment*. New York, NY: Simon & Schuster.

Chödrön, P. (1997). *When things fall apart: Heart advice for difficult times*. Boston, MA: Shambhala.

Dillard, A. (1989). *The writing life*. New York, NY: HarperCollins.

France, P. (1996). *Hermits: The insights of solitude*. New York, NY: St. Martin's Press.

Germer, C. K., Siegel, R. D., & Fulton, P. R. (Eds.). (2005). *Mindfulness and psychotherapy*. New York, NY: Guilford Press.

Gregoriou, S. (2002). *Way of the dreamcatcher: Spirit lessons with Robert Lax, poet, peacemaker and sage*. Toronto, Canada: Novelist.

Grumbach, D. (1994). *Fifty days of solitude*. Boston, MA: Beacon Press.

Heschel, A. J. (1951). *The Sabbath: Its meaning for modern man*. New York, NY: Farrar, Straus and Giroux.

Iyer, P. (2008). *The open road: The global journey of the fourteenth Dalai Lama*. New York, NY: Knopf.

Johnson, S. (1996). *The book of Tibetan elders: The life stories and wisdom of the great spiritual masters of Tibet*. New York, NY: Riverhead.

Kafka, F. (1974). *Letters to Felice*. (J. Stern & E. Duckworth, Trans.). New York, NY: Penguin.

Kaplan, A. (1982). *Meditation and the Kabbalah*. York Beach, ME: Weiser.

Kornfield, J. (2000). *After the ecstasy, the laundry: How the heart grows wise on the spiritual path*. New York, NY: Bantam Books.

Leech, K. (1985). *Experiencing God: Theology as spirituality*. San Francisco, CA: Harper.

Maitland, S. (2008). *A book of silence*. Berkeley, CA: Counterpoint.

Merton, T. (1960). *The wisdom of the desert*. New York, NY: New Directions.

Nouwen, H. (1981). *The way of the heart: The spirituality of the desert fathers and mothers*. New York, NY: Seabury/Harper.

Peterson, C. (2006). *A primer in positive psychology*. New York, NY: Oxford University Press.

Powell, B. (1985). *Alone, alive and well: How to fight loneliness and win*. Rodale, PA: Rodale Press.

Rilke, M. (1934/1993). *Letters to a young poet*. New York, NY: Norton.

Sarton, M. (1973). *Journal of solitude*. New York, NY: Norton.

Storr, E. (1988). *Solitude: A return to the self*. New York, NY: Ballantine Books.

Strand, C. (1998). *The wooden bowl: Simple meditations for everyday life*. New York, NY: Hyperion.

Thoreau, H. (1853/1997). *The writings of Henry D. Thoreau. Journal* (Vol. 5, pp. 1852–1853). P. F. O'Connell (Ed.). Princeton, NJ: Princeton University Press.

Wallach, J. (1996). *Desert queen: The extraordinary life of Gertrude Bell: Adventurer, adviser to kings, ally of Lawrence of Arabia*. New York, NY: Doubleday.

Winnicott, D. (1958). The capacity to be alone. *International Journal of Psycho-Analysis*, 39, 416–420.

REFERENCES

CHAPTER

6

Keeping the Sabbath

Privileging Being Beyond Doing

Jill L. Snodgrass

The candles are lit, blanketing the dinner table in a soft glow, and burning in honor of G-d's commandment to cease work. The smell of warm challah bread fills the air as family and friends come together to eat, to play, and to rest. The sound of children's jubilance fills the air, and a joyous energy is felt as we welcome Shabbat.

In honor of the eighth day, Christians halt their work and worry to join in the worship of God, as the Roman Empire's decree to rest lives on, some 1,700 years later. The muzak that fills the grocer's and stores is forgotten and replaced with the sounds of hymnody and praise. The church bells ring out as the sanctuary empties, sending forth God's children on the Sunday Sabbath.

For some, the rhythm of each week is accented by Shabbat or Sabbath, the rest commanded by the Jewish and Christian traditions. For others, the cacophony of each day blends into the next, spelled only by respite resulting from explicit intention. For many, however, privileging a world away from work is often met with resistance. We protest, saying,

> I have 13 client progress notes yet to record.
>
> If I do not attend the continuing education workshop this weekend, I'll have to do two next month.
>
> I'm the only supervisor who is available to be on call.
>
> If I stop, I won't ever catch up.

The internal and external demands of relationships, parenting, maintaining a home, and living in a society of 24/7 consumption, most often serve only to strengthen such refutations against rest.

According to Hasidic rabbi Zalman Schacter, keeping sabbath is one way of combatting the intense rhythms of life as it invites us "to *be* beyond doing" (as cited in Edwards, 1982, p. 9). Whether in honor of a religious covenant or as a purposeful means of self-care, keeping sabbath is a practice that guides us in pausing our work and toil in order to awaken to joy, rest, and community. This chapter calls us, as clinicians, to consider the implications of keeping sabbath. As an ancient religious discipline, Shabbat- and Sabbath-keeping emerged from a covenant with God to reflect on the work that has been done, as God did with creation, and honor its goodness with a day of rest. The first section of the chapter provides a brief overview of the religious foundations of Shabbat and Sabbath practices. The second section outlines how clinicians can learn to move beyond the incessant need to *do* and honor what it means to *be* through a sabbath practice. Models of keeping sabbath are offered, and the chapter concludes by reflecting on the ways in which this renewal practice contributes to our care of self and client.

Finally, it is important to contextualize briefly the sabbath practice in relation to religion and spirituality before exploring its ancient roots. Religions consist of structured systems of beliefs and practices engaged in by communities of followers. Considered to be a broader term, *spirituality*, one's search for meaning, may be fostered by a faith tradition, but can also be nurtured outside institutionalized religion. Therefore, for some readers, a Shabbat or Sabbath practice lies at the foundation of religious life. For others, whether adherents of faith traditions or not, keeping sabbath is one of many disciplines that facilitates self-renewal. In recognition of the important religious heritage of Shabbat and Sabbath, this chapter does not divorce the practices from their theological and spiritual foundations. For this reason, in referring to sabbath-like practices—practices that require us to rest, to retire, and to renew—the word *sabbath* is not capitalized, thus honoring its significance as a spiritual, but not necessarily religious, practice.

AN ANCIENT RELIGIOUS PRACTICE

Shabbat and Sabbath practice are grounded in the scriptural imperatives outlined in the Torah (or the Pentateuch). Three references to Shabbat can be found in the Torah in the books of Genesis, Exodus, and Deuteronomy. In Genesis, G-d blessed the seventh day and abstained from the work of creation to reflect on the goodness of creation and to rest with a sense of accomplishment (Genesis 2:2 New Revised Standard Version). In the book of Exodus, G-d commands the Israelites to remember the Sabbath and to keep the seventh day holy by refraining from labor (Exodus 20:8–11). Deuteronomy offers the commandment to observe the Sabbath. Moses reminds the Israelites that G-d freed them from slavery that all might rest equally—men, women, children, slaves, strangers, and animals (Deuteronomy 5:12–15). Based on this scriptural foundation, Jews and Christians of various denominations have maintained Shabbat and Sabbath practices for millennia.

In Judaism, Shabbat begins just before sunset on Friday evening with the lighting of the candles, symbolizing the commandment to remember and observe Shabbat. Though the preparations for the 25-hour period of rest begin much earlier in the week, on Friday evening blessings are given to children, the day of rest itself is blessed with wine, and a ritual hand washing occurs. The challah bread is broken and the Shabbat meal enjoyed. Friday evening also features prayers at the synagogue, with many returning to worship again on Saturday morning.

Shabbat is further distinguished from the other 6 days of the week by the 39 prohibited occupations outlined in the Mishnah and recognized by the Talmudists. Though these ancient prohibitions included such tasks as plowing and reaping (Exodus 34:21), loading animals (Nehemiah 13:15), and gathering wood (Numbers 15:32), today Jews contextualize the 39 prohibitions to include tasks like turning on and off lights; using technology such as computers, cell phones, or televisions; carrying anything outside the home; or destroying anything. Cooking also must be finished prior to Shabbat. The 39 prohibitions symbolize the work exerted to build the Temple. Although observant Jews and nonobservant Jews interpret the 39 prohibitions differently, the foundational prohibition is against work, which can be defined as "whatever requires changing the natural, material world" (Bass, 2010, p. 80). Thus, the prohibitions are intended to sanctify the day, creating an atmosphere of rest and time away from work, rather than to impose legalistic punishment, as some perceive.

The chapter returns to the practices and disciplines we are invited to leave behind as well as to adopt in sabbath-keeping; however, first Christian Sabbath practice is differentiated from the Jewish Shabbat. According to the Gospels, Jesus observed Shabbat, but also took liberties to engage in acts he considered acceptable for the day of rest. He healed the sick, an act that as clinicians we may consider a form of work, and stood behind the disciples when they broke Shabbat law by picking corn. In the New Testament book of Mark, Jesus is recounted to have said, "The Sabbath was made for humankind, and not humankind for the Sabbath" (Mark 2:27). Thus, Jesus offered a new conception of Sabbath discipline that influences Christian sabbath-keeping still today.

In 70 C.E., the Romans destroyed the temple at Jerusalem, resulting in a reassertion of faith by the Jews and further changes in the faith practices of those who had followed Jesus (and were then following his ways, prior to the establishment of Christianity). At that time, Jews emphasized the covenant made at Sinai between G-d and Israel and enforced greater restrictions on Shabbat practice. According to Bass (2010):

> At the same time, Christianity was developing a separate identity from Judaism, and many people who were not Jewish were joining the church. Gradually, Christians of Jewish background stopped attending synagogue and observing Jewish law. Over the years, Sunday became their one-day-in-seven for both rest and worship. (p. 82)

Jews and Christians honor the commandments to remember and observe the Sabbath, although the practices today are unique in each tradition. For Christians, Sunday officially became the Sabbath when Emperor Constantine declared Sundays a day of rest in 321 C.E. For centuries in the United States, Sundays were governmentally sanctioned days away from work. Stores were closed. Businesses did not operate. The cultural climate urged families to spend the day in worship and fellowship. Although today some Christians observe the Sabbath on Saturday (for example, adherents of the Seventh-Day Adventist tradition), for many, neither the seventh day (Saturday) nor the eighth day (Sunday) features any deviation from the norms of work and consumption. Government, employers, communities, and coaches all function on Saturday and Sunday in sync with the other days of the week. According to Bass (2010), in an effort to protect the Sabbath, the United States may ultimately have endangered it. She argues that a major influence in no longer protecting Sundays is:

> [I]ncreasing sensitivity to religious diversity—a sensitivity pioneered by the Supreme Court in decisions that forced employers to respect the Sabbath practices of Jews and Adventists. Today, not only the laws but also the customs that once shielded Sunday from most commerce are disappearing, and Christians' day of worship and rest is not automatically "free" for church and family. (p. 84)

Though the Christian Sabbath practice does not necessarily condone or condemn particular acts, as does Shabbat, the Sabbath asks Christians to abstain from work for a day, an abstention that is countercultural to many within a diversity of religious traditions.

A CONTEMPORARY PRACTICE FOR SELF-RENEWAL

With a brief conception of the foundations of Shabbat and Sabbath as religious practices, we now turn to examine how, as clinicians, keeping sabbath can move us beyond a life emphasis on doing, toward a life emphasis on being.

As previously mentioned, for those who already maintain a Shabbat or Sabbath practice, this chapter invites you to reflect on how the religious practice relates to your vocation as a clinician. For those who have never engaged or do not currently engage in regular Shabbat or Sabbath practices, this chapter provides you with models for keeping sabbath and a reflection on how this self-renewal practice influences our clinical work.

Sabbath as a spiritual self-renewal practice is not predicated on the rewards of greater productivity or an increased, balanced client load. Keeping sabbath is not a means to an end; it is a self-renewal practice that invites greater balance *into our lives, for the sake of life*. It is not an effort to do less of one thing in order to do more of another. Abraham Joshua Heschel (1951), a rabbi and leading Jewish philosopher of the 20th century, stated:

> Man [*sic*] is not a beast of burden, and the Sabbath is not for the purpose of enhancing the efficiency of his work [. . .] The Sabbath is not for the sake of the weekdays; the weekdays are for the sake of the Sabbath. It is not an interlude but the climax of living. (p. 14)

As the focus on being rather than doing is in many ways counter-cultural, it helps to understand spiritual models for sabbath-keeping.

MODELS FOR SABBATH-KEEPING

Diddams, Surdyk, and Daniels (2004) offer three models of sabbath-keeping intended to enhance psychological well-being: life segmentation, prescribed meaning, and integrated sabbath. For readers without a current sabbath practice, implementing a 25-hour sabbath each weekend may not be a realistic behavioral change. Life segmentation and integrated sabbath offer two accessible models for intentionally moving beyond our obsessions with doing.

Today, boundaries between the office and home are increasingly blurry. As clinicians, we may spend the weekend taking kids to soccer games, grocery shopping to restock the cupboards, and managing online bill pay, all the while being on call to respond to client crises at any time. With a growing population of telecommuters and advances in technology, we carry a portal to work in our pockets through smart phones and tablets and more. In exploring the shape of our living, Ford (1997) asks:

> Where is the "workplace" if we can be hooked up at home? What happens to the "work day" if we can log in at any time of the day or night and store what we have done for use at another time? The boundaries between work and home, work and leisure, are complexified. But more profoundly our identity as worker is transformed by being part of this network. (pp. 140–141)

Life segmentation is an intentional way of punctuating the chaotic rhythmic melodies of the week. In Judaism, this temporal divide distinguishes holy time from secular time (Smith-Gabai & Ludwig, 2011). According to Diddams et al. (2004):

> People who follow a life segmentation model of Sabbath intentionally segment work from other life arenas and participate in leisure or family activities on a regular basis [. . .] they have "ceased" or "put to an end" by creating boundary conditions between work and other important life domains. (p. 4)

Life segmentation is not meant to be another set of rules to follow and, as we later address more fully, should not be a rigid legalism meant to enhance renewal. Rather, it is the intentional act of demarcating 2, 4, 8, or even 25 hours to rest from work and to focus on the sabbath practices such as those outlined below.

Though contrary to the Shabbat and Sabbath models put forth in the Jewish and Christian traditions, according to Diddams et al. (2004), sabbath-keeping offers even greater renewal when it is integrated within the rhythm of one's week. They write, "Rather than continuing to live a hectic life and attempt to segmentation with Sabbath-keeping, we believe that psychological well-being will be most pronounced when Sabbath-keeping becomes integrated" (p. 6). Integrated sabbath not only entails reserving time for rest on a regular basis, but incorporating sabbath principles of attitude, disposition, and belief into everyday life. Whether segmenting a portion of each week, or incorporating sabbath within each day, the following guidelines clarify what sabbath-keeping asks us to leave behind and what it invites us to adopt. The following suggestions for moving beyond a myopic focus on doing toward the privileging of being can be tailored to both the life segmentation and integrated sabbath models of sabbath-keeping, or may be adapted to fit your current sabbath-keeping disciplines.

Doing Less

Ancient and contemporary Shabbat and Sabbath practices invite clinicians to do less by surrendering five acts or attitudes: legalism, work, self-idolization, consumerism, and worry.

Legalism

Before adopting any sabbath discipline, abandoning a legalistic attitude is imperative. Adopting a sabbath practice can easily morph into a new set of rules and regulations to be adhered to on a daily or weekly basis. Diddams et al. (2004) write:

> It is easy to begin by simply adding rules to their lives: no email, no going to the office, no grading papers, etc. If people add rules to their lives because they decide they *should* slow down, they may feel less in control of their lives than if they had never adopted [a sabbath practice]. (p. 4)

As stated by Jesus in the Gospel of Mark, the Sabbath is in the service of humankind, not the other way around (Mark 2:27). If our sabbath practice is to be renewing, it is essential to leave behind, or never adopt, a rigid, legalistic approach. Abandoning a legalistic attitude also requires foregoing shame as a motivator for disciplined practice. Our clinical background compels us to accept the notion that successful behavioral change results from planning for relapse, anticipating setbacks, and adopting an attitude of grace, not shame, regarding missed opportunities for change.

Work

The most imperative component of any sabbath practice is that of leaving work behind and intentionally choosing rest. We choose rest not because we are weary from toil, not because we simply cannot see one more client, cannot write one more progress note, or cannot spend any more brainpower on insurance claims. We stop work and choose rest because work is an important part of our lives, but it must only be a part. Life balance is only possible through both hard work and respite from it. Moreover, rest affirms that we are not slaves to what we do, to our work.

For many clinicians, helping others is something we were doing long before attending graduate school or pursuing licensure. Many of us feel called to a helping profession as a fulfillment of our identities. Our clinical work is not just a job, but a vocation, "the place where your deep gladness meets the world's deep need" (Buechner, 1993, p. 119). Yet, one lesson we were reminded of again following the recent economic recession is the notion that work must be a part, not the whole, of our lives. We authentically thrive in our vocations only when they are balanced by other life-giving relationships, creative passions, and times of solitude and silence. As noted by Dr. Robert Wicks in Chapter 5, "Valuing and Accessing Alonetime," doing our vocation requires "the crumbs of mindfulness," times for being on "islands of stillness" (Heschel, 1951, p. 29) in the midst of our labor.

Clinical mental health practice is grounded in the belief that growth requires periods of work as well as periods of rest. Changing cognitive distortions, creating new behavioral patterns, and choosing new ways of being are nurtured through times of doing as well as times of being. We most often meet with clients weekly, knowing that on the other 6 days of the week they will encounter periods of working hard on changed thoughts and behaviors, as well as periods of rest from such hard work.

Although work is an important part of our identities and lived experiences, in today's world we more often toil than labor. Toil is labor without rest and, according to Heschel (1951), "labor is a blessing, toil is the misery of man" (p. 28). In a popular *New York Times* op-ed entitled "The 'Busy' Trap," Kreider (2012) argues that the busyness of U.S. life is not an inevitable result of our postmodern context. Rather, it is a choice. Kreider comments on what Ford (1997) calls our "addiction to urgency" (p. 131) when he opines that the "crazy busy" people are not busy out of necessity. He writes:

> Notice it isn't generally people pulling back-to-back shifts in the I.C.U. or commuting by bus to three minimum-wage jobs who tell you how busy they are; what those people are is not busy but *tired. Exhausted. Dead on their feet.* It's almost always people whose lamented busyness is purely self-imposed: work and obligations they've taken on voluntarily, classes and activities they've "encouraged" their kids to participate in. They're busy because of their own ambition or drive or anxiety, because they're addicted to busyness and dread what they might have to face in its absence. (para. 2)

If addiction to urgency and busyness are the result of choice, then it is also our choice to choose sabbath. Prioritizing rest is essential if personal and collective growth and creation are to occur.

Finally, rest affirms that we are not slaves to our work. Rest confirms that we choose to labor but not to toil. As previously noted, in Deuteronomy 5:12–15, G-d commanded the Israelites to observe the Sabbath whether male or female, animal or stranger, slave or free. In this scripture, God is seen as the deliverer of freedom. God frees people—all people—from slavery on the seventh day. According to Bass (2000):

> To keep sabbath is to exercise one's freedom, to declare oneself to be neither a tool to be employed—an *employee*—nor a beast to be burdened [. . .] To insist on sabbath rest is to give testimony to the subversive knowledge that God's bias is in favor of freedom. (pp. 48–49)

Keeping sabbath affirms our freedom. We are not slaves. We are not slaves to our clients, to our computers, nor to our work. As noted by Kreider earlier, our slavery or addiction to busyness is a choice and, according to Deuteronomy, a bondage from which God has already freed us.

Self-Idolization

The third attitude that sabbath-keeping calls us to abandon is self-idolization. For adherents of the Abrahamic faiths, idolization refers to the worship of false idols and, in this case, privileging and honoring ourselves above God. For all of us, regardless of religious tradition, self-idolization is hubris verging on grandiosity. Self-idolization prevents us from keeping sabbath due to the tremendous value we (and/or others) place on our work and contributions. Though somewhat hyperbolized, the fear is that if we stop doing the world will stop turning. "To act as if the world cannot get along without our work for one day in seven is a startling display of pride" (Bass, 2010, p. 86). Failure to see that we can stop and rest results from an inability to recognize that others, many others, are just as capable, if not more, of doing the work that we do. Abandoning self-idolization invites us to think seriously about the value of rest and to reprioritize the importance of our own contributions. It is not a devaluation of our work, but a healthy acceptance of our place in the world. According to Bass (2010), "Overworked Americans need rest, *and* they need to be reminded that they do not cause the grain to grow and that their greatest fulfillment does not come through the acquisition of material things" (p. 88). This leads us to the fourth act to surrender in keeping sabbath, consumerism.

Consumerism

For centuries, blue laws required shopping-free Sundays. Christian Sabbath practices compelled local governments to require shops, restaurants, and other service providers to close, as Sundays were to be spent in worship and fellowship with family. But Sunday-closing laws came under attack in the mid-20th century, as Christian and Jewish practitioners of Saturday Sabbath and Shabbat began to file lawsuits. According to Shulevitz (2010), however, the group responsible for dissolving shop-free Sundays was women. She writes

> As [women] poured into the workforce in the 1960s and the 1970s, they had less time to shop during the week [. . .] [men as well as women] had no choice but to shop on weekends. Businesses quickly perceived the demand for Sunday shopping hours and began lobbying state legislatures to make those hours legal. (p. 192)

Whether brick-and-mortar stores are open or closed, we are invited to consume 24/7. Trading was one of the 39 prohibitions of Shabbat, therefore money, also, is not to be handled. The motivation for this, Bass (2010) contends, is that "buying and spending are closely related to working too much; they depend on work, create the conditions for more work, and often *are* work" (p. 86). Resting from consumerism even one day a week means denying the belief and its lure that our lives will be better when we have more—more time, more money, more stuff. Buying into the belief that happiness requires more results in the desire to work longer and harder. Abstaining even 1 day a week from buying and spending can aid us in cultivating "a degree of spiritual independence from [the] gaudy promises" of consumerism (Bass, 2000, p. 64).

Worry

The final attitude we are invited to abandon during sabbath-keeping is an anxious temperament. Sabbath-keeping not only invites us to rest from work, but to rest from thinking and worrying about work. Sabbath time entails a focus on joy, relationships, and the pleasures of food and our bodies. In keeping sabbath, we are not denying our concerns or repressing thoughts of discordant aspects of our lives. Rather, we are affirming that there is always time for worry, but that the sabbath is an intentional time for rest. According to Smith-Gabai and Ludwig (2011), "One way the Sabbath allows mental rest is through avoidance of thoughts that cause concern or anxiety. Giving up mundane worries for one day can be a relief and a release" (p. 351). We practice the Sabbath with physically restful activities and by cultivating mental rest as well. Calhoun (2005) recommends "letting go of things that stress you out" and "letting the difficult conversations happen another day" (p. 40). As clinicians, we spend much of our week in the presence of others' stress and anxiety. We encounter evidence of the world's darkness and evil in our clients' lives and stories. Keeping sabbath reminds us, much as a good cognitive behavioral therapist would, that we can practice worried thoughts any day and time of the week. But for now, on the sabbath, let us stop. And like our clients, we raise awareness to our automatic thoughts, acknowledge them by letting them pass, and then rest in the joy of being.

Learning to Be

Leaving legalism, work, self-idolization, consumerism, and worry behind creates the space necessary to adopt new attitudes and acts. By doing less in keeping sabbath, we can shift our focus to ways of being. The following four attitudes and acts are not tasks to do or things to check off the list. Only through attention to our ways of being can we change our conception of time, truly connect with others, care for our embodied selves, and accept the goodness of our own creation.

Time

Time is a cultural construction. Nature does not provide us with reminders of when each hour passes. And, although nature does define each day, Alaskan daylight is markedly different in June than it is in January. Though our culture agreed to 60 seconds in a minute, 60 minutes in an hour, and 24 hours in a day, we do not agree on what can or should be accomplished in any given hour or day. What we do agree on, or so it seems, is that there is never enough time.

Clinicians' rhythm of life is dictated by the 50-minute hour. Our days begin and are demarcated into synonymous segments of client suffering, hardship, successes, and growth. This cultural construction furthers faithfulness to society's adage that time is money. The more hours spent in counseling and therapy, the more clients, and thus the more money. Most of us have adhered to this distorted cognition at one point or another. However, what we also know as clinicians is that flexible rather than rigid time is needed for client growth.

Sabbath-keeping asks us to abandon cultural conceptions of time, especially the belief that time is money, and recognize that growth is predicated upon periods of rest and renewal. As noted previously, we should not work in search of rest. Balanced living does not entail striving to "make it to the weekend." According to Ford (1997), keeping sabbath invites us to rest before work. In recounting the sabbath practices of a friend, Ford writes:

> He does not see rest only as a reward for work already done. He takes time off before a specially busy period and just enjoys himself. He treats his day the same way, punctuating it with breaks for exercise or something leisurely. It is an energizing routine, and he gets a great deal done. (p. 131)

Though researchers are still attempting to prove that sleep rejuvenates the body and mind in ways that cannot be accomplished while waking, as clinicians, we already know that emotional health requires sleep. Such rest is not the reward for 6 days spent toiling, but is the time needed in order to create and produce.

Have you ever been on vacation, only to spend the first 5 days trying to wind down and the last two dreading the impending need to gear up? This evidences the need for a changed conception of time. Through life segmentation or integrated sabbath-keeping, we are invited to condition ourselves into more easily stopping the need to do. Practicing times of being every day or every week will alleviate missed opportunities for vacation, as noted earlier. This means less time will be needed to decompress from doing, and more time to be spent simply enjoying being.

Connecting With Others

In Judaism, Shabbat necessitates the coming together of individuals into community. The 25-hour period is spent with family, friends, and neighbors, in homes and at synagogue. Meals are shared. Family and friends gather to take walks. Individuals reconnect with one another in leisurely conversation. According to Goldberg (1986), there is therapeutic value in the connections of the Shabbat. He writes:

> The leisurely evening provides a regular opportunity for family members to become reacquainted with one another and their neighbors, to find security often sought from the therapeutic environment, and

> to realize that there are others to whom one matters and with whom one can share the events and emotions of the week. (p. 240)

As Shabbat is a covenant between G-d and Jews, it entails an assertion of the Jewish identity both as individuals and as a community. According to Diddams et al. (2004), relationships and relatedness are an important aspect of Sabbath and serve to create a sense of belonging that strengthens both one's social identity and ability to cope.

It is no surprise that the individualism rampant in America today delimits our time for connecting with others. Online chat rooms, self-help groups, and congregations are all filled with people seeking connection. Some clients enter counseling not to seek treatment for mental illness, but simply due to a profound need to be heard and understood.

When the majority of our work hours each week are spent giving to others, at times it may seem that the company we keep is determined more by insurance panels than our own prerogative. Keeping sabbath invites us to be intentional about cultivating mutual and reciprocal relationships. In keeping sabbath, we seize the opportunity to care for ourselves, our friends, and our families with the same dedication we give to caring for our clients. By investing in such mutual relationships, we maintain our own support systems, nurture our souls, and gain energy through equitable give and take. Maintaining reciprocal relationships helps to preserve our ethical boundaries and protect us from seeking relational fulfillment through clients.

Embodiment

Many of us spend the majority of our days sitting in front of clients or the computer. Our work requires more mental aptitude and dexterity than physical. Thus, we wrongly assume that our livelihood depends on our brains, not our bodies. Two years ago I pulled a muscle running on the treadmill. As a result, whenever I sat before a client I engaged in an endless routine of shifting and repositioning in search of an elusive comfortable position. I tried about five different chairs and even brought a footstool from home. This experience taught me that I cannot give of my brain or heart without a fully functioning body.

One way that we move beyond fixations with doing toward the privileging of being is by honoring what our bodies are for us, not only what they do for us. Keeping sabbath involves rest and renewal of body, mind, and spirit. According to Heschel (1951), "The Sabbath is not dedicated exclusively to spiritual goals. It is a day of the soul as well as of the body; comfort and pleasure are an integral part of the Sabbath observance. Man in his entirety, all his faculties must share its blessing" (p. 19). Keeping sabbath entails a weekly reawakening to our embodied nature. By taking a walk, swimming, going on a hike, or relaxing in the bath, we are reminded of the pleasure of our physical selves as well as how imperative it is to appreciate and tend to our bodies.

Shabbat practices also include sexual relations. In traditional Jewish thought, husband and wife joined in sexual union to strengthen their intimate bond and to celebrate the sanctity of their embodied nature. Keeping sabbath invites us to embrace our embodiment through both physical rest and energizing exertion. Bass (2000) poignantly reminds us of the importance of caring for our bodies. She writes:

> [Our] bodies will operate, for a while, on mere fuel, which now can be obtained at all hours from the same outlets that sell fuel for motor vehicles. But these bodies cry out for something better than fuel: they cry out for care, for nourishment, for exercise, for rest. (p. 33)

Keeping sabbath helps to remind us that our bodies are not refueled at the filling station.

Accepting the Goodness of Our Own Creation

According to Genesis 2:2, on the seventh day God rested from the work of creation to reflect on the goodness of God's work. Keeping sabbath is not merely abstaining from work in order to rest, or resting in order to work. It is resting with the contentment that what we create through our work is good. In this sense, goodness does not connote worthiness or excellent quality. If this were the case, we might opt on Sabbath to rest in the work we have done with some clients, meanwhile ignoring our work with difficult or stymied clients. Rather, we rest in the acceptance that our work is good because *it is*. We accept creation as good with its flaws, not despite them. In the same way, we reflect on our work of the week before and accept its goodness, with an attitude of gratitude, for the simple fact that *it is*. Mindfulness practices grounded in the Buddhist tradition are predicated on such acceptance. These practices teach us to sit with our shadow sides and our shortcomings and to engage in radical self-acceptance. So too, in sabbath practice, we enter into a separate, holy time, in order to reflect on and accept the goodness of our creation, even when our inner critic is yelling out, "But you didn't finish your progress notes!" "You forgot to get the cups for Sarah's class party!" or "You let Client A rail on for 30 minutes because you really don't care!" Accepting the goodness of our creation compels us to accept, for the sabbath, what *is* without judgment.

So, too, sabbath-keeping invites us to accept our clients for their own goodness in creation. Sabbath-keeping compels us to honor the client we look forward to seeing, as she is insightful and motivated, in the same way that we honor the client we dread, due to his neediness and negativity. We accept clients for the progress they have made, we accept their shortcomings, and we celebrate the progress they are yet to make.

Privileging Being Beyond Doing

What is the rhythm of your week? Perhaps it is like a bass drum, steadily beating out each client appointment, each trip to the grocer's, and each dinner served. Or, perhaps it's like the roll of a snare drum, fast-paced with drive, but syncopated with client crises, emergency medical appointments, and decisions to euthanize the cat. Though there are always factors beyond one's control, truly we are charged with composing the rhythm of our weeks. We are responsible for recapitulating the beat when it gets too fast, or quieting it when it gets too loud. In the rhythmic arrangement of our lives, keeping sabbath is the intentional choice to decide that we are more than what we do, and to privilege our ways and times of being.

The lasting impact of keeping sabbath results not from what we *do* less of, but from the intention we bring to *being*. By recognizing that time is a cultural construction, we then choose how to construct it. By spending time in community, caring for our bodies, and accepting the goodness of ourselves and our work, we remind ourselves that we are not what we do. Changing behaviors is one means of doing something to deepen our being. Therefore, though behavioral changes of sabbath-keeping are essential, it is the cognitive changes, the soul change, that offers us the opportunity not only to renew, but to transform.

REFERENCES

Bass, D. C. (2000). *Receiving the day: Christian practices for opening the gift of time*. San Francisco, CA: Jossey-Bass.

Bass, D. C. (2010). *Practicing our faith: A way of life for a searching people* (2nd ed.). San Francisco, CA: Jossey-Bass.

Buechner, F. (1993). *Wishful thinking: A seeker's ABC*. San Francisco, CA: Harper SanFrancisco.

Calhoun, A. A. (2005). *Spiritual disciplines handbook: Practices that transform us*. Downers Grove, IL: InterVarsity Press.

Diddams, M., Surdyk, L. K., & Daniels, D. (2004). Rediscovering models of sabbath keeping: Implications for psychological well-being. *Journal of Psychology and Theology*, *32*(1), 3–11. Retrieved from http://www.biola.edu/jpt

Edwards, T. (1982). The Christian sabbath: Its promise today as a basic spiritual discipline. *Worship*, 56(1), 2–15. Retrieved from http://www.litpress.org/journals/worship.html

Ford, D. F. (1997). *The shape of living: Spiritual directions for everyday life*. Grand Rapids, MI: Baker Books.

Goldberg, A. D. (1986). The Sabbath as dialectic: Implications for mental health. *Journal of Religion and Health, 25*, 237–244. Retrieved from http://www.jstor.org/stable/27505883

Heschel, A. J. (1951). *The Sabbath.* New York, NY: Farrar, Straus and Giroux.

Kreider, T. (2012, June 30). The busy trap. *New York Times*. Retrieved from http://opinionator.blogs.nytimes.com/2012/06/30/the-busy-trap/

Shulevitz, J. (2010). *The sabbath world: Glimpses of a different order of time*. New York, NY: Random House.

Smith-Gabai, H., & Ludwig, F. (2011). Observing the Jewish sabbath: A meaningful restorative ritual for modern times. *Journal of Occupational Science, 18*(4), 347–355. Retrieved from http://dx.doi.org/10.1080/14427591.2011.595891

CHAPTER

7

Self-Renewal Through Natural Empathy

*Caring for Ourselves and Others**

Cheryl A. Giles

The meditation practice of natural empathy is an invaluable tool for self-renewal for caregivers. In its simplest form, natural empathy is a meditation practice in the tradition of Tibetan Buddhism that focuses on our immediate life experiences in order to nurture compassion and live a more open-hearted life (http://foundationforactivecompassion.org). Meditation offers us the opportunity to see ourselves honestly and to engage more effectively in our life and work. But why is natural empathy important to self-renewal? And how does self-renewal enhance the care we give to others? Quite simply, without self-care, our ability to feel empathy becomes deficient.

As caregivers (i.e., chaplains, doctors, and therapists) we have been taught how to "listen" and how to establish a trusting relationship. Through listening, we model openness, trust, and caring, values that shape our interactions with others and foster well-being. We know that developing a strong alliance or connection with others is necessary for a healthy trusting relationship. However, the relationship we develop with ourselves is just as important. When we are not in touch with our own inner state, our emotional reactivity can confuse us. We can get caught up in reacting to our experience of anger, sadness, fear,

*Based on the teachings of Lama Willa Miller at Natural Dharma Fellowship.

longing, hatred, and guilt. When we ignore or deny these emotions, we risk acting them out unconsciously, sometimes in destructive ways.

Blaming others or blaming circumstances for burnout, compassion fatigue, or depression are ways we may react to the suffering of others when our own self-care is deficient. Some of us make excuses for ignoring self-care, and we are not honest with ourselves that we have chosen to do so. But we alone are responsible for our inner life. When we are mindful of our own emotions, accept them as they are, and learn to let go of the attachment to seeing ourselves in a prescribed way, we can rest in natural empathy. Through the practice of meditation, we can cultivate our capacity to be with suffering without draining our own emotions.

Adapted from the Tibetan Buddhist tradition of Dzogchen or the Natural Great Perfection, natural empathy is the view that our essential being is pure and perfect by nature, though obscured by momentary habits of self-centered thought. The practice of natural empathy meditation offers us a way to connect with our natural state and to learn to accept whatever our experience brings. In *Awakening Through Love: Unveiling Your Deepest Goodness*, John Makransky (2007) offers his insight about the value of meditation practice:

> We practice to become receptive to the tremendous capacity of wisdom and love that is hidden in our being, to let the practice bring these qualities out with such force that they start to release us from the ego-centered causes of suffering in our minds, freeing us finally to become what we had most deeply intended—a real benefactor for the world. (p. 41)

Composed of two essential steps—leaning in (bearing witness, relaxing, and accepting) and communing (working to deepen our compassion and connection to others)—the practice encourages us to open our hearts when we face challenging and difficult circumstances in our everyday experience. Instead of shutting down, we deepen our natural empathy and ability to connect with others, and we renew ourselves in the process. It is this very practice that enables us, as caregivers, to keep giving care without fear of becoming "empty vessels."

Healthy self-care requires that we make a commitment to a spiritual practice, and this practice becomes the foundation for our work and life in the world. The practice of meditation is a path to liberation and freedom, one in which we can learn to live skillfully with discomfort, without resorting to destructive emotions like blame and shame. Empathy grows from deep acceptance of self and others, letting go of the illusion of separation and reminding us that we are interconnected.

Colleagues, patients, students, clients, friends, and our families become our "teachers" when we become angry, feel envy, or simply wish to be left alone. They remind us when we have shut down and when we no longer feel empathy when difficulties and challenges arise. Thoughts and feelings come and go; they are empty though we believe they are solid. They dissolve. Yet sometimes we identify with them, allowing ourselves to be controlled through habit and conditioning. We repeat the same learned patterns.

In my own experience as a teacher, I am often overwhelmed with tasks—phone calls, requests for letters of recommendation, and committee meetings—that pull me away from my "real" work—teaching, writing, and mentoring students. The frustration over the things that "pull" at my attention can dull my ability to feel empathy. At times, I find myself spinning from reacting to the feelings that arise. When I am made aware of and connect with these feelings (which I sometimes realize on my own and sometimes am reminded of by others), I try to stop and take a few deep breaths to stay with what I am feeling in the moment. Breathing creates spaciousness and allows me to get in touch with the natural empathy that already exists.

LEANING IN

When we *lean in*, using the meditation practice of natural empathy, we learn to become aware of our inner states, to welcome what comes, and to accept our experience. Leaning in is the opposite of turning away. We learn to stay with the thoughts and feelings that arise and to look at them with curiosity and without judgment. Leaning in deepens our natural empathy for ourselves and for others. As caregivers, we can learn to experience difficult emotions without identifying with the suffering of others, a key factor in caregiver burnout. By staying present to our everyday experience, we can find the pathway to deepening our empathy.

Teaching offers an opportunity to integrate the concepts of natural empathy with practice on and off the meditation cushion. With this in mind, in 2012 I developed a new seminar, *Buddhism, Community, and Diversity: The Color of Practice*. The goal of the seminar was to explore the impact of racial diversity in Buddhist communities across the United States. This seminar explored the effect of silence and passivity in White Buddhist communities as people of color have joined sanghas throughout the United States in search of enlightenment. As American Buddhism has become more firmly rooted in the United States, issues of diversity need to be in the forefront of conversations about how we embrace the Buddha, dharma (principles or teachings), and sangha, and extend limitless compassion to all. The 12 students who enrolled in the seminar were greeted with a host of expectations: fulfill a requirement for study of other religions in their degree program, take a course focused on diversity and anti-oppression, and complete a seminar to help them integrate the study of Buddhism and diversity.

Most of the students were from major Protestant denominations. Some identified as Christian and Buddhist and one student identified as Buddhist. All of the students had some familiarity with Buddhism from previous coursework at Harvard Divinity School or meditation practice. We began each class with a 3-minute meditation followed by a discussion of the readings.

Hilda Gutierrez Baldoquin's (2004) challenging volume *Dharma, Color, and Culture: New Voices in Western Buddhism* served as one of the key texts in the course. Her critical analysis reflected that Buddhist teachings have become more widespread in a country that is racially heterogeneous and founded by a White majority, "on the unwholesome seeds of colonialism, genocide and slavery" (p. 18). As sanghas embrace the dharma that professes equal access to enlightenment, we find ourselves wrestling with persistent oppression. Prejudice, discrimination, and racism still held by the wider society influences our Buddhist communities, even while our members have the best intentions.

For their first assignment, students wrote a race autobiography that included reflections of their earliest experience of race to the present. They presented these papers in class, followed by deep listening and Council Practice. As explained in *The Way of Council*, written by Jack Zimmerman and Virgina Coyle (1996):

> Participating in council teaches us how to let go of personal expectations and become fully attentive to others. The practice fosters a compassionate response and provides a continuing source of wisdom. Compassion arises naturally when we listen with respect and when we express ourselves with an open heart. Wisdom flows from the wholeness of the circle and reveals itself as the "truth of council." Listening to the voice of council teaches us that the circle's knowledge is greater than the totality of its members' individual knowing. (p. 25)

An example of leaning in can be seen in the Council Practice held in class. After reminding students they could comment only on their *own* experience of what came up for them as they listened to each presentation but not on its content, I asked them to talk about what came up for them. As students reflected on their feelings, the power of deep listening brought forth a range of emotions that for many had been buried deep within themselves.

So what does all this have to do with natural empathy and self-renewal? As a Buddhist practitioner, educator, and clinician, I am powerfully driven to address these issues in my quest to help create a better world. The meditation practice of natural empathy has helped me, and continues to help me, let go of past injuries. When I can offer my best through a clear lens, my students benefit as well. The practice of meditation encourages us to integrate our inner experience with the reflexive process of teaching and learning. By practicing meditation, we develop skillful means and a deep acceptance of who we are, and the natural empathy we rest in becomes more effortlessly available to others.

BEARING WITNESS

Bearing witness is being present to what is happening within us and right before our eyes. When we bear witness, we become one with the situation, and natural empathy arises. Bearing witness is the sacred act of cultivating a deep sense of caring for the suffering of others.

Marsha Linehan, a well-known psychologist, researcher, and the creator of dialectical behavior therapy (DBT), is a striking example of someone who has been quietly bearing witness to others who suffer. She has been a patient suffering from bouts of severe mental illness and an advocate for others like herself. Her work creating dialectical behavior therapy, a treatment model that teaches emotional regulation skills to people who struggle with severe suicidal behaviors, was trailblazing.

Developed in the 1980s, DBT has been widely used to treat borderline personality disorder and mood disorders. It has been a welcome treatment modality for clinicians and improved the lives of countless individuals who suffer from debilitating mental illness. Linehan knew this terrain well as a patient before the treatment existed.

When one of Linehan's patients asked her, "Are you one of us?" she acknowledged that she, too, had been a patient. Speaking at an event at the Institute of Living in Hartford, Connecticut, where she had been treated as an adolescent inpatient more than 50 years previous, she publicly disclosed her own challenges with suicidal behavior. Her story, "Expert on Mental Illness Reveals Her Own Fight" (Linehan, 2011) appeared in the *New York Times* and chronicled her enduring struggle with mental illness and her wish to be free of emotional affliction.

Linehan's journey is remarkable, not only for what she learned about herself but for what she learned about helping others. In the *New York Times* article, Linehan recalled that when she was discharged from the institute, still an adolescent, she vowed to help other patients find the freedom she had won: "I was in hell, and I made a vow when I get out I'm going to come back and get others out of there." Surely, she was not the first person to utter those words, so charged with deeply held feelings of anger, frustration, and, now, renewed hope.

Linehan's vow took shape many years later when she began a doctoral program in psychology and became a clinician to help others who were suffering. Later she created dialectical behavior therapy, a treatment that has helped countless people reconstruct their lives despite the fragility of their fractured personality.

An honest and courageous example of bearing witness, Linehan's story is a reminder that accepting ourselves as we are rather than as we wish to be and acting on our responsibility for self-care is key to sustaining resilience. Before we can bear witness to the pain and misery of others, we must be willing to look into our own hearts and bear witness to what we find there. Sometimes bearing witness to our own experience is the most difficult, and doing so without judging ourselves can feel nearly impossible. It is, however, a worthy and necessary pursuit, not only to connect with our natural empathy but also to attain the peace that comes with resting in the natural state.

RELAXING

We can learn to relax around our resistance to the suffering of others and our wish to make things better. When we are able to let go of our resistance to what we are witnessing, we are able to relax into the natural empathy. By staying with feelings that surface around suffering and not struggling with them, we create the opportunity to be with our experience, relaxing or resting in natural empathy. When we struggle with our resistance to experiencing suffering, our feelings grow stronger.

At a recent intensive weekend continuing education course on Practical Aspects of Palliative Care (Harvard Medical School, 2012), Dr. Muriel Gillick gave a challenging presentation on "Goals of Care: Promise and Pitfalls of the New Paradigm." In it she discussed the need for integrated evidence-based research with practical application of palliative care. During one of the workshops, the discussion focused on self-care and the importance of caregivers being aware of their own feelings as they work with dying patients. One participant commented that the palliative care team on her unit processed the experience of being with dying patients each week, but it was difficult to get the doctors to attend those meetings. Many of the doctors reported feeling too vulnerable to attend and identified two major obstacles: (1) boundary problems with participating as part of a team in which residents they were supervising were present, and (2) feelings of discomfort with openly displaying their deepest feelings after the loss of a patient.

The number of training programs integrating Buddhist practice for caregivers who work with dying patients is growing. As far back as 1972, Roshi Joan Halifax at the Upaya Zen Center in New Mexico has been at the forefront for training healthcare professionals to take care of the dying. This unique program in contemplative care provides clinicians with essential tools to be skillfully present to dying patients and to foster compassion and resilience in themselves as caregivers.

Integrating meditation with other self-care practices helps caregivers to relax and regain the resilience necessary for healthy caregiving. However, despite having this knowledge, some caregivers are reluctant to adopt these practices because their workplace does not support them. When hospitals begin to support these practices by encouraging training in contemplative end-of-life care, doctors will be able to bring balance to their clinical practice with patients.

ACCEPTING

At the November 2012 meeting of the Buddhist Contemplative Care Symposium at Garrison Institute in New York, doctors, social workers, chaplains, nurses, and other health-care clinicians met to discuss how to offer more effective care for the dying. The keynote address, "Aiding the Doctor Who Feels Cancer's Toll," was given by Diane Meier, MD, a palliative care physician at Mt. Sinai Medical Center in New York.

Dr. Meier told the story of a terminally ill patient with advanced cancer who was treated by an oncologist for 3 years. The oncologist had run out of options for this patient and thought the next treatment might be delivering chemotherapy directly to her brain. When Dr. Meier asked the doctor about this risky treatment, the oncologist reported that he did not want his patient to think that he had abandoned her. Meier said "when they run out of ideas and to avoid feeling that they've abandoned their patients, doctors throw procedures at them (patients)."

By confronting the oncologist, Dr. Meier was able to help the doctor see that he was acting out of frustration or inadequacy, and that "what his patient really needed at the end of her life was not more chemotherapy, but for him to sit down with her, to promise to do his best to keep her comfortable and to be there for the rest of her days."

Out of the public eye, doctors often suffer with their dying patients. Two occupational hazards of being with dying patients is burnout and secondary trauma or "compassion fatigue." This kind of stress can have serious health consequences for doctors who rely solely on "doing" or providing treatment to patients rather than "doing" and "being present to patients" where they listen as part of the care they provide.

For many doctors, the stress of caring for their patients combined with a lack of self-care can diminish both their communication with patients and their level of satisfaction with their work. Vicki Jackson, MD, a palliative care doctor at Massachusetts General Hospital, and her colleagues studied 18 oncologists to determine how they provided end-of-life care to their patients. The study, "A Qualitative Study of Oncologists' Approaches to End-of-Life Care," published in the *Journal of Palliative Medicine* (Jackson et al., 2008), explored how oncologists viewed the treatment they provided to their patients.

Doctors who viewed their role as providers of medical and psychosocial care reported feeling satisfied with end-of-life care to patients. Whereas, those who saw their role as primarily medical reported distant relationships with patients, a sense of failure, and a lack of collegial support. Finding sources of renewal is critical to providing good care for self and others.

Learning to practice meditation is one way that doctors can lessen the stress they experience in their work. Focusing on the breath when we feel stress allows the thoughts and emotions to surface. We notice them and then return to the breath. This practice encourages us to be in the present moment without getting involved in the circumstances leading to the stress. We can learn to accept whatever thoughts and feelings arise without judging the experience or ourselves. This simple practice, which is always available to us, can help doctors become more self-aware, empathic, and attentive to their inner life and the emotional suffering of the patients they serve.

COMMUNING

Caregivers who are not self-aware may experience stress, burnout, and secondary trauma as a problem unique to themselves. The practice of natural empathy helps us connect with the suffering of others and reminds us that we are not alone. Communing in the practice of natural empathy helps us to recognize that the pain and suffering that we feel right now is felt by others. We are not unique in our suffering; others suffer as well. When we are able to sit with these feelings, we can allow ourselves to connect with how others feel.

Despite the U.S. values of individualism, self-interest, and competition, communing as a meditation practice reminds us of our interdependence as human beings. Through our own suffering, we are able to recognize and identify with the suffering of others.

When caregivers are able to commune in their meditation practice, they avoid the isolation that comes with feeling that they alone are suffering. This sense of isolation can lead to depression, narcissism, and anxiety.

Dr. Jackson's study (Jackson et al., 2008) highlights that lack of training in providing end-of-life care to patients can lead to burnout and decreased job satisfaction for doctors. But the authors note that finding ways to cope with end-of-life care may be the single most important qualitative factor related to burnout. Jackson and her colleagues reported that despite the evidence that oncologists feel unprepared to care for the dying, little is known about the care they do provide or how they experience and cope with their patients. The study hypothesized that increased support from colleagues, role models, training in effective communication with patients, and time for reflection would improve job satisfaction and end-of-life care with patients.

Oncologists can benefit from practicing natural empathy by facing their discomfort, worry about their patients, and feelings of isolation. By communicating with each other about the challenges they face in the treatment of patients and the emotional stress they experience, doctors might be able to see that they are not alone. In fact, in a profession where inadequacy of any kind is viewed as failure, the knowledge that other doctors suffer might bring genuine relief to them.

COMPASSION

Can we train ourselves to be compassionate? In the past 25 years, there has been a seismic shift in the field of neuroscience. The results have been encouraging according to Emiliana Simon-Thomas, the Science Director for the Greater Good Science Center at UC Berkeley and a researcher who has studied compassion. In "Three Insights from the Cutting Edge of Compassion Research," which appeared on the Greater Good Science Center website in September 2012, she wrote:

> The regular practice of mindfulness—moment to moment awareness of your body and mind—comes more readily if people can be more openly aware of the present moment as it is occurring, particularly in the presence of other's suffering, without reflexive thinking or judgment.

Cultivating compassion through meditation affects parts of the brain system that responds to emotions, like empathy toward others. Richard Davidson, professor of psychiatry and psychology at University of Wisconsin, Madison, and his colleague Antoine Lutz used magnetic resonance imaging (MRI) to study whether positive emotions could be learned like a musical instrument. The MRI scans revealed that parts of the brain were dramatically changed in people who had extensive experience in practicing compassion meditation.

In an article that appeared in the *University of Wisconsin News* March 2008, "Study Shows Compassion Meditation Changes the Brain," Davidson and Lutz reported that they "wanted to see how this voluntary generation of compassion affects the brain system involved in empathy. I think this can be one of the tools we use to teach emotional regulation."

Neuroscience has given us a wealth of information about how the brain can help us to develop our emotional intelligence through meditation practices. Developing compassion is at the heart of this practice. When we have compassion for others we learn to have compassion for ourselves. By opening our hearts to the pain and suffering of people who enter our lives, we come to know that there is no separation between ourselves and others.

Working as a hospice volunteer has deepened my compassion and meditation practice. Facing death is a reminder that the connections we make with one another and the love that we feel opens our hearts wide to our own suffering and that of others. When patients are dying and their families are conflicted over how best to care for them, hospice provides them with the needed support. At times this support may mean making the decision with a family to provide only essential services so that the family can work through the conflicts that exist before the patient dies. This was the situation when I visited John, a middle-aged man, who was dying from a rare form of cancer. After a few canceled appointments, his wife agreed to open her home for a hospice visit. John was rapidly declining after receiving a diagnosis of cancer and having treatment for nearly 2 years. His children were still in a state of shock despite being fully aware of his illness and the prognosis given to them by his doctor.

One of the major stumbling blocks for the family was accepting that further treatment would not prolong their father's life. Their lack of acceptance caused tension among family members since John clearly told them he was ready to die. Hospice visits provided an opportunity for John to voice his concern that he wanted to say good-bye to some members of his family, but refused to see other family members who had caused him pain in his early childhood. His wife was supportive of John's wishes and wanted family members to accept John's decision so that his final days would be free of conflict. John died a few weeks after our meeting. Despite the ongoing conflict around his family's inability to accept that he was dying and his resistance to making peace with people he felt had hurt him, he seemed content.

CONCLUSION

Troops returning home from war in Afghanistan and Iraq have found reentry to civilian life extremely difficult. The rate of suicide throughout the ranks has reached epidemic proportions as many soldiers return home with posttraumatic stress disorder (PTSD; *Boston Globe*, December 2011). In an effort to address this tragic turn of events, a new long-term study funded by the David Lynch Foundation, which provides funds to programs to teach meditation to adults and children who suffer from PTSD, is being offered to first-year cadets, engaging them in meditation twice a day during their training. Researchers hope this will help improve their performance and inoculate them against PTSD.

The *Boston Globe* article, "Study Suggests Meditation May Help Prevent PTSD," states that the study has received high marks for its early success in the well-being of cadets. The article reported that the researchers were surprised by the effectiveness of meditation.

Dr. Carole Bandy, a Norwich University psychology professor and lead researcher, reported that stress, anxiety, and depression decreased significantly for the participants who meditated. Bandy and her colleagues noted that there were improvements in critical thinking and mental resilience, two key elements of overall fitness. Although some cadets reported being mocked by peers, their performance has steadily improved in all areas of their training.

One of Bandy's colleagues, John Dulmage, has been a strong advocate of meditation for all branches of the military. Dulmage, who served as a nurse in the 1991 Persian Gulf War, noted: "They (military) never really helped us with our mental health. We want to send people to war whole and for them to come back whole." Even those who were vocal skeptics have taken notice. Richard Schneider, the president of Norwich University and a retired Coast Guard Admiral, admitted that he was skeptical at the beginning, but after receiving training in meditation he has become a strong supporter:

> We have spent nearly 200 years preparing them physically to be military leaders. What we have never spent any time doing is making them emotionally prepared for battle. We are waiting until the end of the fight. Why not give it to them before they get into the fight? My plan is to make it available to anyone who wants it. I'm not at the point of requiring it but if it works I will be shouting from the rooftop.

My education and training prepared me for work as a chaplain, hospice volunteer, and a clinical psychologist. Though I never planned to become a teacher, that is where my path has taken me. Now, after 16 years of teaching, I find myself reflecting on a journey that has been filled with mostly unexpected joys and challenges. The richness of learning and the growth that comes from interacting with hundreds of students, each uniquely suited to be my "teacher," has been a wonderful surprise and a mutually engaging process. Even more surprising, teaching has given me the opportunity, even forced me, to work with my own fear and uncertainty about what it means to be fully human and to open this same door to my students. But challenges and joys come and go—much the same as students come and go—and without a reliable ground by which to maintain constancy, one can easily be swept away by these transitions.

Over the years, the practice of meditation has sustained me. Cultivating natural empathy, which goes hand-in-hand with meditation, has given me ground and a much-needed tool for self-renewal. The journey is different for everyone. At times, we worry that we are not "doing it right," that others are achieving what we ourselves cannot. We become frustrated. So it is always important to remember that the practice of meditation is precisely that—a practice. It is not perfection nor is it final. It is a lifelong journey that grows and deepens with time, that flows and blends to fill the empty spaces in our hearts, and that helps us to see pain and suffering not as an end but as a blessing that means we are indeed alive.

REFERENCES

Baldoquin Gutierrez, H. (2004). *Dharma, color, and culture: New voices in western Buddhism*. Berkeley, CA: Parallax Press.

Jackson, V. A., Mack, J., Matsuyama, R., Lakoma, M. D., Sullivan, A., Arnold, R. M., . . . Block, S. D. (2008). A qualitative study of oncologists' approaches to end-of-life care. *Journal of Palliative Medicine, 11*(6): 893–906. doi:10.1089/jpm.2007.2480

Linehan, M. (2011, June 23). Expert on mental illness reveals her own fight. *New York Times*.

Makransky, J. (2007). *Awakening through love: Unveiling your deepest good*. Somerville, MA: Wisdom.

Zimmerman, J. & Coyle, V. (1996). *The way of council*. Viroqua, WI: Bramble Books.

CHAPTER

8

Mind and Heart

Mindfulness and Loving-Kindness Meditation for Therapists

Kathleen Gregory, Geoffrey Newbegin, and Margot J. Schofield

OVERVIEW

The practice of psychotherapy for the alleviation of client suffering places high demands on practitioners, since the self of the psychotherapist is instrumental in the healing process. The importance of the psychotherapist's use of self is central not only for person-centered/humanistic counseling approaches (Rogers, 1957), but across a wide spectrum of therapeutic approaches (Duncan, Miller, Wampold, & Hubble, 2010). This healing effect is understood to be facilitated by the psychotherapist's capacity for therapeutic presence, attunement, and responsiveness (Geller & Greenberg, 2011).

Therapeutic presence involves "bringing one's whole self into the encounter with clients by being completely in the moment on multiple levels: physically, emotionally, cognitively, and spiritually" (Geller, Greenberg, & Watson, 2010, p. 599). Unfortunately, this capacity to be empathically attuned with clients in their suffering can also exact a significant emotional toll on therapists, leaving them vulnerable to vicarious trauma and compassion fatigue (Figley, 1995, 2002). Therapists who suffer from compassion fatigue are likely to find it more difficult to bear the suffering of others (Figley, 2002).

It is important to note, however, that compassion fatigue, while a serious risk, does not affect all who work with suffering. Key protective factors against compassion fatigue are self-care (Figley, 1995) and self-compassion (Neff, 2003). This chapter explores the potential of two integrative mind-body methods that may help to bridge the risk of compassion fatigue in therapists due to the therapeutic demands for their empathy, care, and compassion. Specifically, we describe methods known as mindfulness and *metta* or loving-kindness meditation practices. These methods have been utilized for thousands of years in Buddhism as a means to "train the mind" to work both intelligently and compassionately with the suffering of others. We explore the potential of these integrated mind-heart training practices to develop the capacity for psychotherapists to be present with and compassionate toward their clients, while, at the same time, nourishing psychotherapists' own well-being and acting as a protective factor against potential burnout and vicarious trauma.

In the West, there has been increasing recognition of the clinical benefits of mindfulness (Brown, Ryan, & Creswell, 2007). There is also a burgeoning appreciation for the positive impact that mindfulness can have on psychotherapists' capacity to be present with their clients. However, the practice of loving-kindness has only been explored more recently. Following traditional Buddhist explanations, this chapter aims to introduce the dual practices of mindfulness and loving-kindness, suggesting that together they can provide the means for psychotherapists to develop their capacity to be both present and compassionate with their clients. At the same time, the two practices can provide nourishment to their own well-being and protection from potential harmful effects of clinical practice. Thus, it is argued that the combination of mindfulness and loving-kindness practices can assist psychotherapists to both *work well* and *be well at work*, through the development of clarity of mind and warmth of heart.

The authors, experienced psychotherapists and researchers, draw on their long experiences as practitioners within Eastern-inspired spiritual traditions. In this chapter, we suggest that, when the development of a healthy relationship to suffering is made explicit in the practice of mindfulness, then psychotherapists can best serve their own well-being through conjoining the practice of mindfulness with loving-kindness. The chapter explores in more detail what these meditation practices are, the benefits that have been demonstrated through research on these practices, and how they can be incorporated into our lives and our work.

BUDDHIST UNDERSTANDINGS OF MINDFULNESS AND LOVING-KINDNESS

Mindfulness and loving-kindness can be described as representing the mind and the heart respectively. Associated with the two arms of Buddhist practice, wisdom and compassion, they serve as complementary practices. Traditionally, the analogy of a bird needing two wings to fly is used to represent the inseparability of wisdom and compassion on the spiritual path (Kyabgon, 2007, p. 30). Together, wisdom and compassion are the basis for working to alleviate the suffering of others, which remains the spiritual goal within Mahayana Buddhism in particular. The foundation for the development of wisdom is the practice of mindfulness, which is directed toward "making the mind serviceable for the cultivation of insight, presence, clarity, memory, and intelligence" (Wallace, 2011, p. 133). The foundation for the development of compassion is the practice of loving-kindness, which develops the capacity for empathy. When wisdom and compassion are conjoined, one can attend to others effectively with both a "quiet mind and an open heart" (Wallace, 2011, p. 133).

Within Western psychotherapy, and in relation to the training of psychotherapists, the concept of empathy remains difficult to operationalize. Walsh (2008) suggests that, "it is neither a capacity that unfolds naturally nor a skill that develops with a clear and positive trajectory. It may in fact degrade or slip away over time" (p. 75). Yet at the same time, across the spectrum of psychotherapeutic modalities, psychotherapist empathy is valued whether as a "transformative" or "necessary" facilitative condition in the process of client change (Rogers, 1957).

Buddhism, on the other hand, stresses the fact that the development of both wisdom and compassion is reliant on training the mind where notions of refining, increasing, and stabilizing are used to describe the developmental process. In this way mindfulness and empathy are understood as skills, which can be learned and improved through practice (Walsh, 2008, p. 81). This notion of training the mind is the recognition, from the Buddhist view, that human beings cannot simply decide, for example, to be compassionate. Rather, they must exert specific and targeted effort within meditation and contemplative contexts to both cultivate and stabilize compassionate feelings and attitudes, so that compassion can be intelligently and appropriately applied in situations encountered in their outer life.

Buddhism proceeds from the premise that the foundation for genuine and helpful relationships with others begins with the relationship we have with ourselves. Mindfulness practices thus can be understood to help us connect to ourselves; while loving-kindness practice helps us connect to others (Wegela, 2009). From the Buddhist view, the essential connection between self and other is the fact of suffering, the shared condition that links human beings across time and place. This view, encapsulated in the Four Noble Truths, is the central teaching of Buddhism (Gethin, 1998). The first of the Noble Truths, the truth of suffering, often defined as dissatisfaction, attests to the "truth" of the experience of impermanence in the human world. That is, everything is subject to change and as a consequence, is contingent and transient.

However, as the second Noble Truth attests, most human beings do not live their lives within the truth of this condition, which is the cause or origin of much of the suffering they do experience. Rather, human beings are driven by craving, clinging, grasping, and attachment—which are all "exaggerated forms of desire" to want things or, indeed, expect things to be different than the reality of how they are (Kyabgon, 2001, p. 5). Simply, it is exaggerated or excessive desire that makes the human condition worse by increasing the experience of dissatisfaction in the face of inevitable change and impermanence (Kyabgon, 2001, p. 6). From a psychological point of view, Buddhism understands that when we live *outside* or *against* the reality of things as they are, this is a breeding ground for feelings of disappointment, anxiety, anger, depression, and so on.

The context to discover this in relation to one's own experience is the practice of *Shamatha* or calm-abiding meditation; the context to make this understanding part of who one is, is the practice of loving-kindness, which connects one to others in the shared reality of ever-changingness and the accompanying suffering. That is, the barriers between oneself and others are broken down as one realizes certain "truths" through one's own experience: that all human beings want to be happy, all human beings suffer in facing both inevitable change (e.g., aging, sickness, and death) and unexpected change (e.g., loss of relationships, job), and compound their suffering by attachment to a desire for things to be different.

Working from this foundational Buddhist view, this chapter extends commonly held understandings of the practice of mindfulness to one in which the very endeavor to practice mindfulness is a discovery of *human suffering* and when this discovery is conjoined with the practice of loving-kindness, together they become the basis for nourishing both the psychotherapist and his or her work.

BUDDHIST AND WESTERN UNDERSTANDINGS AND PRACTICE OF MINDFULNESS

The translation of these Buddhist understandings into Western psychology has resulted in differing interpretations and a focus on certain aspects at the expense of others. Some have even argued for a decoupling of mindfulness from its origins and treated it purely as a technique or psychological process (Hayes & Shenk, 2004). We suggest that many presentations of mindfulness in Western psychological and well-being contexts have downplayed the complexity of the practice and the paradoxical interplay between adopting the stance of a somewhat detached observer of reality and being the experiencer of reality as it is revealed in the practice. That is, although instructions for practice are detailed and outcomes are established, the actual reality and process of mastering the practice of mindfulness is not so clearly represented.

This reality is the fact of the suffering of an "undisciplined mind," which is described as alternating "between the states of being overwhelmed by habitual agitation and dispersive thoughts and the state of lethargy" (Wallace, 1998, p. 87). From a Buddhist view, mindfulness practice is, in fact, promoted as the context "for seeing all aspects of our mind" (Kongtrul, in Ringu Tulku, 2006,

p. 9). That is, rather than first encountering the peace and calmness associated with a mind stabilized in the steady application of mindfulness, one encounters a wandering, distracted mind "fixated" on experiences, feelings, thoughts, and emotions, and the ensuing suffering that can bring. Meditation is, therefore, a context in which one simultaneously dwells in peace and in the distraction of habitual thoughts and emotions that arise (Kyabgon, 2001).

Thus, Buddhism understands that mindfulness is not easy! It is a context in which the habits of grasping, clinging, craving, and attachments are revealed; it is a place to develop *clarity* and *insight* about one's own propensities and the habits of mind that one begins to be able to identify as keeping one in *cycles of suffering*. This notion of mindfulness (and loving-kindness) as mind trainings highlights the fact that one has to start with "what we are already" (Trungpa, 2005, p. 64) and learn through one's own experience the human capacity to "create" both suffering and peace. When one is able to come to know one's own mind in that way, one can then extend oneself to others not only from the stability of peace that allows one to be "present," but also with a sense of compassion toward others from the encounter with "suffering" within one's own experience and in the difficulty experienced in establishing stable mindfulness. This connection of mindfulness practice to an increased appreciation for suffering allows the "natural" complement of mindfulness and loving-kindness practice to be revealed; wherein experiencing both peace and suffering lays the ground for developing a wish for happiness for self and others.

The cultivation of mindfulness in the practice of meditation is associated with *remembrance*, a process of focusing the mind, again and again, on the object of meditation, for example, the breath, as a present moment experience. External objects such as a candle, a statue, a stone, or a flower can also be used with the similar aim of cultivating a mindful attention, although focus on the breath is regarded as a foundation practice in both Buddhist and Western psychological contexts (see Kabat-Zinn et al., 1992).

Thus, in the context of formal meditation, one cycles through "remembering" and "forgetting" the focus of the breath. One adopts a general attitude of friendliness toward oneself, and intends on whatever arises in meditation without any kind of evaluation, judgment, or expectation; this is the ground Buddhism suggests for developing a *true* relationship with one's experiences based on acceptance. As a consequence, the capacity to be present to experience as it arises becomes available to one; with an emphasis on mindfulness as a way of "being" rather than "doing" (Bien, 2006).

Concomitantly, mindfulness is the foundation for awareness to arise (Wallace, 1998). Awareness, on the one hand, represents our most direct experience of reality (Brown et al., 2007). However, awareness is also understood as a dynamic process whereby direct perceptions of sensory input are rapidly overlaid with cognitive and emotional processes (Brown et al., 2007). Thus, in the context of mindfulness practice, anchoring attention to the breath allows awareness to heighten so one can see what is going on in one's experience in the moment in a purposeful way; a nonjudgmental attitude deters one from getting caught up in what one is experiencing, allowing the inevitable conceptual and emotional experiences that arise, to slowly dissipate (Kabat-Zinn, 2003). Outside of the meditation situation, mindfulness is associated with the capacity to focus our minds on whatever we are doing (Kyabgon, 2001). Thus, meditation provides the training to strengthen *remembering* within daily life.

Translating the Buddhist understanding of mindfulness into the Western psychological context has seen this approach encapsulated in three aspects: attention, attitude, and intention (Shapiro, Carlson, Astin, & Freedman, 2006). *Attention* has been associated with the ability to stay in the present moment with whatever is arising in one's experience. The capacity to experience the moment has psychological benefits as it allows one, for example, to stay with a particular difficult feeling, to examine it more closely, and to observe it in relation to the rising and falling of thought processes. However, the traditional teachings would also emphasize that one should not become fascinated with or start thinking about what is arising in experience; this is regarded as just more conceptual proliferation, which can take one away from the "present" moment.

Attitude is concerned with bringing a sense of openness to the meditation process. Kabat-Zinn (2003) suggests that cultivating a "sense of openheartedness, friendly presence and interest" (p. 145) is the most conducive attitude to the development of a nonjudgmental approach to the practice of mindfulness. Together, attention and attitude help one regulate ruminating thoughts and discomforting feelings as they arise within the practice of mindfulness.

Intention is concerned with the question of purpose, identifying what the goal of practicing mindfulness is. For some, the goal in meditating is to gain enlightenment and compassion for all beings. For others, the intention may be to simply calm the mind. Intention is an important aspect of meditation that will influence both how it is undertaken and what one gains from the process (Shapiro et al., 2006).

In this section we have highlighted the Buddhist emphasis on mindfulness practice in the context of "suffering." With increased awareness of one's own suffering and with increasing capacity to be "present to" one's experience in any given moment, one develops a deeper sympathy and appreciation for one's own condition. It is this, Buddhism suggests, which becomes the basis of a deeper sense of compassion and concern for others (Trungpa, 2005). Thus, for psychotherapists, mindfulness practice extends not only their capacity to be present and attuned with their clients, but is the working basis for their capacity to be compassionate and kind. Furthermore, it nourishes their desire to extend themselves to others in their work in a helpful way. As Trungpa (2005) says, from the practice of meditation one can begin to feel that "you want to do something for others and something for yourself" (p. 59). The practice of loving-kindness serves to deepen and cultivate this motivation.

BUDDHIST UNDERSTANDINGS OF LOVING-KINDNESS

Despite strong interest in Buddhist concepts and practices, there has been less focus in the West on the role of cultivating compassion and loving-kindness, the heart of the practice. Eastern philosophical traditions provide a much richer delineation of heart-related concepts such as the ancient northern Indian concept of *Metta-bhavana*. *Metta* can be translated as loving-kindness, friendliness, goodwill, fellowship, and nonviolence, and refers to love, good intentions, empathy, and establishing connections between people (Payutto, 1995). *Bhavana* means *to develop* or *to cultivate* (Paramananda, 1996). These concepts are brought together in the practice of loving-kindness meditation, which is the cultivation of a genuine wish that others (and oneself) be happy.

Where mindfulness meditation is "nonconceptual" to the extent that thoughts or images are not utilized, loving-kindness is a mental exercise utilizing contemplation to direct thoughts, images, and emotions "intended to transform us by training in thinking about others" (Kyabgon, 2004, p. 117). Paramananda (1996) describes the loving-kindness practice as a process of "encouraging the more expansive and warmer aspects of ourselves" (1996, p. 49).

Loving-kindness practice facilitates a movement toward becoming less self-centered and better able to focus on others; thus it enhances a sense of connectedness, empathy, integration, and wholeness. The development of loving-kindness rests on the Buddhist premise that what is thought and felt influences the views one has of self and others, which establishes the kind of relationships one has with others and the world in general. Thus, loving-kindness practice is concerned with helping one "turn away" from "unwholesome" emotions that result in self-cherishing, and developing an all-encompassing sense of loving-kindness to all without partiality.

First, it is recognized that self-cherishing arises from dwelling on negative emotions such as anger, jealousy, and pride, which can result in a sense of separation from others (Kyabgon, 2004). The practice and cultivation of loving-kindness allows one to more easily let go of the negative experiences of the past and present, and this helps to cultivate a positive and optimistic vision of both oneself and others. Loving-kindness practice is designed to deepen and stabilize positive emotions such as compassion, empathy, tolerance, understanding, and acceptance; as a result, one becomes a more loving and kind human being (Kyabgon, 2004).

Second, as the loving-kindness practice looks outward toward others, it must be done with a sense of impartiality. Rather than being caught up in bias or preference, which can interfere with the capacity to "listen to one another" (Payutto, 1995, p. 236); impartiality is considered an essential principle that supports open-mindedness in relation to *all* others. Thus loving-kindness in itself is "neutral" in relation to who should receive it (Payutto, 1995, p. 236) and is characterized as "all-encompassing" in its reach.

Further, continuing to practice loving-kindness positively impacts not only on one's capacity to give and share with others, but one's life becomes enriched as a result. "Consequently, having loving-kindness for oneself and others can have a stabilizing and strengthening influence on our character and temperament" (Kyabgon, 2004, p. 96). When understood in the context of the self-cherishing tendencies of human beings, the notion of "emotional enrichment" can be elaborated as an outcome of breaking down the perceived divide between self and other, as well as judgments of right and wrong, good and bad, which one imposes on both oneself and others. Loving-kindness is the basis of an all-encompassing attitude to oneself and others that helps to nourish the capacity for compassion (Kyabgon, 2004). Since loving-kindness is directed as a wish that others be happy; there is an implicit recognition that others, like oneself, suffer. Loving-kindness is thus understood to be a "sympathetic and empathic response to the existential condition" (Kyabgon, 2004, p. 105).

It is this basis that allows psychotherapists to be with both their own experience and the experience of the client in the counseling room in a gentle and an all-encompassing manner. That is, one is not just "paying attention" but one is aware of suffering and actual (or potential) happiness, and as a consequence, one is able to extend oneself in a precise and skilful way to the other (Trungpa, 2005).

From a theoretical perspective, there would seem to be much to gain from training therapists in loving-kindness meditation practice to invoke their natural capacity for warmth toward themselves, which allows them to interact with others from a position of warmth, empathy, and compassion. A Buddhist perspective would see such training as providing the framework and stance from which therapists can relate in a healing manner with all manner of people, as well as protecting themselves from potential harm through interaction with disturbed or traumatized clients (Trungpa, 2005).

WESTERN UNDERSTANDINGS AND PRACTICE OF LOVING-KINDNESS

Western scientific traditions have long been preoccupied with the mind/brain at the expense of understanding the role of the heart. Yet, there are now many exciting developments that can focus our attention on the potential for enhanced and more integrated understanding of human behavior and change through positive psychology (Fredrickson, Cohn, Coffey, Pek, & Finkel, 2008; Fredrickson & Losada, 2005; Seligman, Rashid, & Parks, 2006) and neuroscience (Davidson et al., 2003; Lutz, Brefczynski, Johnstone, & Davidson, 2008). Increasingly, understandings from Western science are also being enhanced by the study and integration of Eastern philosophical concepts (Brown et al., 2007). This shift includes a growing interest in core "heart"-related concepts of relevance to psychotherapists' well-being and skill, such as the constructs of compassion, empathy, love, kindness, and mercy (Fredrickson & Losada, 2005; Peterson & Seligman, 2004; Rogers, 1957).

Loving-kindness, as conceptualized in the West, concerns the cultivation of an affective state of unconditional kindness to all people (Hofmann, Grossman, & Hinton, 2011). It has been distinguished from compassion, which is understood as a genuine sympathy for those who experience misfortune, together with an earnest wish to ease their suffering (Grossman & Van Dam, 2011). Loving-kindness has also been associated with the notion of "warmth" toward others because this is recognized as a positive affect, which "stimulates *liking*, affection and feelings of connectedness" (Gilbert, 2005, p. 28). In the West most research has focused on the construct of compassion, especially in relation to the domain of psychotherapy.

The literal meaning of compassion is *to suffer together*. It refers to the feeling that arises in response to another's suffering and that motivates a desire to relieve the other's suffering (Keltner, 2010). Thus, compassion involves a reaching out to another and motivates a desire to altruistically act. Compassion has long been recognized as a core innate quality of the helping professions (Hopkins, 2001), yet there has been little systematic attention on how to teach compassion, or even whether compassion can be taught. Indeed, it could well be argued that the study of compassion has been seriously neglected.

Empathy, a related but different construct, is a central skill identified in most models of counseling and psychotherapy (e.g., Egan, 2010; Rogers, 1957). It differs from compassion, in that the focus in empathy is on the ability to take another's perspective and feel their emotions, but does not include the added component of feeling motivated to relieve their suffering (Keltner, 2010); nor indeed a desired wish for them to be happy, which is the motivation of loving-kindness practice.

There has been a solid body of research suggesting that empathic responding can be taught, at least to a basic level of demonstrating a capacity to understand and feel another's emotions. However, the notion of systematic training and development that builds from a "shared appreciation" of our human existential condition has yet to be realized within the training of psychotherapists. The combined practices of mindfulness and loving-kindness aim to foster such an outcome. It can be said that, to date, psychotherapist training programs have relied too often on basic definitions (e.g., basic versus advanced empathy), and a micro-skills approach to empathic responding. As the traditional Buddhist view shows, empathy, love, and compassion are understood as complex affective responses that arise naturally the closer one is to the reality of human suffering. This is realized first in oneself and then extended to others from the practice of mindfulness.

It is suggested that although there remains potential to explore loving-kindness both as a stand-alone practice and conjoined with compassion, when combined with the practice of mindfulness as a forum to develop an appreciation for human suffering, there is maximum potential to further enhance the positive affective qualities of psychotherapists.

LOVING-KINDNESS PRACTICE

So how can we cultivate *loving-kindness?* The most common three methods are: to turn one's mind to loving-kindness by reflection, to undertake visualizations and use imagination to cultivate all-encompassing loving-kindness, and to use a mantra to create and sustain the wish. If one chooses to practice loving-kindness in the formal context of sitting meditation, it can be helpful to intersperse mindfulness of breath meditation between practices to help ensure one is not overwhelmed by the experience. For example, after each visualization, a few minutes of "relaxing" the mind in meditation is recommended.

Reflecting. Reflecting on one's positive experiences of kindness shown by self and others in the past, and developing an appreciation for the positive attributes in oneself and others, can help to orientate one to the qualities that the practice of loving-kindness is seeking to deepen. In the traditional teachings, remembering the kindness of one's mother in terms of her care and selfless attention to one's needs as one was growing up can be used to help engender the attitude, vision, and feeling state of *loving-kindness*. Granted that many people's experiences of mothering may be problematic and even the notion of "mother" is a culturally bound concept, it is suggested that reflecting on someone else (an aunt, sibling, friend) who loves and cares for one, in the past and present, can be utilized (Khyentse, 2012).

Visualization. Kyabgon (2004) describes the generation of loving-kindness through visualization in relation to three groups of people: one's own loved ones, those who are unknown or "neutral" to oneself, and one's "enemies" or people whom one dislikes or has difficulty with. In the practice, one begins with wanting one's loved ones to be happy, imagining them receiving everything they want on the physical, mental, or spiritual level. One imagines the person visibly affected, being happy, joyous, and content by the love one has generated toward them in this way. After a few minutes, one returns to mindfulness of the breath before then giving rise to the image of a stranger or acquaintance. One imagines them receiving all that they desire or need; that all their dreams and wishes could be fulfilled by the generation of one's love in this way. Again, after a few minutes, one relaxes the mind from the visualization and returns to the mindfulness of breath.

Finally, one thinks of someone one dislikes, and imagines wanting this person to be happy and to have everything they need, want, desire. Even if aversion arises as one perceives the person's aggressiveness, arrogance, or whatever is the source of one's dislike for this person, one can imagine that those aspects or characteristics of the person have become mellowed or softened and that the person can himself become happier and more joyous in both himself and in his relationships with others. After visualizing this for a few minutes, then again one returns to the practice of mindfulness of breath.

As one practices the loving-kindness visualization in this way, over time one can then begin to incorporate an ever-increasing number of people, for example, extending out from those in "one's immediate neighborhood, to one's city, state, country, the world, and even galaxy; including all sentient creatures at the same time" (Kyabgon, 2004, p. 107).

Mantra. Another method to practice loving-kindness is the repetition of a mantra or phrase such as: "May I be well, May I be happy, May I be free from suffering; May others be well, May they be happy, May they be free from suffering." In relation to the self, this mantra can be particularly useful when feelings of despondency arise or one is facing difficult life challenges and situations. When extended to include others, a sense of connectedness is cultivated. Whether bringing to mind a specific other or as a more general motivation, the aim is to cultivate the feeling of genuinely wishing the happiness of self and others to increase. The mantra is not repeated to create a form of self-hypnosis, but rather, it is important that meaning be given to each phrase of the mantra, while allowing time for the mantra to have some effect. "It's as though you take the idea in the form of words and drop it into your heart" (Paramananda, 1996, p. 63).

Regular practice of *loving-kindness* can help to maintain the experience of positive emotions, and the practice can also be applied specifically when negative emotions such as anger, fear, guilt, and sadness arise. That is, the opportunity to practice and develop the experience of positive emotions comes through ongoing encounters with difficult people and situations, which will test the ability to be compassionate, tolerant, and understanding. From the perspective of Buddhism, this is the practice. For psychotherapists, developing the practice of loving-kindness helps in relation to one's own well-being when tired, challenged, or when working with difficult client situations. Generating a feeling of loving-kindness in the work can be helpful when uncertain what to do, or when clients themselves are overwhelmed by affective states. Importantly, the cultivation of loving-kindness helps one "narrow that gap between being and action" (Kyabgon, 2004, p. 116), which itself serves to nourish the motivation of psychotherapists to be of help to others.

This chapter has explored the two meditation practices of mindfulness and loving-kindness in terms of their spiritual and practical origins. The following section reviews some recent research findings on the benefits of both mindfulness and loving-kindness meditation practices, providing a "parallel presentation" to the traditional Buddhist presentation. The aim is to introduce the reader to the fact that there is increasing certainty within Western psychological and well-being contexts about the efficacy of these meditation practices in assisting psychotherapists to work with a wide range of clinical presentations, as well as in fostering positive attentional and affective qualities in the psychotherapists themselves. We propose that the value of current Western understandings and research can be augmented by the traditional Buddhist perspective, which encourages a deeper engagement with the practices of both mindfulness and loving-kindness.

EVIDENCE-BASE FOR MINDFULNESS MEDITATION AND LOVING-KINDNESS PRACTICE

Mindfulness meditation and loving-kindness practice convey a number of measurable benefits, both within and beyond therapy. The benefits and processes of change involved in each of these practices are offered below.

Benefits of Mindfulness Meditation

Reviews and meta-analyses of a substantial and growing body of research support the beneficial effects of practicing mindfulness, in terms of improved physical and psychological health outcomes (Baer, 2003; Brown et al., 2007; Grossman, Niemann, Schmidt, & Walach, 2004). Demonstrated benefits include reduced anxiety, depression, and stress (Baer, 2003; Kabat-Zinn et al., 1992; Reibel, Greeson, Brainard, & Rosenzweig, 2001), reduced suicidal behavior (Williams, Duggan, Crane, & Fennell, 2006), and reduced relapse rates, even for those with more than two depressive episodes (Teasdale et al., 2000). These positive effects have also been found for more complex presentations of individuals with comorbid disorders (Chiesa & Serretti, 2009; Hoffmann, Sawyer, Witt, & Oh, 2010).

Research has also demonstrated that mindfulness improves many aspects of psychological well-being such as self-confidence, happiness, problem solving, acceptance, and tolerance of oneself (Brown & Ryan, 2003; Perez-De-Albeniz & Holmes, 2000). Studies of psychotherapists who practice mindfulness meditation also show improvements in well-being and satisfaction with life (May & O'Donovan, 2007).

Processes of Change in Mindfulness Meditation

The mechanisms underpinning the positive impacts of mindfulness practice have also been investigated. Theoretical assumptions that improved mental health would be achieved through improving the capacity for focused attention, awareness, and emotion regulation have gained support from a growing body of research. For instance, mindfulness meditation has been shown to improve attention (Chambers, Lo, & Allen, 2008; Jha, Krompinger, & Baime, 2007; Valentine & Sweet, 1999; Zeidan, Johnson, Diamond, David, & Goolkasian, 2010) and awareness (Modinos, Ormel, & Aleman, 2010; Siegel, 2007b). It can also reduce distraction (Jain et al., 2007), and improve working memory

(Jha et al., 2007). Thus, the practice of mindfulness seems to improve key metacognitive capacities, and this, in turn, supports the reduction of stress, anxiety, and rumination.

These changes are understood to lead to more effective emotion regulation by reducing negative emotions and enhancing positive ones (Davis & Hayes, 2011). For instance, mindfulness meditation enables people to become less emotionally reactive and more flexible in dealing with situations (Goldin & Gross, 2010; Siegel, 2007a, 2007b). Mindfulness meditators are able to develop a sense of detached self-observation that allows both disengagement from prior experience-based reactions and a greater ability to focus on the present (Siegel, 2007a, 2007b). Mindfulness meditators also seem more open to new experiences compared to people who do not meditate (Brown & Ryan, 2003), and more able to take the perspective of others (Birnie, Speca, & Carlson, 2010). Such changes can lead to improved interpersonal relationships through more mindful responding between people (Barnes, Brown, Krusemark, Campbell, & Rogge, 2007; Block-Lerner, Adair, Plumb, Rhatigan, & Orsillo, 2007), greater skills in identifying and communicating emotions to others, and dealing better with the emotional stressors of relationships (Barnes et al., 2007; Carson et al., 2005; Wachs & Cordova, 2007).

Baer (2003) outlined a number of hypothesized processes that contribute to symptom reduction and changes in behavior. These processes include: *exposure*, where patterns of behavior that are not helpful are allowed to dissipate by observing them nonjudgmentally; *cognitive change*, where mindfulness can allow people to see their thoughts as "just thoughts" rather than as a belief/acceptance of their truth or reality; *self-management*, where mindfulness can improve the range of coping skills for an individual by becoming more aware of thoughts, feelings, and behaviors; *relaxation*, that one of the "side effects" of practicing mindfulness is reduced stress and feeling more relaxed; *acceptance*, that being able to accept thoughts and feelings as they come and go can allow the possibility of change.

More recently, neuroimaging research has shown positive effects of mindfulness meditation on both brain structure and function in ways that are consistent with mindfulness theory (Davidson et al., 2003; Lee et al., 2012; Siegel, 2007a, 2007b). Positive effects include: enhanced sensory processing, increased reflective awareness of sensory experience and audiovisual processing (Kilpatrick et al., 2011); increased attentional focus and regulation (Xue, Tang, & Posner, 2011), increased regional cortical thickness (Xue et al., 2011); increased gray matter in areas related to positive emotions, emotional stability, and mindful behavior (Luders, Toga, Lepore, & Gaser, 2009); denser nerve fibers (white matter) creating larger numbers of brain signaling connections; and an expansion of myelin (protective insulation surrounding the nerves) (Tang, Lu, Fan, Yang, & Posner, 2009). These results, in combination, suggest that practicing mindfulness affects the way the brain functions by assisting in neural integration, self-regulation, and intrapersonal attunement, which, in turn, increases the capacity for attuned relationships (Siegel, 2007a).

Mindfulness Effects in Psychotherapy

Most studies of mindfulness in the psychotherapy context have focused on the training of clients. Of the small number of studies looking at the effects of mindfulness meditation on the therapist, a key outcome has been improved well-being of the therapist. For instance, increased positive affect, decreased negative affect, reduced anxiety and rumination, and increased levels of self-compassion and mindfulness among trained therapists have been reported (Shapiro, Brown, & Biegel, 2007).

There is also a small body of evidence that mindfulness training of psychotherapists may lead to the cultivation of empathy and openness in therapists (Block-Lerner et al., 2007; Lesh, 1970), with flow-on benefits for the therapeutic relationship (Ryan, Safran, Doran, & Muran, 2012). Mindfulness meditation seems to benefit the psychotherapy process by training the therapist in *self-attunement* (Bruce, Manber, Shapiro, & Constantino, 2010; Stern, 2004). Attunement assists the interpersonal process and helps the client achieve greater self-attunement leading to the reduction of symptom severity, greater self-efficacy, and better interpersonal relationships.

Other potentially helpful capacities developed by practicing mindfulness are a stronger sense of "Observing Self" or "Witness" where the psychotherapist can be aware of the thoughts and feelings being experienced and learn not to become attached to them, simply to see them as thoughts and feelings that are separate from themselves (Walsh, 2006). This has the benefit of reducing the intensity of these experiences. Thus, mindfulness training can be beneficial in developing a sense of calmness and clarity in psychotherapists, enabling them to stay present with their clients and to be both empathic and objective. Mindfulness is understood to positively impact upon the therapist's ability to attend to three aspects of the present moment that occur simultaneously in the therapeutic relationship: the therapist's own thoughts and feelings; the client's thoughts and feelings; and the relationship between the two, moment to moment (Stern, 2004).

These benefits suggest that mindfulness may be an effective self-renewal method to reduce the potential of burnout and gives therapists the tools to sit with a client's pain and suffering without feeling overwhelmed by it. At the same time, mindfulness practice allows psychotherapists themselves to be present to their own experiences of discomfort, boredom, or unease that may arise in the therapy work, thus ensuring negative impacts of these experiences are dealt with immediately and gently.

Kristeller and Johnson (2005) suggest that deep engagement in a mindful meditation practice fosters a sense of transcendence of self-focused concerns, and emphasizes an understanding of self as part of a larger humanity, along with the sense of interconnectedness of all. Such a practice may support psychotherapists to remain connected and engaged, and promote a greater sense of compassion for both self and others (Birnie et al., 2010). Furthermore, some research suggests that positive benefits can be achieved from even a small dose of mindfulness training, with as little as a single session of meditation training being found to reduce stress and improve quality of life of health professionals (Prasad, Wahner-Roedler, Cha, & Sood, 2011).

Benefits of Loving-Kindness Meditation

Despite some interest in loving-kindness meditation in popular and spiritual Western literature (Salzberg, 1995), there has been a much smaller body of research on the effects of loving-kindness meditation compared with mindfulness meditation research. Findings to date have generally supported the theory underpinning the practice of loving-kindness, pointing to potential benefits of loving-kindness meditation for decreasing negative emotions and symptoms, and enhancing positive emotions and social connection with others. Demonstrated benefits include: reductions in anxiety, negative mood, anger, and physical and emotional pain across a range of health and clinical samples (Carson et al., 2005; Johnson et al., 2011; Kristeller & Hallett, 1999; Salzberg, 1995). Research has also demonstrated increases in positive social emotions such as love, joy, contentment, gratitude, and self-acceptance toward oneself, an increase in positive emotions toward others, and improved relations with other people (Carson et al., 2005; Fredrickson et al., 2008; Salzberg, 1995). There is also some evidence that positive emotions can be sustained for longer periods after practicing loving-kindness (Fredrickson et al., 2008). However, findings are not always consistent. The study by Fredrickson et al. (2008) found that loving-kindness meditation produced small effects for positive emotions, but no impact on negative emotions, contrary to theoretical predictions.

Recent neuroscience research comparing the effects of focused-attention meditation and loving-kindness meditation on brain structures and functions found evidence of distinct neural activity associated with each form of meditation during sustained attention and emotional processing that was consistent with the specific focus of each form (Lee et al., 2012). The loving-kindness practice was associated with greater activation in emotion-processing regions of the brain and this seems to be the mechanism by which meditators achieve better emotion regulation and more positive emotional states. However, it was noted that some activation of specific emotion-processing areas was observed during attention-focused meditation practice (Lee et al., 2012), supporting the small number of studies that suggest that mindfulness practice can enhance empathy and openness in therapists (Block-Lerner et al., 2007; Lesh, 1970).

In a review of research on loving-kindness and compassion meditation practices, Hofmann et al. (2011) conclude that the loving-kindness practice may be particularly useful for dealing with interpersonal issues such as anger control, whereas compassion meditation may be useful for treating depression and relationship problems. They also noted that across a number of studies, loving-kindness meditation practice produced positive results even with relatively short periods of practice.

Processes of Change in Loving-Kindness Meditation

Recent brain-imaging studies found that the cultivation of positive emotions via compassion and loving-kindness meditations is associated with altered activation of neural circuitries linked to empathy and theory of mind in response to emotional stimuli (Lutz et al. 2008). As well, expert meditators demonstrate stronger effects than novice meditators. Even brief training in loving-kindness meditation can lead to greater positivity toward both strangers and the self (Hutcherson, Seppala, & Gross, 2008). These findings suggest that the practice of meditations like loving-kindness can enhance empathic response to social stimuli. As loving-kindness meditation is increasingly used there will no doubt be further research into the processes and benefits of this heartfelt practice.

ENHANCING PSYCHOTHERAPIST WELL-BEING BY COMBINING MINDFULNESS AND LOVING-KINDNESS PRACTICE

This chapter has described how the meditation practices of *mindfulness* and *loving-kindness* can be equated to wisdom and compassion; the mind and heart. Together they are understood as two wings of a bird; mindfulness without loving-kindness practice may lead to being overly "detached" from others and seeing things only from an intellectual viewpoint. To practice only *loving-kindness*, one may become too "enmeshed" with others and not see situations with clarity. To practice both meditations is to have balance between thought and emotion.

From a psychotherapist's perspective, having both practices to draw on can assist in what Siegel (2007a) described as states of "engaged alignment" and "distanced autonomy" necessary for an effective alliance between psychotherapists and clients. These have been recognized by "master therapists" as core ethical values in the development and maintenance of "interpersonal attachment" in their clinical work (Jennings, Sovereign, Bottorff, Mussell, & Vye, 2005). As has been demonstrated through the research presented, each of the practices contributes to the development and maintenance of these aspects. In this chapter, we have paralleled the research evidence with a review of the traditional Buddhist perspective, which establishes the connection between mindfulness practice and the development of an appreciation for human suffering, and the natural progression from this appreciation to compassion and care for both oneself and others. The loving-kindness practice is identified as the means to nourish one's motivation to be of help to others. Within this view, the combined practices of mindfulness and loving-kindness collapse the divide of "being and action," serving to support the integrity of the psychotherapist in their work.

SUMMARY

This chapter provides an overview and an outline of two traditional Buddhist meditation practices, the mindfulness of breathing and a loving-kindness practice. In parallel, the growing research evidence that these practices support the development and integration of mind and heart in psychotherapists' personal and professional lives has also been presented. However, this chapter has sought to explore the practices from the traditional Buddhist understanding, highlighting that when human suffering is recognized within oneself, naturally one extends out to self and others. Developing oneself in relation to positive qualities such as loving-kindness ensures that one can sustain oneself in the moment with self and others' pain; and hold simultaneously, a hopeful and optimistic view. It is this capacity, the authors suggest, that best acts as a protective process against vicarious trauma and burnout and sustains the well-being of the psychotherapist.

REFERENCES

Baer, R. A. (2003). Mindfulness training as a clinical intervention: A conceptual and empirical review. *Clinical Psychology: Science and Practice*, *10*(2), 125–143. doi:10.1093/clipsy/bpg015

Barnes, S., Brown, K. W., Krusemark, E., Campbell, W. K., & Rogge, R. D. (2007). The role of mindfulness in romantic relationship satisfaction and responses to relationship stress. *Journal of Marital and Family Therapy*, *33*(4), 482–500. doi:10.1111/j.1752–0606.2007.00033.x

Bien, T. (2006). *Mindful therapy: A guide for therapists and helping professionals*. Boston, MA: Wisdom.

Birnie, K., Speca, M., & Carlson, L. E. (2010). Exploring self-compassion and empathy in the context of mindfulness-based stress reduction (MBSR). *Stress and Health*, *26*, 359–371. doi:10.1002/smi.1305

Block-Lerner, J., Adair, C., Plumb, J. C., Rhatigan, D. L., & Orsillo, S. M. (2007). The case for mindfulness-based approaches in the cultivation of empathy: Does nonjudgemental, present-moment awareness increase capacity for perspective-taking and empathic concern? *Journal of Marital and Family Therapy*, *33*, 501–516. doi:10.1111/j.1752–0606.2007.00034.x

Brown, K. W., & Ryan, R. M. (2003). The benefits of being present: Mindfulness and its role in psychological well-being. *Journal of Personality and Social Psychology*, *84*(4), 822–848. doi:10.1037/0022–3514.84.4.822

Brown, K. W., Ryan, R. M., & Creswell, J. D. (2007). Mindfulness: Theoretical foundations and evidence for its salutary effects. *Psychological Enquiry*, *18*, 211–237. doi:10.1080/10478400701598298

Bruce, N. G., Manber, R., Shapiro, S. L., & Constantino M. J. (2010). Psychotherapist mindfulness and the psychotherapy process. *Journal of Psychotherapy Theory, Research, Practice, Training*, *47*(1), 83–97. doi:10.1037/a0018842

Carson, J. W., Keefe, F. J., Lynch, T. R., Carson, K. M., Goli, V., Fras, A. M., & Thorp, S. R. (2005). Loving-kindness meditation for chronic low back pain. *Journal of Holistic Nursing*, *23*(3), 287–304. doi:10.1177/0898010105277651

Chambers, R., Lo, B. C. Y., & Allen, N. B. (2008). The impact of intensive mindfulness training on attentional control, cognitive style, and affect. *Cognitive Therapy Research*, *32*, 303–332. doi:10.1007/s10608–007–9119–0

Chiesa, A., & Serretti, A. (2009). Mindfulness-based stress reduction for stress management in healthy people: A review and meta-analysis. *Journal of Alternative and Complementary Medicine*, *15*(5), 593–600. doi:10.1089/acm.2008.0495

Davidson, R. J., Kabat-Zinn, J., Schumacher, J., Rosenkranz, M., Muller, D., Santorelli, S. F., & Sheridan, J. F. (2003). Alterations in brain and immune function produced by mindfulness meditation. *Psychosomatic Medicine*, *66*, 149–152. doi:10.1097/01.PSY.0000077505.67574.E3

Davis, D. M., & Hayes, J. A. (2011). What are the benefits of mindfulness? A practice review of psychotherapy-related research. *Psychotherapy*, *48*(2), 198–208. doi:10.1037/a0022062

Duncan, B., Miller, S., Wampold, B. & Hubble, M. (Eds.). (2010). *The heart and soul of change: Delivering what works in therapy* (2nd ed.). Washington, DC: American Psychological Association.

Egan, G. (2010). *The skilled helper: A problem-management and opportunity-development approach to helping* (9th ed.). Belmont, CA: Wadsworth.

Figley, C. R. (1995). *Compassion fatigue: Coping with secondary traumatic stress disorder in those who treat the traumatized*. New York, NY: Brunner/Mazel.

Figley, C. R. (2002). Compassion fatigue: Psychotherapists' chronic lack of self care. *Journal of Clinical Psychology*, *58*(11), 1433–1441. doi:10.1002/jclp.10090

Fredrickson, B. L., Cohn, M. A., Coffey, K. A., Pek, J., & Finkel, S. M. (2008). Open hearts build lives: Positive emotions, induced through loving-kindness meditation, build consequential personal resources. *Journal of Personality and Social Psychology*, *95*, 1045–1061. doi:10.1037/a0013262

Fredrickson, B. L., & Losada, M. F. (2005). Positive affect and the complex dynamics of human flourishing. *American Psychologist*, *60*(7), 678–686. doi:10.1037/a0030620

Geller, S. M., & Greenberg, L. S. (2011). *Therapeutic presence: A mindful approach to effective therapy*. Washington, DC: American Psychological Association.

Geller, S. M., Greenberg, L. S., & Watson, J. C. (2010). Therapist and client perceptions of therapeutic presence: The development of a measure. *Psychotherapy Research, 20*(5), 599–610. doi:10.1080/10503307.2010.495957

Gethin, R. (1998). *The foundations of Buddhism*. Oxford, England: Oxford University Press.

Gilbert, P. (2005). Compassion and cruelty: A biopsychosocial approach. In P. Gilbert (Ed.), *Compassion: Conceptualisations, research and use in psychotherapy* (pp. 10–74). London, England: Routledge.

Goldin, P. R., & Gross, J. J. (2010). Effects of mindfulness-based stress reduction (MBSR) on emotion regulation in social anxiety disorder. *Emotion, 10*, 83–91. doi:10.1037/a0018441

Grossman, P., Niemann, L., Schmidt, S., & Walach, H. (2004). Mindfulness-based stress reduction and health benefits. A meta-analysis. *Journal of Psychosomatic Research, 57*(1), 35–43. doi:10.1016/S0022–3999(03)00573–7

Grossman, P., & Van Dam, N. T. (2011). Mindfulness, by any other name . . . : Trials and tribulations of *sati* in western psychology and science. *Contemporary Buddhism, 12*(1), 219–239. doi:10.1080/14639947.2011.564841

Hayes, S. C., & Shenk, C. (2004). Operationalizing mindfulness without unnecessary attachments. *Clinical Psychology: Science and Practice, 11*, 249–254. doi:10.1093/clipsy.bph079

Hofmann, S. G., Grossman, P., & Hinton, D. E. (2011). Loving-kindness and compassion meditation: Potential for psychological interventions. *Clinical Psychology Review, 31*, 1126–1132. doi:10.1016/jcpr2011.07.003

Hofmann, S. G., Sawyer, A. T., Witt, A. A., & Oh, D. (2010). The effects of mindfulness-based therapy on anxiety and depression: A meta-analysis review. *Journal of Consulting and Clinical Psychology, 78*(2), 169–183. doi:10.1037/a0018555

Hopkins, J. (2001). *Cultivating compassion*. New York, NY: Broadway Books.

Hutcherson, C. A., Seppala, E. M., & Gross, J. J. (2008). Loving-kindness meditation increases social connectedness. *Emotion, 8*, 720–724. doi:10.1037/a0013237

Jain, S., Shapiro, S. L., Swanick, S., Roesch, S. C., Mills, P. J., Bell, I., & Schwartz, G. E. R. (2007). A randomized controlled trial of mindfulness meditation versus relaxation training: Effects on distress, positive states of mind, rumination, and distraction. *Annals of Behavioural Medicine, 33*(1), 11–21. doi:10.1207/s15324796abm3301_2

Jennings, L., Sovereign, A., Bottorff, N., Mussell, M.P., & Vye, C. (2005). Nine ethical values of master therapists. *Journal of Mental Health Counseling, 27*, 32–47.

Jha, A. P., Krompinger, J., & Baime, M. J. (2007). Mindfulness training modifies subsystems of attention. *Cognitive, Affective, and Behavioral Neuroscience, 7*(2), 109–119.

Johnson, D. P., Penn, D. L., Fredrickson, B. L., Kring, A. M., Meyer, P. S., Catalino, L. I., & Brantley, M. (2011). A pilot study of loving-kindness meditation for the negative symptoms of schizophrenia. *Schizophrenia Research, 129*, 137–140. doi:10.1016/j.schres.2011.02.015

Kabat-Zinn, J. (2003). Mindfulness-based interventions in context: Past, present, and future. *Clinical Psychology: Science and Practice, 10*(2), 144–156. doi:10.1093/clipsy.bpg016

Kabat-Zinn, J., Massion, A. O., Kristeller, J., Peterson, L. G., Fletcher, K. E., Pbert, L., . . . Santorelli, S. F. (1992). Effectiveness of a meditation-based stress reduction program in the treatment of anxiety disorders. *American Journal of Psychiatry, 149,* 936–943.

Keltner, D. (2010). The compassionate instinct. In D. Keltner, J. A. Smith, & J. Marsh (Eds.), *The compassionate instinct: The science of human goodness* (pp. 8–15). New York, NY: Norton.

Khyentse, D. J. (2012). *Not for happiness: A guide to the so-called preliminary practices.* Boston, MA: Shambhala.

Kilpatrick, L. A., Suyenobu, B. Y., Smith, S. R., Bueller, J. A., Goodman, T., Creswell, J., . . . Naliboof, B. D. (2011). Impact of mindfulness-based stress reduction training on intrinsic brain connectivity. *NeuroImage,* 6, 290–298. doi:10.1016/j.neuroimage.2011.02.034

Kristeller, J. L., & Hallett, B. (1999). An exploratory study of a meditation-based intervention for binge eating disorder. *Journal of Health Psychology,* 4, 357–363. doi:10.1177/135910539900400305

Kristeller, J. L., & Johnson, T. (2005). Cultivating loving kindness: A two-stage model of the effects of meditation on empathy, compassion, and altruism. *Zygon, 40*(2), 391–408. doi:10.1111/j.1467–9744.2005.00671.x

Kyabgon, T. (2001). *The essence of Buddhism.* Boston, MA: Shambhala.

Kyabgon, T. (2004). *Mind at ease: Self-liberation through Mahamudra meditation.* Boston, MA: Shambhala.

Kyabgon, T. (2007). *The practice of Lojong: Cultivating compassion through training the mind.* Boston, MA: Shambhala.

Lee, T. M. C., Leung, M-K., Hou, W-K., Tang, J. C. Y., Yin, J., So, K-F., . . . Chan, C. C. H. (2012). Distinct neural activity associated with focused-attention meditation and loving-kindness meditation. *PLoS ONE, 7*(8), e40054. doi:10.137/journal.pone.0040054.

Lesh, T. V. (1970). Zen meditation and the development of empathy in counselors. *Journal of Humanistic Psychology, 10*(39), 39–81. doi:10.1177/002216787001000105

Luders, E., Toga, A. W., Lepore, N., & Gaser, C. (2009). The underlying anatomical correlates of long-term meditation: Larger hippocampal and frontal volumes of grey matter. *NeuroImage,* 45, 672–678. doi:10.1016/j.neuroimage.2008.12.061

Lutz, A., Brefczynski, J., Johnstone, T., & Davidson, R. J. (2008). Regulation of the neural circuitry of emotion by compassion meditation: Effects of meditative expertise. *PLoS ONE, 3*(3), e1897. doi:10.1371/journal.pone.0001897

May, S., & O'Donovan, A. (2007). The advantages of the mindful therapist. *Psychotherapy in Australia, 13*(4), 46–53.

Modinos, G., Ormel, J., & Aleman, A. (2010). Individual differences in dispositional mindfulness and brain activity involved in reappraisal of emotion. *Social Cognitive and Affective Neuroscience,* 5(4), 369–377. doi:10.1093/scan/nsq006

Neff, K. D. (2003). The development and validation of a scale to measure self-compassion. *Self and Identity,* 2, 223–250. doi:10.1080/15298860309027

Paramananda. (1996). *Change your mind: A practical guide to Buddhist meditation.* Birmingham, AL: Windhorse.

Payutto, P. (1995). *Buddhadhamma: Natural laws and values for life* (G. A. Olson, Trans.). Albany: State University of New York Press.

Perez-De-Albeniz, A., & Holmes, J. (2000). Meditation: Concepts, effects and uses in therapy. *International Journal of Psychotherapy*, *5*(1), 49–58.

Peterson, C., & Seligman, M. E. P. (2004). *Character strengths and virtues: A handbook and classification.* Oxford, England: Oxford University Press.

Prasad, K., Wahner-Roedler, D. L., Cha, S. S., & Sood, A. (2011). Effect of a single-session meditation training to reduce stress and improve quality of life among health care professionals: A "dose-ranging" feasibility study. *Alternative Therapies in Health and Medicine*, *17*(3), 46–49.

Reibel, D. K., Greeson, J. M., Brainard, G. C., & Rosenzweig, S. (2001). Mindfulness-based stress reduction and health-related quality of life in a heterogeneous patient population. *General Hospital Psychiatry*, *23*(4), 183–192.

Ringu Tulku (2006). *The Ri-me philosophy of Jamgön Kongtrul the Great.* Boston, MA: Shambhala.

Rogers, C. R. (1957). The necessary and sufficient conditions of therapeutic personality change. *Journal of Consulting Psychology*, *21*(2), 97–103.

Ryan, A., Safran, J. D., Doran, J. M., & Muran, J. C. (2012). Therapist mindfulness, alliance and treatment outcome. *Psychotherapy Research*, *22*(3), 289–297. doi:10.1080/10503307.2011.650653

Salzberg, S. (1995). *Loving-kindness: The revolutionary art of happiness.* Boston, MA: Shambhala.

Seligman, M. E. P., Rashid, T., & Parks, A. C. (2006). Positive psychotherapy. *American Psychologist*, *61*(8), 774–788. doi:10.1037/0003–066x.61.8.774

Shapiro, S. L., Brown, K. W., & Biegel, C. M. (2007). Teaching self-care to caregivers: Effects of mindfulness-based stress reduction on the mental health of therapists in training. *Training and Education in Professional Psychology*, *1*, 105–115. doi:10.1037/1931–3918.1.2.105

Shapiro, S. L., Carlson, L. E., Astin, J. A., & Freedman, B. (2006). Mechanisms of mindfulness. *Journal of Clinical Psychology*, *62*(3), 373–386. doi:10.1002/jclp.20237

Siegel, D. L. (2007a). *The mindful brain: Reflection and attunement in the cultivation of well-being.* New York, NY: Norton.

Siegel, D. L. (2007b). Mindfulness training and neural integration: Differentiation of distinct streams of awareness and the cultivation of well-being. *Social Cognitive and Affective Neuroscience*, *2*, 259–263. doi:10.1093/scan/nsm034

Stern, D. N. (2004). *The present moment in psychotherapy and everyday life.* New York, NY: Norton.

Tang, Y-Y., Lu, Q., Fan, M., Yang, Y., & Posner, M. I. (2009). Mechanisms of white matter changes induced by meditation. *PNAS*, *109*(26), 10570–10574. doi/10.1073/pnas.1207817109

Teasdale, J. D., Williams, J. M. G., Soulsby, J. M., Segal, Z. V., Ridgeway, V. A., & Lau, M. A. (2000). Prevention of relapse/recurrence in major depression by mindfulness-based cognitive therapy. *Journal of Consulting and Clinical Psychology*, 68, 615–623. doi:10.1037//0022–006X.68.4.615

Trungpa, C. (2005). *The sanity we are born with: A Buddhist approach to psychology*. Boston, MA: Shambhala.

Valentine, E. R., & Sweet, P. L. G. (1999). Meditation and attention: A comparison of the effects of concentrative and mindfulness meditation on sustained attention. *Mental Health Religion and Culture*, 2, 59–70. doi:10.1080/13674679908406332

Wachs, K., & Cordova, J. V. (2007). Mindful relating: Exploring mindfulness and emotion repertoires in intimate relationships. *Journal of Marital and Family Therapy*, 33(4), 464–481. doi:10.1111/j.1752–0606.2007.00032.x

Wallace, B. A. (1998). *The bridge of quiescence: Experiencing Tibetan Buddhist meditation*. Chicago, IL: Open Court.

Wallace, B. A. (2011). *Minding closely: The four applications of mindfulness*. Ithaca, NY: Snow Lion.

Walsh, C. (2006). *Mindfulness training*. Retrieved from http://www.mindfulness.org.au/Benefits.htm#Observer

Walsh, R. A. (2008). Mindfulness and empathy: A hermeneutic circle. In S. F. Hick & T. Bien (Eds.), *Mindfulness and the therapeutic relationship* (pp. 72–86). New York, NY: Guilford Press.

Wegela, K. (2009). *The courage to be present: Buddhism, psychotherapy and the awakening of natural wisdom*. Boston, MA: Shambhala.

Williams, J. M. G., Duggan, D. S., Crane, C., & Fennell, M. J. V. (2006). Mindfulness-based cognitive therapy for prevention of recurrence of suicidal behaviour. *Journal of Clinical Psychology*, 62, 201–210. doi:10.1002/jclp.20223

Xue, S., Tang, Y., & Posner, M., I. (2011). Short-term meditation increases network efficiency of the anterior cingulate cortex. *Cognitive Neuroscience and Neuropsychology*, 22, 570–574. doi:10.1097/WNR.0b013e328348c750

Zeidan, F., Johnson, S. K., Diamond, B. J., David, Z., & Goolkasian, P. (2010). Mindfulness meditation improves cognition: Evidence of brief mental training. *Consciousness and Cognition*, 19, 597–605. doi:10.1016/j.concog.2010.03.014

CHAPTER

9

Zen Therapy

David Brazier

THE ORIGIN OF THE IDEAS OF ZEN THERAPY

Through the 1980s and 1990s I was practicing psychotherapy and concurrently studying Buddhist texts. It became apparent to me that many of the principles and issues that modern psychotherapy deals with were anticipated in these ancient writings. In particular, there is a genre of writing called the *Abhidharma.* Dharma refers to the teachings of Buddha, which were collected together in *sutras* or threads. We still have the word *suture* in English meaning a surgical stitch. Buddha, over the 40 years of his mission, gave threads of teaching mostly in response to specific inquiries, rather as a therapist gives a distinct response to each client. The Abhidharma was a series of attempts to draw out the underlying principles. It was rather as though you had the case histories of a famous therapist and you were trying to work out what his or her system was.

There was a distinct difference of style between the Abhidharma and modern psychological writing. I pondered on this and realized that what the abhidharmikas were trying to do was to classify all the elements in what Buddha taught and did. A science often goes through a classificatory stage. A science like botany is substantially concerned with classifying all the kinds of plants that exist. Only later comes a stage of understanding how plants function. Once I'd realized this, it became apparent that much of the classificatory material could readily be translated into a functional form. I was helped in this last move by a lecture given by a friend, Campbell Purton, who works at the University of East Anglia, who showed that the first element of conditioning listed in the seventh book of the Pali Abhidharma corresponded directly with the necessary and sufficient conditions isolated by Carl Rogers in his seminal theory of humanistic counseling (Rogers, 1961). I immediately became interested to see if the other elements corresponded to modern theories, too, and, lo and behold, there was Jung's association theory and also the basic ideas of behaviorist reinforcement theory and several other intriguing parallels. There was, it seemed, nothing new under the sun. This was exciting stuff and led to the publication of my book *Zen Therapy* (Brazier, 1995).

Now things are rarely entirely straightforward. The ancient Buddhist texts certainly revealed some anticipation of theories that have reemerged in the 20th century in the West and they had the added advantage that what were, in the latter context, often seen as competing and incompatible theories were, in the Buddhist opus, all part of a single unified approach. Here was humanistic, psychodynamic, and behavioral psychology all in a single package. At the same time, not all of the Buddhist categories seemed to have modern equivalents and some of the underlying principles seemed to differ from what tends to be taken for granted in the modern context. In other words, while there were similarities at a theoretical level, there were differences of basic paradigm. This should not be surprising. After all, India in the fifth century before Christ was a very different kind of society from our modern world. In particular, Buddhist psychology as a whole has the following features:

- Ideas of sudden awakening and gradual transformation.
- An emphasis on nobility of character and overcoming of spiritual danger.
- A fundamental notion of emptiness of inherent nature.
- Distinctive views about encounter, relationship, and aloneness.
- A sense that the seeker (client) and guide (therapist) are on essentially similar paths.
- Distinctive ideas about conditioning and causation.
- A nonnormative approach.
- A nonself approach.

I say a little about each of these further on, but first should add that this is just one bit of this particular gold mine. The Buddhist material also contains a huge wealth of practical formulations, many in the form of lists such as the Seven Factors of Enlightenment, the Four Truths of the Noble Ones, the Six Perfections, and any number of others. Again, it became apparent that at least a number of these lists are actually also theories of a functional rather than a merely categoric nature. What I mean by this is that they are listed in order such that the first factor gives rise to the second, the second to the third, and so on. This realization in due course gave rise to my book *The Feeling Buddha* (Brazier, 1997), in which I recast one of the most basic lists, the Four Truths of the Noble Ones, into a new interpretation, showing how it explains how common reactions to stressful circumstances generally turn out to be dysfunctional; yet a more constructive option is available involving faith and courage, which can enable a person to transform disadvantageous circumstances into a constructive spiritual path.

A DISTINCTIVE PARADIGM

The subject of this book is self-renewal. What it is concerned with is the survival of the helper and, more than survival, the arrival of the helper at new growth in wisdom and compassion through the experience of helping and of exposure to the lives and trials of those who are helped. This is similar to the theme of *The Feeling Buddha*. The experienced professional helper has been exposed, at least vicariously, to a wide range of human distress and dysfunction. How can this become a foundation for personal growth, resilience, creativity, and constructive self-transformation?

By way of introduction, let me say a little more about the eight distinctive features that I listed earlier.

1. *Sudden awakening and gradual transformation:* The basic idea here is that change does not happen smoothly. It comes in *eureka!* moments. Life is not a process of change; it is in equilibrium until conditions change, and when they change, things change suddenly. Many people have seized on the idea that Buddhism teaches that everything changes and have taken this to mean that everything is changing all the time. This is not correct. Change happens because conditions change. In all worldly matters, it is inevitable that supporting conditions will change sooner or later so change will come. After such sudden change there is likely to be a series of consequential effects, which gives an appearance of gradual transformation, but even gradual transformation is really just a series of smaller sudden changes. This means that therapeutic effect happens at specific change point times. In principle, wholesale change can happen abruptly. Mere days before his great awakening, the man who became Buddha was in a pretty bad state.
2. *The noble character overcomes spiritual danger:* Danger to spirit means falling into corrupt or inauthentic ways that bring unwholesome life outcomes. In practice this usually means grasping a short-term gain at the cost of a long-term drawback. If all that alcohol did was to help one relax and feel good with no impact on liver health, no next morning hangover, no loss of self-control, and so on, then it would be a wonderful thing. However, the truth is otherwise. The noble character is, therefore, one who takes a longer term view. There is currently a good deal of emphasis on living in the present moment and this is associated with Buddhist teaching, but it seems much truer to the original texts to say that they praise living in the long-term rather than living in the

moment. Again, the noble character is not self-centered, a point we come back to in Point 8, and, most importantly, the noble character is concerned with substance rather than mere appearance, truth rather than passing opinion. Facing the existential truths of life in general and the personal truths of our own life in particular is a key element in transformation.

3. *Emptiness of inherent nature:* It is a recurrent theme in these texts that things are not what they seem. We make sense of the world in our terms, on our terms, but the things we make sense of are not so from their own side. I call this item in front of me *a table* because I use it to put my books and my coffee on, but from its own side, as it were, it is simply what it is. This means, *inter alia*, that it could be many things, an art object, firewood, part of a barricade, raw material for making paper, and so on, yet even all of these are only ideas from the human side. Things have no fixed essential nature. This applies to people, too. In the Buddhist paradigm, there is no essential self or self-nature. Therapy, therefore, is not about being one's true self or anything of the kind. A noble life is a life lived doing noble things, not one lived expressing some kind of essential essence. Spirituality is gratuitous goodness done for its own sake. This means that self-renewal is not, from this perspective, about finding oneself so much as about finding purpose and usefulness. It is a special kind of objectivity.
4. *Encounter, relationship, and aloneness:* Buddhism values aloneness, *ekagata*. This does not necessarily mean physical aloneness. According to the Japanese theorist Tomoda, the purpose of a therapeutic encounter is to facilitate aloneness, to enable the client to experience freedom from conditions (Ryback, Ikemi, Kuno, & Miki, 2001). We tend to carry around internalized others and carry on internal conversations with them. We spend a lot of time looking after our internalized others, imprisoning them and allowing them to imprison us. Zen aims to help us set them free to live their own lives and so let this chatter inside us cease in order that the heart may experience peace. One may then be alone with Buddha and Buddha is silent. This approach has a different flavor from Western ideas about relationship. In Buddhism, the purpose of relationship is, in a sense, to allow each person to experience a kind of aloneness, a state of being clean and empty of tackiness. True encounter is faith, a letting go into the unknown. Where Western thought could be said to be intent on building something together, Eastern though is more concerned with becoming a still pool that naturally nurtures without need for deliberate action.
5. *Similar paths:* Much Western thought about therapy is predicated on the idea that the client needs to be fixed or sorted out in some way because something has gone wrong. Buddhism has a different model. Instead of

thinking that the aberrant must be returned to the right place where others are, the Buddhist sees all as progressing along a path and most as still far from the goal. To be where most people are on this path is not necessarily a gain because most are not far along. The path of the therapist and that of the client are essentially the same. In the therapeutic encounter, both will learn. The client may have more to learn, but the therapist is probably better at learning. Essentially, however, they are companions sharing the journey. The qualification of the guide is simply greater experience in finding a way forward. What lies ahead is unknown. Nonetheless, a guide can, in such circumstances, be vitally useful. Each helps the other, but in implicit ways. The client's problem (koan) triggers that of the therapist. Each is helping to heal the other.

6. *Conditioning and causation:* Buddhism suggests that the human situation is one in which there is an irreducible core of freedom that is rarely realized because of attachment to conditions. Conditioning, here, does not mean what it means in behavioral psychology. In the Buddhist sense, a condition for the table in front of me being where it is is the floor that it stands on. If the floor gave way, the table would move. The movement would be immediate. As long as the floor holds, nothing happens. Humans, unlike tables, can, to an extent, choose conditions. The conditions we choose become props, holding us in a particular posture in relation to life, an identity. Inasmuch as we are dependent on our props they become our masters. If you want something to change, change the things that prop up how it is now. This is a basic therapeutic principle. This is why some of the most creative lives have significant elements of failure or disaster in their history. Such people learned something about liberation that many people avoid learning. Buddhism does not see a nobility or an evil in suffering, merely that affliction is inevitable, but it does see that such inevitable challenge can be a doorway to understanding and deeper conviction. Such may be a liberation.
7. *A nonnormative approach:* Western psychotherapies are largely based on an idea of getting people back to normal whereas Buddhism rests on the idea that the normal state is deluded. The aim of Buddhist cultivation is to rescue people from normality. In this sense, Buddhism is a path of liberation. Normality is seen as somewhere in the middle of a spectrum, which has enlightenment at one end and madness at the other. The normal person is mildly mad. It is interesting to link this to Jung's idea of midlife crisis. In early life a person finds a form of mild madness that works. In later life they have to face the inauthentic aspects of what they have created and try to go beyond them. This is perilous and can involve radical changes in orientation and lifestyle as a person strives for what is true beyond what was sufficient to merely get by. Zen is certainly concerned, not just at midlife, but at every stage, with getting to

what is really true, however unflattering, as a sober basis for genuine living. It tends to see conventional life as more an obstacle than a help in this process. Another way of saying this is that whatever is normal where we are tends to seduce us, and Zen is concerned with helping us to see through and not be caught by that seduction.

8. A *non-self approach:* The essential nature of normal madness is attachment to self, or, we could say, conceit. We act as though we ourselves are a special case, but also rely upon image-management for our self-esteem. Buddhism is not, therefore, concerned with self-building. Society requires us to present a self-image. Zen helps us to see that this is no more than an artificial artifact. Much Western therapy revolves around the idea of promoting self-esteem and self-worth. From a Buddhist perspective this is a waste of time. The remedy for people who have low opinions of themselves is not to give them a high opinion of themselves, but to wean them from so much thinking about self at all. There is a life to live and a job to do and when nothing of the kind calls there is peace to enjoy, none of which requires the investment of energy in maintaining an image of oneself. Such investment only detracts. Effective people are invested in what they do and what they love, not in themselves. The great Zen Master Dogen famously said, "When one studies Buddhism, one studies oneself; when one studies oneself one forgets oneself; when one forgets oneself one is enlightened by everything" (Kennett, 1976, p. 172). Zen encourages realism. Many people think of Buddhism as highly introspective and it certainly has methodologies of introspection, but these exist, rather like surgery, to remove what is troublesome, not as a prescription for healthy living in themselves.

We could go on, but these eight points give some flavor of the difference of paradigm that the original Buddhist texts exhibit. In applying the interpretation of the Four Truths that I gave in *The Feeling Buddha* one can see that setbacks in life can be viewed as the shifts in conditions that initially cause dismay because they threaten the stability of the self-identity structure that one has carefully created, but, from a Zen perspective, it is precisely such disruption that may enable change and liberation. One might, and usually does, in such circumstances, scramble to cobble back together a comfortable self-presentation, but one might just see that the whole self-building exercise is absurd and burst out laughing.

The job of the therapist is not so much to guide the change as to ensure that the lesson of liberation is learned. In this book we are concerned with self-renewal. Obviously, in light of Point 8, applying Buddhist psychology or Zen therapy to this question gives rise to some conceptual complications. The blunt Buddhist response to the question of how to achieve self-renewal would be "Why ever would you want to do that?" In this system "self" is the bad guy.

The term *self* is itself, however, amenable to a variety of interpretations. If we here take it as referring to the potential for a sudden awakening to an enhanced state of liberation, an escape from dulling conditions that have become normal, a rediscovery of the openness and vibrancy through seeing the possibilities along the path of life, then we can proceed.

IT IS ALREADY HAPPENING

If we try to put ourselves into this rather different paradigm, then it may occur to us that our deep-seated concern with professional survival may well itself be half of the problem. The true helper is not attached to being a helper, still less to holding a place in a professional pecking order. A hard look at "Why am I doing this really?" is needed. If we think that the answer is that we really want to help people and we are good at doing it, then the Zen Master is likely to raise an eyebrow. If we look more closely we may find other less flattering motives. Initially we might be well-defended against such honest introspection, wanting to preserve our sense of ourselves as strong, capable, moral, and succeeding. Much popular psychology is concerned with bolstering this sense of self-efficacy and self-worth. Zen has an altogether different strategy.

In fact, from a spiritual point of view generally, not merely a Buddhist one, an essential point is the realization that I am not as wonderful as I am pretending and as the self-help literature endlessly urges me to believe. In life, generally, I am the one being helped. I am supported by innumerable conditions and if I am any use myself in this world then that value will flow from my gratitude for this support. Awakening to the extent of the support one receives and the consequent upwelling of gratitude is a basic ground of East Asian spirituality generally. The foundation stone of renewal is gratitude.

My being whatever I am, and it must ultimately and even in an ordinary sense remain substantially a mystery just what I am, is a result of my being led by some providence. Theists might see here the hand of God while Buddhists assume the working of a natural law, but providence it remains. If this leading has brought me into this troublesome role of being a helper, then it must, in some way, at some level, be for my own good, my own spiritual education. A process of renewal must already be taking place. We cannot renew ourselves, yet we are renewed. Can we cooperate with this? Can we submit to it? Most importantly, can we appreciate it and be moved to a deep thankfulness in relation to our existence?

ENCOUNTERING SOMETHING TERRIBLE AND YET SUBLIME

We are aware of the dangers of compassion fatigue and burnout. I spent some of my childhood in a war zone and have since been a priest, psychotherapist, social worker, community worker, and pilgrim, often traveling the world to places of great distress: the aftermaths of war and typhoon, the presence of poverty and squalor, not to mention the typhoons called *schizophrenia*, *domestic torture*, and *dependent abuse*, so I am well aware of the stress, strain, and shock as well as the joy and satisfaction that such conversations, situations, roles, and encounters bring with them.

Sitting in a dark kitchen in Sarajevo, I heard the story of a woman who had lived through the war that had recently ravaged the Bosnian land. "I did not know that people were capable of being so cruel," she began. Another young man told me of his first experience of war, shaking as he told his account, how at 19 he went out with a party trying to find ways to break the siege and how his first received impact of the reality of war was, when entering a village demolished by bombardment, glancing to the side, he saw a woman's leg, just the leg, the rest of her body having been completely destroyed by explosive. Again, I listened to accounts of people who had been in the zone when the tsunami devastated Japan in 2011, whole villages swept out to sea and lost, the pallor of their faces saying more than words. As a counselor, one is exposed to the horror that others have experienced. One encounters something both terrible and sublime in the midst of such. Before meeting its witnesses one did not really know that people could be so, yet, in one's instinctive depths one had dreamt it and shuddered. Did I help these people? Did I have a technique for them? To think so would be facile. I was with them in the depths of what it is to be human and something happened between us. I know I gained. Whether they did only they know, but really "gain" is not what it is about. It is about being in a situation where reality presses. In our modern insulated lives it can be hard to find such reality.

To be a counselor who attempts a fullness of empathy is to have those depths within stirred and shaken. It is to meet the reality and reality liberates one, or, more precisely, it can awaken one to the actuality of, on the one hand, our complete dependency and vulnerability and, in the midst of this, our irreducible freedom to be what we are, which is, also, to be in the presence of something divine, creative, and vital. The sickness of modern people lies in the very success we have had in distancing ourselves from the reality that we are involved in.

It is as though we live our common lives trying to arrange things so as to shut out this realization. We fill our days with routine, surround ourselves with the familiar, talk mostly to those who agree with us, read only what confirms our prejudices, and go abroad only as "packaged" tourists. Democracy makes majority opinions important, yet majorities are often deluded. They can afford to be. We are creatures of group consensus and even when we rebel, as most of us do in adolescence, we do so in a manner that conforms to our peer group and, if we do not, we run considerable psychological risk. What passes for individuality is mostly simply recycled cliché. We are never empty in the Zen sense. Despite the rhetoric of individualism, we are herd animals. The individuals are mass-produced. Paradoxically, in such a state we experience a comforting sense of assuredness about our own opinions, behaviors, and customs; a sense that it has to be so and we have to be as we are and have what we have (and a little more as soon as we can get it). We are insulated from our own nature and from the reality of the world. Such is normality for people who, like ourselves, live in privileged countries.

I have spent many years accompanying people in their spiritual lives and what I see, both in their and my own cases, is that although we may all benefit from a variety of spiritual practices, what actually liberates is, all too often, the experience of significant disruptions to our business-as-usual existence by factors beyond our control, or of our own unwitting creation. My mother, when she was alive, remembered, as the best time of her life, World War II. At that time people cooperated with one another, pulled together, went out of their way to assist one another, enjoyed sharing one another's joys, tragedies, and privations, and had a depth of feeling for one another that disappeared within a short time of peace breaking out. The question is, how can we have such spirit without the necessity to have wars, tragedies, crises, and disasters? Can we renew ourselves in such a way? We have it in us, but we do not realize it. The helping professional, however, lives a peacetime life that is, in a sense, continually exposed to the "war zones" of her or his clients. This double exposure can make such a life extraordinarily rich. In this circumstance we can either allow the natural process of spiritual actualization to take place or we can reinforce our layers of insulation. All too often what is called *professionalization*, and is presented as a mode of protection for the public, turns out to be, in reality, not much more than an insulation of this kind for the workers, reinforcing their identity and distancing them from the real lives of those they serve.

I am writing as a person imbued in Buddhism particularly, and in Taoism, Sufism, and Christian mysticism to some degree. In these traditions self-renewal is seen in terms of the dying of an old self, or, more precisely, the disappearance of the delusion that there was an "old self," and the emergence of a way of being in which the term *self* has only limited application. When we say "myself" we speak in the singular, as though we were one thing and united, or as though the parts, if there be such, form a single orchestra, harmoniously blending. It is not so. If there is a unity in this cacophony it is not of one's own making except for the courtesy that we have learned to present to our fellow citizens who then reward us for doing so by treating us as a respectable member of society, worthy of its protection and succor. Yet, in reality, we are each many voices and when we open the door of our heart to allow in many more, as we do as therapists, we are multitude. If a single harmony arises from this chorus it is perhaps audible in heaven, but in one's own case, one must endure the passage of complexity, the sudden assaults of disappointment, fear, and rage and, on the other hand, joy and elation, that punctuate the smoother waters of our social presentation. It is not in smooth waters that we find grace so much as in the eye of the storm.

GETTING OUTSIDE OF ONE'S OLD IDENTITY

Here self-renewal means self-overcoming, which means having a fulcrum point that is outside of one's old conceit. We are all born with a measure of omnipotent feeling and as children we live as if immortals. Though children daily confront limitations, they do not believe in their finality. They shall be overcome, they fondly think. It is only later that one learns one is mortal and worse, that one is also capable of "being so cruel"; that one is so made.

A superficial view of spirituality sees it as a path in ascending goodness, but herein lies a great pitfall, for those who believe so almost inevitably fall into the follies of hypocrisy and denial in the attempt to appear to be some approximation of what they think they should be. The "should" becomes mightier than the "is" and in the process, being gives way to fantasy, albeit with the best of intentions. Religion and society impress on us the need to present ourselves as justified in all that we do. Advertising lures us toward pleasure, success, and status. Life in a helping profession tempts us to appear wiser and more skilled than we are. Inevitably we do buy into some of these seductions. Inevitably they erode our integrity. How many layers of pretence do we have to strip off before we can see what we really are? Such pretense is a fundamental source of stress. Self-renewal has to involve a return to a more naive honesty in which we take stock of ourselves more realistically.

Sigmund Freud had the wonderful temerity to disturb Victorian complacency by pointing out that even the most respectable of us is nonetheless substantially motivated by lust, fear, and pride, much as Buddha had done in his time two millennia previously. Freud noticed that often enough we are not our own masters, that "I" contrive some intended project, but something, an "it," prevents me. One is resolved that one lose one's excess weight, but just as one passes the cake shop something else mysteriously takes over and when one wakes up the morsel is already half-consumed. One is proud of being a person of peace, yet finds oneself devoured at times by a fierce loathing toward those who vote for the war party. We deplore sexual abuse, but which of us does not harbor improper lascivious fantasies? We think we are in control of ourselves, but there are other parts. We, therefore, lay stress on the gap between thought and action and practice vigilance over ourselves. This, however, can consume a major portion of our energy.

When Freud was translated from German into English a strenuous attempt was made to medicalize, and so distance, the shocking nature of his suggestion that respectable people could, beneath the veneer of social conformity, be wanton, corrupt, and cruel, and so *der Ich* (the I) became "ego" and *das Es* (the it) became "id." This enabled professionals to be technical about the matter and so watered down the impact. Be that as it may, the idea of a fragile self struggling to stay afloat in a sea of passions may still be a telling image. As psychology has developed, ego has come to indicate control and, within the humanistic project that a person shall be his or her own master, ego-strength has come to be seen as a virtue, but it is a rather martial virtue where Buddhist psychology is aiming for a more genuine inner peace.

Such ordinary stress means that when the initial enthusiasm wears off many competent professional people experience feelings not too distant from breakdown with more than minimal frequency. Such breakdown might possibly involve an access of honesty that proves, surprisingly, a liberation and profound relief, or it may, more commonly, manifest as burnout, dysfunction, depression, or worse. Ordinary folk secure in a niche of family and with less emotionally demanding work may put off this confrontation to a substantial degree until their deathbed, but for those to whom society has delegated the role of softening the edges of its great machine by providing "human services," those who would be counselors of various kinds, there is no way of avoiding the reality of distress and the insoluble manifold paradoxes of mortal life without rendering themselves ineffective in their work.

To be useful and survive as a counselor, in the true sense, one must be more deeply honest, both with oneself and in relation to what confronts one in the life of the client. We ourselves are vulnerable, far from infallible, dependent in many ways, prone to the effects of impulsive passions. Our clients are wading through the mire of failure, disadvantage, betrayal, loss, incapacity, and guilt. Can we face the reality, be changed by it, be willing to be so changed, and be frequently amazed? Can what so often seems awful in the negative sense of the word become a true source of awe in the positive sense? Not just in our professional being does this principle apply. In the real events of one's own life, just as much as in those that one experiences vicariously through the eyes of one's clients, the existential reality of impermanence and emptiness are ceaselessly presenting themselves. One counts oneself among the most fortunate that in being the receiver of so many accounts one vicariously lives far more than a single life within one's span and has at least the opportunity to learn accordingly more in the process.

THE IMPORTANCE OF FAILURE

Buddha's first attempt at the spiritual life was a series of failures. He studied with one guru, learned all he could, realized that it was not enough, and left and went to another. When the same thing happened with the second one he again left and this time took up with a group of ascetics who supported each other in peer-fashion. This did not work either so he went off on his own, sure that by his own effort he could achieve the necessary breakthrough. Carrying his yogic exercises to an extreme he eventually came to a dead end. He was in the gutter, friendless, alienated from his family, starving, and weak. At this point he was helped by a good-hearted passing stranger. He then had a great change of heart, recognized that what he had been doing up to that point was "vain, ignoble and useless" and suddenly arrived at completely new convictions that he then spent the remainder of his days acting upon (Brazier, 1997).

If we look at the life stories of great figures we often see something of this pattern. The early career of Francis of Assisi was a series of setbacks and failures. Dr. Ambedkar, the writer of the Indian constitution, leader of the untouchables, and now a saint to millions, experienced repeated humiliations. Even in less-spiritual domains, Genghis Khan, perhaps the greatest general in history, was, as a young man, orphaned and taken into slavery. Richard Branson, currently one of the most successful entrepreneurs in Britain, failed so badly in his first foray into business that he ended up in jail for revenue fraud. These people lived vigorously, fell hard, and learned crucial things in a manner that impressed itself on them indelibly.

It is, therefore, understandable that the teachings of Buddha begin with a reflection on the inevitability of loss, failure, separation, aging, disease, and death. We might think, "How morbid" and stop listening, but for Buddha, it was the facing of existential realities that led to the discovery of an authentic existence, one in which people act on their own genuine conviction rather than following a formula handed down by others.

We have seen that the Zen Therapy paradigm envisages points of abrupt change. These are often precipitated by events that are at the time experienced as failure. Somehow, therefore, we need an approach that while feeling the full impact of failure still permits learning and life beyond. The best advice for life could be to throw yourself into whatever you choose to do and when that fails, as it usually does, to learn the resulting lesson thoroughly, but this would run totally counter to all conventional advice on career planning.

The general trend toward more and more professionalization, revolving as it does around safety for client and professional alike, may actually make it more difficult for the aspiring to learn the lessons that are so essential to the making of a real therapist. It may, rather, simply make the position of the worker progressively more defensive. However, if we, as the guides, cannot cope with failure in our own lives and professional work, how are we really going to provide a safe environment for the clients who come to us in the midst of their own personal disarray? This is a singularly difficult challenge to us as a profession. A protected education is no education for the job we actually have to do.

The human existential reality is punctuated with episodes of interruption of what we psychologists call "narcissistic supplies": my house, my car, my hot chocolate drink, my bottle of . . . , my holiday, my music, my teddy bear, my friends, my marriage, my professional reputation . . . you name it. We are highly dependent beings. We might think that we should be able to do without such things, but who can? When we have them we feel smug and tend to overestimate our own resilience. As soon as they are threatened, however, we tremble inside and may act out unpredictably. This is the reality that Buddhist psychology refers to as *conditioning*.

Things we rely on are impermanent. The projects we undertake are prone to failure. No amount of positive thinking will make either ourselves or our ventures immortal or infallible. This is the reality of life that Zen points out. Yet it is from these very failures that we, and our clients, can, in the end, learn most and grow most if we are to thrive spiritually; if we are to be renewed. Pretending that we, the clinicians, are immune, only renders us spiritually impotent. Self-renewal is not essentially a different matter for the therapist from what it is for the client. Both are on the path of life where conventional wisdom sooner or later breaks down and both have to go on beyond that challenge into a more genuine life.

Those of us whose profession it is to open ourselves daily to these failures as they have afflicted many others are both especially blessed and cursed to face a cross fire that is unpredictable and deadly. "Self-renewal" means "self-abandon." Buddha's early project failed and so he awakened. The cleverness of the young, idealistic, recently trained professional may give way to the awe and not-knowing of the old hand. Were it not to do so it would simply ossify into a closed heart administering a mechanized formula, though there are enough and more of those in circulation, too.

A DASH OF ZEN

Most of us are probably familiar with the word *Zen* as the name of a form of Buddhism that emphasizes discipline, meditation, simplicity, and a rather provocative style of dialogue. The way that the term is used in this chapter is broader than simply a reference to one school. Rather, here we are referring to a way of the heart that is characteristic of all mystical religions applied not just, nor particularly, to the needs of the spiritual recluse, but rather to the everyday life of ordinary people.

> Zen is simply the awakening of one heart by another, of sincerity by sincerity. Although words can express it and can point to it they cannot substitute for it. It is the authentic experience which occurs when concern with all that is inessential drops away. . . . To grow pearls there has to be some grit in the oyster. Each of us also has our gritty question. All too often, however, we devote our lives to ignoring rather than working on it. According to Zen it is this ignoring which keeps us in the realm of suffering, but it is the grit which gives us the opportunity to liberate ourselves. . . . it is this very [grit] which is our best friend. [It] tells us that we need to do something about ourselves and shows us how, when and where to do it. By working on our own grit we become a "true being," a true pearl. we can be greatly helped in this process by good friends. (Brazier, 1995, p. 13)

The term *Zen* comes from the Indian word *dhyana*, which refers to the cultivation of the spirit through reflection, meditation, recollection, or imagination. Dhyana is to keep something in one's heart, something wholesome and precious that will have a beneficial influence. The heart will be gently tamed and trained by it. By this taming it will arrive at a tranquil abiding and let go of its habitual obstructions, just as a person on a warm day sheds layers of clothing. At some point these intersecting influences will cause the person to "wake up" in apodictic experience that recenters one's existence in a wonderful way. To say that an experience is apodictic means that it impresses itself upon us in a tellingly important way. These are the experiences that one cannot go back from. They are not just for here and now, they are treasures for always that remain in the heart and affect one's behavior explicitly or implicitly according to the situation. We are made what we are by such experience. They are a positive application of the principle that changes of conditions have immediate, lasting effect.

What is the precious thing that one should keep in one's heart that has such transformational power? There is a story about a man who fell asleep and while he was asleep another sewed a jewel into the hem of the man's robe. The man later awoke and went his way, not realizing that he was a rich man. The suggestion of this parable is that we each have our own jewel already, but we are not conscious of its presence in our lives. We do not see the splendor of our existence. We are, in a sense, anesthetized. In our attempts to insulate ourselves from the pain of life, the shame, the discomforts and the setbacks, we also cut ourselves off from its glories.

When we awake in the morning why are we not instantly filled with alacrity? Why do we not realize how rich we are? When we find that we are alive to breathe the precious air, where is the gratitude? Coming to the breakfast table, we meet our companions in this life—what joy! Yet, for so many of us, the sky seems always gray and the heaviness of hurt hangs about us. We have not yet discovered the wish-fulfilling jewel sewn into our coat.

The paradox revealed by the wisdom traditions is that we will not actually find the jewel until we are willing for it to be our master. Although we want the jewel as a support for our own power, we cannot have it. While we think that we ourselves can be strong enough to withstand the stress of life, we will go on living in inner tension. That tension may be greater or lesser depending on circumstances. We may be able to get by or it may all become too much. We oscillate between smugness and dejection because our predominant concerns are self-concerns. In this condition we may gather a kind of spirituality about us, but it is still really just a collection of props holding up the roof of the tunnel we have dug ourselves into. Plato's Socrates speaks of how we all live as if in caves looking at a screen on the back wall thinking that the shadows playing there—our own shadows—are reality and never think to turn around and walk out into the sunshine, which is already shining outside behind us.

TAKING IT ALL UPON ONESELF

Most of us nowadays know a certain amount about self-management. By listening to all the good advice we can find and taking exercise, learning a good relaxation technique, eating a healthy diet, taking holiday breaks, having team support, consuming vitamins, doing Tai Chi, and creating interludes of "quality time," we can certainly manage to cope with more. Many of us do not even do this much, but rather, rely upon TV, alcohol, sleeping tablets, sugar, and tobacco, none of which make the situation any easier in anything but the very short term, and even those of us who do take the wholesome living route may still find ourselves making even this into a further source of stress as we worry about calories, salt, fat, blood pressure, aluminum cooking pots, facilities to do "my practice," and so on. We can soon get to feel deeply guilty that we are not "loving ourselves" in a sufficiently skillful way or be caught in the double bind that trying to balance duty to self and duty to other imposes. I imagine that none of this concerned the Buddha. He did not examine what was put in his bowl to see if it had the right mineral balance. He never thought about exercise regimes. He took no drugs. He was not interested in stress reduction.

Although we live in the most materially privileged part of the world and do not have to fear starvation, physical attack, or exposure to the elements, modern urban people may experience just as much or more anxiety as their apparently less fortunate ancestors due to the social and psychological conditions that we create for ourselves and one another. Self-renewal means turning over a new leaf, but most feel powerless to do anything about the situation that they find themselves in. Strangely the modern, affluent person may feel just as trapped by their affluent lifestyle as poor people do by their poverty, sometimes more so. The poor person, after all, has a certain freedom in having little to lose.

People can act on all the good self-management advice and still start to feel that their life has been hollowed out on the inside because it is distant from reality. Ironically this life of conformity to convention is often called the *real world*; however, the *real* real world is something else. Such a person goes on working, perhaps doing a good job, perhaps helping many other people, ostensibly career-successful, still looking like a good wife or a good family man, ticking all the boxes, perhaps able to give but not receive, inside knowing that they are just going through the motions, becoming a well-performing robot. The tension within is, bit by bit, smothering the heart. Sometimes it will leak out as surges of bad temper, black moods, rash judgments, criticism of others, self-destructive behaviors, mental paralysis, or needless worry, or it will just go on quietly destroying from within, generating hidden bitterness, envy, resentment, and gloom, which cannot help but lead to self-destruction of some kind and take the heart out of their work. I have experienced such black periods myself. The urge to get away may become more and more compelling and may generate symptoms of various kinds of phobia or obsessive behavior. The dark spiral always seems on the edge of getting out of control, often does in small ways, and sometimes with overwhelming effect resulting in breakdown or even suicide.

In this situation, self-management methods are useful, but they are palliative. They do not strike at the core of the problem, which lies in the fact of taking it all on oneself in a mistaken attempt to shore up one's sense of oneself. This taking it on oneself involves a slight of hand, or slight of mind, really, again at two levels. Firstly, the body does have natural responses designed to cope with life-threatening events. Fight-flight mechanisms and all the body alert symptoms that go with them were evolved to cope with situations in which the human organism had to confront savage animals, struggle with hostile enemies, or cope with famine or disease. However, in modern life the same mechanisms are trying to cope with getting a bad report at work, having one's girlfriend leave, failing an exam, moving one's organization up the ratings, getting humiliated in a social situation, or having too many emails in one's inbox. Second, however, there is what we can call the *spiritual level.* Whether the stressors are the old-fashioned ones or the modern ones, sooner or later, some combination of them is going to assail us and often they come in gangs. Such occurrences are make or break situations for the human spirit. They are the danger zones that Buddha called *dukkha.* The more that we take them into ourselves, the more the damage, but although this taking them in is the common response, it is not the inevitable one. It is not the story about oneself that matters.

DUKKHA HAPPENS

In the Buddhist psychology, it is only in such danger zones that real progress actually happens. Buddha said that "dukkha is a truth for noble ones." Dukkha means *affliction.* This means that no matter how spiritually advanced you are, you will still go through these dark passages, but it also means that, paradoxical as it may seem, they are the hidden jewel.

Buddha went on to say that what comes up at such times is also "a truth for noble ones." On the one hand this means that for the spiritually advanced person, just as for the ordinary person, when one gets into this kind of situation, the energy of the passions—all the fight-flight stuff—will uprise. The image of the sage who is above it all and goes through life untouched by the vicissitudes of circumstance is, apparently, a misconception. On the other hand, this also means that it is precisely this energy that is what the "noble one" needs to bring about the needed renewal.

However, he then advocated "pacification-of-uprising-with-dukkha," by which he meant that for the person whose heart is tamed and trained the dukkha situation is one in which they find an even more profound peace than before (Brazier, 1997). How does this happen? By getting real. It is deep acceptance that puts a person on a spiritual path, a path of wholeheartedness.

Buddha delivered this message to a group of six spiritual practitioners. One of them got it. The other five needed more help to understand. A week later, therefore, Buddha gave a second teaching. In this teaching he taught them to use the watchwords "This is not mine, this is not I, this is not myself" (Ñanamoli, 1972, p. 11). This was enough to wake the other five up.

So Zen Therapy is a taming and a training of the heart that comes about through deeply realizing that "This is not me, this is not mine, this is not myself." It is a letting go, which essentially also means a learning of respect for reality that is not oneself. If the house burns down, well, houses do sometimes burn down. If the girlfriend walks out and slanders one all over town, well, they do that sometimes—they have minds of their own. If there is a notice to quit on one's desk when one gets to the office on Monday morning, or a letter from the doctor saying that one's body is now host to a malignant cancer, or the company one has put 20 years' work into is now declared bankrupt, or . . . "This is not me, this is not mine, this is not myself." In fact, all of these things are, in one shape or another, going to happen. They are part of life's lot. Our projects will sometimes fail; our bodies will certainly fail; our lovers will leave; our enemies will sometimes come; governments will change and what we relied on will be there no more. Blame God if you like, but this is how the game plays. At the same time, realizing that this is not me, not mine, not myself, also means that I can stand in awe before this world of wonders and marvel. I can be overwhelmed with great gratitude for my life, for this amazing providence, for sun and cloud, earth and sky, friends and loved ones, and all the myriad complexity of society and evolution that have made the miracle that is this life. We never know what is around the next corner.

There is a time and a tide. There are moments when one can do something and at those times vigor is called for. There are times when one can do nothing and patience is all. We have all read that wisdom is knowing the difference, but can we do it? By no means always, because we are limited, fallible beings: We even have to accept that sometimes acceptance is beyond us, but in this process we learn about our real nature and, little by little, or, sometimes, all at once, we stop pretending and, with the dropping of our cherished denials, energy that has been dammed up for decades can find release, humbling as the process may be.

THE TRANSFORMATION

A key Zen concept is the idea of a *koan*. Originally the word meant a case. Adepts for Zen training would be given the case history of a past Zen master to study. The case would be selected for its aptness to the problems of the student in question. There are a number of histories of the great masters or "ancestors" of the Zen tradition and these typically each show how the master had a besetting problem, fault, or failing that was resolved and transcended through an encounter of some kind. This was often an encounter with another more experienced master, though it might also be an encounter with a natural phenomenon. Thus the Buddha's younger cousin and constant companion, Ananda, was said to be the most erudite of the disciples. He was intelligent, learned, handsome, popular, and sensitive, but he was not enlightened. Eventually the Buddha died. Ananda was still not enlightened. Then, in an encounter with the master Kashyapa, a dialogue took place in which Ananda saw the light. Ananda knew that Kashyapa was enlightened and he kept asking, "Well what was it that the Buddha transmitted to you beside the ceremonial robe?" This is a great question, because it is rather like asking, "Okay, you got your certificate, but what did you actually learn?" Kashapa turned around and said, "Ananda!" Ananda said, "Yes?" and Kashyapa said, "Cut down your flag pole" (Kennett, 1976, pp. 205–210). This was equivalent to saying, "Let go of trying to be something."

This is a very modern koan. Nowadays we come across more and more a desire for formulas, for the trick that will do the job, for the one right argument or idea and, in particular, for the certificate that will tell the world that I am somebody. We think that by knowledge about things we can substitute for or shortcut real life. It does not work. Ananda was already more clever and more learned than Kashyapa, but he still did not have the kind of authenticity that Kashyapa had.

Later on, koans were shortened so that it was just bits of key dialogue like this that were studied. Earlier, among the more literate Chinese, koan study had involved getting a fuller sense of what the whole history of the earlier master involved. How many of us are like Ananda? Quite a few.

From this one example we can see that what Zen is looking for is something that will jolt us out of our artificial life and into the real world. In the case of the koan method, it attempted this by vicarious identification. The adept sensed in the story of the past master the same spiritual barrier as his own. The therapist, too, is daily presented with the koans of her clients. They resonate at a below-conscious level with the koan of the therapist herself. The method, for the Zen adept, had the effect of intensifying the inner struggle. It was certainly not stress reducing, quite the opposite. It pushed him toward a breaking point at which he would stop hanging onto a key prop to his old identity. When this happened there was an awakening, a renewal. All through this struggle the adept was trying to solve the koan. Solving would mean bringing the problem to a resolution within the frame of reference that the adept already had. The breakthrough actually comes at the point where the koan defeats him. We do not solve koans; they defeat us. In that defeat, that point of "I can't," where our existing frame of reference gives way, something other than "I" can take over.

As our social structures, including those of our profession, become more sophisticated, for all their value, they have the effect of making us conform rather than find out deeply. We are concerned with how to avoid burnout, for instance, or how to reduce stress, but if we feel a danger of burnout there is something artificial happening in the way we relate and if we are stressed there is probably a gap between what we truly believe and what we do. The person who acts in a wholly authentic manner may get tired, sad, angry, or elated, but does not get stressed. Renewal is not the same as propping up the old.

Renewal, from the Zen perspective, would be to become, as Master Lin Chi said, "a person of no rank" (Sasaki, 1975). By this he meant that one will be simply what one is, and that what one does will be in line with one's deepest personal convictions. This may well not conform to a standardized formula of how a person in one's position in society should act, but it will be genuine. When a client comes to see a therapist or a seeker comes to meet a sage, various conversations may take place. What is really at stake, however, may not be clear from the words uttered. The client is confronting one of the existential koans of life, its invidious choices, its humiliations, its betrayals or reversals, and, at a deep and generally unspoken level, the clients want to know if the therapist can demonstrate in their being that they have passed through this barrier in their own lived life, and, if not, then whether they can do so now. The dance of therapy revolves around this. Therapist and client can work together to solve the problem, but the real challenge is to break out of the mentality that made this circumstance a problem in the first place.

If we approach the problems of our clients and the issues in our own lives as koans, then we will not be looking for a solution within the old frame, and even less to make things feel better or less stressful. If there is stress then it is a sign that something needs to be done. Stress-reduction techniques may be like giving a person something to reduce the sensation of hunger when what is actually needed is to go and find food.

Every circumstance that life presents is an opportunity for renewal. As therapists we have the particular privilege of being presented with deep revelations by our clients and these give us a virtually unparalleled opportunity to live a life that is endlessly self-refreshing. When what the client presents has such a quality that we realize that it has "got to us" we can be sure that something of immense personal value to both parties is at stake. The veneer of going through the motions of doing therapy has been penetrated and something true is happening between the client and counselor. This something really does threaten the foundations of at least some aspect of the therapist's outlook and identity. This is an opportunity for liberation for both parties. One, other, or both may emerge from this situation having made an important breakthrough to new, deeper conviction. There is, however, nothing certain or predictable about real life. When such renewal actually happens then there is a grounding of life in true experience and from that something wholesome will grow.

From the Zen Therapy perspective, everything in life is a koan, a spiritual challenge that is also a gateway to liberation. Renewal is not a matter of selecting and cultivating the "positive" parts of one's life while discarding or ignoring the "negative." It is a matter of learning to ride the dragon of life's vicissitudes by recovering the whole of one's existence, good, bad, beautiful, and ugly, and finding it to be a miracle. In the darkest parts is often to be found the richest treasures. This is the discovery that turns life around and the gratitude one then feels is the liberation that one needs.

REFERENCES

Brazier, D. (1995). *Zen therapy: Transcending the sorrows of the human mind.* London, England: Constable.

Brazier, D. (1997). *The feeling Buddha.* London, England: Constable.

Kennett J. (1976). *Zen is eternal life.* Emeryville, CA: Dharma.

Ñanamoli. (1972). *Three cardinal discourses of the Buddha.* Kandy, Sri Lanka: Buddhist Publication Society.

Rogers, C. R. (1961). *On becoming a person.* Boston, MA: Houghton Mifflin.

Ryback, D., Ikemi, A., Kuno, T., & Miki, Y. (2001). Japanese psychology in crisis: Thinking inside the (empty) box. *Journal of Humanistic Psychology, 41*, 124–136.

Sasaki, R. F. (1975). *The recorded sayings of Ch'an Master Lin-chi Hui-chao of Chen prefecture.* Kyoto, Japan: Institute for Zen Studies.

PART III

Trauma, Growth, Healing, Patience, Forgiveness, Courage, and the Process of Renewal

CHAPTER

10

Blooming in the Night

Themes of Self-Renewal in Posttraumatic Growth

Mary Beth Werdel

Self-renewal is a term that is used to describe the experience of making an aspect of the self new, or the whole of the self like new. The term is related to experiences such as the restoration of balance, emotional well-being, centeredness, growth, transformation, and self-care. Experiences of self-renewal may allow a person to maintain a perspective in which they may come to find and feel a deeper sense of wisdom relative to understanding new aspects of their self, maintaining a closer connection with others, or holding a greater sense of purpose and meaning in life. In this way, it appears to be that the product of self-renewal (that is to say *being* self-renewed) is arguably intrinsically positive.

However, as is often witnessed in the therapeutic encounter, while the *product* of self-renewal has a positive frame, such may not be true of the *process* of self-renewal. Growing new does not necessarily always feel good. Making time and space for new routines, or the process of forming new understandings, beliefs, and values, does not always come without distress. In fact, sometimes it only comes through the action of enduring distress. Furthermore, while for some, or on some level, a sense of newness may be purposefully sought and the client may come prepared for the pilgrimage toward change, for others, newness or change is not a preconceived goal. For those who come to start on a journey toward self-renewal grounded in painful and drastic life transitions such as divorce, illness, bereavement, war, or physical and sexual abuse, the desired outcome is often not to be self-renewed. Clients who have endured stress and trauma often seek a therapeutic relationship with a desire only for negative psychological symptoms to decrease. However, in the work toward this end, sometimes clients confront major existential questions about the meaning and purpose of their self, of others, and of the whole of life. In meeting existential life questions, sometimes out of necessity, not out of desire, clients find themselves rebuilding, restructuring, or redefining the very assumptions about their self, others, and the world from which they operate, understand, and relate. Sometimes, in this process, it becomes evident that a return to a past experience or a baseline level of functioning is simply no longer possible. Faced with the understanding that they are unable to remake *the* world, to go back to a time pretrauma, clients sometimes find that what is within their power and control is the ability to remake themselves and in doing so remake *their* world in a way that is undoubtedly new and intrinsically positive (Werdel & Wicks, 2012). Although some people's journey toward self-renewal is rooted in the light, many other people's growth is painfully rooted in their night experiences of life.

Perhaps one of the most common images of growth is the blooming plant. Starting as a seedling, given nurturance, attention, the right balance of water, and time, the plant will eventually grow and bloom. Most commonly we think of the necessity of light in the process as well. For almost all plants need light. However, there is a family of plants called *cereus cacti*, sometimes referred to as the *princesses of the night*. The family of plants is unique in that beautiful, large, white fragment flowers bloom not with light but in darkness. While it may feel (and for some it may certainly be) contradictory, sometimes, grounded in the night experiences of life, much like the cereus cacti, clients may experience a psychological bloom.

The idea that growth may come from stress and trauma is not merely Pollyannaish (Werdel & Wicks, 2012). There is a growing, empirically based body of knowledge centered on the phenomena that has been coined posttraumatic growth (Tedeschi & Calhoun, 1996) and the distinct but related terms of stress-related (Park, Cohen, & Murch, 1996) and adversarial (Joseph, 2011; Joseph & Linley, 2006) growth. Based on the research that currently exists, there are at least three primary reasons and one secondary reason why therapists interested in self-renewal should also be knowledgeable and interested in the literature on growth following stress and trauma: (1) suffering can be paradoxical; (2) the posttraumatic growth literature offers a unique vantage point; (3) therapists may unknowingly short-change their clients and secondarily; (4) therapists may short-change their own growth.

A thorough understanding of posttraumatic growth is beyond the scope of this chapter. However, a brief explanation of posttraumatic growth is first provided. This is followed by a discussion of each of the four aforementioned points. For those interested in a more detailed understanding there are a number of resources that are available from a primer (see Werdel & Wicks, 2012), to primary texts and hundreds of research articles (see Calhoun & Tedeschi, 2006; Joseph, 2011).

WHAT IS POSTTRAUMATIC GROWTH?

Briefly, *posttraumatic growth* is a term that was coined by Lawrence Calhoun and Richard Tedeschi (2006). The term refers to the positive psychological changes that a person experiences as a result of enduring a significant stress or trauma. Calhoun and Tedeschi (2006) suggest that posttraumatic growth includes the experiences of changes in the *perception of the self*, changes in *relating to others*, and *philosophical changes of priorities, appreciations, and spirituality*.

Posttraumatic growth is conceptualized to start with a person's pretrauma cognitive schema, which includes a person's global assumptions and goals relative to their individual self and the world. A negative, extremely stressful, or traumatic life event is then experienced, leading a person to form an understanding of the situation or event (a situational assumption) that may be related to the self, others, or the world. If there is a discrepancy or contradiction between global and situational beliefs, a person experiences distress (Park, 2005). For instance, one may hold a belief that the world is a safe place and then experience being physically attacked during a mugging. Now the person has a global assumption (e.g., the world is safe) that contradicts a situational experience (e.g., the physical attack). Distress is experienced when there is a discrepancy between these two different assumptions. Such distress sets people on a course to make sense of the event. To this end, people may experience both automatic (without the will of the person) and deliberate (purposeful) ruminations that may take place either directly after or a longer time after the event (Calhoun & Tedeschi, 2006). As people chew over the conflicting understandings and experiences and attempt to resolve the conflicting belief symptoms and find or make meaning of the experience, they may come to experience changes in their perception of their self (e.g., I am a stronger person than I realized), changes in their perceptions of others (e.g., people are genuinely good as indicated by the fact that after the attack many people gathered around me in deeply kind ways that I had never experienced prior), or philosophical changes of priorities, appreciations, and spirituality (e.g., life is a precious gift; God is a gracious God that has provided me with the strength to move beyond the attack).

Research suggests that the experience of posttraumatic growth is related to a number of factors.

Social Relationships

Human beings are relational beings. The relationships that one has is related to such psychologically positive experiences as the ability to self-regulate emotions (Bowlby, 1988; Karen, 1998), well-being (Henderson & Brown, 1988), and decreased levels of depressive symptoms (Lara, Leader, & Klein, 1997). Knowing this, perhaps it is no surprise that if and how a person experiences growth appears to be dependent in part on one's intrapersonal and interpersonal relationships pre- and post a negative life event (Calhoun & Tedeschi, 1999).

Specifically, the posttraumatic growth literature suggests that relationships may serve to provide new ways of thinking about the world, different ways of perceiving the world, models of coping methods, social support (Calhoun & Tedeschi, 2006); weaken connections between the traumatic experience and negative responses; help to regulate emotional experience; and assist in reappraising cognitive assumptions (Lepore & Revenson, 2006).

Cognitive Processing

After stressful and traumatic events a person may struggle to comprehend or make sense of the experience. In doing so, a person may experience a number of different thoughts related to the event. Research suggests there is a relationship among the type, timing, and content of the thoughts that a person experiences after a traumatic event and whether a person experiences posttraumatic growth. Specifically, research suggests automatic ruminations experienced closely after the event, and more deliberate ruminations experienced sometime after the event is associated with growth (Nightingale, Sher, & Hansen, 2010). Whereas the reverse (deliberate ruminations close after the event and automatic ruminations later) has not been found to be true. Tedeschi and Calhoun (2004) suggest that unless clients cognitively disengage with old worldviews and goals they will not be able to claim a new worldview or form new goals and consequently will not experience posttraumatic growth.

Personality and Personal Attributes

Personality can shape and color how a person sees the world (DeNeve & Cooper, 1998). As such, personality and personal attributes have been found to be a factor related to posttraumatic growth. Specifically, the personality domains of extraversion and openness appear to have the most significant correlations with posttraumatic growth (Werdel & Wicks, 2012). Additional research suggests that the personality attributes of optimism (Stanton, Bower, & Low, 2006), self-esteem (Carpenter, Brockopp, & Andrykowski, 1999) and self-efficacy (Schulz & Mohamed, 2004) have significant correlations to growth (Werdel & Wicks, 2012).

Intensity of Stress

Theories suggest that distress is a necessary factor in the process of posttraumatic growth. The research suggests that growth experiences are greatest for those with moderate levels of distress as a result of enduring the negative event: "those who are not resilient to, but also not flooded by stress" (Werdel & Wicks, 2012, p. 22). For the process of reevaluation and reconstruction of one's basic assumptions is not initiated if one does not feel a certain level of distress relative to having one's global assumptions contradicted or destroyed. However, too much distress, it appears, may create a psychological flooding experience that keeps a person from initiating the search for meaning that is part and parcel of growth.

REASONS TO UNDERSTAND POSTTRAUMATIC GROWTH LITERATURE

There are at least three primary reasons and one secondary reason why it remains important that people interested in the idea of self-renewal understand the literature on posttraumatic growth.

Suffering Can Be Paradoxical

There is no doubt that extreme stress and traumatic experiences are intrinsically negative. Mental health professionals recognize that for some people significant traumatic events may lead a person to experience a diagnosis of posttraumatic stress disorder (PTSD), which includes the symptoms of intrusive recollections, avoidance and/or numbing, and hyperarousal (American Psychiatric Association, 2000). For others events may or may not be traumatic in the sense that it leads to a diagnosis of PTSD; however, one or two of the above traumatic features may be present. Common across all extremely stressful life events, traumatic or not, is that people in their own way desire for the negative psychological symptoms to decrease. It is the primary responsibility of mental health professionals when working with a client who has experienced a traumatic or extremely stressful negative life experience to work with the client to reduce their negative symptoms. Specifically it is the clinician's role to assist in:

- Desensitization.
- Creating a narrative that makes sense of the incidents or at least makes them understandable in some way.
- Re-creating a sense of safety.
- Re-creating a worldview that encompasses what happened as a functional life post trauma (Calhoun & Tedeschi, 1999, p. 53).

For a long time, and for good reason, the way clinicians looked at negative life events was purely with the lens of symptom reduction that is presented above. That is to say decrease negative symptoms and assist clients to reclaim a psychological baseline functioning or as close to it as possible. This type of treatment is necessary and important. It is ethical and empirically warranted. It is always a foundational piece of the work. In fact, sometimes it is all of the work.

However, it is now known that in working toward the above goals, mental health professionals and clients alike may come to realize that for some people a complete return to baseline functioning is neither ideal nor possible.

For some individuals, a stressful or traumatic event has led them to challenge the basic assumptions they hold of life relative to self worth, benevolence, trust, and safety (Janoff-Bulman, 1992). For some people whose experience has been more dramatic, their cognitive foundation has not merely been challenged, it has been destroyed. Understandings of how the world is supposed to work quite simply no longer exist. Such an experience can feel isolating, lonely, threatening, frightening, and even hopeless. Central to their experience is the question of the very meaning of self and life. What does life mean now? Who are they now? The very identity of the self and the purpose of a continued life is held captured in the tension between the mind's drive and the heart's desire to return to a pretraumatic world and an inability to rationally or emotionally do so.

Research from a positive psychological perspective has helped the field to understand that the traditional lens through which stress and trauma have been studied is not complete. Suffering can and does have negative symptoms but enduring suffering *can* lead to positive psychological consequences, too. The posttraumatic growth literature breaks open the possibility that suffering is indeed paradoxical, not merely in theory but in practice. Forms of light (perspective and meaning) can be born in darkness. Without a sensitive awareness of growth, clinicians may miss the opportunity to explore a real and potentially healing place within the client's new schema (Werdel & Wicks, 2012).

With an awareness of the experience of posttraumatic growth, therapists are presented with a risk and a challenge that should not be ignored. The risk associated with the paradox of suffering is that a well-intentioned therapist who holds a desire to help clients may in some way either glorify the trauma or hold an expectation of growth for each of their clients. Research tells us that an expectation of growth on the part of the therapist may serve to cause further distress for the client (Wortman, 2004), which could have negative implications for the client's well-being and the success of therapy. The challenge that the paradox of suffering presents is for clinicians to become highly skilled listeners in regards to growth and hold no preconceived expectations or need for clients to go through the experience (Werdel & Wicks, 2012). Calhoun and Tedeschi (2006) make a call to clinicians to become "expert companions" in the process of working with clients. As Werdel and Wicks (2012) write, a delicate balance is necessary on the part of the therapist who seeks to journey with people who experience stress and trauma:

> The delicate balance requires being open to potential new growth (instead of framing it as denial or avoidance) while not pacing the sessions too fast or providing feedback that indicates to clients they are failures if they don't experience posttraumatic growth. For some, a successful therapeutic experience will be a return to a premorbid phase of functioning; for others new insight and wisdom will occur. (p. 32)

It is only when clinicians engage with the literature on posttraumatic growth that the complex cognitive process of posttraumatic growth and the empirically supported psychological consequences of the paradox of suffering can be incorporated into the ways counselors understand and intervene with clients. Without understanding the literature on posttraumatic growth, the concept of self-renewal following painful life experience may become in practice Pollyannaism. Denial may be mistaken for wisdom. Resistance may be misunderstood as growth.

The Unique Vantage Point of Posttraumatic Growth

Drawing on a number of useful and different psychological theories and movements, the posttraumatic literature offers a unique vantage point for considering the concept of self-renewal. Werdel and Wicks (2012) provide a metaphor to consider the new vantage point provided by the posttraumatic growth literature. Stress and trauma, they write, provide three images that must be acknowledged to understand the complex concept of growth. The first image provided is the image of wreckage and destruction. It is the immediate "after" picture of events: remnants of homes, offices, shopping areas, and faces distorted by pain, grief, and shock (Werdel & Wicks, 2012). Such images are negative and representative of the violence associated with stress and trauma. Homes turned into piles of splintered wood and broken pieces of metal and glass are representative of the shattered assumptions a person once held of how life was supposed to work (Werdel & Wicks, 2012). There is nothing glorious or good about the image of wreckage. To truly understand posttraumatic growth and to work in the area of stress and trauma, a clinician must be able to first hold the negative and painful image of suffering (Werdel & Wicks, 2012).

The second image that is provided in the literature is that associated with growth, one of reaching upward. Images of reaching upward include those of an Olympic medalist raising flowers on an award stand or a mountain climber approaching a summit. "Images of reaching upward are filled with promise and hope; they capture the triumph in a life narrative" (Werdel & Wicks, 2012, p. 27).

The final, and perhaps most important, image that the literature on posttraumatic growth provides is the image of the *relationship* between the two, the idea of rising on the wreckage. Werdel and Wicks (2012) write:

> It is only because of the wreckage left by the destruction of stress and trauma that people have before them a place to climb. In the climbing some people may come to gain a new vantage point, thereby helping them to obtain a new perspective. The world has not changed, but their sadness and woundedness changes their experience of life. (p. 27)

Growth, like self-renewal, is not merely a positive reframe of the stressful or traumatic experience (Neimeyer, 2001). Rather it is a purposeful and deliberate reexamination and reevaluation of life (Werdel & Wicks, 2012). The event remains intrinsically negative; positive psychological consequences exist as a result of enduring the negative event. The unique vantage point can be missed if the nuances are overlooked too quickly and the concept considered merely as a positive reframe. By acknowledging the nuances of the complex process of posttraumatic growth interventions that would otherwise not be considered become possible, one begins to see how a person who re-creates faulty assumptions of life is not "growing up" but rather growing wise.

Therapists May Short-Change Their Clients

One of the leading researchers in the area of posttraumatic growth, Stephen Joseph (2012) in his book *What Doesn't Kill Us: The New Psychology of Posttraumatic Growth*, provides imagery related to the experience of posttraumatic growth in his theory of the shattered vase. Joseph articulates that growth is not about rebuilding the old as best as one can; it is about accepting that an old way of understanding can no longer be reclaimed and so then claiming something new. He writes:

> Imagine that a cherished vase sits on a table in your home . . . imagine that the vase smashes into a thousand tiny shards. . . . Some people will try to put it back together exactly as it was before it fell to the ground. If they are lucky the vase may look just as it used to. Closer examination will reveal the truth, however: It is held together by nothing more than glue and sticky tape. . . . But [this] is not the only strategy: Some people will take the pieces and build something new. They are sad that their prized vase is broken but accept that it can never return to its old form. The question now becomes What to make it next? Perhaps they can use the differently colored pieces to assemble a mosaic, finding a new and useful form to preserve their memories. (p. 105)

There are two questions for clinicians to consider from Joseph's metaphor of the shattered vase. Do therapists see the need to assist a person only in re-creating the broken vase? Or is the therapist open to the idea and knowledgeable about the process of how clients come to create something anew? If they are not open to the idea of growth, then will they not miss opportunities to help clients in the process of making sense of their new understandings of life? Will clients lose the opportunity to nurture and process growth experiences in the therapeutic encounter? Central to the literature on posttraumatic growth is the question of what it is that people come to realize that was not understood prior to the stress and trauma. The experiences that clients have relative to this question may not be intentionally listened for by therapists not engaged with the posttraumatic growth literature. If the possibility of growth after stress and trauma is overlooked or discounted, a therapist may come to "[rob] that individual of the freedom to view life's events from his or her own perspective" (Tedeschi & Calhoun, 1995, p. 101). However, for therapists who are aware of the new vantage point provided by the psychological literature on posttraumatic growth, the possibility of intervening in ways that nurture growth becomes increasingly possible.

Hundreds of studies have demonstrated the positive experiences that may result from enduring stress and trauma. Research suggests that the ability to grow wiser may be felt by persons who experience different and diverse stressful and traumatic life experiences such as HIV/AIDS diagnoses, cancer, bereavement, domestic violence, physical illness, brain injury, or 9/11 type terrorist attacks (Werdel & Wicks, 2012). If therapists limit or neglect the research on posttraumatic growth, they will remain unaware of the clinical considerations associated with facilitating growth, and may unknowingly short-change growth experiences of their clients.

Werdel and Wicks (2012) highlight a number of clinical considerations when working with clients. These considerations include:

- Taking the role of expert companion (Tedeschi & Calhoun, 2006), encouraging reflective cognitive processing of the stressful event in which a clinician helps a client to consider the ways in which a client is reacting to an event.
- Demonstrating authenticity and genuineness by showing a willingness to be emotionally affected by a client's story (Tedeschi & Calhoun, 2006; Werdel & Wicks, 2012).
- Listening to clients' narrative for variations between their global and situational belief systems (Fontana & Rosenheck, 2004; Park & Ai, 2006) and exploring the variations.
- Identifying and supporting clients' ruminations experienced later in the coping process (Taku, Cann, Tedeschi, & Calhoun, 2009) and recognizing how they have been associated with facilitating posttraumatic growth.
- Recognizing the relationship between automatic rumination directly after the event and the relationship it has been found to have with growth (Nightingale et al., 2010).
- When appropriate, considering the use of the cognitive behavioral theory stress management interventions to target low levels of optimism as elevating levels of optimism has been associated with elevations of levels of posttraumatic growth (Antoni et al., 2001).
- Conducting a spiritual assessment as certain religious orientations may serve to aid the work of traumatic growth. Likewise, certain ways of accessing faith traditions may be harmful (Werdel & Wicks, 2012).

Central to the clinical work of posttraumatic growth is an understanding that a therapist must come to honor the growth experiences that clients claim as part of their perspective. Moments will most certainly be missed to assist clients who are ready for work if therapists do not believe in the possibility of posttraumatic growth. As Werdel and Wicks (2012) detail:

> Posttraumatic growth advocates do not presume in any way that new and different experiences, understandings, or perspectives are always positive, but sometimes pieces of them are. Accordingly, the study of posttraumatic growth is not a comparison of pre- and post-lives in the sense that one is better or worse. Instead, it is the study of coming to terms and accepting what is different and about questioning the piece or pieces that are different and determining if they have intrinsically positive qualities that are worthy of being honored for what they are. When these qualities are honored, amazing results become truly possible. Such honoring may begin when we as clinicians and caregivers learn to offer our clients a culture that believes in the possibility of growth. (p. 30)

Therapists May Short-Change Their Own Growth

Lastly, and most certainly secondarily, it is important to know the literature in the area of growth as therapists may unknowingly short-change their own possible growth experiences without it. For research is starting to understand that sometimes in working with clients who have experienced great stress and trauma and subsequently growth, therapists sometimes grow, too.

There is a well-documented phenomenon in stress and trauma work known as vicarious traumatization: the experience that results from emotionally engaging with clients' traumatic experiences that seem to parallel clients' negative experiences (Cohen & Collens, 2012; McCann & Pearlman, 1990). Just as has been indicated in the wider posttraumatic growth literature, while much attention has been given to the negative impacts of vicarious trauma, more recently the potential for positive changes in the way a therapist experiences their self, others, or the world as a result of vicarious traumatization has been explored. There is a small but growing body of research that suggests that clinicians may experience vicarious posttraumatic growth (VPTG) as a result of witnessing posttraumatic growth in a client. In a recent meta-synthesis of 20 qualitative articles that examined VPTG, results suggested that VPTG was indeed a possible experience (Cohen & Collens, 2012). Specifically, research highlighted that therapists have experienced changes in their worldview in regard to human resilience and appreciation of life, changes in values related to the importance of family and friends, changes in their self related to compassion, wisdom, self-awareness, self-worth, and being a better professional, and changes in day-to-day life related to social activism and better parenting.

The research in the area of VPTG is preliminary. Additionally, while it certainly is not a primary reason why a therapist interested in self-renewal would consider posttraumatic growth, the research does suggest that not identifying, naming, and processing growth experiences with clients may limit not only clients' growth but the therapist's growth, too. On the other hand, attending to growth in the client may lead to experiences of self-renewal for the client and the therapist alike.

CONCLUSION

In his 1932 book *Night Flight*, Antoine de Saint-Exupéry wrote, "Even our misfortunes are part of our belongings" (as cited in Werdel & Wicks, 2012). The literature on posttraumatic growth suggests that our misfortunes may be formational life experiences that need to be honored in such a way that they are neither glorified nor disowned. For they hold within them, for some people, under certain circumstances, the ability to lead a person further toward experiences of the self, others, and purpose and meaning in life that is intrinsically positive. Posttraumatic growth and self-renewal share an understanding that is redemptive and necessary to remember. Although a person can move to higher ground to seek safe shelter when hurricanes threaten landfall, no person can stop hurricane-force winds. While a person may exercise and eat a balanced diet to keep from aging poorly, everyone will still age and one day, everyone will die. As bright as the noonday sun may shine, night always falls. While the intention is not one in which people wish night on their self or others, hope lives in the understanding that not all of life withers in the night. When the paradox of suffering is honored by the therapist, some aspects of some people, like some plants, will not merely survive the night. Enduring night, some aspects of some people may bud, may bloom, and even grow.

REFERENCES

American Psychiatric Association (2000). *Diagnostic and statistical manual of mental disorders* (4th ed., text rev.). Washington, DC: Author.

Antoni, M. H., Lehman, J. M., Kilbourn, K. M., Boyers, A. E., Culver, J. L., Alferi, S. M., & Carver, C. S. (2001). Cognitive-behavioral stress management intervention decreases the prevalence of depression and enhances benefit finding among women under treatment for early-stage breast cancer. *Health Psychology, 20*, 20–32.

Bowlby, J. (1988). *A secure base: Parent-child attachment and healthy human development.* New York, NY: Basic Books.

Calhoun, L. G., & Tedeschi, R. G. (1999). *Facilitating posttraumatic growth: A clinician's guide*. Mahwah, NJ: Erlbaum.

Calhoun, L. G., & Tedeschi R. G. (2006). The foundations of posttraumatic growth: An expanded framework. In L. G. Calhoun & R. G. Tedeschi (Eds.), *Handbook of posttraumatic growth: Research and practice* (pp. 1–23). Mahwah, NJ: Erlbaum.

Carpenter, J. S., Brockopp, D. Y., & Andrykowski, M. A. (1999). Self-transformation as a factor of self-esteem and well-being of breast cancer survivors. *Journal of Advanced Nursing, 29*, 1402–1411.

Cohen K., & Collens, P. (2012). The impact of trauma work on trauma workers: A metasynthesis on vicarious trauma and vicarious posttraumatic growth. *Psychological Trauma: Theory, Research, Practice, and Policy, 12*. Advance online publication. doi:10.1037/a0030388

DeNeve, K. M., & Cooper, H. (1998). The happy personality: A meta-analysis of 137 personality traits and subjective well-being. *Psychological Bulletin, 124*, 197–229.

Fontana, A., & Rosenbeck, R. (2004). Trauma, change in strength of religious faith, and mental health service use among veterans treated for PTSD. *Journal of Nervous and Mental Disease, 192*, 579–584.

Henderson, A. S., & Brown, G. W. (1988). Social support: The hypothesis and the evidence. In S. Henderson & G. D. Burrows (Eds.), *Handbook of Social Psychiatry* (pp. 73–85). Amsterdam, The Netherlands: Elsevier.

Janoff-Bulman, R. (1992). *Shattered assumptions: Towards a new psychology of trauma*. New York, NY: Free Press.

Joseph, S. (2011). *What doesn't kill us: The new psychology of posttraumatic growth*. Hoboken, NJ: Wiley.

Joseph, S. & Linley, P. A. (2006). Growth following adversity: Theoretical perspectives and implications for clinical practice. *Clinical Psychology Review, 26*, 1041–1053.

Karen, R. (1998). *Becoming attached: First relationships and how they shape our capacity to love*. New York, NY: Oxford University Press.

Lara, M. E., Leader, J., & Klein, D. N. (1997). The association between social support and course of depression: Is it confounded with personality? *Journal of Abnormal Psychology, 106*, 478–482.

Lepore, S. J., & Revenson, T. (2006). Relationships between posttraumatic growth and resilience: Recovery, resistance, & reconfiguration. In L. G. Calhoun & R. G. Tedeschi (Eds.), *Handbook of posttraumatic growth: Research and practice* (pp. 24–46). Mahwah, NJ: Erlbaum.

McCann, I. L., & Pearlman, L. A. (1990). Vicarious traumatization: A framework for understanding the psychological effects of working with victims. *Journal of Traumatic Stress, 3*, 131–149.

Neimeyer, R. A. (2001). *Meaning reconstruction and the experience of loss*. Washington, DC: American Psychological Association.

Nightingale, V. R., Sher, T. G., & Hansen, N. B. (2010). The impact of receiving an HIV diagnosis and cognitive processing on psychological distress and posttraumatic growth. *Journal of Traumatic Stress, 23*, 452–460.

Park, C. L. (2005). Religion as a meaning-making framework in coping with life stress. *Journal of Social Issues, 61*, 707–729.

Park, C. L., & Ai, A. L. (2006). Meaning-making and growth: New directions for research on survivors of trauma. *Journal of Loss and Trauma, 11*, 389–407.

Park, C. L., Cohen, L. H., & Murch, R. (1996). Assessment and prediction of stress-related growth. *Journal of Personality*, *64*, 71–105.

Schulz, U., & Mohamed, N. E. (2004). Turning the tide: Benefit finding after cancer surgery. *Social Science and Medicine*, 59, 653–662.

Stanton, A., Bower, J. E., & Low, C. A. (2006). Posttraumatic growth after cancer. In L. G. Calhoun & R. G. Tedeschi (Eds.), *Handbook of posttraumatic growth: Research and practice* (pp. 138–175).

Taku, R. D., Cann, A., Tedeschi, R. G., & Calhoun, L. G. (2009). Intrusive versus deliberate rumination in posttraumatic growth across US and Japanese samples. *Anxiety, Stress, & Coping*, *22*, 129–136.

Tedeschi, R. G., & Calhoun, L. G. (1995). *Trauma and transformation: Growing in the aftermath of suffering*. Thousand Oaks, CA: Sage.

Tedeschi, R. G., & Calhoun, L. G. (1996). The posttraumatic growth inventory: Measuring the legacy of trauma. *Journal of Traumatic Stress*, 9, 455–472.

Tedeschi, R. G., & Calhoun, L. G. (2004). Posttraumatic growth: Conceptual foundations and empirical evidence. *Psychological Inquiry*, *15*, 1–15.

Werdel, M. B., & Wicks, R. J. (2012). *Primer on posttraumatic growth: An introduction and guide*. Hoboken, NJ: Wiley.

Wortman, C. B. (2004). Posttraumatic growth: Progress and problems. *Psychological Inquiry*, *15*, 81–90.

CHAPTER

11

Tell the Story

Intergenerational Trauma and Healing

SUZANNE MAYER

Tell the story; the heart from horrors
hardens like ice; pray that words
may melt to tears the heart. Sadako's
friends completed the thousand cranes
to bear away Sadako's poisons.
Imagine those stumbling, ardent fingers,
fingers folding cranes of hope.
Tell the story again and again.

(Spacks, 2009)

The several verses above come from a poem written to commemorate the short life of one Japanese girl, Sasaki Sadako. Born January 7, 1943, Sadako was just 2 years old when the atomic bomb was dropped near her home in Hiroshima, Japan. Spared in the bombing and fires that followed, Sadako succumbed to the aftereffects of the atomic bomb, dying at the age of 12 from leukemia contracted through radiation poisoning. Since her death, this child is remembered through the story of a thousand origami cranes she attempted to fold in the last days and weeks of her life, holding to the legend that to do so would win a wish from the gods and stave off her death (Murty, n.d.).

More than 30 years ago, I met and became great friends with another small Japanese woman named Vanji [pseudonym]. A member of a community of religious women with convents in Japan and Korea, she was in the States along with a number of other young sisters of their province to study at our college and become fluent in English. Their congregation, looking to the future, was training these women for leadership positions with an eye to their need to communicate internationally. One day, along with some sisters from my own community who had returned to receive extended education and formation, we traveled to our retreat house in Stone Harbor on the south Jersey shore. My friend, usually quiet in a warm and gracious way, froze as she stepped out onto the sand and saw the rolling waves of the Atlantic moving toward us. "Cannot! Cannot! Cannot go further. Run, Suzanne, run."

I was stunned as were the other members of my community. Never had any of us heard this petite woman raise her voice, much less scream in the terrified octaves that echoed across that beach. I followed her back into the long shorefront property behind us to find her crumpled on a porch chair, sobbing and shaking. After what seemed a long time of near hysteria, when she could finally talk, Vanji told me that, although she had lived in Nagasaki near to the ocean, no one in her family for as long as anyone could remember went near the sea or even the seaport. "My *obaasan* [grandmother] warn us as she was warned. We must not go near the water. The bomb has made the sea poison. She is a Hibakusha [survivor of the explosion] and she knows. The ocean waters kill."

My friend Vanji is not one of the Hibakusha. She never saw the mushroom cloud rise above her city. She never searched the rubble for the burned bodies of her family and friends. Nor did she, like Sadako, have to watch her own flesh turn purple and waste as the radiation poisoning polluted her blood and crumbled her bones. She is, however, the descendant of a survivor, of a family of survivors, of a cityful of survivors. She bears the scars not from the immediate explosion or even the contaminated remnants of Nagasaki, but from the inheritance passed down to her as intergenerational trauma. As such, she joins the ranks of a growing number of children, men, and women who for generations have been misdiagnosed, undiagnosed, and even mistreated.

When the aftereffects of trauma, whether human-produced or the result of natural catastrophe, were first recognized, the consequences went by sometimes euphemistic, even poetic names. During the Civil War, the term coined was "soldier's heart" to try to characterize the change in behavior and even personality observed in returning troops. In World War I and II, the names ranged from *shell shock* to *combat fatigue* to *survivor's guilt*, to *war neurosis* to *operational exhaustion* (Rooney, 2001, pp. 8–9). With the return of the Vietnam vets and the marked appearance of disorders and dysfunction at times months, even years, after the event, the term posttraumatic stress disorder (PTSD) became the diagnostic category, making it into the *DSM-III-R*. Today the most recent term under discussion is *posttraumatic stress injury*, supported by retired General

Peter Chiarelli, who notes that "no 19-year-old kid wants to be told he's got a disorder" (Jaffe, 2012).

Medically and psychologically, the complex trauma state of PTSD listed in the current *DSM-5/ICD-10* as 309.81/F43.1 is described by Dr. Marcello Maviglia (n.d.), an international expert on trauma and posttrauma treatment, as a constellation of "clinical symptoms following a circumscribed traumatic experience." These symptoms include both intrusive manifestations (e.g., flashbacks, startle response, aggressivity, and nightmares) and numbing presentations (such as withdrawal, avoidance, isolation, reports of meaninglessness, and even suicidal ideation). The complexity of the symptoms are thought to be a product of the alteration of neuronal hyperactivity and hypoactivity, residual effects of the changes within the limbic system, the primitive area of the brain "imprinted" by the trauma (van der Kolk & Saporta, 1991).

However, the reaction of my friend Vanji was not a direct result of PTSD, although this neuropsychological illness could still lay claim to her. Vanji and thousands, perhaps hundreds of thousands, of offspring of first-generation survivors of catastrophic and/or long-term trauma events are suffering from what has come to be called either *historical* or *intergenerational trauma.* Similar in manifestation and, even to some degree in origin, these two syndromes, not yet documented in any handbook or diagnostic reference guide, are the subjects of fertile, ongoing research—studies directed at their resolution and treatment, and ultimately at their reduction and prevention.

The first attempts to operationalize what some more metaphorically term "the wounds of the fathers" passed to future generations occurred with the children of the survivors of one of the greatest of history's horrors, the Holocaust. In the years that followed the emptying of the camps, what was realized by those working with the survivors was that not only the interned themselves, but their children and grandchildren were emotionally scarred. "It became gradually apparent that they had a greater tendency to display emotional problems with respect to the general population . . . and only with the pioneering work of Judith Kestenberg and the findings of a study group set up in 1974 did a picture emerge of the type of psychological condition characteristic" of these later generations (Connolly, 2011, p. 610). Over the decades since, similar observations have been made in the descendants of other groups subjected to attempts at social genocide, destruction of culture, and decimation of their forebears. Studies on such groups as First Nation Americans and Alaskan natives, Canadian indigenous people, New Zealand Maori, and Japanese Americans interned in prison camps during World War II have documented some of the aftereffects passed down to subsequent generations.

Also called *historical trauma*, one of its major researchers, Maria Brave Heart (2005) delineates it as: "the cumulative emotional and psychological wounding over the life span and across generations, emanating from massive group trauma," (p. 4) an extensive suffering that begins with some historical event.

This woman, whose name represents the strength she recognizes in her people, clarifies the difference between historical/intergenerational trauma and other syndromes coming under the heading of complex trauma. She emphasizes that many tribes of Native Americans are:

> [S]urvivors of intergenerational trauma, not just traumas within our lifespan. Our culture and history also influence the way we show our symptoms and the way in which we manifest our symptoms. Our grief is different from the dominant culture's grief. One reason why I say that is true is because the way we mourn in our traditional cultures is a little different. All cultures have their ways of mourning, but in our culture we maintain a connection with the spirit world. The way that we mourned and buried our dead was taken away from us. . . . Then we just got hit with so many things happening to us in history that we didn't have time to heal from one loss, before another occurred. (p. 4)

Some of the major events in the journey of pain of her people extend from the early butchery at Fort Mystic to the infamous Cherokee Trail of Tears, up to the slaughter at Wounded Knee. In a less obvious but perhaps even more destructive way, history is repeated through the thousands of Native American children sent to "Indian boarding schools" to be cleansed of native characteristics, ties, and traditions (Brave Heart, 2005, p. 4).

Some critics have reacted to the aftermath of the horrors held by many of these affected groups with the dismissing term of "emotional baggage," but a description of it from two women working with Aboriginal descendants suggests how significantly deep, destructive, and enduring this suffering is. Wesley-Esquimaux and Smolewski (2004), observing the symptoms and working to heal the patients who come to the many healing centers across Canada, describe "intergenerational or multigenerational trauma" as:

> [T]he effects of trauma that are not resolved in one generation. When trauma is ignored and there is no support for dealing with it, the trauma will be passed down from one generation to the next. What we learn to see as normal when we are children, we pass on to our own children. . . . the unhealthy ways of behaving that people use to protect themselves can be passed on to children without even knowing they are doing so. (p. 2)

The core issue, as they indicate, lies in the phrases "not resolved" and "when ignored." The lack of resolution, the ignoring, the silence that so many observers, clinicians, and researchers have noted surrounding the events, the horror, the images associated with the trauma that are part of the heritage of survivors—all of which are products of neither deliberate avoidance nor even outcomes of defensive denial. The impact on those experiencing the trauma is such that, as Jung (1934) describes it, "whole tracts of our being can plunge into unconsciousness and vanish from the surface for years and decades" (as cited in Connolly, 2011, p. 609). The depersonalization, creating a type of zombie state emotionally and cognitively, removes the sufferer from the field of agony, but at the same time sinks him or her into emotional paralysis. Researchers working the neurological pathways of trauma (Ford, 2009, p. 36), in observing victims of rape and attack as well as war veterans, use terms such as *survival brain*, *frozen responses*, and *exiled parts of the self* to characterize the effect of the shutting down of the prefrontal cortex and other brain areas responsible for higher level functions. Bessel van der Kolk (2009) characterizes the extensiveness of such traumatic aftermath, stating that this shutdown progresses until the trauma once outside becomes "lodged within people's internal experience, in the very sinew and muscles of their organisms" (p. 461).

While the pathways that lengthen the effects of trauma into the lives of children and grandchildren are under much study and some dispute, the sequelae of their impact have been documented. Working from a Freudian perspective, Cathy Caruth (1995) underscores the paradoxical nature of the impact: The "historical power of the trauma is not just that the experience is repeated after its forgetting, but that it is only in and through its inherent forgetting that it is first experienced at all . . . a history [of trauma] can be grasped only in the very inaccessibility of its occurrence" (p. 8). In the words of Auschwitz survivor Eli Wiesel, two of the psychological outcomes of trauma for persons of all sorts, but especially of the most devastating kind that reaches into future generations, is "death . . . of language . . . and of time" (as cited in Connolly, 2011, p. 611).

Taking each of these outcomes separately, even though there exists great overlap, what effect does time erasure have on the sufferers of intergenerational trauma? Alan Young (1995) calls trauma a "disease of time," explaining that "the pathology consists of the past invading the present in re-experiences and re-enactments, and of the efforts to defend oneself from the consequences" such that the "present interpretations of events can continue to impact our lives" (p. 4). A woman, now almost 30 years in recovery who calls herself One Prayer Girl (2009), shares her experience of time loss on her website (http://oneprayergirl.blogspot.com/2009_02_01_archive.html) in her poem "Soul as Dust." In the middle verse she laments: "Wasting away - fading fast / Vibrancy of youth laid flat." and ends: "Time has had its way with/ Stolen minutes of the mind." One Prayer Girl captures here so poignantly what happens to persons caught in trauma, trapped in a morass of past-present-future. I have seen clients exhibit such confusion. Not cognitively impaired or delusional, still they have forgotten how to impose real time boundaries to such a degree that all seems to flow together like a river covering the banks of what exists when. The transmitted memories that descend from one generation to another are sometimes called *memories without experience* or *amalgam memories*, which some researchers suggest:

> [c]onsist not of images but of transmitted sensations and emotions . . . and exactly because these memories are not experienced they acquire their repetitive, static and coercive character . . . over time they accumulate around themselves an amalgam of images taken both from personal experience and from the stereotyped images of family history or the social group." (Neri in Connolly, 2011, p. 612)

Reviewing this explanation, I recall a young woman with whom I worked some time ago. Leticia [pseudonym], a bright and creative student who was on a freshman retreat sponsored by her university, and I met on the first day as partners in reflecting on her retreat experience. I had volunteered to help out with some of the retreatants when several of the originally signed-on spiritual directors were unable to attend. The fruits of my donated time became immediately evident as I grew to know four gifted coeds in earnest about growing in God. Leticia, who asked me to call her Tish, confessed that she struggled with praying. "I can't sit for long and read or think. I get jumbled and all sorts of thoughts come crowding into my head. After a while, I can't sort out today from what I am worrying about tomorrow from mistakes I made yesterday." Time collapse was one of Tish's concerns; the other was an overwhelming phobia she reported. She described how whenever she had to travel any distance by car, especially when she was the driver, she would get highly anxious days before and sometimes come to such a state by departure that she often canceled the trip completely. At the time of Tish's initial sharing, I did not see any strong connection between her two presenting issues, with the exception that anxiety seemed prominent in both.

On the second day of the retreat, Tish reported that she had been doing some writing, a reflective practice I had suggested she might try during her distracted prayer times. She had even attempted doing it with her nonpreferred left hand, although when I first encouraged this she had laughed. Surprising to her were what images had come up several times during the writing; namely, the memory of her Busia, her grandmother. Since she herself was only 8 when her Busia had died, she noted how she could recall only bits and pieces about her. She told how stories of this brave woman had been carried through her family: of her escape from Poland in World War II ahead of Hitler's and Stalin's forces; of her hiding in a truck to cross the borders through several countries after her own brother, a Catholic priest, had been executed; of her traveling to the States from Lithuania on her own after she discovered she was the sole survivor of her seven siblings. Our meeting the next day brought more about her Busia, this time from a spattering of dreams that Tish had experienced during the night. Tish recounted, "I saw her walking, almost endlessly down potholed roads and past burning ruins. A little later, I dreamt of her walking beside a little bedraggled dog, almost like a hobo carrying a stick on which hung a small bundle. Finally, I dreamt of her almost pulling herself up a gangplank to a dirty, listing tramp steamer with hard-looking men leering at her over the rails." When we spoke, Tish assured me that no one as far as she could recall had told her of any events of her Busia's journey. "I really don't think anyone knew any details as she never spoke of it. Once when one of my older brothers had asked her about coming to America, she said simply, 'It was hard but I got here. That is all that matters.' Then she set her mouth in a straight line and we knew not to ask her again." The dream anecdotes that Tish shared and her memory of her grandmother's reaction to being questioned fit well into observations from those who have worked with historically traumatized clients.

In her article "Re-Storying Canada's Past," Christine Woolner (2009), writing for the Beyond Intractability Project, speaks to the etiology of silence in trauma:

> On the other side of "dangerous" stories are stories that are broken, unheard, silenced, or never told. In settings of conflict, especially, the tendency towards collective forgetting or "collective amnesia"—a process through which a society collectively ignores a part of its past instead of dealing with the pain either inflicted to or by this collective—is particularly likely to occur and result in collective narratives that gloss over significant episodes in history—and thus forego the responsibility to deal with injustices. (para. 11)

Tish and her grandmother and many throughout the generations of her Polish American family held the trauma in silence and, like a lid covering a seething cauldron of pain, anguish, secret shame, and more, the containment was crushing more than those who had survived the Polish flight from Axis troops. It was stifling this 21st-century college freshman, holding her captive to her foremother's crises. The truth of this became even more evident as I moved through some systematic desensitization exercises and relaxation techniques to help Tish deal with her phobia for traveling. As we pictured different vehicles in which she might journey she would catch, behind her closed eyes, glimpses of wooden wheeled wagons, battered farm trucks, and even ramshackle cargo ships carrying all types of foreign flags. Slowly, as the images passed, so did her fears, the cold places within her chest where she held the shaking terrors, the accelerated breathing that marked the remembering.

And, as these moved into nontoxic memories, the time in chapel and in prayer grew quieter, gentler, easier. John the Beloved writes: "Perfect love drives out fear" (1 John 4:18, NIV). This apostle, survivor of his own trauma and generations of anti-Semitic suffering before him, held his insights with newborn faith in his Jesus. As he, so Tish came to know the God who loves her without condition or cause. At the end of her retreat, Tish read me a short verse she had written to celebrate her 5 days away: "In stillness he comes / not on little cat feet, / but in the soft whisper of the wind, / and the flutter of the candle flame / in my room / and my heart." With this young woman I celebrated intergenerational trauma at least partly removed.

The chain of broken time and memories became even more personally meaningful, when recently I was doing some work on the novels of an American Irish writer whose stories are built around the history of families descended from the immigrant Irish who poured into the shores of east coast United States following the Great Famine. Researching on systems therapy and diversity, I turned to the internationally acclaimed writer and clinician Monica McGoldrick, drawing on her invaluable collection of essays in *Re-Visioning Family Therapy* (McGoldrick, 2008). In her own chapter, "Finding a Place Called Home," this descendant from the Famine travelers of the 1840s speaks to intergenerational trauma from her personal remembrances. She notes that "There were many things . . . that I grew up without knowing or not knowing that I knew, many issues that were mystified, obscured, or kept invisible by my community, my family, my teachers, and even my professional training" (p. 98). The results that McGoldrick chronicles, which have been passed on from fathers to son and daughters to granddaughters, are numerous. Perhaps none is more striking in her account than a certain kind of homelessness. She describes true home as a "place where we could own our cultural heritage and not have our deepest stories denied. It is about right relations among things" and our search concludes in the place where we come "to be home and to find home" (p. 100). She emphasizes that "Home is a space, where we could all belong—with each other—strengthened by what we take from those who have come before us, creating a safe haven for those who are with us in our time, and insuring that we leave a space for all those who will come after us" (p. 102).

As McGoldrick traced the vestiges of her Irish heritage in the secret keeping, denial, sometimes isolation and even blind obedience to authority that were as real for her as were the members of her family, I had to cry "mea culpa" also. I grew up without even knowing from what part of Ireland my mother's family had come. Not until a sixth-grade geography project necessitated my sending for some soil from my ancestors' homeland did I discover that my mother neither knew nor wanted to know from where on the Old Sod her grandparents had traveled. I ended up having to contact my dad's very distant cousin in Germany for some farmyard dirt. Also, when pressed to do a genogram as a college student, I could go back no farther on my mother's side than her parents. "We don't talk about the 'great hunger,'" she insisted. "They left that bad life behind them and we live a better life now." Regretfully, along with the better life that the immigrants wrestled from the "Irish need not apply" conditions they found in this land of plenty came the blight of "the drink," decades of poverty, and hardworking men crushed during the Depression. I found out only in my 40s that my mother's own dad is listed in one of the census books as a "nomad," who at the death of his young wife, put his young children in the care of relatives and took to the road to look for work. Irish American emigrant Maureen Dezell (2000) notes what she sees as the underlying reason for the Celtic silence across time in her book *Irish America: Coming into Clover*. Quoting James Carroll, she observes, "The Irish learned not to know what happened to them. In their determination to put the savage experience behind them, the survivors of the famine denied its relevance" (p. 220). And the outcome is that their children, and their children's children have been bound with a silence to death and an inclination to denial—of drink, of the drinkers, of the dearth of money, of the stifling of emotions, and of the crushing of hope for the future—all heritage of the Irish spirit reborn.

A modern painter of the stark and real, self-exile to New Mexico, Georgia O'Keeffe captures some of the powerful impotency so familiar to those with this residue of intergenerational trauma: the contrast of life and death against a landscape of silence. In the 1940s and 1950s, after the death of her photographer husband, this woman entered into an almost hermit-like existence in the Southwest, a marked transition from her "personal turmoil" and the "male dominated company" of her New York life (Freed, 2002). In this place of silence, she found her artistic voice. Here the barren sands and dried bones spoke to her of survival and beauty. Like many who have sought stillness in order to "choose life," O'Keeffe allowed what was loss to become her wealth. She said of her work during this time of imposed silence:

> So I brought home the bleached bones as my symbol of the desert. To me they are as beautiful as anything I know. To me they are strangely more living than the animals walking around—hair, eyes and all their tails switching. The bones seem to cut sharply to the center of something that is keenly alive on the desert even tho' it is vast and empty and untouchable—and knows no kindness with all its beauty. (as cited in Freed, 2002)

To be in that place where we can look and not see, know and not speak—such is a description of the void that follows systematic depersonalization and dehumanization that comes with catastrophe. Connolly (2011) invokes the phrase of earlier writers, calling the place "a world without metaphor" to depict the loss of language suffered by survivors and, down through the decades, their descendants (p. 613). Why the silence? Because the words of truth are obliterated by other caustic memories and held feelings, or as Shalamov, a survivor of the Stalin death camps, explains it: The camp had dried up my brain and I could not, I just could not squeeze another word from it . . . not because the gap between my will and Kolyma [Gulag labor camp] was too great . . . but because in those folds of my brain where ecstatic adjectives were stored, there was nothing but hatred (as cited in Connolly, 2011, p. 613). Adding to these explanations is one from Aboriginal survivors:

> Beyond the silence of stories—and perhaps partly as a result of this silence—the often traumatic experience of the Aboriginal's past has led to a fragmentation in their own story and self-understanding. For indigenous cultures in many places . . . original violence might best be understood as the disruption—and far too often—outright destruction—of a people's story. Thus, in the Canadian case, centuries of violence have not simply been ignored/forgotten in mainstream discourse about the past. This violence, compounded by collective forgetting and silencing of Aboriginal voices, has led to a fragmentation and breaking of the Aboriginal's own narratives. (Woolner, 2009)

Each of these explanations touches into a part of the damage done sometimes centuries before, closing minds and lips to a heritage, a culture, sometimes, a creed. The resulting silence crashes in on spoken language, but even more, on "the capacity to create dreams," interrupting the "narrative capacity of the mind in dreaming" through the destruction of "visual metaphors to form a narrative. . . . It is as though the children are forced to dream the nightmares of their parents" (Connolly, 2011, p. 613). Connolly explains this reversal in that "the nightmares so frequently reported by the children and grandchildren of survivors are thus not so much a reflection of the unconscious of the child, but an attempt to represent and come to terms with the reality of the parents' trauma" (p. 614).

A loss of history, a demise of heritage, the destruction of culture, the silencing of voices, the fracturing of time, the crushing of dreams—so much collateral damage carried by descendants of the traumatized. What can be done to help, to heal? Cathy Caruth (1995) states emphatically that the "means to passing out of the isolation" of the wounds of trauma is that "the history of the trauma, in its inherent belatedness, can only take place through the listening of another" (p. 11). The vast research efforts undertaken in the field of healing intergenerational trauma in the past several decades have shown that certain key factors must be in place and are critical to therapeutic interventions. Without examining any modalities in particular, the remainder of this chapter looks at the twofold process that can move the sufferer toward healing and the place of the counselor/caregiver in this process.

Connolly (2011) has underscored both the criticality of the therapist in the process of healing and the impact on the therapist in its undertaking. With a clear vision of both, she writes:

> Working with intergenerational trauma necessitates the recreation of the empathic bond essential for the reconstruction of temporality and

> of language, but this can only be brought about by the capacity of the therapist. . . . This invokes intense anxiety and emotional strain in the analyst and requires a conscious effort on his/her part to overcome the temptation to withhold empathy . . . to be affectively impacted by it without losing his/her capacity for hope and without losing the capacity to distinguish inner and outer reality, past and present. (p. 617)

These demands extend far beyond even awareness of or attention to vicarious or secondary trauma on the part of the counselor/caregiver. This work demands that, in rebuilding the empathic bond destroyed by the generational descent of trauma, the counselor/caregiver become the conduit—open, flexible, and completely connected to the client—without a loss of his or her own creativity, emotional capacity and clarity, and ability for attentiveness.

At the time that recognition of historical/intergenerational trauma was first emerging, a contemporary theologian who had lived through World War II in her native Germany, Dorothee Soelle (1975), plumbed the mystery and mystical truth of suffering against the anguish of the Vietnam War. Examining the pain of past and present conflicts, she identifies "three phases" of suffering within these as the following: "the uncomprehended suffering that makes one mute," marked by isolation and powerlessness (Phase One); the uncovering of "a language of lament, of crying, of pain," whose suffering can move to acceptance (Phase Two); a transcending to grasp the "fulfillment within reach" (Phase Three) (pp. 73–74). Soelle insists that such movement is only possible "(i)n the context of a group of people who share their life—including their suffering with one another" (p. 74).

A trio of collaborators, all of whom are both pastoral ministers and professional caregivers, have paralleled the three stages elucidated by Soelle with the corresponding phase of compassion needed by the one who engages with the sufferer (Headley, Boone, & Sapp, 1993). In the first phase, mute voiceless suffering that locks the anguished within him- or herself can be met by the empathic presence of one who is willing to sit silently in a sufferer's company and wait. Anna Ulanov (2004) calls the sites of such silent presence "the sacred places where our vulnerability and need create a crossing place for the Spirit" (Chapter 9). This crossing place also offers an intersection, much like the famous Fourth and Walnut Streets in Louisville of Thomas Merton's fame (1966), where the client and counselor can experience together their shared humanity and shared divinity, in their kinship as children of an unconditionally loving God. As Merton describes it, it is the point at which he can see:

> [T]he secret beauty of their hearts, the depths of their hearts where neither sin nor desire nor self-knowledge can reach, the core of their reality, the person that each one is in God's eyes. If only they could all see themselves as they really are. If only we could see each other that

> way all of the time. There would be no more war, no more hatred, no more cruelty, no more greed. . . . (p. 153)

The second phase of compassion that can meet with and even touch into the second phase of suffering is called "expressive compassion" (Headley et al., 1993, p. 149). In this phase, in which the beginnings of memories are enunciated, the sufferer's outpourings might be limited to snatched phrases, words of lament, fragmentary images, even primitive wailing. Connolly (2011) warns that the images and content coming from the distressed can "have a nightmarish and fragmentary quality . . . full of presentations of traumatic events" reaching back into distant pasts not of themselves but of their ancestors' worst experiences (p. 619). They emerge from a "psychotic core of nothingness" and in the company of the one who cares and is willing to become the container for the chaos, conflict, and barrenness, the sufferers begin to weave a narrative, one born generations before. They begin to tell the story.

The requirement on the part of the listener is to be able to hold the memories and their almost unspeakable feelings, and focus on the person sharing. Simone Weil in her précis, *Waiting on God* (as cited in Mayer, 1990) describes the intensity of this focused attitude as attenté. With this almost untranslatable word, she describes a contemplative stance defying the fragmentation of time, language, and creativity, the trio of symptoms observed in intergenerational trauma. She writes that attenté, as she expresses it, is neither "rooted in past or present" for to do so is "to confine the mystery of life" (p. 297). Her attitude of attenté includes an active looking for God that penetrates space and time with the burning probe of the visionary and the intense focus of the mystic, as the seer attends to a single point of concentration. In the case of the therapist, the center of concentration is the suffering of the client. Here the counselor, the attentive waiter, assumes the position of the biblical prophet, peering into space and time, uniting then and now, here and there, and discerning in these a future still being fashioned in the company of God. Such a searching vision destroys the hold that traumatized defenses have imposed on the waiter, as client and counselor/caregiver together reach Weil's ultimate, "the truth, the real," on the condition that their attenté be a "looking and not an attachment" (p. 297). Connolly (2011) concludes that "dialogue with a receptive 'other,' is essential for the recreation of the empathic bond and for the possibility of escaping from the imprisonment of the past" (p. 616), for this "recreation of an inner dialogical space and of the empathic bond with the other opens the way to the possibility of a narrative and symbolic reconstruction of the historical reality of the transmitted collective trauma" (p. 622). As this restructuring progresses, words come, stories unfold, narratives are woven and, eventually, truth is born.

The truth emerges, not in full-blown completion, but in ribbons of memory that slowly are woven into a whole. No time warp or amnesia happens in true healing. The reality of the past remains; the factual and corporeal happenings of days, minutes, hours cannot be dissolved in the healing. What occurs is that, having found a voice, even in staggering syllables, meanings emerge that the sufferer him- or herself can claim. Like the crying sobs of a baby, distraught and distressed, are taken in by the loving mother, and in her rocking, her cooing voice, her gentle touch, then returned as soothed, assuaged, and transformed, so the trauma story. The traumatized person shares, the compassionate person receives, and solidarity is formed.

Almost a decade before Alice Walker wrote her famous novel *The Color Purple*, she wrote a womanist essay that celebrates her own race's generations of women sufferers of intergenerational trauma. In this essay, "In search of our mothers' gardens" (1974/2002) she describes the foremothers of her people who, under slave masters' whip and sharecroppers' degradation and bigoted ignorance, struggled to survive. She says of their survival: "They forced their minds to desert their bodies and their striving spirits sought to rise, like frail whirlwinds from the hard red clay. And when those frail whirlwinds fell, in scattered particles, upon the ground, no one mourned. Instead, men lit candles to celebrate the emptiness that remained, as people do who enter a beautiful but vacant space to resurrect a God." Along with mourning the loss of her ancestors, Walker also celebrates the gift that their struggle has brought to her and to future granddaughters. In their trauma these "mules of the world," "matriarchs," "mean and evil women," and "sapphire's bitches" as they have been termed found the capacity to change devastating shame and suffering into meaning and more. They endured, says Walker, because these "crazy Saints and lunatics" planted generative roots. Whether through gospel songs, rag-woven quilts, or as with her mother, in gloriously exotic gardens, they saved themselves and, by so doing, preserved their creative gifts for their female descendants. The inheritance of brutality born and endurance hewn out of poverty is traced in the wealth of their progeny. The breaking of their silence has won not only national and international awards, but pride and honor for the witnesses.

> And so our mothers and grandmothers have, more often than not anonymously, handed on the creative spark, the seed of the flower they themselves never hoped to see: or like a sealed letter they could not plainly read. . . . And so it is, certainly, with my own mother. Unlike "Ma" Rainey's songs which retained their creator's name even while blasting forth from Bessie Smith's mouth, no song or poem will bear my mother's name. Yet, so many of the stories that I write, that we all write, are my mother's stories. Only recently did I fully realize this: that through years of listening to my mother's stories of her life, I have absorbed not only the stories themselves, but something of the manner in which she spoke, something of the urgency that involves the knowledge that her stories—like her life—must be recorded. (Walker, 1974/2002)

REFERENCES

Brave Heart, M. (2005). From intergenerational trauma to intergenerational healing. *Wellbriety!* 6(6). Retrieved from www.whitebison.org/magazine/2005/volume6/wellbriety!vol6no6.pdf

Caruth, C. (1995). *Trauma: Explorations in memory*. Baltimore, MD: Johns Hopkins University Press.

Connolly, A. (2011). Healing the wounds of our fathers: Intergenerational trauma, memory, symbolization and narrative. *Journal of Analytic Psychology*, 56, 607–626.

Dezell, M. (2000). *Irish America: Coming into clover. The evolution of a people and a culture.* New York, NY: Anchor Books.

Ford, J. D. (2009). Overview. In C. Courtois & J. D. Ford (Eds.), *Treating complex traumatic stress disorders: An evidence-based guide* (pp. 31–58). New York, NY: Guilford Press.

Freed, R. (2002). The southwest. In *From skyscrapers to skulls: Georgia O'Keeffe creates the Native American*. Retrieved from http://xroads.virginia.edu/~ma02/freed/okeeffe/intro2.html

Headley, A., Boone, J., & Sapp, G. (1993). Compassion in religious counseling. In G. Sapp (Ed.), *Compassionate ministry* (pp. 123–170). Birmingham, AL: Religious Education Press.

Jaffe, G. (2012, May 5). New name for PTSD. *Washington Post*. Retrieved from www.washingtonpost.com/world/national-security/new-name

Maviglia, M. (n.d.). *Historical trauma and PTSD: The "existential" versus the "clinical."* Retrieved from www.priory.com/ital/fromstates2e.htm

Mayer, S. (1990). The poverty of waiting and its riches. *Spirituality today*, *42*(4), 292–302.

McGoldrick, M. (2008). Finding a place called home. In M. McGoldrick & K. Hardy (Eds.), *Re-visioning family therapy: Race, culture, and gender in clinical practice* (pp. 97–114). New York, NY: Guilford Press.

Merton, T. (1966). *Conjectures of a guilty bystander*. New York, NY: Doubleday.

Murty, D. (n.d.). *Story of the peace crane*. Retrieved from http://www.buddhistcouncil.org/bodhitree/Books/Story_of_the_Peace_Crane.pdf

One Prayer Girl. (2009, February 7). *Soul as dust*. Retrieved from http://oneprayergirl.blogspot.com/2009_02_01_archive.html

Rooney, Rita. (2011, Spring). The invisible wounds of war. *Medicine Bulletin of University of Maryland*, 95(4), 8–13. http://www.medicalalumni.org/wp-content/uploads/2010/10/Bulletin-Spring-2011_web5.pdf

Soelle, D. (1975). *Suffering*. Philadelphia, PA: Fortress Press.

Spacks, B. (2009). *Poem for Sadako*. Sadako Peace Day commemoration on August 6, 2009. (Reprinted with permission.) Retrieved from www.wagingpeace.org/articles/2009/08/20_spacks_sadako_poem.php

Ulanov, A. (2004). *Spiritual aspects of clinical work*. Einsiedlen, Switzerland: Daimon Verlag.

van der Kolk, B. (2009). Afterword. In C. Courtois & J. D. Ford (Eds.), *Treating complex traumatic stress disorders: An evidence-based guide* (pp. 455–465). New York, NY: Guilford Press.

van der Kolk, B., & Saporta, J. (1991). The biological mechanisms and treatment of intrusion and numbing. *Anxiety Research*, *4*, 199–212.

Walker, A. (1974/2002). In search of our mothers' gardens: The creativity of black women in the South. MS. Retrieved from http://www.msmagazine.com/spring2002/walker.asp

Wesley-Esquimaux, C., & Smolewski, M. (2004). *Historic trauma and aboriginal healing*. Ottawa, ON: Aboriginal Healing Foundation.

Woolner, C. (2009). *Re-storying Canada's past: A case study in the significance of narratives in healing intractable conflict*. Retrieved from www.beyondintractability.org/casestudy/woolner-re-storying

Young, A. (1995). *The harmony of illusions: Inventing post-traumatic stress disorder*. Princeton, NJ: Princeton University Press.

CHAPTER

12

Patience and Self-Renewal

Sarah A. Schnitker, Amber E. Blews, and Jessica A. Foss

PATIENCE AND THE PROCESS OF SELF-RENEWAL

Why do we not like to wait? In modern times, waiting has become a nuisance at best and an outright violation of our human rights at worst. How can a culture that values increasingly rapid technology, instant communication, and immediate gratification view patience with any kind of appreciation? Perhaps we have lost sight of what patience is and the benefits to be gained from activation of the virtue. Patience has been defined as the ability to wait calmly in the face of frustration, adversity, or suffering (Schnitker, 2012). According to classical virtue theory, the virtue of patience lies between two vices: sloth and reckless impatience. In essence, sloth, also called *acedia*, is inaction or doing nothing meaningful, whereas reckless impatience implies irritation, aggravation, and provocation (Harned, 1997; Pieper, 1952).

Patience may be enacted during short-term waiting, such as standing in line at the grocery store, or in situations where longer-term patience is required, such as developing a person's acting talent, working on parenting skills, or striving toward self-renewal. Meaningful goals are rarely attained overnight, and obstacles often get in the way of easy progress. Patient endurance allows people to continue pursuing their goals without becoming overly frustrated (falling prey to the vice of reckless impatience) or disengaging from their pursuit (falling prey to the vice of sloth). Patience is a critically important virtue allowing us to deal with life's surprises and disasters in a meaningful way. It is what allows us to walk the often arduous path of self-renewal without losing hope.

The term *patience* is derived from the Greek word meaning *to suffer* and is commonly associated with the concept of longsuffering. Patience and suffering go hand in hand; for it is in the midst of frustrations, trials, and pain that patience must be invoked in order for one to persist despite obstacles. It is this persistence and ability to wait calmly in the midst of suffering, without giving up or losing heart, that promotes the process of self-renewal. Although it may seem counterintuitive that people can be renewed through enduring pain, the concept of growth through suffering is a well-established phenomenon within the empirical mental health literature. Researchers specializing in grief and loss have discovered that renewal through suffering is not an uncommon experience; rather, it is a frequently experienced part of human resiliency that occurs when one is able to successfully and patiently endure hardship (Tedeschi & Calhoun, 2004).

Moreover, suffering does not occur in a vacuum. We suffer with others, and sometimes others cause our suffering. In this chapter, the importance of patience in the process of self-renewal is discussed as it relates to the individual (intrapersonal patience), dyadic relationships (client/therapist, parent/child, marital), and the community (shared experience). We also focus on ways that people can develop their patience in a practical manner based on research findings with the intent that these suggestions be incorporated into practice.

The Great Need for Patience in Therapeutic Contexts

Is patience really needed in our developing world? With abounding opportunities for seemingly immediate self-renewal and healing, why choose to wait? For the average consumer, self-help seems readily available on local bookshelves under titles such as *Happiness Now! Timeless Wisdom for Feeling Good FAST* (2007), along with others, each promising fulfillment and guaranteeing life satisfaction with purchase. For example, when considering mood disorders, there are a plethora of psychotropic medications readily available to treat depression and anxiety, two of the most pervasive mood problems. Prescriptions for antidepressants have greatly increased over the past two decades and continue to increase in number. In a recent article in *Health Affairs*, researchers suggested that the use of antidepressants to treat mild depression has increased twofold or more since 1996 (Mojtabai & Olfson, 2011).[1] Although antidepressants provide much needed treatment to many depressed people, there are many instances where psychotropic medication is overprescribed as a quick fix for mood dysregulation (Mojtabai & Olfson, 2011).

The implications of this "quick-fix phenomenon" for the process of self-renewal in psychotherapy are profound. Counseling often begins with clients presenting multiple problems that they wish to address during therapy. Because the therapeutic course is unique to each person, the time frame can vary

[1]The research did not include data beyond the year 2007, which would likely yield an even greater increase.

from a few short weeks to long-term treatment lasting well over a year. What happens then, when the virtue of patience is not enacted while the therapeutic progression unfolds? According to Miller and Hubble (2011), therapy is ended prematurely. In a recent survey, 50% of all clients ended therapy before they experienced symptom remission. Considering that 90% of people surveyed said they would prefer to talk about their problems rather than take psychotropic medications, the absence of patience in therapy is problematic. Although a person may desire self-renewal, patience is required to sustain the progression, else therapy goals are prematurely abandoned.

Therapy is an ideal example of the self-renewal process because it uncovers the undesirable features of people's lives and brings forth both their desires and options for change. Through this self-reflection, clients begin to examine their self-identity within multiple contexts and at multiple levels, such as mind, body, spirit, and community. Through therapy, clients are better able to understand their identities within these areas and seek to examine what is deemed productive and life-giving, along with that which appears destructive or life-diminishing. Clients may desire renewal of their physical selves, renewal in their relationships, or renewal in their cognitive-emotional functioning. Renewal is often desired in multiple domains, and the renewal process serves to integrate various parts of the self. Thus, activation of the virtue of patience in a therapeutic context allows clients to pursue their therapeutic goals involving self-renewal without becoming overly frustrated.

Individual Patience Leads to Self-Renewal

When considering the therapist/client relationship (or clinician/patient, analyst/analysand, counselor/counselee), patience is activated (or not!) for both people as they work toward the goals of therapy in their distinct roles. Even before the therapist and client are patient with each other, they both must enact intrapersonal patience with themselves in regard to the therapeutic goals.

The Client

First, the client must utilize patience for change to occur. Patience allows people to continue to progress toward their goals, even when they do not feel like they are making progress. This is of particular interest in psychotherapy or counseling because clients often feel worse before their symptoms begin to improve. Professional therapists frequently issue a disclosure statement to potential clients before beginning treatment in an effort to prepare them for what can feel like a lack of progress in therapy (Howes, 2008). Early on in therapy, usually within the first several sessions, clients may experience feelings of doubt related to the effectiveness of their treatment, which may lead them to discontinue therapy. Due to the client's discomfort during this phase, the activation of patience is necessary to persevere and continue therapy.

Let us consider the case of Stan, a man in therapy:

> Stan is a Caucasian male in his fifties who was recently laid off from his job as a quality control manager at a large manufacturing company. He is married and has two children, an 18-year-old son and a 22-year-old daughter. His presenting problem is feeling depressed and anxious because of his recent job loss. He is experiencing a depressed mood most of the day, nearly every day, which he says is a result of his loss of income. He also suffers from intense bouts of worry related to his recent attempts to become employed. Stan has not told his extended family or peers that he was laid off, but has decided to see a therapist to address his emotional distress. Upon entering therapy, Stan wants to know how long it should take before he will feel better. He also expresses his doubts about whether therapy can really help him. In therapy sessions, Stan seems unable to talk about his emotions, particularly those related to his anger and sadness. As Stan discusses his childhood, he remembers how his father would not tolerate his strong emotions such as crying or shouting. He also remembers that his father would often walk out of the room when Stan became upset as a child. Through this personal insight, Stan realizes that though he was not aware of it, he too was hard on his children and discouraged negative emotional expression. He begins to wonder if that is why his children rarely speak to him. Stan notices that he is deeply saddened by the thought that he was not a good father. In one session he cannot control his sadness and he cries in the presence of his therapist. After this session, Stan feels embarrassed about his tearful breakdown and is feeling that therapy may not be able to help him since he feels worse now than when he began. He calls the therapist to cancel his next appointment and she reminds him of the admonition that he would feel worse before feeling better. Stan decides that he can continue his therapy for at least one more appointment. During the next session, he is able to process what happened with the therapist and is surprised that he feels better after the session ends. He decides to schedule another appointment for the following week.

In this example, Stan is faced with unpleasant emotions related to his present and past life experiences. He is embarrassed and troubled by the fact that he does not seem to be "getting well" as quickly as he expected. However, when he is able to express his doubts in the context of therapy, he experiences normalization of his feelings through the therapist's assurance that his feelings are commonplace for clients in therapy. With guidance from his therapist, Stan is able to exert one of his inner strengths—patience—to tolerate the waiting that is inherent to the therapeutic sequence. As he continues to participate in his therapeutic journey, perpetual activation of patience will be required to make progress, to encounter obstacles, and to successfully overcome them.

The Therapist

Inner patience is not only a necessity for clients, but it is also required of therapists. Therapeutic work requires clinicians who can tolerate ambiguity in both their personal and professional lives. Consider the example of Monica, Stan's therapist:

> Monica is a 35-year-old, African-American female. She is married to her college sweetheart, who she wedded 11 years ago. Monica is a licensed clinical psychologist who has recently completed her postdoctoral training and is now part of a small private practice along with two senior clinicians. Monica often experiences self-doubt related to her effectiveness as a therapist. She experiences anxiety and worry related to her position as an independent practitioner who is no longer under supervision and is responsible for facilitating the mental wellness of others. Additionally, she finds her dual roles as both a wife and a professional stressful at times because she feels she cannot give 100% to either one. When she experiences such misgivings related to her professional career, she consults with her mentor, a former supervisor, to discuss client cases that she is struggling with. Through such consultation, she is able to understand her clients' problems in more nuanced ways, allowing her to modify her case conceptualizations and treatment plans. She is also able to recognize that she is continuing to grow as a therapist and that growth requires time. Monica draws upon her virtue of patience to walk through this time of growth. She is beginning to understand that her ability to exercise inner patience toward herself as a developing clinician will allow her to grow as well as model the patience she hopes to impart to her clients.

Monica's struggle to enact patience within herself is one with which many caregivers can identify. Feelings of inadequacy arise when therapists and other caregivers feel they are failing to facilitate improvement in the lives of those who depend upon them. Moreover, caregivers often find themselves conflicted in their dual roles, leading to feelings that one role is sacrificed for the other (Zarit & Zarit, 2011). Through activation of patience, people can successfully navigate their multiple roles, knowing that instant perfection in all facets of life is not a reasonable expectation. Without patience with their own limitations, therapists and caregivers can easily fall prey to insecurity, defensiveness, and hindered practice.

Dyadic Patience in Relationships Leads to Self-Renewal

As helping professionals, we willingly enter into caregiving relationships with our clients, engaging in dyadic interactions that can be stressful and frustrating. We also have a variety of other relationships that can aggravate us. Despite a possibly bleak state of affairs in these relationships, we need to believe that healing and self-renewal will come for those with whom we interact—so long as we can endure through the struggle. Yet, too often, our endurance fails us and we are overcome with exhaustion and discouragement, and quickly overtaken by burnout (Maslach & Jackson, 1982). Caregivers' patience with others must be strengthened in order to help them persist and embrace the growth that comes through suffering, for their clients and for themselves.

In addition, our clients do not live solitary lives. They are involved in a variety of relationships. Quite often, present or past relationships are a cause, symptom, or crux of the presenting problem. Thinking about the ways in which patience has or has not been extended to clients in their past and present lives will provide insight for the therapist and client. Moreover, clients may be encouraged to draw upon their strength of patience in present and future relationships.

To illustrate how patience can promote self-renewal within caregivers' and clients' relationships, three dyads will be explored: (1) the therapeutic dyad between client and therapist, (2) the parent-child dyad, and (3) the marital dyad.

Patience and Self-Renewal in the Therapeutic Dyad

Helping professionals are exposed to a wide spectrum of suffering and are asked to come alongside those who are in pain. As a result, caregivers and therapists often share in their clients' suffering and are required to wait patiently with clients as they endure and sort out life's most challenging adversities. This ability to collaboratively endure with a client who is suffering is the core of psychotherapy. The goal of therapy is to promote health by entering into the suffering of the client and helping them tolerate the process of enduring ambiguity and pain, providing them with coping mechanisms, insight, and empathic understanding along the way. All the while, therapists hold in mind the ultimate trajectory and hope that the client will find self-renewal and growth if they can endure the suffering long enough to overcome it. Although therapists have many tools and techniques to utilize toward this aim, research has shown that the relationship formed by clients and therapists is the most powerful tool in promoting change and the persistence for the achievement of personal growth and healing. In one study, quality of the therapeutic relationship accounted for 26% of the variance in therapeutic success rates (Horvath & Symonds, 1991). In another study, actual therapeutic techniques only accounted for approximately 15% of improvements in psychotherapy, whereas client-therapist relationship factors accounted for approximately 30% of the clients' positive therapeutic outcomes (Lambert & Barley, 2001). Thus, it is evident that the dyadic interaction between therapist and client is central to the client's self-renewal. However, establishing an effective relational context for therapeutic change requires a great deal from both the therapist and the client.

An effective therapeutic relationship requires therapists to be, among other things, warm, accepting, trustworthy, empathic, understanding, and attentive. Unfortunately, however, a strong therapeutic alliance is not easily built with all clients who come to therapy. Clients come to therapy because they are suffering emotionally in some capacity and often struggle interpersonally as a result. Often, clients may seem disagreeable, rude, or annoying. Thus, patience is imperative if therapists are to persist in establishing a strong interpersonal bond with each client while promoting the client's growth. The ability to patiently build rapport with a client and extend unconditional warmth and positive regard requires that therapists be engaged in self-renewal practices so that they can possess the internal resources needed to be emotionally available and accessible to each client. By improving their patience, therapists are improving their ability to remain calm, empathic, relational, and, ultimately, therapeutic to their clients.

Even after a therapeutic alliance has been established, ruptures in that interpersonal bond can happen and may be initiated by the client or the therapist. Recall Stan from the earlier example and his decision to call his therapist and cancel his next session because his symptoms are getting worse and he does not feel that Monica is being helpful. This represents a rupture in the therapeutic relationship because Stan is experiencing disappointment in Monica and is questioning her ability to help him as well as doubting the validity of the therapeutic method in general. This rupture is repaired when Monica is able to remind Stan over the phone of their earlier discussion regarding how symptoms often get worse before getting better. Her ability to empathize and validate Stan's experience as being a normal aspect of the therapeutic course helps strengthen her bond with Stan and enables him to persist in his therapeutic journey toward self-renewal. Monica could have chosen to be impatient with Stan and his slow growth, writing him off and moving on to other clients. Instead, by patiently tolerating the relational rupture and seeking to repair it, Monica is helping Stan to exercise patience and persevere in his journey of personal growth. Her patience allows her to actually feel and exhibit warmth and positive regard to Stan in his moment of weakness. Thus, part of reaping the well-being benefits of being in a relationship, therapeutic or otherwise, requires that both parties be able to tolerate ruptures to the relationship as well as repair attempts to restore the interpersonal bond (Wallin, 2007).

Patience and Self-Renewal in the Parent-Child Dyad

Many therapeutic modalities and helping professions recognize the importance of the parent-child relationship in the formation of the person. Though modalities differ in the extent to which they focus on the clients' relationships with their parents (and perhaps with their own children), it is essential for all therapists to take note of this essential relationship and how it may affect the process of self-renewal in clients.

According to attachment theorists, the parent/child relationship is formative because it influences the way people will approach all subsequent relationships (Hazan & Shaver, 1987, 1994). At an early age, children develop internal cognitive representations of how relationships function, which are often referred to as internal working models (Bowlby, 1969, 1973). These internal working models are theorized to be constructed in part through interactions with the primary attachment figure. Bowlby (1969, 1973) has described secure parent/child attachment interactions as the cyclical process through which the child explores the environment, seeks proximity to the parent after exploration for soothing, and then ventures away from the parent again once the secure base (e.g., parent) has provided the necessary reassurance and security. In insecure parent/child interactions, this cycle breaks down. In the case of what is termed avoidant/dismissive insecure attachment, the child no longer looks to the parent for comfort and security, oftentimes because the parent has previously failed to provide soothing. In anxious/preoccupied attachment, the child seeks the parent for soothing, but due to the parent's inconsistent response, the soothing does not work. The child is not comforted by the parent and is unable to happily explore the environment. In disorganized attachment, the child both approaches and avoids the parent—displaying odd, confused, and unpredictable behavior.

As children fluctuate between seeking proximity and venturing out, the patience displayed by parents plays a crucial role in the developing attachment system. A child needing soothing can be irritating and bothersome, and the time required to sensitively attend to a child's needs is great. Parents acting patiently will be responsive and warm to a child's call for comfort. Conversely, parents acting with reckless impatience may yell or scold the child, and parents acting in slothful impatience may emotionally disengage from the child. Thus, patience is an essential attribute of parenting in the formation of secure attachment patterns. Patience on the part of parents allows children to gain a sense of felt security due to the continual and responsive presence of their caregiver.

According to Bowlby (1969, 1973), children's development of secure internal working models facilitates understanding of their own self-worth and leads to increasingly positive feelings regarding their deservedness of affection and loving-care (Bretherton & Munholland, 2008). It could be argued that this self-acceptance lays the foundation for a person's ability to be patient with others in future relational contexts (Westbrook & Schnitker, 2013). Moreover, if patient interactions are modeled by parents, children will emulate this patience in their interactions with others.

When revisiting the case example of Stan, we can examine the underlying attachment patterns that have affected his ability to create secure attachment patterns in his relationships with his children. If we conceptualize Stan through an attachment framework, he would be categorized as avoidant/dismissive. Due to his father's strict rules prohibiting the expression of negative emotions during childhood, Stan learned to suppress his sad and/or angry feelings. Because he was not even allowed to express his negative feelings to his parents, he did not experience soothing in a relational context and was not the recipient of patience from his parents. Consequently, he would not even allow himself to acknowledge that his sad and angry feelings existed. Later on when he had his own children, Stan did not have a context or script by which to deal with his children's negative emotions and need for soothing. Thus, he followed his father's example and avoided negative emotions. When his children would come to him for soothing, he would be frustrated with them and ignore their needs (or even scold them for wanting comfort). However, there is hope in the therapeutic process as Stan learns to be patient with himself when he experiences strong, negative emotions. If the therapeutic alliance is indeed a model for relationships outside of the therapy room (Yalom, 2002), Stan will learn to tolerate negative emotions and to give and receive soothing with his family. He will begin to pursue healthy relationships with his children. The endeavor will almost certainly require patience on the part of Stan and his children while they learn new ways to communicate with each other. As in individual therapy, the process of reconstructing their relationships will likely feel worse before it feels better, but they will be able to find renewal in their relationships if they are patient with each other.

Patience and Self-Renewal in the Marital Dyad

As professional caregivers, we are more than just our careers. Each of us is engaged in relationships outside of our professional lives that are impacted by the stress and demands placed on us by our profession. The relationships most commonly impacted by such stressors are familial relationships, specifically the marital dyad (Leiter & Durup, 1996). When self-renewal is needed and patience fails, marital satisfaction, success, and longevity suffer. Not surprisingly, interpersonal patience is hypothesized to serve a central role in buffering the negative impact of stress and conflict on a relationship. Interpersonal patience is strongly correlated with a person's own psychological, spiritual, and physical well-being (Schnitker, 2012; Schnitker & Emmons, 2007). When these findings are considered in light of the current relationship research, the importance of patience for both self-renewal and interpersonal renewal becomes evident.

Renowned relationship researcher and psychologist John Gottman can accurately predict marital longevity and satisfaction based on how a couple argues and handles conflict (Gottman & Silver, 1999). Though Gottman identifies a variety of strategies that can help couples promote marital happiness and longevity, three strategies in particular are strongly related to patience and self-renewal: (1) softening your startup, (2) soothing yourself and your partner, and (3) tolerating your partner's flaws. Gottman and Silver (1999) encourage couples to "soften their start-ups," which refers to the ability to gently address a relationship issue with one's partner without using criticism or contempt (p. 161). To control frustration or disappointment with one's spouse when raising a complaint requires a great deal of patience, yet it allows for problem solving, renewal, and reconnection within the relationship. Similarly, soothing the self and partner allows active engagement in the process of self-renewal through the exercise of patience. In times of stress or conflict, to be able to take a break and engage in a self-calming activity can foster patience and self-renewal. This frees emotional resources for soothing the spouse, which promotes relationship renewal and marital happiness. For people to engage in softening their startup or soothing themselves and their partners, they must be able to tolerate their partner's flaws. Patience is pivotal in exercising tolerance for a spouse. Preventing emotional dysregulation and a couple's willingness to work through their relationship problems are strongly implicated in how successful a couple is at improving their marital relationship (Fruzzetti, 2006; Markman, Stanley, & Blumberg, 2001). Patience strengthens people's ability to remain committed and work through the conflict and struggles in marriage by helping to prevent escalation and emotional dysregulation within the marital dyad. However, it should be clarified that patience within the marital dyad does not mean being overly passive nor does it mean accepting abuse from one's partner. Rather, as previously mentioned, patience is the mean between sloth and reckless impatience; it is active (not passive) longsuffering that is aimed at a particular goal.

Returning to the example of Monica, imagine that she has just returned home from a long day of work and is feeling emotionally drained from supporting her clients all day. On coming home Monica notices that the house is still a mess and the one household task she had asked her husband to do has not been completed. When her husband greets her, Monica finds herself feeling frustrated with him and is tempted to start yelling; she feels her muscles tighten and her face begins to feel hot. Instead of exploding with anger, Monica soothes herself by taking a few deep breaths and then reminds herself that she too forgets to do what she is asked sometimes. She brings to mind the stress that her husband has been experiencing at work and finds empathy for him. When her husband asks if everything is okay, instead of accusing him of being unthoughtful and selfish, Monica calmly and patiently tells her husband that she has had a rough day, and then gently requests that he complete his household task when he gets the chance. Thus, as illustrated by this example, interpersonal patience increases well-being (Schnitker, 2012) and promotes self-renewal by improving marital happiness and perpetuating a healthy marital dyad.

Patience in the Community

Professional caregivers are not only involved with and impacted by their clients' lives but also by romantic partners, children, and ultimately a whole community of peers, coworkers, neighbors, and friends. Some may even function as caregivers within a communal setting such as an inpatient program, community mental health program, or retirement home setting. Thus, what follows is an exploration of the ways in which self-renewal can be promoted through involvement with a community of patience as illustrated by examples of patient communities that have positively impacted people's mental health through inclusion and restoration of those who suffer within a group setting.

As previously mentioned, modern U.S. society offers individuals a variety of quick fixes for any ailment that might inflict an individual, whether physical, emotional, spiritual, or psychological. While some of these remedies can be helpful, many of them serve to promote the idea that what one needs when they experience an ailment is *self*-help rather than *communal* help. Within industrialized countries, this emphasis on quickly resolving a problem or engaging in solitary self-help practices has created an environment in which individuals who cannot be helped quickly or be cured are stigmatized and isolated by the community rather than embraced. This unfortunate outcome is perhaps most pervasive within the field of western mental health. For example, the World Health Organization conducted a study comparing the treatment outcomes of individuals with schizophrenia in industrialized versus developing countries (Jablensky et al., 1992). Industrialized countries such as the United States tended to favor individualism and treated the mental illness from a medical model in which schizophrenia was viewed as something to be cured rather than accepted, and individuals with schizophrenia were often excluded from the larger community. In contrast, developing countries tended to treat those with the disorder not as "schizophrenics" who are defined by their disorder, but rather as members of the community who happen to have schizophrenia. Thus, in developing countries, individuals with schizophrenia were embraced by their communities, included in all of the regular communal activities, and, in some instances, were even viewed as favored or gifted because of their uniqueness. These individuals had fewer and less severe symptoms and had a higher level of mental health functioning than their counterparts in industrialized countries. Thus, the community's support of the people with schizophrenia, coupled with patience for their differences, promoted the self-renewal of these individuals by facilitating their mental health and fulfilling their basic human need to connect with and be accepted by others.

Another situation where communal patience has been shown to positively impact self-renewal is in work with those with developmental or physical disabilities. Though not all of us will encounter individuals with schizophrenia, as professional caregivers, we are likely to encounter individuals who have some kind of developmental or physical disability. Perhaps the greatest examples of intentional and patient communities that embrace those with physical and/or mental disabilities are the L'Arche communities. In 1964 Jean Vanier L'Arche created communal living centers in which the abled live with the disabled and share all aspects of life together. Members of the L'Arche communities share meals, participate in social activities, and live in shared spaces together. This approach has had great success in creating an environment in which any inconvenience that may accompany caring for the disabled is far outweighed by the joy gained through rich relationship with such individuals. According to Mr. L'Arche:

> The secret of L'Arche is relationship: meeting people, not through the filters or certitudes, ideologies, idealism or judgments, but heart to heart; listening to people with their pain, their joy, their hope, their history, listening to their heart beats. (L'Arche USA, 2012)

As professional caregivers we can identify with L'Arche's sentiment of listening to our clients' pains and joys as part of their journeys toward self-renewal. However, too often outside of the one-to-one caregiving relationship, these individuals are not surrounded by a community that patiently embraces them and supports their self-renewal as people who can benefit from and be of benefit to other community members. However, to see these benefits, the community members must be patient with each individual's unique gifts and challenges so that they can enter into a relationship with that particular individual and reap the benefits that relatedness brings.

Although we have been using the example of mental and/or physical disabilities, all people encounter their own struggles, which are disabling for a period of time, whether emotionally, physically, relationally, or spiritually. During these times, our clients (or ourselves if we are the ones suffering in some way) could benefit from involvement with a patient and supportive community. Take for example our earlier discussion of Stan who was feeling emotionally immobilized by his financial hardship as indicated by his depression and anxiety. Imagine if Stan had been strongly embedded within a supportive and patient community, such as a church community or sports team, in which he was able to share his experience and emotional suffering with others. Perhaps in sharing his job loss with his community, Stan's friends would have been able to console him, commiserate with his experience, and perhaps even link him to potential job opportunities. Connecting with his community could have accelerated Stan's self-renewal process, and allowed him to experience greater well-being through interpersonal relationships with others as they patiently endured his hardship with him.

Thus, a community's patience with those who are struggling affects self-renewal in two ways. First, it promotes self-renewal by allowing distressed or disabled individuals to glean the mental and physical health benefits of social connection. Second, it allows those who function as caregivers or friends to gain self-renewal through relationship with differently abled individuals who have much to offer the community despite their impairment.

INCREASING PATIENCE TO FACILITATE SELF-RENEWAL

Given the importance of patience for self-renewal—whether operating within the individual, between two people, or in the community—questions surrounding the possibilities and pathways by which we may increase patience are of vital importance. Empirical work provides initial evidence for the efficacy of intentional patience-building activities as well as more general findings on how virtues, which can be both a resource toward and outcome of the self-renewal process, may be acquired (Schnitker & Westbrook, in press). Historically, virtue building has often been located in the realm of spiritual and religious development (MacIntyre, 2007), and patience is a virtue traditionally upheld by the teaching and practices of all major world religions (Schnitker & Emmons, 2007). We explore ways in which spiritual practices facilitate patience, and we examine how patience may enhance a person's ability to connect with the transcendent.

Patience Interventions and Self-Renewal

The empirical study of patience is a relatively new endeavor. To date, one study specifically evaluates the effectiveness of intentional activities to increase the virtue of patience (Schnitker, 2012), but studies on self-control interventions are informative. These intervention studies relate to self-renewal in two ways. First, they provide a way to increase the virtue of patience, which is so instrumental to the intrapersonal and interpersonal processes that promote self-renewal. Second, intentional practices that a person enacts to increase patience and self-control could in and of themselves be seen as a conduit of self-growth and, subsequently, self-renewal.

Patience Intervention Research

In a study by Schnitker (2012), participants attended four 30-minute training sessions (presented as strategies for coping with stress) that included group discussion, individual activities, and guided meditation. Participants in the training condition showed an increase in patience as well as a decrease in depression from pre- to post-test compared to waitlist controls. The content of the sessions was pulled from methods and interventions used by other researchers in the meditation, character strengths, Type A personality, CBT, and self-control literatures. Participants were taught awareness of positive and negative emotion triggers, emotion regulation strategies (both preventive and reactionary), coping strategies for interpersonal stressors, empathy building activities, relaxation meditation, and loving-kindness meditation (see Schnitker, 2012, for full details). For example, in one session participants were given scenarios and asked to write their usual negative reactions to such situations, followed by writing a positive reframe. For example, participants were given the following scenario:

> You are catching a new release at the movies. The person behind you keeps kicking your chair and chewing her popcorn really loudly. As the movie progresses, she proceeds to answer her phone twice.

They were asked to describe their typical negative response (e.g., "People are so annoying! Can't they understand that I'm trying to watch a movie?"), as well as a reframe of the situation (e.g., "I've probably accidentally kicked the chair in front of me before, so maybe it was an accident."). This activity was followed by a loving-kindness meditation (Carson et al., 2005; Fredrickson, Cohn, Coffey, Pek, & Finkel, 2008; Kristeller & Johnson, 2005), which begins with directing positive emotion toward oneself and gradually extending these positive emotions outward to various others. The researchers used loving-kindness meditation because of the highly interpersonal nature of patience.

As noted by Schnitker and Westbrook (in press), future studies on patience interventions (a) need to isolate which of these activities is most instrumental in increasing patience (as opposed to related character strengths and psychological constructs), (b) should include more meaningful control groups, and (c) should move beyond individual outcomes to examine the effects of interventions on interpersonal systems. This initial study provides preliminary support for the idea that increases in patience correspond to self-renewal, as participants in the intervention condition showed a decrease in depression. However, future studies should more directly measure evidence of self-renewal resulting from patience interventions.

Self-Control Interventions Research

Given the limited literature on interventions seeking to increase patience, examination of research on self-control and emotion regulation interventions is useful. To clarify, we maintain that patience and self-control are distinct constructs. Although related to self-control, patience demonstrates discriminant validity from this and other virtues (Schnitker & Emmons, 2007). Patience requires a calm and serene inner state whereas self-control and delay of gratification are more concerned with external behaviors. For instance, delay of gratification typically involves an overt choice between a smaller reward now versus a larger reward later (e.g., Mischel, Shoda, & Peake, 1988). In contrast, patience is often demonstrated in situations where there is no choice about whether to wait—the only choice is *how* one waits. In these situations, there may be no glaring behavioral distinction between an impatient and patient response,[2] but we could distinguish a patient response by assessing the internal state of the individual. In short, people exhibit patience not just by their behaviors (choosing to wait if given that choice), but also by their internal responses to a frustration. In contrast, the concepts of delayed gratification and self-control are essentially defined by behavioral outcomes, without respect to internal states.

Many of the regulatory mechanisms that allow individuals to exert self-control may also increase patience. For example, Metcalfe and Mischel (1999) report that children who utilize attentional deployment strategies wait much longer for larger rewards then those who do not shift attention away from the salient "hot" aspects of the smaller reward. Similarly, people may be able to maintain a patient state if they stop looking at their watches or clocks while waiting. Thus, if people are taught emotion regulation strategies such as attentional deployment or cognitive reappraisal, they may be able to increase their ability and propensity to wait calmly. Therefore, we examine the effects of virtue intervention manipulations on the development of self-control and patience as related—yet distinct—virtues.

In recent years, several intervention studies have supported the muscle metaphor of self-control. Specifically, Muraven and Baumeister (2000) set forth a model of self-regulation by which self-control is conceptualized as a general, limited resource that can be depleted. Laboratory studies have shown that when people exert regulatory strength on an initial task, their performance on subsequent self-regulatory tasks decreases (Baumeister, Gailliot, DeWall, & Oaten, 2006). However, the muscle metaphor of self-regulation extends beyond seeing self-control as a limited resource. Just as physical exercise initially fatigues a muscle but over time makes it stronger, so, too, utilizing self-control may cause immediate losses of regulatory ability but over time can increase self-regulatory capacity, or ego strength.

Several studies have demonstrated the efficacy of self-control practice to increase generalized regulatory strength as evidenced by increased self-regulation in multiple life domains. For example, Oaten and Cheng (2004a) found that adherence to an assigned physical fitness program decreased depletion after regulatory-exertion on a visual tracking task in the lab. Moreover, adherence to the fitness program led to increased self-control in other life domains. Participants reduced cigarette smoking, alcohol consumption, and caffeine intake. They reported increased emotion control and reduced spending; they also reported watching less TV, doing more homework, and improved domestic

[2]Though no glaring behavioral distinctions may be apparent, we would expect more subtle observable differences between a patient and impatient response, such as facial expressions or microexpressions of emotion.

habits (e.g., washing dishes)! In another study, Oaten and Cheng (2004b) assigned participants to a 4-month financial monitoring program whereby they were asked to regulate their spending habits. In addition to increasing the savings rate (from an average of 8% to 38% of income), participants in the financial monitoring program showed lower regulatory depletion in a visual tracking task in the laboratory. In addition, these participants reported decreased psychoactive substance use (with mean reductions of two alcoholic drinks, two cups of coffee, and 15 cigarettes per day), and they demonstrated healthier eating, more emotion control, improved study habits, and improved domestic habits. Participants did not differ from controls on measures of emotional distress, perceived stress, or self-efficacy after the intervention; thus it seems that increased regulatory strength was the primary conduit of improvements. Finally, Denson, Capper, Oaten, Friese, and Schofield (2011) demonstrated that participants in a self-control training condition (using nondominant hand for a week) reacted less aggressively to an insult in the lab given the opportunity to retaliate against the insulter with the blast of a loud noise. The effects of the self-regulation practice were greatest for those who were initially high in trait aggression.

These studies provide a hopeful message for those seeking self-renewal. By engaging in basic exercises to increase self-control in one life domain, a person's regulatory capacity increases for other domains of functioning. Small efforts to change and renew the self by increasing self-control may have beneficial effects beyond the specific activity practiced. Moreover, such self-control strategies and practices may be useful for therapists to suggest to clients as a means of improving self-control and patience, which facilitate self-renewal.

The Formation of Virtuous Habits and Self-Renewal

Our discussion of possible interventions to increase patience and self-control points to the broader topic of virtue formation and self-renewal. The study of virtues and their development has received increased attention in recent years with the advent of the positive psychology movement in the late 1990s (Seligman & Csikszentmihalyi, 2000). Pulling from the virtue ethics literature, psychologists endeavor to test the best ways to build character strengths as a means to increase well-being—both eudaimonic and hedonic. In many ways this quest to increase eudaimonic well-being mirrors efforts toward self-renewal. Concerned with the realization of the "good life" in the fulfillment of human potentials and development of virtues (Kahneman, Diener, & Schwarz, 1999), eudaimonic well-being is acquired through the pathways that often lead to self-renewal—pathways that are often filled with challenges and hardships but lead to inner growth.

Several nuggets of wisdom from the virtue development literature are particularly relevant for self-renewal. First, virtue ethicists, such as Stanley Hauerwas (1981) and Alisdair MacIntyre (2007), stress the importance of developing virtues as habits that are practiced in a community of people who share a common narrative. They emphasize that the formation of virtue is not an individual pursuit. Instead, it must be situated and practiced in a social context. Moreover, moral and virtue formation should not be viewed as a purely cognitive enterprise. In his Social Intuitionist Model of moral development, Jonathan Haidt (2001) stresses the importance of socially shared emotions and intuitions—rather than rational thought—in the construction of our moral systems and behaviors. Numerous studies have shown the importance of emotions, embodiment, and social context in moral development (e.g., Damasio, 1996; Rozin, Lowery, Imada, & Haidt, 1999). Congruently, the process of self-renewal, facilitated by virtue development, should not be thought of as an internal, rational, and individual pursuit. Instead, self-renewal happens in social contexts where people are able to act out, emotionally process, and socially embed their new identities.

Spiritual Practices, Patience, and Self-Renewal

Self-renewal can take place in a variety of contexts. Clinicians often see the therapy room as the prime location for self-renewal, but for many people, self-renewal is situated in religious and spiritual environments. In two unique polls, the Gallup organization found that 92% of Americans said that they believe in God and 55% said that religion is very important in their lives (Newport, 2011). Moreover, 42% of Americans report attending religious services weekly or almost weekly (Newport, 2010), whereas only 3.18% of the U.S. population used any type of outpatient psychotherapy in 2007 (Olfson & Marcus, 2010). Thus, clinicians would do well to examine how patience and self-renewal are operating in religious contexts.

Religious and Spiritual Practices That Foster Patience

The development of virtue—especially patience—has traditionally been situated in religious and spiritual settings. Many world religions instruct their adherents to practice patience. For example, Islamic scriptures enjoin Muslims, "O ye who believe! Persevere in patience and constancy; vie in such perseverance; strengthen each other; and fear Allah that ye may prosper" (Koran 3:200, Shakir Translation), and the Code of Manu from the Hindu tradition says, "He who is persevering, gentle, (and) patient . . . gains if he constantly lives in that manner . . . heavenly bliss" (4:246).

Moreover, religions support these injunctions with a variety of traditions and spiritual disciplines that cultivate patience. Both eastern and western religions instruct followers in prayer and meditative practices. Schnitker and Emmons (2007) found that the prayer fulfillment, universality, and connectedness factors of the Spiritual Transcendence Scale (Piedmont, 1999) were positively correlated with patience, and numerous studies have found relations between meditative/prayer practice and positive individual outcomes that we would associate with self-renewal (Kemeny et al., 2012; Maltby, Lewis, & Day, 1999; Shapiro, Oman, Thoresen, Plante, & Flinders, 2008; Whittington & Scher, 2010). Several mechanisms may be hypothesized to explain how prayer and meditation promote patience. First, meditative practices across different traditions teach people to focus their attention and to calm themselves physiologically, which are essential skills for enacting patience. Second, in more supplicative or intercessory types of prayer, individuals must practice patience as they await the response of a deity or supernatural power. This involves a meaningful context in which patience is seen as noble and praiseworthy rather than as a concession to technological failure. Third, prayer and meditation expand a sense of connectedness with that which transcends the self. This experience of the transcendent may promote patience in that it provides people with a larger, meaningful framework in which to understand their suffering.

Another spiritual practice common across religions that may more directly increase patience and self-control is fasting. Fasting typically involves abstaining from food, drink, or both for a set period of time. Fasting is the fourth of five pillars of Islam and is most notably observed during the holy month of Ramadan. During the month of Ramadan, Muslims abstain from eating, drinking, and sexual intercourse from dawn until dusk. In Christianity, fasting is also a common practice and seen most conspicuously in the Catholic and Eastern Orthodox churches during Lent, a 40-day partial fast. These examples of corporate fasting provide a context to practice self-control and patience in a community. In light of the previously described research on self-control, it seems likely that practices motivating people to exert control in eating/drinking will increase their general resource of regulatory strength (Jarvinen, 2012). This increased self-control and patience will then be available in other life domains, which allows for self-renewal.

Self-Renewal Through Connectedness to a Higher Power

Although spiritual practices such as prayer, meditation, and fasting may increase patience and promote self-renewal, mere psychological or physical self-renewal is not the ultimate aim of these practices within their religious traditions. Instead, these practices are typically seen as a means to spiritual purification and a way to increase connection to the transcendent. Thus, we may want to broaden our understanding of self-renewal to encompass spiritual self-renewal and growth.

Even with this more expansive view of self-renewal, patience is advantageous. By definition, spirituality involves relating to something or someone that transcends the self (Piedmont, 1999). Rarely is knowing the transcendent a quick and easy venture, and patience is needed as humans seek to encounter the transcendent. In the great monotheistic traditions, patience is ascribed to God in his dealings with humans, and it is God's patience that allows for interaction of humans with the deity. For example, Christian scriptures state, "The Lord is not slow in keeping his promise, as some understand slowness. He is patient with you, not wanting anyone to perish, but everyone to come to repentance. . . . Bear in mind that our Lord's patience means salvation" (II Peter 3:9, 15, New International Version). Islamic scriptures also reflect the necessity of Allah's patience in his interaction with humans: "Our Lord! Pour out on us patience and constancy, and take our souls unto thee as Muslims" (Koran 7:126). Thus, at least for Christians and Muslims, God's patience is seen as a prerequisite for genuine spiritual renewal. Similarly, adherents are instructed to wait patiently for God to relate to them. The Jewish Psalms echo the theme of waiting on the Lord with poetic lines such as "I wait for the Lord, my whole being waits, and in his word I put my hope. I wait for the Lord more than watchmen wait for the morning" (Psalm 130:5–6) and "I waited patiently for the Lord; he turned to me and heard my cry" (Psalm 40:1).

In many ways, an analysis of the ways in which patience leads to renewal in a person's relationship with the deity could mirror our previous analyses of patience in other common dyads (therapist-client, parent-child, spouses). Recalling the case of Stan, we may find that his inner self-renewal and relationship renewal with his children extends to spiritual renewal. Stan's patience in learning to accept and endure negative emotions may change the way he relates to God. Although Stan grew up in the Catholic church, he fell away from his faith in college as he was unable to reconcile all the pain and suffering in the world with the idea of a loving and benevolent God. As Stan becomes more comfortable with ambiguity and grows in his patience, he begins to revisit his childhood faith and begins to pray to God about his own suffering and the suffering of others. His prayers provide him comfort and strength because he is patient with God and believes God is patient with him. No longer does he view God as one who, like his childhood father, is cold, distant, and unaccepting of negative emotions. Instead, he sees God as available and willing to patiently endure human foibles. Moreover, his newfound sense of transcendence advances the cycle of self-renewal in other aspects of his life. Because he sees a spiritual authority as patient with him, Stan is able to more readily extend patience to himself and his children. Stan joins a new faith community, where he is provided a meaningful context to build his virtue and be a part of something bigger than himself.

CONCLUSION

Patience is a virtue essential for self-renewal. Renewal requires the ability to withstand suffering for a while—the ability to endure the growing pains of personal development. The inability to patiently endure waiting for change will lead to the premature abandonment of the goals, relationships, and activities that are most instrumental in the process of self-renewal for ourselves and others. Researchers have made great strides in ascertaining the intentional activities, habits, and traditions that nurture patience, self-control, and other virtues. As therapists and caregivers who aim to cultivate renewal, we must utilize this knowledge to foster patience in ourselves, our relationships, and our communities.

REFERENCES

Baumeister, R. F., Gailliot, M., DeWall, C. N., & Oaten, M. (2006). Self-regulation and personality: How interventions increase regulatory success, and how depletion moderates the effects of traits on behavior. *Journal of Personality, 74*, 1773–1801. doi:10.1111/j.1467–6494.2006.00428.x

Bowlby, J. (1969). *Attachment and loss: Vol. 1: Attachment.* New York, NY: Basic Books.

Bowlby, J. (1973). *Attachment and loss. Vol. II. Separation, anxiety and anger.* London, England: Hogarth Press.

Bretherton, I., & Munholland, K. A. (2008). Internal working models in attachment relationships: Elaborating a central construct in attachment theory. In J. Cassidy & P. R. Shaver (Eds.), *Handbook of attachment: Theory, research, and clinical applications* (2nd ed., pp. 102–127). New York, NY: Guilford Press.

Carson, J. W., Keefe, F. J., Lynch, T. R., Carson, K. M., Goli, V., Fras, A. M., & Thorp, S. R. (2005). Loving-kindness meditation for chronic low back pain: Results from a pilot trial. *Journal of Holistic Nursing, 23*, 287–304. doi:10.1177/0898010105277651

Damasio, A. R. (1996). The somatic marker hypothesis and the possible functions of the prefrontal cortex. *Philosophical Transactions of the Royal Society of London, 351*, 1413–1420. doi:10.1098/rstb.1996.0125

Denson, T. F., Capper, M. M., Oaten, M., Friese, M., & Schofield, T. P. (2011). Self-control training decreases aggression in response to provocation in aggressive individuals. *Journal of Research in Personality, 45*, 252–256. doi:10.1016/j.jrp.2011.02.001

Fredrickson, B. L., Cohn, M. A., Coffey, K. A., Pek, J., & Finkel, S. M. (2008). Open hearts build lives: Positive emotions, induced through loving-kindness meditation, build consequential personal resources. *Journal of Personality and Social Psychology, 95*, 1045–1062. doi:10.1037/a0013262

Fruzzetti, A. E. (2006). *The high-conflict couple: A dialectical behavior therapy guide to finding peace, intimacy, and validation.* Oakland, CA: New Harbinger.

Gottman, J., & Silver, N. (1999). *The seven principles for making marriage work.* New York, NY: Three Rivers Press.

Haidt, J. (2001). The emotional dog and its rational tail: A social intuitionist approach to moral judgment. *Psychological Review, 108*, 814–834. doi:10.1037//0033–295X.108.4.814

Harned, D. B. (1997). *Patience: How we wait upon the world.* Cambridge, England: Cowley.

Hauerwas, S. (1981). *A community of character: Toward a constructive Christian social ethic.* Notre Dame, IN: University of Notre Dame Press.

Hazan, C., & Shaver, P. R. (1987). Romantic love conceptualized as an attachment process. *Journal of Personality and Social Psychology, 59*, 511–524. doi:10.1037/0022–3514.52.3.511

Hazan, C., & Shaver, P. R. (1994). Attachment as an organizational framework for research on close relationships. *Psychological Inquiry, 5*, 1–22. doi:10.1207/s15327965pli0501_1

Horvath, A. O., & Symonds, B. D. (1991). Relation between working alliance and outcome in psychotherapy: A meta-analysis. *Journal of Counseling Psychology, 38*, 139–149. doi:10.1037/0022–0167.38.2.139

Howes, R. (2008). Shouldn't psychotherapy make me feel good? *Psychology Today*. Retrieved from http://www.psychologytoday.com/blog/in-therapy/200807/shouldn-t-psychotherapy-make-me-feel-good

Jablensky, A., Sartorius, N., Ernberg, G., Anker, M., Korten, J. E., Cooper, J. E., . . . Bertelsen, A. (1992). Schizophrenia: Manifestations, incidence and course in different cultures, a World Health Organization ten-country study. *Psychological Medicine, 20*, 97.

Jarvinen, M. J. (2012). *Self-regulation and the liturgical practice of Lent: How fasting leads to virtue*. Manuscript in preparation.

Kahneman, D., Diener, E., & Schwarz, N. (Eds.). (1999). *Well-being: The foundations of hedonic psychology*. New York, NY: Russell Sage Foundation.

Kemeny, M. E., Foltz, C., Cavanagh, J. F., Cullen, M., Giese-Davis, J., Jennings, P., . . . Ekman, P. (2012). Contemplative/emotion training reduces negative emotional behavior and promotes prosocial responses. *Emotion, 12*, 338–350. doi:10.1037/a0026118

Kristeller, J. L., & Johnson, T. (2005). Cultivating loving kindness: A two-stage model of the effects of meditation on empathy, compassion and altruism. *Zygon, 40*, 391–407. doi:10.1111/j.1467–9744.2005.00671.x

Lambert, M. J., & Barley, D. E. (2001). Research summary on the therapeutic relationship and psychotherapy outcome. *Psychotherapy: Theory, Research, Practice, Training, 38*, 357–361. doi:10.1037/0033–3204.38.4.357

L'Arche USA. (2012). *Who we are*. Retrieved from http://www.larcheusa.org/who-we-are/

Leiter, M. P., & Durup, M. (1996). Work, home, and in-between: A longitudinal study of spillover. *Journal of Applied Behavioral Science, 32*(1), 29–47. doi:10.1177/0021886396321002

MacIntyre, A. (2007). *After virtue: A study in moral theory* (3rd ed.). Notre Dame, IN: University of Notre Dame Press.

Maltby, J., Lewis, C. A., & Day, L. (1999). Religious orientation and psychological well-being: The role of the frequency of personal prayer. *British Journal of Health Psychology, 4*, 363–378. doi:10.1348/135910799168704

Markman, H., Stanley, S., & Blumberg, S. (2001). *Fighting for your marriage: Positive steps for preventing divorce and preserving lasting love*. San Francisco, CA: Jossey-Bass.

Maslach, C. & Jackson, S. E. (1982). Burnout in health professions: A social psychological analysis. In G. S. Sanders & J. Suls (Eds.), *Social psychology of health and illness* (pp. 227– 244). Hillsdale, NJ: Erlbaum.

Metcalfe, J., & Mischel, W. (1999). A hot/cool-system analysis of delay of gratification: Dynamics of willpower. *Psychological Review*, *106*, 3–19. doi:10.1037/0033–295X.106.1.3

Miller, S., & Hubble, M. (2011). The road to mastery. *Psychotherapy Networker*, *35*, 22–31, 60.

Mischel, W., Shoda, Y., & Peake, P. K. (1988). The nature of adolescent competencies predicted by preschool delay of gratification. *Journal of Personality and Social Psychology*, *54*, 687–696. doi:10.1037/0022–3514.54.4.687

Mojtabai, R., & Olfson, M. (2011). Proportion of antidepressants prescribed without a psychiatric diagnosis is growing. *Health Affairs*, *30*, 1434–1442. doi:10.1377/hlthaff.2010.1024

Muraven, M., & Baumeister, R. F. (2000). Self-regulation and depletion of limited resources: Does self-control resemble a muscle? *Psychological Bulletin*, *126*, 247–259. doi:10.1037/0033–2909.126.2.247

Newport, F. (2010). *Mississippians go to church the most; Vermonters, least: Overall, 42% of Americans attend church weekly or almost weekly*. Retrieved from http://www.gallup.com/poll/125999/mississippians-go-church-most-vermonters-least.aspx

Newport, F. (2011). *Christianity remains dominant religion in the United States*. Retrieved from http://www.gallup.com/poll/151760/Christianity-Remains-Dominant-Religion-United-States.aspx

Oaten, M., & Cheng, K. (2004a). Longitudinal gains in self-control from regular physical exercise. *British Journal of Health Psychology*, *11*, 717–733. doi:10.1348/135910706X96481

Oaten, M., & Cheng, K. (2004b). Improvements in self-control from financial monitoring. *Journal of Economic Psychology*, *28*, 487–501. doi:10.1016/j.joep.2006.11.003

Olfson, M., & Marcus, S. C. (2010). National trends in outpatient psychotherapy. *American Journal of Psychiatry*, *167*, 1456–1463. doi:10.1176/appi.ajp.2010.10040570

Piedmont, R. L. (1999). Does spirituality represent the sixth factor of personality? Spiritual transcendence and the five-factor model. *Journal of Personality*, *67*, 985–1013. doi:10.1111/1467–6494.00080

Pieper, J. (1952). *Leisure: The basis of culture*. (A. Dru, Trans.). London, England: Faber & Faber.

Rozin, P., Lowery, L., Imada, S., & Haidt, J. (1999). The CAD triad hypothesis: A mapping between three moral emotions (contempt, anger, disgust) and three moral codes (community, autonomy, divinity). *Journal of Personality and Social Psychology*, *76*, 574–586. doi: 10.1037/0022–3514.76.4.574

Schnitker, S. A. (2012). An examination of patience and well-being. *Journal of Positive Psychology*, *7*, 263–280. doi:10.1080/17439760.2012.697185

Schnitker, S. A., & Emmons, R. A. (2007). Patience as a virtue: Religious and psychological perspectives. *Research in the Social Scientific Study of Religion, 18,* 177–207. doi:10.1163/ej.9789004158511.i-301.69

Schnitker, S. A., & Westbrook, J. T. (in press). Do good things come to those who wait? Patience interventions to improve well-being. In A. C. Parks (Ed.), *The handbook of positive psychological interventions.* New York, NY: Wiley.

Seligman, M. E. P., & Csikszentmihalyi, M. (2000). Positive psychology: An introduction. *American Psychologist, 55,* 5–14. doi:10.1037/0003–066X.55.1.5

Shapiro, S. L., Oman, D., Thoresen, C. E., Plante, T. G., & Flinders, T. (2008). Cultivating mindfulness: Effects on well-being. *Journal of Clinical Psychology, 64,* 840–862. doi:10.1002/jclp.20491

Tedeschi, R. G., & Calhoun, L. G. (2004). Posttraumatic growth: Conceptual foundations and empirical evidence. *Psychological Inquiry, 15,* 1–18. doi:10.1207/s15327965pli1501_01

Wallin, D. J., (2007). *Attachment in psychotherapy.* New York, NY: Guilford Press.

Westbrook, J. T., & Schnitker, S. A. (2013). *Attachment and the virtuous life: Early attachment's effect on virtue development.* Manuscript submitted for publication.

Whittington, B. L., & Scher, S. J. (2010). Prayer and subjective well-being: An examination of six different types of prayer. *International Journal for the Psychology of Religion, 20,* 59–68. doi:10.1080/10508610903146316

Yalom, I. D. (2002). *The gift of therapy: An open letter to a new generation of therapists and their patients.* New York, NY: Harper Perennial.

Zarit, S. H., & Zarit, J. M. (2011). *Mental disorders in older adults: Fundamentals of assessment and treatment* (2nd ed.). New York, NY: Guilford Press.

CHAPTER

13

Forgiveness and Self-Renewal

Matthew J. Hirshberg and Robert D. Enright

This chapter focuses on forgiveness therapy (FT) and the specific process of forgiveness as a means of self-renewal. In the context of forgiveness, self-renewal intimates the diminution of negative affect and the cultivation of positive psychological attributes such as hopefulness and self-esteem, and sometimes the development of positive behavioral attributes such as increased agency and prosociality as well. The forgiveness process results in self-renewal because unforgiveness, or being unduly affected by anger or resentment, is associated with a host of undesirable psychological and health-related outcomes (see, for example, Waltman et al., 2009; Witvliet, Ludwig, & Vander Laan, 2001; Worthington, Witvliet, Pietrini, & Miller, 2007). Research on forgiveness has demonstrated that forgiving reduces anger and the concomitant deleterious effects that often follow from a personal offense, and supports the cultivation of beneficial psychological dispositions (for a review, see Baskin & Enright, 2004; Lundahl, Taylor, Stevenson, & Roberts, 2008). In short, it is through the forgiveness process of working through negative affect and then cultivating beneficence that the self is renewed.

The past 30 years have seen the emergence and subsequent explosion of forgiveness research. The resulting corpus of rich empirical work and the several millennia old and widely esteemed philosophical tradition postulating the essence of forgiveness will be utilized to explore the theme of self-renewal through forgiveness. The simple mechanistic view presented above, that forgiveness leads to self-renewal by first reducing the anger and resentment that commonly attends to being unjustly treated, and then by cultivating feelings of goodwill toward the one who has been unjust, has been validated by a substantial collection of intervention studies measuring the effect of forgiveness therapy on individuals who have suffered a wide array of personal offense (for a review, see Baskin & Enright, 2004; Lundahl et al., 2008). Interestingly, despite this significant body of empirical data, forgiveness is still frequently misunderstood. Therefore, we begin by defining what forgiveness is and is not.

Defining Forgiveness

Within the academic community, a single consensus definition of forgiveness has not yet been agreed on. At first glance this may seem concerning, but when considering that forgiveness has been examined by diverse domains including social psychology (Exline, Worthington, Hill, & McCullough, 2003), developmental psychology (Park & Enright, 1997), and clinical psychology and psychiatry (Enright & Fitzgibbons, 2000), it is perhaps more understandable. While sharing much in common, the interests in and goals for forgiveness are sometimes domain-specific, and one consequence is difficulty establishing a definitive conceptualization of forgiveness or the forgiveness process. However, despite the extant differences, both definitional and operational, within and between fields investigating forgiveness, the following characteristics are reliably universal:

- Forgiveness involves the person who has experienced injustice forgiving those who perpetrated the unfairness.
- The one who forgives relinquishes resentment, defined as a deep and abiding sense of anger.
- The one who forgives offers goodness of some kind to the offending party.
- The forgiver is motivated by what Kant calls a good will, or what psychologists call a motivation toward beneficence (see McCullough, Fincham, & Tsang, 2003).
- Forgiveness is supererogatory.

Whereas psychologists and philosophers debate the content and operationalization of forgiveness, the general population commonly misunderstands the meaning of forgiveness, conflating it with other, distinct behaviors. Freedman and Chang (2010) demonstrated this by asking a sample of the general population to define forgiveness. They found that the definitions given reliably conflated forgiveness with behaviors such as "forgetting" and "reconciliation." Accordingly, concerns among therapists considering forgiveness during therapy are ubiquitous. In a review, Wade, Johnson, and Meyer (2008) summarize clinician concerns regarding FT as:

- Discussing forgiveness might convey judgment or, worse, express condemnation of the client.

- Promoting forgiveness is promoting reconciliation (and thereby perpetuating cycles of abuse).
- Forgiveness is not helpful beyond the expression of emotions.
- "Discussing forgiveness will invoke religious and moral imperatives" (p. 96).
- There is not enough time allotted for therapy.

Understanding what forgiveness is and is not has practical and clinical import that often overlap. Without first understanding what forgiveness is, it is impossible to differentiate client and clinician concerns predicated on misrepresentations of forgiveness and those concerns that must be genuinely attended to during therapy. First, we must understand the construct of forgiveness clearly. Once that has been accomplished, we can address the concerns formulated by Wade et al. (2008).

What Forgiveness Is and Is Not: Addressing Concerns About Forgiveness Therapy

Forgiveness is not forgetting, condoning, pardoning, or reconciling. These distinctions are operationally essential, and particularly important in the context of the forgiveness being discussed here (i.e., forgiveness in a therapeutic context that presumes the client has suffered an injury). While the forgiveness process may alter the way one remembers the injury, forgetting implies the effect of the offense is mitigated (Enright, 2001). In contrast, FT involves the client developing an awareness of the offense-caused hurt, and the degree to which that hurt has impacted the client's life, perhaps inalterably so. Condoning is excusing the offender and thus mitigating their wrongdoing or being naïve to the injury and the hurt that accompanies it (Baskin & Enright, 2004; Subkoviak et al., 1995). Forgiveness therapy begins with establishing the wrongness of the offense. Pardoning is a legal amnesty for an offense. Forgiveness therapy does not preclude the victim seeking legal justice for their injury. Reconciliation is the reestablishing of normative relations following an injury or conflict. In some situations reconciliation may occur, but in other situations reconciliation is undesirable and even potentially dangerous (Enright & North, 1998; Worthington, 2006). For example, if the client is the victim of continuous physical or emotional abuse, FT is salient in helping the client restore self-worth and diminish negative affect, but reconciliation would likely return the victim to the very context in which they were victimized. Therefore, while in some situations reconciliation or other behaviors commonly conflated with forgiveness may occur, they are distinct from forgiveness.

Forgiveness is supererogatory, not morally obligatory from a philosophical perspective (Enright, 2001; Luskin, 2003). The important role of agency helps distinguish forgiveness from behaviors or cognitions it is commonly conflated with. The singularly essential ingredient in forgiveness is the desire (i.e., agency) to forgive on the part of the injured. Although it has been argued that apology from the offender expedites the forgiveness process (McCullough, Worthington, & Rachal, 1997), it is not essential. This is actually true, because as an internal psychological process, forgiveness is operationally dependent only on the client. But delineating agency clearly in this way has symbolic power as well, as one consequence of deep injustice is often reduced self-esteem (Eaton, Struthers, & Santelli, 2006), establishing the process as client-centered, client-directed, and client-dependent helps to reinforce the intrinsic worth of the client. Convincing arguments also have been made that when forgiveness depends on the apology of the offender, magnification of the original injury is a real possibility, as the ability of the aggrieved to forgive can be held hostage by the intent of the perpetrator (Holmgren, 1993).

Wade and colleagues' (2008) concerns regarding FT can be condensed into three categories: (1) those involving client misperceptions, (2) those based on the skill of the clinician, and (3) concerns about the required duration of therapy. If clinician skill is satisfactory, any concerns relating to client misperceptions are easily remedied. For instance, addressing client misperceptions that may lead to undesirable outcomes (e.g., conflating forgiveness with condoning) can be easily accomplished by a simple, clear conversation defining forgiveness. Concerns about invoking moral or religious imperatives can be assuaged by presenting forgiveness as a secular, philosophical ideal (Enright & Fitzgibbons, 2000).

We should remember that the capacities required of the clinician to successfully lead a client through the forgiveness process are not unique to FT. Skilled clinicians exhibit insight into and the ability to help ameliorate client misperceptions. They display an understanding of client readiness to move forward and the ability to address sensitive issues free of moral imperative and judgment. These are skills clinicians' utilize across the spectrum of psychotherapeutic modalities. In addition, research findings suggest that a large majority of clients are open to forgiveness in therapy (Wade, Bailey, & Schaffer, 2005) and that most individuals have a positive regard for forgiveness (StrategyOne, 2010). Clinicians should not shy away from utilizing forgiveness in therapy simply because they have not used it in the past or feel that they have not been explicitly trained in forgiveness therapy. The process model that is explored in this chapter is intentionally divorced from any one particular therapeutic model and was constructed with ease of use in mind (Enright & Fitzgibbons, 2000).

A final ubiquitous concern about FT is the duration of treatment. This is a challenging topic, as forces outside of client or clinician control can dictate duration of treatment. Experimental data and clinical observation support the contention that forgiveness is a process occurring over time (Enright, 2001; Fitzgibbons, 1986; Freedman & Chang, 2010). Nonetheless, our view is that clinicians, with some ingenuity, can effect positive change utilizing forgiveness for even a short period of time.

Forgiveness as a Virtue

Forgiveness is a virtue (Peterson & Seligman, 2004), and understanding it as such is fundamental to the model of forgiveness therapy we explore. Contextualizing forgiveness in this light is equally essential in operationalizing the self-renewal effect of forgiving. To be clear, establishing forgiveness as a moral virtue is distinct from situating forgiveness as a moral imperative. Moral imperative suggests an obligation to act in a certain way based on externally imposed norms or mores. As a supererogatory behavior, self-renewal through forgiveness depends on the client's ability to sincerely work through the stages of forgiveness. True forgiveness and self-renewal must be generated by the client's desire and decision to forgive.

The sense of virtue used here is founded on the Aristotelian notion of virtue: to affect the good. In the absolute sense, *good* refers to a cognition, affect and/or behavior that benefits the individual and society at large. In the case of FT, we are mostly concerned with transformation at the level of the individual (though more recently forgiveness has begun to be planted within the peace movement and explored as a group phenomenon). By working to release and overcome the anger and sadness that accompanies offense-related injury, the client benefits. By cultivating beneficence toward the offender, the individual is exhibiting a good beyond self-focused intent. Paradoxically, it is precisely when the client transitions from a self-critical reference point to concentrate in a moral way on the offender (e.g., recognizing the intrinsic worth of the person in spite of the injustice), that the client is healed (Enright & Fitzgibbons, 2000). Indeed, Aristotle designated *Agape* love, the variant of love that is "an intentional response to promote well-being when responding to that which has generated ill-being" (Oord, 2005, p. 919), or forgiveness, as the highest human expression of virtue.

FORGIVENESS THERAPY: THE ENRIGHT PROCESS MODEL

Several models seeking to define the stages of the forgiveness process have been proposed. Examples include McCullough's (2000) model that emphasizes empathy as the primary mediator of forgiveness and considers the role of the offender to be a central element of forgiving (McCullough et al. 1997). Worthington's (2006) REACH is a five-stage model that stands for: Recall the hurt, Empathize with the offender, Altruistic gift of forgiveness, Commit to forgiveness, and Hold on to forgiveness. The REACH model primarily involves cognitive and affective components, and also emphasizes empathy as a primary mediator of forgiveness. Here, we focus on the Enright Process Model (Enright, 2001; Enright & the Human Development Study Group, 1991); see Table 13.1.

There are several factors that make the EPM unique from other models of forgiveness. First, it is one of the few to have substantial empirical support

Table 13.1 The Enright Process Model

Uncovering Phase

1. Examination of psychological defenses and the issues involved (Kiel, 1986).
2. Confrontation of anger; the point is to release, not harbor, the anger (Trainer, 1984).
3. Admittance of shame, when this is appropriate (Patton, 1985).
4. Awareness of depleted emotional energy (Droll, 1985).
5. Awareness of cognitive rehearsal of the offense (Droll, 1985).
6. Insight that the injured party may be comparing self with the injurer (Kiel, 1986).
7. Realization that oneself may be permanently and adversely changed by the injury (Kiel, 1986).
8. Insight into a possibly altered "just world" view (Flanigan, 1987).

Decision Phase

9. A change of heart/conversion/new insights that old resolution strategies are not working (North, 1987).
10. Willingness to consider forgiveness as an option (Enright, Freedman, & Rique, 1998).
11. Commitment to forgive the offender (Neblett, 1974).

Work Phase

12. Reframing, through role-taking, who the wrongdoer is by viewing him or her in context (M. Smith, 1981).
13. Empathy and compassion toward the offender (Cunningham, 1985).
14. Bearing/accepting the pain (Bergin, 1988).
15. Giving a moral gift to the offender (North, 1987).

Deepening Phase

16. Finding meaning for self and others in suffering and in the forgiveness process (Frankl, 1959).
17. Realization that self has needed others' forgiveness in the past (Cunningham, 1985).
18. Insight that one is not alone (universality, support) (Enright et al., 1998).
19. Realization that self may have a new purpose in life because of the injury (Enright et al., 1998).
20. Awareness of decreased negative affect and, perhaps, increased positive affect, if this begins to emerge, toward the injurer; awareness of an internal emotional release (Smedes, 1984).

Source: Enright and Fitzgibbons, 2000.

(Al-Mabuk, Enright, & Cardis, 1995; Coyle & Enright, 1997; Freedman & Enright, 1996; Hebl & Enright, 1993; Knutson, Enright, & Garbers, 2008). In addition to experimental and observational support, Denton and Martin (1998) conducted a survey asking more than 100 clinical social workers how they saw forgiveness unfolding in therapy. The surveyed clinicians' presentations of the unfolding of forgiveness closely followed the stages outlined in the EPM. Second, cognition, affect, and behavior are all accounted for in the model, and as such it is a holistic approach, rather than a singularly cognitive, social-cognitive, or behavioral methodology. Third, it is a phase and stage (referred to as units) model. The phases represent the larger, overarching movements of forgiveness, while the stages describe more explicit transformations during the process. The broad strokes of the phases allow for a general accounting of psychological movement toward and readiness for forgiveness, while the detail provided by the component stages can be useful both in explaining forgiveness and in helping clients who become "stuck" refocus (Enright & Fitzgibbons, 2000). It is worth mentioning that the model is intended to be prescriptive rather than descriptive. The stages do not necessarily proceed in uniform order, nor is it uncommon for clients/patients to return to earlier stages already addressed (Knutson et al., 2008). It is important also to bear in mind the idiosyncratic nature of forgiving. It may take a client 2 months to truly decide to forgive, while another client may begin therapy having accepted the impact of the offense and determined to forgive. Although the exact trajectory of forgiveness and the time required to forgive may vary among clients, what is invariant is the requisite decision on the part of the client to forgive.

The Phases of Forgiveness

The phases inform the major goals of the forgiveness process. Phase One, the Uncovering Phase, is a preforgiveness phase that emphasizes the client developing awareness that there was in fact an injustice; that the offense caused pain, and as a result of both the injury and its attendant suffering, the client's life has been altered. The aim of this phase is the construction of an appropriate cognitive framework for the offense and the impact it has had on the client's life. Note that forgiveness is not necessarily discussed in this phase. For those who have been deeply injured, a discussion of forgiveness may be counterproductive at this juncture. As we have seen, forgiveness, while generally viewed favorably, is commonly misunderstood. For those who have suffered deeply, the misperceptions of forgiveness they may carry, or the barriers to forgiveness their unhealed suffering may have erected, can be too encompassing to allow for the notion of forgiveness to take root. The goal here is not to actually forgive, but rather to accept that an injustice has been committed and one has suffered as a result. It is common for clients to express significant sadness in this phase, as they must meet "face to face" the injustice they have been subjected to, and account for the various psychological defenses they may have adopted to handle their hurt. Both because forgiveness is supererogatory and because this is a preforgiveness phase, attainment of a new cognitive framework regarding the injustice is a prerequisite to truly forgiving.

Phase Two is the Decision Phase. Patients/clients comment that this is often the most challenging phase, and represents an epoch of sorts in the forgiveness process and in the process of self-renewal (Knutson et al., 2008). Like Phase One, it represents a cognitive transformation. The emphasis here is on making the decision to forgive. It requires clients to consider whether the strategies they have utilized thus far to mitigate past suffering have been effective. Typically, clients come to the realization that their coping strategies no longer serve them well. Once this understanding has arisen, the client is asked to consider forgiveness as an option. At this point, the therapeutic process incorporates psychoeducational components, as the client must appreciate what forgiveness is (and is not) before moving forward. We recommend clients be introduced to:

- The definition of forgiveness that includes the abandonment of resentment (to which they have a right) and adopting a friendlier attitude (to which the offender may not have a right).
- The paradoxes inherent in the definition.
- The distinction between forgiveness and condoning or excusing, forgetting, and reconciling.
- The concern that to forgive is to make the forgiver a "doormat."
- The interplay between forgiveness and justice seeking (Enright & Fitzgibbons, 2000).

If, after coming to understand what forgiveness is, the client makes the difficult and important decision to forgive, a major step toward forgiveness and self-renewal has been completed: The client has decided to relinquish resentment and anger. Although significant, the deep work of actually forgiving comes next.

The Work Phase, Phase Three, encompasses cognitive and behavioral therapy. The first element of the work phase is to undergo a reappraisal of the offender. Reframing is accomplished by helping the client understand the offender in context. By asking the client, through role taking, to reframe whom the offender is, the client is able to begin to see the larger circumstances in which the client acted wrongly. A series of questions are asked to help stimulate a new view of the offender. Example questions include "What was the offender like as he or she was growing up?," "What was it like for the offender at the time the offense was committed?," "Can you see him or her as a member of the human community?" The exact phrasing of the questions is determined in part by the circumstances of the offense being addressed, and in part through the clinician's understanding of the client.

The first two example questions engage a strictly cognitive reappraisal of the offender. The final example question incorporates cognitive reappraisal of affective elements as well. By asking clients to consider whether they can see the offender as a member of the human family, we are asking that they acknowledge the inherent worth of that person, in spite of the injuries inflicted. Establishing the inherent worth of all people helps the client distinguish between a person's actions and the intrinsic value of that person. This is a transformative moment in the process of self-renewal because, to reiterate, the paradox of self-renewal through forgiveness is that it is when clients shift focus off of the self in a critical way to the offender in a moral way that they are healed (Enright & Fitzgibbons, 2000).

It may be appropriate to reaffirm the distinction between forgiveness and reconciliation, and forgiveness and condoning at this point. The former will help assuage discomfort among clients who do not wish to reconcile, and the latter exemplifies the coexistence of justice, the naming of that which is wrong as wrong and the right to seek redress for wrongs, and forgiveness.

An outgrowth of having recognized the inherent worth of the offender is the organic arising of empathy or compassion for the offender (McCullough et al., 1997). Empathy, the ability to feel what another person feels or more colloquially, to enter into another's shoes, cannot be forced. This process encourages its emergence, but clients show different levels of readiness when attempting to feel empathy, and for a variety of reasons, some are able to more easily access it (Davis, 1983). Interpreting client readiness can be a challenge, but clinicians familiar with forgiveness often observe that when clients can understand who the other is without overadulation or distortion, it is indicative of successful reframing and a readiness to move toward empathy and compassion (Enright & Fitzgibbons, 2000).

The experience of empathy or compassion toward the offender, founded on the client's capacity to view the offender in a moral way, is integral to the cultivation of positive affect and possibly prosocial behaviors that mark self-renewal through the forgiveness process. As with all of the stages of this process, clients must move at their own pace. Mounting evidence suggests that empathy and compassion can be trained (Lutz, Brefczynski-Lewis, Johnstone, & Davidson, 2008; Weng et al., 2013), and so, assuming client readiness, we suggest a "fake it until you make it" mentality while working toward a genuine feeling of goodwill toward the offender.

Before the Work Phase is complete, the client is asked, with this new, reframed appraisal of the offender and the offense, to bear or accept the pain (Bergin, 1988). By this courageous readiness to accept the offense-related pain, clients are accepting the impact the offense has had on their life and acknowledging that they are able to carry on in spite of it (Enright & Fitzgibbons, 2000; Kaufman, 1984). This can be a challenging and extremely rewarding realization. As noted earlier, one common negative effect of offense-related injury is low self-esteem. Clients who are able to "bear the pain" often experience a revelation of their resilience and strength in the face of adversity (see, for example, Freedman & Enright, 1996).

The final stage of the Work Phase is giving a moral gift to the offender. Giving a moral gift actualizes the second half of forgiveness: responding with beneficence to the offender. Recall the distinction between forgiveness and reconciliation, pardoning, or condoning. Giving a moral gift is concerned with the internal, cognitive, and affective response one has to being the recipient of an offense. It is an act that can be accomplished without any interaction between client and offender. The importance of the gift is that in giving it, the client has moved to transcend, at least to some degree, the negative affect resulting from the injury.

The final phase of the forgiveness process is the Deepening Phase. As the name suggests, the Deepening Phase revisits many of the stages and themes of earlier phases. As a general movement, this phase asks clients to expand on their perception of the events they have forgiven and to consider more universally the meaning of suffering and forgiveness for themselves and others (Frankl, 1959). One way to look at this aspect of the Deepening Phase is as an attempt to write suffering and forgiveness, with utility and meaning, into the client's narrative and worldview. Some clients come to therapy with an ontology supportive of this aim while others will have a more difficult time logically incorporating suffering and forgiveness into their narrative of self and the world. Contemplating the effect the hurt has had on one's life and the transformations effected through forgiveness, and incorporating these experiences into one's altered self-narrative allow meaning making out of the pain that is founded on client agency rather than victimhood. Some clients gain from this meaning making a new purpose in life, and experience emerging positive affect toward the offender. A poignant example can be found in the Freedman and Enright (1996) incest survivor study, where one participant expressed a desire to counsel other incest survivors (Enright & Fitzgibbons, 2000).

MEASURING SELF-RENEWAL THROUGH FORGIVENESS

Now that the phases of forgiveness have been explored, we turn our attention to the notion of self-renewal. Building off what was written earlier in the chapter, self-renewal takes on a specific and circumscribed meaning with the context of forgiveness. It is understood by the quantifiable outcomes that can be reliably and consistently measured in those who have undergone forgiveness therapy. As has been discussed, self-renewal as understood in the paradigm of FT describes the process of relinquishing negative affect and cognitions (anger and resentment) and cultivating beneficence (forgiveness, empathy, and compassion). Although various psychometrics exist to measure these two movements (away from the negative and toward the positive), each with its own unique construct, four major domains of self-renewal are implicated through forgiveness: (1) a reduction of negative affect and cognition, and increases in (2) self-esteem, (3) hopefulness for the future, and (4) forgiveness. Examples of intervention findings can be found in Table 13.2.

Forgiveness is a temporal process. As the process model outlines, the first areas addressed relating to self-renewal fall under Category One. By working to relinquish anger and resentment, the client also begins to diminish the deleterious and concomitant cognitions and affective states. Although no study has yet deconstructed the process model to determine at which point specific effects (e.g., a diminution of anger, or a reduction in depression) manifest, it is reasonable to posit that negative affective states and cognitions begin to diminish first. As these negative affective and cognitive dispositions begin to subside (especially inwardly directed ones), self-esteem begins to improve. Rosenberg (1965), author of one of the most commonly employed self-esteem inventories, describes self-esteem as "the totality of the individual's thoughts and feelings with reference to himself as an object" (p. 38).

Encompassing both cognitive (thoughts/appraisals/judgments) and affective (valence/positive or negative) components, self-esteem has been shown to be central to systems affecting internal and external experience. For example, low self-esteem has been shown to correlate positively with heightened anxiety and depression (Subkoviak et al., 1995). Conversely, high self-esteem correlates positively with happiness and life satisfaction. Furthermore, Collins (1982) demonstrated that in children grouped according to math ability (low, medium, high), high self-esteem predicted resiliency and performance on difficult problems more accurately than innate ability (as cited in Bandura, 1993). Increasing self-esteem is thus an important marker of one's overall emotional health and can impact on cognitive performance as well. Forgiveness interventions have demonstrated statistically significant, and often large magnitude, effects for increasing self-esteem (for a review, see Baskin & Enright, 2004; Lundahl et al., 2008).

Similarly, hopefulness for the future indicates the level at which one expects positive experiences in the future. Like self-esteem, high hopefulness is positively correlated to more positive emotionality and negatively correlated to anxiety and depression. It is another indicator of macro-level emotional functioning. Finally, forgiveness itself is a strong predictor of self-esteem, hopefulness for the future, and positive emotionality. Anxiety (Al-Mabuk et al., 1995; Hebl & Enright, 1993), anger (Gambaro, Enright, Baskin, & Klatt, 2008), and depression (Al-Mabuk et al., 1995; Freedman & Enright, 1996) have been shown to diminish as forgiveness increases. Gambaro et al.'s (2008) research with high trait anger middle school adolescents suggests that forgiveness therapy may also decrease antisocial behavior measured as conduct citations in school.

Table 13.2 Forgiveness Therapy Intervention Studies

Author	Category	Design	Sample size	Outcome
Al-Mabuk et al. (1995)	Parentally Love-Deprived College Students	Randomized Control Trial	Study 1: $N = 48$	Forgiveness group showed significant increases beyond controls in hopefulness and willingness to forgive.
			Study 2: $N = 45$	Forgiveness group showed significant increases beyond controls in forgiveness, hope, attitude toward fathers, and self-esteem; significant decreases relative to controls in trait anxiety.
Hebl and Enright (1993)	Elderly Females	Randomized Active Control Trial	$N = 24$	Forgiveness group showed significant increases relative to controls in forgiveness and willingness to forgive. Both treatment and controls showed significant decreases from pre- to posttesting in trait anxiety and depression.
Freedman and Enright (2006)	Incest Survivors	Randomized Active Control Trial	$N = 12$	Forgiveness group showed significant improvement relative to controls in anxiety, depression, hope, and forgiveness.
Coyle and Enright (1997)	Postabortion Men	Randomized Wait-List Control Trial	$N = 10$	Forgiveness group showed significant improvement relative to controls in anxiety and forgiveness. Wait-list controls turned treatment group showed significant within-subjects improvement in anxiety, forgiveness, and grief.

Lin, Mack, Enright, Krahn, and Baskin (2004)	Inpatient Substance Abuse Clients	Randomized Active Control Trial	$N = 14$	Forgiveness group showed significant improvement relative to controls in anger, anxiety, depression, forgiveness, self-esteem, and vulnerability to drug use.
Reed and Enright (2006)	Emotionally Abused Women	Randomized Active Control Trial	$N = 20$	Forgiveness group showed significant improvement relative to controls in trait anxiety, depression, post-traumatic stress symptoms, forgiveness, self-esteem, environmental mastery, and finding meaning in suffering.
Waltman et al. (2009)	Patients With Coronary Heart Disease	Randomized Active Control Trial	$N = 17$	Forgiveness group showed significantly fewer anger-recall induced myocardial perfusion defects and a significant increase in forgiveness relative to the control group.
Hansen, Enright, Baskin, and Klatt (2009)	Forgiveness During Palliative Care	Randomized Wait-List Control Trial	$N = 20$	Forgiveness group showed significant improvement relative to controls in forgiveness, hope, quality of life, and anger.
Osterndorf, Enright, Holter, and Klatt (2011)	Adult Children of Alcoholics	Randomized Active Control Trial	$N = 12$	Forgiveness group showed significant improvement in forgiveness, self-esteem, depression, anger, and positive relations with others relative to active controls.

In concert, these four categories express significant qualities of research participants' present emotional and cognitive disposition, and their expectations for what the future holds in store. As these qualities become increasingly positive, marked by hope and positive expectancy, affective valence transforms in kind. It is through this transformation from hopelessness to hopefulness, from expectations of the negative to expectations of the positive, and from self-criticism to self-worth that self-renewal is realized through the forgiveness process.

An Example of Adult Self-Renewal Through Forgiveness

Forgiveness therapy has demonstrated efficacy in remediating negative affect and developing positive psychological health among individuals suffering from a wide range of injuries. For example, married couples (Orathinkal & Vansteenwegen, 2006), emotionally abused women (Reed & Enright, 2006), elderly women (Hebl & Enright, 1993), elderly in palliative care (Hansen, Enright, Baskin, & Klatt, 2009), adult children of alcoholics (Osterndorf, Enright, Holter, & Klatt, 2011), incest survivors (Freedman & Enright, 1996), and parentally love-deprived college students (Al-Mabuk et al., 1995) have all shown a significant diminution of negative affect and corresponding increase in positive emotional health after having undergone FT. Work done with adolescents (Al-Mabuk et al., 1995; Gambaro et al., 2008) and children (Enright & Fitzgibbons, 2000) demonstrate promise for FT at many points along the life span. To understand more specifically the degree to which FT affected the individuals in these groups, let us explore in some detail the Freedman and Enright (1996) study involving incest survivors.

A Forgiveness Intervention With Incest Survivors

Incest must be regarded as one of the most heinous and grievous injuries a human being can commit on another human being. Concomitant with such a severe offense is trauma that is encompassing, stable over time, and can manifest as biological, behavioral, social, and psychological impairment (Courtois, 2010). Working through a violation of trust as deeply rooted as incest poses incalculable challenges for therapist and client. Indeed, the research literature shows that clinician skill alone is rarely sufficient in helping clients suffering from incest find lasting psychological and emotional improvement (Freedman & Enright, 1996).

In Freedman and Enright's (1996) study, 12 females, all Caucasian between the ages of 24 and 54, met the criterion of having been sexually abused by a male family member. Participants were then yoked to form pairs that aligned as closely as possible along the dimensions of nature of abuse, abuser, current age, education level, and socioeconomic status. One person within each matched pair was randomly assigned to the experimental group (FT) and the other to a wait-list control group, receiving FT after posttesting.

Pretest measures for both experimental and control participants revealed elevated negative affect (e.g., anxiety, depression) and decreased self-esteem, hopefulness, positive affect, and low levels of forgiveness. The experimental intervention consisted of weekly, one-on-one FT sessions based on the process model of forgiveness discussed earlier. Mean duration of therapy was 14.3 months.

The experimental group participants showed statistically significant changes relative to the waitlist control group in psychological health after FT. State and trait anxiety and depression were reduced, while hope and forgiveness increased. Self-esteem among these participants showed no statistically significant improvement but was trending in the expected direction, pointing to a generally significant improvement in overall emotional health. Control group participant scores were then compared before and after receiving FT. Among this cohort, as with the experimental group, state and trait anxiety and depression were reduced, while hope and forgiveness increased at a statistically significant threshold. In addition, the experimental group's trend toward self-esteem reached statistical significance for the wait-list control group.

These results, coupled with the findings cited in Table 13.1, offer convincing support for the assertion that forgiveness therapy can lead to self-renewal. Observational data reported by participants offer further validation, suggesting the quantified changes had real and substantive impact on participant lives. In addition to the survivor mentioned earlier, another participant described how the process of forgiveness helped her realize that her partner was not offering her what she required and broke off the relationship. Finally, one participant forgave so deeply that she reconstituted relations with her formerly estranged father, the perpetrator of the incest—offering a moral gift that the offender did not deserve (Freedman & Enright, 1996).

NEW APPLICATIONS: FORGIVENESS AND PEACE

The empirical findings on FT have led to a general recognition that forgiving can benefit emotional health. This understanding has directed researchers to begin to evaluate new applications for forgiveness. One such exciting trend is to study the effects of forgiveness on children exposed to violence and/or deprivation. Children exposed to violence and deprivation, such as those living in extreme poverty in the United States or in regions marred by continual violence as are found in Northern Ireland, display many of the same adverse psychological manifestations as adults who have suffered personal injury. Heightened anxiety, anger, and depressive symptoms are exhibited, conduct disorders are common, forgiveness is low, and generally hopefulness for the future is also impaired (Bolger, Patterson, Thompson, & Kupersmidt, 1995;

Enright et al., 2007; McLeod & Shanahan, 1996; Samaan, 2000). As a vulnerable population, children exhibiting these symptoms ought to be a major cause for concern.

The ability of forgiving to counteract the negative environmental effects and, in the case of conflict societies, plant a seed of peace that will hopefully effect positive change in the future, although a relative new domain of inquiry, has yielded encouraging results. Forgiveness education implemented by teachers once a week for 15 weeks was sufficient to significantly reduce anger among primary school (U.S. equivalent of first grade) students in Belfast, Northern Ireland from clinically significant to average levels (Enright, Knutson Enright, Holter, Baskin, & Knutson, 2007). In a second, concurrent study, Enright et al. (2007) found that the same intervention, adjusted for age-appropriateness, significantly reduced anger and depression, and significantly increased forgiveness in a sample of older primary school students (U.S. equivalent of third grade). Forgiveness was not measured in the younger children because a pilot study showed that the measurement instrument was not age appropriate for this younger cohort.

Holter, Magnuson, Knutson, Knutson Enright, and Enright (2008) replicated the above studies in Milwaukee's Central City, one of the poorest areas in the United States. First graders who received forgiveness education showed significant reductions in anger. While third graders receiving forgiveness education did not differ significantly from controls in anger reduction, within-groups analysis revealed both control and experimental group participants significantly reduced anger from pre- to posttesting. A more sophisticated forgiveness education intervention was also given to fifth graders. As with first graders, at the fifth grade level the experimental group showed a significant reduction in anger relative to the control group, which increased in anger from pre- to posttesting (Holter et al., 2008).

Overall, the effectiveness of forgiveness education was on par with adult FT interventions, with an average effect size for anger of Cohen's *d* between .28 and .73, and for depression .30 (Enright et al., 2007). These findings represent a significant shift in the trajectory of emotional and psychological development for these children, and offer hope for renewal at a time when development is still extremely plastic, although longitudinal work is needed to determine the stability of these changes.

The teachers who delivered the forgiveness curriculum overwhelmingly rate as positive the effects on student behavior and classroom environment. For instance, among Milwaukee teachers, 78% observed student improvement in cooperation. 72% witnessed a reduction in overall student anger, and 71% reported that students generally improved academically as well. Interestingly, the teachers reported that they felt their teaching improved as a result of forgiveness education (91%). Moreover, and with implications for community and society, 93% of teachers also stated that they felt they had become a better person as a result of incorporating forgiveness education into the classroom (International Forgiveness Institute, 2012). Research on clinician renewal through directing FT has not yet been conducted, but perhaps the same will prove to be true about clinicians who incorporate FT into their practices.

CONCLUSION

Forgiveness is a process of self-renewal that begins with the individual relinquishing the anger and resentment that attends to being unjustly treated, and then learning to focus on the offender in a moral way. This latter movement of beneficence toward the offender serves as balm on the wound, offering a new reference point for the injustice and the resulting suffering—making meaning from the pain. The exact temporal moment at which the stages of forgiveness account for the outcomes that have been recorded remains unknown, but it is evidenced by the range of injustices positively affected by FT and the magnitude of the effects, that forgiveness is a powerful process for healing emotional suffering and thereby renewing the self. The recent work outlined on forgiveness education offers new hope for establishing more positive developmental trajectories among children whose life experiences are already having deleterious impact, consequences which, if left unaddressed, are predictive of future maladaptive outcomes. Although the long-term impact of these interventions requires additional research, there is hope that the improvement children demonstrated will continue, and having a positive impact on the communities in which they live.

REFERENCES

Al-Mabuk, R. H., Enright, R. D., & Cardis, P. A. (1995). Forgiveness education with parentally love-deprived late adolescents. *Journal of Moral Education*, *24*, 427–444. doi:0.1080/0305724950240405

Bandura, A. (1993). Perceived self-efficacy in cognitive development and functioning. *Educational Psychologist*, *28*(2), 117–148. doi:10.1207/s15326985ep2802_3

Baskin, T. W., & Enright, R. D. (2004). Intervention studies on forgiveness: A meta-analysis. *Journal of Counseling and Development*, *82*(1), 79–90. doi:10.1002/j.1556–6678.2004.tb00288.x

Bergin, A. E. (1988). Three contributions of a spiritual perspective to counseling, psychotherapy, and behavior change. *Counseling and Values*, *33*(1), 21–31. doi:10.1002/j.2161–007X.1988.tb00733.x

Bolger, K. E., Patterson, C. J., Thompson, W. W., & Kupersmidt, J. B. (1995). Psychosocial adjustment among children experiencing persistent and intermittent family economic hardship. *Child Development*, 66(4), 1107–1129. doi:10.2307/1131802

Collins, J. L. (1982). *Self-efficacy and ability in achievement behavior.* Paper presented at the annual meeting of the American Educational Research Association, New York, New York.

Courtois, C. A. (2010). *Healing the incest wound: Adult survivors in therapy* (2nd ed.). New York, NY: Norton.

Coyle, C. T., & Enright, R. D. (1997). Forgiveness intervention with postabortion men. *Journal of Consulting and Clinical Psychology*, 65, 1042–1046. doi:10.1037/0022-006X.65.6.1042

Cunningham, B. B. (1985). The will to forgive: A pastoral theological view of forgiving. *Journal of Pastoral Care*, 39, 141–149.

Davis, M. H. (1983). The effects of dispositional empathy on emotional reaction and helping: A multidimensional approach. *Journal of Personality*, *51*(2), 167–184. doi:10.1111/j.1467-6494.1983.tb00860.x

Denton, R. T., & Martin, M. W. (1998). Defining forgiveness: An empirical exploration of the process and role. *American Journal of Family Therapy*, 26, 181–192. doi:10.1080/01926189808251107

Droll, D. M. (1985). Forgiveness: Theory and research. *Dissertation Abstracts International B*, 45(8), 2732.

Eaton, J., Struthers, C., & Santelli, A. G. (2006). Dispositional and state forgiveness: The role of self-esteem, need for structure, and narcissism. *Personality and Individual Differences*, *41*(2), 371–380. doi:10.1016/j.paid.2006.02.005

Enright, R. D. (2001). *Forgiveness is a choice: A step-by-step process for resolving anger and restoring hope*. Washington, DC: American Psychological Association.

Enright, R. D., & Fitzgibbons, R. P. (2000). *Helping clients forgive: An empirical guide for resolving anger and restoring hope*. Washington, DC: American Psychological Association. doi:10.1037/10381-000

Enright, R. D., Freedman, S., & Rique, J. (1998). The psychology of interpersonal forgiveness. In R. D. Enright & J. North (Eds.), *Exploring forgiveness* (pp. 46–62). Madison: University of Wisconsin Press.

Enright, R. D., & the Human Development Study Group. (1991). The moral development of forgiveness. In W. Kurtines & J. Gewirtz (Eds.), *Handbook of moral behavior and development* (Vol. 1, pp. 123–152). Hillsdale, NJ: Erlbaum.

Enright, R. D., Knutson Enright, J. A., Holter, A. C., Baskin, T., & Knutson, C. (2007). Waging peace through forgiveness in Belfast, Northern Ireland II: Educational programs for mental health improvement of children. *Journal of Research in Education*, *3*, 63–78.

Enright, R. D., & North, J. (1998). *Exploring forgiveness.* Madison: University of Wisconsin Press.

Exline, J., Worthington, E. R., Hill, P., & McCullough, M. E. (2003). Forgiveness and justice: A research agenda for social and personality psychology. *Personality and Social Psychology Review*, *7*(4), 337–348. doi:10.1207/S15327957PSPR0704_06

Fitzgibbons, R. P. (1986). The cognitive and emotive uses of forgiveness in the treatment of anger. *Psychotherapy*, *23*, 629–633. doi:10.1037/h0085667

Flanigan, B. (1987, September). *Forgiving.* Workshops conducted at the Mendota Mental Health Institute, Madison, Wisconsin.

Frankl, V. (1959). *The will to meaning: Foundations and applications of logotherapy*. New York, NY: World.

Freedman, S., & Chang, W. (2010). An analysis of a sample of the general population's understanding of forgiveness: Implications for mental health counselors. *Journal of Mental Health Counseling, 32*(1), 5–34.

Freedman, S. R., & Enright, R. D. (1996). Forgiveness as an intervention goal with incest survivors. *Journal of Counseling and Clinical Psychology, 64*(5), 983–992. doi:10.1037/0022–006x.64.5.983

Gambaro, M. R., Enright, R. D., Baskin, T. W., & Klatt, J. (2008). Can school-based forgiveness counseling improve conduct and academic achievement in academically at-risk adolescents? *Journal of Research in Education, 18*, 16–27.

Hansen, M. J., Enright, R. D., Baskin, T. W., & Klatt, J. (2009). A palliative care intervention in forgiveness therapy for elderly terminally-ill cancer patients. *Journal of Palliative Care, 25*, 51–60.

Hebl, J., & Enright, R. D. (1993). Forgiveness as a psychotherapeutic goal with elderly females. *Psychotherapy: Theory, Research, Practice, Training, 30*(4), 658–667. doi:10.1037/0033–3204.30.4.658

Holmgren, M. R. (1993). Forgiveness and the intrinsic value of persons. *American Philosophical Quarterly, 30*(4), 341–352.

Holter, A. C., Magnuson, C. M., Knutson, C., Knutson Enright, J. A., & Enright, R. D. (2008). The forgiving child: The impact of forgiveness education on excessive anger for elementary-aged children in Milwaukee's Central City. *Journal of Research in Education, 18*, 82–93.

International Forgiveness Institute. (2012). *Forgiveness education in Milwaukee's Central City: Executive summary*. Retrieved from http://www.internationalforgiveness.com/data/uploaded/files/Teacher%20Evals%20Four%20Year%20Averages.pdf

Kaufman, M. E. (1984). The courage to forgive. *Israeli Journal of Psychiatry and Related Sciences, 21*, 177–187.

Kiel, D. V. (1986). I'm learning how to forgive. *Decisions*, 12–12.

Knutson, J., Enright., R. D., & Garbers, B. (2008). Validating the developmental pathway of forgiveness. *Journal of Counseling and Development, 86*(2), 193–199. doi:10.1002/j.1556–5678.2008.tb00497.x

Lin, W., Mack, D., Enright, R. D., Krahn, D., & Baskin, T. W. (2004). Effects of forgiveness therapy on anger, mood, and vulnerability to substance use among inpatient substance-dependent clients. *Journal of Consulting and Clinical Psychology, 72*(6), 1114–1121. doi:10.1037/0022–006X.72.6.1114

Lundahl, B. W., Taylor, M., Stevenson, R., & Roberts, K. (2008). Process-based forgiveness interventions: A meta-analytic review. *Research on Social Work Practice, 18*(5), 465–478. doi:10.1177/1049731507313979

Luskin, F. (2003). *Forgive for good.* New York, NY: HarperOne.

Lutz, A., Brefczynski-Lewis, J. A., Johnstone, T., & Davidson, R. J. (2008). Regulation of the neural circuitry of emotion by compassion meditation: Effects of meditative expertise. *PLoS ONE, 3*(3), e1897. doi:10.1371/journal.pone.0001897

McCullough, M. E. (2000). Forgiveness as a human strength: Theory, measurement, and links to well-being. *Journal of Social and Clinical Psychology, 19*(1), 43–55. doi:10.1521/jscp.2000.19.1.43

McCullough, M. E., Fincham, F. D., & Tsang, J. (2003). Forgiveness, forbearance, and time: The temporal unfolding of transgression-related interpersonal motivations. *Journal of Personality and Social Psychology, 84*(3), 540–557. doi:10.1037/0022–3514.84.3.540

McCullough, M. E., Worthington, E. L. Jr., & Rachal, K. C. (1997). Interpersonal forgiving in close relationships. *Journal of Personality and Social Psychology, 73*, 321–336. doi:10.1037/0022–3514.73.2.321

McLeod, J. D., & Shanahan, M. J. (1996). Trajectories of poverty and children's mental health. *Journal of Health and Social Behavior, 37*(3), 207–220. doi:10.2307/2137292

Neblett, W. R. (1974). Forgiveness and ideals. *Mind, 83*, 269–275.

North, J. (1987). Wrongdoing and forgiveness. *Philosophy*, 62, 499–508.

Oord, T. J. (2005). The love racket: Defining love and *agape* for the love-and-science research program. *Zygon, 40*(4), 919–938.

Orathinkal, J., & Vansteenwegen, A. (2006). The effect of forgiveness on marital satisfaction in relation to marital stability. *Contemporary Family Therapy: An International Journal, 28*(2), 251–260. doi:10.1007/s10591–006–9006-y

Osterndorf, C. L., Enright, R. D., Holter, A. C., & Klatt, J. (2011). Treating adult children of alcoholics through forgiveness therapy. *Alcoholism Treatment Quarterly, 29*, 274–292. doi:10.1080/07347324.2011.586285

Park, Y., & Enright, R. D. (1997). The development of forgiveness in the context of adolescent friendship conflict in Korea. *Journal of Adolescence, 20*(4), 393–402. doi:10.1006/jado.1997.0095

Patton, J. (1985). *Is human forgiveness possible?* Nashville, TN: Abingdon.

Peterson, C., & Seligman, M. P. (2004). *Character strengths and virtues: A handbook and classification.* Washington, DC: American Psychological Association.

Reed, G. L., & Enright, R. D. (2006). The effects of forgiveness therapy on depression, anxiety, and posttraumatic stress for women after spousal emotional abuse. *Journal of Consulting and Clinical Psychology, 74*(5), 920–929. doi:10.1037/0022–006X.74.5.920

Rosenberg, M. (1965). *Society and the adolescent self-image.* Princeton, NJ: Princeton University Press.

Samaan, R. A. (2000). The influences of race, ethnicity, and poverty on the mental health of children. *Journal of Health Care for the Poor and Underserved, 11*(1), 100–110.

Smedes, L. B. (1984). *Forgive and forget: Healing the hurts we don't deserve.* San Francisco, CA: Harper & Row.

Smith, M. (1981). The psychology of forgiveness. *The Month, 14*, 301–307.

StrategyOne. (2010). *Survey of love and forgiveness in American society.* Retrieved from Fetzer Institute website: http://www.slideshare.net/fetzerinstitute/fetzer-institutesurveyonloveandforgiveness

Subkoviak, M. J., Enright, R. D., Wu, C., Gassin, E. A., Freedman, S., Olson, L. M., & Sarinopoulos, I. C. (1995). Measuring interpersonal forgiveness in late adolescence and middle adulthood. *Journal of Adolescence, 18*, 641–655. doi:10.1006/jado.1995.1045

Trainer, M. F. (1984). Forgiveness: Intrinsic, role-expected, expedient, in the context of divorce. *Dissertation Abstracts International B*, *45*(04), 1325.

Wade, N. G., Bailey, D. C., & Schaffer, P. (2005). Helping clients heal: Does forgiveness make a difference? *Professional Psychology: Research and Practice*, *36*(6), 634–641. doi:10.1037/0735–7028.36.6.634

Wade, N. G., Johnson, C. V., & Meyer, J. E. (2008). Understanding concerns about interventions to promote forgiveness: A review of the literature. *Psychotherapy: Theory, Research, Practice, Training*, *45*(1), 88–102. doi:10.1037/0033–3204.45.1.88

Waltman, M. A., Russell, D. C., Coyle, C. T., Enright, R. D., Holter, A. C., & Swoboda, A. C. (2009). The effects of a forgiveness intervention on patients with coronary artery disease. *Psychology and Health*, *24*, 11–27. doi:10.1080/08870440801975127

Weng, H. Y., Fox, A. S., Shackman, A. J., Stodola, D. E., Caldwell, J. Z. K., Olson, M. C., . . . Davidson R. J. (2013). Compassion training alters altruism and neural responses to suffering. *Psychological Science*.

Witvliet, C.V.O., Ludwig, T. E., & Vander Laan, K. L. (2001). Granting forgiveness or harboring grudges: Implications for emotion, physiology, and health. *Psychological Science*, *12*(2), 117–123. doi:10.1111/1467–9280.00320

Worthington, E. L. Jr. (2006). *Forgiveness and reconciliation: Theory and application*. New York, NY: Brunner/Routledge.

Worthington, E. R., Witvliet, C. V. O., Pietrini, P., & Miller, A. J. (2007). Forgiveness, health, and well-being: A review of evidence for emotional versus decisional forgiveness, dispositional forgivingness, and reduced unforgiveness. *Journal of Behavioral Medicine*, *30*(4), 291–302. doi:10.1007/s10865–007–9105–8

CHAPTER

14

Psychological and Spiritual Aspects of Courage for Self-Renewal

Cynthia L. S. Pury and Kaye N. Glennon

Self-renewal is an act of transformation. In some cases, it requires reaching a point in one's life where the old paradigms, behaviors, and modes of operating are no longer working. Life is no longer fulfilling—personally, emotionally, or spiritually. For transformation to occur, one must be prepared to let go, to shed the old skin that no longer fits, and step forward into new ways of being. One must be ready to change, even if the change creates real or apparent risk.

People in helping professions may recognize the need for personal self-renewal, but face special challenges in embarking and managing that path to their higher self. Helping others is often fraught with darker, more difficult times that will drain one of energy and resources. How does one continue to give to others when there is little to give? Clergy face a unique challenge that their growth may lead them to a deeper understanding of God that their parishioners are not yet ready to embrace, while those in helping professions are not expected to show weakness. They are expected to have their own lives figured out so that they can then help others. People can feel inadequate in helping others when they are struggling to find their own way.

In this chapter, an academic psychologist and a Christian pastor explore courage and its relationship to self-renewal from both a psychological and a spiritual viewpoint. Although little to no empirical research has been conducted on psychological methods to increase courage, research on the basic psychology of courage suggests targets for intervention. These targets intersect with centuries-old spiritual traditions that can be used to encourage self-renewal.

PSYCHOLOGY AND COURAGE

How do we define and understand courage? Are some types of courage different from others? How is courage developed, strengthened, or accessed by individuals? These and other important questions are considered in the following section.

What Is Courage?

An early formulation of courage, proposed by Lord in 1918, describes courage as the process of the base sentiment of fear being overcome by a more noble sentiment. However, as behaviorism became a more dominant paradigm in psychology, this internal process became replaced with a definition borrowing heavily from externally observable phenomena. Rachman and his colleagues (e.g., Cox, Hallam, O'Connor, & Rachman, 1983; McMillan & Rachman, 1987, 1988; O'Connor, Hallam, & Rachman, 1985; Rachman, 1983, 2010) define courage as experiencing the subjective/cognitive and psychophysiological experience of fear, yet approaching the feared object rather than engaging in flight or avoidance. A similar definition of courage as acting despite fear appears in other, more recent empirical research as well (Muris, 2009; Muris, Mayer, & Schubert, 2010; Norton & Weiss, 2009).

While courage does commonly act in opposition to fear, viewing courage as only a specific response to fear is incomplete in two ways. First, some types of courage may not require the presence of fear. Ratings of how courageous an action is compared to the way most other people act correlate with actors' feelings of efficacy, but not their feelings of fear (Pury, Kowalski, & Spearman, 2007). Individuals who have been hailed as extremely courageous by society show reduced levels of fear when exposed to laboratory stress, thus suggesting they are more fearless than courageous (Rachman, 1983).

A second problem with viewing courage as standing up to fear is that it does not consider why the person is taking action. Consider two people who, despite great fear, run into a burning building. One runs in to save a baby; the other runs in to save a favorite pair of shoes. It is likely that the first may be heralded as courageous and the second called a fool. Scales designed to measure this ability to stand up to fear have a strong positive correlation with sensation seeking (Muris, 2009).

Rate and colleagues conducted a series of studies to explore implicit theories of courage (Rate, 2010; Rate, Clarke, Lindsay, & Sternberg, 2007). They found that three main factors define courage: (1) taking a voluntary action, (2) despite personal risk, (3) in pursuit of a noble or worthwhile goal (Rate, 2010). This definition recaptures the goodness of intent found in Lord (1918). It also avoids the conundrum of fear in courage: Fear frequently, but not always, accompanies risk. Finally, and perhaps most importantly for self-renewal, it describes courage as something one can choose or not choose, rather than a state of being or an automatic response.

Types of Courage

Two of the three components of a courageous action, the risk and the worthwhile goal, can vary in ways that produce recognizable subtypes of courage. Since the time of Plato, scholars have differentiated physically courageous actions, such as running toward an armed enemy or facing danger at sea, from morally courageous actions, such as standing up for one's convictions (Plato, 1961). Physical and moral courage, in this analysis, are alike in the voluntary nature of their action but are different in the risks borne and the goals pursued. Physical courage, by definition, requires some sort of physical risk assumed by the individual. Commonly (but not always), physically courageous acts involve saving someone else from the same physical danger—the soldier takes on the armed enemy so that the enemy does not kill others, the lifeguard faces the riptide to save the drowning swimmer. Moral courage, on the other hand, requires that the goodness of the action derives from its congruence with the actor's values. The risks involved in moral courage typically are social rejection by others, but in extreme cases can involve additional risks, such as the financial risk of a whistleblower losing a job or the physical risk of a civil rights advocate being attacked or even killed.

Philosopher Dan Putman proposes a third type of courage, *psychological courage* (Putman, 1997, 2004). Psychological courage involves the courage to face psychological instability, including uncertainty or emotional distress. His prototypic example of psychological courage, undergoing psychotherapy despite the fact that it might cause emotional distress, mirrors Rachman's (1984) observations of early behavior therapy patients as being terrifically courageous in facing their fears. In our analysis, psychological courage involves facing an internal risk, commonly for personal growth. Psychological courage can also involve a broader concept of stepping outside one's comfort zone—to attend a school far from home, to take on a challenging new work assignment despite the risk of failure (see Pury et al., 2007), or to engage in self-renewal.

Another key implication of Rate's (2010) definition is that the danger of the risk and value of the goal are judged subjectively, with reference to both the actor and the observer (Pury & Starkey, 2010). Thus, Pury et al. (2007) found a distinction between *general courage*, or actions that would be courageous for anyone, and *personal courage*, or actions that are courageous if taken by a particular actor. Actions high in general courage are those in which the risks would be dangerous for anyone—such as drowning or losing one's job. They also involve goals that most people would find laudable—such as saving another human being from harm or standing up for commonly shared values. Actions high in personal courage, on the other hand, involve actions that are risky for that particular actor—such as facing a private fear or personal limitation. They might also involve goals that are more valuable or worthwhile for that particular actor—such as pursuit of a personal goal or standing up for oneself. Actions high in general courage are more likely to be accompanied by feelings of self-efficacy or confidence in the actor; actions high in personal courage are more likely to be accompanied by feelings of fear (Pury et al., 2007). Self-renewal, we suspect, is far more likely to be an act of personal courage.

A third distinction suggested by a subjective approach to risks and goals is courage as an accolade and courage as a process (Pury & Starkey, 2010). Accolade courage occurs when observers look at an action and see voluntary action for goals they support despite risks they appreciate. Medals and other public honors bestowed on courageous actors are a clear example of accolade courage, but so is a simple acknowledgment by another—"That was a brave thing to do." Process courage, on the other hand, occurs within the actor and represents the process of overcoming a subjective sense of risk to pursue what (at the time) seems a noble goal. The risks might be objectively minimal or nonexistent, such as a phobic fear of spiders or excessive concern about others' opinions of you. The value of the goal may change with time—what seems to be a worthwhile goal at one point in life may seem trivial or even detrimental in a decade. For example, a young couple might be quite courageous in risking everything to be together only to find out they are not suited for a long-term relationship. A more noble goal makes both the accolade of courage and the process of taking the action more likely; a more dangerous or certain risk makes the accolade of courage more likely but the process of actually taking the action less likely. Because of its personal nature, acts of self-renewal are likely to meet the definition of process courage but are not likely to meet everyone's threshold for accolade courage. Observers *might* view pursuing a career in music, completing a marathon, or becoming a more attentive person as a valuable goal. The comfort and ease of old patterns that need to be abandoned, or the scariness of trying this particular new way of being may not be apparent. Thus, the self-renewer should not expect to receive praise from others as courageous. The important thing is how courageous the individual sees him- or herself for making these changes.

Becoming More Courageous

Value of the goal and subjective sense of risk also come into play when people are asked if they have tried something to make themselves more courageous. The most common answers involve focusing on the goal and reducing either the actual or felt risk. A third category, increasing the likelihood that the action will succeed, may be related to the sense of efficacy needed for voluntary action (Pury, 2008). These three areas are also commonly used when we encourage others. We encourage our children to do well in school by talking about their future plans. We encourage a friend who is facing a frightening medical condition by telling them it will be alright. Most of all, we encourage everyone from small children to adults by stating our belief in their efficacy: "You can do it."

Courage might also be fostered by the individual adopting a particular persona. Using Mischel and Shoda's (2000) Cognitive-Affective System (CAPS) theory of personality, Hannah, Sweeney, and Lester (2010) propose that people act courageously when they are in a mind-set that requires it. In this model, different mindsets, or roles, have different cognitions, goals, values, self-regulatory plans, affects, and expectancies. Drawing on your specific role—parent, soldier, lifeguard, or even good person—may help you to become more courageous. Combining this theory with Rate's (2010) three-part model, we might think of different mind-sets causing us to weigh the goals and risks of a situation differently. For example, parents may value the well-being of their child more highly than their own well-being. Different mindsets might also cause differences in efficacy—a role in which one is strong, powerful, and successful can lead to a greater sense that one will succeed and weather any risks.

Ethnographic interviews of courageous people around the world suggest other ways courage might be accomplished (Biswas-Diener, 2012). Reminding oneself of the importance of goals may be augmented by focusing on feelings of anger or defiance. Reducing felt risk might be accomplished through reducing uncertainty, relaxation, getting angry, identifying oneself as defiant [a mind-set change, in Hannah et al.'s (2010) model], or being willing to fail. Increasing felt efficacy may be accomplished by teaching oneself to see success and drawing on one's beliefs in supernatural influences, including spirituality.

SPIRITUALITY AND COURAGE

More formally, spirituality and religious traditions suggest many ways to become courageous and many reasons to do so, particularly to transform or renew the self. Spirituality is an interior experience of "something more." Known by many names, this "something more" is our Source, the Divine, God, Goddess, Loving Energy, Authentic or Higher Self—call it by whatever you will. Healthy spirituality trusts that this "something more" is loving and desires each person to live life authentically and abundantly. In the Christian scriptures, Jesus is quoted as saying, "I came that they may have life and have it abundantly" (John 10:10). Courage for self-renewal and transformation is often found when an individual connects with the Divine. Through different spiritual practices one remembers that one is not alone on their journey and that this loving being or energy is present to lead and guide them in a self-renewal process that will bring them ever closer to their authentic self and fulfillment. Even if one's goal is to shed the worn out pieces of their lives that no longer work, which is a lofty and admirable goal, people are rarely apt to jump in with both feet, unless unavoidable. In self-renewal there is no clear pathway, no clear knowledge of who we are becoming. What will this change require of us?

Sue Monk Kidd (1990), in her book *When the Heart Waits*, says, "We have within us a deep longing to grow and become a new creature, but we possess an equally strong compulsion to remain the same—to burrow down in our safe, secure places," (p. 101). Many people who have embarked upon a journey of self-renewal, and relied on the strength of their relationship with the Divine to see them through, have been disheartened to find themselves in what has come to be known as the "dark night of the soul." In this experience, the person feels bereft of God, they feel alone and may even be unable to pray. They feel that no matter what they do, they cannot feel the presence of the Divine as they used to, and so may even question their faith altogether. Alas, this is a risk that one must take in their quest for self-renewal. Sometimes the process of transformation requires serious self-reflection, a slaying of the dragons of the past, dumping our old heavy baggage and packing lighter in a new bright green backpack. Courage is absolutely necessary if one is to go forward. We cannot slay the dragon until we confront it in all its ferocity. And we cannot dump the baggage until we have sorted through it and determined once and for all that we do not want to keep it. The pain and grief this often elicits may sink a person into the darkest nights of loneliness and despair. It is important to recognize at this point that this can be a normal part of any transformative process. Hopefully, the deeply spiritual person will recognize that, even though they may feel that God has abandoned them, this simply isn't the case. One should remain focused on their goal and trust that God constantly desires whatever is for their highest good and will work to lead and guide them.

Spiritual Practices to Foster Courage

There are a number of spiritual practices that can help a person to bolster their courage and continue the road toward self-renewal. Prayer, scripture, metaphor, and spiritual stories, and becoming involved in a spiritual community are simply a few that we explore.

Prayer is perhaps the most common way that one can connect with the Divine and draw courage. Christian theologian Matthew Fox asserts, "Prayer is the process of rerooting oneself" (Fox, 2001, p. 77). Prayer, or meditation, means connecting to the God-spark within us, and that God-spark is connected energetically to all of creation. It is like logging on to the World Wide Web where we have a vast network of resources, a huge pool of energy to draw from and learn from. One can find strength, comfort, peace, clarity, and courage for the journey. The work of the Divine is itself transformational, helping each person to live authentically and the world to live in harmony. God uses what God has to work with . . . when we pray we change ourselves, and so change what God has to work with.

There are many people in this world who are stuck in bad situations, in unfulfilling lives and yet are resistant to change. Perhaps the biggest thing that keeps a soul stuck is the belief that—because of who a person is, or what they have done, or what they have not done—they are unlovable, even by God. This belief holds one in the power of guilt, shame, hurt, blame, and feeling unworthy. But the truth is that God is love—pure, unbounded, unconditional love. It is the very essence of God, and no one can be bad enough to change the essence of God.

In prayer or meditation, when we are rerooted in the Eternal One, we are nourished, as a tree by water, by the unconditional love of God. Connecting with this love sets one free from the fear of being unlovable and unworthy—the risk is gone. Perfect love casts out fear. If a person dwells in that love and knows the depth of that love, if they know they are cradled, guided, and strengthened by that love, then where is the fear? It begins to dissipate and courage grows. In the words of the great 13th-century Sufi mystic, Jalal ad-Din Rumi:

> Oh soul,
> you worry too much.
> You have seen your own strength.
> You have seen your own beauty.
> You have seen your golden wings.
> Of anything less,
> why do you worry?
> You are in truth
> the soul, of the soul, of the soul.
>
> *(Rumi & Shiva, n.d.)*

Within each spiritual tradition one can find stories in its sacred scripture that will inspire courage. For example, in Christianity there is the story of the hemorrhaging woman (Mark 5:25–34) who dares to touch the hem of the great Teacher's garments. In Judaism there is the story of Shiprah and Puah (Exodus, 1:8–21), the midwives who refused to obey Pharaoh and kill the Hebrews' baby boys as they were born. In Hinduism, we have the tale of Ramayana in which Hanuman the monkey symbolizes the power of faith and devotion to overcome human frailties, and Sita who undergoes a trial of fire to prove her fidelity to her husband (Fisher, 2012, p. 53). These stories reinforce both good action and the worth and value of taking good action. They also instill efficacy—others have successfully taken risks to pursue the good. Spiritual leaders may be able to guide people in finding a story that has meaning for them and can be used to summon courage when it wanes.

Specific metaphors in spiritual traditions may also be useful in helping one gain understanding and courage for their own process of becoming. As self-renewal often requires the deconstruction of oneself only to live for an unspecified amount of time in an uncomfortable place where things are not re-created yet, the metaphor of the wilderness journey may be helpful. Both Christian and Jewish traditions count this story among their sacred stories. In the book of Exodus, Moses helped the Hebrews escape from slavery in Egypt only to find themselves wandering in the desert for 40 years before coming to the land promised to them by God. However, they are not alone in the wilderness. God provides manna, bread from heaven (Exodus 16:4), for them to eat fresh each day, and guides them with a pillar of cloud by day and a pillar of fire by night (Exodus 13:21). How similar this might be to a person who has left behind a life they may have felt they were a "slave" to, only to wander and struggle to "find themselves" before finally coming to a better, more fulfilling place in their lives. Being lost is not as risky as it might seem. In the midst of that struggle, it is important to remember the abiding presence of the Divine bringing them nourishment and direction, often in unexpected ways, for the long journey.

Archetypes are universal symbols of the human spirit which, when identified and understood, may bring one to deeper awareness. They may also be tools for change, transformation, and self-renewal. Identifying with these archetypes can be seen as a form of taking on a courageous mind-set, in Hannah et al.'s (2010) CAPS model. Jean Shinoda Bolen, psychiatrist and author of *Goddesses in Everywoman* and *Gods in Everyman*, suggests that "Identifying the god and goddess archetypes at work within each of us will help us tap their power and become better heroes and heroines in our own life stories" (Bolen, 2004, p. 335). Because most traditional religion is patriarchal, women especially may find power and courage by exploring goddess archetypes in their own lives. A woman seeking a resource for courage might consider invoking one of the three ancient Greek Virgin Goddesses: Artemis, Athena, and Hestia. All three of these goddesses "represent inner drives in women to develop talents, pursue interests, solve problems, compete with others, express themselves articulately in words or through art forms, put their surroundings in order, or lead contemplative lives" (Bolen, 2004, p. 35). And a woman who has one of these goddess archetypes actively at work in her will be "one-in-herself, she will be motivated by a need to follow her own inner values, to do what has meaning or fulfills herself, apart from what other people think" (Bolen, 2004, p. 36). A man, on the other hand, might consider evoking the Greek god Hermes, considered by some to be the father of alchemy, that elusive science of turning lead into gold. Metaphorically, when engaging in self-renewal, the alchemist can work within spiritual and psychological struggles to bring about transformation. Bolen (1989) suggests that "we invite Hermes to be with us whenever we are willing to venture into new territory with an attitude of exploration and openness" (pp. 170–171).

Becoming active in a healthy spiritual community is another way to boost courage for the task of self-renewal. A healthy spiritual community will be based in the love of the divine and in compassion for one another and will understand the value of personal reflection, transformation, and renewal. Alcoholics Anonymous is a good example of a spiritual community that does not dictate what one needs to do or believe, but allows each person their own experience of the divine and supports them in their process of becoming sober. Spiritual writer Anne Lamott (1999) in her book *Traveling Mercies* talks about her own struggle to re-create her life, and her penchant for getting lost. As a child, she once found herself literally lost and the policeman drove her around town trying to find her house when she spotted her church and told him, "This is my church . . . I can always find my way home from here" (p. 55). As one metaphorically attempts to find their way home to their authentic self, that church or temple or mosque or support group can be a very important source of encouragement.

Finally, spiritual advice and wisdom can also be found in the world's sacred scripture. They can be used to keep focus or gain courage when said as a mantra, taped to the refrigerator, or written in lipstick on the bathroom mirror. The Bhagavad Gita states, "The worried mind tends to veer from the only real goal—realizing the Atman, uniting with Divinity, the True Self Within," ("The Bhagavad Gita," Hawley, 2001, 2:47). Lao-tzu (1988) in the *Tao Te Ching* questions, "Do you have the patience to wait till your mud settles and the water is clear? Can you remain unmoving till the right action arises by itself?" (p. 15). In the Christian Old Testament, or Jewish Scriptures, Joshua 1:9 states: "[B]e strong; be courageous! Don't be afraid or discouraged, for Yahweh your God is with you wherever you go" (Priests-for-Equality, 2007, p. 125). Such inspirational quotes can function like the verbal talismans recommended by Biswas-Diener (2012).

CONCLUSION

Spiritual and religious traditions suggest many reasons to take on the courageous task of self-renewal and many paths to get there. Psychology has come lately to courage, but can suggest an overall framework for both secular and spiritual courage for self-renewal: value of the goal, reduction of felt or actual risk, and the efficacy to act.

We close this chapter with additional verbal talismans to encourage your own renewal:

> New life is born in the state of total vulnerability—this is the mystery of love. Power kills. Weakness creates. It creates autonomy, self-awareness, and freedom. It creates openness to give and receive in mutuality. And finally it creates the good ground on which new life can come to full development and maturity. (Nouwen & Durback, 1997)

What "real artists" have is courage. Not enormous gobs of it. Just enough for today. . . . Courage, after all, is a matter of heart, and hearts do their work one beat at a time. (Cameron, 1996, pp. 200–201)

[I]n the search for your True Self, you have to find the courage to enter a great absurdity. . . . This means leaning out into the unknown spaces of faith and risk. (Kidd, 1990, p. 72)

You may feel tempted to change your relationship, your career, or any area of life that feels difficult or frustrating. Some new choices may be appropriate or even overdue, but the heroic choice often means taking responsibility for where you are now and participating fully and intentionally, with greater presence and passion than ever before. (Millman, 1995, p. 23)

REFERENCES

Biswas-Diener, R. (2012). *The courage quotient: How science can make you braver*. San Francisco, CA: Jossey-Bass.

Bolen, J. S. (1989). *Gods in everyman: Archetypes that shape men's lives*. San Francisco, CA: HarperCollins.

Bolen, J. S. (2004). *Goddesses in everywoman: Powerful archetypes in women's lives*. San Francisco, CA: Harper.

Cameron, J. (1996). *The vein of gold: A journey to your creative heart*. New York, NY: Tarcher/Putnam.

Cox, D., Hallam, R., O'Connor, K., & Rachman, S. (1983). An experimental analysis of fearlessness and courage. *British Journal of Psychology, 74*(1), 107–117. doi:10.1111/j.2044–8295.1983.tb01847.x

Fisher, M. P. (2012). *A brief introduction: Living religions* (3rd ed). Upper Saddle River, NJ: Prentice Hall.

Fox, M. (2001). *Prayer: A radical response to life*. New York, NY: Tarcher/Putnam.

Hannah, S. T., Sweeney, P. J., & Lester, P. B. (2010). The courageous mind-set: A dynamic personality system approach to courage. In C. L. S. Pury & S. J. Lopez (Eds.), *The psychology of courage: Modern research on an ancient virtue* (pp. 125–148). Washington, DC: American Psychological Association.

Hawley, J., Trans. (2001). *The Bhagavad Gita*. Novato, CA: New World.

Kidd, S. M. (1990). *When the heart waits*. San Francisco, CA: Harper.

Lamott, A. (1999). *Traveling mercies: Some thoughts on faith*. New York, NY: Anchor Books.

Lao-Tzu. (1988). *Tao Te Ching* (S. Mitchell, Trans.). New York, NY: HarperCollins.

Lord, H. G. (1918). *The psychology of courage*. Boston, MA: Luce.

McMillan, T. M., & Rachman, S. J. (1987). Fearlessness and courage: A laboratory study of paratrooper veterans of the Falklands War. *British Journal of Psychology, 78*(3), 375–383. doi:0.1111/j.2044–8295.1987.tb02255.x

McMillan, T. M., & Rachman, S. J. (1988). Fearlessness and courage in paratroopers undergoing training. *Personality and Individual Differences*, 9(2), 373–378. doi:10.1016/0191–8869(88)90100–6

Millman, D. (1995). *The laws of spirit: A tale of transformation*. Tiburon, CA: Kramer.

Mischel, W., & Shoda, Y. (2000). A cognitive-affective system theory of personality: Reconceptualizing situations, dispositions, dynamics, and invariance in personality structure. In E. T. Higgins & A. W. Kruglanski (Eds.), *Motivational science: Social and personality perspectives* (pp. 150–176). New York, NY: Psychology Press.

Muris, P. (2009). Fear and courage in children: Two sides of the same coin? *Journal of Child and Family Studies*, *18*(4), 486–490. doi:10.1007/s10826–009–9271–0

Muris, P., Mayer, B., & Schubert, T. (2010). "You might belong in Gryffindor": Children's courage and its relationships to anxiety symptoms, Big Five personality traits, and sex roles. *Child Psychiatry and Human Development*, *41*(2), 204–213. doi:10.1007/s10578–009–0161-x

Norton, P. J., & Weiss, B. J. (2009). The role of courage on behavioral approach in a fear-eliciting situation: A proof-of-concept pilot study. *Journal of Anxiety Disorders*, *23*(2), 212–217. doi:10.1016/j.janxdis.2008.07.002

Nouwen, H., & Durback, R. (1997). *Seeds of hope: A Henri Nouwen reader*. New York, NY: Image Books.

O'Connor, K., Hallam, R. S., & Rachman, S. (1985). Fearlessness and courage: A replication experiment. *British Journal of Psychology*, *76*(2), 187–197. doi:10.1111/j.2044–8295.1985.tb01942.x

Plato. (1961). Laches (B. Jowett, Trans.). In E. Hamilton & H. Cairns (Eds.), *The collected dialogues of Plato, including the letters* (pp. 123–144). Princeton, NJ: Princeton University Press.

Priests-for-Equality. (2007). *The inclusive Bible: The first egalitarian translation*. Lanham, MD: Rowman & Littlefield.

Pury, C. L. S. (2008). Can courage be learned? In S. J. Lopez (Ed.), *Positive psychology: Exploring the best in people. Vol. 1: Discovering human strengths* (pp. 109–130). Westport, CT: Praeger/Greenwood.

Pury, C. L. S., Kowalski, R. M., & Spearman, J. (2007). Distinctions between general and personal courage. *Journal of Positive Psychology*, 2(2), 99–114. doi:10.1080/17439760701237962

Pury, C. L. S., & Starkey, C. B. (2010). Is courage an accolade or a process? A fundamental question for courage research. In C. L. S. Pury & S. J. Lopez (Eds.), *The psychology of courage: Modern research on an ancient virtue* (pp. 67–87). Washington, DC: American Psychological Association.

Putman, D. (1997). Psychological courage. *Philosophy, Psychiatry, & Psychology*, 4(1), 1–11. doi:10.1353/ppp.1997.0008

Putman, D. (2004). *Psychological courage*. Dallas, TX: University Press of America.

Rachman, S. J. (1983). Fear and courage among military bomb-disposal operators. *Advances in Behaviour Research & Therapy*, 4(3), 99–165.

Rachman, S. J. (1984). Fear and courage. *Behavior Therapy*, *15*(1), 109–120. doi:10.1016/s0005–7894(84)80045–3

Rachman, S. J. (2010). Courage: A psychological perspective. In C. L. S. Pury & S. J. Lopez (Eds.), *The psychology of courage: Modern research on an ancient virtue* (pp. 91–107). Washington, DC: American Psychological Association.

Rate, C. R. (2010). Defining the features of courage: A search for meaning. In C. L. S. Pury & S. J. Lopez (Eds.), *The psychology of courage: Modern research on an ancient virtue* (pp. 47–66). Washington, DC: American Psychological Association.

Rate, C. R., Clarke, J. A., Lindsay, D. R., & Sternberg, R. J. (2007). Implicit theories of courage. *Journal of Positive Psychology*, *2*(2), 80–98. doi:10.1080/17439760701228755

Rumi, J. a.-D., & Shiva, S. (n.d.). *Rumi Poems by Shiva*. Retrieved from www.rumi.net/rumi_by_shiva.html

PART

IV

Theoretical Approaches to Self-Renewal: Group, Marital, and Family System, Dialectical, Behavioral, and the Ways Paradigm

CHAPTER

15

The Group as a Medium for Personal and Professional Renewal

Virginia Brabender and Courtney Slater

The weary traveler entered the forest to find food. He discovered the berries were too high in the trees to reach. Another weary traveler came his way and together they tried to capture the berries, but to no avail. Even with one man on the other's shoulders, they lacked the stature to reach the fruity prize. Finally, a posse of four wayfarers, no less hungry, joined them. The men looked up wistfully at the berries. Surely with one man standing on the shoulders of another, and another higher still, they would merely topple over reaching not a single berry. Then the smallest man said, "Place me on top—with you three strong men at the bottom, and two on you. I can reach the forest canopy." And so he did, and a berry dinner they enjoyed.

Like our traveler, the individual journeying through life needs sustenance to take each successive leg of the trip. Our own creativity, problem-solving skills, and ingenuity may serve us well in finding that sustenance—be it physical, intellectual, or emotional—for ourselves. However, as our contexts become more complicated and challenging—as in the case of those high-hanging berries—sustenance may require something more than our own individual efforts: It may require a collaborative relationship. However, those difficulties that are sufficiently great to deprive individuals of sustenance over a period of time often require a range of human resources. Our weary traveler was ultimately able to eat because he had in his midst men who could serve as supports and a man who was lithe enough to climb to the top of the structure. In other words, what our traveler needed was a group, and it is often a group that helps those lacking emotional sustenance.

This chapter discusses the distinctive role of groups in contributing to those seeking to renew themselves. We define renewal as emotional and intellectual refueling, allowing the individual to partake of the growth opportunities of the developmental period in which he or she resides. We see the medium of group as having renewal potential for virtually anyone in need of reinvigoration. Yet, we believe its contribution to the mental health professional is particularly important in helping that professional to cope creatively with the stressors that attend clinical work. In this chapter, we talk about three different types of groups—and their unique contributions—to the layperson and the mental health professional: the self-help group, the support group, and the psychotherapy group. Additionally, we consider the role of the peer supervision group in the ongoing rejuvenation of the therapist. Renewal is not a phenomenon limited by age. In this chapter, we provide the example of a very young person in need of renewal and someone considerably older.

RENEWAL IN LATE ADOLESCENCE/EARLY ADULTHOOD

Renewal is an opening to truth, vitality, freedom, and confidence and a washing away of pessimism, rigidity, and lifelessness. These shifts can be seen in the case of Dani:

> Dani was an 18-year-old Italian-American woman beginning her first year at college. She identified as Catholic, straight, and middle to upper class. In the fall of her freshman year she felt both excited to explore her independence and anxious about breaking from her family. By the third week of classes she appeared at the college counseling center at the urging of her mother who was distressed by Dani's frequent calls home and effusive crying. Dani explained to the intake clinician that she was homesick and having trouble fitting in. She desperately wanted acceptance from the peers living in her residence hall, but after a boy down the hall called her "pint-sized" and others decided to adopt "Pint" as a nickname, she felt self-conscious about her petite body and alienated from her peer group. During the initial evaluation, Dani also explained that another stressor was her long-distance relationship with her boyfriend, Troy.
>
> Dani began dating Troy in high school and upon graduation, they made plans to stay together while attending different universities and living about two hours from each other. She said that the entire

> relationship had been tumultuous, but it grew worse after moving to college. Troy would call Dani, crying and stating that he needed to see her, so she began driving to see him on the weekends, which further limited her connection with her peers in her residence hall. As the semester progressed, Troy grew more distressed by the distance, afraid that he was losing Dani, and paranoid about Dani's connection to other men at college. He began making threats that he would hurt himself if she cheated on him. Dani was alarmed and felt responsible for his safety, but she was also tired of carrying his life in her hands. Although Dani had always been a very good student, she began to feel uninterested in her course material. During classes, she was preoccupied with her recent communications with Troy. She felt a kind of dullness and deadness as she tried to approach her assignments outside of classes. She also stopped attending mass and told the clinician that she was still Catholic, but not like "real Catholics."

Dani was in the midst of many developmental issues, especially involving issues of identity and intimacy. As a young adult, she was developing cognitively, emotionally, and socially, which was allowing her to reflect on herself, compare herself to others, and experiment with new ways of being. She experienced such a strong desire for acceptance from her peers that she was willing to sacrifice her values and morals to achieve a sense of closeness. She was also enthralled with romantic intimacy, excited to explore sexuality and connection with her partner. The excitement of being emotionally and sexually intimate with Troy was enthralling and almost intoxicating to Dani.

These developmental issues were paired with a history of loss and a resulting depressive personality. Dani had a tendency to internalize negative qualities, including the negative aspects of others and the environment. Feeling inferior to others and a pervasive sense of guilt led to passivity in relationships and a timid demeanor. Furthermore, she seemed ready to receive rejection and criticism. When relating to others, Dani felt responsible for others' well-being and compelled to repair those who were suffering. Therefore, when her boyfriend insisted that she visit him, it was ego-syntonic to believe that she would be culpable if he hurt himself.

Group therapy was a preferred method of treatment for Dani because group offered Dani a group of peers to whom she could relate within a structure that promoted safety and healing. This is important primarily because her presenting symptoms included homesickness, which was alleviated as she experienced validation and grew more comfortable with her peer group at college. While secondary to the issues related to her presenting symptoms, the challenges and issues inherent to young adulthood made group therapy a preferred option for Dani. Young adulthood is filled with social comparison and experimentation; Dani was forming a sense of self by comparing herself to others her age. Peer opinion was likely to hold more weight than that of an individual therapist who may be seen as similar to a parental figure. The structure of group therapy provided an intentional and safe place for Dani to work out these issues with peers who were interested in a similar process.

Group therapy can be a treatment of choice not only for the alleviation of symptoms, but also for regeneration and life. Dani achieved symptom relief quickly, through the validation and encouragement from the other group members. Her homesickness declined as she began to share and she felt appreciated. Her relationship distress also waned, because members shared their perspectives on her situation, which included shock that she would feel responsible for Troy's well-being. Cognitive space opened up for Dani to see herself and her relationship in a new way; she no longer felt compelled to be Troy's ultimate caregiver. She also saw others as potential sources of support and encouraged Troy to get professional help.

Not only is group therapy helpful in alleviating presenting symptoms, it can also be a rich environment for personal growth and development. As Dani's distress alleviated, her mental and emotional energy was freed up and she began a process of engaging her intra and interpersonal dynamics. Through the process of group therapy, she gained new awareness into feelings of fear and a resulting constriction. Exploring and experimenting with these feelings resulted in rejuvenation and she developed a fresh energy for life.

> For a few weeks in a row Dani noticed that she had headaches while in group. She brushed them off, but the other group members reflected that they had also noticed a change in her. The therapist invited Dani to try an experiment. She invited Dani to tune in to her headache and act out, with her body, what the headache was expressing. Dani crossed her arms and her legs and squeezed her body so tight that it looked painful to the rest of the members. Then the therapist asked Dani if she would be okay with the other members also taking that posture. She said okay and the whole group crossed their arms and legs and squeezed. Afterwards, each member talked about what it felt like for him or her and what it was like to see others in that position. They expressed feeling constricted, tied up, and tense. Dani added that it felt dark, but safe.
>
> This turned the discussion to Dani wanting safety and realizing that she generally felt unsafe. Next, the therapist wondered if each member could express with their bodies the opposite body position. Dani felt uncomfortable with this exercise and stayed in her chair, but other members stood, stretched out their arms, and moved freely. To Dani, this looked frightening, but the members who stood said it felt great. This sparked a discussion about feeling free and how sometimes they each, in different ways, constrict themselves rather than experience

freedom. Before this session, Dani had never realized that she felt unsafe and constricted, because she was focused on maintaining others' safety. Through group, she accessed underlying feelings and through the help of others, she was able to see a new way of being and begin to explore what that might be like for her. Slowly, Dani experienced a sense of renewal. Her headaches ceased and she regained a sense of freedom to acknowledge, explore, and integrate lively parts of herself, such as her love of her family, her religious practices, and her friendships. Tuning in to her body allowed Dani to access underlying and unconscious feelings, which served in her overall sense of self-knowledge, integration, and life.

The somatic psychology literature suggests that the integration of bodily and sensory experiences into the cognitive and affective work of group therapy can facilitate personal growth, coherence of the self, and satisfaction in relationships (Cohen, 2011). Neuroscientists studying the embodiment of emotion observe that when we embody the emotion we are attempting to communicate and when the recipient of the information also embodies the emotion, then communication and comprehension are increased (Niedenthal, 2007). Processing embodied emotion in group therapy facilitates awareness, understanding, and empathy. Similarly, attachment theory posits that the earliest relationships depend on embodied attunement to create safety and security (Schore, 2001). Showing an experience through the use of movement and gestures in group therapy allows the members who have difficulty using words express themselves more freely (Cohen, 2011). Other group members can share in the experience and mirror it back, which further enhances self-awareness and insight.

Furthermore, Niedenthal (2007) suggests that the emotion we embody has an effect on subsequent behavior. For example, if a group member finds his heart racing and slumps in his chair while another group member is relaxed and sitting upright, the one who is sitting upright and relaxed is more likely to engage in session and is more likely to report positive experiences in group. Although this is probably not surprising, it is a reminder that neglecting sensory experiences and bodily communication can hinder treatment. When a group is attentive to and supportive of somatic expression, each member is more likely to engage and benefit from the therapy.

Using somatic material in group therapy is especially useful when the group experiences confusion or feels stuck, because somatic processing goes beneath the words and the linear process of thinking to access the unconscious (Cohen, 2011; Shields, 2012). Through nonjudgmental curiosity and experiments in the here-and-now moment of group therapy, material unfolds expressing underlying conflicts, tension, and emotion. Through this process, confusion can be clarified and impasses worked through.

Dani was well served by an experiential process group focused on understanding the self and others. The environment was supportive while providing ample space for the group process to develop. As a young adult, having a group of peers met her developmental need of developing of her unique identity by comparing herself to others her age. Meeting with a group of people, each offering a different perspective, helped open Dani's eyes to many different ways of relating and increased her thoughtfulness and intentionality in relationships. Finally, group therapy helped Dani integrate her emotions, thoughts, and bodily experiences, which not only alleviated her symptoms, but also facilitated greater self-awareness, insight, and renewal.

PROFESSIONAL CASE

The process of renewal plays a special role in the lives of professionals who themselves are responsible for the mental health of others. Therapists' restorative self-transformations are likely to have cascading positive effects in the lives of those they treat. Yet, the depth of the renewal depends on therapists' recognition and use of a medium that targets the sources of therapist depletion.

> June had been practicing as a therapist for 20 years. She had just seen her last child of three get married. This daughter had lived at home until the wedding and they had been extraordinarily close. Not only did they confide in one another but also spent many leisure time activities together. June's husband had died 5 years prior, and although she had grieved deeply, she had been too occupied with her children's activities and important life events to pause and fully reckon with the loss. Even after her daughter left home, she found that she was fairly well occupied with seeing her clients, pursuing continuing education activities, and consulting with other professionals. She thought about dating but convinced herself that she simply did not have the time to devote it. In fact, she did not even have time to spend with her close friends. Still, she noticed that whereas her early years of practice were characterized by a passionate engagement with her work, presently her sessions were characterized by a blandness that left her unfulfilled. At times, she was so beset by feelings of sleepiness in her sessions that she obtained a medical evaluation. No evidence of physical illness was obtained. Even though her clients ostensibly were making progress, June wondered whether they were deriving all of the benefit that they might. She also worried that perhaps they could sense a change in her and be perplexed by it.
>
> June talked about the pallid quality of her work in consultations with colleagues and they reassured her that such periods of

> disengagement are not unusual and that clinical practice has a natural ebb and flow. They described periods of their own in which their spirits took a downward turn. They assured her that their spirits rose without their having to take any particular action. They also noted that because June had been so busy with family the last number of years, her experience of a void at this time was natural. They expressed confidence that as June moved into the world more, her verve would return. However, June herself felt that this period was unlike any that she had had in her two decades of practice, and that perhaps something more was involved than just the natural waxing and waning of interest in her work. She also felt a level of fatigue that precluded her following her friends' advice to increase her social activity.

June's colleagues were correct in observing that clinicians, over the course of their professional lives, have varying levels of emotional engagement with their work. Yet, they may have been less than helpful in portraying her current psychological state as a natural phenomenon that should be endured rather than addressed constructively. Their laissez-faire attitude manifested toward June's waning interest in her work and their own similar distress is not unusual in mental health professionals in their stance toward their own difficulties. Research shows that mental health professionals are prone to ignore their own emerging problems (e.g., Sherman, 1996).

The Benefits of Therapists' Help Seeking

A more active response is potentially useful for several reasons. First, in psychotherapy, therapists are the medium through which interventions are delivered so that, as Elman (2007) stated, "The personal is the professional" (p. 608). To the extent that the therapist carries an emotional burden, he or she is less likely to be helpful to the client. For example, Guy, Poelstra, and Stark (1989) found that one third of all psychologists who described themselves as experiencing distress saw their psychological pain as adversely affecting their clients. Second, if June is like the vast majority of mental health professionals who enter their professions with a notion of making a contribution to others, her failure to enjoy deeply her work is likely to compromise her overall well-being. In her case, in particular, the departure of her daughter makes her work even more important as an arena in which to experience gratification. Third, although some psychological states are passing, no guarantee exists that this one will not be long-lived. Moreover, a risk in failing to grapple actively with this change in investment may lead to its intensification, to the detriment of both June and her clients.

June gave evidence of struggling with a life developmental issue. The past decades of her life were devoted to active parenting. She was called on to make a transition to an era in which parenting is less hands-on, and in which space exists for other types of relationships to achieve prominence in her life. June found this transition to be challenging. After all, the extent of her focus on family may have left little foundation for establishing other relationships as focal points in her life. June may also have emphasized family relationships as an avoidance of other kinds of intimacies that seemed more threatening. If so, this transition to a life with alternate intimate connections is likely to be especially daunting.

> June wisely viewed her current professional malaise as something worthy of investigation, but initially, felt that the question that arises is how to go about such an exploration. June consulted with a supervisor with whom she had worked for many years. The supervisor noted that as an individual therapist herself, her natural bent may be to pursue some type of individual-centered intervention. The supervisor pointed out to June three considerations that may lead to the conclusion that June would be well served by moving outside of the individual, dyadic paradigm.
>
> The first reason is that whereas June had learned to navigate around in the individual therapy situation, group psychotherapy offered greater novelty and, therefore, a stronger stimulus for change. A second reason the supervisor offered was that sharing her experiences with others in the group could ameliorate June's loneliness. She described group as entailing an intense emotional sharing that can provide a radical removal from a position of isolation. The supervisor's third reason was that group therapy offers a milieu in which June can make progress on the very particular difficulties that have sapped her life of joy and felt productivity. She is missing an intimate tie that could sustain her through the next developmental stage of life. Her insistence that she lacks the time to develop relationships suggests a defensive avoidance of closeness, possibly rooted in fear. The microcosmal aspect of group ensures that whatever apprehensions June has—nascent or fully palpable—are likely to emerge in her relationships with group members. They will be available for exploration and potentially, modification. After the discussion with the supervisor, June felt that participation in a group might be a good path to self-renewal. However, she wondered what type of group might be optimal for her needs.

Types of Therapeutic Groups

Broadly, three different therapeutic options are available to individuals seeking renewal: a psychotherapy group, a support group, or a self-help group. A fourth alternative that would specifically address her work as a therapist is a peer supervision group. Each of these types of groups can make a contribution to the process of renewal.

Self-Help Group

In a self-help group, individuals who share a particular difficult life situation meet together to share their painful feelings and obtain relief. Often, the members themselves convene these groups. If they have a facilitator, it rarely will be a mental health professional. The lack of a professional person reduces the power differential in a way that can empower members. However, for June, this absence of a professional leader could create a void that she might easily fill. The potential exists that, ultimately, she would emphasize her caretaking of other members to the neglect of her own needs. Although this same dynamic could play out in a traditional group, the mechanisms are much more fully in place for addressing it. Additionally, were June to consider the appropriateness of this type of group for her, she might recognize that her difficulties are not well-defined; in part, her task is to figure out what is underpinning her professional malaise. This circumstance, the amorphousness of her problem, would make it difficult for her to find a relevant self-help group. When June's husband died, certainly this option would have been available to her, and might have set her on a somewhat different path than the one she pursued following this loss.

Support Group

A support group is similar to a self-help group in that it revolves around a particular difficulty or problem. Support groups, like self-help groups, are designed to lessen the suffering of members, increase their ability to cope with their difficulties, and intensify their hopefulness about their futures (Brabender, Fallon, & Smolar, 2004). Unlike self-help groups, support groups are typically organized and conducted by a mental health professional. This feature enables some selection and composition considerations to be made in organizing the group. For example, the professional facilitator can consider whether some individuals have psychological needs that are so great as to lie outside of the group's scope. In contrast to traditional groups, in support groups, encouragement exists for members to provide support to one another outside of group. For a professional person seeking help, the fluid boundaries of contact can expand the potential for ethical dilemmas to arise. For example, the therapist may legitimately fear encountering a client through another support group member. Although such risks for boundary crossings can exist in traditional groups, they are lessened by the typical prohibition or regulation of extra-group contact. Also, as in the case of self-help groups, the nebulous nature of June's concerns would make the identification of an appropriate group difficult.

Both support and self-help groups, while perhaps not being ideal for June, have an aspect that is highly compatible with the notion of renewal. Neither of these types of groups assumes that the participant has a diagnosable condition. Often, individuals enter these groups because of their situations, not their persons. In fact, individuals frequently involve themselves in these groups without any expectation that they will receive insurance coverage for doing so. Fortunately, these types of groups are typically low cost or free so that insurance is not as critical as for participation in other formats. A difficulty can occur when an individual does warrant a diagnosis but does not obtain services at the level of intensity needed to address it.

Psychotherapy Group

In this type of group, members undertake the task of self and interpersonal exploration for the purpose of lessening suffering, improving relationships, and moving toward a higher level of well-being. These goals are, in most psychotherapy groups regardless of theoretical orientation, pursued through the use of process. That is, members focus on their relationships with one another as the means by which learning occurs. Mental health professionals conduct psychotherapy groups. Their training prepares them to select appropriate members, prepare members for their group experience, and facilitate the group in such a fashion that members can make systematic progress toward their goals (Brabender, 2011). The psychotherapy group enables members to take greatest advantage of that group's resource critical to psychological growth—group process or the flowering of patterns of interaction among members (Yalom & Leszcz, 2005). Although process will emerge in any group circumstance—including groups outside of the therapeutic realm—it is only if the therapist has the skill to harness it for the group's exploration that its potential is realized. However, the therapist's skill is insufficient to ensure progress: The group members must make a commitment to the kinds of interpersonal goals that the use of group process serves. Grappling with group process enables group members to deepen their understanding of their own experiences and those of others in a way that enables them to move to more effective ways of relating to others, thereby enhancing their potential for interpersonal fulfillment.

June did indeed join a psychotherapy group, and met with the therapist to craft three goals. First, what prevents June from achieving intimate relationships with men and possibly women? Recall that June had some ambivalence toward dating and she made time for her friends rarely. Second, what hinders June from maintaining a high level of engagement in her work? Third, is sleepiness a way of responding to events occurring in relationships? If so, what does the sleepiness mean and how else might she react to relational events? Let us look at each of these questions in relation to specific exchanges that June had in the group that might help her with each difficulty.

THREE VIGNETTES

The following three vignettes show how June's group work aided her in progressing toward her therapeutic goals. The group she joined was a mixed-gender, long-term group run from a psychodynamic orientation.

Vignette I

> June had been present in her group for a month. She had been reticent in the initial group sessions, but increasingly, was verbalizing her reactions to other members' communications. Often, her contributions took the form of a careful, sensitive questioning of members, getting them to disclose far more than they otherwise might have. June, however, disclosed very little. Members were very appreciative of her contribution and revealed that they felt nurtured by her.
>
> As the group progressed, Emile became increasingly pessimistic about his chances of succeeding in any area important to him. June became more and more active until the session in large part became an interaction between the two of them. The therapist asked to entire group to comment on the interactional pattern that had been developing. Members expressed their notion that Emile did not seem to be getting any better, and they felt concern for June who was so greatly exerting herself for him. They wondered what June was receiving in return. They worried that she might decide to leave the group because it wasn't meeting her needs. However, they also admitted they weren't sure what her needs were. They noted that June rarely put herself in a position wherein others could be helpful to her.

In this vignette, we see June begin to address the manner in which she structures her relationships with others. Although many aspects are yet to be developed, it would appear that June embraces a caregiver role to an extent that may leave her depleted. Her eschewal of her friendships outside the group may be somewhat akin to her avoidance of peer-level contact within the group. Furthermore, we see that June persists in her efforts with others even when they do not seem to take hold. Is this something that occurs in her life outside of the group, for example with her clients?

Vignette II

June has now been in the group for 3 months and has generally been experiencing a high level of comfort in, and support from, the group:

> June was quiet during the beginning of a particular session. Because during this phase of the group she had been consistently vocal, members wondered whether she was preoccupied with an issue. She said she had had an argument with her daughter right before she came to the group, but she felt that that happening was "out of the room," and her understanding was that they were to focus on their relationships with one another. The therapist observed June was correct in noting that much of the group's work was in the room by design. However, she also reminded June and the other members that no prohibition existed in members' making forays outside the group, and in fact, often these were useful.
>
> Tommy said he did not want to pressure her to share information about what had happened between June and her daughter but felt that if she would share more about her life outside the group, it would make her less of an enigma to him. Sarah said that she thought June hid behind rules and what she saw as proper boundaries. June sighed and commented that the interaction with her daughter was "dreadfully dull" because it was so repetitive. Her daughter had wanted June to go on a shore vacation with her family and June had insisted that her work would not permit a week off. She confessed to the group that she found her daughter's husband irritating. She worried that over a week's period of sustained contact, her irritation would show. Cindy observed that June avoided the intimate contact with her daughter in the way she did with them—by assuming an "It's all business" attitude. In this instance, we see Cindy drawing the kinds of parallels between in-the-room and out-of-the-room interpersonal behaviors that help members in general, and June in this instance, to transfer the learning from the group to their everyday situations. She wondered if in fact irritation was a problem for June in both places: by keeping distant, June could prevent herself from ever seeming annoyed, or impatient, or anything of that sort.

This moment in group life is important for June in two ways. First, another member is drawing a parallel between how June responds in and outside of the group, a parallel that will help June transfer learning in therapy to everyday situations. Second, the exploration of the parallel enables Cindy to propose a hypothesis for June's lack of intimate connection—a possible effort on her part to prevent emotions that she sees as negative from revealing themselves as she interacts with others.

Vignette III

June has been in the group 6 months and a new member, Darius, a young man of 26 years, has recently joined the group.

> Darius came into group talking about a new romantic relationship he had formed with a somewhat older woman. Darius was afraid to tell his parents about the relationship, fearing their disapproval. Still, he found this woman to be extremely compelling. As he talked about the relationship, it became clear that this woman provided him with a measure of structure and direction that abetted his functioning. Other members spoke of making "a go" of relationships that seemed odd or inappropriate to others. Although June customarily became quite active when Darius spoke, she was reticent during Darius's exploration of this topic with the other group members. Cindy noticed this fact, and June responded that her fatigue prevented her from concentrating more than minimally on the exchanges. She hardly knew what they were talking about. Members vocalized sympathy that June would be so tired. The therapist then speculated that this sleepiness was a response to what was occurring in the group. Tommy observed that what had been going on in that session was new and different in that Darius usually turned to June to solve his problems but now, it seemed less necessary for her to help him in the same way. He seemed more independent of her. June acknowledged that she found herself worrying about Darius—perhaps this relationship was not a healthy, constructive one, and it sounded as though it were moving too quickly. Cindy wondered aloud whether June had some worry about her own well-being: Did Darius's new involvement take away from how June participated in the group? June said it wasn't something she liked to think about. However, it was true that her sleepiness intensified after her daughter left their home. She liked having someone to care for, and her patients didn't satisfy this need totally. It made her feel at loose ends.
>
> The therapist noted that within the group, members took on familiar roles that provided comfort. She pointed out that when members face opportunities to step out of these roles, anxiety ensues and takes different forms, with sleepiness as being one form. Darius chimed in saying, "Yes, I get dizzy when that happens—when I can't be the little kid." The group laughed and other members admitted to finding solace in the predictable ways in which they interacted with one another. June seemed to be following this part of the conversation closely.

This vignette demonstrates the potential for groups to examine and ultimately understand the linkages between bodily experiences and members' feelings, urges, cognitions, and fantasies. This information is helpful because it strengthens members' abilities to discern that bodily reactions can be signposts to difficult internal reactions. For June, the linkage between sleepiness and anxiety empowered her to look beneath the sleepiness—to treat it as social information.

This session also highlights the benefit of groups to examine the roles they adopt in social interaction. Jacob Moreno (1940, 1959) wrote that psychological problems invariably entail fixity of the role a person adopts across social situations. June, who consistently maneuvers herself into a caregiving role, provides illustration of this point. To the extent that the environment allows her to function in this way, she functions comfortably; otherwise, she is ill at ease and avoids that circumstance through various means such as sleepiness. The identification of this role and the exploration of its limitations in providing fulfilling relationships enable the individual to move toward greater spontaneity and flexibility.

Peer Group Supervision

Although psychotherapy groups, support groups, and self-help groups offer emotional relief, social support, and interpersonal insight for individuals seeking self-renewal, a fourth alternative that would specifically address June's work as a therapist is a peer supervision group. A peer supervision group is a group of trusted colleagues who meet regularly to discuss clinical issues in a supportive and confidential setting (Kassan, 2010). The term peer *supervision* group implies a power differential with a supervisor that is responsible for the supervisee's patients. Many times peers choose to meet together for consultation purposes, without assuming responsibility for each other's cases. To be technically correct, these groups are peer *consultation* groups, although these labels are often used interchangeably.

Although research on the effects of participation in a peer supervision group is scant, many clinicians and professional organizations have noted that peer supervision groups have great potential to enhance the self-care of June and other therapists, as well as their care of their clients (American Psychological Association [APA], 2005; Kassan, 2010). One primary benefit of peer group supervision could be very important for June: reducing the isolation of private practice. However, other potential, positive consequences of peer consultation groups might also enhance her professional and personal functioning: recognizing a wide spectrum of solutions to clinical problems, preventing clinical burnout, reducing shame about errors and personal limitations, providing networking opportunities and referrals, and offering a forum for continuing learning and experience (Counselman & Weber, 2004).

The emotional support provided in peer consultation groups can be especially helpful in professional renewal, given that therapists face multiple occupational hazards and emotional vulnerabilities by meeting with people who are distressed. Therapists are vulnerable to stress due to professional burnout, vicarious traumatization, a tendency to overwork, unrealistic expectations, and the challenge of managing professional boundaries with clients (APA, n.d.). The consequences of ignoring these occupational hazards can range from personal distress, such as mood disturbances, relational difficulties, and reactivity, to professional impairment or clinical errors. In some cases, ignoring burnout and emotional distress can lead to poor clinical decision making and even ethical violations (APA, n.d.). Consulting with peers can normalize, validate, and broaden understanding, which can lead to better outcomes for both the therapist and client.

For those looking to form a new peer consultation group, APA notes a number of topics that should be addressed, including group membership, structure, content, size, and schedule (APA, 2005). When discussing group membership, it is important to consider the size of the group. Smaller groups allow for more sharing, while larger groups offer more perspectives. For someone like June whose personal difficulties are affecting her work, the former might be more suitable. It is also important that group members feel comfortable with each other, so when making decisions about who is invited to join the group, factors such as range of experience, theoretical orientation, and member expectations should be considered.

Next, the group must consider the structure of the group. Some groups take a formal structure with a group member presenting a case each meeting. Other groups prefer to remain informal, which allows group members to share cases and information more spontaneously. Finally, a decision also has to be made regarding leadership for administration and group process. While having a leader can aid in clarity and structure, many groups remain leaderless to increase the sense of investment in the group and cohesion between members.

The group must also come to agreement on the schedule. Depending on the needs of the members, the group could meet weekly, biweekly, or monthly. It could be open-ended or time-limited. And it could be a closed group or open, with new members coming at any time. Establishing a strong frame can promote safety and clear expectations, which create reliability and effectiveness.

Once the structure, size, and schedule have been worked out, the group must decide on the range of issues that will be discussed in consultation. Challenging cases, practice management problems, and professional or ethical dilemmas are common issues discussed in supervision groups, but quality supervision often goes beyond content to include process. Therefore, a supervision group where members agree to participate in discussion around their own emotional responses, impairments, enactments, and associations can promote additional learning and insight. This type of process requires trust and vulnerability, which takes time and experience to develop (Counselman & Weber, 2004).

When professionals meet together to discuss the challenges associated with being a therapist, the support and dialogue can alleviate a host of emotional and professional concerns. Peer supervision groups can also offer preventative care to help keep professionals at the top of their game and prevent future problems by providing a forum for sustained dialogue and renewal.

In fact, many therapists use peer supervision groups as a staple in self-care, rather than a solution to be activated when problems arise. Peer supervision groups can be useful whether an individual is experiencing difficulty and regardless of the other forms of group or individual therapy that an individual chooses to engage in. Long after the therapist's therapy is over, membership in a peer consultation group can be usefully continued. In a case like June's, she may have been well served by a peer supervision group that could have helped her notice the change in herself as she experienced it. The group could have also helped her think about additional resources to add when she experienced professional malaise. Especially for those professionals who work in isolation, peer supervision groups can offer a place to observe, talk about, and problem-solve issues as they come up.

PRINCIPLES OF GROUP PSYCHOTHERAPY FOSTERING RENEWAL

The two cases that were presented in this chapter are very different from one another. Dani is a very young person; June, well advanced in years. Dani has a history of psychological difficulties, whereas June has enjoyed a relatively high level of psychological health. Dani still has many crucial life decisions ahead of her whereas June has set many elements of her personal and professional course. Despite these differences, we see both as benefiting from group psychotherapy, and a renewal focus within the group. Four features characterize group treatment serving the goal of renewal.

The first feature is that the goal of the group, the enhancement of the well-being of the individual, does not require that the individual have a set of symptoms corresponding to a formal diagnosis. In considering Dani's presentation, we could well imagine that she would qualify for a symptom-based diagnosis in a standard diagnostic system. However, June may fall short of meeting the criteria for a diagnosis. Both of these individuals could undergo renewal through participation in group psychotherapy.

The absence of diagnosable disorder has implications for the financing of group participation in that third-party payment almost always requires a diagnosis. Fortunately, group treatment can be more readily paid out-of-pocket given that the per-session fee tends to be about half of what is charged for individual therapy. In some groups, a sliding fee scale increases its accessibility to members across the economic continuum (Brabender, 2002). Whatever the monetary arrangement is, the terms must be clear and explicit in the informed consent.

The second feature is that the focus of the group is holistic. An emphasis on renewal requires the instigation of change in multiple sectors of the person—emotional, cognitive, motivational, spiritual, and somatic. We saw the somatic focus in both cases. With time, the group would have helped Dani to explore any lingering issues related to her lessening tie with Catholicism. A focus on this range of areas entails the assumption is made that growth in one area can instigate development in another. A requirement on the part of the member who is joining group for the purpose of renewal is receptiveness to exploring multiple domains. A member holding the position "I only came here to work on" would soon become frustrated with other members' seemingly irrelevant excursions.

A third element is that because the aim of the work is holistic, it often requires a myriad of types of interventions, with each type being geared to abet the functioning of a particular system. For example, in Dani's case, the therapist did not use merely verbal interventions, but also introduced a somatic component into the treatment in order to ameliorate Dani's headaches. In June's case, working with her sleepiness via interpretation proved to be sufficient to making an alteration in this somatic reaction. As Shields (2012) points out, attention to the somatic elements of experiences can be a route to the identification of unconscious wishes that are informing the individual's everyday social behaviors. Although a wide range of theoretical orientations may be compatible with a renewal focus, the therapist may find him- or herself dipping into the interventional repertoire of another orientation to accommodate the members' needs.

A fourth element of renewal group therapy is that it encompasses the notion that over the course of one's life, an individual will encounter periods in which the revitalizing effects of a group are helpful. Frequently, difficulty passing from one developmental stage to another can precipitate the need for psychological stance. This stance affects the decision process in relation to termination in that it reduces the stakes. The member need not ascertain whether he or she is ready to be separated from the group into perpetuity. Rather, the invitation is made clear that the member is able to return to the group whenever the member perceives it to be helpful in resolving life issues. Were such a return to be made, it would be celebrated as an act of self-care rather than lamented as a sign of regression. Although a more traditional group psychotherapeutic experience does not preclude a member's return, in a group conducted within a renewal framework, this invitation is made more explicit.

CONCLUSIONS

Individuals who experience depletion or stasis require an infusion of resources that group treatment can provide on the road to self-renewal. As the berry-seeking traveler from our opening parable learned, what a group offers is not only a multitude of resources, but also different types of socioemotional provisions. The spectrum of perspectives and relating styles in treatment groups are key to accommodating the diversity of needs with which members present. Moreover, as we see in this chapter, groups themselves are diverse in format; they may be structured as psychotherapy, support, or self-help groups, with each providing somewhat different renewal opportunities. For mental health professionals, peer supervision groups foster a kind of renewal that can enhance a therapist's satisfaction in her work, lessen her vulnerability to professional hazards, and improve her effectiveness with her clients.

REFERENCES

American Psychological Association, Board of Professional Affairs' Advisory Committee on Colleague Assistance (n.d.). *Professional health and well-being for psychologists.* Retrieved from http://www.apapracticecentral.org/ce/self-care/well-being.aspx

American Psychological Association, Communications Staff. (2005). *Not going it alone: Peer consultation groups.*

Brabender, V. (2002). *Introduction to group therapy.* New York, NY: Wiley.

Brabender, V. (2011). Group psychotherapies. In S. B. Messer & A. S. Gurman (Eds.), *Essential psychotherapies: Theory and practice* (3rd ed., pp. 460–493). New York, NY: Guilford Press.

Brabender, V., Fallon, A., & Smolar, A. (2004). *Essentials of group therapy.* New York, NY: Wiley.

Cohen, S. (2011). Coming to our senses: The application of somatic psychology to group psychotherapy. *International Journal of Group Psychotherapy*, *61*(3), 397–413.

Counselman, E. F., & Weber, R. L. (2004). Organizing and maintaining peer supervision groups. *International Journal of Group Psychotherapy*, *54*(2), 125–143.

Elman, N. S. (2007). Who needs self-care anyway? We all do! *Professional Psychology: Research and Practice*, *38*(6), 608–610.

Guy, J. D., Poelstra, P. L., & Stark, M. J. (1989). Professional distress and therapeutic effectiveness: National survey of psychologists practicing psychotherapy. *Professional Psychology: Research and Practice*, *20*, 48–50.

Kassan, L. D. (2010). *Peer supervision groups: How they work and why you need one.* New York, NY: Aronson.

Moreno, J. L. (1940). Mental catharsis and psychodrama. *Sociometry*, *3*, 209–244.

Moreno, J. L. (1959). The scientific meaning and the global significance of group psychotherapy. *Acta Psycotherapeutica*, *42*(7), 148–167.

Niedenthal, P. M. (2007). Embodying emotion. *Science*, *316*, 1002–1005.

Schore, A. N. (2001). The effects of early relational trauma on right brain development, affect regulation, and infant health. *Infant Mental Health Journal, 22*, 201–269.

Sherman, M. D. (1996). Distress and professional impairment due to mental health problems among psychotherapists. *Clinical Psychology Review, 16*, 299–315.

Shields, W. (2012). On Suzanne Cohen's (2011) paper: "Coming to our senses: The application of somatic psychology to group psychotherapy." *International Journal of Group Psychotherapy, 62*(1), 143–145.

Yalom, I., & Leszcz, M. (2005). *The theory and practice of group psychotherapy* (5th ed.). New York, NY: Basic Books.

CHAPTER

16

Renewal in Marital and Family Systems

Paul Giblin

INTRODUCTION

Family specialist Dolores Curran published the results of a survey, *Stress and the Healthy Family*, in 1985. To my knowledge it is the only study that had more responses than questionnaires originally sent out. Family members photocopied the questionnaire and gave it to friends. Families were eager to talk about their experiences with stress. A surprising finding of the study was that family members rank ordered specific stress items quite differently, while overall agreeing to high levels of stress in their lives.

Author and psychologist Mary Pipher (1997) believes that the stresses contemporary couples and families face are both toxic and unknown to generations past:

> For the first time in history, children are not being socialized by their parents. Our children are being raised by TVs and other appliances. Multinational corporations have become the culture's storytellers, teaching children what life is all about. . . . We have families isolated in their homes, each member in a different room with their appliance of choice: a television, computer, a stereo. (p. 27)

Fast forward from the mid-1980s and mid-1990s to 2013. I suggest that levels of couple-family stress and anxiety have only increased. The need for couple-family self-care and renewal is all the more dramatic. In this chapter we explore the meaning and practice of self-care and renewal for couples and families and attempt to answer five questions: What is meant by the term *renewal*? What images or metaphors might accurately convey this process? What is involved in the process of *renewal*? With what major stressors, threats, and/or obstacles are contemporary couples-families struggling? And finally, with what intervention strategies might clinicians and educators assist couples-families in their struggles?

Definition of Terms

Curiously, the term *renewal* rarely surfaces in the clinical marital-family literature. "Family resilience," "marital and family enrichment," yes, but not "renewal." One renews a license, membership, subscription, acquaintance, or vows. What does it mean to renew a marriage or family? Terms that come to mind include: to care for, refresh, reform, revive, regenerate, rebalance, recharge, replenish, reconnect, remember, return; to energize, empower, strengthen, to take perspective, to take refuge. Sometimes it is enlightening to contrast a term with its opposite. For example, the opposite of renewal might be: to be spent, depleted, exhausted, fragmented, empty, lost, unbalanced, disempowered, disconnected, weakened, stressed or burnt out, having lost perspective. What terms come to your mind?

What images or metaphors speak to renewal? Consider the following: to drink from a well or spring; to find refuge in a harbor; to gather around the fireplace/hearthside; to check one's compass or North Star. How might a couple or family be assisted by developing their own image of renewal, that is, what or where is their well or North Star?

Elements of Renewal

What is involved in the process of couple-family renewal? I suggest that at least three key processes occur. First they are *reconnecting*. The pace and busyness of life pull couples and families apart. Pipher (1997) notes:

> Ten years ago, I would spend a lot more time talking with families about their feelings about each other and their family-of-origin than I do today. I would have focused on the way people communicate with each other and so on. These days I spend much of the time treating people's schedules. I find that the problems most families bring into therapy today are directly or indirectly related to time. (p. 31)

Pipher (1996) goes on to describe strategies for helping families find ways to connect, to spend time with each other, share meals, and spend time outdoors in nature. Attachment theorists and emotion-focused marital therapists like Susan Johnson, Leslie Greenberg, and Rhonda Goldman all view marital and family conflict to be a falling out of connection (Greenberg & Goldman, 2008; Johnson,

2004, 2008). Couples and families find ways to connect, reconnect, and stay connected, first with themselves, then with each other, and finally with a supportive community beyond themselves.

A second element of marital and family renewal is *repairing*. Breaks in emotional connection are inevitable. Differences, disappointments, disagreements, and misunderstandings are givens in intimate relationships. How to understand the cause of breaks varies according to the theoretical orientation of the practitioner. The question is not whether such breaks will occur, but rather how quickly they will be repaired. Many marital authors assert that without breaks and conflict there is no impetus for growth (Hendrix, 1988; Levine & Levine, 1995; Welwood, 1990, 1997). To repair is to find understanding, to apologize and forgive, and to return hope to the relationship. Failure to develop ongoing repair strategies is a significant divorce predictor (Gottman, 1999).

A third element of marital and family renewal is the process of *revisioning*, returning to an original, perhaps discarded vision for the meaning and direction of their lives together. Couples return to their founding hopes, dreams, and visions. This may be a short-term, daily, or weekly process. This is the engaged couple who meets each Thursday for breakfast to review the week past and discuss the week to come. They agree to air issues, concerns, and resentments and to carry no baggage forward into the next week. This is the married couple who revisits and/or revises their vows each anniversary, or the couple who makes seasonal or annual trips to family-of-origin special places or other sacred spaces. This is the family who, for one dinner a week, has a "family meeting" to discuss and/or negotiate activities and schedules. Revisioning often means recommitting to each other, to the couple or family relationship, and to a broader purpose for their lives (Shem & Surrey, 1999; Welwood, 1990, 1997). Marriage and marital therapy researcher John Gottman (1999) suggests that marital stalemate often results from couple disconnection from their hopes, dreams, and visions.

Couples and families that fail to consciously articulate their own vision then default to the cultural "dominant narrative" and find that such a vision with its related values fails to sustain a vibrant life (Covey, 1997; Doherty, 1997, 2001; Hendrix, 1988; Sheras & Koch-Sheras, 2006). I am reminded of the saying from Proverbs, 29:18 "Where there is no vision the people perish" (21st Century King James Version, 1994). Let us return to these three elements of renewal as they play out in intervention strategies. Meanwhile, let us explore the importance of renewal in couple and family life.

Need for Renewal

Why is renewal so important for couples and families? What are the stresses, pushes and pulls, the obstacles and threats, that couples and families encounter today? I suggest they are legion. Here I focus on four stresses in particular, that is, those associated with time, values, loss of ritual, and ambivalence about the body.

Time Stress

The busyness and pace of life, the competing demands for time, family member extracurricular activities, the challenge to balance work-family-self time, family members carrying more than one job, the contagion of "hurry sickness," the attractiveness of multitasking, all present considerable stress for families today. Family members communicate with texts and messages left on the refrigerator! Mary Pipher treats people's schedules. John Gottman (1999) argues that the difference between happy, satisfied couples and dissatisfied couples is "five magic hours." That is happy, satisfied couples take time to connect with each other at the beginning and end of each day (partings and reunions), share admiration, appreciation, and affection, and have a regular date each week, totaling 5 hours each week.

Marital and family therapist Peter Fraenkel, in *Synch Your Relationship, Save Your Marriage* (2011) observes that marital conflict often results from "couple arrhythmia," partners being out of sync with each other. Fraenkel helps spouses become aware of and negotiate their different rhythms in pace, punctuality, and orientation to time. He notes that stress highlights such differences.

In *The Medical Marriage: A Couple's Survival Guide* (2000) and *Beat Stress Together: The Supercouple Syndrome* (1998), authors Wayne and Mary Sotile address the busyness and time dilemmas of dual career and especially medical couples. Too often couples fail to live in the present and suffer from a psychology of postponement. They believe things will be better following: graduation from medical or law school, completion of residency, passing board exams, or making partner. Couples fail to appreciate that their marriage is an organic reality that needs ongoing nurture, especially in its early stages. Their profession's demand for time easily compromises marital and family life. Fatigue, sleep deprivation, lack of time together, loneliness, isolation, and constant interruptions all stress such relationships. Such couples suffer from the "hurry sickness."

It is New Year's Day as I write (rewrite!) this paper. My wife and I spent last evening at the lovely condominium of friends. The husband collects clocks, old, beautiful, mostly wooden, working clocks. There were four clocks in the bathroom. Not helpful. There were clocks small and large in the halls and in every room. There were several extraordinary grandfather clocks. I asked of his interest at dinner but did not receive a satisfactory answer. I wondered (to myself) if his many clocks serve to reduce time pressures, certainly he "has plenty of time," and increases his sense of control.

Psychiatrist Stephen Rechtschaffen (1996) introduces the image of "timeshifting" in a book of the same name. With this wonderful image he asserts the need to be able to shift gears/time perspectives, as situations warrant. He describes the interesting phenomenon of "entrainment," that is, the process by which rhythms fall into synchronization with each other:

> For the last hundred years or so, Western society has set an overly fast rhythm, a rhythm that varies only in that it is continually getting faster,

> urging us to do more, produce more, learn more. This rhythm of fast and still faster is a relatively new phenomenon, and no one seems to know how to vary it. Most of us don't even think of varying it, because society judges it "productive," and because we as individuals are so entrained with it that we don't consciously realize we want to change it. Even if we recognize that something is wrong, we don't know how to change the rhythm, how to entrain with something slower, more "human." Most of us don't know how to shift time. . . . We don't know how to pause for contemplation, to take time for ourselves, to go from the frenetic to the peaceful, to truly relax, to take note, to feel. (p. 27)

Value Stress

Strong marriages and resilient families are guided by a clear belief system and consensual set of values. They are able to make meaning of adversity, maintain hope and unity in the face of crisis, and continue to connect with a sense of purpose beyond their individual, daily needs (Walsh, 2006). However, it is increasingly difficult for couples and families to articulate and live according to such a value base. Pipher (1997) likens contemporary family life to a house without walls. Families are bombarded with a materialist, consumerist, individualist vision and values from the media that parents have less and less control over:

> I am much more likely to talk to people about their values—that is the North Star that orients their life—rather than their feelings or communication style. . . . For the first time in history, children are not being socialized by their parents. Our children are being raised by TVs and other appliances. Multinational corporations have become the culture's storytellers, teaching children what life is about. We have families isolated in their homes, each member in a different room with their appliance of choice: a television, a computer, a stereo. No one's talking. (p. 31)

By our choices we define ourselves. Are we healthier and happier by virtue of the abundance of choices made available to us today? In *The Paradox of Choice* (2004), author Barry Schwartz describes the dilemma of "choice overload" that leads to increasingly challenging decision making: not settling for good enough, seeking only the best, buyer's remorse, postdecision regret, reversible decisions, all of which contribute to increased stress and decreased satisfaction. Author Sheena Iyengar in *The Art of Choosing* (2010) continues this theme as she analyzes the process of decision making. "We assume that if having choice is good, having more must be better. For all of its positive qualities, however, a wide variety of choice can also be confusing and overwhelming" (p. 179).

Research regularly identifies commitment as a key component of strong marriages and healthy family functioning (Giblin, 2011; Sheras & Koch-Sheras, 2006). However, contemporary attitudes toward relationship commitment are in significant flux. Commitment requires maturity, self-knowledge, willingness to sacrifice, investment in the relationship, ability to cooperate and collaborate, as well as carry a long-term view of marriage (Carter & Sokol, 1998; Haughey, 1975; Stanley, 1998). However, long-term commitment as a societal and relationship value seems to be losing ground. See, for example: increasingly visible extramarital affairs, commitment violations seen in work and financial sectors, corporate mergers wherein employees lose their jobs and/or pensions, and Ponzi schemes wherein people lose their life savings. Long-term commitment and the trust on which it is based are increasingly called into question.

Stress Associated With Loss of Marital and Family Ritual

Healthy ritual life is an essential element of marital and family well-being (Cox, 1998; Imber-Black & Roberts, 1992). Typically rituals serve to connect, heal, establish and reinforce identity, and facilitate stability and transition, among other functions. However, given increased mobility, increased time stresses, increased emphasis on individualism, and decreased institutional affiliation, family ritual life is threatened. This is not a recent phenomenon. In 1950, Bossard and Boll published their 10-year study, *Ritual in Family Living.* They concluded that family rituals were indeed changing, from more religious to secular, public to private, prescribed to more individually constructed, adult-centered to child-centered, and neighborhood to isolated families. They lamented that instead of gathering around the hearthside and generating song, story, or other entertainment, family members were interacting less and were focused on the Victrola.

Marital and family therapist William Doherty addresses the diminishment of marital and family ritual in *The Intentional Family* (1997) and *Take Back Your Marriage* (2001). Doherty is from Minneapolis and lives adjacent to the Mississippi River. He draws analogies to the river when he (1997) notes,

> If you get married or have a child without a working plan for your family's journey, you will likely head "south" toward less closeness, less meaning, and less joy over time. A family, like a canoe, must be steered or paddled, or it won't take you where you want to go. The natural drift of family life in contemporary America is toward slowly diminishing connection, meaning, and community. (pp. 7–8)

Doherty's answer to this problem is to work at becoming a more ritualizing intentional family. He focuses in particular on rituals of connection and healing, and rites of passage. In *From Beginning to End: Rituals of Our Lives* (1996), minister and author Robert Fulghum addresses this same diminishment of family rituals surrounding birth, weddings, and death and the accompanying psychological price that is paid.

Stress/Ambivalence Associated With the Body

Family therapist pioneer Virginia Satir (1972) asserted that everyone needs eight hugs a day for maintenance, not growth. When we connect with the body, we are energized (Borysenko, 2011), find wisdom (Whitehead & Whitehead, 2001), receive clarity for decision making (Cornell, 1996), locate blocks to healing (Cornell, 1996; Schwartz, 1995, 2008), reduce anxiety and stress (Kabat-Zinn, 1990), and find pleasure and relaxation (McCarthy & McCarthy, 2004). Yet our society is entirely ambivalent, confused, and polarized about the body, pleasure, and that which is sexual. Society deifies the young, beautiful body and pleasure, while church institutions deify relationship, commitment, and are suspect of pleasure. In both circles "sexual" is reduced to genital activity. Lost in the conversation are the gender, personality, emotional, and affectional dimensions of sexuality. Lost in the conversation is the broader understanding of eros or the erotic as the drive for connection, unity, beauty, and creativity. It is no wonder that sexuality and the body fail to serve as meaningful resources in marital and family life. Theologian Marva Dawn (1993) notes how easily social intercourse, the desire for emotional closeness with another, is so easily confused with sexual intercourse, in a society that fails to understand the broader meaning of eros. She invites the reader to attend to his or her needs for community, social connectedness, and attachment.

STRATEGIES FOR RENEWAL

I have suggested that renewal in marital and family systems involves at least three interrelated processes, that is, reconnecting, repairing, and revisioning. Renewal is a process of looking back as well as looking ahead. There is a critical need for marital and family renewal, be it daily, weekly, seasonally, or longer. The stresses and threats to contemporary marital and family life are multiple. Four particular areas of stress were examined: busyness, pace, and imbalance of contemporary life; struggles related to whose vision and values guide marital and family life; diminishment/loss of ritual life; and failure to receive the body as a resource. In the final section of this chapter I focus on intervention strategies that follow from these major areas of stress.

Time Strategies

Couples and families who "don't have time" need to learn ways to create time. Couples and families who know only two speeds, fast and faster, need to learn to "timeshift." Couples and families out of sync with each other need to adjust their rhythms and perspectives. Couples and families living in the future, that is, "the psychology of postponement" need to learn to come into the present. Buddhist monk and activist Thich Nhat Hanh (1999) defines meditation as the process of stopping, calming, and going inside. How do couples-families stop, calm, and go inside? It begins with making time and spending time with each other. This does not have to involve a large amount of time. The absolute amount of time is less important than the perception that some quality time is being spent together. This is the dual career couple who do the dishes together each evening in spite of having five able-bodied teenage sons. When asked why the sons do not do dishes they explained it was the only time each day they had to talk with each other, and if they were interrupted, the violator had to do the dishes. They were never interrupted. This is the Marriage Encounter (Berger & Hannah, 1999; Hunt, Hof, & DeMaria, 1998) trained couple who take 20 minutes each evening to journal about their feelings of the day, then share and discuss their journals, that is, "10 and 10."

Couples often report how easily they are caught up in daily/weekly routines. "We get up in the morning . . . go to work . . . come home . . . go to bed, get up the next morning, and start the same thing all over again." "I feel like I live most of my life in a trance." How are couples and families to encounter their lives with greater vitality and awareness? The spiritual practices of centering prayer (Keating, 1986; Reininger, 1998) and mindfulness meditation (Hanh, 1999; Kabat-Zinn, 2005; Kornfield, 1993) offer possible answers. Stephen Levine, a hospice therapist and Buddhist practitioner, wondered why his patients, who had a finite time to live, all had a higher quality of life than those of us who do not know our end time. So he and his wife lived for 1 year "as if" they would die at the end of that time (Levine & Levine, 1998). The quality of their lives increased as they engaged each day with greater intentionality and attentionality. They paid more attention to life's details and to the desires with which they approached each day. To live life "in a trance" is to be out of touch with one's heart's desires. The daily practices of mindfulness meditation, body relaxation, and yoga were the center of the Levines' spiritual practice. Paradoxically, they felt sad as the yearlong experiment neared its end. Knowing they were going to live, they feared losing the vitality of the "as if" year!

Couples and families need to find strategies to "come into the now," to live in the present, not in the future, not in the "psychology of postponement." What would it be like to put aside one's watch, clocks, and other electronic devices for a day or week? Some people do so 1 day a week (i.e., Sabbath). A fellow I know took the dramatic step of removing the second, minute, and hour hands of his watch and in their place posted the word "now." He continued to wear his watch and every time he checked it he came into the "now"! A small town in rural New Hampshire agreed to put away every clock and watch for 1 week. Their intention was to free themselves from clock-determined time and live according to nature's clock and their own internal sense of time. They reported being more relaxed, energized, and aware, enjoyed themselves and each other more, and were generally "on time" for their commitments (newspaper source unknown).

Many religious couples and families, Jewish and Christian, find "keeping Sabbath" a deeply meaningful strategy for "timeshifting," for creating "time out of time." Sabbath (or sabbathing as a verb) creates special time (kairos) in the midst of ordinary time (chronos); it introduces a helpful and healthful rhythm to life. In *Keeping the Sabbath Wholly* (1989), theologian Marva Dawn focuses on four Sabbath practices: ceasing, resting, embracing, and feasting. It is about *ceasing* work, productivity, accomplishment, anxiety, acquisitiveness, and the need to be in control. It is about *resting* spiritually, physically, emotionally, and intellectually. Dawn tells the story of a wagon train on its way from St. Louis to Oregon. They were in the habit of celebrating Sabbath. As winter approached, half the group decided to push on and no longer honor Sabbath. This group was in fact the latter to arrive at the destination. Sabbath is about *embracing* intentionality, values of the faith community, time, caring, giving, vocation, and wholeness. And Sabbath is about *feasting* in worship, on the eternal, with music, beauty, food, and affection. Sabbathing is a countercultural practice in a culture that prizes itself on multitasking, productivity, speed, and access 24/7/365.

Vision and Values

Couples do well to regularly assess their marital/family vision and values. Where do they stand relative to their North Star? As mentioned above, Sabbath practice is designed to renew one's vision and values grounded in a faith community. Giving is valued over receiving, appreciating above striving after, slowing down above speed and multitasking, resting in God's embrace above individualism and self-sufficiency. Sabbathing invites couples and families to enter into community with like-minded couples and families.

Aids to facilitate couples and families in a vision/values clarification process are found in several sources. Marital and family therapists Sheras and Koch-Sheras (2006) provide suggestions for couples to create a shared couple vision. They suggest that spouses regularly update/rewrite their marriage vows. They believe that marital therapy needs to begin with clarification of a couple's marital vision and commitment, and only after that move to communication and conflict resolution. The authors share their vision that marriage has a purpose and meaning beyond the needs and happiness of the spouses. Without commitment to something greater than themselves, typically expressed as spiritual beliefs and practice, a couple will not create or maintain a vital life together. Buddhist marital therapist John Welwood articulates this point well in *Journey of the Heart: Intimate Relationship and the Path of Love* (1990):

> In its final outreach, conscious love leads two lovers beyond themselves toward a greater connectedness with the whole of life. Indeed, two people's love will have no room to grow unless it develops this larger focus beyond themselves. The larger arc of a couple's love reaches out toward a feeling of kinship with all of life, what Teilhard de Chardin calls "a love of the universe." Only in this way can love, as he puts it, "develop in boundless light and power." (p. 206)

Couples and families benefit from a regular return to and exploration of their founding vision and related values. I am convinced that many couples and families today suffer from a lack of vision and imagination. Helpful resources for assisting couples in this reflective process are found in Hendrix (1988) and Covey (1997).

Rituals and Routines

Rituals contribute to a sense of marital and family meaning, identity, and belonging. They facilitate communication, stability and change, and healing. Family rituals buffer the stresses associated with parental alcoholism (Wolin & Bennet, 1980, 1984), death (Giblin & Hug, 2006), poverty, and divorce (Fiese, 2006). Rituals and routines have a self-righting function, helping families get back on track when exposed to risk; rituals provide predictability, consistency, and self-efficacy, all of which are compromised as family stress increases. Families in which there is emotional cutoff are often good candidates for ritual development (Fiese, 2006).

Rituals (VanderHart) are "prescribed symbolic acts that must be performed in a certain way and in a certain order and may or may not be accompanied by verbal formulas" (as cited in Fiese, 2006, p. 109). Couples and families can be assisted in exploring their beliefs about rituals and routines. When spouses share similar views on the importance of routines and rituals, especially religious celebrations, for example, they typically are happier in their marriage. Ritual assessment explores beliefs and practices. "Tell me about the rituals and routines in your marriage (family). Mealtimes, holidays, seasons, birthdays, anniversaries, vacations, bedtime?" This is diagnostic and typically an engaging line of inquiry. In doing genograms it is informative to inquire about rituals surrounding births, deaths, and normative and nonnormative changes in client lives. Families can be helped to retrieve treasured rituals, to discard rituals that have been outgrown, to balance skewed ritual life that favors only one side of a family, and to create new rituals as needed.

Researcher and family therapist Barbara Fiese (2006) notes that threats to maintaining family rituals are increasing, especially related to technology. She notes that home space is becoming less communal and more individual, that 36% of households with children 0–6 years of age have televisions in their bedrooms, and this number increases to 43% for children 4–6 years old. Parents are reading less to children, have less face to face interaction, and family members are more isolated. John Gottman (1999) offers a similar observation: "It is a sad fact that less than a third of U.S. families eat dinner together regularly, and more than half of those that do have the television on during dinner. This effectively ends conversation during dinner" (p. 250). Fiese (2006) suggests that clinicians focus on one routine/ritual that can be preserved or developed that might have a powerful effect on the couple/family. She cites the example of a family meal, which need not take more than 20–30 minutes, four times a week. Pipher (1996) suggests turning off all electronic devices for some periods of couple/family time, including meals, and spending time with each other, especially outdoors. Gottman (1999) urges couples to pay attention to their rituals surrounding partings, reunions, admiration and appreciation, affection, and weekly dates. He found that couples who devoted an extra 5 hours a week to these areas had dramatically improved marriages. In *Sleeping With Bread: Holding What Gives You Life* (1995), Dennis, Sheila, and Matthew Linn adapt the spiritual practice of the Ignatian Examen to family life. They suggest that family members share their answers to two questions at dinner each evening. The questions are: "what gave you life today, energized you, for which you are most grateful, i.e., your high?" and "what drained you today, what you struggled with the most, what you feel least grateful for, i.e., your low?" Families and couples report this to be a powerful ritual of connection.

Ambivalence About the Body

In this final section of the chapter I suggest that the body is a largely underutilized resource for marital/family renewal. How might the body serve to reconnect, repair, and reorient relationships? Gottman's (1999) multimethod research is again informative. In clinical and observational laboratory sessions he tracks spousal physiological responses to conflict. As conflict and anxiety increase spouses become "emotionally flooded," and "emotionally hijacked." Flight/fight hormones course through their blood. Their perceptual world narrows as does their problem-solving capability. They become reactive more than reflective. Gottman's findings as related to men are intriguing. Men's physiology reacts more quickly and returns to calm more slowly than that of their wives. Men sooner experience "flooding" and respond by shutting down, withdrawing, and becoming defensive than their female partners.

Couples, parents, and families need body-based skills to manage their stress responses. Gottman (1999) helps bring couples into greater body awareness through the use of feedback monitors attached to their wrists. Welwood (1990, 1997) invites partners to pay attention to two overall body senses, when they feel open, receptive, flexible; and when they feel closed, rigid, and defensive. Partners practice breathing and relaxation exercises. When sessions become heated, they are encouraged to use their body awareness and practices to bring themselves back into calm. When family therapist Schwartz (1995, 2008) added body awareness to his parts work in *Internal Family Systems Therapy*, the depth of the work increased dramatically. Greenberg and Goldman (2008) describe calming and relaxation skills, that is, self-soothing and partner-soothing as essential to their approach of *Emotion-Focused Couples Therapy*. In a largely autobiographical work, *Fried: Why You Burn Out and How to Revive*, psychologist Joan Borysenko (2011) writes about the essential role body work, that is, meditation, body scan, yoga, and movement exercises, played in her encounters with stress and burnout.

Buddhist practitioners Stephen and Ondrea Levine (1995), in *Embracing the Beloved: Relationship as a Path of Awakening*, provide spouses with a series of wonderful comeditation exercises. The "dyadic bonding meditation" facilitates connection. One spouse lies down on the floor while the other sits adjacent to him/her. The seated partner observes the other's breathing, places his or her hand on their abdomen, and seeks to come into resonance, entrainment, with the partner. The "soft belly meditation" is designed to facilitate release of toxic emotions and encourage healing. Partners learn to recognize "hard belly" where they carry defensiveness, pain, fear, and anger and shift to "soft belly" where spaciousness and compassion reside. Partners explore the costs of "hard belly," emotional armoring and the benefits of "soft belly" openness.

Touch is a basic human need. We need to be held and seen. Attachment behavior is mediated by touch and physical proximity. Anthropologists have noted that cultures that are comfortable, if not extravagant with touch tend to be nonviolent, while cultures that tend to be "hands off" tend to be more violent. Affection is easy and frequent early in a relationship. It can tend to get lost in favor of sexual intercourse. Touch is a nonverbal way of communicating love and belonging (Chapman, 1992; Satir, 1972). Gottman's research suggests that affection is a key factor distinguishing happy from unhappy marriages. In doing genogram work clinicians are encouraged to explore family and cultural histories surrounding comfort with and practices of affection and touch.

How essential is sex for marital well-being? It is a key component of reconnection, repair, and revisioning. Sex is one form of intimacy and needs to be part of an integrated sense of intimacy. Other forms of intimacy include emotional, spiritual, intellectual, leisure and recreation, social, aesthetic, and work commitment (Dyer & Dyer, 1991). When a couple's sexual life carries too much responsibility for these other areas of intimacy, it becomes overburdened. This is especially true for men who overidentify with work, are emotionally restricted, and lack an extended friendship system. Theologian Marva Dawn (1993) observes that "social intercourse" is often confused with "sexual intercourse" in cultures like ours. When social connection is a basic need and a culture is characterized by isolation, then sexual intercourse is sought when in fact many are in search of social intercourse.

Theologian Christine Gudorf (1992) offers the following introduction to a provocative article about marital sexuality: "Ever consider that sex—good, frequent, mutually pleasurable—is as vitally important to the vocation of marriage, as reception of Eucharist is to the membership in the church community" (p. 6). Marital sex "prompts companionship, creates intimacy, spurs bonding; . . . friendship and commitment are conveyed in sexual form; . . . sex helps partners feel more real, alive, more loving, and more at peace with themselves and each other" (p. 8). A couple's sexual relationship generates an energy of attraction, unity, and creativity. The erotic is an invitation to appreciate the pleasures of beauty, art, nature, food, music, and the senses (Moore & Gillette, 1993). Couples are encouraged to explore the sexual dimension of their relationship as a profound source of renewal, reconnection, repair, and revision. Sex therapists Barry and Emily McCarthy (2004) note that 15% to 20% of marital satisfaction is attributed to sex in happy and healthy marriages. On the other hand, 50% to 70% of unhappiness in conflicted couples is attributed to an unhappy sex life. When couples do not have a vital sexual life it can make a big difference. Clinicians are encouraged to do a sexual genogram and timeline with couples (DeMaria, Weeks, & Hof, 1999) in order to assess spouses' history and satisfaction with their sexual practices and beliefs.

One final reflection on body, the corporate body, the community is important. Couples and families cannot make it alone. Yet there is much isolation within families and in the broader community today. Couples and families need to be part of a larger community, a body of supportive and challenging companions. They benefit from the wisdom and modeling of those who have gone before them, they are enriched by the feedback, advice, and ideas from other couples and families, and they share common experiences (Sheras & Koch-Sheras, 2006). The offering of hospitality to others, looking out for and sharing responsibility for each other's children, and offering service to the broader community all deepen and renew couple and family life. "Because we had experiences both as a family and as individuals that went beyond our family, we had more to talk about when we were together. Our commitments outside the family strengthened our common identity" (Rubio, 2003, p. 183). A couple/family's interaction with the communal body of neighborhood, faith, ethnicity, if not nation, is important to their ongoing well-being. When missing, couples and families can be helped to find if not create healthful community.

CONCLUSION

"Renewal" is not directly discussed in the marriage and family literature, yet it is a critically important concept. This chapter examines synonyms, antonyms, images, and metaphors for renewal. At least three psychological processes are suggested to be included in renewal—reconnecting, repairing, and revisioning. Renewal is thought to be a prospective, forward-looking process as well as a retrospective, backward-looking process. Stresses related to *time*, *values*, *loss of ritual*, and *ambivalence about the body* were examined.

The chapter concludes with intervention strategies that address four areas of marital-family stress.

Clinicians were invited to help couples and families "stop, calm, and go inside," to take time with/make time for each other, especially at the beginning and end of the work day, to explore their rhythm and pace differences and perspectives on time, to turn off electronic devices regularly and come into the now with each other, and to practice "time shifting."

Clinicians were invited to help couples and families reflect on the vision and values, that is, their compass or North Star; to critique the cultural definition of their values; and explore of the role of spirituality in their lives.

Clinicians were invited to explore couple and family ritual belief and practice, including retrieving lost but treasured rituals, abandoning meaningless rituals, and creating new rituals as needed; to explore practices for stopping, calming, and going inside, including "sabbathing" practices of ceasing, resting, embracing, and feasting.

Clinicians were invited to explore the wisdom and "felt sense" of the body in self/couple-awareness, decision making and healing, as a resource in lowering stress and anxiety, and as a source of pleasure and deep unity.

REFERENCES

Berger, R., & Hannah, M. (1999). *Preventive approaches in couples therapy*. Philadelphia, PA: Brunner/Mazel.

Borysenko, J. (2011). *Fried: Why you burn out and how to revive*. New York, NY: Hay House.

Bossard, J., & Boll, E. (1950). *Ritual in family life*. Philadelphia: University of Pennsylvania Press.

Carter, S., & Sokol, J. (1998). *Getting to commitment: Overcoming the 8 greatest obstacles to lasting connections*. New York, NY: Evans.

Chapman, G. (1992). *The five love languages: How to express heartfelt commitment to your mate*. Chicago, IL: Northfield.

Cornell, A. (1996). *The power of focusing: A practical guide to emotional healing*. Oakland, CA: New Harbinger.

Covey, S. (1997). *The 7 habits of highly effective families*. New York, NY: Golden Books.

Cox, M. (1998). *The heart of a family: Searching America for new traditions that fulfill us*. New York, NY: Random House.

Curran, D. (1985). *Stress and the healthy family*. New York, NY: Harper & Row.

Dawn, M. (1989). *Keeping the Sabbath wholly: Ceasing, resting, embracing, and feasting*. Grand Rapids, MI: Eerdmans.

Dawn, M. (1993). *Sexual character: Beyond technique to intimacy*. Grand Rapids, MI: Eerdmans.

DeMaria, R., Weeks, G., & Hof, L. (1999). *Focused genograms*. Philadelphia, PA: Brunner/Mazel.

Doherty, W. (1997). *The intentional family: Simple rituals to strengthen family ties*. New York, NY: Avon Books.

Doherty, W. (2001). *Take back your marriage: Sticking together in a world that pulls us apart*. New York, NY: Guilford Press.

Dyer, P., & Dyer, G. (1991). *Growing together: Couple workbook*. Minneapolis, MN: PREPARE/ENRICH.

Fiese, B. (2006). *Family routines and rituals*. New Haven, CT: Yale University Press.

Fraenkel, P. (2011). *Synch your relationship, save your marriage*. New York, NY: Palgrave.
Fulghum, R. (1996). *From beginning to end: The rituals of our lives*. New York, NY: Ivy Books.
Giblin, P. (2011). Men making and keeping commitments. *American Journal of Family Therapy*, *39*, 124–138.
Giblin, P., & Hug, A. (2006). The psychology of funeral rituals. *Liturgy*, *21*(1), 11–19.
Gottman, J. (1999). *The seven principles for making marriage work*. New York, NY: Crown.
Greenberg, L., & Goldman, R. (2008). *Emotion-focused couple therapy: Dynamics of emotion, love and power*. Washington, DC: American Psychological Association.
Gudorf, C. (1992). Why sex is so good for your marriage. *U.S. Catholic*, November, 6–13.
Hanh, T. N. (1999). *The miracle of mindfulness: An introduction to the practice of meditation*. Boston, MA: Beacon Press.
Haughey, J. (1975). *Should anyone say forever: On making, keeping and breaking commitments*. Garden City, NJ: Doubleday.
Hendrix, H. (1988). *Getting the love you want: A guide for couples*. New York, NY: Harper & Row.
Hunt, R., Hof, L., & DeMaria, R. (1998). *Marriage enrichment: Preparation, mentoring, and outreach*. Philadelphia, PA: Brunner/Mazel.
Imber-Black, J., & Roberts, J. (1992). *Rituals for our times: Celebrating, healing, and changing our lives and relationships*. New York, NY: HarperCollins.
Iyengar, S. (2010). *The art of choosing*. New York, NY: Twelve.
Johnson, S. (2004). *The practice of emotionally focused couple therapy: Creating connection*. New York, NY: Brunner-Routledge.
Johnson, S. (2008). *Hold me tight: Seven conversations for a lifetime of love*. New York, NY: Little, Brown.
Kabat-Zinn, J. (1990). *Full catastrophe living: Using the wisdom of your body and mind to face stress, pain, and illness*. New York, NY: Delta.
Kabat-Zinn, J. (2005). *Wherever you go there you are*. New York, NY: Hyperion.
Keating, T. (1986). *Open mind, open heart*. New York, NY: Amity House.
Kornfield, J. (1993). *A path with heart: A guide through the perils and promises of the spiritual life*. New York, NY: Bantam Books.
Levine, S., & Levine, O. (1995). *Embracing the beloved: Relationship as a path of awakening*. New York, NY: Doubleday.
Levine, S., & Levine, O. (1998). *A year to live: How to live this year as if it were your last*. New York, NY: Bell Tower.
Linn, D., Linn, S., & Linn, M. (1995). *Sleeping with bread: Holding what gives you life*. New York, NY: Paulist Press.
McCarthy, B., & McCarthy, E. (2004). *Getting it right the first time: Creating a healthy marriage*. New York, NY: Brunner-Routledge.
Moore, R., & Gillette, D. (1993). *The lover within: Accessing the lover in the male archetype*. New York, NY: Avon Books.
Pipher, M. (1996). *The shelter of each other: Rebuilding our families*. New York, NY: Putnam.
Pipher, M. (1997). The family unplugged. *Psychotherapy Networker*, January/February, 24–33.

Rechtschaffen, S. (1996). *Timeshifting: Creating more time to enjoy your life*. New York, NY: Doubleday.

Reininger, G. (1998). *Centering prayer in daily life and ministry*. New York, NY: Continuum.

Rubio, J. H. (2003). *A Christian theology of marriage and the family*. New York, NY: Paulist Press.

Satir, V. (1972). *Peoplemaking*. Palo Alto, CA: Science and Behavior Books.

Schwartz, B. (2004). *The paradox of choice: Why more is less*. New York, NY: HarperCollins.

Schwartz, R. (1995). *Internal family systems therapy*. New York, NY: Guilford Press.

Schwartz, R. (2008). *You are the one you've been waiting for: Bringing courageous love to intimate relationships*. Oak Park, IL: Trailheads.

Shem S., & Surrey, J. (1999). *We have to talk: Healing dialogues between men and women*. New York, NY: Basic Books.

Sheras, P., & Koch-Sheras, P. (2006). *Couple power therapy: Building commitment, cooperation, communication and community in relationships*. Washington, DC: American Psychological Association.

Sotile, W., & Sotile, M. (1998). *Beat stress together: The supercouple syndrome*. New York, NY: Wiley.

Sotile, W., & Sotile, M. (2000). *The medical marriage: A couple's survival guide*. New York, NY: Birch Lane Press.

Stanley, S. (1998). *The heart of commitment*. Nashville, TN: Nelson.

Walsh, F. (2006). *Strengthening family resilience*. New York, NY: Guilford Press.

Welwood, J. (1990). *Journey of the heart: The path of conscious love*. New York, NY: HarperCollins.

Welwood, J. (1997). *Love and awakening: Discovering the path of intimate relationships*. New York, NY: Harper.

Whitehead, E., & Whitehead, J. (2001). *Wisdom of the body: Making sense of our sexuality*. New York, NY: Crossroad.

Wolin, S., & Bennett, L. (1980). Disrupted family rituals: A factor in generational transmission of alcoholism. *Journal of Studies of Alcohol*, *41*, 199–214.

Wolin, S., & Bennet, L. (1984). Family rituals. *Family Process*, *23*, 401–420.

CHAPTER

17

A Dialectical Behavior Therapy Approach to Self-Renewal

Maria Mouratidis

> To be worn out is to be renewed.
>
> —Lao Tzu (Laozi & Chan, 1988)

How is it possible to be both worn out and renewed at the same time? These concepts seem contradictory and seem impossible for both to be true at the same time. Lao Tzu, a sixth-century BC Chinese philosopher, seems to suggest that somehow being worn out renews us (Laozi & Chan, 1988). Elements of both acceptance and change are embedded in this apparent contradiction. Perhaps the process of being worn out or spent gives rise to new perspectives, new priorities, and new beginnings. Motivation to grow may also arise out of being worn out. The synthesis of the tension, otherwise known as dialectic, may be what brings about change (McMain, Korman, & Dimeff, 2001). Most people tend to seek psychotherapy when feeling worn out, conflicted, and/or suffering along with the hope, sometimes the size of a mustard seed, that there is a path toward healing and wholeness.

Dialectical Behavior Therapy (DBT) was originally developed as a treatment for suicidal behavior (Dimeff & Koerner, 2007; Dimeff & Linehan, 2001; Linehan, 1993a, 1993b). DBT has been found to treat difficulties and disorders related to emotion dysregulation (McMain et al., 2001), such as borderline personality disorder, eating disorders, trauma spectrum disorders, and substance abuse disorders (Dimeff et al., 2007; Dimeff & Linehan, 2001; Harned, Banawan, & Lynch, 2006; Linehan, 1993a). Components of DBT, such as mindfulness, have been developed into treatments for disorders such as Major Depressive Disorder (Segal, Williams, & Teasdale, 2002). Although DBT principles and practices have been empirically supported to have clinical utility, they are also practical for healthy living. DBT is ultimately focused on "getting a life worth living" and directly focuses on quality of life-interfering behaviors as treatment targets once life-threatening and therapy-interfering behaviors have been managed (Linehan, 1993a, 1993b; McMain et al., 2001).

Dialectical Behavior Therapy (DBT) theory and technique may offer perspectives and strategies related to self-renewal. Cultivating motivation is a key feature of DBT. Motivation may be a central mechanism for moving from being worn out to being renewed. DBT approaches can be used during a stressful time, recovery from a stressful event, or when one might find the need or desire to refresh oneself. DBT comes from a vantage point of personal responsibility. Linehan (1993a) has been quoted saying that although we may not have caused all of our problems, they are ours to solve. DBT encourages motivation and an internal locus of control where we have the capacity to change our thoughts and change our behaviors. In particular, self-renewal from a DBT perspective may involve the management of emotional resources. Managing emotional resources involves balancing the loss of emotional resources and gaining of more emotional resources. Practicing self-renewal from a DBT perspective might decrease vulnerability to negative emotions and increase positive emotional experiences. In other words, DBT offers a way of thinking and behaving that may decrease our becoming depleted and increase our replenishment, both of which contribute to our self-renewal. Awareness of oneself, responding to one's needs, and taking time for oneself are inherent in the concept and practice of self-renewal. These ideas are very much related to DBT in terms of concepts of awareness, validation, and the development and practice of skillful behaviors.

DBT is formulated as a framework (Dimeff et al., 2007). As a model, DBT is supported by four pillars: (1) the philosophy of the dialectics; (2) the biosocial theory; (3) Eastern approaches; and (4) technology of cognitive behavioral theory and therapy (CBT). The technology of how to think and behave differently is built on these pillars with the intention of helping people behave more effectively and to cultivate a life worth living. The spirit of the synthesis of the dialectic involves merging the "technologies of acceptance" offered by Eastern approaches with the "technologies of change" offered by crisis and behavior theories (Dimeff & Linehan, 2001, p. 10; Linehan, 2000).

The concept of the dialectics originated in philosophy as early as the 5th century BC in the works of Zeno of Elea who wrote about "paradoxes" (Plato & Scolnicov, 2003). Later, the concept of the dialectics was discussed in the works of Kant and Hegel (Popper, 1940). It is based on logic arguments where there is a thesis and antithesis with the goal of arriving at synthesis. The synthesis may lead to a new thesis, and ultimately a new dialectic (Dimeff et al., 2007; Harned et al., 2006). According to Popper (1940), an antithesis is generated by the thesis because the thesis is incomplete or lacking. DBT might understand this concept as the opportunity to develop motivation and new capabilities (Linehan, 1993a). One goal of synthesis might be to create a more whole, more accurate view of reality. Popper (1940) argued that the synthesis combines the best elements of the thesis and the antithesis. The fundamental idea of reality is that two, seemingly opposite, things or ideas can be true at the same time and that the synthesis of those opposites might lead to a whole greater than the sum of its parts. For example, many patients have trouble when their psychotherapist goes on vacation and it is also true that psychotherapists need and deserve to go on vacation. Both the needs of the patient and the psychotherapist are valid at the same time and one need does not negate the other. It is possible that both people's needs could get met leading to a overall greater benefit to the relationship as a whole. Try a simple experiment. Substitute the word "and" for "but" in a sentence and see how it changes the meaning. The word "but" negates the first part of the sentence. For example, "I studied really hard, *but* I did poorly on the test" as opposed to "I studied really hard, *and* I did poorly on the test." Both things are true: You studied really hard and you did poorly on the test. Just because you did not do well on the test does not negate that you studied hard. There is an implicit judgment here, that if you studied hard that you would do well on the test. Judgments, positive or negative, within or outside of our awareness, implicit or explicit, can directly affect our appraisal of a situation and subsequently affect our feelings.

Adopting a dialectical philosophy reduces the propensity for judgments and supports a stance of acceptance. Although there can be an inherent tension in two seemingly opposing things being true at the same time, it is possible that acceptance of that fact of reality can reduce the tension. Failure to accept reality creates suffering (Linehan, 1993b). Pain is part of life, but suffering is optional. One important part of psychotherapy is helping the person to decrease needless suffering. Once we accept reality, we can start to deal with it and start to see our options more clearly.

According to the biosocial theory, which is a second pillar of DBT, emotion dysregulation results from being born with a sensitive nervous system coupled with growing up in an invalidating environment (Linehan, 1993a). According to this theory, problems with emotional dysregulation can also occur as a result of having a nervous system that is easily perturbed and/or a nervous system that has difficulty with regulation and may take a long time to return to its baseline or normal state (Dimeff & Koerner, 2007; Linehan, 1993a). Although we do not have control over what nervous system we were born with (nature) or the environment we were raised in (nurture), understanding these influences and their impact on us can help us focus on how to more effectively deal with our emotional experiences. Understanding the biosocial theory also helps to reduce feeling of fault for emotional difficulties. In the spirit of the dialectic, we may not have caused our problems *and* (not "but") they are ours to solve (Linehan, 1993a).

A third pillar, Eastern approaches, is related to the spirit and discipline of acceptance. Acceptance is an often-misunderstood term. Accepting something does not mean it is okay that it happened, does not mean you agree, does not mean that it does not matter, and does not mean there is nothing that can be done about it. Resignation is giving up. Acceptance is an active process (Brach, 2003). Acceptance is the willingness to acknowledge a circumstance, a feeling, or a reality without fighting against it. As long as the emotional energy is trapped into refusing to accept reality, there are limited emotional resources available to actually deal with it. Willingness is a spirit and an attitude that puts us in the position to do whatever is needed in the moment (Linehan, 1993a).

Cognitive behavioral theory and therapy, as a fourth pillar, focuses on changing one's thinking and behavior. Cognitive theory is predicated on the notion that thoughts come before feelings (Beck, 1970). Presumably, if we change the way we think then we can change the way we feel. An important component of cognitive theory is related to cognitive appraisal. Cognitive appraisal is how we evaluate and what meaning we assign to a particular event (Beck, 2008). It is the meaning we assign that determines how we feel. The behavioral component is related to learning theory and skill acquisition. We learn through making associations (classical conditioning) or through reinforcements (operant conditioning). Our learning otherwise, thought of as experience, contributes to the likelihood of a behavior occurring, being maintained, or not occurring. Learning occurs through observing others, known as modeling, or psychoeducation where specific skill sets are taught and practiced. DBT, consistent with CBT, focuses on decreasing all or nothing thinking (or black-and-white thinking) and on challenging irrational beliefs and replacing them with more rational responses. Modifying cognitions, or thoughts, can be achieved through employing dialectical thinking, moving from black-and-white thinking to seeing shades of gray (Dimeff & Koerner, 2007). Skill acquisition and generalization is a key component of DBT where people learn to develop skills to manage their emotions and their relationships more effectively.

DBT involves balancing acceptance and change (Dimeff & Koerner, 2007; Linehan, 1993a, 1993b; McMain et al., 2001). Acceptance begins with self-validation. Self-validation or validation strategies help people see that their feelings or reactions "make sense" in a given situation (McMain et al., 2001, p. 190). There are instances when there are circumstances that cannot be changed and accepting reality helps to decrease suffering. Other times, skillful behavior can help to change circumstances resulting in more effective behavior and reduced pain and suffering. Skillful behavior results from learning new skills or capacities and practicing skills through exposure, opposite action, and response prevention (Linehan, 1993a, 1993b; McMain et al. 2001). It is difficult to begin to change without first accepting reality. Discerning when an acceptance skill versus a change skill is effective in a given moment is a skill in and of itself and pivoting between acceptance and change skills generates movement, integration, and synthesis (Linehan, 1993a). Movement, integration, and synthesis may be mechanisms that transition us from a state of being worn out to being renewed. There are four major skill sets in DBT (Linehan, 1993a, 1993b). Mindfulness and distress tolerance are acceptance skills whereas emotion regulation and interpersonal effectiveness are change skills (Linehan, 1993a, 1993b). All four skill sets are integral to DBT and are relevant to cultivating self-renewal. Homework is an important part of DBT because practice is required for a new skill to be acquired.

MINDFULNESS

Mindfulness is an acceptance skill and is considered the core skill in DBT (Linehan, 1993a, 1993b). Mindfulness involves (1) awareness; (2) a nonjudgmental attitude; (3) wise mind; and (4) a spirit of self-compassion and loving-kindness. Awareness is needed in order to use a skill or to change one's thinking.

1. Mindfulness is about awareness, specifically, awareness of and in the current moment. As an age-old practice in the Eastern tradition, much has been written about what it is and how to do it. Noticing is the vehicle of awareness. Mindfulness is the tool or gauge that lets us know how we are feeling. The first step in cultivating self-renewal is noticing that we are running low and the earlier we notice that, the better. It stands to reason that the sooner we intervene to either decrease being depleted or increase replenishment, the better we will feel. Recognizing where we are relative to our emotional resources at any given moment is a task of acceptance. We cannot really change how "filled up" we are at the moment, but noticing our gauge of emotional resources helps us ensure that we do not run on empty. It is no accident that *most* people never have or rarely ever run out of gas in their cars. We monitor the gas gauge and we ensure that we fill up before we end up stranded somewhere with no gas. When we notice that we are running low on gas, we can make a decision and take action that will ensure that we will not run out of gas. If our gas gauge was broken or if we did not pay attention to it, we would likely end up on the side of a road somewhere, a road that would almost definitely lead to distress. Mindfulness is like a gauge of how many emotional resources we might have at a given moment in time. This awareness is the gateway to taking action to minimize the debit of emotional resources and/or to generate more emotional resources.
2. Judgments, especially self-judgments, tear down the self. The subtexts of judgments are that we are not as good as other people, that our needs

are not as valid, and that somehow we are less deserving. Judgments are also linked to our expectations of ourselves, of others, or of how we have decided how the world "should" be. "Shoulds" and related words, such as "supposed to be," are hallmarks of a judgment. Expectations may be within our awareness or they may be automatic. Expectations can be influenced by previous experiences (learning) or values and may take the form of irrational beliefs or dysfunctional thoughts leading to negative emotions. Checking the facts (Linehan, 1993b) is one emotion regulation technique that can be used to assess the veracity of the expectation or judgment.

3. Often, people make the differentiation between their head and their heart. DBT language characterizes this idea as reasonable mind and emotional mind. Mindfulness helps to synthesize both of these valuable and necessary parts of ourselves into "wise mind" (Linehan, 1993a; Linehan, 1993b). Wise mind is where our reasonable mind and our emotional mind overlap and is thought to be the place from which wise and balanced interpretations and decisions emerge. A sense of peace is one way of knowing whether you are in wise mind. Using mindfulness to enter into wise mind can help us feel less dragged around by our emotions or torn between how we think and how we feel. Having a firm place to stand within ourselves, on the platform of wise mind, can help us feel more grounded and gain our bearings, contributing to an experience of self-renewal. Sitting in wise mind generates a sense of peace.
4. Approaching ourselves with a spirit of self-compassion and lovingkindness is central to self-renewal. Accepting ourselves, our whole self, as we are in the present moment is an important part of taking care of ourselves. Refusal to accept our pain or ourselves causes suffering (Linehan, 1993a). Instead of pushing away painful feelings, embracing them and comforting them in the moment can lead to relief and renewal. Embracing painful emotions may seem unpalatable because we may prefer to see our pain as separate from us, not part of us. Denying a part of ourselves, no matter how painful, prevents us from being whole and prevents peace. The Greek word *eirini* and the Hebrew word *shalom* both mean peace and both define peace as wholeness. Self-renewal may be understood as reaching peace and wholeness, which suggests that it is a process we go through many times over the course of life.

Many mindfulness exercises use the breath as a focal point. The idea is that you watch your breath, with an attitude of acceptance and dignity, without trying to control or manage your breath. In many ways, focusing on your breath is simple and you always have it with you. The breath may hold symbolic value as well. Our breath may be a symbol of life and of spirit. Our breath grounds us and with each inhalation renews us by bringing vital oxygen to each of our individual cells. Nothing precludes us from being more aware of our breath and from consciously taking more breaths.

Homework

Set a timer for 5 minutes. Cloak yourself with an attitude of acceptance and dignity. Take a moment to feel the grounding of the earth beneath your feet, the support of the chair under and behind you, and the support of the breath within you. Count your breaths up to 10 and then back down to zero. As thoughts, worries, feelings, and distractions grab your attention, notice that and invite your attention back to your breath. Repeat this process until the timer sounds. Take a moment to notice what you noticed.

DISTRESS TOLERANCE

Distress tolerance, as an acceptance skill, helps us to endure difficult moments. Accepting and tolerating painful emotions as opposed to fighting them minimizes emotional suffering, thereby preserving emotional resources. Radical acceptance is an important aspect of distress tolerance. Radical acceptance means that you are willing to accept the pain of the present moment. This does not mean that you agree with what is happening or that it does not matter how you are feeling. Brach (2003) discussed how radical acceptance opens the door to change. Willingness, a spirit of doing whatever is needed in the present moment, is borne out of radical acceptance. Willfulness, which is the opposite of willingness (and otherwise known as stubbornness) is a refusal to accept the present moment as it is, digging in one's heels, and giving up. According to Brach (2003), "the sacred pause" becomes the "fertile ground for wise action" (p. 66). According to Linehan (1993a, 1993b), distress tolerance skills include (1) distraction skills, (2) self-soothing skills, and (3) skills to improve the moment. Distress tolerance skills can help to manage difficult emotions so they do not cause unnecessary drain of emotional reserves as well as help to refuel emotional resources.

1. Distraction skills involve behaviors such as volunteer work and being involved in activities. Being active generates self-renewal, which may seem counterintuitive, because activities take energy. The same premise applies to exercise, for example. Although we exert energy with exercise, the more we exercise, the more energy we generally have. Volunteer work and being involved with activities often involves interaction with other people and to contributing, both of which help to build ourselves back up and distract us from our current worries, even for just a moment.
2. Self-soothing skills involve employing the use of our five senses: vision, hearing, smell, taste, and touch (Linehan, 1993a, 1993b). Engaging with

Table 17.1 Distress Tolerance Examples (adapted from Linehan, 1993a, 1993b)

Sense	Examples
Vision	Looking at photos of loved ones or special moments Gazing on a nature scene Having fresh flowers around
Hearing	Listening to favorite or soothing music Listening to nature sounds Listening to the laughter of children
Smell	Smelling cookies baking in the oven The scent of a candle The scent of a hand or body lotion The scent of body wash The smell of coffee brewing
Taste	Enjoying the taste of chocolate melting in your mouth Enjoying a cup of coffee or tea Enjoying a bowl of ice cream
Touch	Petting your dog or cat A hug Massage Wearing soft clothes The feel of a hot shower or a warm bath Putting on hand cream The feel of grass

stimuli related to our senses is one quick and easy way to rejuvenate ourselves. Here are some examples:

Avoid mood- or mind-altering substances for self-soothing purposes. You might be tempted to think alcohol would be soothing, but it actually causes more discomfort and problems. Combining as many senses as possible in the activity will increase the potential benefit. For example, using a scented hand cream involves both smell and touch or enjoying a cup of coffee involves smell and taste.

3. Improving the moment involves skills such as using (a) imagery, (b) finding meaning, (c) prayer, and (d) relaxation (Linehan, 1993a, 1993b).
   a. Imagery is useful to help you imagine either a time where you felt good or to imagine a place where you feel more comfortable or happy. The place you use in the imagery exercise can be either real or imagined.
   b. Finding meaning helps us to feel that our pain is not in vain or senseless. It is natural for our minds to want to make sense of what is happening around us and within us. Our cultural and spiritual beliefs

influence the meaning we make out of what happens. Embracing rituals and our value system can help us to find meaning in difficult circumstances and with difficult feelings.

c. Prayer, across religious traditions, helps to both curtail the leaking of emotional resources and to help nourish our spirit. Praying helps us to acknowledge and accept that everything is not up to us alone, that there is someone, some entity, bigger than we are. Prayer offers us a pathway to express our feelings and needs, to receive a spirit of comfort and guidance, and a way to connect with others when praying together.
d. Relaxation exercises have been proven to soothe the nervous system. Relaxation exercises activate the body's parasympathetic nervous system, which is responsible for calming the body. Neurologically calming the body both decreases distress and supports renewal. Relaxation exercises such as deep breathing, progressive muscle relaxation, and imagery can be used throughout the day to renew a moment.

Homework

Put together a self-soothing kit. Find a respectable container, such as a nice box or a basket. Put in several items related to each sense. Have it readily available to use regularly and as often as needed.

EMOTION REGULATION

Emotion regulation is a change skill according to dialectical behavior theory (Linehan, 1993a, 1993b). Emotion regulation is closely tied with self-regulation. Emotion dysregulation occurs when one's emotions are either too extreme/expansive or too restricted. Part of emotion regulation is directly linked to the physiological characteristics of the nervous system with which you were born. Some nervous systems are easily jarred and take longer to return to baseline, whereas others are more unflappable (Dimeff & Koener, 2007; Linehan, 1993a). You may notice that some people tend to get upset more easily and it takes them longer to calm down than others. Knowing this about yourself is important so you can develop skills to better manage your emotions.

There are physiological and psychological components to emotions. Emotion regulation and self-renewal both begin with biological regulation. Six strategies for biological regulation include (Linehan, 1993b):

1. Getting enough rest. Lying down or decreasing activities can be restful if you are having trouble sleeping.
2. Taking in nutrients. We are not hungry for food; we are hungry for nutrients. Water is a powerful nutrient.

3. Getting some exercise. Just taking a 15-minute walk can be helpful.
4. Avoid mood- or mind-altering substances.
5. Treat any physical pain or ailments. Take any medication as your doctor prescribes.
6. Stay hydrated. Remember that caffeine is a diuretic and is dehydrating.

Balancing and managing our physiology can make us less emotionally vulnerable and may help us to reboot or reset ourselves as the basis of self-renewal. Although it may seem easy to say that one should get enough sleep, eat well, and exercise, these things can be difficult to do or to do consistently. Changes in priorities and changes in behaviors may be necessary to begin the path toward self-renewal.

DBT suggests that emotion regulation involves increasing positive/pleasant events and decreasing emotional suffering (Linehan, 1993a, 1993b). Self-renewal can be facilitated through engaging in more activities that are pleasurable and through letting go of painful emotions. Becoming engaged in pleasant activities may involve making time to do the things that you enjoy doing or in exploring a new hobby. Letting go of painful emotions usually involves recognizing that you are not your emotion, but your emotion is part of you (Linehan, 1993a, 1993b). Being mindful of your painful emotion and taking care of it instead of fighting it can decrease suffering and foster self-renewal. Taking care of your emotion means practicing lovingkindness toward your emotion and toward yourself. There is a common mindfulness exercise inspired by the 13th-century's poet Rūmī's poem, "The Guest House," translated by Barks (Jalāl al-Dīn Rūmī & Barks, 1996).

You are invited to try this exercise:

> Close your eyes. Imagine that you are sitting in your favorite chair. You hear a knock at the door. You open the door to find, lo and behold, your most unpleasant emotion. Notice what your first thoughts, feelings, and instincts are. You decide to invite in your most unpleasant emotion. You offer it your favorite chair and a cozy blanket. You ask if you can make it a cup of tea. You share a cup of tea with your most unpleasant emotion. You ask it, "Why have you come?" You listen. You ask it, "What are you asking me to let go of?" You ask it, "What do you need in order to feel better?" and you listen for what you can do to make your most unpleasant emotion feel more comfortable. You offer to make your favorite meal for your most unpleasant emotion. You share the meal together. What do you talk about? After dinner, your most unpleasant emotion asks you to dance. How do you feel? What is the dance like? After the dance, your most unpleasant emotion thanks you and says that it is time to go. As it moves toward the door, it offers you a beautifully wrapped gift. As it walks out the

door, it reminds you that it will be back. You sit in your favorite chair and you open the gift. What do you find inside? How does your most unpleasant emotion feel now? What is your relationship like now with your most unpleasant emotion compared to when you first opened the door?

This exercise is an example of how to separate yourself from your emotion, with grace and honor, how to sit with your emotion without being consumed by it, and how to practice lovingkindness. Suffering will be decreased if we accept our emotions and take care of them as opposed to denying them or fighting against them. Self-renewal can occur when we learn from what our emotions are telling us. This can be valuable information to help us determine what is compromising our emotional resources and how to augment or sustain them.

Increasing positive events and letting go of painful emotions will likely require problem solving (Linehan, 1993a). The task is to accept our emotions in the moment and then determine what circumstances may be useful to change in order to bring about a change in our emotions. Problem solving is also part of DBT's model of emotion regulation (Linehan, 1993a, 1993b). Our thinking or something concrete may need to change in our lives in order to support our self-renewal. There are at least two components to problem solving related to self-renewal: (1) identifying what is causing our depletion and stopping the drain, and (2) identifying how to fill ourselves up. There are two ways to keep water in a bathtub: You can fill it from the spigot or you can plug the drain. If you are trying to fill a bathtub full of water and keep it filled, it is most effective to do both. Similarly, there may be relationships that are draining that may need to be ended or there may be some relationships that are nurturing to be further developed. Balancing your time so that you might have more time for yourself or to spend with loved ones may require becoming less overextended at work. Problem-solving skills help you to take care of what needs to be done without adding unnecessary stress or suffering to yourself.

Homework

(1) Engage in at least one pleasant event each day for the next week; and (2) welcome and take care of at least one pleasant emotion of the day.

INTERPERSONAL EFFECTIVENESS

Interpersonal effectiveness is a change skill (Linehan, 1993a, 1993b). It is probably the most difficult skill because it involves another person. We might be skillful; however, the result of the interpersonal interaction is also dependent on someone else's choices and reactions. According to Linehan (1993a, 1993b), interpersonal effectiveness involves attending to relationships, balancing wants and shoulds, balancing priorities and demands, and developing mastery and self-respect. Three planets of interpersonal effectiveness are in constant orbit with one another: (1) objective effectiveness; (2) relationship effectiveness; and (3) self-respect effectiveness. Self-renewal involves balancing all three of these elements of interpersonal effectiveness. They are prioritized in a particular order depending on what is most important to you. For example, if you are calling the help desk to get your computer fixed, your objective is likely most important. You are probably not trying to develop or preserve a relationship with the technician and your interaction is not likely to involve your self-esteem. On the other hand, if there is something you would like your significant other to do, you might put the relationship effectiveness first, and then the self-respect, and then the objective effectiveness last. Ultimately, maintaining objective, relationship effectiveness, and self-respect simultaneously is ideal; we typically need to order the three of them based on each situation.

1. Objective effectiveness is about getting what you want (Linehan, 1993a). Being clear on what you want is central to achieving your objective. What do you want in order to achieve self-renewal? Are you doing what you *want* to do or what you *should* do? Although as responsible adults, there are things that we should and must do, this does not mean that we cannot do things that we want to do. Some people have trouble allowing themselves to do that they want. This often gets tied up with cognitive distortions of not feeling worthy or deserving of what one wants. Part of self-renewal can involve becoming in touch with what you do want at this point in your life and finding a way to incorporate that want into your life. Linehan (1993b) offers the **DEAR MAN** skills to help us achieve our objective effectiveness. She suggests that we **D**escribe what we need or want, **E**xpress our feelings, **A**ssert ourselves, **R**einforce the person ahead of time for giving us what we are asking for, being **M**indful of our objective, **A**ppear confident, and be willing to **N**egotiate.
2. Relationship effectiveness is about taking care of the relationship. Linehan (1993b) suggests the **GIVE** skills to help us maintain relationships, especially during times of interpersonal stress or conflict. The **GIVE** skills involve using a **G**entle manner with the other person, being **I**nterested in what is important to the other person, **V**alidating the person, and using an **E**asy manner with humor. Relationships are key to self-renewal because many of our needs become met through relationships. Healthy relationships are nourishing to both people and are key sources of support, especially during difficult times or during times of transition.
3. Self-respect and self-renewal may share an interesting relationship. Compromising our self-respect could likely impact our emotional reserves. Developing greater self-respect effectiveness may contribute toward self-renewal. According to Linehan (1993a, 1993b), the **FAVE** skills help develop self-respect effectiveness. Being **F**air to oneself can

foster self-renewal. This would involve having reasonable expectations of ourselves, taking care of ourselves, not overextending ourselves, and acknowledging that we are as valid as everyone else. Make no **A**pologies for what you need or want. Our desires, needs, values, and goals are just as valid as anyone else's. Maintain your **V**alues, even when they seem to be at odds with someone else's value system. Compromising your values can be emotionally costly and undermine self-renewal efforts. Part of the self-renewal process involves reflecting on your current values and determining how congruent they are with your current needs and goals. There is no need to **E**xaggerate your point of view in order to have your needs met. They are valid just as they are and they deserve to be met. Self-respect effectiveness is most central to self-renewal because it is very difficult to develop, maintain, or renew one's personal resources without a balanced sense of self that is informed by an awareness and acceptance of one's own worth and personal value system.

Homework

(1) Ask for something you need from someone without compromising your value system and without compromising the relationship; (2) do at least one thing to nurture a relationship that you value.

DBT is ultimately about getting a life worth living (Linehan, 1993a). All of the DBT skill sets come together leading to improved relationships, better self-regulation, and more quality of life with practice. Decreasing all-or-nothing thinking and seeking synthesis where there is tension may increase the opportunity to feel peaceful, better connected with others, and well. Mindfulness is the key tool in helping us notice that we are in need of self-renewal. It is also key in helping to reduce feeling overwhelmed or depleted by staying in the moment. Self-renewal may not be about restoring oneself, but may be more akin to transforming oneself. It may not be about mending a broken part, but having that part become new again. One does not have to be emotionally bankrupt to need or benefit from self-renewal. A creative process whereby the self is revitalized, redesigned, and renewed from a platform of strength and wholeness may foster continued growth toward self-actualization. DBT offers a pathway for more balanced thinking and more skillful behaviors that can contribute toward personal transformation and quality of life.

REFERENCES

Beck, A. T. (1970). Cognitive therapy: Nature and relation to behavior therapy. *Behavior Therapy*, *1*(2), 184–200.

Beck, A. T. (2008). The evolution of the cognitive model of depression and its neurobiological correlates. *American Journal of Psychiatry*, *165*(8), 969–977. doi:10.1176/appi.ajp.2008.08050721

Brach, T. (2003). *Radical acceptance: Embracing your life with the heart of a buddha*. New York, NY: Bantam Books.

Dimeff, L., & Koerner, K. (2007). *Dialectical behavior therapy in clinical practice: Applications across disorders and settings*. New York, NY: Guilford Press.

Dimeff, L., & Linehan, M. (2001). Dialectical behavioral therapy in a nutshell. *California Psychologist, 34*, 10–13.

Harned, M. S., Banawan, S. F., & Lynch, T. R. (2006). Dialectical behavior therapy: An emotion-focused treatment for borderline personality disorder. *Journal of Contemporary Psychotherapy, 36*(2), 67–75. doi:10.1007/s10879–006–9009-x

Jalāl al-Dīn Rūmī, M., & Barks, C. (1996). *The essential Rumi/translated by Coleman Barks, with John Moyne, A.A. Arberry, Reynold Nicholson*. San Francisco, CA: Harper.

Laozi, & Chan, W. (1988). *The way of Lao Tzu (Tao-te ching) / translated with introductory essays, comments, and notes, by Wing-tsit Chan*. New York, NY: Macmillan.

Linehan, M. (2000). The empirical basis of dialectical behavior therapy: Development of new treatments versus evaluation of existing treatments. *Clinical Psychology: Science and Practice, 7*, 113–119.

Linehan, M. M. (1993a). *Cognitive behavioral treatment of borderline personality disorder*. New York, NY: Guilford Press.

Linehan, M. M. (1993b). *Skills training manual for treating borderline personality disorder*. New York, NY: Guilford Press.

McMain, S., Korman, L., & Dimeff, L. (2001). Dialectical behavior therapy and the treatment of emotion dysregulation. *Journal of Clinical Psychology, 57*, 183–196.

Plato & Scolnicov, S. (2003). *Plato's Parmenides [electronic resource]/translation with introduction and commentary by Samuel Scolnicov*. Berkeley: University of California Press.

Popper, K. (1940). What is dialectic? *Mind, 49*(196), 403–426.

Segal, Z. V., Williams, J. G., & Teasdale, J. D. (2002). *Mindfulness-based cognitive therapy for depression: A new approach to preventing relapse*. New York, NY: Guilford Press.

CHAPTER

18

Self-Renewal and the Ways Paradigm

Sharon E. Cheston

When you go through the tumbler of life, you can come out crushed or polished.

—Elisabeth Kübler-Ross (1995, p. 73)

INTRODUCTION

Being a mental health professional can be perilous to your health. Our job is to assure that we are walking the path of keeping ourselves mentally and emotionally tuned up, physically fit, and spiritually connected in order to endure the appalling stories that are revealed in our presence. While clients' stress and experiences do not belong to us, the very act of listening to distressing stories or situations that seem to be intractable can take a toll on our minds, bodies, and spirits. For example, a client who describes images of her rape evokes bodily triggers and summons mental images that we would rather not experience. However, seeing these images, hearing information, and experiencing the client's pain is necessary for us to be empathic, to understand the depth of terror, and to induce elucidations that will lead to appropriate, and sometimes brilliant, interventions. However, these images and knowledge now reside in our heads, bodies, and spirits. Without the purposeful act of self-renewal, we can become as depleted as the clients who come to us for help.

According to Gentry (2002), self-care is the "ability to refill and refuel oneself in healthy ways" (p. 48). While I agree with Gentry's definition, I would add the caveat that one should attend to self-renewal before burnout, not after we are depleted.

THE WAYS PARADIGM

The Ways Paradigm (Cheston, 2000) was developed in the late 1990s to assist in teaching new counselors how to integrate a variety of theoretical approaches that seemed to be in contradiction to each other and therefore confused students as they prepared for clinical work. While a theoretically eclectic practice is becoming the "theory" of choice, students were grasping at concepts that were sometimes in opposition to each other. The paradigm has helped bring clarity to students' confusion by offering them a template from which they could engage clients in a theoretical, structured manner but also allowed them to use a variety of theories and techniques. In this chapter the Ways Paradigm is being stretched to define and organize our self-renewal process.

A Way of Being refers to the counselor's presence in the counseling room and how to "establish an atmosphere in which change can occur" (Cheston, 2000, p. 256). A Way of Understanding involves the body of counseling theory and knowledge that explains personality and human behavior and also how people change, form belief systems, assimilate culture and values, and develop symptoms. The area also includes gaining knowledge of client's strengths, resources, and personal skill sets. A Way of Intervening is the work of therapy. Most theories explain not only how change occurs but also what techniques enhance the movement toward a desired clinical goal. The therapist assists the client to interrupt self-defeating cycles, to look at situations from a different perspective, to create healthier ways of thinking or believing concerning their dilemmas, and to enact purposeful steps toward health. These steps can include not only cognitive and behavioral movement but also altering belief systems, gaining insight, allowing grieving, or seeking other supportive people who can assist clients on the path toward health. In other words, one can be theoretically eclectic and still be carefully structured in clinical work with a variety of clients and presenting problems.

THE WAYS PARADIGM AND SELF-RENEWAL

Encouraging students to ask the following questions assists them in gaining a sense of the theory that they want to embrace in each counseling situation. What do I need to understand? How do I want to "be" while in the situation? What do I want to say or do?

However, engaging more broadly and prophylactically in self-renewal, the questions become more focused. How do I want to *be* with myself and others each day in order to enhance self-renewal? How do I understand and conceptualize life's crises, tragedies, and frustrations so I can be sane in what feels, at times, like an insane world? What intervention strategies do I want to use so that I lessen the impact of negativity I experience in the therapy room and in life? How do I intervene each day so that others are safe in my presence, I am safe in the world, and I feel that I have done what God has requested of me without allowing the challenges to drain the joy out of life? The answer should not surprise us that some of the very therapeutic strategies we use as clinicians to help clients can assist us in our search for renewal. Dr. Robert Wicks in his beautifully crafted book *The Resilient Clinician* (2008) calls helpers to consider that the very interventions, suggestions, and experiences we encourage clients to use are also available to us and should be used to ameliorate our own pain and stress so that we can continue to help others.

WAY OF BEING

> Sometimes the most important thing in a whole day is the rest we take between two deep breaths, or the turning inwards in prayer for five short minutes.
>
> —Etty Hillesum, Holocaust survivor (cited in Hillesum, Smelik, & Pomerans, 2002, p. 305)

In the original article, the Ways Paradigm proffered a way of being as the professional manner that counselors brought to the clinical relationship. In other words, how they connected with and attended to the client. Today professionals are using the word *attune* to describe the interpersonal connection that is established with a client. In the search for a way of being with our self that creates renewal, attunement describes a healthy personal relationship with our self that includes adaptation, accommodation, and regulation. Attunement as our Way of Being calls us to adjust and regulate our internal processes as needed to garner the best of what we have to offer ourselves and, by extension, others.

I frequently tell my clients that they are the only people who travel womb to tomb with themselves. The same is true for our personal journeys as clinicians. We are the only ones who will make that journey from birth to death. Parents will die, friendships will fade, children will grow up and leave home, and colleagues will leave to take other jobs. However, we are our constant companions and how we engage ourselves, talk to ourselves, or love ourselves will create or destroy our presence on this planet.

Self-renewal, therefore, becomes our imperative as professionals. Without our continued attention to our being with ourselves, we make the mistake of believing and behaving as if we do not need to attend to ourselves the way we suggest clients do. This lack of self-attention to health and well-being is an ironic self-absorption and belief that we do not have to do what we are encouraging others to do. Narcissism becomes our guide as we pretend we do not need to do the pedestrian things that others must do.

As an example, I ask you to think of a time when you were angry at yourself. Perhaps you dropped something that shattered, or forgot something at the grocery store, or made a decision that did not work out well. How did you talk to yourself? What did you feel about your error? Irritated? Disappointed? Blaming? Now think about how you would have handled a similar situation if a 5-year-old had made the same mistake. We tend to blame ourselves as adults more than we do a child. However, is that fair to ourselves? We have the weight of the world in our backpacks. Clients require that we give them our best, universities demand our improvement year after year, licensing boards require us to improve our skills every year, and our everyday tasks are enormous. So why do we not allow ourselves to make pedestrian mistakes? We would tell our clients that they are entitled to stumble, err, fall, so why cannot we? The first step in being with ourselves in a loving and tender way is to recognize that we are fallible and yet live in a world that demands perfection. Anything less than perfection is a setup for personal diminishment. Improving this one area will allow for a more loving and forgiving presence with ourselves. So instead of saying "I am a clumsy dolt!" when you drop something, use the cognitive-behavioral tool of reframing and say, "Oops, perhaps you need to slow down, sweetheart."

Another tool that I was given more than 20 years ago was the gift of being alone for extended periods of time. The first time I took a vacation by myself, I was unsure if that decision was the right one. I started off thinking of all the things that could go wrong and ended up having to do thought-stopping just to get out of the driveway. However, that initial 5-day trip changed my life. I became my best friend and connected spiritually in ways that I never thought I could. What I discovered was that my shutting up, slowing down, and looking inward rather than outward brought insight and allowed an opening for God to lead.

I am a believer in prayer, meditation, and quiet reflection. However, I am not good at planning for that time. My life just seems to have 20 things going at once and all of them are vying for my attention. However, when I have 1 minute waiting in a parked car, or when the electricity goes off, or when standing in line at an airport, I use that time for me and God. It is the greatest, soothing balm for my harried world. When I do speaking engagements, I am frequently asked how I know that God really exists. These quiet, alone times when my cell phone is off, my Kindle needs recharging, and my computer is not "on" . . . I know. Therefore, closing off the world is key to self-renewal. How can you renew yourself if the world is constantly encroaching on your time and talents? Simply, you cannot. When will the world stop demanding our time and talents? Simply, never. So what do we do? We need to take charge and establish the same boundaries that we recommend to our clients. The task is to say no, not now, contact me later, or I don't want to. Saying the word *no* is hard, but can also be essential for our self-renewal. An excellent, ancient metaphor about how a sword is crafted is frequently used to demonstrate how important stress is in our formation. This metaphor refers to a sword becoming stronger, better, more honed when it is thrust into the fire for curing. Each time the sword is pummeled with a mallet and thrust into the fire, it becomes more polished, durable, and valuable. However, what is frequently left out of the metaphor is that the sword is removed from the fire also and allowed to cool and harden before being thrust into the fire once again. Sometimes we have no control over the fire that is burning nor when we are being thrust into it to increase our tungsten. However, there are the times that we have the power to remove ourselves from the fire and heal. During this time, the power of *no* is essential for us to use. At times, when I am being buffeted around with demands I erroneously believe that I have no power over the circumstances, but in those moments, when I remember to say no, I find that my no to others becomes a yes for me. In conclusion, be as compassionate with yourself as you are with others: by saying no when you are overwhelmed with life, by loving yourself enough to spend time by yourself, by closing off the world, and by speaking lovingly to yourself.

WAY OF UNDERSTANDING

> As health care professionals, we recognize the privilege of sharing so deeply in the lives of our clients. We devote considerable energy, resources, love, and time to relieving their suffering. Yet often we do not devote similar care and attention to ourselves. To put patients' welfare above our own is not skillful and can lead to deleterious consequences. (Shapiro, Brown, & Biegel, 2007, p. 107)

In his research article "Helping Till It Hurts? A Multimethod Study of Compassion Fatigue, Burnout, and Self-Care in Clinicians Working With Trauma Survivors," Killian (2008) states that there is a "burgeoning interest in secondary traumatic stress, compassion fatigue, and self-care in the helping professions. Data shows that therapists detect job stress through bodily symptoms such as sleep disturbances, distraction, increased difficulty concentrating" (p. 32). Another theme that Killian observed from interviews with therapists was their ability to identify stress via bodily symptoms such as muscle tension, headaches, and lack of energy (p. 35). The workplace contributors to stress or burnout included high caseloads, workaholism, lack of support in the work environment, as well as anemic social networks and isolation. The more personal issues that arose in the research as contributors of stress and recovery from stress included a personal history of trauma, social isolation, the clinician's worldview (e.g., self-awareness, optimism, or cynicism), and the ability to recognize and meet one's own needs.

Jevne and Williams (1998) found that identifiers of potential burnout include feeling "less." For example, when burnout occurs there is less enthusiasm and fewer feelings of being valued in addition to viewing oneself as having less capability, connectivity, energy, and creativity. Professionals who are burning out begin to feel a sense of disillusionment, detachment (evidenced as loneliness, isolation, or withdrawal), dread, depression, worry, despair, and hopelessness. In addition, they begin to complain of a variety of physical symptoms, such as poor or decreased sleep, lowered immunity, increased aches and pains, digestive problems, or sexual dysfunction.

As helpers who know how to work with the stress and burnout of others, why do we fall into the same pitfalls as our clients and become stressed, frazzled, irritated, and tense? Some authors indicate that vicarious or secondary traumatization initiates a process by which a professional's inner experience is negatively transformed through empathic engagement with clients' trauma material (Cunningham, 1999; McCann & Pearlman, 1990; Pearlman & MacIan, 1995). In this process, trauma, and possibly other negative experiences that are the topics of therapy, are transferred from clients to the therapist. When this occurs the helper becomes susceptible to psychological distress and Posttraumatic Stress Disorder (PTSD) symptoms (Figley, 2002; Nelson-Gardell & Harris, 2003). Further, other authors conclude that therapists' compassion stress can and does permeate other aspects of a therapist's life and accumulates over time if one does not attend to the symptoms (Carbonell & Figley, 1996; Pearlman & MacIan, 1995). Lest one feels that we should quit our jobs as helpers and become plumbers, the literature also reveals that there is a positive outcome to being a compassionate helper. The job as therapist also contains a healthy dose of compassion satisfaction, which includes a feeling of reward and competence (Figley, 2002).

The question that then begs for an answer is how do helpers increase their compassion satisfaction and reduce their compassion fatigue? In some of the literature, the transfer of stress from client to counselor almost sounds like catching a virus from another person. How does one keep from catching the fatigue virus and build a healthy compassion immune system?

One way to begin the journey is to stop seeing the external world as bequeathing happiness. Happiness is internal, not external. If we buy a new car, we might be happy about that for a few months until the next newest car emerges in the marketplace and then the cycle of want and dissatisfaction starts all over again. About 6 years ago, I was seeing a client who was miserable with her job, her financial situation, and her personal relationships. Then she won a great deal of money playing the lottery and she beamed for a few weeks. She was now out of debt, she had a nest egg for her daughter's education, she had a new car, she changed jobs, and she felt free for the first time in her life, so she quit therapy. Six months later she called for an appointment. She found out that others, who were claiming to be her friends, were taking advantage of her. The "issue" that brought her back to therapy was that her three best friends would ask her to go to dinner and then assume she would pick up the tab. She allowed this to occur a couple of times and then she became angry and felt used. The next time they were at dinner, she suggested splitting the bill and they became irate and said that she was being selfish with her "new wealth" and walked out in unison, leaving her with the check. She decided she would not see them again. Now she was without friends and, yet, she had what she always wanted, a comfortable lifestyle. Before her windfall, her lifestyle was uncomfortable but she had friends. She assumed that after she won the lottery that everything would stay the same except that she would have more money. She had not counted on the personal ramifications. Before her winning the lottery, her friends had seen her as a dependent person who needed them as emotional crutches. After she won the money, they saw her as a dependent person who still needed them as crutches but this time she could pay for her crutches and for their needs, too. She was angry and devastated and blamed herself for being foolish and allowing them in her life in the first place. She lived in the "what if" of life. She reified her friends as those who could give her salvation from the cold world. She believed that money solved *all* problems. She believed her life was hard, joyless, and a difficult journey because she struggled financially. The key to her health was found in her ability to let go of her assumptions about life. She found that money does not solve everything and her view of herself needed to change to someone who focused on strength, growth, and caring for others. For the first time, she started to work on herself rather than complaining about the rest of the human race. She saw life as a journey of impermanence and each day she looked at life as having something new to offer her and, most importantly, celebrated life, even if the new offering was a difficult challenge. In other words, she began to understand that she needed to enjoy living today instead of always focusing on changing her life tomorrow. I learned much from her about how disappointment, stress, demands, and money impact our lives. And I learned that wonderful changes do not always solve our problems but can simply reveal new ones that need our attention.

WAY OF INTERVENING

> A famous Vedic verse says, "It is our duty to the rest of mankind to be perfectly healthy, because we are ripples in the ocean of consciousness, and when we are sick, even a little, we disrupt cosmic harmony." (Chopra, 2000, p. 374)

Gardner (1995) echoes this cosmic importance of self-renewal. "If a society hopes to achieve renewal it will have to be a hospitable environment for creative men and women. It will also have to produce men and women with the capacity for self-renewal" (p. xxi). Further, Gardner indicates that "Renewal is not just innovation and change. It is also the process of bringing the results of change into line with our purposes" (p. 6).

The Way of Intervening is the "work" of therapy and therefore the work of self-renewal. In therapy, it refers to the means by which a counselor interrupts the client's cycle of dysfunction and allows for the practicing and processing of healthier alternatives of thinking, feeling, and behaving. In both therapy and self-renewal, the process involves practicing, reviewing, repeating, and affirming the desired changes. Interventions can also include reframing feelings, changing attitudes, altering belief systems, gaining insight, grieving, or staying with painful feelings in the presence of another supportive person.

Elsewhere in this text are chapters that capture a variety of specific techniques or interventions for self-renewal such as the use of cognition, solitude, supervision, forgiveness, and exercise. Therefore, this section only mentions how those items fit into the Ways Paradigm and I leave the specifics to my colleagues who will flesh out the interventions more thoroughly. This chapter therefore describes the Ways of Intervention for self-renewal, which are similar to those used in counseling and psychotherapy, knowing that no one technique or idea fits all. Ways of Intervening therefore would include reframing, practicing positive self-care, and altering our attitudes and belief systems when they no longer work for us. An example of such an altering experience occurred to a supervisee who was afraid of acupuncture. She was not afraid of needles but she was afraid of the process of someone "messing with my energy." She suffered from a mild but chronic disorder that manifested as exhaustion and had plagued her most of her life. She had engaged in several interventions that she felt had minimal effect in relieving her fatigue. When her medical doctor recommended acupuncture she was stunned but decided to try this intervention. After three treatments she pronounced herself a "believer in acupuncture" and now has treatments regularly and advocates for the procedure to all who will listen. She found the intervention that helped her but what works for one person does not work for everyone so our intervention strategies need to adjust depending on the situation and our life circumstances. There is a cost to doing clinical work, so the key factor is for each of us to choose the self-renewal techniques that feed and enhance our lives.

> Counseling is one of the most taxing endeavors known to mankind. There is nothing that compares to confronting human misery hour after hour and bearing the responsibility for easing that misery using only one's mind and mouth. At its best it is tremendously uplifting, as you watch the client open up, breathe, let go of the pain. At its worst, it is like surfing in a cesspool, struggling for balance while being slapped with wave after putrid wave. (Author Unknown)

While in that cesspool, our task therefore is to be at our best with each client; however, we are also responsible for being at our best with ourselves and with those who care about us. Because this text is replete with excellent examples, I have briefly described some intervention strategies that are my personal favorites or have been embraced by others or demonstrated in the literature to enhance well-being.

Supervision or Peer Consultation

Killian (2008) proffers several self-care strategies including processing or debriefing with peers or supervisor (p. 36). However, Jevne and Williams (1998) and Evans and Villavisanis (1997) not only embrace consultation and supervision for ongoing support, but further recommend that we broaden this strategy to include networking (including more people, resources, and new ideas in our circle of renewal), continuing education to further increase our knowledge base and therefore become less stuck in our therapeutic routine, and reaching out to other professionals to share concerns and provide encouragement, possibly in a regular, structured group format.

Personal Therapy and Self-Knowledge Enhancement

As therapists, our imperative of self-care requires that we are self-knowledgeable enough to know when we are in need of a tune-up in our personal lives and engage in prophylactic therapy to enhance our growth and healing. Our experiences and life struggles create a self-awareness and knowledge that can be the best "textbook" for therapy that one can read. Through our own pain and suffering, we learn how to be human. This learning cannot only become a source of wisdom and healing for ourselves but can inform our work with others. However, to become the wise healer we need to enter into the very experience that we offer others. The pain and suffering that we endure mimics the pain and suffering of our clients and is part of the very core of being human. The belief that reentrance into therapy from time to time as needed is expressed beautifully by Shapiro, Brown, and Biegel (2007): "The heart pumps blood first to itself, before pumping blood to the rest of the body. If it didn't, it would die, and then the rest of the body would die. The art of caring for others is learning how to first care for yourself " (p. 108).

Forgiveness

Frederic Luskin, a senior consultant at Stanford University, in his book *Forgive for Good* (2002) contends that forgiveness yields health benefits and that people who forgive experience fewer symptoms of stress such as backaches, muscle tension, and upset stomachs. His research indicates that those who forgave others experienced improvements in appetite, sleep, energy, and feelings of well-being. In other words, forgiving is physically healthy and will lead to a sense of liberation.

Failure to let go of our negative feelings that occur when we do not forgive interferes in our ability to help others move on from their hurt and pain when they have experienced unfair actions. In addition, we have been told that the best practice when someone hurts us is to "forgive and forget." The problem with this statement is that the probability that a person is going to forget a painful experience is slim. Yet, we continue to pressure ourselves to do the unattainable. I do not know who first linked forgiving and forgetting together, but forgetting is often not in our best interest. Forgetting means that we will not see the warning signs the next time someone is hurting us. Luskin (2002) has developed a modified way to use forgiveness that engages people not only at the intellectual and emotional levels but also at the physical and rational levels. His idea is that hurts are like planes circling the field and cannot land because we cannot let go of them. So they continue to circle, taking up space that should be available to us for the good things in life. When we fail to let go and instead tell the same painful stories over and over, we expend too much mental and physical energy and therefore cannot move forward with the positive aspects of life.

As clinicians we see the patterns of clients who repeat the same story of a past hurt that cannot be forgotten. We patiently listen to the same story hoping that the client will become tired of retelling the story. But do we do the same thing? We can be just as guilty of keeping hurts alive, which makes us prone to illness and stress that can hurt us physically and can also keep us from being compassionate helpers.

The Gratitude Attitude

The Positive Psychology movement has increased our awareness of gratitude as a positive, healthy attitude and skill that mentally healthy people employ on a routine basis.

In a study of gratitude as predictor of bringing closure to unpleasant memories, Watkins, Grimm, and Kolts (2004) found that feeling gratitude in processing unpleasant memories did reduce impact and also brought closure. Further, in a study by Rollison, Cheston, O'Grady, Fialkowski, and Cho Kim (2011), gratitude was found to be a predictor of physical, psychological, and spiritual benefits to individuals. Likewise, Seligman, Steen, Park, and Peterson (2005) and Emmons and McCullough (2003) provided strong empirical evidence that counting "three good things" or "blessings" (grateful events) each day led to significant and sustained improvements in mood, well-being, and health habits. In addition, Watkins et al. (2004) found that grateful people are more likely to remember pleasant memories and also found that the processing of unpleasant memories using gratitude may reduce negative impact and create closure (Watkins et al., 2004). Those who engaged in using gratitude instead of complaining or remembering negative events reported appreciating themselves, others, and (sometimes) God more (Rollison et al., 2011). Although this research is a strong endorsement of how gratitude is able to improve our clients' lives, the essential gift of this research is to remind us to use gratitude to enhance self-renewal in our own lives.

Gratitude may also add benefits to a mindfulness practice, which is long associated with reducing stress, creating a sense of well-being, and in improving perspective. Kashdan, Uswatte, and Julian (2006) noted that gratitude is generated when one is overtly being mindful of positive experiences and this mindfulness then appears to broaden an individual's cognitive and behavioral repertoire of reactions. This finding was supported by Rollison et al. (2011) where participants also observed a connection between gratitude and mindfulness (p. 137).

Spirituality, Prayer, Meditation, and Mindfulness

Carl Jung kept the following saying on the wall of his consulting room where he saw his patients: *Vocatus Atque Non Vocatus, Deus Aderit*. Bidden or unbidden, God is present (Calhoun, 2005, p. 30). Recently, the fields of counseling, psychology, and social work have included spirituality, mindfulness, meditation, and prayer as important tools in helping clients to address cognitions, behaviors, and feelings that are disturbing, repetitive, critical, and self-defeating. The Buddhist belief that we are best served by detaching from our thoughts and observing dispassionately with clarity while being mindful and aware allows us to overcome chronic feelings like anger. The Dalai Lama noted that the most powerful influences on the mind come from within our own mind (Begley, 2007, p. 229).

Killian's (2008) research found that the therapists cited spirituality as playing a major role in their self-care and that most of the interviewees referred to *spirituality* as a worldview that situates their focus as outside the "individual." In other words, spirituality was seen as a relationship with a larger force that guides them in their overall life and more specifically, their practices (p. 37).

Creating Boundaries

As has been stated previously, the helping fields can be hazardous to your health. The creation of boundaries can assist you in separating yourself from the pain and suffering that is experienced each day in the therapeutic environment and help alleviate the feeling that there are painful psychic viruses that follow us as we exit the office after a long day of listening to others' problems. One supervisor suggested that I draw a line at the threshold of my door at the end of the day. Mentally seeing the pain of each client being left behind the door as the door is being exited and locked can assist us in facilitating a transition from the therapeutic environment to the next place we inhabit, be it home, school, or the gym.

Being in the Moment—Breathwork

One self-renewal task that involves separating from the moment is breathwork. The task is to empty oneself of frequently unconscious, self-imposed barriers or impediments like defenses, repressed material, or body memories. "Sustained conscious breathing provides a bridge between the conscious and unconscious, allowing transparent beliefs to come into the conscious awareness, where they can be examined intentionally and subsequently transformed" (Young, Cashwell, & Giordano, 2010, p. 115). Interventions include breathing deeply, quickly, and fully, allowing one to experience altered states of consciousness through which emotional information and spiritual beliefs can come to awareness. This altered state of consciousness provides a vehicle for relaxation and a focus on current stressful issues. Be aware that reentry needs to be gentle and gradual or the calming effect may disappear abruptly and create a feeling of discomfort. Having another person present can assist in the process and keep the discomfort at a minimum.

A similar practice that can create a sense of renewal is a technique borrowed from the Buddhist tradition but is in fact one that all religions use to connect with the holy. This technique uses focusing and concentration to quiet the mind and close out the surroundings so that one can focus on feelings, thoughts, and beliefs. The key to relaxing and renewing is to see the feelings, bodily sensations, thoughts, and beliefs as part of the self and then not a part of the self. The next step is to allow any images, sensations, ideas, and beliefs to enter and often these focus on a relationship with our creator.

Cinema Therapy

What is your favorite feel-good movie . . . the one that takes you away and allows you to release all the stress of this world for a couple of hours? One of my clients told me that whenever she gets stressed she watches *Dr. Zhivago*. While I nodded, acknowledging that I had seen it, I could not fathom using this movie to relax. I remembered the war, the betrayal, the sadness, and the tragic ending. However, she said, "That movie taught me to let go of my puny problems. So when my kids are acting up and my husband is playing golf all day leaving me to fend for myself, I turn on that movie and say, 'See, life is not so bad,' and I can manage better."

I had to admit, she had a point. So now I stop and watch *The Princess Bride* no matter what I am doing and laugh my woes away.

The idea that a film can take us away from the current world for a couple of hours and give us a respite from worry and stress while calming the tension can be seen as a welcomed change. A good book, journaling, a long walk alone, digging in the garden are similar respites, however brief. However, what can lead to a more permanent change?

Another related idea is to write or create a movie or book of our life. I have found that simply naming a book or movie allows for insight into how I am living life. Issues then emerge that can then be addressed. For example, if your life was a novel what would the title be? Relax and create a title and then some dialogue that goes along with the title. Next, change the title to what you want life to be and now change the dialogue so that it matches what you want to happen.

Social Interest

To see with the eyes of another, to hear with the ears of another, to feel with the heart of another. For the time being, this seems to me an admissible definition of what we call social feeling. Alfred Adler (as cited in Ansbacher & Ansbacher, 1964, p. 42).

Leak (2006) states, "The essence of social interest is the valuing of something outside of the self without ulterior motives: a true absence of self-centeredness" (p. 59). However, in the case of self-renewal for clinicians, the question becomes "Is not this caring the very activity that drained us to the point of needing self-renewal?" Probably, however Adler and other therapists have observed that there is a relationship between embracing social interest and emotional health (Adler, 1938).

The Adlerian concept of social interest as a basic inclination of human beings and, therefore, a necessary component of mental health, involves a feeling of belongingness and a willingness to engage in activities that seek to serve the common good. From this vantage point, Adler considers those with high social interest as embracing a wellness model that would encourage self-care. This book affirms the importance of self-renewal for therapists. The very title leads helpers to the conclusion that we need to take time away from the interaction of clients and engage in self-reflection, self-healing, and caring for ourselves. However, Adler turns the seeking of self-renewal upside down when he promotes engaging with others as a way toward personal health. This does not mean that we are to give ourselves emotionally away to everyone and keep nothing for ourselves but he does encourage us to view life from a vantage point of care for self *and* care for others. He believes that we need both imperatives to be truly human and truly healthy. When you think of a time when you have gone out of your way to help another you will probably say that giving to another actually made *you* feel good. That is the idea from an Adlerian point of view. We need to take care of ourselves *and* others. Both types of care-taking are instrumental in mental health.

In his book *The Conscious Universe*, Dean Radin (1997) quotes Claude Levi-Strauss, "Just as the individual is not alone in the group, nor anyone in society alone among others, so man is not alone in the universe" (p. 159). In other words, isolation from others is not possible. An overview of the major world religions reveals that helping others is a common theme and imperative to being a holy person who is doing the work of the creator. However, helping others has an ironic twist. Helping others makes us feel better about ourselves. And in the gratitude literature, for example, Rollison et al. (2011), there seems to be a relationship between gratitude and prosocial behavior that creates reciprocity and encourages social bonding. In addition, Bartlett and DeStano (2006) and Tsang (2006) demonstrate in their research that participants who received a favor would be more likely to reciprocate to both benefactor and strangers. In other words, to quote a popular movie title . . . *Pay It Forward.*

Have we come full circle? As helpers we have a tendency to assist others with problems and do not always care for ourselves in that process. And now a famous clinical theorist, Alfred Adler, says use social interest and you will be exercising not only helping others but also engaging in self-renewal. According to Radin (1997) and Chopra (2000), what is probable is that we are all one. So when we are acting in ways that create self-renewal, we are more available to take care of others and when we take care of others we are also engaging in social interest, which is a form of self-care and renewal, and thus we are engaging in a cosmic love fest.

In my work with clients I have noticed that when a client does a kindness for someone else, she reports an increased feeling of self-worth. So how does this concept of social interest help us to achieve renewal when our job is to help others and in doing so we can become part of the walking wounded community? The theorists are not asking us to put forth even more energy to help others with their emotional problems, but to redirect our energy to first heal ourselves and then to look outward and help others in a different way than we do as clinicians helping clients. To elucidate this dilemma a bit more, Sweeney (2009) proposes that persons with high social interest think and act differently from those with low social interest. Sweeney uses the analogy of a sport or game. He indicates that people with high social interest usually focus on the enjoyment or process as opposed to those with lower social interest who tend to focus on the outcome of the game. In other words, those with high social interest tend to enjoy the game while those with low social interest focus on winning or losing. So in this day of managed care and focus on outcome measures, perhaps one way we can help ourselves is to focus on the "being" with clients and the enjoyment and satisfaction we get when we observe/experience a client making an impressive turn toward health in sessions. In addition, our nonclinical focus should be on enjoying the game of life rather than seeing ourselves as people who must fix the world and if we do not . . . we lose. The very effort should be seen as a social contribution.

Many see social interest as a Christian imperative (love your neighbor as yourself) pointing to the model of the Good Samaritan who helped a man who was left to die at the side of a road. However, most faith groups promote the imperative of helping others. In the Jewish tradition the value Tikkun Olam means repairing the world. More recently, Mahatma Ghandi stated to those who would listen, "You may never know what results come from your action. But if you do nothing, there will be no results." Another example is found in the beliefs of the Cree Indians. . . . All beings in the universe are intimately knitted together in a pattern of interconnectedness. Finally in Zen therapy, we are encouraged to re-create what Buddhists call *harmonious* community.

When we are experiencing a drag on our lives, which can foster feelings of being overwhelmed or exhausted, we often turn inward and become inactive or aloof. However, Adler (1938) recommends that we turn outward and engage in activities that are based on being a part of a community to gain a lift in our emotional state.

This aid to others would best be served outside of the mental health field from whence comes our exhaustion and the activity need not absorb a lot of time or energy. The key is for the activity to take us away from our emotional exhaustion or personal drain and focus on another person or a task that is different from therapy. Cheer on a kid, smile at a stranger, help an elderly person with his groceries, wave to your neighbor, but do all of this with the knowledge that this is not only good for others but healthy for you as well.

PROFESSIONAL OBLIGATION

Although there is an awareness of our need to take our self-care and self-renewal seriously from a purely personal perspective, we are also under the obligation to care for ourselves from a professional perspective. The American Counseling Association's 2005 Code of Ethics identifies self-care as a professional mandate. "Counselors engage in self-care activities to maintain and promote their emotional, physical, mental, and spiritual wellbeing to best meet their professional responsibilities" (ACA, 2005, p. 9). There are similar mandates in the Codes of Ethics of the Association for Marriage and Family Therapy and of the American Psychological Association.

A more colloquial way to see this mandate is from Figley and Figley (2007) who suggest that self-care should be seen as a similar experience to airline travelers. Do not forget to put on your oxygen mask before you help others to put on theirs. We cannot attend to others' needs if we do not attend first to our own needs.

In conclusion, self-renewal does not require a lot of time and energy. One can simply be with oneself in a healthy way. One can understand the importance of daily self-renewal and one can use intervention strategies on a regular basis that are simple and do not require a lot of time and energy. Observe a sunset, help a neighbor, be mindful of our processing, forgive, or be grateful. Bober and Regehr (2006) found no association between the use of *specific* self-care strategies and reduction in stress. In other words, it is not what you do for self-renewal but that you do something that fits with your life.

REFERENCES

Adler, A. (1938). *Social interest*. London, England: Faber & Faber.

American Counseling Association. (2005). *Code of ethics*. Alexandria, VA: Author.

Ansbacher, H. L., & Ansbacher, R. R. (Eds.). (1964). *Superiority and social interest: A collection of later writings. "Brief comments on reason, intelligence & feeble mindedness."* Evanston, IL: Northwestern University Press.

Bartlett, M. Y., & DeSteno, D. (2006). Gratitude and prosocial behavior: Helping when it costs you. *Psychological Science, 17*, 319–325. doi:10.1111/j.1467–9280.2006.01705.x

Begley, S. (2007). *Train your mind, change your brain: How a new science reveals our extraordinary potential to transform ourselves*. New York, NY: Ballantine Books.

Bober, T., & Regehr, C. (2006). Strategies for reducing secondary or vicarious trauma: Do they work? *Brief Treatment and Crisis Intervention*, 6, 1–9.

Calhoun, A. A. (2005). *Spiritual disciplines handbook: Practices that transform us*. Downers Grove, IL: InterVarsity Press.

Carbonell, J. L., & Figley, C. R. (1996). When trauma hits home: Personal trauma and the family therapist. *Journal of Marital and Family Therapy, 22*, 53–58.

Cheston, S. E. (2000). A new paradigm for teaching counseling theory and practice. *Counselor Education and Supervision, 39*(4), 254–269.

Chopra, D. (2000). *Perfect health: A complete mind body guide*. New York, NY: Three Rivers Press.

Cunningham, M. (1999). The impact of sexual abuse treatment on the social work clinician. *Child and Adolescent Social Work Journal, 16*, 277–290.

Emmons, R. A., & McCullough, M. E. (2003). Counting blessings versus burdens: An experimental investigation of gratitude and subjective well-being in daily life. *Journal of Personality and Social Psychiatry, 84*, 377–389. doi:10.1037/0022–3514.84.2.377

Evans, T. D., & Villavisanis, R. (1997). Encouragement exchange: Avoiding therapist burnout. *Family Journal, 5*, 342–345.

Figley, C. R. (2002). *Treating compassion fatigue*. New York, NY: Brunner-Routledge.

Figley, C. R., & Figley, K. R. (2007). Put the oxygen mask on yourself. *Family Networker*, 6, 8–11.

Gardner, J. W. (1995). *Self-renewal: The individual and the innovative society*. New York, NY: Norton.

Gentry, J. E. (2002). Compassion fatigue: A crucible of transformation. *Journal of Trauma Practice, 1*(3/4), 37–61.

Hillesum, E., Smelik, A., & Pomerans, A. J. (2002). *Etty: The letters and diaries of Etty Hillesum 1941–1943*. Grand Rapids, MI: Eerdmans.

Jevne, R. F., & Williams, D. R. (1998). *When dreams don't work: Professional caregivers and burnout*. Amityville, NY: Baywood.

Kashdan, T. B., Uswatte, G., & Julian, T. (2006). Gratitude and hedonic and eudaimonic well-being in Vietnam war veterans. *Behavior Research and Therapy, 44*, 177–199. doi:10.1016/j.brat.2005.01.005

Killian, K. D. (2008). Helping till it hurts? A multimethod study of compassion fatigue, burnout, and self-care in clinicians working with trauma survivors. *Traumatology, 14*, doi:010.1177/1534765608319083

Kübler-Ross, E. (1995). *Death is of vital importance: On life, death, and life after death*. Barrytown, NY: Stationhill.

Leak, G. K. (2006). An empirical assessment of the relationship between social interest and spirituality. *Journal of Individual Psychology, 62*(1), 59–69.

Luskin, F. (2002). *Forgive for good: A proven prescription for health and happiness.* New York, NY: HarperCollins.

McCann, L., & Pearlman, L. A. (1990). Vicarious traumatization: A framework for understanding the psychological effects of working with victims. *Journal of Traumatic Stress, 3*, 131–149.

Nelson-Gardell, D., & Harris, D. (2003). Childhood abuse history, secondary traumatic stress, and child welfare workers. *Child Welfare, 82*, 5–26.

Pearlman, L. A., & McIan, P. S. (1995). Vicarious traumatization: An empirical study of the effects of trauma work on trauma therapists. *Professional Psychology: Research and Practice, 26*, 558–565.

Radin, D. (1997). *The conscious universe: The scientific truth of psychic phenomena.* New York, NY: HarperCollins.

Rollison, D., Cheston, S., O'Grady, K., Fialkowski, G., & Cho Kim, (2011). *Grace in grateful: Exploring gratitude's potential influence on faith maturity and stress-related growth.* Unpublished Dissertation.

Seligman, M. P., Steen, T. A., Park, N., & Peterson, C. (2005). Positive psychology progress: Empirical validation of intervention. *American Psychologist, 10*, 410–421. doi:10.1037/0003–066x.60.5.410

Shapiro, S. L., Brown, K., & Biegel, G. (2007). Self-care for health care professionals: Effects of MBSR on mental well being of counseling psychology students. *Training and Education in Professional Psychology, 1*(2), 105–115.

Sweeney, T. J. (2009). *Adlerian counseling and psychotherapy: A practitioner's approach.* New York, NY: Routledge.

Tsang, J. (2006). Gratitude and prosocial behaviour: An experimental test of gratitude. *Cognition and Emotion, 20*, 138–148. doi:10.1080/02699930500172341

Watkins, P. C., Grimm, D. L., & Kolts, R. (2004). Counting your blessings: Positive memories among grateful persons. *Current Psychology, 23*, 52–67. doi:10.1007/5121 44–004–1008–2

Wicks, R. J. (2008). *The resilient clinician.* New York, NY: Oxford University Press.

Young, J. S., Cashwell, C. S., & Giordano, A. L. (2010). Breathwork as a therapeutic modality: An overview for counselors. *Counseling and Values, 55*, 113–125.

PART

V

Spirituality and Self-Renewal

CHAPTER

19

Spiritual Coping Resources for the Self-Renewal of Clients and Therapists

MELISSA D. FALB AND KENNETH I. PARGAMENT

INTRODUCTION

Engaging in mental health endeavors, whether as a client or a clinician, is a demanding task. It requires a vast amount of personal, emotional, and—for some people—spiritual resources. Those familiar with the therapeutic process know that participation in psychotherapy is a sign of strength rather than weakness. Indeed, personal change requires a great deal of effort and dedication. Especially for those struggling with more difficult issues, such as trauma, abuse, or loss, recognizing and putting words to one's problems is only the beginning of the path to growth and change. To engage in the therapeutic process fully, one can no longer go it alone, but must reach out to others. One must also be willing to experience an intense range of emotions, including frustration and joy, loneliness and intimacy, pain and relief, anger and gratitude.

For good reason, the treatment relationship focuses on change and growth among counseling and psychotherapy clients. However, clinicians undergo similar processes, mirroring those of their clients. They experience their own ups and downs—drained by the needs and emotions of their clients, energized by clients' insights and successes, worn out after investing their hearts and minds fully into the problems and narratives they have been privileged to witness, or overcome with paperwork and other secondary responsibilities. Despite the many rewards of this path, all clinicians experience varying degrees of career-related stress, burnout, "compassion fatigue," or "vicarious traumatization" (Canfield, 2005). Even the most dedicated clinicians experience difficulties at times in the pursuit of their vocation. Because of these challenges, self-renewal is critical for both clients and clinicians. In particular, spiritual renewal can be a vital resource for maintaining one's effectiveness and commitment to the path of mental and emotional change of self or others. This chapter summarizes how spirituality, religion, and spiritual coping can be effective in the process of self-renewal. The chapter first briefly reviews the concept of coping generally, then describes the benefits (and risks) of spiritual/religious coping and what it offers above and beyond secular strategies, and, finally, discusses specific examples of spiritual resources that may contribute to self-renewal within the psychotherapeutic endeavor.

WHAT IS COPING?

A vast psychological literature suggests that how individuals adjust to a stressor depends on the coping methods they utilize in response to that stressor. Coping, generally, is defined as the "constantly changing cognitive and behavioral efforts to manage specific external and/or internal demands that are appraised as taxing or exceeding the resources of the person" (Lazarus & Folkman, 1984, p. 141). This model contains the important idea that coping methods serve as mediators between stressful experiences and outcomes. In other words, a stressor does not invariably bring about predetermined outcomes; rather, the impact of a stressor is related to the characteristics of the individual in transaction with the situation and his or her environment. For example, how individuals understand and interpret their experiences can have a significant impact on the outcomes of particular stressors. In particular, more adaptive coping strategies can reduce the negative effects of stressors (and subsequent distress), whereas maladaptive coping responses can intensify the negative effects of stressors. Clearly, the choices individuals make about their interpretation and response to stress are at least as important as, if not more important than, the actual events that people experience.

Anecdotally, we all understand this phenomenon. We witness the differing ways in which our friends and neighbors deal with similar types of adversity. For example, one friend responds to the loss of her job with a pervasive attitude of fear, anger, and despair. Another experiences the same event yet is able to maintain an attitude of hope, gratitude, and growth. One relative responds to chronic disease by blaming God; another beseeches Him for strength and support. One colleague responds to divorce by gaining weight, remaining bitter, and swearing off intimacy completely, while another develops new interests, takes better care of himself, and considers the qualities he desires in a future partner. We see these contrasts in the ways people approach their work, their health, their relationships, and virtually all aspects of their lives.

Research shows that the choice of coping methods can have significant effects. For example, more problem-focused, active, or goal-oriented coping strategies (planning, seeking social support) tend to be effective in reducing stress by allowing individuals to achieve a sense of mastery over a stressor and divert energy and attention away from a problem. On the other hand, emotion-focused coping strategies (related to managing, controlling, or regulating emotional distress) are less effective (Penley, Tomaka, & Wiebe, 2002). A third style of coping, avoidance coping (wishful thinking, self-distraction, mental disengagement) has more mixed results. While avoidance coping appears to be generally negative, it may be useful in dealing with short-term distress, such as noise or uncomfortable medical procedures (Suls & Fletcher, 1985).

These conclusions about patterns of coping and their effects are necessarily generalizations. Overall, coping is affected by the individual (e.g., personality) in dynamic interaction with the situation and the larger context (e.g., environment), such that helpful coping strategies for one person or in one situation may be harmful for another person or in another context. For instance, while emotion-focused coping is generally less adaptive than problem-focused coping, emotion-focused coping has been shown to be useful under low-control situations where active strategies are unlikely to be successful. (For a fuller examination of this topic, see Park, Armeli, & Tennen, 2004, and Park, Folkman, & Bostrom, 2001.)

In this book, as well as in other places, readers are presented with a wide range of coping strategies. From the start of their training, clinicians are provided with numerous ideas about how to deal with the inevitable stresses of their chosen profession. Among the most common suggestions include strengthening one's support system, maintaining personal boundaries, engaging in one's own therapy, practicing healthy habits (e.g., exercise, diet, sleep), and balancing social, leisure, and family activities with career demands. In addition, at one point or another, effective clinicians are likely to talk to their clients about the importance of self-care in maintaining good physical and mental health. In early sessions, especially, they may question clients about their support system, health habits, and other methods of managing stress and mitigating psychological symptoms. Clinicians routinely practice such methods in sessions with clients (e.g., relaxation training) or use specific therapeutic orientations to pursue more effective ways of managing thoughts (e.g., Cognitive Behavioral Therapy) and emotions (e.g., Dialectical Behavior Therapy), ideally leading to more effective, problem-focused types of coping.

Generally, most of the coping strategies suggested for both clients and clinicians are secular ones. Nonetheless, spirituality and religion play an important role in the lives of most Americans (Pew, 2007). Although mental health practitioners tend to be less religious and spiritual than the clients they serve

(Shafranske & Cummings, 2013), they, too, can benefit from spiritual coping techniques. Even nonreligious clients may be open to such strategies.

SPIRITUAL/RELIGIOUS COPING AND SPIRITUAL SELF-CARE

This section examines the types of coping strategies that are spiritual or religious in nature and that could make a useful addition to the typical list of strategies personally used and recommended to clients by mental health practitioners.

Spiritual/Religious Coping

Although spirituality and religion are frequently neglected as sources of coping, an increasing number of studies have assessed the role religious and spiritual factors can play in the coping process. Spiritual and religious coping refers to sacred methods, which individuals use to find significance (e.g., meaning, comfort, sense of control, spiritual connectedness) in difficult circumstances (Pargament, 1997). It can draw on cognitions, beliefs, and theologies, as well as on emotions and behaviors. Spiritual and religious coping can refer to numerous strategies such as seeking spiritual support and community, engaging in practices and rituals (praying/meditating, reading religious texts, rites of passage, etc.), making religious appraisals, expressing spiritual discontent, and pursuing positive virtues (e.g., compassion, forgiveness, acceptance). As with coping generally, the effects of spiritual and religious coping have been shown to depend on the types of coping strategies utilized. A range of studies supports the notion that spiritual and religious coping can yield both helpful and harmful effects, depending on the types of coping strategies employed.

Specifically, the literature on spiritual and religious coping demonstrates that it can be related to a range of positive coping functions, including intimacy (Johnson & Mullins, 1989), personal growth and actualization (Park & Cohen, 1993), meaning-making (Park & Folkman, 1997), and a search for the sacred (Pargament, Magyar, & Murray-Swank, 2005). In addition, however, spiritual and religious coping has been related to a range of detrimental effects, including anxiety, depression, PTSD symptomology, and other forms of distress including suicidal ideation and values confusion (see Exline, 2013, for a review). Generally, positive spiritual and religious coping—which reflects a more secure relationship with the sacred and with other people—tends to be related to positive outcomes, while negative spiritual and religious coping—which reflects a spiritual struggle with self, others, or the sacred—tends to be related to negative outcomes (see Ano & Vasconcelles, 2005; Pargament, 2011, for a review).

For example, several studies have found a relationship between positive religious coping and health outcomes. In one study utilizing a spiritually focused treatment with cancer patients, Cole (2005) found that positive religious coping was correlated with greater physical well-being and reduced pain severity. Similarly, in a study of cardiac surgery patients, Ai, Peterson, Bolling, and Rodgers (2006) reported a relationship between positive coping strategies prior to surgery and overall functioning after surgery. In addition, positive religious coping has been shown to be related to mental and emotional outcomes. For example, Harris et al. (2008) found a relationship between positive religious coping and posttraumatic growth in individuals struggling with a range of negative life events, including death of a loved one, childhood sexual abuse, assault, accidents, and natural disasters.

On the other hand, robust links have been reported between negative religious coping (i.e., spiritual struggle) and negative physical and mental/emotional outcomes. Spiritual struggles have been defined as tensions, stress, and strain within oneself, with others, and with God about spiritual matters (Exline, 2013). For example, Trevino et al. (2010) found spiritual struggle to be related to reduced emotional and physical functioning in HIV/AIDS patients. This included lower quality of life, increased depressive symptoms, and greater HIV symptoms and detectable viral load. Similarly, Ai, Seymour, Tice, Kronfol, and Bolling (2009) studied cardiac patients and reported that spiritual struggles were related to negative effects, including increased plasma interleukin-6, a marker of inflammation-immune system functioning. With regard to mental health outcomes, McConnell, Pargament, Ellison, and Flannelly (2006) showed that spiritual struggles were related to various forms of psychopathology including anxiety, depression, paranoid ideation, obsessive-compulsiveness, and somatization.

In summary, spiritual and religious coping is not necessarily beneficial, although in many instances it can be. Instead, the types of coping methods utilized in times of stress play a role in how individuals are affected by difficult life events. The choice to use positive versus negative coping strategies can yield differential effects. As with coping generally, spiritual and religious coping methods can lead to either burnout and exhaustion or, alternatively, to self-renewal and revitalization.

Spiritual Self-Care

Spiritual self-care is a similar concept relevant to the current discussion. The idea of self-care is widely researched in nursing and health care, although less so in the field of psychology. Self-care is conceptualized as a prerequisite for healthy physical, mental, and social well-being, but does not specifically include the idea of spirituality. Spiritual self-care incorporates this idea and can be defined as "the set of spiritually-based practices in which people engage to promote continued personal development and well-being in times of health and illness" (White, Peters, & Schim, 2011).

Spiritual self-care includes introspection and reflection, values clarification, virtues such as love, joy, and happiness, and spiritual emotions. It can rely on practices such as praying, meditating, attending religious services, reading religious/spiritual/inspirational texts, volunteering, engaging in personally relevant group activities and relationships, and spending time in nature. Spirituality is important to the concept of self-care, because spirituality can be a motivator for individuals to engage in various self-care behaviors. For example, spirituality may influence choices related to diet, relationships, and personal goals/values, among other things. For the purposes of this chapter, spiritual coping and spiritual self-care are not distinguished.

THE IMPORTANCE OF SPIRITUAL COPING AND SPIRITUAL SELF-CARE

Now that we have briefly defined the concepts of spiritual coping and spiritual self-care, several questions arise. What can spiritual coping and self-care offer above and beyond secular strategies? How is spiritual coping relevant to the psychotherapeutic endeavor? This section attempts to address these questions, in particular by looking again at the empirical evidence.

While secular forms of coping and self-care offer benefits to health and well-being, there is some indication that spiritual approaches may be incrementally beneficial. For example, the psychology of spirituality research offers evidence of the potential value of explicitly spiritual practices compared to similar nonspiritual ones. In one study, Wachholtz and Pargament (2008) assigned migraine sufferers to one of four conditions: spiritually based meditation, internally focused meditation, externally focused meditation, and progressive muscle relaxation. They found that spiritual meditation led to greater improvements in a number of areas, including frequency of migraines, pain tolerance, negative affect, anxiety, and existential well-being. Another study compared a manualized Buddhist-based therapy (Spiritual Self-Schema or 3-S; Avants & Margolin, 2004) to a comparison condition in treating addiction and HIV risk behaviors (Margolin et al., 2007). Individuals in the 3-S group experienced greater decreases in impulsivity and intoxicant use and greater increases in spiritual practices, motivation for abstinence, medication adherence, and HIV prevention than those in the comparison condition.

Several other programs provide evidence that spiritually based interventions may be helpful for individuals coping with a range of issues including spiritual struggles (Gear et al., 2008), childhood sexual abuse (Murray-Swank & Pargament, 2003), serious mental illness (Phillips, Lakin, & Pargament, 2002), bereavement (Azhar & Varma, 1995), anxiety (Azhar, Varma, & Dharap, 1994), and drug addiction (Gruner, 1984). Even among nonclinically distressed populations, such interventions appear to provide a positive means of coping with stress (Oman et al., 2007). Research is ongoing in this area, even among traditionally nonreligiously affiliated groups such as the military (Pargament & Sweeney, 2011).

Finally, there is evidence that spirituality plays a role in coping with the stresses of working in the mental health professions. Several studies have shown—unsurprisingly, given the low religiosity of mental health practitioners—that spirituality is rated by mental health practitioners as an infrequently utilized coping resource (Stevanovic & Rupert, 2004; Turner et al., 2005). Nonetheless, Stevanovic and Rupert (2004) found that highly satisfied psychologists (those in the top quartile with regard to professional satisfaction) were significantly more likely than their less satisfied counterparts (those in the bottom quartile) to turn to their spiritual beliefs to cope with the stresses of their profession. This suggests that although spirituality is less frequently used as a coping method than other secular strategies, it is effective in maintaining career satisfaction for those who access it to help sustain themselves in their professional lives.

Overall, these studies indicate that the use of spiritual coping/spiritual self-care strategies is important to the process of self-renewal, above and beyond secular coping strategies. Whether coping with life changes and transitions as a therapy client or attempting to alleviate the stress, which can arise due to working in the sometimes emotionally draining mental health professions, spiritual resources are a vital tool for coping. The remainder of this chapter delineates a range of specific spiritual coping techniques that might be utilized as a means of self-care for both clients and clinicians.

SPIRITUAL SELF-CARE STRATEGIES

A diverse range of spiritual coping strategies and techniques can be effective in self-care. These include practices related to specific religious beliefs and formal religious systems, spiritual practices that are not related to formal beliefs and systems, and interpersonal practices that help cultivate the spiritual qualities inherent in the connections between people—which is especially relevant for partners in the therapeutic relationship. This section describes a variety of these specific types of practices that can be useful for self-renewal. Although there is considerable overlap between these categories, specific practices are listed in the area in which they seem to fit most appropriately or where they are found most commonly.

Practices Related to Specific Religious and Spiritual Beliefs/Systems

First we consider self-care practices that stem directly from specific spiritual and religious beliefs and systems. These are perhaps the most well-known and common of spiritual self-care methods and are generally used by practitioners of the spiritual or religious tradition(s) from which they derive. One of the most familiar is prayer, a common element of many religious traditions and certainly of the dominant Christian tradition in the United States and in the West. While there are many forms of prayer, including those with more ritualistic qualities (see section on ritual for a description of these characteristics), prayers in response to life events or those that express gratitude and thanksgiving may be especially useful for fostering self-renewal.

Several research studies have looked at the effects of prayer on health and well-being. Despite some mixed results, due perhaps in part to more distressed or ill individuals using prayer more frequently, several studies show prayer to be related to positive outcomes. These outcomes include increased posttraumatic growth (Harris et al., 2010; VandeCreek, Pargament, Belavich, Cowell, & Friedel, 1999) and decreased psychological distress (Rajagopal, Mackenzie, Bailey, & Lavizzo-Mourrey, 2002). In addition, prayer appears to yield positive physiological effects, such as stabilizing respiration rates and increasing cardiovascular rhythms (Bernardi et al., 2001). Praying is a strategy that is easy to implement, familiar to most people, and takes little time or resources to practice, making it a simple but effective mechanism for self-care/renewal.

Another example of a self-care practice related to specific beliefs/systems is reading of religious texts. Although no empirical studies have evaluated the use of reading scripture as an intervention, several case studies provide anecdotal evidence of the healing benefits of using sacred texts to deal with emotional distress and psychological symptoms. For example, Garzon (2005) describes various ways the Bible can be effectively incorporated into therapeutic work with Christian clients. These include many out-of-session (homework) techniques for clients, such as reading scripture between sessions and considering ways it applies to their situation, and repeating soothing Bible phrases (e.g., "the Lord is my shepherd") for reducing anxiety or stress. Some in-session techniques can also be useful, including discussing pertinent passages together and having clients imagine themselves as Biblical characters who possess current or ideal qualities of the client. The exercises can be modified to use sacred texts from other religious traditions as well. Certainly, these techniques can also be useful for clinicians as well as clients. Like prayer, this strategy can be relatively quick and simple and can be practiced at almost any time and place, making it another effective method of self-renewal.

Participation in religious services and with spiritual communities is a third example of a spiritual self-renewal strategy, which stems from specific spiritual and religious beliefs/systems. In addition to providing support for one's personal beliefs, attendance at religious events also contains a social element, which offers participants a sense of community and connectedness with others who share similar values. Several research studies provide evidence of the physical and mental health benefits of participation in religious services. For instance, Maselko, Gilman, and Buka (2009) found religious service attendance to be correlated with reduced risk of major depression, and Rasic, Robinson, Bolton, Bienvenu, and Sareen (2011) showed it to be related to decrease suicide attempts. These types of benefits are experienced even after accounting for the effects of similar secular support. For example, Krause (2006) showed that church-based emotional support was related to fewer negative health effects from financial strain as compared to support from family and friends. Similarly, in a meta-analysis looking at religious community involvement, Chida, Steptoe, and Powell (2009) found decreased mortality rates among physically healthy samples who attended religious services regularly as compared to those who did not. Thus, for individuals who hold to specific spiritual and religious beliefs, participation with a religious community appears to be an effective strategy for self-care and self-renewal.

Finally, participation in rituals—most of which take place within an explicitly spiritual or religious context—can be a helpful strategy for self-care and renewal. Rituals refer to formalized practices that involve words and physical actions, are constant in the details of their performance, often take place in special places, create a time set apart from everyday life, and offer the potential for contact with the sacred (Idler, 2013). Many rituals are enacted in group settings, and thus provide similar benefits to other spiritual and religious group activities and events, especially the sense of creating community identity and shared experience. Many of these shared rituals occur within participation in religious events (weddings, funerals, communion, coming-of-age ceremonies, etc.); however, rituals can also be performed individually.

Studies that have assessed the physical and mental health effects of rituals show a range of positive outcomes. For instance, a recent study by Tewari, Khan, Hopkins, Srinivasan, and Reicher (2012) showed that participants in a month-long pilgrimage event experienced increased well-being and decreased symptoms of ill health as compared to nonparticipating controls. In another study, looking at physical effects of ritual, Maislos, Abou-Rabiah, Zuili, Iordash, and Shany (1998) showed that daily fasting among Bedouin Muslims during Ramadan increased "good" (HDL) cholesterol levels, at least in the short term. Several studies have even shown decreased mortality in the time period leading up to ritualistic celebrations and holidays, especially among religiously observant individuals and groups (see Idler, 2013, for a summary).

Although many rituals take place within a communal, religious context, individuals might also create their own personal rituals, either those mimicking social rituals or more individualized ones. For instance, on the anniversary of a loved one's death, many people find it healing to look at pictures of their loved one, to remember special times together, to visit a gravesite, or some other meaningful ritual similar to that which might occur at a more public funeral service or interment ceremony. Personal rituals include utilizing a sacred space, shrine, or altar for praying, meditating, reading religious texts, or engaging in other spiritual/ religious activities. Other personalized rituals make use of the cleansing powers of water or light, incorporate meaningful pictures or symbols, or pay homage to religious and spiritual leaders or role models. The type and number of these rituals are limited only by the individual imagination, but they may have healing power. As such, they are another simple tool for self-renewal.

Practices Stemming From Religious and Spiritual Beliefs/Systems

The second main category of spiritual self-renewal strategies is those that are generally not practiced as part of a formal belief system. The most familiar, and increasingly popular of these, are the Eastern practices of yoga, qi gong, tai chi, and other mind-body practices, as well as various forms of meditation, including mindfulness. Although generally divorced from a context of spirituality and religious belief systems, these self-renewal techniques clearly originate from within specific spiritual and religious traditions.

For example, Chinese qi gong and tai chi chuan are rooted in centuries-old spiritual traditions including Taoism, Confucianism, and Buddhism. Similarly, most yogic traditions trace their roots back thousands of years to Hindu belief systems. While the physical aspects are most prominent in Western adaptations of these practices, the techniques themselves are naturally meditative and often practiced by individuals interested in spiritual endeavors. They can be found in temples and monasteries across the world, including in the United States. They are seen as a complement to other spiritual endeavors and have a tendency, when practiced with intention and attention, to develop calmness of both body and mind. Despite these spiritual roots and aspects, many individuals engage in these practices from a purely secular frame of reference and find them beneficial.

In recent decades, a number of empirical studies have examined the implications of these practices and reveal positive effects in a range of domains. Several review studies of tai chi chuan (Jimenez, Melendez, & Albers, 2012; Wang et al., 2010), for instance, have shown benefits with regard to stress, anxiety, depression, sleep, pain, physical functionality, and numerous other conditions. Similarly, review studies of yoga (Büssing, Michalsen, Khalsa, Telles, & Sherman, 2012; Meyer et al., 2012) suggest positive effects over a range of physical and mental outcomes, including depression, fatigue, anxiety, epilepsy, cancer-related fatigue and distress, and pain. Although less research has assessed the effects of qi gong, a few recent studies show positive preliminary results in the treatment of individuals with diabetes (Liu, Miller, Burton, Chang, & Brown, 2011) and hypertension (Lee, Lee, Kim, & Choi, 2004).

With regard to meditation and mindfulness practices, empirical research has exploded over the past several decades. A mere 90 articles on this topic were published between 1990 and 1999; however, in the first 2 years of the most recent decade alone, 710 articles were published. Studies have assessed mindfulness-related treatments and practices among patients struggling with a wide array of mental and physical conditions and found a range of positive effects. This includes, for example, patients struggling with medical conditions such as diabetes (Gregg, Callaghan, Hayes, & Glenn-Lawson, 2007) and cancer (Shennan, Payne, & Fenlon, 2011), as well as psychological disorders including anxiety/depression (Hofmann, Sawyer, Witt, & Oh, 2010) and substance abuse (Witkiewitz & Bowen, 2010).

Some caution is warranted in interpreting these findings due to methodological limitations of many of these studies (e.g., lack of control groups, unstandardized practices, and small sample sizes), as well as to the range of different forms and practices, which might fall under the same name (e.g., "yoga") despite vast differences in technique. Nonetheless, the empirical evidence provides preliminary support for the idea that these practices are effective in reducing a range of physical and mental health symptoms and conditions. Indeed, their increasing popularity suggests that many individuals find benefit from using them. As such, physical practices such as yoga, tai chi, and qi gong, as well as more explicitly meditative practices including mindfulness, appear to help reduce physical and emotional suffering for some individuals. Thus, these techniques may be effective spiritual self-care strategies for people from all walks of life, including clients and clinicians, regardless of spiritual and religious affiliations.

Practices Unrelated to Religious and Spiritual Beliefs/Systems

The third type of spiritual self-renewal strategies are those that do not originate within a formal religious context. Nonetheless, these practices tend to develop spiritual qualities and attitudes. Common self-renewal techniques in this category could include taking walks in nature, creating art, listening to music, reading inspirational works, writing or talking about one's deepest values and aspirations, or engaging in volunteer/service activities. Other practices unrelated to formal spiritual and religious belief systems include those that focus on interpersonal interactions. They indirectly emphasize the spiritual nature and interconnectedness of all human beings (Falb & Pargament, 2012), creating a type of intimate "I-Thou" relationship, such as that envisioned by Martin Buber (1987). The remainder of this section focuses on these less well-known and practiced interpersonal techniques.

For the purposes of this section, we call these interpersonal practices *relational mindfulness*. Although not all of them derive from mindfulness traditions, they share many of the qualities of mindfulness and involve deliberate attention to another person. Relational mindfulness is an emerging concept, although similar techniques and practices have existed for some time, especially within and derived from clinical psychology and psychotherapy practice (e.g., Gestalt, Imago, Focusing, Co-Counseling). In simplest terms, relational mindfulness can be defined as practicing mindfulness in interactions with one or more other people. In contrast to the solitary, generally silent, mode of traditional mindfulness, relational mindfulness integrates words with silence and brings mindful qualities into interpersonal interactions, such as speaking and listening.

Relational mindfulness techniques can take a range of different forms. Although some of them derive from mindfulness traditions (Buddhism), the techniques do not exist in their current form in these traditions. Practices that derive explicitly from mindfulness/meditation include Insight Dialogue (a form of dialogic meditation based on Vipassana meditation; Kramer, 2007) and the related Interpersonal Mindfulness Program (a training program based on Insight Dialogue taught to therapists). A brief outline of the Insight Dialogue guidelines (Kramer, 2007) is provided in Table 19.1 as an example to give the reader a better understanding of what such practices can look like. Other relational

Table 19.1 Insight Dialogue Basic Guidelines

Guideline	Qualities Cultivated	Basis Intentions for Guideline
Pause	Mindfulness	To be in the present moment with immediate experience during listening and speaking; to interrupt the mind's habit of reactivity and forward pressure
Relax	Tranquility, acceptance	To counter agitation; to replace tension of mind and body with ease; to keep awareness soft, gentle, receptive, and kind
Open	Relaxation, spaciousness	To extend relaxed mindfulness from the internal to the external, from self to other; to increase mutuality; to soften the boundary between self and other
Trust Emergence	Flexibility, letting go	To remain present with change, instability, and impermanence; to set aside judgments, expectations, prediction, and plans; to release goals for interactions with others in favor of the present moment
Listen Deeply	Receptivity, attunement	To listen fully and receptively to one's partner without any agenda; to seek understanding; to attend to the flow, direction, and nuance of communication; to develop wisdom, compassion, and discernment
Speak the Truth	Integrity, care	To speak from one's values (generosity, love, wisdom, etc.); to maintain awareness of the present moment and of mental/emotional processes and habits while speaking; to maintain mindful qualities during interactions with others

mindfulness practices take the form of simple interpersonal interactions such as engaging in prolonged eye gazing (Levine & Levine, 1995), shared breathing (Co-Meditation; Boerstler & Kornfeld, 1995), or brief, formal exchanges ("What would you like to tell me?," "If you really knew me . . ."), which deliberately emphasize nonreactive, present-moment awareness of self and other.

There is limited evidence to date about the effects of these practices. One informal study suggests that Insight Dialogue can help ease social anxiety (Kim & Kramer, 2002) and anecdotal evidence indicates that the practice may cultivate empathy, therapeutic presence, and other traits relevant to interpersonal relationships (Kramer, Meleo-Meyer, & Turner, 2008). One study of a more formal interpersonally oriented mindfulness protocol with psychotherapists-in-training showed that relational practices decreased stress, increased social connectedness, increased emotional intelligence, and reduced anxiety (Cohen & Miller, 2009) as compared to a control group. Informal relational mindfulness practices have not yet been evaluated, although practitioners and participants provide enthusiastic reviews.

Due to the novel nature of these practices, gaining experience with them may be difficult. In larger cities, insight dialogue, focusing, or co-counseling groups may be available to interested participants. In such instances, these can be effective self-renewal strategies, especially for clinicians who are already skilled in the art of listening, but do not have their own mindful listening partner. Less formal practices, which require minimal training, may be more accessible and require primarily an interested partner, as well as a bit of self-study and practice. In these instances, the reader is referred to books such as Levine and Levine (1995)—especially suited for intimate partners—or Geller and Greenberg (2012) and Surrey (2005)—both especially suitable for therapists. For readers in the Los Angeles area, the Mindful Awareness Research Center (MARC) at UCLA frequently offers relational mindfulness groups. As awareness of and interest in these practices grows, opportunities for learning and practicing them are likely to increase.

SUMMARY OF SELF-RENEWAL

As this chapter has illustrated, individuals cope or seek self-renewal in a variety of ways, including using spiritual practices and techniques. This choice of strategies can have a profound impact on the effects of stress. Within coping theory generally, it is clear that individuals and their context are as important as the stressors a person experiences. As a result, the strategies individuals utilize for dealing with stress may be more or less effective depending on a variety of personal, social, and situational factors. What works for one person may not work for another. What works in one situation may not work in the next. Thus, having a wide range of coping strategies, including spiritual and religious ones, is optimal.

Spiritual and religious self-renewal strategies derive from a range of contexts—some are explicitly religious and rely on formal religious beliefs and systems, whereas others derive from spiritual traditions, but do not rely on specific belief systems. Still other renewal strategies are not related to spiritual and religious practices, yet cultivate spiritual qualities. As such, among the described techniques, many options exist, which may or may not fit for a given individual. Those who belong to a specific religious system may select different forms of spiritual coping than those who draw loosely from a variety of religious traditions (e.g., the "spiritual but not religious"). Those who consider themselves atheist or eschew all formal belief systems may choose yet other options.

People will also vary in the ways they apply these practices. Many of them can be implemented individually, outside of clinical work. Others could be used therapeutically in session. Yet others might be best instituted in the context of a religious counseling setting. Some practices are best carried out on one's own, but others naturally fit into a context of social interactions. Some spiritual techniques will be appropriately learned and practiced within a religious community. Other spiritual renewal skills can be gained by taking classes or workshops through universities, hospitals, community centers, private organizations, or in an informal or grassroots context. Because of this wealth of practices and contexts, each individual can find the methods most suitable for him or her. Certainly, there is no shortage of techniques and practices that psychotherapy clients and clinicians can choose from in order to find spiritual self-renewal.

REFERENCES

Ai, A. L., Peterson, C., Bolling, S. F., & Rodgers, W. (2006). Depression, faith-based coping, and short-term postoperative global functioning in adult and older patients undergoing cardiac surgery. *Journal of Psychosomatic Research*, *60*, 21–28. doi:10.1016/j.jpsychores.2005.06.082

Ai, A. L., Seymour, E. M., Tice, T. N., Kronfol, Z., & Bolling, S. F. (2009). Spiritual struggle related to plasma interleukin-6 prior to cardiac surgery. *Psychology of Religion and Spirituality*, *1*(2), 112–128.

Ano, G. G., & Vasconcelles, E. B. (2005). Religious coping and psychological adjustment to stress: A meta-analysis. *Journal of Clinical Psychology*, *61*(4), 461–480.

Avants, S. K., & Margolin, A. (2004). Development of spiritual self-schema (3-S) therapy for the treatment of addictive and HIV risk behavior: A convergence of cognitive and buddhist psychology. *Journal of Psychotherapy Integration*, *14*(3), 253.

Azhar, M. Z., & Varma, S. L. (1995). Religious psychotherapy as management of bereavement. *Acta Psychiatrica Scandinavica*, *91*, 233–235. doi: 10.1111/j.1600–0447.1995.tb09774.x

Azhar, M. Z., Varma, S. L., & Dharap, A. S. (1994). Religious psychotherapy in anxiety disorder patients. *Acta Psychiatrica Scandinavica*, *90*, 1–3. doi:10.1111/j.1600–0447.1994.tb01545.x

Bernardi, L., Sleight, P., Bandinelli, G., Cencetti, S., Fattorini, L., Wdowczyc-Szulc, J., & Lagi, A. (2001). Effect of rosary prayer and yoga mantras on autonomic cardiovascular rhythms: Comparative study. *British Medical Journal, 323*, 1446–1449.

Boerstler, R. W., & Kornfeld, H. L. (1995). *Life to death: Harmonizing the transition: A holistic and meditative approach for caregivers and the dying*. Rochester, VT: Healing Arts Press.

Buber, M. (1987). *I and Thou* (2nd ed.). New York, NY: Scribner's.

Büssing, A., Michalsen, A., Khalsa, S. B. S., Telles, S., & Sherman, K. J. (2012). Effects of yoga on mental and physical health: A short summary of reviews. *Evidence-Based Complementary and Alternative Medicine, 2012*. doi:10.1155/2012/165410

Canfield, J. (2005). Secondary traumatization, burnout, and vicarious traumatization: A review of the literature as it relates to therapists who treat trauma. *Smith College Studies in Social Work, 75*, 81–88. doi:10.1300/J497v75n02_06

Chida, Y., Steptoe, A., & Powell, L. H. (2009). Religiosity/spirituality and mortality. *Psychotherapy and Somatics, 78*, 81–90. doi:10.1159/000190791

Cohen, J. S., & Miller, L. J. (2009). Interpersonal mindfulness training for well-being: A pilot study with psychology graduate students. *Teachers College Record, 111*(12), 2760–2774.

Cole, B. S. (2005). Spiritually-focused psychotherapy for people diagnosed with cancer: A pilot outcome study. *Mental Health, Religion & Culture*, 8, 217–226. doi:10.1080/13694670500138916

Exline, J. J. (2013). Religious and spiritual struggles. In K. Pargament, J. Exline, J. Jones, A. Mahoney, & E. Shafranske (Eds.), *APA handbook of psychology, religion, and spirituality*. Washington, DC: American Psychological Association.

Falb, M. D., & Pargament, K. I. (2012). Relational mindfulness, spirituality, and the therapeutic bond. *Asian Journal of Psychiatry*, 5, 351–354. doi:10.1016/j.ajp.2012.07.008

Garzon, F. (2005). Interventions that apply scripture in psychotherapy. *Journal of Psychology and Theology*, 33, 113–121.

Gear, M. R., Faigin, C. A., Gibbel, M. R., Krumrei, E., Oemig, C., McCarthy, S. K., & Pargament, K. I. (2008). The winding road: A promising approach to addressing the spiritual struggles of college students. *Spirituality in Higher Education Newsletter*, 4, 1–8.

Geller, S. M., & Greenberg, L. S. (2012). *Therapeutic presence: A mindful approach to effective therapy*. Washington, DC: American Psychological Association.

Gregg, J. A., Callaghan, G. M., Hayes, S. C., & Glenn-Lawson, J. L. (2007). Improving diabetes self-management through acceptance, mindfulness, and values: A randomized controlled trial. *Journal of Consulting and Clinical Psychology, 75*, 336–343. doi:10.1037/0022–006X.75.2.336

Gruner, L. (1984). Heroin, hashish, and hallelujah: The search for meaning. *Review of Religious Research*, 26, 176–186. doi:10.2307/3511701

Harris, J. I., Erbes, C. R., Engdahl, B. E., Olson, R. H. A, Winskowski, A. M., & McMahill, J. (2008). Christian religious functioning and trauma outcomes. *Journal of Clinical Psychology*, 64, 17–29. doi:10.1002/jclp.20427

Harris, J. I., Erbes, C. R., Engdahl, B. E., Tedeschi, R. G., Olson, R. H., Winskowski, A. M. M., & McMahill, J. (2010). Coping functions of prayer and posttraumatic growth. *International Journal for the Psychology of Religion, 20*, 26–38. doi:10.1080/10508610903418103

Hofmann, S. G., Sawyer, A. T., Witt, A. A., & Oh, D. (2010). The effect of mindfulness-based therapy on anxiety and depression: A meta-analytic review. *Journal of Consulting and Clinical Psychology*, *78*(2), 169–183. doi:10.1037/a0018555

Idler, E. L. (2013). Rituals and practices. In K. Pargament, J. Exline, J. Jones, A. Mahoney, & E. Shafranske (Eds.), *APA handbooks in psychology: APA handbook of psychology, religion, and spirituality*. Washington, DC: American Psychological Association.

Jimenez, P. J., Melendez, A., & Albers, U. (2012). Psychological effects of tai chi chuan. *Archives of Gerontology and Geriatrics*, *55*, 460–467. doi:10.1016/j.archger.2012.02.003

Johnson, D. P., & Mullins, L. C. (1989). Religiosity and loneliness among the elderly. *Journal of Applied Gerontology*, 9, 110–131.

Kim, J., & Kramer, G. (2002). Insight dialogue meditation with anxiety problems. *Gestalt!*, 6(1). Retrieved from www.g-gej.org/6–1/insightdialogue.html

Kramer, G. (2007). *Insight dialogue: The interpersonal path to freedom*. Boston, MA: Shambhala.

Kramer, G., Meleo-Meyer, F., & Turner, M. L. (2008). Cultivating mindfulness in relationship: Insight dialogue and the interpersonal mindfulness program. In S. F. Hick & T. Bien (Eds.), *Mindfulness and the therapeutic relationship* (pp. 195–214). New York, NY: Guilford Press.

Krause, N. (2006). Exploring the stress-buffering effects of church-based and secular social support on self-rated health in late life. *Journal of Gerontology*, *61B*, S35–S43.

Lazarus, R. S., & Folkman, S. (1984). *Stress, appraisal, and coping*. New York, NY: Springer.

Lee, M. S., Lee, M. S., Kim, H., & Choi, E. (2004). Effects of qigong on blood pressure, high-density lipoprotein cholesterol and other lipid levels in essential hypertension patients. *International Journal of Neuroscience, 114*, 777–786. doi:10.1080/00207450490441028

Levine, S., & Levine, O. (1995). *Embracing the beloved: Relationship as a path of awakening*. New York, NY: Doubleday.

Liu, X., Miller, Y. D., Burton, N. W., Chang, J., & Brown, W. J. (2011). Qi-gong mind-body therapy and diabetes control: A randomized controlled trial. *American Journal of Preventative Medicine*, *41*, 152–158. doi:10.1016/j.amepre.2011.04.007

Maislos, M., Abou-Rabiah, Y., Zuili, I., Iordash, S., & Shany, S. (1998). Gorging and plasma HDL-cholesterol—The Ramadan model. *European Journal of Clinical Nutrition*, *52*, 127–130. doi:10.1038/sj.ejcn.1600526

Margolin, A., Schuman-Olivier, Z. S., Beitel, M, Arnold, R. M., Fulwiler, C. E., & Avants, S. K. (2007). A preliminary study of spiritual self-schema (3-S+) therapy for reducing impulsivity in HIV-positive drug users. *Journal of Clinical Psychology*, 63, 979–999. doi:10.1002/jclp.20407

Maselko, J., Gilman, S. E., & Buka, S. (2009). Religious service attendance and spiritual well-being are differentially associated with risk of major depression. *Psychological Medicine, 39*, 1009–1017. doi:10.1017/S0033291708004418

McConnell, K. M., Pargament, K. I., Ellison, C. G., & Flannelly, K. J. (2006). Exploring the links between spiritual struggles and symptoms of psychopathology in a national sample. *Journal of Clinical Psychology, 62*, 1469–1484. doi: 10.1002/jclp.20325

Meyer, H. B., Katsman, A., Sones, A. C., Auerbach, D. E., Ames, D., & Rubin, R. T. (2012). Yoga as an ancillary treatment for neurological and psychiatric disorders: A review. *Journal of Neuropsychiatry and Clinical Neurosciences, 24*, 152–164. doi:10.1176/appi.neuropsych.11040090

Murray-Swank, N., & Pargament, K. (2003, April). *Solace for the soul: A psycho-spiritual intervention for female survivors of sexual abuse*. Paper presented at the meeting for the International Center for the Integration of Health and Spirituality, Bethesda, Maryland.

Oman, D., Shapiro, S. L., Thoresen, C. E., Flinders, T., Driskill, J. D., & Plante, T. G. (2007). Learning from spiritual models and meditation: A randomized evaluation of a college course. *Pastoral Psychology, 55*, 473–493. doi:10.1007/s11089–006–0062-x

Pargament, K. I. (1997). *The psychology of religion and coping: Theory, research, practice*. New York, NY: Guilford Press.

Pargament, K. I. (2011). Religion and coping: The current state of knowledge. In S. Folkman (Ed.), *Oxford handbook of stress, health, and coping* (pp. 269–288). New York, NY: Oxford University Press.

Pargament, K. I., Magyar, G. M., & Murray-Swank, N. (2005). The sacred and the search for significance: Religion as a unique process. *Journal of Social Issues*. doi:10.1111/j.1540–4560.2005.00426.x

Pargament, K. I., & Sweeney, P. J. (2011). Building spiritual fitness in the Army: An innovative approach to a vital aspect of human development. *American Psychologist, 66*, 58–64. doi:10.1037/a0021657

Park, C. L., Armeli, S., & Tennen, H. (2004). Appraisal-coping goodness of fit: A daily Internet study. *Personality and Social Psychology, 30*, 558–569. doi:10.1177/0146167203262855

Park, C. L., & Cohen, L. H. (1993). Religious and nonreligious coping with the death of a friend. *Cognitive Therapy and Research, 17*, 561–577.

Park, C. L., & Folkman, S. (1997). Meaning in the context of stress and coping. *Review of General Psychology, 1*, 115–144.

Park, C. L., Folkman, S., & Bostrom, A. (2001). Appraisals of controllability and coping in caregivers and HIV+ men: Testing the goodness-of-fit hypothesis. *Journal of Consulting and Clinical Psychology, 69*, 481–488. doi:10.1037//0022–006X.69.3.481

Penley J. A., Tomaka, J., & Wiebe, J. S. (2002). The association of coping to physical and psychological health outcomes: A meta-analytic review. *Journal of Behavioral Medicine, 25*(6), 551–603.

Pew Forum on Religion & Public Life. (2007). *U.S. religious landscape survey*. Retrieved from http://religions.pewforum.org/reports

Phillips., R. E. III, Lakin, R., & Pargament, K. I. (2002). Development and implementation of a spiritual issues psychoeducational group for those with serious mental illness. *Community Mental Health Journal*, 38, 487–495. doi:10.1023/A:1020832218607

Rajagopal, D., Mackenzie, E., Bailey, C., & Lavizzo-Mourrey, R. (2002). The effectiveness of a spiritually-based intervention to alleviate subsyndromal anxiety and minor depression among older adults. *Journal of Religion and Health*, *41*, 153–166. doi:10.1023/A:1015854226937

Rasic, D., Robinson, J. A., Bolton, J., Bienvenu, O. J., & Sareen, J. (2011). Longitudinal relationships of religious worship attendance and spirituality with major depression, anxiety disorders, and suicidal ideation and attempts: Findings from the Baltimore epidemiologic catchment area study. *Journal of Psychiatric Research*, *45*, 848–854. doi:10.1016/j.jpsychires.2010.11.014

Shafranske, E. P., & Cummings, J. P. (2013). Religious and spiritual beliefs, affiliations, and practices of psychologists. In K. Pargament, J. Exline, J. Jones, A. Mahoney, & E. Shafranske (Eds.), *APA handbooks in psychology: APA handbook of psychology, religion, and spirituality*. Washington, DC: American Psychological Association.

Shennan, C., Payne, S., & Fenlon, D. (2011). What is the evidence for the use of mindfulness-based interventions in cancer care? A review. *Psycho-Oncology*, *20*(7), 681–697. doi:10.1002/pon.1819

Stevanovic, P., & Rupert, P.A. (2004). Career-sustaining behaviors, satisfactions, and stresses of professional psychologists. *Psychotherapy: Theory, Research, Practice, Training*, *41*, 301–309. doi:10.1037/0033–3204.41.3.301

Suls, J., & Fletcher, B. (1985). The relative efficacy of avoidant and non-avoidant coping strategies: A meta-analysis. *Health Psychology*, *4*, 249–288. doi:10.1037/0278–6133.4.3.249

Surrey, J. L. (2005). Relational psychotherapy, relational mindfulness. In C. K. Germer, R. D. Siegel, & P. R. Fulton (Eds.), *Mindfulness and psychotherapy* (pp. 91–110). New York, NY: Guilford Press.

Tewari, S., Khan, S., Hopkins, N., Srinivasan, N., & Reicher, S. (2012). Participation in mass gatherings can benefit well-being: Longitudinal and control data from a North Indian Hindu pilgrimage event. *PLoS ONE*, *7*(10). doi:10.1371/journal.pone.0047291

Trevino, K. M., Pargament, K. I., Cotton, S., Leonard, A. C., Hahn, J., Caprini-Faigin, C. A., & Tsevat, J. (2010). Religious coping and physiological, psychological, social, and spiritual outcomes in patients with HIV/AIDS: Cross-sectional and longitudinal findings. *AIDS and Behavior*, *14*, 379–389. doi:10.1007/s10461–007–9332–6

Turner, J. A., Edwards, L. A., Eicken, I. M., Yokoyama, K., Castro, J. R., Tran, A. N., & Haggins, K. L. (2005). Intern self-care: An exploratory study into strategy use and effectiveness. *Professional Psychology: Research and Practice*, 36, 674–680. doi:10.1037/0735–7028.36.6.674

VandeCreek, L., Pargament, K., Belavich, T., Cowell, B., & Friedel, L. (1999). The unique benefits of religious support during cardiac bypass surgery. *Journal of Pastoral Care*, 53, 19–29.

Wachholtz, A. B., & Pargament, K. I. (2008). Migraines and meditation: Does spirituality matter? *Journal of Behavioral Medicine*, *31*, 351–366. doi:10.1007/s10865–008–9159–2

Wang, C., Bannuru, R., Ramel, J., Kupelnick, B., Scott, T., & Schmid, C. H. (2010). Tai Chi on psychological well-being: Systematic review and meta-analysis. *BMC Complementary and Alternative Medicine*, *10*, 1–16. doi:10.1186/1472–6882–10–23

White, M. L., Peters, R., & Schim, S. M. (2011). Spirituality and spiritual self-care: Expanding self-care deficit nursing theory. *Nursing Science Quarterly*, *24*, 48–56. doi:10.1177/0894318410389059

Witkiewitz, K., & Bowen, S. (2010). Depression, craving and substance use following a randomized trial of mindfulness-based relapse prevention. *Journal of Consulting and Clinical Psychology*, *78*(3), 362–374. doi:10.1037/a0019172

CHAPTER

20

Religion and Spirituality

A Source of Renewal for Families

GINA M. BRELSFORD AND JAELYN R. FARRIS

A frequent source of renewal in families is the use of religion or spirituality. More than 80% of families indicate that religion and spirituality were important in their family of origin and more than 75% of Americans surveyed indicate that their family relationships are strengthened through religion (Gallup & Lindsay, 1999). However, scholars continue to debate specific definitions of religion and spirituality, but the impact of religious and spiritual worldviews on family functioning is evident in research and practice (see Mahoney, 2010). Some families find that religious or spiritual frameworks are the backbone of their lives, which guide their life choices and daily interactions; whereas other families have traces of religious or spiritual rituals that fade into view when needed, frequently in times of crisis. In either case, religious and spiritual sources of support can facilitate renewal in times of deep despair or can lift family members up when feeling uncertain about life paths. On the other hand, religion and spirituality can also be a source of deep divide and conflict for families, which can hamper renewal and growth. Thus, regardless of whether religion and spirituality are causing families pain and division or are facilitating growth and stability, exploring and understanding families' religious and spiritual worldviews is an important and useful way to achieve renewal.

In this chapter we provide definitions for renewal, religion, and spirituality to highlight the complexity of these constructs. We then briefly discuss how different family therapy theories can work to encourage renewal in families. A focus on family structure and functioning, including communication, is presented next, followed by an exploration of specific sources of religious and spiritual renewal for families. The chapter closes with a discussion of how providers can use these sources of renewal in and for their own families.

DEFINING RENEWAL

Renewal can refer to the maintenance of well-being in periods of stress or bouncing back to typical functioning after a period of distress. In this fashion, renewal is similar to the construct of resilience (Luthar, 2003). For the purposes of this chapter, we use the term *renewal* in a broad sense to refer to the ability to overcome obstacles, bounce back, recover strength, or reclaim a more positive outlook in periods of strife. The process of renewal can be especially valuable in times of stress, change, or transition, and can apply to both personal and professional well-being.

Renewal is essential in allowing for optimal physical, emotional, and cognitive functioning. Focusing on renewal can be an important way to prevent burnout, defined as a state of depletion characterized by helplessness and hopelessness, or impairment, defined as an extreme state of depletion, which prevents people from being effective in their personal and/or work lives (Corey, Corey, & Callanan, 2007). Early signs of burnout can include poor health habits in the areas of nutrition, exercise, and other self-care regimes; a withdrawal from relationships with friends and family; failing to recognize the personal impact of stressful situations; or resisting opportunities for help in times of distress. In any of these situations, it is critical to pursue renewal in order to maintain or return to optimal functioning.

Renewal can be achieved in a variety of ways. One method of working toward renewal is to determine which activities are energizing or evoke positive emotions, and then make a point to engage in those activities on a regular basis. For some, these activities may include participating in exercise programs, spending time with friends, reading books, or taking vacations. Regardless of the source of renewal, it should be noted that these activities can be pursued either as an individual or as a group. One way that many individuals and families can attain renewal is through the use of religion and spirituality.

DEFINING RELIGION AND SPIRITUALITY

The debate regarding a definition of religion and spirituality extends to whether religion and spirituality are similar, different, or have small yet significant overlapping aspects (Pargament, 1999). Some prominent definitions of religion include: a faith community with religious teachings that enhance a search for the sacred (Pargament, 1997); an organized belief systems that encompasses shared views about God or a Higher Power (Walsh, 1999); or institutionalized doctrines related to the worship of the sacred (Burr, Marks, & Day, 2012). These definitions have similarities in that they focus on an organized form of worshipping the sacred that is typically institutionalized and involves rituals, beliefs, and doctrine.

Spirituality is often thought to be one's search for meaning as related to ultimate concerns (Tillich, 1959); a unity with all of life, including nature and the universe (Stander, Piercy, MacKinnon, & Helmeke, 1994); and transcending the physical to focus on one's "spirit" (Frame, 2003). Spirituality can imply less focus on organized religious practices and more focus on connections with others or a connection to the sacred (Zinnbauer, Pargament, & Scott, 1999). Spirituality can be associated with a Higher Power or the transcendent, but this association is not necessary. Notably, some scholars suggest that no matter how religion and spirituality are defined there is no one perfect way to capture the multidimensional aspects of these constructs (Moberg, 2002). As such, for the purposes of this chapter, we do not attempt to determine whether religion and spirituality are separate constructs, but rather do assume that they are interrelated constructs, which can operate differently for various individuals and families.

In this chapter, the phrase "religion and spirituality" refers to the intersection of these two constructs, which involves "a search for the sacred, a process through which people seek to discover, hold on to, and when necessary, transform whatever they hold sacred in their lives" (Hill & Pargament, 2003, p. 65). Using this definition, both religion and spirituality have a "sacred" connection. One's search for the sacred can occur in a religious context, such as a church, synagogue, mosque, or other place of religious worship or may not occur within the context of a particular religion (Pargament, 1997). The sacred can include the divine or God, but can also include any aspect of life that takes on divine significance or character (Pargament & Mahoney, 2005), which can include the family. For those families who find that religion and spirituality impact their lives, either can be a source of resilience and renewal that can be accessed if and when the family chooses to do so.

FAMILY THERAPY THEORIES

Family therapy theories differ based on their focus on structure, hierarchy, mechanisms, and intervention targets. The central focus of family systems theory is to allow family members to develop a differentiation of self, which entails distinguishing between thinking and feeling (McGoldrick & Carter, 2001). This ability allows one to understand how their emotional reactions are separate from their cognitions, which facilitates being able to engage in a family system without losing objectivity and flexibility. Further, the transgenerational approach of Bowen's family systems theory emphasizes that change can occur through working with only one individual rather than with the family as a whole (Kerr & Bowen, 1988). In fact, Kerr and Bowen (1988) indicate that to alter the family's emotional system, sometimes working with the most highly differentiated individual will be the most successful endeavor. At times, seeing the entire family can impede the progress of one family member or another. As such, the strongest gains may be made for the family by working with only one individual.

Other family therapy theories, however, emphasize the necessity to focus on the entire family unit as a whole, suggesting that change or growth can only occur when working with the entire family. In particular, structural family therapy emphasizes that changes to the family hierarchy are integral to altering the family system (Minuchin, Lee, & Simon, 1996). Structural family therapy is a contextual approach to the therapeutic process where the focus is on family stability during times of change. In families who are not functioning well, renewal can occur when boundaries are clearly delineated, there is little enmeshment, and family subsystems function effectively (Minuchin & Nichols, 1993).

The strategic view of family therapy supports understanding how family rules, homeostasis, and feedback loops impact family and individual functioning (Keim, 1998). Strategic family therapy evolved out of communication theory, which discusses the processes of family disputes rather than the content. Thus, in strategic family therapy, the key is to move from a question of *what* is occurring to *why* it is occurring. In other words, communication between family members is viewed as the target of intervention, with family interactions being the primary focus for avenues of change (Keim, 1998).

Other family systems theories have different targets such as behaviors within the family unit and/or cognitions about the family (see Dattilio, 2001; Forgatch & Patterson, 1998; Jacobson & Christensen, 1996). However, regardless of the family therapy technique or conceptualization, one could argue that worldviews of the individual family members and norms within the family system remain impactful. Thus, mental health professionals can take cues from many different types of family therapies to suggest that individuals' religious or spiritual worldviews can impact the family system, or that the family system itself may have a guiding religious or spiritual philosophy that can impact individual family members. For the purposes of this chapter we will discuss family structure and family function—defined in terms of communication and homeostasis—as two key aspects of families that may be relevant to their use of religion and spirituality as a source of renewal.

FAMILY STRUCTURE

Family structure refers to the composition of the family. In other words, family structure refers to who is defined as being part of the family. In the United States today, family can mean a variety of things to a variety of people. The traditional, Westernized notion of family often refers to nuclear families with two parents, a couple of children, and a moderate level of involvement with extended family in the form of grandparents, aunts/uncles, and cousins. Societal changes, cultural diversity, and periods of economic hardship over the past several decades have brought changes to the idea of family, most notably in the domains of the increased age at first marriage, high rate of divorce, increased age at birth of first child, and greater acceptance of homosexual lifestyles. With these changes have come a proliferation of various family structures, such as those in which children are reared by single parents, blended families with stepparents and half-/stepsiblings, same-sex couples with or without children, extended families who choose to live in a single household to save money, adults who choose to remain single and carve out a family of friends, and adults who cohabitate with or without children. In addition, advancements in technology have made it easy for families to remain connected across a distance without massive expenses, so moving away from one's family of origin no longer means separation from the family and its dynamics. These changes highlight the idea that family structure today is flexible and is not limited to a family of origin or a nuclear family. Thus, family is what someone wants it to be, and the way that families function and pursue renewal can vary based on any given family's structure.

As families change over time, roles evolve. Sometimes this evolution occurs naturally and painlessly, whereas at other times struggles can ensue. When families move into different roles (e.g., from being single to being part of a couple, from being a childless couple to one with children, from being a couple with young children to a couple with adolescents, to being "empty nesters," or from being coupled to single), worldviews are often tested. This highlights the importance of considering family functioning in the process of renewal, which we refer to using the key constructs of communication and homeostasis.

FAMILY FUNCTIONING

One of the primary ways that families function is through their communication with each other. Family communication is defined as ways of relating with other family members both verbally and nonverbally. There are various motives for the ways that families communicate, and these motives influence how family members choose to communicate with others. Family communication patterns are associated with mental well-being and also predict conflict styles, which can lead to either the need for renewal or the seeking of support from religion and spirituality in an effort to renew themselves. Clearly, good family communication, which centers on openness and affection, is associated with more positive outcomes. Clients and clinicians can work on optimizing their family communication patterns in order to attain self- and family renewal.

When families find that religious and spiritual worldviews diverge, a source of disagreement can emerge. These religious and spiritual differences can cause division in the family or, surprisingly can bring a family much closer together.

Families who engage in open discussions in a warm and supportive fashion are likely to find that they feel more comfortable talking about divisive issues. In relation to religion and spirituality, families who have open discussions about closely held beliefs related to religiousness and spirituality tend to have lower levels of destructive forms of conflict resolution and more frequent constructive resolutions of difficulties (Brelsford, 2010; Brelsford & Mahoney, 2008).

When families who are experiencing changes feel free to openly discuss them, they may find there are more sources of agreement than disagreement, or that there are misunderstandings that have resulted in conflict and division. Thus, when applying these open conversations to religious and spiritual issues, family members may feel especially vulnerable, particularly if family members are readily aware of known religious and spiritual differences. However, if families can move beyond these fears and have frank conversations, they can find a sense of growth and renewal as a result.

A second salient aspect of family functioning is a family's level of homeostasis, defined as "seeking a balance between stability and change" (Goldenberg & Goldenberg, 2004, p. 71). This construct is especially relevant to clinicians who are attempting to work with families. If a family member seeks help from outside the family, the family system may feel threatened if they perceive that their homeostasis is impacted. Alternatively, if the family is involved in working with a mental health professional, the goal is often to alter the family's homeostasis to bring about a new normal. This may be challenging if religious or spiritual worldviews are hampering this process. Conversely, changing patterns of ineffective behavior and irrational cognitions may more easily be accomplished if religious or spiritual worldviews support the importance of the family as a place for comfort, support, and love. Thus, mental health professionals need not only to understand a family's perception of their family structure and evaluate family communication patterns, but also assess the religious and spiritual worldviews of those with whom they work. Even if the professional may not feel competent in providing religious or spiritually integrated mental health services, it is important to consider these worldviews as they may be integral to the family's search for and attainment of renewal during times of distress.

RELIGION AND SPIRITUALITY AS SOURCES OF FAMILY RENEWAL

Whether at home or in the context of family therapy, many families engage in religious or spiritual practices that facilitate renewal. Some individuals even experience family relationships as taking on divine significance by association with the sacred, which invariably links their own spiritual and religious views to their family lives (Mahoney, Pargament, Murray-Swank, & Murray-Swank, 2003). Regardless of their specific theistic views, however, families may be able to use religion and spirituality as a source of renewal through the use of rituals.

Family therapists frequently call on the use of ritual as a source of comfort for families (Imber-Black, Roberts, & Whiting, 2003). Secular rituals, such as bedtime stories for children or date night for couples, reinforce the stability of the family and tend to require that family members engage in positive communication and close family interactions. There is a sense of familiarity with rituals that bring a person "home" and provide a foundation in times of difficulty. Families who call on their religious and spiritual worldviews as sources of renewal or supportive mechanisms in times of flux or crisis may find that rituals such as praying together, reading scripture, meditating as a family, or attending religious services provide a source of comfort and strength (Walsh, 2009).

A common family ritual is the use of prayer, which can occur in the family context or in a more personal individual setting. Using prayer can reorient individuals and their family to how they are connected to one another through God or the transcendent and reinforce views of what is sacred. Family rituals that involve prayer could include prayers at bedtime, prayers before meals, or prayer while attending religious services. Prayer during these times could be used to assist family members with difficult issues by reminding families of their close ties to the sacred or providing a foundation for growth and renewal.

Families can also find that bringing God or a transcendent being into conflictual or difficult family situations can allow for faster resolution and easier return to optimal functioning (Mahoney, 2005). The act of bringing God into the family in a positive way, called *theistic mediation*, can occur in an outward way through openly suggesting or requesting that God come into the relationship (Brelsford & Mahoney, 2009). Theistic mediation could include praying to God together, encouraging the other person to see what God would do in the situation, or suggesting that God wants the dyad or multiple family members to be patient with each other (Brelsford, 2011). Conceptually, this positive form of triangulation may have a beneficial impact on parent-child or marital relationships. In a few exploratory studies, mothers, fathers, and college-age children who endorsed greater use of theistic mediation tended to have higher levels of relationship satisfaction and more frequent use of constructive conflict resolution (Brelsford, 2011; Brelsford & Mahoney, 2009).

APPLICATIONS TO HELPING PROFESSIONALS

Family therapists and others who work with families spend much of their time helping others who are in need, and some of this helping may result in difficulties for the helper and his/her family. Helping professionals are at especially high risk for burnout or impairment given the nature of their work, yet often are unprepared to take steps to maintain their vitality (Corey et al., 2007). Personal and professional vitality are prerequisites to functioning effectively as a professional helper, and therefore it can be considered an ethical obligation. Helping professionals must acquire and regularly practice self-care and wellness strategies. One of the key ways of accomplishing this is for helping professionals to utilize religious and spiritual renewal strategies aimed at their own selves and families when feeling depleted, when bolstering is needed, or simply on a regular basis to prevent burnout or impairment.

The first essential step in this process is for helpers to explore their own religious and spiritual roots and beliefs (Walsh, 2009). Therapists and mental health workers may not realize that these fundamental religious or spiritual beliefs impact their work with families and their own well-being. Some therapists, particularly those trained in the integration of religion and spirituality in clinical settings, may find they are drawn to the spiritual as a source of renewal for their clients and themselves. However, others may not realize that themes uncovered in therapy either overtly or covertly may trigger reactions from their own religious or spiritual backgrounds. Bringing these themes to life through reflection and open conversations can lessen their deleterious impacts and allow for growth in areas that may not have been realized to date.

To reflect fully on how religious and spiritual landscapes impact the functioning of helping professionals, conversations in the family unit should be undertaken. These conversations can include open discussions about how religious and spiritual themes emerge in each family member's life or how the family unit is impacted by religious and spiritual worldviews. There may be conflicts that are uncovered within the family that have not been explicitly discussed, which could hamper therapists' renewal efforts. General exploration of religious or spiritual worldviews may also reveal dissonance between strongly held sacred beliefs and choices in life.

Another effective technique would be to draw a spiritual genogram of the family. When drawing a spiritual genogram careful attention is paid to intergenerational interactions and spiritual roots within the family unit (Hodge, 2001). Some questions therapist may ask themselves are: (1) What type of religious affiliation characterized each family member? (2) What religious or spiritually significant events have occurred in the family? and (3) What are the similarities and differences between family members' religious beliefs and their practices? (Limb & Hodge, 2011). Knowledge of familial interactions related to one's religiousness and spirituality can facilitate a better understanding of how religious and spiritual worldviews have evolved for the individual and in the family, and how they impact current functioning. The act of drawing a spiritual genogram can bring to mind conflicts in the family unit or untapped family resources that have gone unutilized over time. Bringing relationships and spiritual histories to the forefront can reinforce open communication and illuminate difficulties that can hamper a family's renewal.

Just as recommended for application to clients, helping professionals may benefit from engaging in religious or spiritual rituals. Attending religious services, praying or meditating together as a family, or engaging in other rituals such as giving thanks before a meal can facilitate a connection to the sacred that anchors a family and can facilitate renewal during times of difficulty. The use of religious and spiritual rituals, especially in conjunction with other uses of religion and spirituality, can enhance the family's connection to each other and provide support during times of need.

Overall, the importance of reflecting on one's own past and present family and the application of religious and spiritual practices can have a positive impact on renewal. When therapists tap into relationship networks, such as the family, they can find a safe place for healing and renewal. Further, if a family has a sacred anchor or tie, calling on it in times of difficulty or crisis can be a lifeline to resilience. If there are less obvious threads of religion and spirituality woven into family life, asking oneself if religious or spiritual themes need to be uncovered to fully explore sources of renewal can also be helpful.

CONCLUSION

Regardless of their worldviews and structure, virtually all families can benefit from using religion and spirituality as a source of renewal. Religion and spirituality can play a role in how well families communicate, which can predict their overall level of satisfaction or harmony. Religion and spirituality can be used as a source of support or comfort when homeostasis is threatened, thereby leading families to grow as a group of interconnected individuals who are seeking growth, rather than interfering with that individual's or family's development.

Specific applications of religion and spirituality in the renewal process can include the use of rituals, spiritual genograms, open discussions of religious/spiritual beliefs and values, and theistic mediation, to name a few. Clinicians can apply these approaches to virtually all families, including their own family, regardless of the individual's or family's specific worldviews. Doing so can help the family establish greater harmony and cohesion, leading to the prevention of some difficulties and opportunities for renewal in periods of discord or crisis.

To maintain their personal well-being and professional effectiveness, helping professionals should also attend to their own family's religious and spiritual landscape. There may be unspoken religious or spiritual conflicts that emerge when working with clients that trickle over into a helper's family life. When therapists can better understand their own religious and spiritual lenses they can better address clients' issues and be aware of how their own belief systems are triggering reactions to various clinical situations. If renewal is the focus of both the therapist and the client, gains can be made more effectively and efficiently when religion and spirituality are incorporated into the healing process.

REFERENCES

Brelsford, G. M. (2010). Interpersonal spirituality between college students and fathers. *Research in the Social Scientific Study of Religion, 21*, 27–48.

Brelsford, G. M. (2011). Divine alliances to handle family conflict: Theistic mediation and triangulation in father-child relationships. *Psychology of Religion and Spirituality, 3*, 285–297.

Brelsford, G. M., & Mahoney, A. (2008). Spiritual disclosure between older adolescents and their mothers. *Journal of Family Psychology, 22*, 62–70.

Brelsford, G. M., & Mahoney, A. (2009). Relying on God to resolve conflict: Theistic mediation and triangulation in relationships between college students and mothers. *Journal of Psychology and Christianity, 28*, 291–301.

Burr, W. R., Marks, L. D., & Day, R. D. (2012). *Sacred matters: Religion and spirituality in families*. New York, NY: Routledge.

Corey, G., Corey, M. S., & Callanan, P. (2007). *Issues and ethics in the helping profession* (8th ed.). Belmont, CA: Cengage Brooks/Cole.

Dattilio, F. M. (2001). Cognitive-behavior family therapy: Contemporary myths and misconceptions. *Contemporary Family Therapy, 23*, 3–17.

Forgatch, M. S., & Patterson, G. R. (1998). Behavioral family therapy. In F. M. Dattilio (Ed.), *Case studies in couple and family therapy: Systemic and cognitive perspectives*. New York, NY: Guilford Press.

Frame, M. W. (2003). *Integrating religion and spirituality into counseling*. Pacific Grove, CA: Thomson.

Gallup, G. Jr., & Lindsay, D. M. (1999). *Surveying the religious landscape: Trends in U.S. beliefs*. Harrisburg, PA: Morehouse.

Goldenberg, I., & Goldenberg, H. (Eds.). (2004). *Family therapy: An overview* (6th ed.). Pacific Grove, CA: Thomson Brooks/Cole.

Hill, P. C., & Pargament, K. I. (2003). Advances in the conceptualization and measurement of religion and spirituality: Implications for physical and mental health research. *American Psychologist, 58*, 64–74.

Hodge, D. R. (2001). Spiritual genograms: A generational approach to assessing spirituality. *Families in Society, 82*, 35–48.

Imber-Black, E., Roberts, J., & Whiting, R. (Eds.). (2003). *Rituals in families and family therapy* (2nd ed.). New York, NY: Norton.

Jacobson, N. S., & Christensen, A. (1996). *Integrative couple therapy: Promoting acceptance*. New York, NY: Norton.

Keim, J. (1998). Strategic family therapy. In F. M. Dattilio (Ed.), *Case studies in couple and family therapy: Systems and cognitive perspectives*. New York, NY: Guilford Press.

Kerr, M. E., & Bowen, M. (1988). *Family evaluation: An approach based on Bowen theory*. New York, NY: Norton.

Limb, G. E., & Hodge, D. R. (2011). Utilizing spiritual ecograms with Native American families and children to promote cultural competence in family therapy. *Journal of Marital and Family Therapy, 37*, 81–94.

Luthar, S. S. (Ed.). (2003). *Resilience and vulnerability: Adaptation in the context of childhood adversities*. New York, NY: Cambridge University Press.

Mahoney, A. (2005). Religion and conflict in marital and parent-child relationships. *Journal of Social Issues*, *61*, 689–706.

Mahoney, A. (2010). Religion in families, 1999–2009: A relational spirituality framework. *Journal of Marriage and Family*, *72*, 805–827.

Mahoney, A., Pargament, K. I., Murray-Swank, A., & Murray-Swank, N. (2003). Religion and the sanctification of family relationships. *Review of Religious Research*, *40*, 220–236.

McGoldrick, M., & Carter, B. (2001). Advances in coaching: Family therapy with one person. *Journal of Marital and Family Therapy*, *27*, 281–300.

Minuchin, S., Lee, W-Y., & Simon, G. M. (1996). *Mastering family therapy: Journeys of growth and transformation*. New York, NY: Wiley.

Minuchin, S., & Nichols. M. P. (1993). *Family healing: Tales of hope and renewal from family therapy*. New York, NY: Free Press.

Moberg, D. (2002). Assessing and measuring spirituality: Confronting dilemmas of universal and particular evaluative criteria. *Journal of Adult Development*, *9*, 47–60.

Pargament, K. I. (1997). *The psychology of religion and coping: Theory, research, and practice*. New York, NY: Guilford Press.

Pargament, K. I. (1999). The psychology of religion and spirituality? Yes and no. *International Journal for the Psychology of Religion*, *9*, 3–16.

Pargament, K. I., & Mahoney, A. (2005). Sacred matters: Sanctification as a vital topic for the psychology of religion. *International Journal for the Psychology of Religion*, *15*, 179–198.

Stander, V., Piercy, F. P., MacKinnon, D., & Helmeke, K. (1994). Spirituality, religion, and family therapy: Competing or complementary worlds? *American Journal of Family Therapy*, *22*, 27–41.

Tillich, P. (1959). *Theology of culture*. New York, NY: Oxford University Press.

Walsh, F. (Ed.). (1999). *Spiritual resources in family therapy*. New York, NY: Guilford Press.

Walsh, F. (Ed.). (2009). *Spiritual resources in family therapy* (2nd ed.). New York, NY: Guilford Press.

Zinnbauer, B., Pargament, K., & Scott, A. (1999). The emerging meanings of religiousness and spirituality: Problems and prospects. *Journal of Personality*, *67*, 889–919.

PART VI

Topics in Self-Renewal

CHAPTER

21

Self-Renewal With African Americans in Psychotherapy

Deborah G. Haskins

INTRODUCTION: SELF-RENEWAL AND AFRICAN AMERICANS

Addressing self-renewal themes with all clients is valuable. Incorporating these themes with African American clients and other clients who are racially, ethnically, and culturally diverse is equally important, since many of these individuals and communities experience challenges with maintaining mental health wellness and experience disparities in mental health services (U.S. Department of Health and Human Services, 2001).

SELF-RENEWAL: DEFINITIONS AND WELLNESS COMPONENTS

What is self-renewal? How do African Americans define self-renewal? These and other important themes are addressed in this section.

Self-Renewal Definitions

Gardner (1981) discusses many principles and considerations of self-renewal for the individual and society. The author says no one knows why some persons seem capable of self-renewal while others do not. Gardner states what is most important *is to remove the obstacles to individual fulfillment* and says this means "removing the gross inequalities of opportunity imposed on some citizens by prejudice, poverty, and other handicaps" (p. 12). African Americans suffer many gross inequalities and their wellness is affected. What also compounds self-renewal is that many African Americans are just trying to survive; daily survival includes maintaining an intact cultural and psychological self during stressful life experiences. Practitioners will engage African Americans more in psychotherapy if they create a safe place for the African American client to share these experiences. Therapy can be a place where the client can process and heal. This chapter offers self-renewal recommendations with specific racial and cultural applications.

How Do African Americans Define Self-Renewal?

This is a good question, because psychological literature has not always reflected the "voices" of African American perceptions regarding wellness and renewal. The term *self-renewal* is not necessarily even part of an African American vocabulary. African American culture is a communal culture. Therefore, the first word, "self," is not necessarily the first focus within the culture. While African Americans are individuals, a key part of their worldview is communal and relational (Constantine, Redington, & Graham, 2009). Communalism emphasizes the valuing of human relationships and the interrelatedness of people; it recognizes the value and uniqueness of every member of the community and places an emphasis on unity and not uniformity (Coakley, 2005). This is a cultural community where relationships with others and focus on self and others is a core value.

For example, one prospective African American consumer called this author inquiring about counseling. She said, "I was referred to you by a friend who sought counseling from you. I have never been in counseling before. I am African American, 47 years old, and a Christian. I am feeling depressed because I'm tired of caring for everyone else and no one is taking care of me. I have two adult sons and a granddaughter I'm helping my son to raise. I am sick and tired of caring for everyone else—I can't keep living like this!" This caller was struggling with self-renewal. While she attached to her religious faith positively and reported that her faith helped to renew her, especially when facing challenges in life and on her job, her church and religious faith did not attend to all of her emotions and difficulties. This prospective counselee struggled with the concept of focusing on herself. She, like many African Americans, valued caring for others but did so sometimes at the risk of not focusing on her own self-renewal. Therefore, one of the first issues that many helping professionals may experience is that the notion of focusing on *self* and *renewing self* may be a foreign concept. The Western model of psychology emphasizes self and independence (Grills, 2002). African-centered psychology is the opposite. Effective culturally informed helping professionals are those who will *explore and facilitate the meanings and strategies* that African Americans already consider for self-renewal. How does your African American client consider wellness and self-renewal? While there may be universal themes across cultures regarding self-renewal, *culturally nuanced interpretations* also exist. Exploring self-renewal meanings and interpretations, both at the individual and community level, will be important to integrate in psychotherapy. Much has been written about wellness, but how do African Americans view wellness?

This author emphasizes key cultural intentionality attitudes and behaviors for mental health professionals. This chapter first discusses the term *African American*, shares this chapter author's cultural identity and importance of cultural context when discussing culturally diverse members, provides suggested cultural competency reflections before beginning self-renewal focused psychotherapy with African Americans, briefly summarizes cultural context issues as practitioners attempt self-renewal psychotherapy, and concludes with knowledge and tools for incorporating spiritual, mental health, cognitive, and behavioral self-renewal themes in psychotherapy with African Americans.

Definition of African American

First, it is important to define the term *African American* so that practitioners and health professionals do not make assumptions about the African American client seeking services or about human behavior. Too often persons view skin color and other physical features and make assumptions about the person's race, ethnicity, or cultural identities (Brooks, Haskins, & Kehe, 2004; Helms & Cook, 1999). Hall (2005) states that the term *African American* identifies a citizen of the United States with lineage that can be traced to Africa, south of the Sahara. African Americans' history is connected to the transatlantic slave trade and does not include White South Africans and Black people from the Caribbean or Africa who have attained citizenship through the immigration naturalization process. Children of these parents who are born in the United States are typically identified as African Americans. Ethnicity, however, is understood as a shared culture or way of life, displayed through language, attire, religion, food, music, literature, and art (Johnson, 2000) and should not be confused with race (Hall, 2005).

Readers are cautioned not to make a judgment that the client *self-identifies* as African American or is American born (or is attached to African culture). Persons from Africa or the West Indies (e.g., Jamaica) may identify with their ethnicity and nationality more (McGoldrick, Giordano, & Garcia-Preto, 2005). They may be unfamiliar with the African American experience and socialization and may identify more with the immigrant experience if that is their experience (Brooks et al., 2004). One West Indian woman shared, "I am West Indian. When I came to the United States, all of a sudden I'm now viewed as an African American. I don't know or understand the African American experience. I'm just learning what that experience is; yet many think I have the same experience . . . however; I'm now being treated like I am African American. Maybe I need to learn more about what this experience is since that's how I'm being viewed/treated." This person is now thinking about the shifts in her identity, and particularly how others view her as she is transitioning culturally. Parham (2002) emphasizes that viewing African American people as a homogenous group instead of seeing the richness of their heterogeneity is limited. He states, "There is not a clear understanding of whom or what constitutes an African American. The journey from colored to Negro, to Black, to Afro-American, to African American, to now persons of African descent represents an identity transformation of sorts and a change from accepting imposed definitions to asserting a posture of self-determination and self-definition" (p. 26). This is important exploration during psychotherapy.

African American Identity, Intersections of Therapist's Racial/Cultural Identity, and Impact on Self-Renewal Process

How an African American defines his or her identity can also intersect with the therapist's own race and identity to influence a client's behavior in the therapy session (Parham, 2002). Why, then, is it important to talk about identity and race, including the therapist's race and culture? Because for many African Americans, self-renewal includes attending to race and culture as one relates to self and the world. Self-renewal with African Americans cannot, therefore, exclude race and culture. Mental health professionals must increase their understanding, comfort, and competency in addressing the dynamics of race (and culture) in the therapy process. If practitioners are not comfortable addressing the role of race and culture within African American clients' lives as well as understanding how race and culture influence the therapeutic relationship, then self-renewal focused psychotherapy may not be possible. For example, when supervising a European American counselor trainee, who was engaged in his first experience at a substance abuse treatment agency servicing primarily African American males, this author observed how race became a huge projection (Comas-Diaz & Jacobsen, 1991) in therapy, similar to how race is experienced in human relationships in the United States. The trainee formerly worked as a police officer in the city but then went into the military and now was transitioning as a counselor. The trainee would often become very frustrated during therapy with the African American clients. He would report during supervision, "I don't understand why these African American clients won't just follow the rules. If they followed the rules, they wouldn't get into trouble, they wouldn't become addicts, and now they won't even follow the rules of substance treatment." This trainee was struggling with his own racial and cultural identities as well as his occupational identity shifts. He was leaving the military. He previously left police work because, he reported, "I need structure and need to be in a place where people followed the rules. The military offered that." What the trainee lacked was increased awareness around his own racial identity and privileges as a White American (McIntosh, 1989). His ability to connect relationally with his African American clients intersected with *his own racial identity and cultural experiences*. Fortunately, he had a culturally competent supervisor (this author) who understood her own racial identity and the racial experiences of others, and could invite him to begin this process during clinical supervision. This self-reflection was necessary so that he could effectively support his African American clients' self-renewal goals as they abstained from substances and developed more healthy identities and behaviors. How can therapists approach these conversations with client?

Suggested Script to Explore Cultural Identity

One important strategy that practitioners can use to broach race, ethnicity, and culture (Day-Vines et al., 2007) and explore the saliency of culture and self-renewal with African American clients (including if there is a void in self-renewal because of inattention to race and culture) is to ask the client *directly:* Is race, ethnicity, and/or culture important to you? What is important in your identity? For example, one African American woman called for psychotherapy services and stated at the beginning of the phone call: "I am looking for an African American therapist who understands African spirituality. I am transitioning to African spirituality and am also in the process of changing my name to reflect my new spirituality. It is important for me to find a therapist who can understand my cultural experiences." This author shared that I am African American and while I was not entirely familiar with African spirituality that I could respect her cultural values and invited her to share her spirituality in psychotherapy. I also asked her if she wanted me to begin using her future name. Respecting the culture right at the beginning of psychotherapy helps to strengthen the helping alliance. The client was beginning self-renewal work and needed to know "up front" that there would be a counselor willing to work with her in the ways she valued renewal—African spirituality. Even if we do not know or fully understand the cultural aspects of self-renewal, therapists must demonstrate openness to clients' sharing cultural experiences of renewal. Constantine, Redington, and Graham (2009) stated that raising the issue of race early in the therapeutic relationship conveys cultural sensitivity and may address clients' concerns about a racially different counselor. Part of addressing self-renewal with African American clients includes helping professionals' disclosures of how race and culture is part of their own or others' renewal experiences. Clinical training has emphasized neutrality; however, cultural competency includes appropriate counselor self-disclosure, especially around culture (Sue & Sue, 2008).

My Cultural Identity and Importance of Cultural Context for Understanding African Americans While Engaging in Self-Renewal Therapy

Multicultural competency education highlights that sometimes being a well-intended psychotherapist may not be enough for the African American client (and other cultural communities). Culturally diverse counselees evaluate therapist credibility differently (Sue & Sue, 2008). Often as a counselor educator and trainer, students and learners will say, "I try to help my clients work on self-growth (or renewing transformation) but I feel like something is getting in the way. I often feel that my client just isn't opening up to me." It may be that the African American client perceives that the therapist (or healer) is not in sync relationally with them; therefore, no renewal work can be done. It is imperative that practitioners understand cultural context first so that they can incorporate self-renewal themes more effectively. Therapists can begin with creating a relationship with the African American client where the client feels "safe" opening their hearts, souls, and minds to another person outside of the culture, particularly relationships with White or European Americans—persons with whom many African Americans report painful experiences from racism and racial microaggressions (Helms & Cook, 1999; Pierce, 1975; Sue & Sue, 2008). Grills (2002) stated, "To truly embrace an African-centered approach, clinicians must be willing to make a *shift* in the lens through which the world is seen, how reality is defined, and how human behavior is understood" (p. 11). Further, Landrine (1992) stated that, "Cultural differences are not primarily differences in behavior, but rather in the *meanings attached* and attributed to the same behaviors" (p. 401). These authors' emphasis is that we are more effective when we explore the meanings African Americans attach to behaviors and experiences.

This Author's Lens and Self-Renewal Commitment

I often say, "When I look through my lens, I see culture!" I am an American-born person of African descent and self-identify as an African American. Race and culture are part of my ongoing self-renewal and wellness. As a young child, my family, like many African American families, included race and culture during childrearing. During my graduate counselor education, I lamented that the training reflected only Western psychology or European American cultural contexts. I would continually ask myself, my professors, and peers, "How does this theory and/or technique apply or fit with an African American population?" There were many unique cultural values that I knew warranted inclusion. Growing up I was exposed to cultural self-renewal themes such as the valuing of religious faith and teachings (Cook & Wiley, 2000), contributions of the African American community (or tribe) who "takes a village approach to raising African American children," (Boyd-Franklin, 1989; Parham, 2002), the strengths and contributions of an African American extended family network (Boyd-Franklin, 1989, 2005; Helms & Cook, 1999), the role of African American parents in socializing their children for achievement (McAdoo, 1994), the availability of African arts and music to affirm racial identity (e.g., "Say it Loud, I'm Black and I'm Proud" by James Brown), and many other African American enculturation experiences.

Fortunately, I did not have to rely on printed literature or media for African American cultural education; however, just by living in American society, I was exposed to distorted or biased miseducation—education that often challenges self-renewal practices. Cross (1991) and Tynes and Ward (2009) document that this miseducation impacts White Americans and Persons of Color; many incorporate these negative images into their personal identities and relationships. I could reject the deficit or pathological perspectives regarding persons of African descent because my family education (and personal experiences) contradicted the negative portrayals disseminated. I also personally knew of the many cultural strengths African Americans possessed. Many clients, however, will not be as fortunate. Families encourage the development of self-esteem and positive racial identity (Boyd-Franklin, 2005), but there is no guarantee how negative racial conditioning will affect a child's or adult's development in the achievement of a healthy, positive self-concept. A strengths-focused approach is highlighted in this chapter, and suggested therapist self-reflections are offered to assist you as you provide cultural-context meaningful psychotherapy.

Cultural Competency Reflections for Effective Self-Renewal Psychotherapy Establishing Therapeutic Relationships With African Americans

Because mental health professionals, too, may begin psychotherapy with images and unconscious biases about African Americans, the following self-reflections are suggested for self-monitoring before, during, and after psychotherapy with African American clients:

- What perceptions, attitudes, beliefs, and experiences do I have regarding African Americans?
- Which perceptions, attitudes, beliefs, and experiences are possibly influenced by miseducation regarding African Americans (e.g., family, culture, society, media, education)?
- Might my views be distorted by the negative portrayals of African Americans, and will these views influence my approach and relationship stance?
- Am I flexible in acknowledging the diversity that exists within African American culture and strive to discover the uniqueness of *this African American client* (instead of relying on generalizations about African Americans)?

- Do I recognize that there may be variations between the experiences of African Americans born within the United States and other African-descent members (e.g., West Indians, persons immigrating from Africa)?

Why are the above reflections important for self-renewal psychotherapy with African Americans? African Americans as a culture differ in nonverbal communication (Andrews & Majors, 2004). Clients may notice if the psychotherapist does not appear comfortable "being in the room" with them. Therefore, since many African Americans value the spirit force (Grills, 2002; Parham, 2002; Taylor, Chatters, & Levin, 2004), mental health professionals are encouraged to display congruent attitudes and behaviors demonstrating genuine interest and energy in working with African Americans. Often, when African Americans ask me for a referral for counseling, they will say, "How do I know that this counselor will be a good fit for me?"

I will encourage clients to trust their "spiritual-knowing" and say, "Ultimately, you will know once you sit with this person: *Is this a person I can feel safe with or stay in the room with?*" Broadley (2000) described the concept *presence* and emphasizes that therapists have presence when they are not *just in the room with the client* but also brings forth one's *abilities to attend to and be engaged by the client*. Therefore, this presence will be important since self-renewal exploration may not evolve if the African American client assesses that the therapist lacks a capacity to interact with the client. Many young people will say, "Keep it real" or "keeping it hundred." This means "Are you being honest, upfront, loyal, or sincere?" Understanding the African American's culture will assist practitioners in effectively achieving self-renewal psychotherapy goals.

The following reflection questions focus on the professional's openness to cultural interpretations of self-renewal:

- Do I understand how social class may affect self-renewal practices, especially among African Americans who lack material resources? For example, do I expect that persons who lack finances will engage in the same type of wellness/renewal activities compared to persons who are more materially privileged?
- How do African Americans participate in mental health wellness? Do they value counseling or psychotherapy? For example, because I value psychotherapy do I believe that everyone (even communities, like African Americans, who may not embrace psychotherapy) will see therapy as the way to take care of emotional or mental health concerns?
- Can I be open to African American clients' expressions of the ways they renew themselves, including cultural ways that I may not be familiar with, practices that may be integrated during psychotherapy, such as African dance, Hip-Hop music, sitting on the porch with neighbors, playing "pick-up" basketball in the neighborhood, or spending social time with

family/friends (e.g., family/friend card games, house parties), line dancing, church or spiritual activities, and cultural activities (e.g., African-descent cultural arts and history, African poetry or "open mike")?
- Do I understand indigenous healing practices and explore how local or native practices could be valued?

The following is a suggested script for beginning the conversation:

> Hi, ______. I am glad that you are taking an important step to care for yourself. I believe counseling and psychotherapy can be a gift one gives self. Therapy can be a place where persons can be cared for also. For some persons, including African Americans, a culture gifted in caring for others, this may be a new and different process to begin. I am open to hearing about your experiences, including cultural experiences.

Again, these types of direct exploration by the practitioner can set the stage for the client's perception that the clinician is open to his or her African American cultural identity and experiences.

Spiritual Self-Renewal

Because the foundation of African Americans' "being" is spiritual, I begin the self-renewal themes discussion on the topic of spiritual self-renewal. In traditional African cultures, there is no separation of mind, body, and spirit. All human existence is viewed as spiritual at its core (Grills, 2002; Parham, 2002). While Western psychotherapy models typically emphasize emotions and mental processes, in the African American worldview, spirit and spirituality are emphasized and tend to be more familiar to persons of African descent. While religion and spirituality share some common features, the constructs and experiences are not the same (Richards & Bergin, 2000); the expression and relationship with spirituality and religious faith vary depending on the African American's values and identification of his or her spiritual core. There may be persons who adopt a religious faith identity and expression while others may adopt a spiritual-based identity and expression. Also, there may be African Americans who possess indigenous beliefs, values, and practices. Indigenous psychology is defined as psychological knowledge that is native, that is not transported from another region, and that is designed for its people (Kim, 1990). Practitioners are cautioned not to assume that there is *one* experience and take time to explore those native, or indigenous, spiritual and psychological values and practices; one can then use the client's unique spiritual experiences for coping, problem solving, and supportive resources.

For example, this author is a gambling addictions specialist and when the City of Detroit opened casinos during the late 1990s, problem gambling leaders recognized they needed a cultural clinical consultant to train counselors to counsel African American problem gamblers using a culturally competent addictions framework. The European American leader recognized that many professionals lacked cultural knowledge regarding how to help counselors provide treatment to a largely African American consumer population. I was told right away, "We seem to have really good success with our African American female gamblers especially. Many of the European problem gamblers or African American males tend to take longer to connect to the spiritual base of gambling addiction recovery; the African American women rapidly connect and they tend to do better in treatment. It does not appear to take them as long." Practitioners will discover that many of your African American clients may be open to spiritual exploration. Persons who have abandoned spiritual wellness can also be invited to participate, and may discover their clients are open even if spirituality has been neglected. Early assessment during the initial intake will be useful.

Religious and Spiritual Assessment

Because there are diverse religious and spiritual practices, practitioners must assess their African American clients' valuing of religion and/or spirituality (Richards & Bergin, 2000). Some may connect with formal religious identities and communities, some may identify only with a spiritual self and not practice a formal religion, and some will not identify with either. Taylor, Chatters, Jayakody, and Levin (1996) found that 69.9% of Black Americans stated they were both spiritual and religious, 3.1% were spiritual only, 6.7% were religious only, and 21% were neither religious nor spiritual. While the basis of African culture, community, and families typically functions from a spiritual place, it does not mean that African American clients will identify with and relate as a spiritual self.

Smith (1981) noted that psychotherapy is not readily available or helpful to the materially poor or uneducated, including African American populations. Consequently, many African Americans found that identifying with and participating in the church was more affirming of their mental health than participating in psychotherapy (Brooks, Haskins, & Kehe, 2004). Often, African Americans find racial, cultural, and psychological validation through their religious faith communities. When attending church, they could "be at home" and because of their shared cultural experiences, many African Americans find solace and support by being connected socially with others who understand their experiences. Further, the "Black Church" has included civil rights as a key mission of the church life. Members could voice, hear, and address liberation from social injustice (Taylor et al., 2004). So what are strategies that mental health professionals can use when integrating spiritual self-renewal themes in psychotherapy?

Comfort With Exploring Spiritual Themes

First, practitioners must be comfortable exploring spiritual themes. If the practitioner is not comfortable with the notion of spirit, spirituality, and/or religion, one's effectiveness will be diminished. Many religious and spiritual African Americans are ambivalent about professional mental health services (Cook & Wiley, 2000; Washington, 2012). If they notice that the psychotherapist is not comfortable accepting and validating a part of the African American's identity, such as religion and/or spirituality, then the client may terminate psychotherapy. Washington (2012) found that African American respondents reported seeking help from family, friends, and pastors as a first resource. Only a small percentage reported seeking help from mental health professionals.

Second, practitioners should spend some time during the rapport-building phase to inform your client that you are aware that many African Americans value spirituality. Let the client know that you are interested in hearing more about whether spirituality and/or religion is important for him/her. A conversation starter could include:

> Hi, ______. I am learning that African Americans, like many cultures, value religion and spirituality. I don't want to make assumptions and would like to hear if and how you connect to spirituality and/or religion. Would you be comfortable sharing what is important for me to know about this part of your life?
>
> I have also learned that sometimes a person may have been raised in a religious faith or spiritual practice but then later discovered an identity separate from what they experienced as a child. I'm open to hearing anything you believe may help me support you during our work together.

Practitioners should also know that African Americans, like other cultures, may have negative or uncomfortable experiences with formal religions. Some may report feeling abandoned or rejected by God or their faith community. Again, it is important not to jump to conclusions and to gather information from the client so that you can best explore spiritual themes, including conflicts with one's spiritual self. If a person has negative experiences, then the individual (or family) may not be open to integrating spiritual themes in psychotherapy. For example, in addictions recovery work, an important part of the recovery model includes the identification of a Higher Power. This Higher Power can be a formal God object or "A God of your own understanding." Sometimes, addictions professionals may expect (especially novice professionals) that a client will engage in this spiritual identity work early in recovery treatment. Sometimes, this spiritual relationship discovery takes a long time for some clients, and clients may be resistant to this exploration due to past experiences, including formal religions. For example, one former African American male client, Sam (name is changed) participated in substance abuse recovery treatment where I was the doctoral intern. Sam struggled to explore spiritual themes during his substance abuse treatment. When I asked Sam how connected he felt to God or to a Higher Power, he said, "I don't believe in God." I asked him if he identified with a Higher Power. Sam remarked, "My Higher Power is nature." At the time, this author had not been trained in how to support clients who use nature as a Higher Power (this author's training is in pastoral counseling). I remember being unsure how to proceed but due to my training in psychoanalytic and psychodynamic psychotherapy, I decided to explore Sam's religious and spiritual history. What I discovered through Sam's narratives is that Sam rejected God because as he described:

> My mother put me and my siblings in foster care and I was raised by my grandmother. My grandmother was the best and loved me to death. However, my mother got my siblings back while my grandmother kept me. I don't understand how my mother could give me up and not get me back. I had to grow up and watch my mother raise my siblings while I lived with my grandmother. Don't get me wrong. I am very thankful for my grandmother's support. But I had to grow up and wonder why me? Was there something wrong with me? Maybe that is why my mom did not take me. I used to ask God and He never gave me an answer. What kind of God would allow that to happen? So, no, God isn't my Higher Power! Nature is. I can't count on God but I can count on nature.

So Sam's history with religion was one where he felt abandoned by his mother and by his God. Therefore, he was not open to exploring a spiritual self-renewal experience that included God; but he would be open to exploring connecting to nature. This author began to explore with Sam how using narcotics in effect conflicted with nature. I said, "Nature focuses on growth, replenishment, 'renewal'—using cocaine damages your spirit, psyche, and body." I worked with Sam to explore how he could use nature as renewal. This case demonstrates the challenge of exploring spiritual themes without exploring Sam's "story" further. We must be open to understanding the client's use of "spirit" even if different from our own.

The following are suggested spiritual self-renewal probes:

- Describe what the word *Spirit* (also spirituality, religion) means to you.
- Do you find your religion or spirituality to be renewing? Do you experience limitations in being renewed/refreshed/spiritually "whole?" (e.g., one person described being a member of a church where single women were not free to date; this practice was not self-renewing to her.

Ultimately, she began exploring other churches where as a single woman she could feel refreshed and encouraged to date).

- What are the ways you use religion and/or spirituality to renew yourself as an African American?
- Describe your family's experiences with religion and/or spirituality.
- What are your earliest recollections of religion and/or spirituality? Have any of these memories influenced who you are?
- Do you have positive experiences with religion and/or spirituality? Describe the ways these experiences influence your life positively.
- Do you have (or have you had) negative experiences with religion and/or spirituality? Describe the ways these experiences affected you and influence you in your life.
- Is this an area you need more help/support with?

Again, it may be useful for practitioners to explore the client's developmental history and journey. Research documents that when clients perceive that the mental health professional affirms his/her spiritual identity, the client is more likely to engage in psychotherapy (Richards & Bergin, 2000). Readers are encouraged to consult the wealth of spirituality literature that exists in the literature.

Third, how should practitioners respond if the client *is not* interested in exploring spiritual self-renewal themes? From a bio-psycho-social perspective, professionals understand the importance of focusing on the "whole" person and the limits of attending to only *one* part of identity. However, there will be times when a client has a conflicted spiritual identity; or the client's psychological self may be vulnerable and he/she may struggle with accessing the spiritual self. For example, when providing counseling services to sexual abuse survivors, many persons have conflicted spiritual identities. Research documents that men and women, but particularly women, are survivors of incest and sexual abuse. African American women, too, suffer child sexual abuse and may not receive psychotherapy until adulthood (Fontes, 2005; Wyatt, 1985). By this time, psychological and spiritual functioning may be damaged. Additionally, LGBT members also report rejection from their religious communities regarding sexual orientation and may abandon a religious identity during their sexuality journey (Fischer & DeBord, 2007). When this author conducts counselor professional development sessions on religion and spirituality, one of the most frequently asked participant questions is: How can I help clients who are LGBT and clients with sexual abuse experiences attend to their spiritual selves? Many describe hurtful/rejecting experiences by their religious families and communities. These workshop participants often shared that they felt unprepared in responding (and report they are also working through their own religious and spiritual identity conflicts and/or lack sufficient training). Sexual abuse recovery work and working through sexual orientation identities can be complex and require knowledgeable practitioners to do this work; however, we must be prepared to take time and seek education and supervision (and/or consultation) because often conflicted spirituality will result from hurtful experiences, including abuse.

Fourth, many African Americans renew self by being involved in the community and giving service. Community service and altruism is an important African American (and African culture) value (Grills, 2002; Parham, 2002). The community, including religious and spiritual institutions, uses volunteerism as self-help resources (Taylor et al., 2004). Explore with your client whether altruism and service are valued. Is self-renewal challenged because they are not participating in this part of their identity? Is self-renewal compromised because altruism and service is imbalanced? Assess this area and incorporate altruism and service to the community (and world) as counseling goals. For example, if you go into many African American churches, you will see a large community of African American women. However, sometimes the women may be overinvolved and neglect other key parts of their life (relationships, health). Is this involvement imbalanced because the African American female is escaping emotional distress, and this participation distracts her from painful (or life) experiences? Again, self-renewal work will include seeking harmony even with altruistic and community valuable experiences.

An example: One African American male client who sought voluntary psychotherapy due to major depression and substance addiction shared how important service was to his identity. The client was a very loving husband and father, mentored younger males on his job, and offered support and help to his family members. This client shared that while he was raised within a religious faith community, as an adult he stopped attending church and began asking his own questions about what was important in life—existential meanings about his existence. He expressed having no desire to adopt a formal religious faith and even struggled to describe himself having a spiritual self. However, if he could consider any spirituality, it was when he was in service to others. He owned a home repair business and expressed joy in offering subsidized services to his customers and community. He felt he did not make a lot of money (and he could) but found it more important to be in service to others. This was his way of renewing spiritually. This client felt less depressed when he could help others through giving his time, resources, and mentoring. Interestingly, he questioned how valid this practice of service was. He would say, "Am I stupid? I'm giving away money by not charging and my family has needs." I wondered if he would have questioned less if he was a female? Was he questioning his masculinity also? This counselor found that exploring gender (and cultural) notions of service and his identity was beneficial. Giving to others distracted him from focusing on the areas in his life that contributed to his sadness. Service was how he felt renewed. Service is important across cultures, but understanding cultural interpretations of altruism and service can be valuable and validating.

Last, another important spiritual self-renewal resource to include is prayer. African Americans are praying people (Cook & Wiley, 2000) and use prayer as a central coping source (Ellison & Taylor, 1996). The National Survey of American Life reported that 3 out of 10 Black Americans prayed at least once a day, and that they prayed more frequently than Whites (Taylor et al., 2004). African Americans rely on prayer, especially in difficult situations. When you inquire about spiritual coping strategies, prayer may be commonly cited, even among persons who may not be religious. Many therapists have been trained in behavioral techniques, such as systematic desensitization to alleviate anxiety (Wolpe, 1958). Prayer can also be used to help African American clients inhibit fear and anxiety. For example, the previously described female client who initiated counseling regularly used prayer to address anxiety and fears. She was anxious about: Will I have enough money to help raise my granddaughter? Will my son do what he's supposed to do? Will I ever have a loving relationship? Will I be able to succeed as a Black woman manager in this organization where I do not see many persons of color like me in management? We began examining how she could use prayer (a spiritual self-renewal strength she already used) to face her many fears. Prayer could inhibit the anxiety she faced. What we often discover is that clients' psychological mind-set (e.g., cognitions) will invade their prayer life. Persons will begin to use negative beliefs even in their prayer life. While little research on prayer is available (Taylor et al., 2004), health providers can consider incorporating prayer in psychotherapy.

Spiritual themes in psychotherapy are such an important theme and topic. A book chapter is insufficient to explore this theme completely and readers are encouraged to let their African American clients share their experiences, their values, and their goals. Most important, however, is for the practitioner to have a "way of being" that presents a person who is in touch with his or her own spiritual self so that the African American client is comfortable. I have had individuals say to me, "I feel comfortable in your presence." This comfort contributes to the person's "coming back" to psychotherapy. Ultimately, the counselor's spiritual self will be important. Even without directly addressing spiritual themes, one's spiritual presence as a healer will contribute to persons establishing a trusting relationship with the practitioner.

Emotional Self-Renewal

So what can mental health practitioners and other health professionals anticipate as you assist African Americans with emotional self-renewal? There are many cultural considerations as you focus on supporting clients with emotional self-renewal. The following are illustrative scenarios of the challenges and opportunities:

> Scenario 1: African American gambler. Dr. Haskins, I am interested in counseling. My wife has told me she can't take it anymore and

may leave me if I don't stop gambling. I've been gambling for 8 years. I keep trying to stop on my own, but I keep going back. I've never seen a counselor before and am not sure this is going to help. I go to work every day on this dead-beat job and gambling is the only way I feel like I have a break and I may win! My dream is to retire and live by the water; I love fishing and after this physically draining work, that's what I want to do.

Scenario 2: "Orphaned" brothers: Parents are deceased but the mother, before her death, initiated family counseling with her two young adult sons after her husband had a massive heart attack and died. Mom needed the boys to "step up and help more" because she was in kidney failure and waiting for a donor kidney. "They are not consistent, and I can't always depend on them but I have no one else." The mother eventually died from transplant complications. Because we had a secure therapeutic alliance, the sons would often call the counselor to schedule an appointment when they needed emotional support.

Oldest son, 24-year-old African American male: Young man struggles to find his way after his dad died. He struggles with responsibility and tends to overspend instead of paying his bills; he uses money for self-renewal; however, he has a difficult time identifying his emotions. He appears to think a lot and is very sociable. When attempting to explore what's troubling him, he has difficulty getting in touch with his emotions. He comes in for one session at a time and does not want to commit to ongoing counseling. He appears to find these solo sessions helpful, despite the counselor questioning how helpful they are.

Youngest son, 20-year-old African American male: He is a golfer and finds golf to be the most renewing activity in his life; he is focused on pursuing a professional golf career (despite his mom's concern that this is not a realistic goal even though he has won awards as an amateur golfer). He reports that "When I am on the golf course, I don't have any worries. I can forget about all my troubles and not only that—I'm really good."

What do the above persons of African descent have in common? While they each possess varied journeys with emotional, spiritual, cognitive, and behavioral experiences, they face opportunities and challenges with self-renewal. More importantly, many of these persons were unfamiliar with psychotherapy, did not embrace psychotherapy as a typical coping strategy, were ambivalent about the benefits of psychotherapy, and already had cultural strengths and resources that could also foster healthier identities and renewed selves. Therefore, what are important cultural considerations as you integrate this self-renewal theme?

Cultural Influences on African American Mental Health and Experiences

The above scenarios are also classic portrayals of many African Americans who call for help and seek professional counseling or psychotherapy. Often, these persons (or their family members) have *never* sought help from someone outside of the family or community. Psychotherapy is not an experience that African Americans typically value and recommend (Brooks et al., , 2004; Helms & Cook, 1999; McGoldrick et al., 2005; Sue & Sue, 2008). African Americans tend to rely on traditional support systems (Boyd-Franklin, 1989, 2005; Brooks et al., 2004; Helms & Cook, 1999; McGoldrick et al., 2005) such as older relatives, community elders (e.g., ministers, church deacons, and teachers) or other persons seen as having wisdom (Parham & Parham, 2002). Therefore, the first hurdle for many professionals will be to encourage African Americans *to take this step of using psychotherapy as a tool for self-renewal*, a process that actually *is not viewed or trusted* as a form of self-renewal.

Historically and even today, African Americans viewed mental health treatment as something to fear since it was provided by Europeans or Whites; many African Americans would not seek services by a system/organization/professional that they (and the community) mistrusted due to historical oppression (Boyd-Franklin, 2005; Brooks et al., 2004; Helms & Cook, 1999). Even years later, as documented in the Surgeon General's Report on Mental Health (U.S. Department of Health and Human Services, 2001), African Americans were more likely to use hospital emergency rooms when experiencing mental distress rather than more traditional outpatient mental health services. The case of the gambler (Scenario 1) above illustrates how African Americans are quite resilient and survived tremendous challenges. The gambler actually sought previous psychiatric attention for his anxiety symptoms, but never participated in pathological gambling treatment or self-help addictions programs. The family (Scenario 2) had not sought counseling before. The mother sought counseling after her husband died, and she experienced a caregiving challenge while they all were at varying places in their grief journeys. Even after the mother's death, the sons tended to seek therapy only when they needed advice and emotional support. Now that they were "orphaned" as young adults, they needed emotional support from someone. Since mom and dad were gone, they would contact me for help in the same way they would call mom or dad in times of crisis.

African Americans often use natural ecosystems (Boyd-Franklin, 2005; Harvey, 1996) such as religious faith and/or spirituality, family, and extended family networks (such as friends, neighbors), for coping and problem resolution (Brooks et al., 2004; McGoldrick et al., 2005; Washington, 2012). Therefore, many will be unfamiliar with or ambivalent about psychotherapy. What are suggestions as you integrate emotional themes?

Explore Ambivalence Regarding Help-Seeking

As stated earlier, one first step for practitioners is to explore what are the client's perceptions about getting professional help? How does the client (or family) view mental health? Are they feeling ambivalent about this process? Do they actually see psychotherapy as a process of wellness? Is the psychotherapy considered anti-cultural or anti-spiritual or religious? Because African Americans often experience a cultural conflict when seeking help outside of the family or community (Boyd-Franklin, 1989, 2005; Brooks et al., 2004), and they may believe therapy means "I am really crazy!" (Martin, 2002), African Americans' ambivalence may reflect the perspective that therapy is not a renewing experience. Therapists will need to explore these emotions and cognitive beliefs in order to offer alternative beliefs to support them in therapy.

For example, one African American client sought psychotherapy after her pastor referred her to this writer for pastoral counseling services. By the time she presented for therapy, this client had moderate clinical depression. A lot of the initial psychotherapy work included working with her psychological and cultural constructions (particularly religious) regarding her view of mental health. The psychological constructions included ideas such as "If I need psychotherapy, then this must mean something is wrong with me." Some of her cultural constructions included: As an African American woman, I am supposed to be strong. As a Christian, I am supposed to have strong religious faith. If I have a problem, I should be able to rely on God and my faith entirely. If I need professional help, does this mean I am not faithful as a Christian? If I seek psychotherapy, does this mean I am not relying on God to help me?" When I asked the client if any of her family members knew she was in psychotherapy, she answered, "No! I told my sister who I am very close to that I am coming to choir rehearsal when I come here"; thereby creating more internalized conflict because she was not being honest. So while the beginning work included doing respectful exploration of both her psychological, cognitive, and cultural beliefs and constructions, we eventually evolved to a place in therapy where the client created a view of mental health that her psychological and cultural self could tolerate. Eventually, this client got healthier and her sister took notice. She reported, "My sister wants to join the choir now because she thinks choir participation is what's contributing to my improvement! What do I tell her now?!" We both chuckled and began exploring how she could now share that therapy was self-renewal time, just as participating on the choir was.

Integrate Cultural Understanding of Individual as Community of Selves

Grills and Ajei (2002) discuss Western psychology's perspective of the referential self as a separate, encapsulated self that is presumed to be the originator, creator, and controller of behavior and uses concepts such as self-awareness, self-actualization, self-fulfillment, and self-change. In the Afrikan-centered perspective, using this definition of self results in alienation, disconnectedness, and confusion, and ultimately contributes to more suffering. An Afrikan analysis of self discusses the concept of self as community and suggests that Afrikans view the individual as a "community of selves" and that absence of community integration contributes to persons who are not genuine (Ogbonnaya, 1994). Self is not an independent, individually guided or initiated construction, but is deeply rooted in a historical, cultural, and sociopolitical context that is full of meaning. Self communicates multiple levels of connectedness and the outcomes on the interpersonal, political, and economic levels typically look different from those that emerge from Western constructions of self. Therefore, practitioners are more effective when approaching self-renewal differently.

African Americans may have difficulty when sources of their challenges include relationships (e.g., the Scenario 2 mother). Like Ogbonnaya's (1994) explanation of an individual as a "community of selves," the Scenario 2 mother's identity was a community of selves: her husband, her sons, her church, her neighborhood, and so on. She often talked about wanting to be sure that her spirit would help others even after her death. Self was interpreted as an intrapsychic community. Ask your client about family, extended family networks, and community relationships. Doing so signals to your client that you are aware of flexibility in cultural relationships (Boyd-Franklin, 1989, 2005; McGoldrick et al., 2005).

Acknowledge Racism and Its Toll on Mental Health and Self-Renewal

Racism is well documented to affect mental health and contributes to tremendous stress (Williams & Williams-Morris, 2000). Self-renewal psychotherapy must acknowledge that African American mental health includes an ability to manage racism as a stressor (Speight, Blackmon, Ogugu, & Steele, 2009). Clinical and health training does not always include stress management for negotiating racism as psychological stressors. The Brother #2 in Scenario 2 called this writer one day after his mother had died and the family had long terminated therapy. He had experienced an episode of "driving while Black." He called this author very upset and needed emotional support to process this traumatic experience. The client was upset and did not report to work the next day. He described being pulled over by a police officer and detained at a station for hours. By the time he was released (and there was no legal basis for arresting and detaining him), he was so emotionally shaken up that he could not go to work. We scheduled an emergency appointment. The session focused primarily on providing a safe place for this African American young male to "vent "and therapeutically process the traumatic event. This counselor affirmed him and validated the client, expressed cultural and psychological empathy, and helped him to access coping strategies. The difficult part of this experience for both the client and the counselor was the knowledge that "this would not be the last time; there would likely be many other racial microaggressions." This African American male especially did not have the freedom to function in society without experiencing racism. Therefore, self-renewal work includes not only attending to "emergencies" such as this illustration but also to provide cultural validation and coping strategies for African Americans. I remember one challenge this Scenario 2 brother shared was that he also had to take sick leave for not reporting to work. He reported needing to provide official documentation that he was "sick." After processing his cognitions and emotions related to how his employer would perceive his report (and whether he felt safe to disclose this, especially since he also shared that he suffered racism in the organization and did not really feel safe to honestly disclose what occurred and that his sick leave use would be viewed as valid), we worked out a support plan for processing the current traumatic event and future ones. Remember this client did not have parents anymore. Who does he go to with these experiences? Where do African Americans take their experiences of racism and other culturally laden stressors? Many will never come in to therapy but for those who do, clinicians will need to be prepared and not "gloss over" or overlook these experiences (particularly if we do not feel competent and may address/attend other self-renewal goals but exclude racial/cultural stressors). In sum, professionals must be ready to respond to these events. If the mental health professional cannot provide cultural empathy and skillfulness in addressing racism (and race or cultural-related) events, then a referral to a culturally competent clinician is ethically and professionally warranted.

Integrate Renewal With Challenging Relationships

Like the brothers in Scenario 2, the African American client may want (and need) to address wellness with family, extended network, and/or community relationships. Many African Americans may share, "I feel renewed or energized when I am connected to the people I care about: my family, my community, my culture." However, sometimes, these relationships minimize feelings of renewal, and the African American client may be conflicted about the relationship. In my work with African American clients, the client may come to psychotherapy because her or his relational life is imbalanced (e.g., Mary lacked a love relationship where she could be cared for and also struggled with her caregiver roles as mom, grandmother, and Christian servant). The client may experience affective, cognitive, and spiritual dissonance because of this conflict.

However, the process may not be as simple as setting boundaries with loved ones, limiting involvements with certain persons, or reorganizing relationships. Because aspects of self include community, often some of the self-renewal psychotherapy will be complicated due to this community-of-self. Practitioners are cautioned not to use prescriptive self-renewal strategies that may be valid for some and not for others. Instead, explore the African American's valuing of self and community. For example, in my gambling addictions recovery services for consumers, one of the challenges the addictions professional faces when counseling the gambler's family members is educating them about providing financial "bail outs." An African American client may perceive *not helping* the individual with their financial struggles as a demonstration *of not loving and supporting* the person. Because of the communal valuing, the family may experience an impasse. Part of the self-renewal work includes a focus on balance, and there are ways that practitioners can support the African American with achieving communal harmony.

What are other emotional and cognitive self-renewal considerations?

Attend to Bicultural Identity/Experiences

We know that holistic health is accomplished when persons validate themselves completely. African Americans live bicultural lives: They live in the Eurocentric world and expectations while navigating the African American world. Parents socialize their children to live in both worlds (McAdoo, 1994). Some accomplish this bicultural identity well, while others struggle. Self-renewal work can invite the African American client to address these bicultural challenges. For example, one couple bought their adolescent daughter to therapy. The mother was African American while the father was West Indian. The parents' shared that the teenage daughter was not doing well in school—she struggled educationally (and at home) with attention difficulties. When speaking with the daughter, she shared that she got confused moving between the two cultures of West Indian and African American culture. The daughter was also functioning in a culture where she navigated the expectations of the "White world" as a student. She stated, "When I am with my mom's family, they are quiet but then when I go to my dad's everything is louder, animated, lively. I am having trouble focusing . . . I can't get my work done and I struggle with how I'm supposed to behave when each family has different expectations." Emotionally, this teen (and her parents) navigated three cultures: one was the experience of an African American, the other was as an immigrant West-Indian culture, and the third was the culture of European Americans. It was no surprise to me why this young person had trouble balancing the various stimuli across these diverse experiences that held varying roles and expectations. Therapy provided a time for self-renewal work to explore the families' cultural identities and the educational culture so that the daughter could develop more emotional and cognitive balance. The work was not simply addressing "attention deficits" from a clinical perspective. The teen's challenges included managing the variety of typical and cultural stimuli. Psychotherapy included collaborating with the family to explore not only the standard psychological (and educational) concerns but also cultural considerations that challenged the young adolescent and family. Cultural broaching contributed to moving beyond the surface to the core issues, which also included culture.

African American Women

African American women seek therapy for similar reasons as other cultures. Many will report to therapy challenged with balancing self-renewal with their other roles and identities. Counselors can explore the relationship between roles/experiences and emotional and cognitive responses with them. Many African American women experience the "blues" or clinical depression. However, their experiences may not always be similar to White women's. Barbee (1993) interviewed 15 African American women about their ideas and experiences with dysphoria. The author found the women's view of dysphoria differed from the typical clinical presentation of dysphoria. These respondents reported that the "blues" is both a transition mood between feeling down and depression and a signal that they need time for self. Many African American women may notice when their emotional moods become sad and may engage in a coping response other than psychotherapy. If African Americans seek help with experiences of loss (such as sexual abuse, domestic violence, trauma, identity, relationships, parenting, substance use, and many other concerns), practitioners can examine times when self-renewal strategies work and when they do not work. Most practitioners will discover that often these women will triumph through painful emotional and difficult experiences; practitioners can provide opportunities like psychotherapy or include self-renewal opportunities such as using psychoeducation in community settings (e.g., offering workshops at churches, spiritual settings, recreation centers, work settings) to demystify and destigmatize psychotherapy but also to affirm that there are times when African American women can renew themselves without seeking professional services. Mental health professionals will need to leave the traditional office settings and consider offering self-renewal resources in nontraditional formats.

Additionally, African American women are culturally viewed as matriarchs of the family and nurturers (Boyd-Franklin, 2005; Brooks et al., 2004; Robinson, 1983). It may be hard for African American women to focus on self or take time for self. Self-care may be viewed as "selfish" or they may say "I just don't have time," (and this may be true because of their circumstances). Like the persons portrayed in Scenario 1 and 2, African American women will typically struggle with permitting themselves to focus on self. One self-renewal beginning (which is not often easily internalized) is for the therapist to tell the African American female to view psychotherapy as self-renewal time where someone can care for her. This image and view can be hard for the African American female because "I do the caring for." The person's identity may be strengthened when they care for others, even when these experiences are draining. For example, in Scenario 2, the mother with kidney failure had to now depend on her sons for her caregiving. She did not have control over doing simple household tasks or even driving to dialysis. She depended on her sons now for everything. Despite her limitations, she wanted to control how they took care of her. Some of the psychotherapy work included her hearing from them that she needed to trust they could care for her even if this caring did not evolve "exactly like you want it to be."

Gender Considerations With African American Men and Women

As we might anticipate, there may be differences in how African American men and women focus on self-renewal. Practitioners can expect that it is uncommon for African American men to voluntarily seek psychotherapy. In my private practice work during the past 15 years, I can count on two hands how many African American males sought voluntary psychotherapy. Many African American men who do seek services (voluntary or mandated) have untreated mental health issues from early on that are now being addressed in adulthood. In many cases, men experienced legal or criminal justice problems and obtained mental health treatment beyond childhood; the psychological (and other) symptoms and behaviors intensified over time.

Mental health professionals will benefit from reading Dr. A. Franklin's work on the *invisibility syndrome of the African American male* (Franklin, 2004) for an in-depth overview on the challenges facing African American males, particularly an examination of their psychological and mental health concerns including the invisibility syndrome these men experience in American culture. Dr. Franklin notes that Black men face life in a world where they are feared and treated as invisible; this invisibility creates numerous internal conflicts, which originate from environmental and societal injustices and microaggressions. These microaggressions and conflicts limit self-renewal. Some psychological issues include depression, anxiety, hopelessness, conflicted racial identities, anger, and other emotional, cognitive, spiritual, and behavioral responses. Therapy requires practitioners to engage in their own cultural consciousness and adoption of congruent attitudes and behaviors where the African American male client is respected and visible during psychotherapy or health services, especially since race and culture may be sources of stress and challenges to the African American male's health. Sometimes verbal or traditional talk therapy may be limited in addressing their self-renewal needs. Practitioners are encouraged to be flexible in considering a range of formats and interventions.

Expressive Arts

Expressive arts such as music, poetry, dance, and art can be incorporated into psychotherapy. For example, when facilitating a substance abuse treatment group with primarily men and women of color, many of these consumers were African Americans. I began incorporating music as part of the self-renewal group interventions, because the clients, particularly men, often struggled with sharing their emotions during group therapy. Music is very important and healing in African culture. Music can be identified to parallel the renewal recovery themes highlighted during therapy. Clients can also be invited to identify music that represents an absent self-renewal area in their lives. For example, if they needed to spend more time developing intimacy in their relationships, the clients would select songs that "spoke to their heart" on this issue. They were more inclined to share their emotional awareness after listening to the music (or asking them to identify music they can use outside of therapy) than if solely using traditional talk-therapy. Because many African American males wear masks as a cultural survival strategy (Franklin, 2004), it may take time for them to address emotional issues. They are not going to let the world see how their experiences of racial misunderstanding and mistreatment strips away their masculinity and identity as a Black man (Franklin, 2004). Yet, this strong exterior comes at a huge self-renewal cost. We all have an opportunity to support them and practitioners are encouraged to consider creative ways (including psychoeducation as an intervention) to support African American men and women.

To summarize, begin psychotherapy with asking and exploring how this African American *client views their identity as an African American* and include how being African American or African descent is valued and internalized. Also, understand that not all clients will be attached to race and/or ethnicity (Cross, 1995; Helms, 1995). Once the helping alliance is more secure, practitioners can probe further. If the client does not incorporate race, ethnicity, or culture into identity, we can explore the explanations. This information will be useful in knowing who your client is.

SUMMARY

Focusing on holistic self-renewal with African Americans provides rich opportunities for persons who have rarely participated in psychotherapy. Because many will engage in this process for the first time, the journey may not always be smooth. However, when clients encounter "healers" who are committed to their own self-renewal discovery, possess cultural consciousness and flexibility, and apply a strengths-focused attitude, knowledge, and skills approach with their African American clients, then the outcomes tend to be life changing. I always tell my clients "I want to encourage you to stay in the process . . . even when you do not always want to . . . we see change when we approach this as a journey." I invite mental health professionals to also embrace the journey of continually using a cultural lens as you collaborate with your African American clients in self-renewal growth together.

REFERENCES

Andrews, V. L., & Majors, R. G. (2004). African American nonverbal culture. In R. L. Jones (Ed.), *Black psychology* (4th ed., pp. 313–351). Berkeley, CA: Cobb & Henry.

Barbee, E. L. (1993). Healing time: The blues and African American women. *Healthcare for Women International, 15*, 53–60.

Boyd-Franklin, N. (1989). *Black families in therapy: A multisystem approach*. New York, NY: Guilford Press.

Boyd-Franklin, N. (2005). *Black families in therapy: Understanding the African American experience*. New York, NY: Guilford Press.

Broadley, B. T. (2000). Personal process in client-centered therapy. *Person-Centered Journal, 1*, 37–48.

Brooks, L., Haskins, D., & Kehe, J. (2004). Counseling and psychotherapy with African American clients. In T. Smith (Ed.), *Practicing multiculturalism: Affirming diversity in counseling and psychotherapy* (pp. 145–166). Boston, MA: Pearson/Allyn & Bacon.

Coakley, K. O. (2005). Racial(ized) identity, ethnic identity, and Afrocentric values: Conceptual and methodological challenges in understanding African American identity. *Journal of Counseling Psychology, 52*, 517–526.

Comas-Diaz, L., & Jacobsen, F. (1991). Ethnocultural-transference and countertransference in the therapeutic dyad. *American Journal of Orthopsychiatry, 61*, 392–402.

Constantine, M. G., Redington, R. M., & Graham, S. V. (2009). Counseling and psychotherapy with African Americans. In H. A. Neville, B. M. Tynes, & S. O. Utsey (Eds.), *Handbook of African American psychology* (pp. 431–444). Thousand Oaks, CA: Sage.

Cook, D. A., & Wiley, C. Y. (2000). Psychotherapy with members of African American churches and spiritual traditions. In P. S. Richards & A. E. Bergin (Eds.), *Handbook of psychotherapy and religious diversity* (pp. 369–396). Washington, DC: APA Books.

Cross, W. E. (1991). *Shades of Black: Diversity in African American identity*. Philadelphia, PA: Temple University Press.

Cross, W. E. (1995). The psychology of nigrescence: Revisiting the Cross model. In J. G. Ponterotto, J. M. Casas, L. A. Suzuki, & C. M. Alexander (Eds.), *Handbook of Multicultural counseling* (pp. 93–122). Thousand Oaks, CA: Sage.

Day-Vines, N. L., Wood, S. M., Grothaus, T., Craigen, L., Holman, A., Dotson-Blake, K., & Douglass, M. (2007). Broaching the subjects of race, ethnicity, and culture in the counseling process. *Journal of Counseling and Development*, 85(4), 401–409.

Ellison, C. G., & Taylor, R. J. (1996). Turning to prayer: Religious coping among black Americans. *Review of Religious Research*, 38, 111–131.

Fischer, A. R., & DeBord, K. A. (2007). Perceived conflicts between affirmation of religious diversity and affirmation of sexual diversity: That's perceived. In K. J. Bieschke, R. M. Perez, & K. A. DeBord (Eds.), *Handbook of counseling and psychotherapy with lesbian, gay, bisexual, and transgender clients* (2nd ed., pp. 317–339). Washington, DC: APA Books.

Fontes, L. A. (2005). *Child abuse and culture: Working with diverse families*. New York, NY: Guilford Press.

Franklin, A. J. (2004). *From brotherhood to manhood: How black men rescue their relationships and dreams from the invisibility syndrome*. Hoboken, NJ: Wiley.

Gardner, J. W. (1981). *The individual and the innovative society*. New York, NY: Norton.

Grills, C. (2002). African-centered psychology: Basic principles. In T. Parham (Ed.), *Counseling persons of African descent: Raising the bar of practitioner competence* (pp. 10–24). Thousand Oaks, CA: Sage.

Grills, C., & Ajei, M. (2002). African-centered conceptualizations of self and consciousness: The Akan model. In T. Parham (Ed.), *Counseling persons of African descent: Raising the bar of practitioner competence* (pp. 75–99). Thousand Oaks, CA: Sage.

Hall, L. E. (2005). *Dictionary of multicultural psychology: Issues, terms, and concepts*. Thousand Oaks, CA: Sage.

Harvey, M. R. (1996). An ecological view of psychological trauma and trauma recovery. *Journal of Traumatic Stress*, 9, 3–20.

Helms, J. (1995). An update of Helms' white and people of color racial identity models. In J. Ponterotto, J. M. Casas, L. A. Suzuki, & C. M. Alexander (Eds.), *Handbook of multicultural counseling* (pp. 181–198). Thousand Oaks, CA: Sage.

Helms, J., & Cook, D. A. (1999). *Using race and culture in counseling and psychotherapy: Theory and process*. Boston, MA: Allyn and Bacon.

Johnson, A. (2000). *The Blackwell dictionary of sociology* (2nd ed.). Malden, MA: Blackwell.

Kim, U. (1990). Indigenous psychology: Science and applications. In R. W. Brislin (Ed.), *Applied cross-cultural psychology* (pp.142–160). Newbury Park, CA: Sage.

Landrine, H. (1992). Clinical implications of cultural differences: The referential versus the indexical self. *Clinical Psychology Review*, *12*, 401–415.

Martin, M. (2002). *Saving our last nerve: The Black woman's path to mental health*. Roscoe, IL: Hilton.

McAdoo, H. (1994). Racial attitudes and self-concepts of Black preschool children. In L. Gary (Ed.), *Social research and the Black community* (pp. 66–75). Washington, DC: Howard University Press.

McGoldrick, M., Giordano, J., & Garcia-Preto, N. (Eds.). (2005). *Ethnicity and family therapy* (3rd ed.). New York, NY: Guilford Press.

McIntosh, P. (1989, July/August). White privilege: Unpacking the invisible knapsack. *Peace and Freedom*, 8–10.

Ogbonnaya, A. O. (1994). Person as community: An African understanding of the person as an intrapsychic community. *Journal of Black Psychology*, *20*, 75–87.

Parham, T. A. (Ed.). (2002). *Counseling persons of African descent: Raising the bar of practitioner competence*. Thousand Oaks, CA: Sage.

Parham, T. A., & Parham, W. D. (2002). Understanding African American mental health: The necessity of new conceptual paradigms. In T. A. Parham (Ed.), *Counseling persons of African descent: Raising the bar of practitioner competence* (pp. 25–37). Thousand Oaks, CA: Sage.

Pierce, C. (1975). A report on minority children. *Psychiatric Annals*, *5*, 244–246.

Richards, P. S., & Bergin, A. E. (2000). *Handbook of psychotherapy and religious diversity*. Washington, DC: APA Books.

Robinson, C. R. (1983). *Black women: A tradition of self-reliant strength*. London, England: Haworth Press/Taylor-Rutledge.

Smith, A. (1981). Religion and mental health among Blacks. *Journal of Religion and Health, 20*, 264–287.

Speight, S. L., Blackmon, S. M., Ogugu, D., & Steele, J. C. (2009). Conceptualizing mental health for African Americans. In H. A. Neville, B. M. Tynes, & S. O. Utsey (Eds.), *Handbook of African American psychology*. Thousand Oaks, CA: Sage.

Sue, D. W., & Sue, D. (2008). *Counseling the culturally diverse: Theory and practice* (5th ed.). Hoboken, NJ: Wiley.

Taylor, R. J., Chatters, L. M., Jayakody, R., & Levin, J. S. (1996). Black and White differences in religious participation: A multisample comparison. *Journal of the Scientific Study of Religion, 36*, 403–410.

Taylor, R. J., Chatters, L. M., & Levin, J. (2004). *Religion in the lives of African Americans: Social, psychological, and health perspectives*. Thousand Oaks, CA: Sage.

Tynes, B. M., & Ward, L. M. (2009). The role of media use and portrayals in African Americans' psychosocial development. In H. A. Neville, B. M. Tynes, & S. O. Utsey (Eds.), *Handbook of African American psychology* (pp. 143–158). Thousand Oaks, CA: Sage.

U.S. Department of Health and Human Services. (2001). *Culture, race, and ethnicity: A supplement to mental health: A report of the Surgeon General*. Washington, DC: Author.

Washington, L. D. (2012). *The sense of divine control, locus of control, education and socio-economic status as predictors of religious coping and attitude toward seeking professional psychological help among African American Christians* (Unpublished dissertation). Loyola University Maryland, Baltimore, Maryland.

Williams, D. R., & Williams-Morris, R. (2000). Racism and mental health: The African American experience. *Ethnicity & Health, 5*, 243–268.

Wolpe, J. (1958). *Psychotherapy by reciprocal inhibition*. Stanford, CA: Stanford University Press.

Wyatt, G. E. (1985). The sexual abuse of Afro-American and White American women in childhood. *Child Abuse and Neglect, 9*, 507–519.

CHAPTER

22

Clergy Self-Renewal Themes in Clinical Practice

Thomas E. Rodgerson

The theme of self-renewal is rarely the presenting problem for clergy seeking therapeutic help. The presenting problem more often will be marital issues, family problems, sexuality issues, depression, anxiety, job loss or conflict, career change, or substance abuse issues, with which the theme of self-renewal is coterminous and connected to the unique cultural, or subcultural, context of the clergyperson. This unique context confronts the clinician with a variety of environmental hazards, exceptional resources, and even ambivalence in the understanding of the self often not found in other treatment populations. As we see, engaging the "otherness" in this unique population becomes an invitation to a new level of wisdom for the therapist in clinical practice.

THE CONGREGATIONAL CONTEXT

Clergy work and live in a number of contexts, each of which has resources and limitations. In the section that follows, the limitations of a congregational understanding of clergy self-renewal and the hazards of the congregational context are explored.

Limitations

To speak of "clergy self-renewal" implies a more ecumenical than interfaith discussion. While Buddhist and Hindu traditions may have teachers, gurus, or masters with disciples who gather in *sanghas* or *ashrams*, and Muslim traditions may have Imams who teach and preach to those who gather in communities for prayer, clergy are usually associated with congregations. To speak of congregations naturally limits the interfaith nature of this discussion to Jewish and Christian faith traditions. Within those two faith traditions clergy are variously referred to as priests, pastors, ministers, or rabbis, and they are employed in a full-time or part-time capacity in a variety of Jewish traditions (Reformed, Orthodox, Conservative, etc.) and Christian denominations (Roman Catholic, Orthodox, Baptist, Lutheran, Presbyterian, Episcopalian, Pentecostal, Evangelical, Nondenominational, etc.). In some traditions and denominations, clergy can be male or female, but in many cases clergy are limited to the male gender. Likewise, in some traditions and denominations, sexual orientation can vary, but in many cases clergy are limited to being heterosexuals who are either married or celibate.

Within the congregational context, it is easy to become reductive and forget that there is uniqueness to every congregation and for every clergyperson. In the clinical interaction with any clergyperson, it is best to remember the words that came out of early anthropological studies (Kluckhohn & Murray, 1948) and were variously applied to the counseling context (e.g., Augsburger, 1986)—namely, that every person is in certain respects like all others, like some others, and like no other. This can be said equally of the individuals who present for treatment and of the individual congregations in which they find themselves. While it is natural within this chapter, for reasons of space limitations, to approach clergy self-renewal themes from the position of "like all others" or "like some others," it is important to remember the unique clergy personality and congregational interaction that is "like no other" for every clergyperson who presents for clinical treatment.

In some of the earliest literature written on the topic of burnout for helping professionals, convincing arguments were made implying, on the one hand, that there were certain types of individuals who were more susceptible to burnout (Freudenberger & Richelson, 1980; Pines & Maslach, 1978) and, on the other hand, that there were certain environmental characteristics that might lead to burnout in any individual (Maslach, 1978). Research along these lines has continued for decades, suggesting to the clinician concerned with self-renewal in clergy that one must seek to understand both the inner world of the clergyperson, and also the inner dynamics of the congregation.

Congregational context matters, if for no other reason than to understand the nature of authority and power within the system. For instance, is there a congregational polity or an ecclesiastical polity operating in the congregation? Does the local congregation "hire and fire," or can a bishop intervene in times of trouble? Is the clergyperson expected to be heterosexual and married needing to support a family, or is the clergyperson expected to be celibate and living in a religious community? All of this affects an understanding of the self-in-context and may require the clinician to seek consultation on the particularities of the congregational context. Having done this, the clinician must press on to understand the unique congregation that is "like no other" because each congregation has a history and an operating system that in some sense functions like the "DNA" of the congregation. How the congregation came into being, historical accidents in the congregation or surrounding community, or past history of clergy malpractice and how it was handled by the congregation all affect the local operating system of the congregation. When the unique operating system of the congregation interacts with the unique worldview of a clergyperson, it can be like a marriage or deep friendship with profound implications for clergy self-renewal, or the lack of it.

Occupational Hazards

As is the case with other treatment populations in clinical practice, it is easy to focus on diagnosing what is wrong and overlook the positives in any given situation. The occupational hazards of congregational life are legendary. Yet, there is plenty of anecdotal evidence to indicate the positive aspects of being a priest, pastor, or rabbi. One clergyperson said, "I actually get paid to be able to study scripture and use it to positively influence the lives of people." Another person said, "This has been the most safe and nurturing environment possible in which to raise my kids. It's like they have 100 doting grandparents!" Being able to answer a "higher calling," to engage people in the most meaningful parts of their lives, to provide help to others, and to bring about change in the local community and the world are just some of the positives that draw people to and keep people in the work of congregational life.

But the opposite can also be true. In researching clergy self-care, Oswald (1991) said that clergy, "have gone like lambs to the slaughter because they have not been offered even minimal survival skills in their training for ministry" (p. ix). The often quoted study by the Fuller Institute of Church Growth (Pastors in Covenant, 2003; Zettersten, 1993) found that: (a) 90% of pastors work more than 46 hours a week; (b) 80% believe pastoral ministry has affected their families negatively; (c) 33% say being in the ministry is an outright hazard to their family; (d) 75% report a significant stress-related crisis at least once in their ministry; (e) 50% feel unable to meet the needs of the job; (f) 90% feel they were inadequately trained to cope with ministry demands; (g) 70% say they have a lower self-image now than when they started; (h) 40% report a serious conflict with a parishioner at least once a month; (i) 37% confess having been involved in inappropriate sexual behavior with someone in the church; and (j) 70% do not have someone they consider a close friend. Other surveys corroborate these findings, such as the 1998 report by Focus on the Family (as cited in Pastors in Covenant, 2003) that found 80% of pastors and 84% of their spouses are discouraged or are dealing with depression, and 40% of pastors and

47% of their spouses are suffering from burnout, frantic schedules, and unrealistic expectations. Anecdotal evidence of this kind is often found, such as the pastor who said, "I'm done with ministry. Let me be a janitor somewhere. I feel abandoned by God." Or, the pastor who said, "I want to teach, preach, and care for others, but I simply hate the pettiness of people in their church power struggles that make me anxious and unable to sleep at night."

A meta-data analysis of mental health issues among clergy (Weaver, Larson, Flannelly, Stapleton, & Koenig, 2002) found similar results with clergy reportedly working on average 56.2 hours per week in ministry and 12 evenings a month away from home on church duties. The study found that ministers with the highest level of stress were most susceptible to sexual misconduct. Various studies cited in this meta-data analysis showed sexual misconduct rates among clergy at 5.8% of the clergy population and 11% to 17% of the professionals accused of sexual misconduct. In addition, Clodfelter (2011), citing health statistics from the Duke Divinity School Health Initiative, reported that on average clergy show higher rates of obesity, high blood pressure, asthma, and depression than the general population.

On the one hand, understanding the occupational hazards of congregational life may be similar to understanding the phenomenon of acute secondary stress, vicarious posttraumatic stress, or compassion fatigue experienced by many helping professionals (Wicks & Ciarrochi, 2000). But, on the other hand, clinicians attempting to understand the theme of self-renewal in clergy must not overlook the unique congregational context, colloquially referred to as living in a "stained glass fish bowl" (Hunt, 1990). In a classic study, Sanford (1982) described nine special circumstances that make clergy susceptible to burnout: (1) the job of the ministering person is never finished; (2) the ministering person cannot always tell if his or her work is having any results; (3) the work of the ministering person is repetitive; (4) the ministering person is dealing constantly with people's expectations; (5) the ministering person must work with the same people year in and year out; (6) because he or she works with people in need, there is a particularly great drain on the energy of the ministering person; (7) the ministering person deals with many people who come to him or her or the church not for solid spiritual food but for "strokes"; (8) the ministering person must focus a great deal of the time on his or her "persona"; and (9) the ministering person may become exhausted by failure. As witnessed by the current author, the experience of clergy in ministry is like one who becomes a "lightning rod for other people's pathology" owing to the fact that people with problems (those who know they have problems and those who are unaware of their problems) are attracted to churches for help and often expect the clergyperson to do something about their problems. Added to all of this is the fact that in the wider culture, clergypersons have gone from having a relatively high-status, high-paying job to a relatively low-status, low-paying job (Arena, 1992). Wicks and Ciarrocchi (2000) go further to note an anticlericalism now extant in the culture with clergy being the recipients of negative transferences, whereas in an earlier time clergy were treated with deference and given a place of honor.

The Necessity of Self-Care

The unique occupational hazards of congregational life necessitate self-care disciplines by clergy—body, mind, and soul—just as if they were athletes preparing for the running of a marathon. In this regard, clinicians can serve as "coaches" who hold clergy accountable to the rigorous training of self-care, using educational, solution-focused, cognitive-behavioral, systemic, or dynamic forms of therapy.

Body

From many years of working with clergy, Van Lant (2011) speaks pointedly about the need for self-care when he says, "As a pastor, it is imperative that you are attuned to, and care for, the body, mind, and spirit that God has blessed you with. If you are overweight, exhausted, and out of shape, you must begin to take seriously the spiritual discipline of caring for your body" (p. 425). Clergy are no different from the general population when it comes to the benefits of a diet that reduces the consumption of sugar, salt, white flour, and saturated fat. Oswald (1991) comments that clergy often experience intense emotions in their lives as they deal with the unique hazards of ministry, and when combined with poor eating habits this provides a double assault upon the body. He says, "When our bodies are assaulted by battering rams of emotional turmoil all day, and then we assault them even more with caffeine, sugar, salt, fat, alcohol, and refined flour, it is like a one-two punch" (p. 152).

Likewise, clergy are no different from others in benefiting from some form of regular exercise. A wide body of research indicates that exercise can reduce symptoms of depression and anxiety, increase mental alertness, and improve immune system functioning (Seligman, Rashid, & Parks, 2006; Van Lant, 2011). The general rule of thumb is to have an exercise regimen of at least three times a week for 20 minutes in which the heart rate gets up to about 120 beats per minute. Any exercise program should be developed in consultation with a medical doctor, such consultations themselves being a form of self-care often overlooked by clergy.

Congregational life can both help and hinder clergy in the development of disciplines around the body. The flexibility of their work schedule gives the opportunity to create space for taking a walk, going to the gym, or taking time to eat a balanced meal. Scriptures that point to the body as the temple of God are often taken as positive motivators for the care of the whole person, such as I Corinthians 3:16, which says, "Do you not know that you are God's temple and that God's Spirit dwells in you?" (Revised Standard Version). At the same time, much of community life in congregations revolves around food, from potluck dinners before business meetings, to personal invitations to dinner, and even to the "paying" of ministers with food in rural settings or small congregations. Such congregational practices can work to undermine self-care disciplines around diet.

Similarly, the 24/7 lifestyle of congregational life for the clergy can work to undermine a regular schedule of exercise. Established routines for self-care can be interrupted at any time by a family crisis in the life of a congregant, a sudden tragic death, or an impromptu meeting. Regular congregational services, weddings, and funerals make it hard to establish regular times for rest and relaxation. There are usually no "weekends" for clergy, and even vacations can be interrupted by the sudden death of an important member of the congregation. Questions such as, "How are you sleeping?," "Are you taking your day off?," or "Do you regularly take vacation time?" are important diagnostic questions in the work with clergy. The establishing of regular "Sabbath time," even with the motivation from scripture, can be difficult in practice but vitally necessary to the health of those in congregational ministry. Clinicians who understand the unique context of congregational life can be of real value to clergy as they educate, help with goal setting, provide a place of accountability, and maintain an atmosphere of curiosity about the successes and failures of the care of the body.

Mind

Such curiosities will often lead to self-care that begins to focus on the mind. Helping the clergyperson to become cognizant of the underlying cognitions and self-talk about the body, one's body image, and one's sexuality could follow traditional cognitive-behavioral approaches to therapy (e.g., Burns, 1980). Catching sex-negative cognitive distortions engendered by congregations who often see clergy as nonsexual beings, or catching negative self-talk about the body begins a process of renewing the mind.

Yet, renewing the mind pertaining to how one thinks about the body is only the beginning. Just as living in a marriage or any close relationship brings into bold relief patterns of behavior and ways of thinking about others, so the emotion-laden environment of congregational life provides the stage on which automatic ways of thinking and behaving, default ways of relating and loving, and repetitive ways of reacting to anxiety, fear, and stress are played out. In speaking of clergy self-care, Oswald (1991) says, "There are some internal messages or self-perceptions that keep us on a treadmill that leads to our own destruction. Uncovering these hidden drives, these distorted self-images, usually requires the aid of an objective outsider" (p. 159). Whatever the presenting problem, and whether the clinician uses a cognitive-behavioral, psychodynamic, or family systems approach to therapy, the unique congregational context provides a laboratory for experimenting with new ways of thinking and behaving that can renew the mind.

For example, Perry (2003) found in a study focused in one denomination that clergy candidates had a higher need for others' affirmation than 90% of the people in the general population, and that affirmation was often missing in congregational life, creating stress in the life of the clergyperson and resulting in more illness from stress than 90% of the general population. Self-care relating to keeping the body in good shape through diet and exercise would be one approach that a clinician could use to help cope with this situation, but obviously the bigger form of self-care would involve being curious about the need for affirmation and how the mind processes such needs.

One approach often used to investigate such patterns of behavior is that of family systems. The work of Bowen (1978) was most directly applied to congregational life by Friedman (1985) with a number of authors making further application to health and leadership issues (e.g., Richardson, 2005; Steinke, 2006, 2007). In introducing his book, Richardson (2005) says, "Our development within our family of origin is a major but usually hidden component of how we function emotionally within our congregations as pastors" (p. ix). Friedman's (1985) major thesis was that "all clergymen and clergywomen, irrespective of faith, are simultaneously involved in three distinct families whose emotional forces interlock: the families within the congregation, our congregations, and our own" (p. 1). Stress for clergy, he would go on to say, was less the result of "overwork" and more the "effect of our position in the triangle of our families" (p. 1).

Focusing more on process than content, Friedman (1985) applied five basic concepts of family systems thinking (identified patient, homeostasis, differentiation of self, the extended family field, and emotional triangles) to congregational life. Following the trail of anxiety, monitoring our reactivity, noticing patterns of overfunctioning or underfunctioning, attending to emotional fusion or emotional cutoffs, are all ways of looking at the self in the family system of the congregation. Taking ownership of how the self functions in the system, and how this often repeats patterns of survival within one's family of origin and even one's current family becomes a primary means of self-care through the renewal of the mind as the clergyperson chooses to monitor his or her anxiety and change the way of thinking and behaving in the congregation. Friedman (1985) says, "What is vital to changing any kind of 'family' is not knowledge of technique or even of pathology, but, rather, the capacity of the family leader to define his or her own goals and values while trying to maintain a nonanxious presence within the system" (p. 2). He goes on to say, "If we must conceive of leadership in terms of expertise rather than self-definition, none of us will ever feel adequately prepared. The disintegration of self that threatens all clergy today is due less to the structure of our lives than to the way we are expected to organize our thinking" (p. 3).

The clergyperson who was the "family hero" in an alcoholic family of origin and who survived by ignoring inner feelings of guilt, by overfunctioning in parenting her parents, and by learning a style of perfectionism that masked inner insecurity may quickly find that this style of functioning actually creates stress, conflict, and burnout in ministry. The clergyperson who was a middle child and peacemaker in an angry family, and who ignored his own need for nurture and affirmation, may quickly find that this style of functioning becomes impossible to maintain in a conflicted congregation. Using the unique congregational context as a laboratory for experimenting with different thinking and behaving, the clinician can help clergy identify family patterns, monitor their own anxiety, and react differently to any situation, using a therapeutic approach that enhances self-care through a renewal of the mind.

Motivation for such a renewal of the mind may come negatively through the experience of emotional pain and failure in congregational life. But motivation for such a renewal of the mind is also part and parcel of the spiritual traditions to which the clergyperson has been called. The proclamation that God desires to have "my law within them, and I will write it upon their hearts" (Jeremiah 31:33) speaks to the deepest kind of alteration of human thinking and behaving. Likewise, the admonition of the Apostle Paul to "not be conformed to this world but be transformed by the renewal of your mind that you may prove what is the will of God, what is good and acceptable and perfect" (Romans 12:2) is often an underlying goal of many clergy. Self-care of the mind, then, often aligns naturally with the clergyperson's highest personal goals and values.

Soul

Attending to the self-care of the soul will have the added benefit of supporting any self-care of the body and self-care of the mind. By "self-care of the soul" it is meant the spiritual practices or disciplines that give significance to, awareness of, and development of a person's inner life. In speaking of that "inner life" for counselors (defining "counselors" as all psychotherapists and caregivers whether professional or not), Wicks (2012) says:

> There is the *gestalt* of the core elements responsible for the way through which all of the counselor's daily and professional encounters are experienced—what we may call here the *inner life*, a "place" that should be explored and nourished through the understanding and practice of mindfulness. (p. ix)

"Mindfulness" comes from the eastern religious traditions and is simply defined by Thich Nhat Hanh (1975) as "keeping one's consciousness alive to the present reality" (p. 11), which he documents as coming from the Buddhist Sutra of Mindfulness, where it says in part:

> When walking, the practitioner must be conscious that he is walking. When sitting, the practitioner must be conscious that he is sitting. When lying down, the practitioner must be conscious the he is lying down. . . . No matter what position one's body is in, the practitioner

> must be conscious of that position. Practicing thus, the practitioner lives in direct and constant mindfulness of the body. (p. 7)

Such mindfulness would be extended to a similar awareness of one's breathing and, then, to an awareness of all activities of life (e.g., when one is washing the dishes to be completely aware that one is washing the dishes). Being aware in this way changes the inner *gestalt* of a person, and, in turn, changes the way that one engages others and all of life. In the psychotherapeutic literature, this mindful way of being has proven to be helpful in the treatment of a number of mental health disorders, as well as being helpful for the vitality of the clinician (Baer, 2003; Kabat-Zinn, 1994; Kornfield, 2000; Linehan, 1993; Segal, Williams, & Teasdale, 2002).

While mindfulness training may be of great value in the self-care of the soul for clergy, not every person in congregational life will be attracted to spiritual practices from the eastern religions. Again, the congregational context, and the unique individual who is "like no other," matters. Wicks' (2009) use of the term *prayerfulness*, which he defines as "being in the present with your eyes wide open to experiencing God and life in dynamic ways" (p. vi), develops the same theme, but with language that can appeal to a wider audience. He stresses that this is not the mastery of a set of techniques, but an ethos to be absorbed and an attitude to be cultivated. "Prayerfulness is the openness to let life get 'into your bones, under your skin'" (Wicks, 2009, p. 10).

Similarly, the term *watchfulness* is a term that emerged from early (4th century to 15th century) Christian literature, grounded in Christian texts like I Thessalonians 5:6, "So, then let us not sleep, as others do, but let us keep awake and be sober." Watchfulness is the "opposite to a state of drunken stupor; hence spiritual sobriety, alertness, vigilance. It signifies an attitude of attentiveness, whereby one keeps watch over one's inward thoughts and fantasies, maintaining guard over the heart and intellect" (Palmer, Sherrard, & Ware, 1979, p. 367). The early desert fathers developed a way of inward prayer that would lead to an inner stillness (*hesychia*) that contained the idea of inner tranquility and silence, but also the idea of "being seated, fixed, and so of being concentrated" (Palmer et al., 1979, p. 15). Such ideas were built on long-existing ways of praying seen in the Hebrew scripture where there was a focus upon learning to wait upon God. For example, Psalm 62:5 says, "For God alone my soul waits in silence, for my hope is from him." Or, Psalm 130:5–6 says, "I wait for the Lord, my soul waits, and in his word I hope; my soul waits for the Lord more than watchmen for the morning, more than watchmen for the morning."

Commenting that spiritual depth is often the antidote to burnout for clergy, Oswald (1991, p. 92) reminds the clergyperson that there are many ways to develop the spiritual discipline of prayer. His preference is for a way of praying that combines the benefits of meditation techniques such as Benson's (1984) relaxation response with repetitive "mantras," which have been used in religious traditions for centuries. Such mantras might include the following: "Lord have mercy"; "Come Lord Jesus"; "Yahweh, Yeshua, Ruach"; "Kyrie Eleison"; "I am, Thou art." He goes on to say, "The quality of my day is different when I take fifteen minutes before I rush out the door to move into this meditative space. . . . I try to keep the practice going throughout the day by attaching it to a certain trigger, e.g., sitting at a red light, or in an airplane ready to take off" (Oswald, 1991, p. 99).

Self-care of the soul is not limited to prayer. Oswald (1991) suggests other spiritual disciplines and exercises such as journaling, fasting, chanting, body prayer, retreats, days of silence, or talking to a spiritual friend. Foster (1978) reminds us that there are inward spiritual disciplines (meditation, prayer, fasting, study), outward spiritual disciplines (simplicity, solitude, submission, service), and corporate spiritual disciplines (confession, worship, guidance, celebration).

Not that the clinician working with clergy for self-renewal must be an expert in the various spiritual disciplines. In fact, the clinician may choose to refer the clergyperson to a certified pastoral counselor (see the American Association of Pastoral Counselors) or to a spiritual director (see Spiritual Directors International). Yet, there are a number of approaches that can be incorporated into therapy by most clinicians to assist in the self-care of the soul. First, introducing relaxation techniques or times of stillness/silence into a therapy session begins to build the capacity for the inner life. Second, for those clinicians trained in mindfulness techniques, these approaches can also be introduced into therapy, with the caveat that the language may need to be adjusted, or the parallels drawn to ancient spiritual practices compatible with the unique congregational context (as demonstrated above). Inclusive in this approach might be an invitation to and education about spiritual practices and ways of praying/meditating that have been shown by research to be beneficial to both the body and the mind (Hagerty, 2009; Newberg & Waldman, 2009). Third, clinicians can be aware of the great irony amongst clergy that they are constantly attending to the spiritual life and growth of others, but often forget to attend to their own spiritual/inner life. For example, to preach on a scriptural text is not the same as quietly listening to a scriptural text. To teach others how to pray is not the same as taking time for quietness in one's own life. As a part of any routine assessment, clinicians can inquire as to the spiritual practices in the life of the clergyperson, helping to make the distinction between pastoral work with others and the nurture of one's own inner life.

Fourth, in any routine assessment, clinicians can evaluate if the spiritual practices of the clergyperson contribute to positive mental health outcomes or hinder positive outcomes. For instance, research has shown that there are clear, patterned forms of religious coping when it comes to dealing with life problems or illness. Pargament (1997) identifies three major spiritual/religious methods of coping (self-directing, deferral, collaborative) that define styles of reaching out to God or interacting with God in times of need. These styles are not positive or negative themselves, but depend on the scope of the individual's power to influence the course of the illness in the context of a specific situation (Mohr & Huguelet, 2009). When the style of religious coping leads to spiritual meaning-making that includes appraisals of God's benevolence and power, there are often positive outcomes for mental health. To the contrary, when this leads to appraisals of God as punishing or having no power, the outcomes tend to be negative (Mohr & Huguelet, 2009).

Fifth, the clinician can help clergypeople not to compartmentalize their spiritual life, but to develop spiritual practices that, on the one hand, can be attended to throughout the day (being able to use relaxing mantras at stop lights or in the midst of business meetings; seeing work itself as a form of prayer) and, on the other hand, are transformative of being and not simply obligatory spiritual rituals. Speaking to the first point, Rupp (1999) understands the tension between the work of ministry and spiritual solitude/prayer as a "tension of opposites" where growth can occur as one develops eyes to recognize God as a part of who one is and what one is doing at all times. Speaking to the second point, Wicks (2012) describes the development of the inner life in such a way that it becomes a way of "standing" in the world. He says, "It is not the amount of darkness in the world that matters. It is not even the amount of darkness in *ourselves* that matters. Instead, in the end, it is how we stand in that very darkness that makes the ultimate difference" (p. x).

There is a Sanskrit word, *sthita*, from the Hindu scriptures that means *standing firm* or *taking a position*, which Simmons (2000) understands as "finding a stillness in the midst of life's calamitous downhill rush" (p. 113). From the Christian scripture there is a passage that talks about a variety of spiritual goals and disciplines that ultimately are to help one stand:

> Therefore take the whole armor of God, that you may be able to withstand in the evil day, and having done all, to stand. Stand therefore, having girded your loins with truth, and having put on the breastplate of righteousness, and having shod your feet with the equipment of peace; above all taking the shield of faith. . . . And take the helmet of salvation, and the sword of the Spirit, which is the word of God. Pray at all times in the Spirit, with all prayer and supplication. To that end keep alert. (Ephesians 6:13–18)

Self-care of the soul, then, ultimately is about how clergypeople will "stand" in this world. The task of clinicians is to assess the spiritual practices and to pay attention to how they help them "stand" in ministry and in the world. As well, the task of the clinician is to attend to the integration of the spiritual disciplines with psychological theory, being on the lookout for spiritual practices that help change metacognitions (cognitive-behavioral theory), that help engender a nonanxious presence or self-differentiation (systems theory), and that help lower defenses, make the unconscious conscious, or engage the task of individuation (psychodynamic theory). Regarding the latter, Jung (1959), in his chapter on the self, finds the task of individuation to be completely compatible with the Christian concept of redemption, having mutual goals of wholeness or completeness. Spiritual practices that accept the work of making the unconscious conscious avoid the unhappy consequences of repressed individuation and the acting out of an inner conflict. But if a person voluntarily takes the burden of completeness on himself, he need not find it "happening" to him against his will in a negative form. "This is as much to say that anyone who is destined to descend into a deep pit had better set about it with all the necessary precautions rather than risk falling into the hole backwards" (Jung, 1959, p. 70).

Those "necessary precautions" are a part of appropriate spiritual practices important to the self-care of the soul, and, as we discuss below, are essential for self-care that leads to self-renewal.

THE AMBIVALENCE TOWARD SELF

One of the necessary precautions to be addressed in clergy self-care is the ambivalence of many clergy to the recognition, sustenance, and care of the self.

Resistance to Self-Care

Despite the plethora of information on the importance of and the "how-to" of self-care available within the wider culture and often disseminated through denominational wellness programs or clergy benefit boards, data such as that mentioned above on clergy health problems and stress rates suggest a significant resistance to the incorporation of self-care into the clergy lifestyle. It could be argued that this is no different from the general population where there is often seen an inherent and multifaceted resistance to change of any kind, variously explained in terms of the power of *defenses*, the powerful pull of *homeostasis*, or simply the difficulty of overcoming *bad habits*. Clergy could easily blend in with the multitudes that make New Year's resolutions about diet, exercise, and improved habits for self-care, only to find the resolutions broken within weeks.

However, clergy resistance to self-care has an added dimension that is important to understand—namely, an embedded ambivalence toward the very understanding of the self. This ambivalence toward the self is a part of the wider culture and is a part of the unique religious subcultures extant in congregational life. As leaders within the culture and within religious subcultures, clergy often embody this ambivalence, and it is suggested that this ambivalence contributes to the resistance to self-care and self-renewal.

Cultural Ambivalence

Baumeister (1991), alluding to the work of Rosenthal (1984), comments how the very usage of the word *Self* as seen in the Oxford English Dictionary changed from the Middle Ages to the Romantic era. In the 1680 edition, the usage of the word had the example of "Self is the Anti-Christ and Anti-God in the world," whereas the 1870 edition offered, "respect to self and its ultimate good pertains to the very nobility of man's nature." Baumeister (1991) says, "Thus, in two centuries, *self* went from the ultimate bad to the ultimate good" (p. 112). Beyond this, well into the 20th century, social morality was defined by what was best for the welfare of the group and usually meant overcoming self-interest condemned as selfishness, greed, or egoism. Virtue meant conquering self-interest. Vice meant putting the self first and acting on desires and impulses of the self counter to the best interest of the community.

> Thus, self-interest and moral values created a balance of opposing forces. But in the 20th century this balance has been destroyed. Morality has become allied with self-interest. . . . The modern message is that what is right and good and valuable to do in life is to focus on yourself, to learn what is inside you, to express and cultivate these inner resources to do what is best for yourself, and so forth. Now, instead, there is an increasingly moral imperative to do the opposite. To live one's life properly and achieve the highest forms of human fulfillment, it was once considered necessary to know about God. Now it is considered vital to know about yourself instead. . . . Many Americans today can no longer accept the idea that love requires sacrificing oneself or making oneself unhappy or doing things that do not (at least eventually) serve one's individual best interests. (Baumeister, 1991, p. 113)

In the core meaning-making activity of the culture there are profound shifts occurring regarding the self. As leaders within the culture, it is suggested that clergy may embody the cultural shifting and ambivalent understandings of the self, contributing in part to a resistance to focus on the self for the purpose of self-care.

Friedman (2007) notes that there is ambiguity and ambivalence associated with the very word *Self*, as seen in the varied and contradictory ways in which it is used in the English language. When "ish" is added to many words (e.g., *bookish, reddish, faddish, Jewish)* it simply means "having the quality of." But when "ish" is added to *self*, it becomes a pejorative term. The word *Self* can be used in a purely reflexive mode (*self-explanatory, self-evident, self-expression*), it can be added to a neutral word and make it negative (*self-centered, self-justified, self-congratulatory*), or it can be added to words indicating a positive quality because of the absence of *Self* (*self-denial, self-sacrifice, self-less*). "How can it be good to be both self-sufficient and self-less, self-made and self-effacing, self-respectful and self-denying . . . ? Actually, the word *self* has trouble retaining its self" (p. 175). Friedman (2007) goes on to say that this ambiguity and ambivalence contributes to a "failure of nerve" by leaders who (when seen from a systems perspective) cannot get the balance right between individuality and togetherness. In systems of chronic anxiety, the force for individuality is suspect in human institutions, which results in an overemphasis on togetherness often leading to tribalism, anarchy, tyranny, or (at the cellular level) tumors. He says that to be true leaders, leaders must get past the pathologizing of the self:

> It is only when self is valued that leaders can be less at the mercy of the data/technique deluge, no less its addictive properties. It is only when leaders value self that their cortex can be kept from the service of the reptilian brain and their cerebration can be true thinking. It is only when leaders value self that they can recognize the importance of making their own self-definition more crucial than feeling for others. . . . It is only when leaders value self that they can muster the self-regulation necessary for countering the sabotage that will greet them. (Friedman, 2007, p. 173)

Especially when there is chronic anxiety within the culture or within a congregation, clergypersons as leaders will embody this pull toward togetherness and the tendency to pathologize the self. It is suggested that this will be a unique part of the resistance to a focus on the self, which is a necessary part of self-care and self-renewal.

Finally, within the culture there is not always a clear definition of what constitutes the Self. "Ego," "personality," and the "Self" are often used interchangeably and seen as evolving (Kegan, 1982). The self can be seen as partly related to the ego, but bigger than the ego, "consisting of the sum of conscious and unconscious processes" (Jung, 1959, p. 189). In the psychological world, "ego" and "Self" have largely come to replace the word *soul* (Muller, 2010) and this, too, may generate in clergy an innate ambivalence about a focus on the self instead of a focus on the soul.

Religious Subcultural Ambivalence

The cultural ambivalence about the self is only compounded within the religious subculture and within the context of congregational life. Not only are the terms *care of the soul*, concern for the *heart*, or *spirit* more familiar than and more scripturally relevant than the term *Self*, focus on the self can be seen as either narcissistic or weak. Oswald (1991) says, "In seminars with pastors, I often feel the tension in the room rise when the subject of self-care comes up. . . . Some unconscious tapes play in their minds telling them that taking care of the self is somehow unChristian or at least unnecessary" (p. 4).

Foucault (1988) suggests that "taking care of oneself" was important in early Christianity just as it was for Greek and Roman philosophers. However, owing to the fact that it is hard to base rigorous morality on giving ourselves more care, Christian asceticism introduced alternative ideas of self-renunciation and self-exposure or self-revelation for the purpose of abasing, nullifying, or destroying the self. This was combined with giving control of the self to another (such as a spiritual director) often resulting in the self's domination and diminishment. Capps (1993), commenting on Foucault's conclusions, says that the Christian ascetic tradition seems to have been all too successful and "that the time has come for us to recognize that taking care of our selves . . . is emphatically not a self-indulgence, but a moral imperative" (p. 168).

At some level, clinicians will need to engage the seeming contradiction and ambivalence embedded in the religious subculture and embodied in the clergyperson's resistance to self-care where one is called both to "love one's neighbor as one's self" (Leviticus 19:18; 19:34; Matthew 19:19; 22:39)—implying that there is an appropriate love of self—and to "humble the self," "hate the self," or "crucify the self" (Luke 14:11,26; Galatians 2:20). Learning to "stand" in that ambivalence and not overfocus on self (which can lead in the overfocus to narcissistic self-interest, breaking of boundaries, inappropriate power over others, overconcern for performance) or underfocus on self (which can lead in the underfocus to tribalism, the inability to think for oneself, or appropriately love the self), may actually lead the clergyperson from self-care to the deeper aspects of self-renewal.

BEYOND SELF-CARE TO SELF-RENEWAL

Hidden within the reality of the embedded cultural and religious ambivalence about self-care is a gift. It is a gift that guards against the potential superficiality of self-care. Questioning whether or not the language of self-care is even appropriate for clergy, Miller-McLemore (2011) comments that self-care as often discussed in developed countries is appropriate only for the affluent. He says, "Who has time or resources for self-care in the developing world or the inner city? Do ministers in Haiti talk about their provisions for self-care? . . . In an affluent culture, can we trust our self's desire for care to show us the way to good ministry" (Miller-McLemore, 2011, pp. 120–122)? In the context of congregational life and the calling of clergy to their life work of transforming unjust systems and transforming the deepest meaning-making systems of a person's life, self-care (at best) is a preparation for the far deeper work of self-renewal. Self-care of the body can provide the energy, and self-care of the mind and soul (as discussed earlier) can open the door, but it is important in the clinical work with clergy to see that the gift in clergy ambivalence about self-care is at some level a call to move beyond self-care to the deeper work of self-renewal.

Psychological Language for Self-Renewal

Any language for self-renewal depends on one's understanding of the self. Lewis (1990) notes the wide range of possibilities for understanding the concept of the self, from a materialistic understanding that sees the self as a part of the body (perhaps the brain), to behaviorism that sees the self as prescribed tendencies or dispositions, to philosophers and theologians who see the self as larger than experiences—even a "pure self," which is also the Supreme Self in some forms of mysticism.

From a constructive-developmental perspective, Kegan (1982) can speak of an evolving self. He can speak of a "zone of mediation where meaning is made," which is "that most human of 'regions' *between* an event and a reaction to it—the place where the event is privately composed, made sense of, the place where it actually *becomes* an event for that person" (p. 2). "The zone of mediation where meaning is made is variously called by personality psychologists the 'ego,' the 'self,' the 'person'" (p. 3). To Kegan (1982), this self is always in motion and moves through stages in life, developing through the Incorporative Self, the Impulsive Self, the Imperial Self, the Interpersonal Self, and the Institutional Self. At each stage there is an "evolutionary truce," which gives defined and patterned meaning to understanding subjects and objects, inclusion and distinctness, or ways of "seeing" the world. As a person moves through life, he or she must renegotiate the evolutionary truce, suffering a loss of meaning-making in one way in order to grow into meaning-making in another way.

In describing the stages of life and the movement of growth and loss from one stage to the other, Kegan (1982) looks closely at "those periods in a life when the terms of our evolutionary truce must be renegotiated. These terms *are* the self. Their renegotiation is a natural emergency" (p. 110). Self-renewal in this case, then, would be the renegotiation of the self's constructed evolutionary truce and way of meaning-making at a particular stage of life development. Fowler (1981, 1984) proposes that there are similar stages of faith that occur in adult development and need to be renegotiated. The "natural emergencies" that occur in stage development may be a part of that which brings clergy to therapy. The "natural emergencies" may manifest in terms of anger, anxiety, depression, marital issues, and so on, but the deeper work is renegotiating how the self constructs an understanding of the world or an understanding of faith.

Using the language of developmental psychology would not be the only possible psychological language for understanding self-renewal. Again, it depends on how one defines the self. For instance, Jung (1959) says, "I have suggested calling the total personality which, though present, cannot be fully known, the *self*. The ego is, by definition, subordinate to the self and is related to it like a part to the whole" (p. 5). Or again, he can define the self by drawing on mystical literature about the Anthropos, which he describes as "the greater more comprehensive Man, that indescribable whole consisting of the sum of conscious and unconscious processes. This objective whole, the antithesis of the subjective ego-pscyhe, is what I have called the self, and this corresponds exactly to the idea of the Anthropos" (p. 189).

At the risk of a gross over-simplification, self-renewal in Jungian terms might be described as the assimilation of unconscious contents to the ego, "even though this approximation must be a never-ending process" (Jung, 1959, p. 23). Integrating unconscious material (e.g., anima, animus material) intellectually and according to its feeling value opens the way "to a higher union, a *coniunctio oppositorum*. This is an indispensable prerequisite for wholeness" (Jung, 1959, p. 31). Describing this journey to wholeness and quoting from the Christian scriptures, Jung (1959) says, "The individual may strive after perfection ('Be you therefore perfect . . . as also your heavenly Father is perfect') but must suffer from the opposite of his intentions for the sake of his completeness. 'I find then a law, that, when I would do good, evil is present with me'" (p. 69). This is often the case with clergy who are frequently put on a pedestal of perfection by those in the congregation or, in their own self-determination, strive for righteousness, only to be surprised by some of their own contradictory actions that seem to come out of nowhere. Examples would be of the clergyperson who preaches about moral purity and then is caught viewing pornography on his computer, or the pastor who preaches on love but is violently angry in his own home.

These examples also illustrate reasons why clergy might present for clinical treatment. In Jungian terms, they are examples of unconscious material attempting to become conscious. Jung (1959) uses the symbol of the sucking-fish, *Echeneis remora*, which attaches itself to other fish or to the bottom of ships by means of the sucker on top of its head, and tells the story of how a remora attached itself to the rudder of the ship of emperor Caligula, bringing it to a standstill, delaying his arrival in Rome, and contributing to his murder on his arrival. He says, "In this way the remora came to symbolize that extremely small thing in the vastness of the unconscious which is charged with such fateful significance: it is the self, the *atman*, 'smaller than small, greater than great'" (p. 144). The unexplainable and contradictory behavior of clergy will sometimes bring them into treatment. It is like something from the unconscious has attached itself to the "rudder of their ship" and brought their life to a standstill. Self-renewal in this case is coming to understand the deeper significance of their behavior and working to name and integrate unconscious material that has come from seemingly nowhere out of the depths. Such integration would be a true renewal of the self, and clergy may intuitively know that the real work of therapy lies at this level of renewal—beyond the work of self-care when it is more superficially understood.

Theological Language for Self-Renewal

In this deeper work of self-renewal it can be helpful if the clinician is "bi-lingual" because the first language used in the congregational context is the language of theology and not psychology. As one conservative pastor once said at the beginning of treatment, "I hope that you are not planning to do psychotherapy with me." Obviously psychology was not his first language and the work of therapy had to be translated into a language he could understand. In his first language of theology, however, he already had the language for and an intuitive understanding of the depth of change that was needed in his life, which can be understood in this case as self-renewal.

While the language of *coniunctio oppositorum* may not resonate at all in the congregational context, the story of David who experienced unexpected and contradictory behavior in a relationship with Bathsheba and the murder of her husband, Uriah, would certainly be familiar. This was David's "remora," which attached to the "rudder of his ship" and brought his life to a standstill. Psalm 51 records David's desire for self-renewal after he was confronted by Nathan the prophet. David can write to God, "Behold, thou desirest truth in the inward being; therefore teach me wisdom in my secret heart. . . . Create in me a clean heart, O God, and put a new and right spirit within me" (Psalm 51:6, 10). If the language of exploring the unconscious does not resonate, exploring what it means to have "wisdom in the secret heart" or even exploring what the "secret heart" is in the first place could get at the same thing. Self-renewal in this case would take on the deeper character of "creating in me a clean heart."

While the language of evolutionary development might not resonate in the congregational context, the Hebrew understanding of life as a journey involving Exodus, Wilderness, and Promised Land, and the Christian understanding of the journey of Sanctification imply that life is always in process and that there are stages in the journey. Renegotiating evolutionary truces would rarely be understood in the congregational context, but the call in the Hebrew scripture to have an "uncircumcised heart" (Jeremiah 9:26) or to have the Covenant "written upon the heart" (Jeremiah 31:33), and the call in the Christian scripture to "crucify the ego" (Galatians 2:20) or "lose the self to find it" (Luke 9:24), or to "empty the self" (Philippians 2:7) all refer to a similar process of self-renewal at a core level.

Using the language of a nonintegrated or unassimilated ego would not be the first language in the congregational context, but the language of the false self and the true self spoken of by theologians would be more easily understood. Keating (1994) essentially defines the false self as maladaptive egoic functioning when he says the false self is:

> The self developed in our own likeness rather than in the likeness of God; the self-image developed to cope with the emotional trauma of early

> childhood. It seeks happiness in satisfying the instinctual needs of survival/security, affection/esteem, and power/control, and bases its self-worth on cultural or group identification. (p. 163)

Keating (1994) goes on to define the true self as "The image of God in which every human being is created; our participation in the divine life manifested in our uniqueness" (p. 166). Using this language, self-renewal would be the work of moving from living a life driven by the false self to a life lived out of the true self. Certainly this understanding of self-renewal would be beyond that of self-care understood in a more superficial sense, and using this kind of language in understanding the self would help to overcome any ambivalence embodied by clergy in the congregational context. Whatever the presenting problem in clinical treatment, at some level (intuitively known by the clergy) this is sanctification work and moving from the false self to the true self. Self-care of the body may provide the energy, and self-care of the mind and soul will give strategies and techniques that help to open to the deeper work, but self-renewal is ultimately about the transformation of the core meaning-making functions of the person: the renewal of the heart.

The Translator as Traitor

There is a saying sometimes used by those who work on translating languages that the translator is always a traitor. This means in part that something is always lost in translation and that some concepts are almost impossible to convey from one language to another. In this case, the phrase reminds us that concepts from psychological language and theological language are not necessarily equivalent. Gerkin (1984) says, "Just as German and English or French and Swahili can only be to a limited degree translated back and forth across cultural and language barriers, so the language of psychology and of theology remain discrete and point to different meaning worlds" (p. 19).

The work of self-renewal with clergy allows for, and actually calls for, a bilingual approach where theological and psychological concepts are seen to have a striking similarity and where a dialogue occurring within the clinician between psychology and theology can generate the wisdom necessary for understanding and facilitating the transformational work of the self. However, it would behoove the clinician to remember that the meaning-world of self-renewal is much broader within the theological world and ultimately has different goals than that of psychology; goals variously described as having only Christ in me, or deification, or reaching completeness/*teleos*, or unitive consciousness, or apophatic awareness, or transcending the ego.

Bourgeault (2004) reminds us that "wellness" in spiritual terms is more than the relief of neurotic symptoms, because in that case the ego is still in its comfort zone. She says, "Classic spiritual work, no matter what the religious tradition, is about transcending the ego. It seeks to awaken within a person something that is recognized as 'true self,' or higher Self" (p. 102). She goes on to say, "Whatever 'true self' may look like when described theologically, *operationally* it involves the shift to a different kind of consciousness (called non-dual or 'unitive' in classic Christian terminology), which flows out from that deeper place within us, described earlier as our 'apophatic awareness'" (p. 104).

The word *apophatic* comes from the distinctions made in prayer between kataphatic and apophatic approaches to prayer. Kataphatic approaches to prayer, known as the *via positiva*, means "with images," and kataphatic praying focuses on things like beauty of nature, the Gospels, the symbols of faith in the creed, an affective relationship with Christ, and participation in the liturgical life of a faith community. Apophatic prayer, known as the *via negativa*, strips away all of the attitudes, mental images, and ideas that are considered to stand in the way of a relationship with God because God transcends all human language. It is the "unsaying" (*apophasis*) of language for God, and it leads eventually from the negation of knowing to the "negation of negation," where the mind shifts beyond knowing to an inexpressible, hidden union with God (Rodgerson, 2012).

Even this theological language would not always be used or even understood in certain congregational contexts. But the invitation to a place of mystery, stillness, unity, and ultimate peace would be understood. Intuitively, spoken or unspoken, this would be a goal in therapy no matter what the presenting problem. It is the ultimate in self-renewal. The clinician can actually offer this "apophatic awareness," with or without theological or psychological language, by attending to the silence in the room and by coming from a place of stillness in the clinician's own life. Working with clergy at some level, then, is an invitation to the clinician to find this stillness in his/her own life so that it might be a part of the clinical work with clergy in which clergy and clinician join at some unitive, unspoken level.

CONCLUSION

In the clinical work with clergy, perhaps it is best to think of an interplay between self-care and self-renewal. Self-care, when taken seriously and done effectively, can provide the energy for the deeper work of self-renewal. At the same time, when there is resistance to self-care or the obvious lack of self-care, this can be taken as a signal that there is ambivalence about the self or the need for self-renewal, which goes beyond self-care.

For instance, the failure of a clergyperson's self-care of the body is not significant simply because the physical body is out of shape and needs attention, but more importantly because it is a signal alerting the clergyperson to the necessity of attending to the deeper work of self-renewal and to an examination of the clergyperson's core motivating forces of life. Failure around diet may have to do with deeper concerns about how one is nurtured in life (or not). Failure to reign in one's workaholism may be pointing to deeper issues of needing to please or needing affirmation. Failure to get a handle on reactivity may be pointing one to core patterns of self-regulation, or residual anger. Essentially, all of this demonstrates where one is not finished yet in the ongoing development of self or in the journey of sanctification. Then, in the interplay, when the deeper work of self-renewal is attended to, the energy comes full circle and self-care is more possible.

REFERENCES

Arena, R. (1992, May). A satisfying, fulfilling call. *American Baptist*, 20–21.

Augsburger, D. (1986). *Pastoral counseling across cultures*. Philadelphia, PA: Westminster Press.

Baer, R. (2003). Mindfulness training as a clinical intervention: A conceptual review. *Clinical Psychology: Science and Practice*, *10*, 123–143.

Baumeister, R. (1991). *Meanings of life*. New York, NY: Guilford Press.

Benson, H. (1984). *Beyond the relaxation response*. New York, NY: Times Books.

Bourgeault, C. (2004). *Centering prayer and inner awakening*. Lanham, MD: Cowley.

Bowen, M. (1978). *Family therapy in clinical practice*. New York, NY: Aronson.

Burns, D. (1980). *Feeling good*. New York, NY: New American Library.

Capps, D. (1993). *The depleted self: Sin in a narcissistic age*. Minneapolis, MN: Fortress Press.

Clodfelter, M. (2011, June). Numbers don't lie: The truth about clergy health. *Door Post: The Newsletter of the Center for Congregational Health*. Retrieved from http://www.healthychurch.org/doorpost-june-20–2011

Foster, R. (1978). *Celebration of discipline: The path to spiritual growth*. San Francisco, CA: Harper & Row.

Foucault, M. (1988). Technologies of the self. In L. Martin, H. Gutman, & P. Hutton (Eds.), *Technologies of the self: A seminar with Michel Foucault*. Amherst: University of Massachusetts Press.

Fowler, J. (1981). *Stages of faith*. New York, NY: Harper & Row.

Fowler, J. (1984). *Becoming adult, becoming Christian*. San Francisco, CA: Harper & Row.

Freudenberger, H., & Richelson, G. (1980). *Burn-out: The high cost of high achievement*. New York, NY: Bantam Books.

Friedman, E. (1985). *Generation to generation: Family process in church and synagogue*. New York, NY: Guilford Press.

Friedman, E. (2007). *A failure of nerve: Leadership in the age of the quick fix*. New York, NY: Seabury Books.

Gerkin, C. (1984). *The living human document*. Nashville, TN: Abingdon Press.

Hagerty, B. (2009). *Fingerprints of God*. New York, NY: Riverhead Books.

Hanh, Thich Nhat. (1975). *The miracle of mindfulness*. Boston, MA: Beacon Press.

Hunt, H. (1990). *The stained glass fishbowl*. Valley Forge, PA: Ministers Council.

Jung, C. (1959). Aion: Researches into the phenomenology of the self. In H. Read, M. Fordham, G. Adler, & W. McGuire (Eds.), *The collected works of* C. G. *Jung* (Vol. 9, Part II). Princeton, NJ: Princeton University Press.

Kabat-Zinn, J. (1994). *Wherever you go, there you are*. New York, NY: Hyperion.

Keating, T. (1994). *Intimacy with God*. New York, NY: Crossroad.

Kegan, R. (1982). *The evolving self*. Cambridge, MA: Harvard University Press.

Kluckhohn, C., & Murray, H. (1948). *Personality in nature, society, and culture*. New York, NY: Knopf.

Kornfield, J. (2000). *After the ecstasy, the laundry: How the heart grows wise on the spiritual path*. New York, NY: Bantam.

Lewis, H. (1990). Self, philosophy of. In R. Hunter (Ed.), *Dictionary of pastoral care and counseling*. Nashville, TN: Abingdon Press.

Linehan, M. (1993). *Skills training manual for treating borderline personality disorder*. New York, NY: Guilford Press.

Maslach, C. (1978). The client role in staff burn-out. *Journal of Social Issues*, *34*(4), 111–124.

Miller-McLemore, M. (2011). Revaluing "self-care" as a practice of ministry. *Journal of Religious Leadership*, *10*(1), 109–134.

Mohr, S., & Huguelet, P. (2009). Religious and spiritual assessment in clinical practice. In P. Huguelet & H. Koenig (Eds.), *Religion and spirituality in psychiatry* (pp. 232–243). New York, NY: Cambridge University Press.

Muller, R. (2010). Soul. In G. Asquith Jr. (Ed.), *The concise dictionary of pastoral care and counseling* (pp. 30–34). Nashville, TN: Abingdon Press.

Newberg, A., & Waldman, M. (2009). *How God changes your brain*. New York, NY: Ballantine Books.

Oswald, R. (1991). *Clergy self-care: Finding a balance for effective ministry*. Washington, DC: Alban Institute.

Palmer, G., Sherrard, P., & Ware, K. (Eds.). (1979). *The Philokalia* (Vol. 1). London, England: Faber and Faber.

Pargament, K. (1997). *The psychology of religion and coping: Theory, research, and practice*. New York, NY: Guilford Press.

Pastors in Covenant. (2003). *Clergy fact sheet*. Retrieved from http://www.pastorsincovenant.com/clergyfact.htm

Perry, C. (2003). First look: What brings clergy candidates into ministry and what happens when they don't get it. *Journal of Pastoral Care and Counseling*, *57*(1), 15–25.

Pines, A., & Maslach, C. (1978). Characteristics of staff burnout in mental health settings. *Hospital and Community Psychiatry*, *29*(4), 233–237.

Richardson, R. (2005). *Becoming a healthier pastor*. Minneapolis, MN: Fortress Press.

Rodgerson, T. E. (2012). Apophatic attending: An essential for pastoral diagnosis. *Journal of Pastoral Care and Counseling*, 66(1), 4:1–8.

Rosenthal, P. (1984). *Words and values: Some leading words and where they lead us*. New York, NY: Oxford University Press.

Rupp, J. (1999). Rediscovering God in the midst of our work. In R. Wicks (Ed.), *Handbook of spirituality for ministers* (pp. 259–273). Mahwah, NJ: Paulist Press.

Sanford, J. (1982). *Ministry burnout*. New York, NY: Paulist Press.

Segal, Z., Williams, M., & Teasdale, J. (2002). *Mindfulness-based cognitive therapy for depression*. New York, NY: Guilford Press.

Seligman, M., Rashid, T., & Parks, A. (2006). Positive psychotherapy. *American Psychologist, 61*(8), 774–788.

Simmons, P. (2000). *Learning to fall: The blessings of an imperfect life*. New York, NY: Bantam Dell.

Steinke, P. (2006). *Congregational leadership in anxious times*. Herndon, VA: Alban Institute.

Steinke, P. (2007). *Healthy congregations: A systems approach*. Herndon, VA: Alban Institute.

Van Lant, K. (2011). The minister's meltdown: Getting help for yourself. In C. Franklin & R. Fong (Eds.), *The church leader's counseling resource book* (pp. 417–427). New York, NY: Oxford University Press.

Weaver, A., Larson, D., Flannelly, K., Stapleton, C., & Koenig, H. (2002). Mental health issues among clergy and other religious professionals: A review of research. *Journal of Pastoral Care and Counseling*, 56(4), 393–403.

Wicks, R. (2009). *Prayerfulness: Awakening to the fullness of life*. Notre Dame, IN: Sorin Books.

Wicks, R. (2012). *The inner life of the counselor*. Hoboken, NJ: Wiley.

Wicks, R., & Ciarrocchi, J. (2000). *Psychotherapy with priests, Protestant clergy, and Catholic religious: A practical guide*. Madison, CT: Psychosocial Press.

Zettersten, R. (1993, January). Ministering to your pastor. *Focus on the Family*, 14.

CHAPTER

23

Self-Renewal Among Gay and Lesbian Adults

ELIZABETH A. MAYNARD AND KATIE E. KATUZNY

Are self-renewal themes different among gay men and lesbian women than among adults of other sexual orientations? What are the unique stressors faced by queer adults, and the characteristic strengths forged in response to them?

In recent years, clinicians have become increasingly aware of the needs and challenges of gay men and lesbian women. Further, both research and social advocacy efforts have led to increased sensitivity to and awareness of the characteristics and needs of bisexual men and women, transgender youth and adults, asexual individuals, those born with intersex conditions, and many who consider themselves "queer" or questioning. The term *queer* has been transformed by many from a slur to a term of empowerment and inclusion. It is in the latter sense that the term is used here—a descriptor used to include youth and adults from myriad sexual orientations and gender identities.

Queer individuals may belong to one group (e.g., gay) or many simultaneously (e.g., transgender lesbian). While the queer umbrella is large enough to include a wide variety of individuals, it is important to also recognize that gay men and lesbian women often have different social and psychological experiences. However, most are well acquainted with social stigma and one or more forms of marginalization. This marginalization can range from explicit discrimination or violence, to more subtle forms of marginalization such as silence. Thus, although queer individuals may have much in common, and self-renewal themes may also share common threads, the wise clinician recognizes the varied experiences and forces at work in the lives of both individuals and specific communities.

Historically, one's personal identification as gay, lesbian, or bisexual, and one's decision to "come out" was seen as an important developmental step, and essential to self-renewal. However, traditional notions of sexual orientation, while often important to those who came of age in the latter half of the 20th century, have changed for many queer youth and young adults today. Many queer youth reject categorization of both sexual orientation and gender identity, choosing a queer identity over a more specific gay, lesbian, or bisexual identity or conventional ideas about gender. For this reason, previous research on LGBTQ individuals may not apply to some of today's queer adolescents who are growing up in social environments often very different from those experienced by previous generations of LGBTQ youth (Johnston & Stewart, 2011). At the same time, identification as lesbian, gay, or bisexual remains an essential aspect of identity for many adolescents and adults.

Is being "out" an essential element of self-renewal? Although it can be extremely psychologically and socially freeing for individuals to make the choice to be open with themselves and others about their sexual orientations and the nature of their relationships, the ethics of outing themselves and others are highly complex (Mayo & Gunderson, 1994; Swartz, 2011). The most elemental aspect of this situation appears to be the *choice* whether to be out or to retain one's privacy, rather than the *specific direction* of the choice. In other words, one's sense of choice about how to understand and describe oneself is often more important in self-renewal than the specific definitions (gay, lesbian, bisexual, transgender, queer) one adopts.

Self-renewal for clients may involve the adoption of a gay, lesbian, bisexual or queer identity and sexual behaviors; a heterosexual identity and sexual practices; or celibate sexuality. This range of options for clients may be a challenge for both clinicians and clients to accept. Self-renewal also involves the weighing of the benefits and drawbacks of coming out to oneself, one's family, and one's community, and electing to which individuals and in which contexts to be out (family, friendship groups, workplace, spiritual community). Clinicians can play a vital role in helping LGBTQ individuals navigate these difficult decisions and situations clients face as they build their identities throughout the life span.

COMING OUT ACROSS THE LIFE SPAN

Because many queer adolescents and adults have experienced exclusion or abuse, it may be difficult in some situations for queer clients to distinguish between elements of their experience that are common to youth and young adults of all sexual orientations (e.g., feeling odd or excluded, discerning how autonomous and connected to be) and those that are related specifically to being queer. For example, most adolescents are exquisitely attuned to rejection by peers, and often engage in behaviors to either fit others' expectations or to flout them. This appears to be true no matter what the adolescent's sexual orientation, though the nature of the conformity or countercultural actions may be different for queer youth. Thus, growing up queer involves both universal or near-universal stresses and challenges, and those particular to the experiences of sexual minorities.

The coming out process, should it be pursued, also may look quite different at different stages in the life span. To come out at puberty often involves quite different responses from peers and family members than coming out in midlife. Youth and young adults often receive mixed responses of support and discouragement from family members concerned about potential harm that may come to the client (related to health behaviors or discrimination from others), or concerns about shaming the family. Those coming out in midlife may be negotiating relationships with former or current heterosexual spouses and children of varying ages.

Further, the era and cultural context in which the individual comes out can have significant implications for both wellness and self-renewal. That is, the experience of a young man coming out in New York City in the 1970s was often quite different than that of his rural peer, and the coming out experience of a teenage girl with affirming parents and a supportive religious community is quite different from that of the teen who remains closeted at home with a legitimate fear of being kicked out of the house and only finds a supportive community online.

Men and women often differ in sexual orientation across the life span. While gay men often report consistency in sexual orientation across the life span, some women report more flexibility in sexual orientation between youth and old age. Some young women report participation in same-sex relationships primarily during adolescence and early adulthood, followed primarily by heterosexual relationships in later adulthood; others report primarily heterosexual relationships until or unless they encounter a person of the same sex to whom they feel particularly drawn. Women in the latter situation often report that their attraction to particular individuals is more important than the gender or sexual orientation of the person to whom they are attracted.

SELF-RENEWAL AND WELLNESS

Self-renewal among queer adults is a multidimensional phenomenon, involving the physical, intellectual, emotional, occupational, social, and spiritual dimensions of well-being.

Physical Self-Renewal

Physical well-being and self-renewal are important elements of self-care, particularly for queer youth and adults who may have limited access to health care. Members of the LGBTQ community are less likely to seek medical care than their heterosexual counterparts for a variety of reasons. Some are uncomfortable coming out to their physicians and others may not have access to health care because LGBTQ individuals are less likely to have health insurance than heterosexuals (Cochran, Sullivan, & Mays, 2003). Even if one member of a same-sex couple has health care benefits, the benefits often do not extend to a same-sex partner, unless they live in a state with same-sex marriage or work for an employer with inclusive benefits policies. This is particularly problematic because members of the LGBTQ community are more likely to have HIV/AIDS (especially gay and bisexual men) and substance abuse problems than heterosexuals (Cochran et al., 2003). If they do not feel comfortable talking to health care providers or mental health professionals, or do not have the financial freedom to see medical professionals, these and other conditions often remain undertreated.

Clinicians can assist their clients in this area by providing information about low-cost health care services and discussing possible barriers that may prevent their clients from seeing a doctor regularly. Clinicians can also do their part to help LGBTQ clients with substance abuse issues to prevent the psychological and physical complications that are associated with drug and alcohol abuse. Further, clinicians may refer clients to knowledgeable and accepting health care providers familiar with health concerns common to queer youth and adults.

Another health concern that faces the LGBT community is the lack of education about sex between members of the same sex. Throughout most of the country, children and young adults frequently remain uninformed and receive inaccurate information about gay sex and safe sex practices. As a result, HIV/AIDS continues to be a major problem for the gay male community. This, coupled with internalized homophobia (often correlated with compulsive sexual behavior) are issues that clinicians can focus on to prevent the spread of STIs/STDs within the LGBTQ community (Ross, Rosser, & Neumaier, 2008). They can ask their sexually active queer clients about their safe-sex practices and provide information about safe practices.

Clinicians may also promote self-renewal among queer clients by more fully seeking to understand their sexual experiences. This involves not only learning about the client's sexual orientation and gender identity, but also the client's number and type of partners. While teens and adults often choose romantic and sexual partners consistent with their sexual orientation, there are frequent exceptions to this practice. For example, a male client may be straight-identified and prefer women as partners, but have sex with men when a desirable female partner isn't available. Further, a lesbian woman may experience surprise (or distress) when she falls in love with and finds herself sexually attracted to a man. Clients may not volunteer this type of sexual information if they are concerned that the clinician will judge them for these disclosures, so the thoughtful clinician routinely gathers a thorough sexual history from all clients. Self-renewal may be promoted by the clinician acknowledging the unfolding identity and reality of the client, whether or not that fits common or accepted paradigms.

Physical health is a particularly important topic for those who are transgender. Transgender people feel that their biological sex is not consistent (fully or partially) with their internal, psychological sex. Some members of the transgender community go through the process of gender reassignment surgeries to create a match between their internal identity and external sex. Clinicians may play a unique role in this process because those who decide to undergo gender reassignment surgeries must undergo psychological evaluation by a mental health professional before a physician will perform the procedures. Clinicians serving transgender clients must be sensitive to the difficulties involved in the client's decision to pursue gender reassignment surgeries. They should also be aware of any prejudices or their own internal beliefs about the reassignment process so that they may serve as a helpful companion to the client in the decision-making process.

Also, clinicians who treat children may encounter parents who are concerned when their children exhibit cross-gender play and behavior. In this case the clinician, parent(s), and child must determine whether the child actually feels as if he or she is the other sex or if it is only a play activity. It may also be the job of the clinician to help parents realize that their child could possibly be gay, which would be more likely assessed and self-identified during early adolescence. When it is clear that the child's biological sex is fundamentally different from her or his psychological identity, it is possible to advocate for hormonal medications that can prevent the process of puberty so that secondary sex characteristics do not develop; a decision to undergo gender reassignment surgery may then be easier in the future (Wren, 2000). Although this is usually an extremely challenging decision for a family to make, it can lead to less internal and external conflict for both the individual and the family. Clinicians may support the self-renewal of these clients and families by acknowledging the biological, psychological, social, financial, and spiritual complexities of these decisions.

For a transgender client, self-renewal may be promoted by the pursuit of one or more medical treatments to create a match between the individual's internal experience and outward appearance. Self-renewal may also involve deciding which procedures to pursue and may not involve a complete change. For some clients, self-renewal may also involve little to no change to physical attributes and may emphasize an internal reconciliation and acknowledgement of the complexity of gender identity and biological sex. The client may decide to let go of an either/or (male/female) conception of gender in favor of a more complex, multifaceted, or nuanced sense of self (e.g., "I am a man with breasts" or "I am a woman with a penis").

Emotional Self-Renewal

At the heart of emotional self-renewal for queer adults are several important questions. Who am I? How do I want to understand myself? What or who is authoritative in my life as I understand myself? Whom do I want to be? How do I want to live out my identity? What is my vision for an emotionally healthy, thriving person? How do I choose to respond to the stresses of living as a sexual minority?

Gay, lesbian, bisexual, transgender, and queer teens and adults face discrimination ranging from subtle exclusion to anti-gay violence (Herek, 1991). Surveys of gay men and lesbians in the 1990s indicated that more than 90% had been targets of anti-gay verbal abuse or threats, and up to a quarter had experienced victimization because of their sexual orientation (Herek, 1989, 1993; Herek, Gillis, & Cogan, 1999; Herek, Gillis, Cogan, & Glunt, 1997). Common reactions to these types of experiences are heightened levels of depression, anger, anxiety, posttraumatic stress, vulnerability, and crime-related fears (Garnets, Herek, & Levy, 1990). Thus, queer adults not only face the everyday stresses inherent in the human condition, but also experience emotional stresses related to living in often discriminatory or hostile environments. These heightened stresses and mental health concerns may lead to higher rates of suicide, substance abuse and dependence, and relational/family violence for queer teens and adults.

Queer adults often encounter those with homonegative and homophobic sentiments expressed either directly or subtly. In many ways, homophobia remains a "permissible" prejudice (Hoffman et al., 2000; Patel, Long, McCammon, & Wuensch, 1995). Homonegativity is sometimes classified into two forms: old-fashioned and modern. Old-fashioned (traditional) homonegativity reflects moral or religious objections to homosexual behaviors or gay and lesbian people, while modern homonegativity is characterized by the idea that gay men and lesbians make unreasonable demands to change the status quo or that discrimination is no longer relevant because lesbians and gays have received special treatment or consideration by social institutions (Morrison & Morrison, 2011; Morrison, Morrison, & Franklin, 2009). Higher levels of modern homonegativity are often expressed toward gay men than toward lesbians (Morrison & Morrison, 2011), likely due to more rigid social norms for men. For this reason, the clinician may assist clients in exploring the impact of and desired responses to both traditional and more subtle forms of homonegativity.

Past research has demonstrated relationships between homonegativity and other personality features such as patriotism, nationalism, social dominance, and political conservatism (Morrison, Kenny, & Harrington, 2005). Some forms of religiousness have also predicted homonegativity, including religious fundamentalism (Laythe, Finkel, & Kirkpatrick, 2001; Malcomnson, Christopher, Franzen, & Keyes, 2006). Although some individuals note a difference between "hating the sin" and "hating the sinner," and conclude that moral evaluations do not necessarily represent prejudice (Bassett et al., 2000; Fulton, Gorsuch, & Maynard, 1999), gay men and lesbians often experience both positions as equally homonegative (Maynard & Gorsuch, 2001). Further, men, older persons, and less-educated individuals tend to express more homonegativity than women, younger persons, more educated adults and political liberals (Jenkins, Lambert, & Baker, 2009). While ethnicity may sometimes play a role in one's level of acceptance of homosexuality, American Black and White adults tend to have very similar antidiscrimination attitudes toward gay men and lesbians (Jenkins et al. , 2009; Lewis, 2003). That is, some studies have suggested that African Americans are more likely than Whites to express homonegative attitudes, but the two cultural groups are similar in the levels of active discrimination that they endorse.

Homonegative attitudes appear to be strongest among those who believe that sexual orientation is a choice (Malcomnson et al., 2006). This becomes more complex in situations where sexual orientation is considered inherent and/or immutable, but sexual behaviors are chosen. Some queer adults experience this perspective as freeing ("I am who I am, my sexual orientation is not a choice; I, like people of all sexual orientations, choose my behaviors"), while others experience this perspective as a deeper bind ("My sexual orientation isn't something I chose, but my community expects me to only choose heterosexual sex or celibacy"). At heart, this gets to the debate about whether sexual orientation is a fundamental, unchanging aspect of the individual (the essentialist position) or whether sexual orientation is socially constructed and changeable (the constructivist perspective). Mental health professionals most often endorse an essentialist position, though there is considerable variety among positions.

Although it can be difficult to cope with homonegativity expressed by others, it can be even more disabling when the homonegativity has become internalized and the person experiences a sense of shame, low self-worth, anger, anxiety, and depression. Emotional self-renewal for queer adults thus requires exploration of both homonegativity received from others (external) and internalized homonegativity. Research suggests that internalized homonegativity has a strong relationship with psychological distress, conservative versus liberal ideology, the degree to which one is integrated into the gay community, one's level of identity development, and one's religious orientation (Szymanski, Kashubeck-West, & Meyer, 2008; Tozer & Hayes, 2004; Wagner, Serafini, Rabkin, Remien, & Williams, 1994). One's level of internalized homonegativity is also related to one's likelihood of seeking conversion therapy to change one's sexual orientation (Tozer & Hayes, 2004). Conversion or "reparative" therapy occurs when a lesbian, gay, or bisexual-identified or questioning individual seeks treatment to identify as heterosexual. As the terms suggest, these approaches view sexual orientation as a phenomenon that can be changed; the latter approach assumes that the repair of early psychological wounds will lead to the development of a heterosexual identity. The American Psychological Association has clearly rejected these approaches.

Although not all queer individuals need to be "out," or to be out in every setting, clients report that the coming-out process can yield a number of important emotional benefits. Many clients experience an enhanced sense of confidence and personal efficacy after coming out. Further, the self-exploration necessary in a coming-out process can yield both a clearer and more positive sense of self. This enhanced clarity about the self (Who am I? How do I feel about who I am?) can represent some resolution of the questions of identity and roles that all persons are called to address. Coming out is also seen by many as a process of claiming an identity, which may be an inherently empowering act.

Coming out is also a potentially self-renewing act, particularly when the individual has felt pressured to adopt roles or a public persona that are not authentic matches for her or his true self. That is, the individual is renewed by letting go of once necessary expressions of identity (e.g., passing as straight) and renewed in the claiming of an element of identity that is experienced as more true, whether it meets with the approval or acceptance of others.

Coming out can also bring the emotional benefits of release and relief. Many queer individuals feel forced into an extended period of uncertainty, both as they question their own identity and also as they may make compromises to please important others. For example, many religious youth receive social support in their faith communities when they report that they are "struggling" with their sexual orientation, but may be rejected when they come out with a lesbian, gay, or bisexual identity. Thus, it can be a release to be able to claim an identity, even if it may mean some dislocation from a valued community. For others, the fear of being found out as queer can produce tremendous stress, and the process of coming out can lead to renewal as the individual no longer carries the fear of being outed. Many individuals feel an enhanced sense of personal pride after facing the fear of coming out. Queer individuals also often feel some relief upon coming out. Even if they are rejected by important others, there can still be a new security in knowing where others stand.

Because so many individuals experience coming out (to self, if not to others) as a struggle, those who make a decision about how to identify themselves may experience increased confidence, as they see themselves as having succeeded in a major struggle or challenge. The client's self-renewal may also be supported as the clinician accepts that it may not be authentic or advisable for a client to come out; it may be self-renewing for the client to be supported in a continued exploration of identity, or a decision to remain undeclared. It is often a challenge for clinicians to support and accept a client who has decided not to decide, has confirmed an orientation but elected not to come out, or has elected a sexual orientation with which the clinician is either uncomfortable or unfamiliar. This can be a particular challenge for clinicians who have been trained that the only healthy outcome for a client is to be both decided and out. It can also be a challenge for a clinician who embraces the position that same-gender attraction represents disordered psychological or spiritual processes and who believes that the goal of self-renewal is the emergence of a heterosexual identity and behaviors. In both situations, clinicians are encouraged to seek consultation or supervision from an experienced colleague or peer consultation group to identify both potential areas of countertransference and to discern ethical and evidence-based ways to proceed with clients.

Occupational Self-Renewal

One of the most common concerns for LGBTQ clinicians and clients is the decision to reveal one's sexual orientation or come out in the workplace. LGBTQ individuals must judge the climate of their workplace and be aware of potential repercussions that may occur if their supervisors or colleagues are unwelcoming or express prejudice toward them. Although the number of states with antidiscrimination laws that protect LGBTQ employees is increasing, some states do not have these policies in place. Thus, it is still possible to be fired from a job for being queer. Overall, LGBTQ employees tend to be happier at work if they are out and if they perceive their company to be supportive of gay people (Griffith & Hebl, 2002), but this is not the case for many employees.

Queer clients may be harassed or intimidated by others, passed over for promotion or other professional opportunities, or more subtly excluded from workplace policies or events. It can be helpful for queer employees to be aware of their rights and protections within their companies. The benefits and rights available for LGBTQ employees and their families can often be confusing because they were likely written with heterosexual families in mind. LGBTQ employees should be encouraged to consult with their human resources department for the full details of their benefits.

Workplaces vary greatly in terms of benefits for families of LGBTQ employees. It is often the case that health care benefits are only applicable for married couples and in some cases heterosexual domestic partners. Companies also may not allow employees with same-sex partners the same leave time for the birth of a child (except in cases where the employee is the birth mother) or medical leave to care for an ill same-sex partner.

Clinicians should be aware that it is not always in the best interest of their clients to be out in the workplace, and it is not always a sign of acceptance of their identity if they are out. Clinicians may help their clients weigh the costs and benefits of being out at work. Some benefits of coming out include the positive feelings associated with openly discussing aspects of their personal lives with colleagues, reduction in stress produced by concealing their sexual orientation and/or gender identity, and increases in self-esteem by taking pride in their identities. Some negative outcomes of coming out at work may include negative reactions from colleagues or supervisors, loss of employment, or covert discrimination. Subtle exclusion may also be present in the absence of discussion of the needs of same-sex families or queer employees not being asked about family life when this is a common topic among heterosexual peers.

There are some cases, however, where it may be necessary for an LGBTQ client to leave a job if it is dangerous or damaging to him or her. Although it would be best to involve a supervisor or human resource staff member when there is harassment or discrimination related to an LGBTQ employee's sexual orientation and/or gender identity, it may not always be possible. If these issues become serious enough to endanger the safety of the client, it may be necessary to leave the job. Legal action in such a situation may or may not be possible based on the state's laws (which often do not include queer adults in employment protections). As a clinician, it will be important to consistently assess the client's safety and their plan of action. It may be an act of self-renewal for a client to decide to leave a job, to decide whether to pursue legal action if discriminated against, or to remain in a stressful or challenging job by choice in service to other values.

Coming out may lead to more occupational success in some fields, and some fields are more supportive of coming out than others (i.e., college student affairs, psychology, interior design, hairdressing, construction). The overall climate of the client's field may be an important determinant in whether it is wise to come out, and may also impact the number of available queer role models to whom she or he may turn.

Issues such as acceptance and benefits are often difficult to handle and can cause a great deal of added stress to the lives of those affected. In some cases it may be helpful for an LGBTQ client to talk to supervisors and explain how their situation is as valid as their heterosexual peers'. This process may take multiple attempts and be time consuming, but in the end the reward may be enjoyed by LGBTQ employees throughout the company or organization. In states where these rights are not granted to LGBTQ people, it could be rewarding and cathartic for these employees to either lobby or write to legislators about how the lack of equal rights affects their families.

A possible self-renewal opportunity for LGBTQ employees is to create an LGBTQ group within their company. This could allow LGBTQ employees to connect with their LGBTQ coworkers to create a community that fosters a safe environment for all. Also, these organizations can function to advocate for equal rights of LGBTQ employees for equivalent maternity/paternity leave, financial benefits, health benefits, and nondiscrimination policies. In these nondiscrimination policies, it is important to address the LGBTQ community as a whole and include sexual orientation and gender identity/expression. A survey of bisexuals found that they felt safer at work if their employers' antidiscrimination policies included gender identity and gender expression (Green, Payne, & Green, 2011). Therefore, the key to drafting these types of policies would be to provide a forum to address the individual needs of employees. This may not be possible or advisable in all work environments. Clients may be unaware of workplace advocacy options and the clinician may be helpful in identifying possibilities with the client.

Many suggestions for self-renewal that apply to clients are also applicable to clinicians, but there are some unique issues for clinicians to consider. The decision to come out at work is particularly interesting for clinicians because they need to consider the implications of being out to both their clients and colleagues (Newman, Bogo, & Daley, 2008). Clinicians possess a wide range of beliefs about self-disclosure in therapy, influenced by both personal beliefs and theoretical orientation. Also, the stigma attached to clinicians who self-disclose being transgender may be worse than those who self-disclose a gay or lesbian sexual orientation (Mathy, 2006). Clinicians who are out must also weigh the decision to be openly LGBTQ-affirmative with the reality of the possible financial loss of homonegative or homophobic clients; however, some LGBTQ-identified clinicians and allies may find that providing an open and accepting source of support will foster opportunities for self-renewal for both the clinician and clients. For financial reasons, it may be easier for clinicians with established practices or those who are part of a large clinic to be out and openly LGBTQ-affirmative than those who are just starting to build an independent practice. However, in some situations being out or affirming can lead to a greater number of client referrals. The decision to be out to colleagues is also separate from the choice to be openly LGBTQ-affirmative. In this way they can achieve the benefits of being authentic with peers in the workplace while remaining neutral with clients.

Heterosexual clinicians may elect not to disclose sexual orientation to clients if they are concerned that clients may not be as open about sexual orientation concerns to straight-identified clinicians as they may be with queer clinicians. Clinicians vary considerably in their positions, both on the ethics of outing oneself to clients and whether or not the clinician should be open with the client about his or her model of mental health for queer clients ("affirming," "transformative," or other models).

Social Self-Renewal

The stigma associated with homosexuality can be profoundly injurious, both to those who fit societal stereotypes and those who are not highly visible but can "pass" as heterosexual (Hammersmith, 1987). While those who fit the stereotypes of their cultural or social group are often the first targets of homonegative comments and discrimination from others, those who are less visible often experience constraint due to reluctance to be identified with the stigmatized group. The necessity of "passing" or remaining closeted in one or more environments often limits the individual's expression of self within important relationships. Queer youth usually grow up in heterosexual families and peer groups, and often lack positive role models. Role models may allow the young person to see sexual orientation in perspective as one of many facets of adult life and identity.

Often when LGBTQ people come out they lose relationships with some family members and friends to whom they had previously been very close. To counteract those losses, they must often work to create "families of choice" to replace those that have been lost or significantly changed (Dewaele, Cox, Van den Berghe, & Vincke, 2011). LGBTQ individuals must also learn to navigate a new community or communities, build friendships, and find relationships in often unfamiliar contexts. The process of creating this new family and community of choice is one of the first sources of renewal for LGBTQ persons. They can feel empowered and accepted by those who are part of their newly chosen family. Fortunately, not all those who come out to their families face a negative reaction, and those who come out to supportive parents often experience better health outcomes than those with parents who react negatively (Rothman, Sullivan, Keyes, & Boehmer, 2012).

To facilitate well-being in LGBTQ clients, clinicians should be aware that they may have alternative families that they created on their own, and they may have lost contact with their families of origin. In many cases clinicians may need to help their LGBTQ clients cope with the loss of these relationships while also helping them find ways to meet people who are accepting. One outlet for this to occur is to suggest that LGBTQ clients attend LGBTQ support groups in the community. This is a possible forum for them to form friendships and build their identities in a positive way. Clinicians should also be aware that the primary place for LGBTQ people to meet each other is often still in bars and clubs (though the Internet has emerged as a place for many to build community). For this reason, it is often important to monitor substance use, especially for those just coming out, as they may be vulnerable to greater use due to depression, anxiety, and social pressures. LGBTQ adolescents who feel accepted by their parents are less likely to abuse substances (Padilla, Crisp, & Rew, 2010), so clinicians who focus on strengthening bonds between LGBTQ adolescents and their parents may decrease the likelihood that they will use substances.

Clinicians should practice asking their clients questions about how they define their families and if they have a partner(s) or children. During the clinical interview it is important that clinicians ask questions in an inclusive way, instead of questions created for heterosexual individuals and families (such as questions about husbands or wives), and to understand that LGBTQ individuals can have children in a number of different ways. If the clinical interview is conducted in an inclusive way, it may build trust in the therapeutic alliance. Also, LGBTQ families may have many other legal struggles to handle, especially with regard to children, which may require the assistance of a clinician to manage. For example, clients may be managing care and custody of children from a previous heterosexual or same-sex relationship; they could experience a legal battle over custodial rights between a birth mother and nonbirth mother after the breakup of a same-sex relationship. Clinicians should have a clear understanding of their state's laws regarding same-sex marriage and second-parent adoptions to successfully work with LGBTQ families.

LGBTQ clinicians are often faced with a personal and professional dilemma when they work with queer clients, especially in smaller communities. Except in very large urban areas, it is likely that LGBTQ clients and clinicians will see each other in social settings on multiple occasions. It will be necessary for LGBTQ clinicians to determine how and when to keep their social life separate and private from their LGBTQ clients who are likely to know the same people and even to have mutual friends. In some cases it may be necessary to refer clients to other clinicians if the clinician's ties in the community are extensive.

Spiritual Self-Renewal

Finding rapprochement between one's sexual orientation and religious beliefs has often been a challenging process for queer youth and adults. Some queer adults believe that they must make a choice between their religious faith and sexual orientation (Kelly, 1995; Lynch, 1996; Maynard & Gorsuch, 2001; Wagner et al., 1994), abandoning one's faith, attempting to change one's sexual orientation, pursuing celibacy, or a combination of strategies to create a meaningful identity (Haldeman, 1996). Some in the American Bible Belt have described their experiences as gay men and lesbians being "spirit crushing" (Barton, 2010, p. 465) and conservative religious beliefs have been linked in the research to higher levels of shame, guilt, and internalized homophobia (Sherry, Adelman, Whilde, & Quick, 2010). While religiosity predicts seeking conversion therapy, one's level of internalized homonegativity accounts for much of this relationship (Tozer & Hayes, 2004). However, integrating one's religion with one's sexual orientation may be a weapon against internalized homonegativity for some queer adults (Wagner et al., 1994), and clinicians may help clients recover religion as a helpful coping resource (Bozard & Sanders, 2011). Strict moral and religious neutrality in clinical work is both difficult and problematic for clinicians, who need clarity about their own moral and religious assumptions (Nelson, 1981).

Many religious traditions, particularly those in North America and Europe, have become increasingly accepting of homosexuality and bisexuality, and affirming groups within established religious traditions or parallel to them (parachurch organizations such as Dignity and Integrity) are increasingly common. However, many queer adults have been raised in and find their primary spiritual identities and sustenance in communities that expect or prioritize heterosexual identity and behaviors. The importance of these belief systems and supports must be grasped by the clinician to promote the client's self-renewal. Queer clients often report a sense of forced choice between an orienting faith system and a queer identity. Self-renewal may involve such a choice for the client, but may also involve the brokering of a new identity that prizes both dimensions. Individual therapy, group therapy, pastoral counseling and psychotherapy, and secular therapies may all be helpful venues for this exploration (Heermann, Wiggins, & Rutter, 2007; Yarhouse & Beckstead, 2011).

Studies of religious gays and lesbians suggest that these adults demonstrate many of the same features of their heterosexual counterparts (Maynard & Gorsuch, 2001). Queer adults often participate in religious and spiritual activities, both for the inherent value of those activities and for the social support and involvement that religious participation provides. In fact, some queer adults are more out in their religious communities than elsewhere in their lives, particularly when they experience their faith communities as safe (Maynard & Gorsuch, 2001).

Clients may find spiritual support within their existing traditions and are often surprised to discover a variety of perspectives toward homosexuality within individual traditions (Nelson, 1981). Individual religions, denominations within religions, and individual groups may hold differing perspectives on homosexuality. Johnson (2006) identified seven common theological positions that represent a range of religious approaches to homosexuality (prohibition, toleration, accommodation, legitimation, celebration, liberation, and consecration), many of which may be unfamiliar to clients and clinicians. When clients express interest in maintaining or reclaiming religion, it can be helpful for knowledgeable clinicians to educate them about the range of acceptance offered by the community's religious communities.

Clients may find support in their traditions through established programs or communities, parachurch and similar organizations, or new traditions and communities. For example, the formal teaching in many churches emphasizes sex within heterosexual marriage. Some queer adults remain in their religious communities (which may or may not be affirming); some choose affirming spiritual communities within their own or a neighboring area; some choose to participate in a parachurch organization; others choose to leave the individual church, denomination, or faith entirely for another faith tradition, agnosticism, or atheism. Any of these choices may be self-renewing for an individual client, though each includes its own losses and benefits.

SELF-RENEWAL THEMES FOR LGBTQ ADULTS: STRENGTHS BORN OF CHALLENGE

Queer youth and adults face the challenges common to people of all sexual orientations, as well as challenges unique to sexual minorities. Although these challenges and stresses are often debilitating, and can lead to significant mental health concerns such as depression, anxiety, substance abuse, relational stress, family violence, and spiritual crisis, these experiences may also lead to the development of signature strengths born from these challenges.

Among the most salient strengths and self-renewal themes are a broadened sense of family and community, increased sense of self-confidence, a release from fear, an enhanced sense of self-efficacy, pride, self-esteem, renewed and intimate relationships with others, and the rejection of false dichotomies or inauthentic selves. Choice is at the heart of self-renewal for queer clients: the choice of one's identity, one's partner(s), one's family and community, the choice to be fully or partially out, and with whom and when to be out. Clinicians may promote self-renewal by helping the client explore the range and consequences (both gains and losses) of choices and the impact of these choices on the client's physical health, and emotional, social, and spiritual well-being. Finally, clinicians are called to manage their own anxieties if and when clients make choices that differ from their values and visions of self-renewal. It is the companionship with clients as they explore their own decisions that clinicians are most likely to support genuine transformation and health.

REFERENCES

Barton, B. (2010). "Abomination"—Life as a Bible Belt gay. *Journal of Homosexuality*, *57*, 465–484. doi:10.1080/00918361003608558

Bassett, R. L., Hodak, E., Allen, J., Bartos, D., Grastorf, J., Sittig, L., & Strong, J. (2000). Homonegative Christians: Loving the sinner but hating the sin. *Journal of Psychology and Christianity*, *19*(3), 258–269.

Bozard, R. L., & Sanders, C. J. (2011). Helping Christian lesbian, gay, and bisexual clients recover religion as a source of strength: Developing a model for assessment and integration of religious identity and counseling. *Journal of LGBT Issues in Counseling*, *5*, 47–74. doi:10.1080/15538605.2011.554791

Cochran, S. D., Sullivan, J. G., & Mays, V. M. (2003). Prevention of mental disorders, psychological distress, and mental health services use among lesbian, gay, and bisexual adults in the United States. *Journal of Consulting and Clinical Psychology*, *71*(1), 53–61. doi:10.1037/0022–006X.71.1.53

Dewaele, A., Cox, N., Van den Berghe, W., & Vincke, J. (2011). Families of choice? Exploring the supportive networks of lesbians, gay men, and bisexuals. *Journal of Applied Social Psychology*, *41*, 312–331. doi:10.1111/j.1559–1816.2010.00715.x

Fulton, A. S., Gorsuch, R. L., & Maynard, E. A. (1999). Religious orientation, antihomosexual sentiment, and fundamentalism among Christians. *Journal for the Scientific Study of Religion*, 38(1), 14–22. doi:10.2307/1287580

Garnets, L., Herek, G. M., & Levy, B. (1990). Violence and victimization of lesbians and gay men: Mental health consequences. *Journal of Interpersonal Violence*, 5(3), 366–383.

Green, H., Payne, N. R., & Green, J. (2011). Working bi: Preliminary findings from a survey on workplace experiences of bisexual people. *Journal of Bisexuality*, *11*, 300–316. doi:10.1080/15299716.2011.572007

Griffith, K. H., & Hebl, M. R. (2002). The disclosure dilemma for gay men and lesbians: "Coming out" at work. *Journal of Applied Psychology*, *87*, 1191–1199. DOI:10.1037/0021–9010.87.6.1191

Haldeman, D. C. (1996). Spirituality and religion in the lives of lesbians and gay men. In R. P. Cabaj & T. S. Stein (Eds.), *Textbook of homosexuality and mental health* (pp. 881–896). Washington, DC: American Psychiatric Press.

Hammersmith, S. K. (1987). A sociological approach to counseling homosexual clients and their families. *Journal of Homosexuality*, *14*(1–2), 173–190. doi:10.1300/J082v14n01_13

Heermann, M., Wiggins, M. I., & Rutter, P. A. (2007). Creating a space for spiritual practice: Pastoral possibilities with sexual minorities. *Pastoral Psychology*, *55*, 711–721. doi:10.1007/s11089–007–0085-y

Herek, G. M. (1989). Hate crimes against lesbians and gay men: Issues for research and policy. *American Psychologist*, *44*(6), 948–955. doi:10.1037/0003–066X.44.6.948

Herek, G. M. (1991). Stigma, prejudice, and violence against lesbians and gay men. In J. C. Gonsoriek & J. D. Weinrich (Eds.), *Homosexuality: Research implications for public policy* (pp. 60–80). Newbury Park, CA: Sage.

Herek, G. M. (1993). Documenting prejudice against lesbians and gay men on campus: The Yale sexual orientation survey. *Journal of Homosexuality*, *25*(4), 15–30. doi:10.1300/J082v25n04_02

Herek, G. M., Gillis, J. R., & Cogan, J. C. (1999). Psychological sequelae of hate-crime victimization among lesbian, gay, and bisexual adults. *Journal of Consulting and Clinical Psychology*, *67*(6), 945–951. doi:10.1037/0022–006X.67.6.945

Herek, G. M., Gillis, J. R., Cogan, J. C., & Glunt, E. K. (1997). Hate crimes victimization among lesbian, gay, and bisexual adults. *Journal of Interpersonal Violence*, *12*(2), 195–215. doi:10.1177/088626097012002003

Hoffman, L. G., Hevesi, A. G., Lynch, P. E., Gomes, P. J., Chodorow, N. J., Roughton, R. E., . . . & Vaughan, S. (2000). Homophobia: Analysis of a "permissible" prejudice: A public forum of the American Psychoanalytic Association and the American Psychoanalytic Foundation. *Journal of Gay and Lesbian Psychotherapy*, *4*(1), 5–53. doi:10.1300.J236v04n01_02

Jenkins, M., Lambert, E. G., & Baker, D. N. (2009). The attitudes of Black and White college students towards gays and lesbians. *Journal of Black Studies*, *39*(4), 589–613. doi:10.1177/0021934707299638

Johnson, W. S. (2006). *A time to embrace: Same-gender relationships in religion, law, and politics*. Grand Rapids, MI: Eerdmans.

Johnston, L. B., & Stewart, C. (2011). Rethinking GLBTQ adolescent spirituality: Implications for social workers in the twenty-first century. *Journal of GLBT Family Studies*, *7*(4), 388–397. doi:10.1080/1550428X.2011.592967

Kelly, E. W. (1995). *Spirituality and religion in counseling and psychotherapy: Diversity in theory and practice*. Alexandria, VA: American Counseling Association.

Laythe, B., Finkel, D., & Kirkpatrick, L. A. (2001). Predicting prejudice from religious fundamentalism and right-wing authoritarianism: A multiple-regression approach. *Journal for the Scientific Study of Religion*, 40(1), 1–10. doi:10.1111/0021–8294.00033

Lewis, G. B. (2003). Black-white differences in attitudes toward homosexuality and gay rights. *Public Opinion Quarterly*, *67*, 59–78. doi:0033–362X/2003/6701–0006

Lynch, B. (1996). Religious and spirituality conflicts. In D. Davies & C. Neal (Eds.), *Pink therapy: A guide for counsellors and therapists working with lesbian, gay, and bisexual clients* (pp. 199–207). Buckingham, England: Open University.

Malcomnson, K. M., Christopher, A. N., Franzen, T., & Keyes, B. J. (2006). The Protestant work ethic, religious beliefs, and homonegative attitudes. *Mental Health, Religion and Culture*, 9(5), 435–447. doi:10.1080/13694670500264068

Mathy, R. M. (2006). Self-disclosure: A dance of the heart and a ballet of the mind. *Journal of Gay & Lesbian Psychotherapy*, *10*, 109–121. doi:10.1300/J236v10n01_10

Maynard, E. A., & Gorsuch, R. L. (2001). Gay and lesbian Christians: Faith and coping in the church. In H. N. Malony (Ed.), *Pastoral care and counseling in sexual diversity* (pp. 59–70). New York, NY: Haworth Press.

Mayo, D. J., & Gunderson, M. (1994). Privacy and the ethics of outing. *Journal of Homosexuality*, *27*(3/4), 47–65. doi:10.1300/J082v27n03_04

Morrison, M. A., & Morrison, T. G. (2011). Sexual orientation bias toward gay men and lesbian women: Modern homonegative attitudes and their association with discriminatory behavioral intentions. *Journal of Applied Social Psychology*, *41*(11), 2573–2599. doi:10.1111/j.1559–1816.2011.00838.x

Morrison, M. A., Morrison, T. G., & Franklin, R. (2009). Modern and old-fashioned homonegativity among samples of Canadian and American university students. *Journal of Cross-Cultural Psychology*, *40*(4), 523–542. doi:10.1177/0022022109335033

Morrison, T. G., Kenny, P., & Harrington, A. (2005). Modern prejudice toward gay men and lesbian women: Assessing the viability of a measure of modern homonegative attitudes within an Irish context. *Genetic, Social, and General Psychology Monographs*, *131*(3), 219–250. doi:10.3200/MONO.131.3.219–250

Nelson, J. B. (1981). Religious and moral issues in working with homosexual clients. *Journal of Homosexuality*, *7*, 163–175. doi:10.1300.J082v07n02_16

Newman, P. A., Bogo, M., & Daley, A. (2008). Self-disclosure of sexual orientation in social work field education: Field instructor and lesbian and gay student perspectives. *Clinical Supervisor*, *27*, 215–237. doi:10.1080/07325220802487881

Padilla, Y. C., Crisp, C., & Rew, D. (2010). Parental acceptance and illegal drug use among gay, lesbian, and bisexual adolescents: Results from a national survey. *Social Work*, *55*, 265–275. doi:10.1093/sw/55.3.265

Patel, S., Long, T. E., McCammon, S. L., & Wuensch, K. L. (1995). Personality and emotional correlates of self-reported antigay behaviors. *Journal of Interpersonal Violence*, *10*(3), 354–366. doi:10.1177/088626095010003008

Ross, M. W., Rosser, B. R. S., & Neumaier, E. R. (2008). The relationship of internalized homonegativity to unsafe sexual behavior in HIV seropositive men who have sex with men. *AIDS Education & Prevention*, *20*(6), 547–557.

Rothman, E. F., Sullivan, M., Keyes, S., & Boehmer, U. (2012). Parents' supportive reactions to sexual orientation disclosure associated with better health: Results from a population-based survey of LGB adults in Massachusetts. *Journal of Homosexuality*, 59, 186–200. doi:10.1080/00918369.2012.648878

Sherry, A., Adelman, A., Whilde, M. R., & Quick, D. (2010). Competing selves: Negotiating the intersection of spiritual and sexual identities. *Professional Psychology: Research and Practice*, *41*(2), 112–119. doi:10.1037/a0017471

Swartz, M. (2011, June 16). Living the good lie: Should therapists help God-fearing gay people stay in the closet? *New York Times*.

Szymanski, D. M., Kashubeck-West, S., & Meyer, J. (2008). Internalized heterosexism: Measurement, psychosocial correlates, and research directions. *Counseling Psychologist*, *36*(4), 525–574. doi:10.1177/0011000007309489

Tozer, E. E., & Hayes, J. A. (2004). Why do individuals seek conversion therapy?: The role of religiosity, internalized homonegativity, and identity development. *Counseling Psychologist*, *32*, 716–740. doi:10.1177/0011000004267563

Wagner, G., Serafini, J., Rabkin, J., Remien, R., & Williams, J. (1994). Integration of one's religion and homosexuality: A weapon against internalized homophobia? *Journal of Homosexuality*, 26(4), 91–110. doi:10.1300/J082v26n)4_06

Wren, B. (2000). Early physical intervention for young people with atypical gender identity development. *Clinical Child Psychology and Psychiatry*, 5, 220–231. doi:10.1177/1359104500005002007

Yarhouse, M. A., & Beckstead, A. L. (2011). Using group therapy to navigate and resolve sexual orientation and religious conflicts. *Counseling and Values*, 56, 96–120. doi:10.1002/j.2161–007x.2011.tb01034.x

CHAPTER

24

Renewing One's Ethical Sensibilities

Jeffrey E. Barnett

Each of the helping professions has a keen focus on professional ethics. This is consistent with the roles we serve in, the potential impact we may have on others' lives, and the obligations we have to those we interact with professionally and to the public at large. The codes of ethics of each of the helping professions emphasize the professional responsibilities and obligations to act and function ethically so that the best interests of those we serve are met, to ensure that they are not exploited or harmed, and so that we do not lose the public's trust and faith in our professions and the services we offer.

Yet, over the course of our careers we may lose our focus on achieving the highest ethical ideals of our respective professions. We may become preoccupied with keeping up with the many demands of our busy professional and personal lives and we may lose touch with the fundamentals of ethical practice and not even give them ongoing consideration. Even the most well-trained, thoughtful, and moral people can lose this focus over the course of their career. Unless we make a conscious decision to give these issues our attention, we may slowly over time drift off our ethical course in our professional work. It is for these reasons that each of us must take the time to carefully consider the foundations of ethical practice, how we may integrate them into our professional lives once again, and how to apply them effectively in the many situations we experience in our professional roles. Doing so will assist us to renew our ethical sensibilities and assist each of us to fulfill our shared goal of achieving the highest possible standards of ethical practice.

This attention to the process of renewing our ethical focus requires self-awareness, self-reflection, and a conscious effort to attend to these important issues. Further, ethical self-renewal should not be seen primarily as a single event engaged in as a form of remediation for wayward professionals who have lost their focus. Rather, this is a process of active engagement that each of us will hopefully participate in on an ongoing basis throughout our careers. This process of renewal of our commitment to ethical practice and to providing the best possible services to our clients will hopefully help us to reconnect with the reasons we each had for entering a helping profession, resulting in deeper and more meaningful relationships with our clients and a greater sense of fulfillment from our professional work.

UNDERLYING VALUES OF THE MENTAL HEALTH PROFESSIONS

Each helping profession is built on a set of common values that are intended to guide its members in their professional activities. These values are typically articulated in each of these profession's codes of ethics that are based on a set of core values, or what Beauchamp and Childress (2001) describe as the underlying virtues of the helping professions. These virtues include:

- Beneficence: Helping others and working to provide them with benefit in all our professional interactions with them.
- Nonmalfeasence: Preventing harm to, and exploitation of, those we serve, actively taking steps to minimize the risk of these occurring.
- Fidelity: Being true to, and fulfilling, our commitments to others, both those that are explicit such as those in the informed consent agreement and those that are implicit such as those things others may reasonably expect from us.
- Autonomy: Working to promote our clients' autonomy over time and not engaging in actions that would promote their continued dependence on us.
- Justice: Providing all individuals with fair and equitable treatment, not singling out certain individuals for better or worse care. This also involves providing all individuals with equal opportunities for access to needed services.
- Self-care: Taking adequate care of ourselves and managing the stressors and challenges in our professional roles and personal life to prevent the development of burnout and problems with professional competence.

These underlying virtues form the foundation for the ethics codes of the helping professions and are seen in their core values and ethics standards. For example, the American Psychological Association's Ethical Principles of Psychologists and Code of Conduct (APA Ethics Code; APA, 2010) articulates that its intent is "to guide psychologists toward the highest ideals of psychology" through its aspirational principles and its "enforceable rules for conduct" (p. 1). Further, the APA Ethics Code "has as its goals the welfare and protection of the individuals and groups with whom psychologists work and the education of members, students and the public regarding ethical standards of the discipline" (p. 2). Further, the underlying values of this profession are clearly evidenced in the APA Ethics Code's General Principles of Beneficence and Nonmaleficence, Fidelity and Responsibility, Integrity, Justice, and Respect for People's Rights and Dignity.

These values are consistent with those held within the other helping professions. For example, the National Association of Social Workers' (NASW's) Code of Ethics (NASW, 2008), which is representative of the codes of the other helping professions, articulates that "The primary mission of the social work profession is to enhance human wellbeing and help meet the basic human needs of all people, with particular attention to the needs and empowerment of people who are vulnerable, oppressed, and living in poverty" (para. 5). Further, the NASW Code lists the profession's core values as service, social justice, dignity and worth of the person, importance of human relationships, integrity, and competence. Similarly, the American Counseling Association's (ACA's) Code of Ethics states that the American Counseling Association's mission is "to enhance the quality of life in society by promoting the development of professional counselors, advancing the counseling profession, and using the profession and practice of counseling to promote respect for human dignity and diversity" (ACA, 2005, para. 1). In speaking of the profession's focus on its values and their connection to a focus on ethics, the ACA further states that "professional values are an important way of living out an ethical commitment" (para. 3). It is through engagement in the process of ethical self-renewal that we can ensure that we retain the needed focus on these values of our profession over the course of our career.

A COMMITMENT TO ETHICAL PRACTICE

Living out this ethical commitment, based on each helping profession's core values, is fundamental to the very nature of being in the helping professions. Most individuals who enter these professions do so out of a commitment to serving and helping others (Norcross & Guy, 2007) and we are inculcated with a focus on ethical conduct in all aspects of our professional training. Students and trainees are instructed in the importance of ethical conduct and they learn the principles and standards in their profession's ethics code. But learning to be an ethical professional goes far beyond familiarity with the ethics code or even memorizing a list of rules and standards.

As Jordan and Meara (1990) emphasize, the ethical professional must go beyond asking the question "What shall I do?" and ask the important question of "Who shall I be?" This distinction raises the notion of thinking, reasoning, and being ethical, rather than focusing on a rule-based approach to ethics. Helping professionals who focus on the rule-based approach of principle ethics are likely to engage in rote memorization of an ethics code, efforts to rigidly apply it, and an emphasis on meeting minimal standards of conduct. Those who eschew this approach and ascribe to virtue ethics will work to integrate the underlying virtues of their profession into all they do in their professional roles.

Also of relevance to the development of an ethical helping professional is each helping professional's personal values. Our personal values may or may not be consistent with our profession's core values. Handelsman, Gottlieb, and Knapp (2005) explain in their ethics acculturation model that each person entering a helping profession brings with them their personal values (along with their beliefs, biases, and prejudices). These must be examined in light of the profession's core values to ensure consistency and to resolve any discordance or conflict between the two. It is proposed that this process of self-reflection and self-exploration results in a process of ethics acculturation that has four possible outcomes; integration, assimilation, separation, and marginalization (Handelsman et al., 2005).

The educational and self-reflective process that all ethics training should involve will hopefully result in ethics integration on the part of the helping professional. This individual looks for consistency between his or her personal values and his or her profession's core values with the goal of integrating the two and achieving a seamless integration in their approach to ethics and ethical decision making. The self-reflective process should also assist the helping professional to become aware of any inconsistencies between personal and professional values with the hope that these will be resolved prior to acting on them.

Ethics assimilation, separation, and marginalization are each less desired and more problematic styles of ethics acculturation. Ethics assimilation involves helping professionals fully immersing themselves in and accepting the profession's values, while perhaps overlooking or rejecting any personal values they may have. These helping professionals may be at significant risk of unethical behavior as a result of an inflated sense of competence and confidence in their judgment due to what may be a naïve overreliance on and confidence in strictly following their profession's ethics code. This may result in what Handelsman and colleagues (2005) describe as "empty, legalistic, and overly simplistic applications of our ethical principles" (p. 61) in the absence of a thoughtful and sophisticated approach to ethical decision making and judgment.

Ethics separation involves a primary focus on one's personal values and a failure to integrate them with the profession's values. This reliance on one's personal values, beliefs, and perspectives places the helping professional at great risk for unethical behavior as well. The helping professional who ignores the dictates of the profession's ethics code and makes decisions based on personal beliefs and values may act with good intentions, but inconsistently with accepted professional standards, possibly resulting in harm to those impacted by their decisions and actions.

Ethics marginalization is present when the helping professional lacks an awareness of, and connection to, both professional and personal values. Handelsman and colleagues (2005) suggest that these helping professionals may be at greatest risk for engaging in unethical behavior, making decisions that are perhaps motivated by their personal needs and interests, failing to understand their professional obligations to others, and lacking in the personal values needed to guide appropriate decision making. These individuals are unlikely to be considered well suited for participation in the helping professions.

A COMMITMENT TO EXCELLENCE

Although an ethics acculturation approach clearly is desired, even those professionals who have integrated their personal values with the core values of their profession may not be fulfilling the ethics ideals of their profession. Consistent with the approach presented by Jordan and Meara (1990), it is vital that helping professionals not assume that meeting minimal standards set in their profession's ethics code is necessarily consistent with their profession's core values. Authors such as Knapp and VandeCreek (2006) describe positive or aspirational ethics as an alternative to the rules based approach that focuses on meeting minimal requirements. In positive or aspirational ethics the objective is for the helping professional to do the best he or she can in each situation. Rather than asking oneself if a certain action meets minimal expectations, we should ask instead questions such as "How can I best meet my obligations?"

As an example, rather than working to meet minimal standards of competence, it is hoped that the helping professional will work continually to develop and enhance his or her clinical competence. With this approach, one is never done; we can always do more, such as to read another journal article, attend another workshop, seek consultation with a colleague, and the like. While not taking these actions would not necessarily constitute unethical behavior, the avoidance of unethical behavior is not the goal. The goal is to continually work toward improvement so that clients and others receive the best services we can reasonably offer.

Mental health professionals who take an aspirational approach to ethics understand the minimal standards that must always be met, but the goals they set far exceed these minimal expectations. They embrace the objective of continual self-improvement in the service of ever-improving services to those they interact with professionally. One never achieves perfection and thus, one is never done working toward these aspirational goals. But these goals provide the helping professional with clear guidance on a direction to move in and hopefully with clear guidance on those actions to take.

By engaging in the self-reflective process of renewal of our ethical sensibilities we are provided with the opportunity to reflect on how and if we are working to fulfill this obligation in our varied professional roles and activities. Thoughtful consideration of our approach to ethical practice, to how we interact with each client, and to what we view our role as being (e.g., instructor, supporter, guide) are each important elements of this process. Through renewal we can re-engage with our goals and make changes in our approach to our professional responsibilities and relationships; a process likely to be mutually beneficial to ourselves as well as to those we serve.

ETHICAL DILEMMAS AND PROBLEMS

Even the most well-intentioned, caring, and competent helping professionals may at times find themselves confronted by ethical dilemmas. In fact, it is often those with the best of intentions and the highest level of care and competence who are most likely to experience ethical dilemmas in their work with clients. Ethical dilemmas are those situations that have no obvious correct or incorrect course of action. Ethical dilemmas arise in the normal course of clinical practice and are an expected part of our professional work. In contrast, an ethical problem is a situation in which there are clearly correct and incorrect (ethical and unethical, respectively) courses of action available to the helping professional.

An example of an ethical problem is considering if I should initiate an intimate relationship with a current client to whom I am attracted. Another example is deciding if I should discuss an interesting client's difficulties with friends or family members. There is no dilemma in these situations. Both of these actions would violate the core values of my profession and violate specific enforceable standards of my profession's ethics code. Alternatively, I might be faced with the decision of providing clinical services to a friend, acquaintance, or business associate in my local community. While this also would constitute a multiple relationship situation, I would need to go through a thoughtful decision-making process, weighing a number of factors, to determine if this is the most appropriate course of action. Similarly, if I received a request to disclose information about a minor client to his or her parent, I would also need to work through a decision-making process to determine the most appropriate course of action in this situation. This appropriate course of action may vary depending on the facts of the situation, your perception of the client's best interests, your motivations for taking particular actions, the client's clinical issues and needs, what was agreed to in the informed consent agreement, reasonably available options and alternatives, and their relative risks and benefits, among other factors and considerations.

It is vital that we consider the core values of our profession when confronted by such dilemmas. Thoughtful helping professionals can ask themselves questions based on these values such as "Will taking this action be helpful to this client?," "Will this action increase the risk of exploitation or harm to this individual?," "Is taking this action in keeping with my responsibilities to this client?," "Will this action promote my client's independence of me?," "Am I treating this individual justly and fairly?," and "Are there any personal factors that may be impairing my objectivity or judgment in this situation?" Honestly reflecting on the answers to these questions can be a good start to a decision-making process as well as a reflection of our commitment to the core values of our profession. Further, participation in this process is a reflection of our commitment to an aspirational approach to ethics in our professional roles and interactions.

ETHICAL DECISION MAKING

Helping professionals with a commitment to the ethical ideals of their profession will acknowledge that they do not have all the answers, that they at times will need to consult with colleagues to seek input and assistance, and that they will need assistance in successfully navigating through the many ethically challenging situations that arise in the course of our professional activities. When faced with ethical dilemmas, in addition to engaging in a self-reflective process and asking the questions described above that are based on the ethics virtues and core values of the helping professions, thoughtful professionals will also utilize one of many available ethics decision-making models to arrive at an appropriate course of action.

A wide range of ethical decision-making models are available for use by helping professionals (see Clause & Cottone, 2000, for a review of many of these models). No one model is superior to the others, but each may emphasize different factors or focuses that may be of relevance when selecting a model for use. For example, numerous authors have integrated feminist perspectives to include autonomy, equality, and justice, into ethical decision-making models (e.g., Hill & Glaser, 1998; Rave & Larsen, 1995). Similarly, Houser, Wilczenski, and Ham (2006) have proposed a culturally informed decision-making model that takes into consideration various cultural perspectives and values in an effort to help make decisions that are most appropriate for individuals of diverse backgrounds. In the field of social work, Abramson (1996) integrated principle-based ethics, virtue ethics, feminist ethics, and Afrocentricity to create a holistic model of ethical discernment and decision making.

Other decision-making models focus on addressing dilemmas in particular situations or contexts. For example, one model focuses on balancing autonomy rights with the need for protection when making judgments about decisional capacity in HIV-positive youth (Chenneville, Sibille, & Bendell-Estroff, 2010). Alternatively, Younggren and Gottlieb (2008) developed a decision-making model that is designed to be applied to dilemmas regarding multiple relationship situations between helping professionals and their clients. Edwards, Delaney, Townsend, and Swisher (2011) developed a decision-making model they call the Ethical Reasoning Bridge, which is designed to promote the core value of justice by assisting helping professionals to better make decisions when deciding about health care access and distribution decisions.

Within the nursing field, Park (2012) conducted a review of more than 20 ethical decision-making models and based on this review developed a representative integrated approach to ethical decision making. This model includes six steps:

1. The identification of an ethical problem.
2. The collection of additional information to identify the problem and develop solutions.
3. The development of alternatives for analysis and comparison.
4. The selection of the best alternatives and justification.
5. The development of diverse, practical ways to implement ethical decisions and actions.
6. The evaluation of effects and development of strategies to prevent a similar occurrence.

This model represents a rational-analytic approach (Davis, 1997) and provides a rational step-by-step approach for working through ethical dilemmas. This model is similar to Barnett and Johnson's (2009) more comprehensive rational-analytic ethical decision-making model, which includes 10 steps:

1. Define the ethical dilemma or conflict clearly.
2. Determine who will be impacted and in what ways.
3. Consult the principles and standards of the profession's ethics code.
4. Refer to relevant laws, regulations, and professional guidelines.
5. Reflect honestly on personal feelings and competence as they are relevant to the situation.
6. Consult with trusted colleagues in an honest and forthright manner.
7. Formulate alternative courses of action to consider.
8. Consider the possible outcomes based on alternative actions considered.
9. Engage in further consultation with colleagues as well as with ethics committees and when relevant, with legal professionals.
10. Implement the plan decided on and then monitor the outcome. Reengage in this decision-making process as needed and modify the action plan accordingly.

Regardless of the ethical decision-making model used, it is hoped that helping professionals will consider how to best apply a deliberative thought process when faced with ethical dilemmas. Perhaps of tantamount importance is the need for helping professionals to realize when an ethical dilemma is present.

This will require a sense of humility, knowledge of one's limitations, and an openness to seeing and understanding the complexities of each clinical situation with which we are presented.

ETHICAL CHALLENGES AND PITFALLS

Helping professionals may face ethical dilemmas in a wide range of situations. Each area of practice may present its own unique challenges and dilemmas. The diverse roles in which helping professionals may function, the settings in which we may serve, and the various groups with whom we may work, each present unique challenges. Thus, ethical dilemmas may be seen in different roles such as counseling, assessment, research, teaching, clinical supervision, administration, as well as others. Settings may vary from inpatient to outpatient settings; working for government agencies, hospitals, clinics, prisons, schools, the courts, and in private practice; and working in urban, suburban, and rural areas. Professional services may be provided to individuals, couples, families, groups, and organizations; and those served may be children, adolescents, adults, and even agencies. While not exhaustive, the following review highlights some of the areas in which dilemmas may arise for helping professionals and about which we must be vigilant.

Clinical Competence

Clinical competence is an essential requirement for all helping professionals. Interestingly, competence is both an aspirational principle and an enforceable standard. Thus, we should be constantly striving to enhance and increase our competence so that we may provide the best professional services possible. But we must also never allow our competence to fall below minimal professional standards.

It is important to understand that competence is not an all or nothing phenomenon (Barnett, Doll, Younggren, & Rubin, 2007). One may be competent in some aspects of practice and not in others, with some populations and not with others, and with some techniques and not with others. Thus, a helping professional may possess the needed competence to effectively provide individual counseling to older adults, yet providing assessment services to young children may be outside of that practitioner's expertise. Additionally, one may be competent at one point in time and not at a later date. I may have been competent in using a certain assessment or treatment technique when I left graduate school, but if I have not practiced that technique over the years and if I have not kept current with relevant developments in this field, I may no longer be competent in this aspect of professional practice. Thus, one's clinical competence may degrade over time, what we have learned may become outdated, and we are unlikely to remember all we have previously learned, especially without ongoing review and practice.

Helping professionals are not limited to using those techniques and to providing those services that we learned during our graduate education and training. We may expand our scope of practice into new areas throughout the course of our careers. This may be due to the needs of the community we serve, job requirements, changing professional interests, and other relevant factors. Regardless of the reason, we must each follow appropriate ethical standards when considering providing professional services in new areas, ensuring that we obtain the needed education and clinical training to provide these new services ethically and competently.

The requirement to first develop needed competence before offering new services is seen in each of the helping professions' ethics codes. For example, the NASW Code of Ethics (NASW, 2008) makes it clear in Standard 1.04, Competence, that "Social workers should provide services in substantive areas or use intervention techniques or approaches that are new to them only after engaging in appropriate study, training, consultation, and supervision from people who are competent in those interventions or techniques" (para. 34). But self-awareness, honesty, and sensitivity to the impact of our level of competence on those we serve is essential for making thoughtful decisions about our education and training needs. For example, in Standard C.2, Professional Competence, of the ACA Code of Ethics (2005) it states that "Counselors continually monitor their effectiveness as professionals and take steps to improve when necessary" (p. 9). Further, the Code of Ethics for Nurses (American Nurses Association [ANA], 2011) states that "Continual professional growth, particularly in knowledge and skill, requires a commitment to lifelong learning" (Standard 5.2).

We must each continually monitor our competence, honestly reflecting on our training needs, carrying out continual self-assessment (ANA, 2011). When we are unsure of our needs for additional education and training, we should consult with colleagues who are recognized experts in that area of practice, review relevant practice guidelines, and consider the most current research literature available. Taking these actions is consistent with a commitment to the aspirational approach to ethics as well as with the core values of each of the helping professions.

Informed Consent and Assent

Informed consent sets the foundation of the professional relationship that is a requirement set in each of the helping professions' codes of ethics. It involves the sharing of sufficient information with the other individual so that he or she may make an informed decision about participating in the professional relationship (Beahrs & Gutheil, 2001). This is consistent with and an important aspect of respecting and promoting each client's self-determination and autonomous functioning (ANA, 2011, Standard 1.14, The Right to Self-Determination).

Informed consent should be an ongoing process that begins with the first contact with the client and continues throughout the professional relationship. Potential benefits of the informed consent process include promoting the client's autonomy, promoting a collaborative working relationship, and helping to minimize the risks of exploitation of or harm to the client (Snyder & Barnett, 2006).

It is possible for helping professionals to overlook important aspects of informed consent and to become complacent about its appropriate implementation. It is important that we first give careful consideration to each individual's competence to provide informed consent. We must actively assess if clients are legally and cognitively/emotionally competent to provide their own consent. Thus, to ensure legal competence we must be familiar with relevant laws in our jurisdiction such as the age of majority. We also need to determine if the individual's rights have been modified by the courts. With regard to cognitive and emotional competence we must again assess the client's ability to provide fully informed consent. A client with dementia or active psychosis, for example, may not be able to understand what they are agreeing to and thus would not be providing informed consent.

The informed consent process must be conducted in a manner that ensures that consent is given voluntarily and no coercion occurs, the information must be presented verbally and in writing at a level the client can reasonably be expected to understand, we must actively ensure each client's understanding of the information being provided to them, and sufficient information must be presented so that the client may make an informed decision about participation in the professional relationship (Fisher & Oransky, 2008). Decisions about the amount and type of information to be shared should be based on the dictates of the professional's ethics code and licensing law, as well as be based on the criterion of what information clients would want to have in advance that might impact their decision to participate in this service (Barnett, Wise, Johnson-Greene, & Bucky, 2007). Examples include fees and financial arrangements, limits to confidentiality, options and alternatives reasonably available and the relative risks and benefits of each, and the like.

Further, each helping profession's ethics code emphasizes the importance of sensitivity to cultural and other diversity factors when engaging in the informed consent process. For example, the ACA Code of Ethics (2005) necessitates that counselors utilize the services of interpreters when needed to ensure that the client fully understands the information being shared (Standard A.2.c., Developmental and Cultural Sensitivity).

For those clients unable to give consent for legal or cognitive/emotional reasons, it is recommended that consent be obtained from an appropriate third party (e.g., NASW Code of Ethics Standard 1.03c, Informed Consent) and that assent be given. Assent involves the sharing of information with the client at a level that can be expected to be understood by the client. While the client may not have the legal right to decline participation, it is still important to engage in this process for all the reasons cited above regarding the benefits of informed consent (Fisher, Hatashita-Wong, & Greene, 1999).

Boundaries and Multiple Relationships

Boundaries are the ground rules that set the parameters of the professional relationship. They may include factors such as touch, self-disclosure, interpersonal space, location, fees, and gifts (Gutheil & Gabbard, 1993). Boundaries may be avoided, crossed, or violated. A boundary crossing is considered to be clinically relevant, ethically appropriate, and an important part of the client's treatment; a boundary violation is inconsistent with the client's treatment needs, it is exploitative or harmful, and it is unethical (Smith & Fitzpatrick, 1995). Thus, one may work on an inpatient unit that has an absolute "no touching" rule (avoiding the boundary), one may shake the hand of a client who extends it in greeting (boundary crossing), or one may enter into a sexually intimate relationship with a client (boundary violation).

But boundary situations in real life are not always so clear-cut. Would it be ethical and appropriate to hug a grieving client? With regard to multiple relationships, would it be appropriate to provide professional services to a work colleague or friend in the community? Such situations arise with great frequency and there are a number of factors helping professionals will need to be aware of, sensitive to, and consider. The American Psychological Association's Ethics Code (2010) states that:

> A psychologist refrains from entering into a multiple relationship if the multiple relationship could reasonably be expected to impair the psychologist's objectivity, competence or effectiveness in performing his or her functions as a psychologist, or otherwise risks exploitation or harm to the person with whom the professional relationship exists. (p. 6)

Other factors that must be considered include the setting in which one is practicing (e.g., urban versus rural), reasonably available options and alternatives, one's theoretical orientation, the client's mental health history and treatment needs, how the actions are intended, how the actions are likely to be interpreted by the client to include attention to cultural and other diversity factors, and prevailing professional standards.

A strict avoidance of boundaries and multiple relationships in the clinical setting in an effort to avoid potentially unethical behavior may result in a sterile therapeutic environment and a poor treatment alliance (Zur, 2007). The ethics codes of each of the helping professions prohibits sexual intimacies with those to whom we provide professional services and their significant others due to the exploitative and harmful nature of these multiple relationships along with their ability to alter our objectivity and professional judgment. Yet, if an action is not motivated by our personal needs but instead by the client's treatment needs, if it is not likely to be harmful, and if it is consistent with the client's best interests, a multiple relationship may not only be appropriate, to not engage in it may be the unethical course of action. Thus, we each must engage in a thoughtful decision-making process prior to crossing boundaries and entering into multiple relationships.

An additional issue we each must honestly consider is the "slippery slope" (Gutheil & Gabbard, 1993). Historically, it was seen that sexually intimate relations with clients was preceded by a series of increasingly intrusive and inappropriate actions on the part of the helping professional. This sequence of behaviors often began with apparently benign boundary crossings that over time led to increasingly inappropriate boundary violations and then ending in the exploitative and inappropriate sexual relationship. This process of moving through these increasingly inappropriate behaviors was termed the slippery slope. It was believed that because all inappropriate multiple relationships were preceded by this pattern, that all boundary crossings should be avoided so that the unethical boundary violations would be prevented. But this thinking overlooked the fact that boundaries can be crossed without one being on the slippery slope (Gottlieb & Younggren, 2009). In fact, as has been highlighted, to avoid all boundary crossings would be inconsistent with the core values of the helping professions. But professionals must consider their intentions when considering crossing boundaries, engage in honest self-reflection, seek consultation, and when unsure of the potential impact of an action on the client, an open discussion with the client before taking the action is recommended.

Confidentiality

Confidentiality is an essential aspect of all professional relationships that helping professionals have with those they serve. Its importance is reflected in the ethics codes of each of the helping professions. For example, the ACA Code of Ethics (2005) states "Counselors respect client rights to privacy" and that "Counselors do not share confidential information without client consent or without sound legal or ethical justification (p. 7). Yet, a number of issues are relevant to this legal and ethical justification that each helping professional must consider that make confidentiality issues a potentially challenging area of practice.

By and large, clients have been reported to expect that everything they share with their helping professional to be completely confidential (Miller & Thelen, 1986). Yet, as we know, this often is not the case and we must inform clients of the limits of confidentiality as part of the informed consent agreement. There are a number of potential limitations to confidentiality of which the helping professional must be aware. As is stated in the ANA Code of Ethics (2011), confidentiality is "not absolute and may need to be modified in order to protect the patient, other innocent parties and in circumstances of mandatory disclosure for public health reasons" (p. 6).

Clients should be informed of these potential disclosures of confidential information prior to the confidentiality being breached. As the NASW Code of Ethics (2008) states, "Social workers should inform clients, to the extent possible, about the disclosure of confidential information and the potential consequences, when feasible before the disclosure is made" (para. 46).

Numerous other issues are relevant to respecting and protecting each client's confidentiality. Examples include how client records are stored, how access to them is controlled, and how they are disposed of; how staff members and subordinates are trained to protect each client's confidentiality such as not discussing confidential information with others; how various technologies such as computers and the Internet are used; how the helping professional responds to requests for records to include only disclosing confidential information with appropriate consent and only releasing the information necessary to meet the request; how the helping professional responds to subpoenas and court orders; when legal requirements to release confidential information are relevant to a particular client's situation, and many others. As should be evident, it is easy to become lax in each of these areas.

It is recommended that helping professionals have written office policies regarding confidentiality, that staff be appropriately trained and supervised, and that confidential information be protected to the fullest extent allowed by law (Fisher, 2009). When considering the importance of protecting and preserving each client's confidentiality, ensuring that clients understand all limits to confidentiality, and that they are informed of potential disclosures prior to them being made, helping professionals are advised to bear in mind the ACA Code of Ethics (2005) statement that "Counselors recognize that trust is the cornerstone of the counseling relationship" (p. 7). In all actions taken with regard to each client's confidentiality, whether it be to protect it or in making disclosures, whether mandated or with the client's consent, it is essential that helping professionals keep this focus on not violating our clients' trust paramount.

Clinical Supervision and Delegation to Subordinates

Helping professionals often have responsibility for the work of subordinates, both clinically and administratively. In their roles as clinical supervisors, helping professionals may significantly impact the professional growth and development of trainees and students. Clinical supervisors provide education, training, evaluation, and oversight, as well as serve in an important gatekeeper function with trainees. Yet, helping professionals who are tasked with clinical supervision duties may not always be well equipped for this role.

It is imperative that those serving as clinical supervisors possess the needed competence in both the areas of practice to be supervised and in the methods and techniques of clinical supervision. As the NASW Code of Ethics (2008) states, "Social workers who provide supervision or consultation should have the necessary knowledge and skill to supervise or consult appropriately and should do so only within their areas of knowledge and competence" (para. 105). Additionally, supervisors will need to ensure that each supervisee's training needs are adequately addressed, that sufficient oversight is provided, and that timely and effective feedback is provided to the supervisee (Bernard & Goodyear, 2014). As the ACA Code of Ethics (2005) states, "A primary obligation of counseling supervisors is to monitor the services provided by other counselors or counselors-in-training. Counseling supervisors monitor client welfare and supervisee clinical performance and professional development" (p. 13).

An essential point for all supervisors to keep in mind is the trainee's potential impact on current and even future clients. As a result, we must be vigilant about our obligations and responsibilities to all parties involved, ensuring that competent and effective services are provided to those our supervisees serve. When concerns about supervisee competence and suitability for functioning in this role arise, it is important that we address these issues directly, provide the trainee with opportunities for remediation, keep the supervisee's training program informed, and when necessary, not pass the trainee on to the next stage of training (Johnson et al., 2008).

It is recommended that supervisors conduct an assessment of each supervisee's training needs from the outset and to then tailor the training provided as well as the nature and intensity of the supervision to be provided based on the supervisee's clinical competence and experience. Supervisors should realize their responsibility for the quality of the services provided to clients by their supervisees and be guided by this responsibility when making decisions about the nature and extent of supervision provided. As the ANA Code of Ethics (2011) states, "Through assignment of nursing care activities to learners [supervisors] share responsibility and accountability for the care provided" (p. 9). The ANA Code of Ethics (2011) also emphasizes the importance of ensuring "that the knowledge and skills of the learner be sufficient to provide the assigned nursing care and that appropriate supervision be provided to protect both the patient and the learner" (p. 9).

When considering administrative supervision, helping professionals should consider the appropriateness of the subordinate carrying out the appointed duties. When considering the delegation of tasks to subordinates, the APA Ethics Code (2010) requires that psychologists "authorize only those responsibilities that such persons can be expected to perform competently on the basis of their education, training or experience, either independently or with the level of supervision being provided" (p. 5). Thus, administrative staff should not have clinical activities delegated to them in an effort to reduce the helping professional's workload or to expand billable clinical activities. Further, the APA Ethics Code (2010) requires that tasks not be delegated if the psychologist's objectivity and judgment may reasonably be at risk of impairment due to the presence of a multiple relationship or conflict of interest situation.

Clinical supervisors have a unique opportunity to influence and impact their supervisees both through formal instruction and through role modeling. How the supervisor interacts with the supervisee and the issues the supervisor focuses on or overlooks quite powerfully demonstrate to the supervisee which issues are important and worthy of our consideration and which ones are not. Accordingly, clinical supervisors have the opportunity to teach supervisees about the importance of self-awareness, self-reflection, and the value and need of a career-long process of self-renewal. Supervisors may openly discuss with supervisees their own process of renewing their ethical sensibilities on an ongoing basis throughout their careers, emphasizing the importance of beginning this process now. This helps to promote engagement in this process from the start of one's career and helps emphasize the importance of ethical self-renewal as a preventative process one chooses to engage in for reasons consistent with the values of our profession.

Termination and Abandonment

Once the professional relationship has been initiated, the helping professional has an obligation to the client to continue providing the professional services until agreed upon goals have been achieved or if the client has discharged the helping professional from his or her duties. Although there is not a need to continue treating a client indefinitely, helping professionals do have an obligation to address their clients' ongoing treatment needs even when they cannot personally continue providing needed services (Davis & Younggren, 2009). Potential reasons for this occurring include a client's inability to continue paying for services as had previously been agreed, the client's treatment needs changing and no longer fitting the helping professional's areas of clinical competence, the development or discovery of an inappropriate multiple relationship or conflict of interest situation that will likely adversely impact the professional's objectivity and judgment, and of course as a result of a decision by the client to pursue treatment elsewhere such as due to moving one's residence from the local area.

In general, it is recommended that issues relevant to the ending of the professional relationship be addressed as part of the ongoing informed consent agreement. It is hoped that the termination of professional services is planned for and anticipated by the client and helping professional. Relevant issues to be addressed from the outset include the possibility of financial limitations on the client's part to include limits to insurance coverage, anticipated periods of unavailability on the part of the helping professional, and if the terms of one's employment raise the possibility that the helping professional may withdraw from the treatment site prior to the client's treatment being completed.

As the NASW Code of Ethics (2008) states, "Social workers should take reasonable steps to avoid abandoning clients who are still in need of services" (para. 58). Abandonment may occur at the end of the professional relationship, such as failing to provide agreed-upon services to a client in need, as well as when the helping professional is not accessible or available in between scheduled appointments for a client who may be in crisis (Younggren & Gottlieb, 2008). Thus, helping professionals will need to make appropriate advance arrangements with clients for how to contact them when the need arises. Further, helping professionals should anticipate periods of absence and unavailability, making arrangements for coverage by appropriately trained colleagues to ensure that clients' ongoing clinical needs are met.

When making decisions about ending professional relationships, helping professionals need to consider the multiple obligations they have to their clients. Decisions made may be different depending on the reasons for ending the professional relationship. The ACA Code of Ethics (2005) articulates that "Counselors terminate a counseling relationship when it becomes reasonably apparent that the client no longer needs assistance, is not likely to benefit, or is being harmed by continued counseling" (p. 6). But these circumstances are not absolute and require careful forethought with a focus on the client's needs and best interests. Further, open discussion with the client about such concerns when they become evident and consultation with colleagues are both appropriate and, at times, necessary.

THE COMPETENT COMMUNITY AND COMMUNITARIAN ETHICS

To promote the achievement of the highest ethical ideals of the helping professions and to help ensure that ethics issues are present in helping professionals' minds, Johnson, Barnett, Elman, Forrest, and Kaslow (2012) have proposed a focus on communitarian ethics. This focus involves actively working as a community of colleagues in the service of promoting ethical conduct. Data repeatedly demonstrate that professionals are not well suited to assessing their own competence and that we often overestimate our abilities and level of functioning (e.g., Dunning, Johnson, Ehrlinger, & Kruger, 2003). In fact, making decisions about our own competence, when our ability to accurately self-assess is a component of that which may be impaired, presents a great paradox for the professional who aspires to be ethical. The use of consultation when faced with ethical dilemmas has previously been emphasized, but this may not even be considered when helping professionals are not aware that a dilemma is present or when their ability to thoughtfully and effectively make such decisions is impaired.

Johnson and colleagues (2012) propose that one cannot be ethical when isolated from one's community. Further, they argue that participating in a professional community that is committed to the ethical conduct of each member of the community is essential for achieving ethical practice. Care for others is emphasized as essential for the achievement of the greater good. If fact, it is believed that helping professionals cannot truly be ethical over time when isolated from the larger professional community. In addition to our obligation to those we serve, we have an obligation to each other. Fulfilling this obligation to our larger professional community, promoting ethical conduct among our colleagues will assist us to collectively better meet the needs of those we serve. It is further recommended that we infuse a communitarian focus on ethics in how students are trained, in how trainees are supervised, and in how we function throughout each phase of our careers. By accepting and fulfilling our obligations to each other we can help ensure ethical practice for ourselves and for our professions. Each helping professional is further encouraged to develop a "competence constellation"; a "network or consortium of individual colleagues, consultation groups, supervisors, and professional association involvements that is deliberately constructed to ensure ongoing multisource enhancement and assessment of competence" (Johnson et al., 2012, p. 11). Actively utilizing one's competence constellation can be a key step in promoting ethical functioning throughout each phase of our careers. Engaging with it nondefensively and actively participating in this collegial network to promote ethical conduct are essential.

REVITALIZING YOUR ETHICAL FOCUS

Over the course of one's career it is possible to grow complacent with regard to a focus on ethics. We each may become preoccupied with earning a living, relationships in our personal lives, and a wide range of life challenges and activities. It is easy to lose our focus on the core values of our profession. It is vital that we regularly take the time to reflect on these core values and consider how we are working to achieve them in all our professional roles and activities. Keeping in mind our original motivations for entering a helping profession, what our obligations are to those we serve and to our profession, and how we are living the embodiment of these values are essential to maintain our ethics focus.

It is also important to consider relevant factors that may be degrading or chipping away at our ethics focus and ethical conduct. The many stresses of our personal lives and the many challenges in our professional roles can combine over time to result in burnout and problems with professional competence. Attending to these issues on an ongoing basis and engaging in proactive activities are important for preventing the development of these difficulties.

Positive actions we may all take include:

- Participate in a competence constellation and utilize this resource fully. This may include participation in personal psychotherapy, clinical supervision, consultation, participation in peer supervision and support groups, and actively reaching out to individual colleagues to reduce professional isolation.

- Openly and honestly share with colleagues your challenges, difficulties, and failures. When we only share about our great successes we limit our ability to learn and grow. Actively seek out and rely on colleagues to provide feedback on your competence and do not rely solely on self-assessments.
- Reflect on the core values of your profession, your personal values, and your present level of ethics acculturation. Make decisions on changes needed in your approach to ethics with the input, guidance, and support of your competence constellation.
- Periodically conduct a review of your ethical practices. This can include a review of how you conduct the informed consent process, how you protect and maintain each client's confidentiality, how you delegate tasks to subordinates and the level and types of oversight you provide to them, and how you monitor and manage boundaries and multiple relationships, among others. Ensure that these ethical practices are consistent with the core values of your profession, relevant standards of your profession's ethics code, and applicable laws and regulations.
- Attend to personal needs and issues, remaining cognizant of how they may impact your objectivity and judgment. Be wary of rationalization, self-justification, and efforts to avoid sharing your motivations and actions with your ethics constellation colleagues.
- Carefully consider the impact of diversity factors on your professional work and honestly reflect on and then address any biases and prejudices you may have.
- Utilize a comprehensive ethical decision-making model when faced with ethical dilemmas, freely consulting with colleagues, and being available to serve as a consultant to them when asked.
- Actively participate in lifelong learning and ongoing professional development activities. These may include reading relevant journals and books, attending continuing education courses and participating in advanced clinical training and certification programs, attending and giving presentations at professional conferences, and active participation in one's professional association.
- Accept and embrace the need to fully engage in this process and accept that ethical practice results from a proactive, deliberative process. It is not automatic and should not be taken for granted. This is an aspirational activity that requires an ongoing commitment and our active participation throughout our careers.

It is hoped that by actively engaging in the process described above, each of us may renew our ethical sensibilities. This active process should be viewed as an essential professional responsibility for all mental health professionals. The need to engage in these activities should not be considered an indication of a weakness, flaw, or problem that is in need of remediation; rather, it should be seen as an essential professional activity that each of us engages in repeatedly throughout our careers. Doing so will enable each of us to continually renew our ethical sensibilities and as a result, to have the best possible chance of achieving the highest ethical standards in all our professional roles and activities.

REFERENCES

Abramson, M. (1996). Toward a more holistic understanding of ethics in social work. *Social Work in Health Care, 23*(2), 1–14.

American Counseling Association. (2005). *ACA code of ethics*. Retrieved from http://www.counseling.org/Resources/CodeOfEthics/TP/Home/CT2.aspx

American Nurses Association. (2011). *Code of ethics for nurses*. Retrieved from http://ana.nursingworld.org/MainMenuCategories/EthicsStandards/CodeofEthicsforNurses.aspx

American Psychological Association. (2010). *Ethical principles of psychologists and code of conduct*. Retrieved from http://www.apa.org/ethics

Barnett, J. E., Doll, B., Younggren, J. N., & Rubin, N. J. (2007). Clinical competence for practicing psychologists: Clearly a work in progress. *Professional Psychology: Research and Practice, 38*, 510–517.

Barnett, J. E., & Johnson, W. B. (2009). *Ethics desk reference for psychologists*. Washington, DC: American Psychological Association.

Barnett, J. E., Wise, E. H., Johnson-Greene, D., & Bucky, S. F. (2007). Informed consent: Too much of a good thing or not enough? *Professional Psychology: Research and Practice, 38*, 179–186.

Beahrs, J. O., & Gutheil, T. G. (2001). Informed consent in psychotherapy. *American Journal of Psychiatry, 158*, 4–10.

Beauchamp, T. L., & Childress, J. F. (2001). *Principles of biomedical ethics* (5th ed.). New York, NY: Oxford University Press.

Bernard, J. M., & Goodyear, R. K. (2014). *Fundamentals of clinical supervision* (5th ed.). Boston, MA: Pearson.

Chenneville, T., Sibille, K., & Bendell-Estroff, D. (2010). Decisional capacity among minors with HIV: A model for balancing autonomy rights with the need for protection. *Ethics & Behavior, 20*, 83–94.

Clause, R. E., & Cottone, R. R. (2000). Ethical decision-making models: A review of the literature. *Journal of Counseling and Development, 78*, 275–283.

Davis, A. H. (1997). The ethics of caring: A collaborative approach to resolving ethical dilemmas. *Journal of Applied Rehabilitation Counseling, 28*, 36–41.

Davis, D. D., & Younggren, J. N. (2009). Ethical competence in psychotherapy termination. *Professional Psychology: Research and Practice, 40*, 572–578.

Dunning, D., Johnson, K., Ehrlinger, J., & Kruger, J. (2003). Why people fail to recognize their own incompetence. *Current Directions in Psychological Science*, *12*, 83–87.

Edwards, I., Delaney, C. M., Townsend, A. F., & Swisher, L. L. (2011). Moral agency as enacted justice: A clinical and ethical decision-making framework for responding to health inequities and social injustice. *Physical Therapy*, *91*, 1653–1663.

Fisher, C. B., Hatashita-Wong, M., & Greene, L. I. (1999). Ethical and legal issues. In W. K. Silverman & T. H. Ollendick (Eds.), *Developmental issues in the clinical treatment of children* (pp. 470–486). Boston, MA: Allyn & Bacon.

Fisher, C. B., & Oransky, M. (2008). Informed consent to psychotherapy: Protecting the dignity and respecting the autonomy of clients. *Journal of Clinical Psychology: In Session*, *64*, 576–588.

Fisher, M. A. (2009). Ethics-based training for non-clinical staff in the mental health setting. *Professional Psychology: Research and Practice*, *40*, 459–466.

Gottlieb, M. C., & Younggren, J. N. (2009). Is there a slippery slope? Considerations regarding multiple relationships and risk management. *Professional Psychology: Research and Practice*, *40*, 564–571.

Gutheil, T. G., & Gabbard, G. O. (1993). The concept of boundaries in clinical practice: Theoretical and risk-management dimensions. *American Journal of Psychiatry*, *150*, 188–196.

Handelsman, M. M., Gottlieb, M. C., & Knapp, S. J. (2005). Training ethical psychologists: An acculturation model. *Professional Psychology: Research and Practice*, *36*, 59–65.

Hill, M., & Glaser, K. (1998). A feminist model for ethical decision making. *Women & Therapy*, *21*(3), 101–122.

Houser, R., Wilczenski, F. L., & Ham, M. A. (2006). *Culturally relevant ethical decision-making in counseling*. Thousand Oaks, CA: Sage.

Johnson, W. B., Barnett, J. E., Elman, N. S., Forrest, L., & Kaslow, N. J. (2012). The competent community: Toward a vital reformulation of professional ethics. *American Psychologist*, *67*, 557–569.

Johnson, W. B., Elman, N. S., Forrest, L., Robiner, W. N., Rodolfa, E., & Schaffer, J. B. (2008). Addressing professional competence problems in trainees: Some ethical considerations. *Professional Psychology: Research and Practice*, *39*, 589–599.

Jordan, A., & Meara, N. (1990). Ethics and the professional practice of psychologists: The role of virtues and principles. *Professional Psychology: Research and Practice*, *21*, 106–114.

Knapp, S. J., & VandeCreek, L. D. (2006). *Practical ethics for psychologists: A positive approach*. Washington, DC: American Psychological Association.

Miller, D. J., & Thelen, M. H. (1986). Knowledge and beliefs about confidentiality in psychotherapy. *Professional Psychology: Research and Practice*, *17*, 15–19.

National Association of Social Workers. (2008). *Code of ethics of the National Association of Social Workers*. Retrieved from http://www.naswdc.org/pubs/code/default.asp

Norcross, J. C., & Guy, J. D. (2007). *Leaving it at the office: A guide to psychotherapist self-care*. New York, NY: Guilford Press.

Park, E-J. (2012). An integrated ethical decision-making model for nursing. *Nursing Ethics, 19,* 139–159.

Rave, E., & Larsen, C. (Eds.). (1995). *Ethical decision making in therapy: Feminist perspectives.* New York, NY: Guilford Press.

Smith, D., & Fitzpatrick, M. (1995). Patient-therapist boundary issues: An integrative review of theory and research. *Professional Psychology: Research and Practice, 26,* 499–506.

Snyder, T. A., & Barnett, J. E. (2006). Informed consent and the process of psychotherapy. *Psychotherapy Bulletin, 41,* 37–42.

Younggren, J. N., & Gottlieb, M. C. (2008). Termination and abandonment: History, risk, and risk management. *Professional Psychology: Research and Practice, 39,* 498–504.

Zur, O. (2007). *Boundaries in psychotherapy: Ethical and clinical explorations.* Washington, DC: American Psychological Association.

CHAPTER

25

Sexual Attraction and Self-Renewal in Psychotherapy

Stephen W. Simpson and Jonathan D. Reeves

The mere mention of sexual attraction between client and therapist typically elicits outrage. Such responses are easy to understand. Sexual boundary violations in psychotherapy can inflict lasting damage on clients who come to therapy looking for safety and support (Gutheil & Gabbard, 1992; Somer & Nachmani, 2005). Pope (2001) found that about 4.4% of therapists (7% male, 1.5% female) have violated sexual boundaries with a client. But the damaging consequences of crossing sexual boundaries mask the potentially reparative potential of sexual dynamics in the therapeutic relationship. While sexual attraction must be handled with gentleness in the confines of legal and ethical boundaries, sexual feelings in therapy are not unilaterally dangerous. Rather, sexual feelings are powerful. Like most powerful forces, they are dangerous when handled with recklessness and selfishness. Uncontained sexual attraction corrupts psychotherapy. When the therapist and client incorporate sexual attraction into the healing process, however, it can be a powerful force for growth and self-renewal.

THREE UNAVOIDABLE ASPECTS OF THE THERAPEUTIC RELATIONSHIP

In clinical training, supervisors frequently treat sexual or romantic attraction in psychotherapy as an aberration. When the client has sexual feelings for the therapist it is "diagnostic." Clinicians often cite it as evidence of a personality disorder, one of the most damning and stigmatizing diagnostic categories. It raises far more concern, however, if a therapist admits to being attracted to a client. Supervisors or colleagues may think the therapist irresponsible, unethical, impulsive, and a danger to his or her client. Though the difference between acknowledging feelings and acting on them is great, most therapists will not admit feeling attracted to a client because of the accusations that may result.

Such stereotypes are unfortunate. We should not be surprised that feelings of sexual attraction arise in therapy. Feelings of attraction are difficult to avoid due to three unavoidable foundational elements of psychotherapy.

The Nature of the Relationship

The therapeutic relationship is unlike any other. From the outset, the goal of one person is the explicit support, understanding, growth, and healing of the other. People are not accustomed to such unidirectional care. Even if the therapist employs a directive model that emphasizes technique over the relationship, the client might experience levels of attention and care that are unusual outside of childhood. Even in romantic relationships and parent-child relationships, seldom does one person give his or her exclusive attention to the other without expectation or condition. Early in therapy, the client comes to understand that social formalities are not necessary. Clients learn that they do not need to ask about the therapist's well-being at every meeting. Though the client must pay the fee and respect the therapist's time, the experiential aspect of the relationship is unidirectional.

Many clients experience such attention as a powerful form of intimacy. This can be especially true if the client has limited experiences with attention and affection. The less affection and warmth the client has received in life, the more powerful it will feel in the therapeutic relationship. For clients who did not experience regular nonsexual intimacy during childhood, the experience of warmth and attention in therapy might be sexualized. Physical intimacy is affection made tangible. If the client lacked attention during crucial phases of development, they may only be able to experience affection in adulthood if it is sexualized.

The client is not the only one who may feel special in this situation. Therapists can also experience affection from the client. A negative framing of the situation might propose that the therapist enjoys the feeling of power and is in danger of abusing that power. Sometimes this is the case. More often, however, therapists might enjoy a type of appreciation that they experience nowhere else. The therapist plays a role in the client's life that no one else does. The client reveals things to the therapist that they might reveal to no one else. The client grants the therapist a place of privilege and trust that is rare in even the most intimate relationships. It is easy to see why anyone would feel special while occupying such a role in the life of another.

Clients frequently idealize their therapists. Being on the receiving end of this idealization can be just as powerful for the therapist as the unidirectional attention is for the client. The client does not see the therapist's flaws. Clients seldom, if ever, see therapists lose their temper or hear a controversial opinion. Therapist do not expose their annoying or unsavory habits (most of the time). Just as the clients get to be uniquely understood, therapists get to be uniquely perceived in a positive light. Just like the clients, they get to feel special.

The client and therapist may experience their special relationship as intimate and/or sexual. The structure of psychotherapy pushes this potential for intimacy even further.

The Structure of Therapy

Therapy works because it is not a natural social structure (Wachtel, 1993). Although the boundaries of therapy limit the opportunities for a sexual relationship, they create the potential for intense intimacy. Free from the demands of an ordinary relationship, both client and therapist can expend more energy on the relationship during the therapeutic hour. The client can share more and be more emotionally vulnerable. No awkward moment will arrive when the client sees the therapist at the office or a family gathering. The client can enter the relationship with abandon. This makes the therapist feel special. They are discovering things about the client that no one else can, pioneering territory that even beloved family and friends cannot access.

This cordoned-off relationship also increases the potential for fantasy. Client and therapist experience each other within the confines of the therapist office during the therapeutic hour. Everything beyond this is fantasy, a blank canvas onto which both may paint any picture they imagine.

One of my (SS) clients saw me at the gym one morning. She gave me a quick wave. I smiled and nodded in response. Normally, I would have waved back, but she seemed distressed by our encounter, so I followed my instincts and kept my response minimal. It happened that we had a session later that day. As soon as the session began, the client described how seeing me at the gym "all sweaty, in shorts, with your hair all messy" disrupted her fantasy of me as a "well-groomed, poised gentleman." There was no logical reason for her to think I would not go to the gym and get a little sweaty, but fantasies do not reside in the realm of logic. She imagined that I was the same outside of therapy as I was in therapy. Seeing me at the gym contaminated that fantasy.

The structure of therapy also contains an implicit contract. Client and therapist agree to avoid other potential relationships with each other. A client and therapist tacitly agree to forgo romance, business, friendship, and the pursuit of common interests. By shutting down all of these possible realities, they open each to the realm of fantasy. For example, in ordinary romantic relationships, people date and get to know each other before falling in love. While dating, they learn things that help them make an informed decision about their potential as a couple. A therapeutic relationship has no such avenue for realistic exploration. The fantasy dominates, and this fantasy can fuel feelings of intimacy and sexual attraction.

Fortunately, we have been aware of the role of fantasy since psychotherapy's inception (Hayman, 1989). When understood and examined, the fantasies of both the client and therapist can be tools rather than landmines.

The Reality of Sexuality

This third component is not unique to psychotherapy. It is a common feature of human experience. People are sexual. To pretend that therapists and clients are asexual is naïve. Both have sexual drives and desires, and there is widespread consensus as to who is attractive (Langlois, Ritter, Casey, & Sawin, 1995). Sometimes, clients and therapists will be attracted to each other. This is neither healthy nor pathological. How the client and, especially, the therapist manage these sexual feelings makes all the difference. Poor management can result in enduring hurt and dire consequences. Wise, intentional management, however, can reap rewards for both the client and the therapist.

THE PROCESS OF ATTRACTION IN THE THERAPEUTIC RELATIONSHIP

The process of attraction in the therapeutic relationship is worthy of exploration. Attraction is connected to the goals and process of therapy.

Attraction and the Goals of Therapy

Even a cursory examination of the therapeutic process reveals that a therapist should not be surprised when feelings of attraction arise in therapy. Consider just a few of the things therapy encourages.

Intimacy

Many clients come to therapy because they have problems with intimacy. Even if this is not the presenting problem, it often proves to be an underlying source of depression, anxiety, substance abuse, and a range of dysfunctional behaviors. A goal of therapy is to enhance intimacy, whether the therapist names it as such or calls it "improving interpersonal communication." The work usually begins inside the therapeutic relationship. In almost any therapeutic model, from psychoanalytic to cognitive-behavioral to humanistic, the client practices some form of intimacy with the therapist (Hill, 2005). Even if the therapist focuses on skill building, it occurs in a relational context. The therapist frames feelings of warmth, attachment, and communication as positive. It is difficult to imagine the therapeutic relationship remaining exempt from this positive focus on intimacy.

Emotional Expression

Therapy encourages the expression of almost every single emotion. In fact, it is difficult to imagine an emotion that is off the table. In more relational models of therapy, the therapist encourages clients to express any and every emotion they might have about the therapist . . . except for love and sexual attraction. The therapist who welcomes anger, envy, fear, disappointment, disillusionment, idealization, frustration, and suspicion becomes alarmed if the client one day says, "Sometimes I wonder what it would be like to kiss you." Many a therapist will applaud a client's free expression of feelings toward the therapist until attraction is disclosed. Then suspicion of personality disorders and concern about healthy boundaries emerge as if the therapist did not play a key role in opening this Pandora's Box. Increased emotional expression is a key part of psychotherapy, and love is a key emotion.

Healthy Risk-Taking and Vulnerability

Many people come to therapy because they are shut down. Life has become frightening. The client fears irrational consequences for acting on reasonable desires. Rejection seems catastrophic. Failure feels overwhelming. Fear of disappointment destroys relationships. Frequently, part of the therapeutic process involves discovering that such fears are false. Testing such fears in the real world may be too frightening at first, so clients often test them in the secondary world of psychotherapy. As the client gradually discovers that the therapist accepts them regardless of the feelings they express, they take more emotional risks in the therapy room. One of the greatest risks a client can take (and one of the most powerful ways they can test the acceptance of their therapist) is to reveal feelings of attraction for the therapist. The client might not even be looking for reciprocation; indeed, reciprocation might even be unwelcome or frightening. Expressing the attraction and feeling safe is the important thing. Most therapists labor long and hard in the service of creating safety. They should not be surprised when this is successful.

Where Attraction Appears in Psychotherapy

Attraction on the part of the client or therapist can show up in several different aspects of the therapeutic process, some more obvious than others.

Transference/Countertransference During the Session

This is the most well-documented domain of attraction in psychotherapy. The classical psychoanalytic tradition defines transference as the projection of feelings about a past primary object, usually a parent, onto the therapist. Countertransference occurs when the therapist projects such feelings onto the client. A broader understanding of transference and countertransference includes any feelings about the therapist/client that are not a product of the actual relationship. An even broader understanding includes any feelings that are not relevant to the treatment goals.

The attraction that appears during psychotherapy proper is the most easily identified and understood. For example, a client's sexual desire for the therapist may represent unresolved needs for affection from a parent. The therapist may develop sexual feelings for a client as a result of unmet intimacy needs in their current life. These are both common forms of attraction in therapy.

Selection of Client/Therapist

The client usually has several options in choosing a therapist. Certainly factors such as goodness of professional fit, specialization, experience, and expertise impact the pairing of client and therapist. However, research demonstrates that more subjective factors, such as finding the therapist likeable, also influence clients' selection (Alexander, Barber, Luborsky, Crits-Cristoph, & Auerbach, 1993). There is some evidence that physical attraction plays a role in selection of therapist (Lo Pinto, 2000). Physical attraction might not be the only influential dynamic, however. Attractive features of the therapist or client's personality or features that elicit transference or countertransference might play a role. Regardless, attraction may be a dynamic in psychotherapy from the very beginning.

The Edges of Therapy

Attraction is often most evident in the spaces surrounding the psychotherapy hour. If the client pays in advance, brings gifts, calls or emails outside of session, or compliments the therapist on anything from attire to their latest publication, they might be expressing attraction toward the therapist. If the therapist allows the client a few extra minutes, permits the client to accrue a large balance, does not charge for missed sessions, makes jokes or chitchat at the end of session, or discloses more of their personal life than they do with other clients, then this could be a sign of attraction toward the client. Any of these incidents in isolation might be unremarkable, but consistent occurrences indicate some form of attraction. Therapists and higher functioning clients with good defenses are most likely to demonstrate attraction in these subtle ways. A client with good boundaries, insight, and social skills will be too embarrassed to admit feelings of attraction. The client is much more likely to let such feelings leak out at the edges of therapy. Likewise, any therapist who values ethics and professionalism may never admit, even to him- or herself, that he or she feels attracted to a client. Even if they are aware of such feelings, they will usually be too embarrassed to admit this to a colleague and, unless they are foolish and reckless, will never share their feelings with the client. Instead, they will take satisfaction from small attention-seeking maneuvers and tiny displays of affection surrounding the formal work of therapy.

Assessing Attraction in Therapy

Attraction in psychotherapy can contribute to self-renewal only under certain conditions. Assessing these conditions involves slightly different criteria for the therapist and client.

For the Client: Ego Strength and Reality Testing

For the client to weather feelings of attraction in psychotherapy and experience self-renewal, they must have good *ego strength* and good *reality testing*. Ego strength is the capacity to tolerate psychological pain with one's identity intact. Someone with high ego strength can tolerate constructive criticism. Normal life stress does not seem overwhelming. This is not to say that the person does not feel pain, anxiety, sadness, anger, and so on. Someone with high ego strength can still be sensitive. However, they do not experience emotional pain as catastrophic and threatening to their identity and self-worth.

A client needs good ego strength to discuss feelings of attraction with a therapist who cannot reciprocate. It does not need to be exceptionally high, but it cannot be low. Spending hours exploring feelings of affection, much less sexual desire, with people who reveal nothing about how they feel would be trying for anyone. A client who has a fragile sense of self will have difficulty experiencing self-renewal by working through feelings of attraction for his or her therapist.

It is important to make a distinction between low ego strength and feeling pain. Everyone feels pain. Rejection always hurts. Individuals with poor ego strength, however, lose their psychological moorings when they experience rejection or criticism. Their self-esteem plummets. They can act out toward others or themselves in destructive ways. Their identity can fragment. They may hate the therapist for whom they felt love only moments before. It is difficult to begin the work of self-renewal while trying to cope with such painful extremes of emotion.

A competent therapist can sometimes manage attraction when a client has low ego strength, but the work of self-renewal cannot begin until the client's ego strength improves. However, if a client with low ego strength expresses attraction toward the therapist and finds the strength to stay in the therapeutic relationship and work through the pain, he or she will begin to develop higher ego strength. This, in itself, is a form of self-renewal that lays the groundwork for further growth.

Reality testing is the degree to which a client accurately perceives and interprets the physical world, relationships, and people. People with good reality testing accurately perceive the real world and their relationship to it. This is the *sine qua non* of working with attraction in therapy. If the client believes that the therapist, despite statements to the contrary, is secretly in love with him or her, there is no hope of corrective experience. Such delusions most commonly occur in psychotic disorders and severe mood disorders.

It is important to distinguish poor reality testing from fantasy. The client may have fantasies that the therapist is attracted to him or her, but these are different than delusions. Fantasies can be anything from daydreams to beliefs. Beliefs based in fantasy crumble when confronted with a contradictory reality. Someone with poor reality testing will fight for delusional beliefs, but clients entertaining fantasies will grieve their loss when confronted with the truth.

For the Therapist: Referral and Consultation

Good ego strength and reality testing are also necessary for the therapist to experience self-renewal from feeling attracted to a client. One hopes that the number of mental health professionals with poor ego strength and/or poor reality testing is very low. In addition to these requirements, the therapist must meet two others.

First, there is the referral question. The therapist must ascertain whether his or her feelings of attraction have an iatrogenic effect on the client's therapy. If the therapist's feelings of love or sexual attraction become too strong for him or her to provide sound psychotherapy, then the therapist has an ethical obligation to refer the client to another therapist. The therapist does not have to reveal the reasons for making the referral. Instead, it is better for the therapist to be vague or lie about the reason for the referral. To tell a client, "I have to refer you to another therapist because I find you sexually attractive" could be traumatic for the client. Deciding whether one needs to refer a client is difficult to do without professional consultation. This brings us to the second requirement.

To experience self-renewal, the therapist must discuss with someone else his or her feelings of attraction. This person should not be a spouse, a partner, or a friend who is not a therapist. Ideally, the therapist should work through such feelings in his or her own psychotherapy. If this is not possible, the therapist should discuss the issue with a colleague. The colleague should be someone the therapist trusts, ideally someone with whom the therapist consults on a regular basis. The therapist should not choose his or her consultant lightly. Although there is a wide gulf between sexual attraction and sexual behavior, too many mental health professionals wrongly associate the two. Pope, Sonne, and Greene (2006) call this "guilt by association." A therapist who is attracted to a client should consult with someone who understands the difference between sexual feelings and sexual actions. Ideally, the therapist will confide in someone who understands the potential for self-renewal buried beneath confusing, shameful feelings of attraction.

SEXUAL ATTRACTION AND SELF-RENEWAL

The dangers of crossing ethical and professional boundaries due to romantic and sexual desires have been well documented. We do not discuss the damaging consequences of boundary violations here. Rather, we turn our attention to the possibility of self-renewal that can result from attraction in psychotherapy.

Self-Renewal for the Client

The stereotype of attraction in therapy, perpetuated by myriad examples from popular culture, is therapy becoming undone by the client falling in love with the therapist. It is hard to erase the mental image of the powerful, intimidating Tony Soprano rising from his client's chair to kiss his psychiatrist, Dr. Jennifer Melfi. However, attraction in therapy can awaken the process of self-renewal in psychotherapy just as easily as it can cause harm.

Although clients with more acute symptoms may have poor boundaries and difficulties with impulse control, many clients seek therapy as a result of hurt, trauma, or neglect that shuts down healthy desires. Many clients associate intimacy with pain. As a result, they develop efficient psychological mechanisms that prevent further suffering by muting feelings of love and attraction. When such clients spend a significant amount of time in a safe relationship with a therapist, feelings of attraction may begin to blossom once more. Indeed, therapy may provide the only relationship that is safe enough for feelings of attraction to develop.

Often, the client need not have experienced past trauma for feelings of attraction to be repressed. Some clients may have been required to play a parent role or another role that required them always to be strong. Such clients expect others to be too weak to care for them, too needy to be attractive. After spending time in a relationship with the therapist who provides a strong, steady presence, they feel free to experience desire for the first time in their adult lives.

Such situations open the door to self-renewal in many ways. Sometimes, this process begins in the therapy room when the client reveals feelings of attraction to the therapist. Though the therapist created the safe space for this to happen, such a revelation is an act of courage on the part of the client. Once clients become aware of their feelings for the therapist, they wrestle, sometimes for weeks or months, with the decision to share their feelings with the therapist. The confession is nothing less than a leap of faith. It flies in the face of crystallized survival skills from childhood that now stand as obstacles to adult intimacy. Ignoring alarms that warn of humiliation, rejection, and shame, the client courageously shares feelings that place them at their therapist's mercy.

The crucial element of self-renewal is that clients do not reveal such desires in hope of reciprocation. They do it for the hope of growth. They do not even understand how they will grow; rather, they trust that the proclamation of affection or desire will take them to a new place that will result in healing.

Many believe that a client must confess feelings of attraction in therapy in order to experience growth. There is no evidence that this is the case. Clients might find someone other than the therapist attractive and desirable, or they might bypass the therapist in favor of someone with whom they can have a "real" relationship. This is just as powerful as expressing feelings of attraction in therapy. In some cases, it represents the client learning to swim by jumping into the deep end of the pool. The client knows, consciously or not, that the therapist will neither reciprocate nor abandon him or her. They know that the real risk, the real step forward, lies in taking a chance with a person who might reject them.

Clients almost certainly feel attracted to their therapists more than they admit. The safety of the therapeutic relationship allows dormant feelings, once regarded as dangerous, to emerge with the therapist as their object. But perhaps clients also bypass their therapist more than we know. Too often, therapists think they are the primary object in a client's life. While this is sometimes the case, higher functioning clients will "practice" with their therapists but "field test" feelings and desires with primary objects outside the therapy room. Therapy provides a foundation for self-renewal, but clients do the real work on their own.

Self-Renewal for the Therapist

If sexual attraction and self-renewal for the client is a controversial topic, it is all but taboo for the therapist. At best, the therapist understands and contains feelings of attraction. Many regard as ludicrous the idea that the therapist might embark on a path of growth as a result of feeling desire for a client. Given the potential pitfalls of uncontained sexual attraction, such a position is understandable. However, we feel that both the frequency of therapist attraction to clients is underreported, and the potential for self-renewal underexamined.

Pope, Keith-Spiegel, and Tabachnick (1986) found that 87% of the therapists they surveyed had felt sexually attracted to a client at some point. The incidence of reported boundary violations, however, is much lower. While it is a relief that most therapists never act on their feelings of sexual attraction, it is unfortunate that most therapists seldom discuss such feelings with a colleague or supervisor. Yet, it is understandable. The mental health culture has a somewhat unbalanced emphasis on legal and ethical issues. Note that we did not say there is an overemphasis. It is crucial that all mental health professionals possess a thorough knowledge of ethical guidelines and the laws that govern their profession. The first order of creating safety in the therapeutic relationship is full compliance with the highest legal and ethical standards. However, too many mental health professionals emphasize the possible over the probable. If a colleague or a trainee admits to having sexual feelings for a client, is it possible that they will act on such feelings? Yes. Is it probable? According to Pope et al.'s

(1986) research, no. Too many supervisors and colleagues react as if a boundary violation is probable rather than possible, though the admission of attraction to another professional in itself signals that a boundary violation is improbable. This culture of fear must change if more therapists are to explore the meaning of their feelings.

Exploration with a colleague or supervisor is crucial. It is difficult for the therapist to achieve the first step toward self-renewal alone. The first step requires understanding the attraction. That the client is physically attractive is seldom the lone reason (Celenza & Gabbard, 2003). An attractive client might be a distraction for the therapist at the beginning, but it soon diminishes as the therapist begins to focus on the work. The attraction takes hold only if it meets some other need. If the therapist can understand this need, the work of self-renewal can begin.

There are two primary sources of enduring attraction for the therapist.

Intimacy Needs

The therapist whose life lacks intimacy is most likely to become attracted to a client. The therapist who lacks physical intimacy will develop sexual feelings for an attractive client. The therapist who needs emotional intimacy will feel drawn toward the warm client who reciprocates the therapist's attention. Therapists who need social intimacy will find themselves self-disclosing to a client with similar interests.

Countertransference

Unmet needs from childhood can result in reenactments for both the therapist and the client. If clients are meeting needs from childhood, the therapist may become entwined by powerful feelings of attraction they don't understand. Countertransference is harder to identify than adult intimacy needs, which makes consultation even more crucial.

Unmet intimacy needs from adulthood and countertransference are not mutually exclusive. They often emanate from the same source and result in similar symptoms. If therapists can identify one, they would be wise to look for the other.

Attraction leads to self-renewal for the psychotherapist by revealing the unresolved needs described above. While unexamined attraction can wreak havoc if left unchecked, scrutinized attraction highlights unmet needs. This leads to self-renewal.

Self-Renewal: A Therapist's Story

A colleague of ours spent the final summer of his postdoc year in relative isolation. His girlfriend was traveling abroad, friends and family were scattered across the country, and he was living in an apartment without a roommate for the first time in his life. Working in a private-practice setting, he maintained a full caseload. More than half his clients were women, but he had never felt attracted to any of them.

The first thing he noticed that summer was increased self-disclosure. He started sharing more of his life, especially with his female clients. He shared only innocuous details about movies he had seen or music he enjoyed, but it was conspicuous because it was something he had seldom done before. He worked from a psychoanalytic model that restricted self-disclosure. He believed in the model and was surprised by his impulsive departures from it.

Next, flirtation appeared at the end of sessions. He would make jovial chitchat with certain female clients while they were writing the check. Sometimes he would linger in the doorway, conscious of his attempts to elicit a smile or laughter.

When he began having sexual fantasies about certain clients, he knew that it was time to seek consultation. He returned to the therapist with whom he had done several years of work. It only took them one session to assess the situation. Our colleague was more isolated than he had been in his entire life. His only social outlet was his clientele. He knew he was lonely, but he thought his professional boundaries were too strong for the loneliness to affect his work. He did not realize how much emotional harm months of isolation had done.

The next day, he took 2 personal days and embarked on a long weekend trip to visit friends a few hours away. Two weeks later, he took vacation time to visit his girlfriend in Europe. He had previously told her that he could not afford the trip—but now he decided he could not afford *not* to go.

Sexual Attraction and Self-Renewal

Self-renewal can begin only after one realizes something has been depleted. Attraction in psychotherapy accentuates unmet needs, old and new wounds, emerging strengths, a longing for growth, and a desire for freedom. It is a compass for self-renewal, pointing the way toward growth for love and sexuality. Love and sexuality bring joy and wonder, but they can also bring fear and pain. We know how love and sexuality can bring fear and pain to psychotherapy. If we never forget that, we can make room for joy and wonder.

REFERENCES

Alexander, L. B., Barber, J. P., Luborsky, L., Crits-Christoph, P., & Auerbach, A. (1993). On what bases do patients choose their therapists? *Journal of Psychotherapy Practice and Research*, *2*, 135–146.

Celenza, A., & Gabbard, G. O. (2003). Analysts who commit sexual boundary violations: A lost cause? *Journal of the American Psychoanalytic Association*, *51*(2), 617–636. doi:10.1177/00030651030510020201

Gutheil, T. G., & Gabbard, G. O. (1992). Obstacles to the dynamic understanding of therapist-patient sexual relations. *American Journal of Psychotherapy*, *46*, 515–525.

Hayman, A. (1989). What do we mean by "phantasy"? *International Journal of Psychoanalysis*, *70*, 105–114.

Hill, C. E. (2005). Therapist techniques, client involvement, and the therapeutic relationship: Inextricably intertwined in the therapy process. *Psychotherapy: Theory, Research, Practice, Training*, *42*, 431–442. doi:10.1037/0033–3204.42.4.431

Langlois, J. H., Ritter, J. M., Casey, R. J., & Sawin, D. B. (1995). Infant attractiveness predicts maternal behaviors and attitudes. *Developmental Psychology*, *31*, 9. doi: 0012–1649/95

Lo Pinto, L. A. (2000). Effects of gender, attractiveness, and disorder on perceptions of therapists. *Dissertation Abstracts International: Section B: The Sciences and Engineering*, *60*(7-B), 3620.

Pope, K. S. (2001). Sex between therapists and clients. In J. Worell (Ed.), *Encyclopedia of women and gender: Sex similarities and differences and the impact of society on gender* (pp. 955–962). Retrieved from http://kspope.com/sexiss/sexencyc.php

Pope, K. S., Keith-Spiegel, P., & Tabachnick, B. G. (1986). Sexual attraction to clients: The human therapist and the (sometimes) inhuman training system. *American Psychologist*, *41*, 147–158. doi:10.1037/1931–3918.s.2.96

Pope, K. S., Sonne, J. L., & Greene, B. (2006). *What therapists don't talk about and why: Understanding taboos that hurt us and our clients*. Washington, DC: American Psychological Association.

Somer, E., & Nachmani, I. (2005). Constructions of therapist-client sex: A comparative analysis of retrospective victim reports. *Sexual Abuse: Journal of Research and Treatment*, *17*, 47–62. doi:10.1177/107906320501700106

Wachtel, P. (1993). *Therapeutic communication: Principles and effective practice*. New York, NY: Guilford Press.

Going Forward

A Brief Epilogue

Robert J. Wicks and Elizabeth A. Maynard

The goal of this book has been a simple one: to *begin* a more in-depth and broader discussion as to how using the lens of self-renewal can enrich the psychotherapy process as well as the clinician's personal and professional life. Going forward there is so much more to be written, reflected about, and shared. However, this is one of the first steps we felt needed to be taken.

The emphasis on the clinician's own self-renewal in the beginning was a conscious choice on the part of the editors. It is an outgrowth of their belief that while technique and the therapeutic relationship are of paramount importance in the treatment encounter, there is a third element that is of profound import as well: the modeling by the therapist of a respect for, and involvement in, seeking a healthier lifestyle.

In this light, a clinician's self-care is not viewed solely as benefiting the therapist alone, although the direct benefit to the helper is certainly a goal. It is also seen as having a subtle but powerful impact on the therapy process itself.

Understanding the benefits, challenges, resistances to, and results of self-care and a healthy lifestyle allows clinicians to be sensitive to their presence in their clients as well. Similarly, a case can be made for appreciating mindfulness in this regard.

Being in the now with a sense of awareness not only makes life more enjoyable and fulfilling for the therapist's own life, it provides a clinical tone to the sessions, in which a nonjudgmental attitude toward seeking clarity becomes more prevalent and eventually, increasingly collaborative.

With clinician self-care and mindfulness as a bedrock of self-renewal then, the remainder of the chapters just read were designed to provide new insights and perspective on self-renewal in terms of client growth and healing, therapeutic techniques, spirituality, different populations, ethics, and other challenges. Yet, from our comments, as can be surmised, in going forward the positive impact of this information is not limited to a present *specific* benefit (i.e., how can I put this knowledge in play with my caseload?) alone. In a broader sense, the previous sections are designed as well to draw on the experience and wisdom of the clinicians reading this material by prompting them to also ask such questions as:

- How can I more productively use the frame of "self-renewal" with different populations and presenting problems?
- What topics were *not* covered in this initial effort at discussing self-renewal and clinical practice that you might develop more clearly going forward?
- What are the most pressing issues that intrigue, challenge, and reward you in your own personal and professional journey that would significantly enhance your self-renewal process?
- How can your own self-renewal plan be developed further—not as a duty in being healthier but as part of a pilgrimage in enjoying life—including one's clinical practice in a much fuller way *now*?

These are but a few questions if truly, honestly, nonjudgmentally, and comprehensively faced may well lead to alter and enrich how we as clinicians can involve ourselves in the process. Peterson (2006) notes:

> Like many academics, I spent my young adult years postponing many of the small things that I knew would make me happy, including reading novels for pleasure, learning to cook, taking a photography class, and joining a gym. I would do all of these things when I had time—when I finished school, when I had a job, when I was awarded tenure, and so on. I was fortunate enough to realize that I would never have time unless I made the time. And then the rest of my life began.

The impact, and living out, of such an insight changes the clinician and how therapy is undertaken. The lyrics (theory and technique) of the treatment may remain fairly unaltered. However, the music (modeling, relational aspects, and sense of mindfulness in play) of the clinical work may profoundly be changed, ending in surprisingly gratifying results. Once again, self-renewal is a gift therapists can give themselves. But, in the end, it is a gift that can open up those they treat to open up so much more in their lives as well and, in its essence, isn't this what therapy is truly about?

REFERENCE

Peterson, C. (2006). *A primer in positive psychology*. Oxford, England: Oxford University Press.

Author Index

Subject Index